PLAYFAIR
FOOTBALL
ANNUAL 1993-94

PLAYFAIR FOOTBALL ANNUAL 1993-94

EDITED BY JACK ROLLIN

HEADLINE

First published in 1993
by HEADLINE BOOK PUBLISHING LTD

10 9 8 7 6 5 4 3 2 1

Cover photograph Left: David Hirst (Sheffield Wednesday); right: Mark Hughes
(Manchester United) (*Colorsport*)

ISBN 0 7472 4103 1

Typeset by BPCC Whitefriars Ltd,
Tunbridge Wells

Printed and bound in Great Britain by
BPCC Hazell Books Ltd
Member of BPCC Ltd

HEADLINE BOOK PUBLISHING LTD
A member of the Hodder Headline PLC Group
Headline House
79 Great Titchfield Street
London W1P 7FN

CONTENTS

Other Football

Information and Records

EDITORIAL

Only a year after the demise of Aldershot as a Football League club, Barnet appeared on the brink of being thrown out of the League themselves because of a lack of finance.

Incidentally reorganised on a purely local basis as Aldershot Town, the Hampshire club made a successful comeback in the Diadora League, Division Three, finishing as champions and enjoying a fine level of support.

But Barnet's plight was all the more remarkable when you realise that the Hertfordshire club had won promotion to the Second Division in only their second season as a League club.

They were saved in the first instance by insufficient numbers of other clubs turning up for the meeting to dismiss them and those who were present, did not present enough votes for the resolution to remove them.

For a well-supported club, the fact that Barnet had reached this stage was hard to believe. But in the summer months, eleven of their players were given free transfers by the League, because of non-payment of wages over a period.

Somehow what was left of the club carried on trying to seek the right kind of financial guarantees which would satisfy the League. This was forthcoming before the deadline imposed by the new club chairman at Barnet.

This meant no reprieve for Halifax Town, who thus lost their status and will play this season in the GM Vauxhall Conference. They were original members of the old Division Three (Northern Section) when it was formed in 1921.

At the other end of football's finances, the transfer records were broken in both England and Scotland, as the market appeared to be moving out of recession. Duncan Ferguson was transferred to Rangers from Dundee United for 4 million, while Roy Keane moved from Nottingham Forest to Manchester United in a 3.75 million deal.

But another British player, England captain David Platt, found himself in the unlikely position of being the world's most expensive player in terms of transfer fees paid for his services during a career. By being transferred from Juventus to Sampdoria for £5.2 million, his aggregate transfer value rose to £17.4 million following moves from Crewe to Aston Villa in 1988 for £200,000, to Bari in 1991 for £5.5 million and to Juventus in 1992 for £6.5 million.

Sponsorship changes for the 1993–94 season will see new names on the main domestic competitions: The FA Carling Premiership and the Endsleigh Insurance League, replace the FA Premier League and Barclays League of last season.

Adams, Tony A.
Bould, Stephen, A.
Campbell, Kevin J.
Carter, James, W. C.
Davis, Paul V.
Dickov, Paul.
Dixon, Lee, M.
Flatts, Mark M.
Heaney, Neil A.
Hillier, David.

Jensen, John.
Keown, Martin R.
Limpar, Anders.
Linighan, Andrew.
Lydersen, Pal.
Marshall, Scott R.
Merson, Paul C.
Miller, Alan J.
Morrow, Stephen, J.
Parlour, Raymond,

Read, Paul C.
Seaman, David A.
Selley, Ian.
Shaw, Paul.
Smith, Alan M.
Webster, Kenneth D.
Will, James A.
Winterburn, Nigel.
Wright, Ian E.

League Appearances: Adams, T.A. 33(2); Bould, S.A. 24; Campbell, K.J. 32(5); Carter, J.W. 11(5); Davis, P.V. 6; Dickov, P. 1(2); Dixon, L.M. 29; Flatts, M.M. 6(4); Groves, P. (1); Heaney, N.A. 3(2); Hillier, D. 27(3); Jensen, J. 29(3); Keown, M.R. 15(1); Limpar, A. 12(11); Linighan, A. 19(2); Lydersen, P. 7(1); Marshall, S.R. 2; McGowan, G.G. (2); Merson, P.C. 32(1); Miller, A.J. 3(1); Morrow, S.J. 13(3); O'Leary, D.A. 6(5); Parlour, R. 16(5); Pates, C.G. 2(5); Seaman, D.A. 39; Selley, I. 9; Smith, A.M. 27(4); Winterburn, N. 29; Wright, I.E. 30(1).
League (40): Wright 15, Merson 6, Campbell 4, Smith 3, Carter 2, Dickov 2, Limpar 2, Linighan 2, Bould 1, Hillier 1, Parlour 1, Winterburn 1.
Coca Cola Cup (15): Wright 5 (1 pen), Campbell 4, Smith 2, Linighan 1, Merson 1, Morrow 1, Winterburn 1.
FA Cup (18): Wright 10 (1 pen), Adams 2, Campbell 1, Linighan 1, Merson 1, Parlour 1, Smith 1, own goal 1.
Ground: Arsenal Stadium, Highbury, London N5. Telephone 071–226 0304.
Record attendance: 73,295 v Sunderland, Div 1, 9 March 1935.
Manager: George Graham.
Secretary: K. J. Friar.
Honours –
Football League: Division 1 Champions – 1930–31, 1932–33, 1933–34, 1934–35, 1937–38, 1947–48, 1952–53, 1970–71, 1988–89, 1990–91.
FA Cup winners 1929–30, 1935–36, 1949–50, 1970–71, 1978–79, 1992–93.
Football League Cup winners 1986–87, 1992–93.
European Competitions:
Fairs Cup winners: 1969–70.
Colours: Red shirts with white sleeves, white shorts, red stockings.

Atkinson, Dalian R.
Barrett, Earl D.
Beinlich, Stefan.
Berry, Trevor J.
Blake, Mark A.
Boden, Christopher D.

Bosnich, Mark.
Breitkreutz, Mattias.
Carruthers, Martin G.
Cox, Neil J.
Crisp, Richard I.
Daley, Anthony M.

Davis, Neil.
Ehiogu, Ugochuku.
Farrell, David.
Farrelly, Gareth.
Fenton, Graham A.
Froggart, Stephen J.

Houghton, Raymond, J.   Richardson, Kevin.   Teale, Shaun.
Kubicki, Darisz.   Saunders, Dean N.   Williams, Lee.
McGrath, Paul.   Small, Bryan.   Yorke, Dwight.
Oakes, Michael C.   Spink, Nigel P.
Parker, Garry S.   Staunton, Stephen.

League Appearances: Atkinson, D.R. 28; Barrett, E.D. 42; Beinlich, S. 1(6); Blake, M.A. (1); Bosnich, M. 17; Breitkreutz, M. 2(1); Carruthers, M. (1); Cox, N.J. 6(9); Daley, A.M. 8(5); Ehiogu, U. 1(3); Farrell, D. 1(1); Froggart, S.J. 16(1); Houghton, R.J. 39; McAvennie, F. (3); McGrath, P. 42; Parker, G.S. 37; Regis, C. 7(6); Richardson, K. 42; Saunders, D.N. 35; Small, B. 10(4); Spink, N.P. 25; Staunton, S. 42; Teale, S. 39; Yorke, D. 22(5).

League (57): Saunders 13 (1 pen), Atkinson 11, Parker 9 (1 pen), Yorke 6, McGrath 4, Houghton 3, Daley 2, Richardson 2, Staunton 2, Barrett 1, Cox 1, Froggatt 1, Regis 1, Teale 1.

Coca Cola Cup (7): Atkinson 2, Saunders 2, McGrath 1, Richardson 1, Teale 1.

FA Cup (5): Saunders 2, Cox 1, Houghton 1, Yorke 1.

Ground: Villa Park, Trinity Rd, Birmingham B6 6HE. Telephone 021-327 2299.

Record attendance: 76,588 v Derby Co, FA Cup 6th rd, 2 March 1946.

Manager: Ron Atkinson.

Secretary: Steven Stride.

Honours –

Football League: Division 1 Champions – 1893–94, 1895–96, 1896–97, 1898–99, 1899–1900, 1909–10, 1980–81. Division 2 Champions – 1937–38, 1959–60. Division 3 Champions – 1971–72.

FA Cup: Winners 1887, 1895, 1897, 1905, 1913, 1920, 1957.

Football League Cup: Winners 1961, 1975, 1977.

European Competitions:

European Cup winners: 1981–82

European Super Cup winners: 1982–83.

Colours: Claret shirts, blue trim, white shorts, claret and blue trim, blue stockings, claret trim.

BARNET   DIV. 2

Alexander, Timothy M.   Horton, Duncan.   Naylor, Dominic J.
Barnett, David.   Howell, David C.   Payne, Derek R.
Bodley, Michael J.   Hunt, Jonathan R.   Phillips, Gary C.
Bull, Gary W.   Huxford, Richard J.   Showler, Paul.
Carter, Mark C.   Lowe, Kenneth.   Wilson, Paul R.
Evans, Nicholas J.   Lynch, Anthony J.

League Appearances: Barnett, D. 36; Bodley, M.J. 33; Bull, G.W. 41; Carter, M.C. 26(15); Cooper, G.V. 17; Evans, N.J. 5(13); Hayrettin, H. (2); Hoddle, C. 5(14); Horton, D. 28; Howell, D.C. 23; Hunt, J.R. 10(9); Huxford, R.J. 33; Lowe, K. 29(7); Lynch, A.J. 6(2); Naylor, D.J. 24(1); Oxbrow, D.W. 1; Payne, D.R. 37; Phillips, G.C. 42; Showler, P. 30(2); Sorrell, A.C. 8; Stein, B. 17(23); Willis, R.C. 6; Wilson, P.R. 9.

League (66): Bull 17 (3 pens), Carter 11, Stein B 8, Payne 5, Showler 5, Evans 4,

9

Barnett 2, Bodley 2, Hoddle 2, Lowe 2, Sorrell 2, Huxford 1, Lynch 1, Willis 1, own goals 3.
Coca Cola Cup (2): Bull 2 (2 pens).
FA Cup (0).
Ground: Underhill Stadium, Barnet Lane, Barnet, Herts EN5 2BE. Telephone 081–441 6932.
Record attendance: 11,026 v Wycombe Wanderers. FA Amateur Cup 4th Round 1951–52.
Manager: Gary Phillips.
Secretary: Bryan Ayres.
Honours –
FA Amateur Cup winners 1945–46.
GM Vauxhall Conference winners 1990–91.
Colours: Amber shirts, black shorts, amber stockings.

BARNSLEY   DIV. 1

Archdeacon, Owen D.
Biggins, Wayne.
Bishop, Darren C.
Bullimore, Wayne A.
Burton, Marc A.
Butler, Lee S.
Currie, David N.
Davis, Steven P.
Eaden, Nicholas J.

Fleming, James G.
Godfrey, Warren P.
Graham, Deiniol W. T.
Gridelet, Philip R.
Harriott, Marvin L.
Jackson, Christopher D.
Liddell, Andrew M.
Morgan, Gregory D.
O'Connell, Brendan.

Rammell, Andrew V.
Redfern, Neil D.
Robinson, Jamie.
Taggart, Gerald P.
Watson, David N.
Whitehead, Philip M.
Williams, Gareth G.

League Appearances: Archdeacon, O.D. 37(1); Bennett, T. 2; Biggins, W. 32(2); Bishop, D.C. 43; Bullimore, W.A. 10(7); Burton, M.A. 5; Butler, L.S. 28; Connelly, D. (1); Currie, D.N. 23(12); Davis, S.P. 10(1); Eaden, N.J. 1(1); Feeney, M.A. (2); Fleming, J.G. 46; Godfrey, W.P. 1(7); Graham, D.W. 9(6); Gridelet, P.R. 2; Hendon, I.M. 6; Jackson, C. 1(2); Liddell, A.M. 16(5); O'Connell, B. 35(5); Pearson, J.S. 21(1); Rammell, A.V. 27(3); Redfern, N.D. 46; Robinson, J. 8; Robinson, M.J. 28(1); Smith, M.C. 3(1); Taggart, G.P. 44; Watson, D.N. 5; Whitehead, P.M. 13; Williams, G.J. 4(4).
League (56): Biggins 14, Rammell 7, Archdeacon 6 (1 pen), O'Connell 6, Williams 5, Currie 4, Taggart 4, Pearson 3, Redfearn 3, Liddell 2, Graham 1, Robinson M 1.
Coca Cola Cup (2): Liddell 1, Redfearn 1.
FA Cup (7): Rammell 3, Redfearn 2, Archdeacon 1, own goal 1.
Ground: Oakwell Ground, Grove St, Barnsley. Telephone Barnsley (0226) 295353.
Record attendance: 40,255 v Stoke C, FA Cup 5th rd, 15 February 1936.
Player-Manager: Viv Anderson.
Secretary: Michael Spinks.
Honours –
Football League: Division 3 (N) Champions – 1933–34, 1938–39, 1954–55.
FA Cup: Winners 1912.
Colours: Red shirts, white trim, white shorts, red stockings.

BIRMINGHAM CITY   DIV. 1

Beckford, Jason N.
Clarkson, Ian S.
Donowa, Brian L.
Dryden, Richard A.
Fenwick, Paul J.
Frain, John W.
Gayle, John.
Gosney, Andrew R.

Hiley, Scott P.
Mardon, Paul J.
Matthewson, Trevor.
Moulden, Paul A.
O'Neill, Alan.
Parris, George.
Peer, Duncan.
Peschisolido, Paolo P.

Potter, Graham S.
Rodgerson, Ian.
Rogers, Darren J.
Rowbotham, Darren.
Saville, Andrew V.
Smith, David.
Sturridge, Simon A.
Tair, Paul R.

League Appearances: Beckford, J.N. 3; Catlin, R. 8; Clarkson, I.S. 25(3); Cooper, M.N. 3(3); Donowa, B.L. 18(3); Dryden, R.A. 11; Fenwick, P.J. 3(7); Fitzpatrick, P.J. 7; Foy, D.L. 3; Frain, J.W. 45; Gayle, J. 17(2); Gleghorn, N.W. 11; Gosney, A.R. 21; Hicks, M. 16(2); Hiley, S.P. 7; Holmes, P. 12; Mardon, P.J. 18(3); Matthewson, T. 40; Moulden, P.A. 13; Parris, G. 13; Peer, D. 13; Peschisolido, P. 16(3); Potter, G.S. 16(2); Quinn, S.J. 1(3); Rennie, D. 15(3); Rodgerson, I. 24(7); Rogers, D.J. 14(3); Rowbotham, D. 10(4); Sale, M.D. 9(6); Saville, A.V. 10; Scott, R.P. 1; Sealey, L.J. 12; Smith, D. 13; Speedie, D.R. 10; Sturridge, S.A. 15(5); Tait, P.R. 28; Thomas, M.R. 5.

League (50): Peschisolido 7, Saville 7, Frain 6 (3 pens), Moulden 5, Gayle 3, Donowa 2, Matthewson 2, Potter 2, Rennie 2, Rodgerson 2, Rowbotham 2, Speedie 2, Tait 2, Beckford 1, Gleghorn 1, Mardon 1, Peer 1, Smith 1, Sturridge 1.

Coca Cola Cup (1): Sale 1.

FA Cup (0).

Ground: St Andrews, Birmingham B9 4NH. Telephone 021–772 0101.

Record attendance: 66,844 v Everton, FA Cup 5th rd,11 February 1939.

Manager: Terry Cooper.

Secretary: Alan Jones BA, MBA

Honours –

Football League: Division 2 Champions – 1892–93, 1920–21, 1947–48, 1954–55.

Football League Cup: Winners 1963. **Leyland Data Cup:** Winners 1991.

Colours: Royal blue and white shirts, white shorts, blue stockings with white trim.

BLACKBURN ROVERS   FA PREMIER

Andersson, Patrik J.
Atkins, Mark N.
Berg, Henning.
Brown, Richard A.
Burnett, Wayne.
Collier, Darren.
Cowans, Gordon S.
Dewhurst, Robert M.
Dickins, Matthew J.
Dobson, Anthony J.

Gallacher, Kevin W.
Hendry, Edward C. J.
Irland, Simon P.
Le Saux, Graeme P.
Makel, Lee R.
Marker, Nicholas R. T.
May, David.
Mimms, Robert A.
Moran, Kevin B.
Newell, Michael C.

Ripley, Stuart E.
Scott, Andrew M.
Shearer, Alan.
Sherwood, Timothy A.
Talia, Frank.
Tallon, Gary T.
Thorne, Peter L.
Wilcox, Jason M.
Wright, Alan G.

11

League Appearances: Andersson, P.J. 6(5); Atkins, M.N. 24(7); Berg, H. 2(2); Brown, R.A. 2; Cowans, G.S. 23(1); Dobson, A.J. 15(4); Gallacher, K.W. 9; Hendry, E.C. 41; Hill, K.J. (1); Ireland, S.P. (1); Le Saux, G.P. 9; Livingstone, S. 1(1); Makel, L.R. 1; Marker, N.R. 12(3); May, D. 34; Mimms, R.A. 42; Moran, K.B. 36; Newell, M.C. 40; Price, C.J. 2(4); Ripley, S.E. 38(2); Shearer, A. 21; Sherwood, T.A. 38(1); Wegerle, R.C. 11(11); Wilcox, J.M. 31(2); Wright, A.G. 24.

League (68): Shearer 16 (3 pens), Newell 13, Ripley 7, Atkins 5, Gallacher 5, Moran 4, Wegerle 4, Wilcox 4, Sherwood 3, Cowans 1, Hendry 1, May 1, own goals 4.

Coca Cola Cup (19): Shearer 6, Newell 5, Wegerle 4, Andersson 1, Atkins 1, May 1, own goal 1.

FA Cup (9): Newell 3, Ripley 2, Wegerle 2, Livingstone 1, Moran 1.

Ground: Ewood Park, Blackburn BB2 4JF. Telephone Blackburn (0254) 55432.

Record attendance: 61,783 v Bolton W, FA Cup 6th rd, 2 March, 1929.

Manager: Kenny Dalglish MBE.

Secretary: John W. Howarth FAAI.

Honours –

Football League: Division 1 Champions – 1911–12, 1913–14. Division 2 Champions – 1938–39. Division 3 Champions – 1974–75.

FA Cup: Winners 1884, 1885, 1886, 1890, 1891, 1928.

Full Members' Cup: Winners 1986–87.

Colours: Blue and white halved shirts, white shorts, blue stockings.

BLACKPOOL   DIV. 2

Bamber, John D.
Bonner, Mark.
Briggs, Gary.
Burgess, David J.
Cook, Mitchell.
Davies, Michael J.
Eyres, David.
Gore, Ian G.

Gouck, Andrew S.
Horner, Philip M.
Leitch, Grant.
Martin, Lee B.
McIlhargey, Stephen.
Mitchell, Neil N.
Murphy, James A.
Murray, Mark.

Robinson, David J.
Rodwell, Anthony.
Sinclair, Trevor L.
Speak, Christopher.
Spooner, Stephen A.
Stoneman, Paul.
Watson, Andrew A.

League Appearances: Bailey, N. 7(1); Bamber, J.D. 24; Beech, C. 1; Bond, R. (1); Bonner, M. 8(7); Briggs, G. 33; Burgess, D.J. 20; Cook, M. 9; Davies, M.J. 30; Dickins, M.J. 19; Duffield, P. 3(2); Eyres, D. 46; Garner, A. 4(1); Gore, I.G. 30; Gouck, A.S. 27(2); Harvey, R.G. 4(1); Horner, P.M. 46; Leitch, G. 11(6); Martin, L.B. 24; McIlhargey, S. 3; Mitchell, N.N. 6(6); Murphy, J.A. 28(5); Murray, M. 1; Robinson, D.J. 12(2); Rodwell, A. 19(1); Sinclair, T.L. 45; Speak, C. (1); Spooner, S.A. 2; Stoneman, P. 8(2); Stringfellow, I.R. 3; Thornber, S.J. 21(3); Ward, A.S. 2; Watson, A. 10(5).

League (63): Eyres 16 (6 pens), Bamber 13, Sinclair 11, Horner 7, Gouck 4, Robinson 2, Watson 2, Briggs 1, Davies 1, Duffield 1, Leitch 1, Mitchell 1, Rodwell 1, Stringfellow 1, Ward 1.

Coca Cola Cup (:4): Eyres 1, Murphy 1, Robinson 1, own goal 1.

FA Cup (1): Mitchell 1.

Ground: Bloomfield Rd Ground, Blackpool FY1 6JJ. Telephone Blackpool (0253) 404331.

Record attendance: 38,098 v Wolverhampton W, Division 1, 17 September 1955.

Manager: Bill Ayre.
Secretary: D. J. Allan.
Honours – Football League: Division 2 Champions – 1929–30.
FA Cup: Winners 1953.
Anglo-Italian Cup: Winners 1971.
Colours: Tangerine shirts with navy and white trim, white shorts, tangerine stockings with white tops.

BOLTON WANDERERS   DIV. 1

Branagan, Keith G.
Brown, Phillip.
Burke, David I.
Clarke, Christopher J.
Darby, Julian T.
Fisher, Neil J.
Green, Scott P.

Kelly, Anthony G.
Lee, David M.
Lydiate, Jason L.
McAteer, Jason W.
McGinlay, John.
Oliver, Darren.
Parkinson, Gary.

Patterson, Mark A.
Roscoe, Andrew R.
Seagraves, Mark.
Spooner, Nicholas M.
Stubbs, Alan.
Walker, Andrew.
Winstanley, Mark A.

League Appearances: Branagan, K.G. 46; Brown, M.A. 4(2); Brown, P. 40; Burke, D.I. 43; Came, M.R. 3(1); Darby, J.T. 18(3); Fisher, N.J. 3(1); Green, S.P. 33(8); Kelly, A.G. 33(3); Lee, D.M. 32; Lydiate, J.L. 6; McAteer, J.W. 19(2); McGinlay, J. 31(3); Oliver, D. 3; Parkinson, G. (2); Patterson, M.A. 35(2); Philliskirk, A. 9(1); Reeves, D. 10(4); Seagraves, M. 36(1); Spooner, N.M. 6; Storer, S.J. 1(2); Stubbs, A. 37(5); Walker, A. 31(1); Winstanley, M.A. 27(2).
League (80): Walker 26 (3 pens), McGinlay 16 (2 pens), Green 6, Brown P 5, Lee 5, Seagraves 5, Darby 4, Kelly 2, Patterson 2, Philliskirk 2, Stubbs 2, Reeves 1, Spooner 1, Winstanley 1, own goals 2.
Coca Cola Cup :(5): Stubbs 2, Green 1, Philliskirk 1, Walker 1.
FA Cup (13): McGinlay 5, Walker 4, Green 1, McAteer 1, Reeves 1, Seagraves 1.
Ground: Burnden Park, Bolton BL3 2QR. Telephone Bolton (0204) 389200.
Record attendance: 69,912 v Manchester C, FA Cup 5th rd, 18 February 1933.
Manager: Bruce Rioch.
Secretary: Des McBain.
Honours –
Football League: Division 2 Champions – 1908–09, 1977–78. Division 3 Champions – 1972–73.
FA Cup winners 1923, 1926, 1929, 1958.
Sherpa Van Trophy: Winners 1989.
Colours: White shirts, navy blue shorts, red stockings, blue and white tops.

AFC BOURNEMOUTH   DIV. 2

Bartram, Vincent L.
Fletcher, Steven M.
Masters, Neil B.
McGorry, Brian P.
Mean, Scott.
Mitchell, Paul R.

Morrell, Paul D.
Morris, Mark J.
Moss, Neil G.
Murray, Robert J.
O'Driscoll, Sean M.
Pennock, Adrian B.

Pulis, Anthony.
Rowland, Keith.
Shearer, Peter A.
Watson, Alexander F.
Wood, Paul A.

13

League Appearances: Bartram, V.L. 45; Beadle, P.C. 9; Butler, S. 1; Cooke, R.E. 8(4); Ekoku, E. 14; Fletcher, S.M. 29(2); Holmes, D.G. (1); Lovell, S.J. 3; Masters, N.B. 19(1); McElhatton, M. (1); McGorry, B.P. 36(1); Mean, S. 6(9); Mitchell, P.R. 3(2); Morgan, N. 6; Morrell, P.D. 20(1); Morris, M.J. 43; Moss, N.G. 1; Mundee, D.W. 23(3); Murray, R.J. 5(20); O'Driscoll, S.M. 38(4); Pennock, A.B. 43; Regis, D. 6; Rowland, K. 31(4); Scott, P.R. 9(1); Shearer, P.A. 34; Smith, D. 1; Watson, A.F. 46; Williams, D.M. (1); Wood, P.A. 27.

League (45): McGorry 8, Ekoku 7, Fletcher 4, Murray 4, Shearer 4, Wood 4, Beadle 2, Mundee 2 (1 pen), Regis 2, Rowland 2, Mean 1, Morgan 1, Morris 1, Pennock 1, Watson 1, own goal 1.

Coca Cola Cup (1): Morris 1.

FA Cup (7): Mundee 2, Ekoku 1, Lovell 1, McGorry 1, Morgan 1, Shearer 1.

Ground: Dean Court Ground, Bournemouth. Telephone Bournemouth (0202) 395381.

Record attendance: 28,799 v Manchester U, FA Cup 6th rd, 2 March 1957.

Manager: Tony Pulis.

Secretary: K. R. J. MacAlister.

Honours –

Football League: Division 3 Champions – 1986–87.

Associate Members' Cup: Winners 1984.

Colours: Red shirts with white V shape & reverse V shape 3" pattern, black shorts with white piping, black stockings with red/white turnback.

BRADFORD CITY   DIV. 2

Blake, Noel L.	McCarthy, Sean C.	Stapleton, Francis A.
Duxbury, Michael.	McHugh, Michael B.	Tomlinson, Paul.
Heseltine, Wayne A.	Oliver, Gavin R.	Torpey, Stephen D. J.
Hoyle, Colin R.	Partridge, Scott M.	Williams, Gary.
Jewell, Paul.	Reid, Paul R.	
Lawford, Craig B.	Richards, Dean I.	

League Appearances: Blake, N.L. 31(1); Bowling, I. 7; Duxbury, L.E. 42; Duxbury, M. 36; Heseltine, W.A. 40(2); Hoyle, C.R. 33; Jenkins, I. 6; Jewell, P. 45(1); Lawford, C.B. 5(3); MacDonald, D.H. 7; Margerison, L. 1(2); McCarthy, S.C. 40(2); McHugh, M.B. 10(6); Oliver, G.R. 39(1); Partridge, S.M. (4); Pearce, C. 9; Reid, P.R. 44; Richards, D.I. 1(2); Stapleton, F. 8(5); Tinnion, B. 24(3); Tomlinson, G.M. 24; Torpey, S.D. 17(7); Whitehead, P.M. 6; Williams, G. 31.

League (69): McCarthy 17, Jewell 16, Reid 6, Duxbury L 5, Torpey 5, McHugh 4, Blake 3, Tinnion 3 (1 pen), Williams 3 (1 pen), Oliver 2, Stapleton 2, Heseltine 1, Hoyle 1, Lawford 1.

Coca Cola Cup (3): Jewell 1, McCarthy 1, Reid 1.

FA Cup (6): Jewell 2, McCarthy 2, Blake 1, Tinnion 1 (pen).

Ground: Valley Parade Ground, Bradford BD8 7DY. Telephone Bradford (0274) 306062 (Office); (0274) 307050 (Ticket Office).

Record attendance: 39,146 v Burnley, FA Cup 4th rd, 11 March 1911.

Manager: Frank Stapleton.

Secretary: Angie Harrison.

Football League: Division 2 Champions – 1907–08. Division 3 Champions – 1984–85. Division 3 (N) Champions – 1928–29.
FA Cup: Winners 1911.
Colours: Claret and amber shirts, black shorts, amber stockings.

BRENTFORD   DIV. 2

Allon, Joseph B.
Bates, Jamie.
Bennett, Michael R.
Benstead, Graham M.
Birch, Paul A.
Blissett, Gary P.
Booker, Robert.
Buckle, Paul J.

Chalmers, Grant L.
Dickens, Alan W.
Evans, Terence W.
Gayle, Marcus A.
Jones, Murray L.
Kruszynski, Zbigniew.
Manuel, William A. J.
Millen, Keith.

Peters, Robert A. A.
Peyton, Gerald J.
Ratcliffe, Simon.
Smillie, Neil.
Statham, Brian.
Stephenson, Paul.
Westley, Shane L. M.

League Appearances: Allon, J.B. 17(7); Bates, J. 24; Bayes, A.J. 2; Bennett, M.R. 34(4); Benstead, G.M. 25; Blissett, G.P. 46; Booker, R. 1(2); Buckle, P.J. 4(1); Chalmers, G.L. 9(2); Dickens, A.W. 13(2); Evans, T.W. 11; Gayle, M.A. 31(7); Godfrey, K. 9(12); Hughton, C. 20; Jones, M.L. 6(10); Kruszynski, Z. 5(1); Luscombe, L.J. 19(10); Manuel, W.A. 39(2); Millen, K. 43; Mortimer, P.H. 6; Peters, R.A. (1); Peyton, G.J. 19; Ratcliffe, S. 25(5); Rostron, J.W. 19; Sansom, K.G. 8; Smillie, N.18(3); Statham, B. 45; Stephenson, P. 11; Westley, S.L. 15(2).
League (52): Blissett 21 (2 pens), Allon 6 (3 pens), Bennett 4, Gayle 4, Millen 4, Luscombe 3, Ratcliffe 2, Chalmers 1, Dickens 1, Manuel 1, Smillie 1, Westley 1, own goals 3.
Coca Cola Cup (7): Blissett 4, Bates 1, Booker 1, Millen 1.
FA Cup (0):
Ground: Griffin Park, Braemar Rd, Brentford, Middlesex TW8 0NT. Telephone 081-847 2511.
Record attendance: 39,626 v Preston NE, FA Cup 6th rd, 5 March 1938.
Manager: David Webb.
Secretary: Polly Kates.
Honours –
Football League: Division 2 Champions – 1934–35. Division 3 Champions – 1991–92. Division 3 (S) Champions – 1932–33. Division 4 Champions – 1962–63.
Colours: Red and white vertical striped shirts, black shorts, red stockings.

BRIGHTON & HOVE ALBION   DIV. 2

Bissett, Nicholas.
Chapman, Ian R.
Clarkson, David J.
Codner, Robert A. G.
Edwards, Matthew D.

Farrington, Mark A.
Funnell, Simon P.
Kennedy, Andrew J.
McCarthy, Paul J.
Munday, Stuart C.

Nogan, Kurt.
Wilkins, Dean M.
Wilkinson, Darron.

League Appearances: Beeney, M.R. 42; Bissett, N. 12; Byrne, J.F. 5(2); Chapman, I.R. 32(2); Chivers, G.P. 43; Codner, R.A. 43; Cotterill, S. 11; Crumplin, J.L. 27(5); Digweed, P.M. 4; Edwards, M.D. 24(9); Farrington, M.A. 3(5); Foster, S.B. 35; Funnell, S.P. (2); Gallacher, B. 14; Kennedy, A.J. 26(4); Macciochi, D.A. (2); McCarthy, P.J. 30; Moulden, P.A. 11; Munday, S.C. 7; Myall, S.T. 7; Nogan, K. 30; Robinson, J.R. 6; Walker, C. 36(2); Wilkins, D.M. 32(3); Wilkinson, D. 26(1).
League (63): Nogan 20, Kennedy 8, Moulden 5, Cotterill 4, Foster 4, Codner 3, Walker 3, Wilkins 3, Wilkinson 3, Byrne 2, Edwards 2, Farrington 2, Chapman 1, Crumplin 1, own goals 2.
Coca Cola Cup (3): Wilkins 2, Edwards 1.
FA Cup (6): Codner 2, Kennedy 2, Crumplin 1, Edwards 1.
Ground: Goldstone Ground, Old Shoreham Rd, Hove, Sussex BN3 7DE. Telephone Brighton (0273) 739535.
Record attendance: 36,747 v Fulham, Division 2, 27 December 1958.
Manager: Barry Lloyd.
Assistant Secretary: Amanda Stewart.
Honours –
Football League: Division 3 (S) Champions – 1957–58. Division 4 Champions – 1964–65.
Colours: Royal blue shirts with white pin stripe, royal blue sleeves, royal blue shorts with white and royal trim, royal blue stockings with red/white trim.

BRISTOL CITY   DIV. 1

Aizlewood, Mark.
Allison, Wayne.
Atteveld, Raymond.
Bent, Junior A.
Benton, Stephen.
Brown, Ian O.
Bryant, Matthew.
Dziekanowski, Dariusz P.
Edwards, Robert W.

Gavin, Mark W.
Harrison, Gerald R.
Kamara, Abdul S. A.
Leaning, Andrew J.
Llewellyn, Andrew D.
McIntyre, James.
Morgan, Nicholas.
Munro, Stuart.
Osman, Russell C.

Pennyfather, Glen J.
Rosenior, Leroy D. G.
Scott, Martin.
Shail, Mark E. D.
Shelton, Gary.
Thompson, David.
Tinnion, Brian.
Welch, Keith J.

League Appearances: Aizlewood, M. 19(1); Allison, W. 22(17); Atteveld, R. 5(2); Bent, J.A. 13(7); Bryant, M. 41; Cole, A.A. 29; Connor, T.F. 2(3); Dziekanowski, D. 24(2); Edwards, R.W. 14(4); Fowler, J.K. (1); Gavin, M.W. 16(3); Harrison, G.R. 24(9); Kristensen, B. 4; Leaning, A.J. 1; Llewellyn, A.D. 12; Melon, M.J. 7(3); Mitchell, C.B. 15(1); Morgan, N. 10; Munro, S. 16; Osman, R.C. 33(1); Pennyfather, G. 14; Reid, N.S. 3(1); Rosenior, L.D. 29(9); Scott, M. 35; Shail, M.E. 3(1); Shelton, G. 42; Thompson, D. 17; Tinnion, B. 11; Welch, K.J. 45.
League (49): Cole 12, Rosenior 7, Allison 4, Shelton 4, Bent 3, Dziekanowski 3, Morgan 3, Scott 3 (2 pens), Tinnion 2 (1 pen), Bryant 1, Gavin 1, Harrison 1, Mellon 1, Pennyfather 1, own goals 3.
Coca Cola Cup (7): Cole 3, Allison 1, Edwards 1, Rosenior 1, Scott 1 (pen).
FA Cup (0):
Ground: Ashton Gate, Bristol BS3 2EJ. Telephone Bristol (0272) 632812 (5 lines).
Record attendance: 43,335 v Preston NE, FA Cup 5th rd, 16 February 1935.
Manager: Russell Osman.

Secretary: Jean Harrison.
Honours – Football League: Division 2 Champions – 1905–06. Division 3 (S)
Champions – 1922–23, 1926–27, 1954–55.
Welsh Cup winners 1934.
Anglo-Scottish Cup: Winners 1977–78.
Freight Rover Trophy winners 1985–86.
Colours: Red shirts, white shorts, red and white stockings.

BRISTOL ROVERS   DIV. 2

Alexander, Ian.	Hardyman, Paul G. T.	Stewart, Marcus P.
Archer, Lee.	Kelly, Gavin J.	Taylor, Gareth K.
Browning, Marcus T.	Maddison, Lee R.	Taylor, John P.
Channing, Justin A.	Mehew, David S.	Tillson, Andrew.
Clark, William R.	Parkin, Brian.	Tovey, Paul W.
Cross, Stephen, C.	Pounder, Antony M.	Waddock, Gary P.
Davis, Michael V.	Reece, Andrew J.	Yates, Steven.
Evans, Richard W.	Saunders, Carl S.	
Gurney, Andrew R.	Skinner, Justin.	

League Appearances: Alexander, I. 41; Archer, L. 1(1); Beasley, A. 1; Browning,
M.T. 17(2); Channing, J.A. 23(2); Clark, W.R. 19(5); Cross, S.C. 6(5); Davis, M.V.
(1); Evans, R.W. 6(5); Hardyman, P.G. 36(1); Jones, V. 12; Kelly, G.J. 19;
Maddison, L.R. 12; Mehew, D.S. 14(10); Moore, K.T. 4; Parkin, B. 26; Pounder,
A.M. 17(1); Reece, A.J. 22(4); Saunders, C.S. 33(8); Skinner, J. 12; Stewart, M.P.
27(11); Taylor, J.P. 39(3); Tillson, A. 29; Twentyman, G. 7(1).
League (55): Taylor 14, Saunders 11 (1 pen), Stewart 11 (2 pens), Hardyman 4,
Channing 3, Mehew 3, Reece 2, Alexander 1, Archer 1, Browning 1, Clark 1, Davis
1, Moore 1, Pounder 1.
Coca Cola Cup (1): Reece 1.
FA Cup (1): Browning 1.
Ground: Twerton Park, Twerton, Bath. Telephone: 0272 352508.
Record attendance: 9464 v Liverpool, FA Cup 4th rd, 8 February 1992 (Twerton
Park). 38,472 v Preston NE, FA Cup 4th rd, 30 January 1960 (Eastville).
Manager: John Ward.
Secretary: R. C. Twyford.
Honours –
Football League: Division 3 (S) Champions – 1952–53. Division 3 Champions –
1989–90.
Colours: Blue and white quartered shirts, white shorts, blue stockings with two white
rings on top.

BURNLEY   DIV. 2

Beresford, Marlon.	Conroy, Michael K.	Dowell, Wayne A.
Campbell, David A.	Davis, Stephen M.	Eli, Roger.
Clayton, John.	Deary, John S.	Farrell, Andrew J.

Francis, John A.   McKenzie, Paul.   Pickering, Nicholas.
Harper, Steven J.   Measham, Ian.   Randall, Adrian J.
Heath, Adrian P.   Monington, Mark D.   Thompson, Leslie.
Howarth, Neil.   Mullin, John.   Welch, Brian J.
Lancashire, Graham.   Painter, Peter R.   Williams, David P.
Livingstone, Richard.   Pender, John P.   Wilson, Paul A.
McKay, Paul W.   Penny, Steven A.   Yates, Mark J.

League Appearances: Beresford, M. 44; Campbell, D.A. 7(1); Clayton, J. 3; Conroy, M.K. 38(1); Davis, S.M. 37; Deary, J.S. 32; Donowa, B.L. 4; Eli, R. 2(9); Farrell, A.J. 40(2); Francis, J.A. 9; Harper, S.J. 33(1); Heath, A.P. 43; Jakub, Y. 31(1); Lancashire, G. 2(1); Measham, I. 39; Monington, M.D. 22(9); Mooney, B.J. 6; Painter, P.R. 7(10); Palin, L. 1; Pender, J.P. 44; Penny, S.A. 10(1); Pickering, N. 4; Randall, A.J. 19(4); Slawson, S.M. 5; Sonner, D.J. (1); Thompson, L. 2(1); Williams, D.P. 2; Wilson, P.A. 20; Yates, M.J. (1).
League (57): Heath 19 (2 pens), Conroy 6, Harper 5, Farrell 4, Pender 4, Deary 3, Penney 3, Davis 2, Monington 2, Slawson 2, Clayton 1, Francis 1, Randall 1, own goals 4.
Coca Cola Cup (2): Pender 1, Sonner 1.
FA Cup (9): Conroy 3, Heath 3, Monington 1, Pender 1, own goal 1.
Ground: Turf Moor, Burnley BB10 4BX. Telephone Burnley (0282) 427777.
Record attendance: 54,775 v Huddersfield T, FA Cup 3rd rd, 23 February 1924.
Manager: Jimmy Mullen.
Secretary: Mark Blackbourne.
Honours –
Football League: Division 1 Champions – 1920–21, 1959–60. **Division 2 Champions** – 1897–98, 1972–73. **Division 3 Champions** – 1981–82. **Division 4 Champions** – 1991–92.
FA Cup winners 1913–14.
Anglo Scottish Cup: Winners 1978–79.
Colours: Claret shirts with sky blue sleeves, white shorts and stockings.

BURY   DIV. 3

Adekola, David.   Kearney, Mark J.   Rigby, Antony A.
Anderson, Lee C.   Kelly, Gary A.   Robinson, Spencer L.
Daws, Nicholas J.   Knill, Alan R.   Stanislaus, Roger E. P.
Gorton, Andrew W.   Lyons, Darren P.   Stevens, Ian D.
Hughes, Ian.   Mauge, Ronald C.   Valentine, Peter.
Hulme, Kevin.   Reid, Andrew.   Ward, Derek.

League Appearances: Adekola, D. 14(2); Anderson, L.C. 13; Branch, G. 3(1); Daws, N.J. 35(1); Esdaille, D. 1(5); Fitzpatrick, P.J. 8(1); Gardner, S.G. 1; Greenhalgh, L. 2; Hughes, I. 11(4); Hulme, K. 32; Kearney, M.J. 37(2); Kelly, G.A. 42; Kilner, A.W. 4(1); Knill, A.R. 38; Lyons, D.P. 14(12); Mauge, R.C. 12(1); McKee, C. 2; Mike, A.R. 5(2); Morris, P.I. (1); Norman, J. 1(1); Reid, A. 25(4); Rigby, A.A. 21; Robertson, P. 3; Robinson, S.L. 14; Scott, I. 7(2); Sonner, D.J. 5; Stanislaus, R.E. 23(1); Stevens, I.D. 28(4); Valentine, P. 35(1); Ward, D. 25; White, E.W. 1(1).

18

League (63): Stevens 14, Hulme 9, Adekola 8, Robinson 6 (1 pen), Knill 5 (2 pens), Lyons 3, Sonner 3, Valentine 3, Kearney 2, Rigby 2, Scott 2, Branch 1, Daws 1, Kilner 1, Mauge 1, Mike 1, own goal 1.
Coca Cola Cup (6): Hulme 2, Valentine 2, Kearney 1, Robinson 1.
FA Cup (4): Hulme 1, Knill 1 (pen), Mauge 1, Robinson 1 (pen).
Ground: Gigg Lane, Bury BL9 9HR. Telephone 061-764 4881.
Record attendance: 35,000 v Bolton W, FA Cup 3rd rd, 9 January 1960.
Manager: Mike Walsh.
Assistant Secretary: J. Neville.
Honours – Football League: Division 2 Champions – 1894–95. Division 3 Champions – 1960–61.
FA Cup winners 1900, 1903.
Colours: White shirts, navy blue shorts, navy stockings.

CAMBRIDGE UNITED   DIV. 2

Bartlett, Kevin F.
Butler, Stephen.
Chapple, Philip R.
Cheetham, Micahel M.
Claridge, Stephen E.
Clayton, Gary.
Daish, Liam S.
Danzey, Michael J.

Dennis, John A.
Fensome, Andrew B.
Fowler, John A.
Heathcote, Michael.
Kimble, Alan F.
Leadbitter, Christopher J.
Lyne, Neil G. F.
O'Shea, Daniel E.

Parkhill, Philip R. B.
Raynor, Paul J.
Rowett, Gary.
Sheffield, Jonathan.
Smeeth, Jamie F.
Wilkins, Richard J.

League Appearances: Ainsworth, G. 1(3); Atkins, I.L. 1(1); Bartlett, K.F. 3(5); Butler, S. 23; Chapple, P.R. 16(2); Cheetham, M.M. 16(1); Claridge, S.E. 29; Clayton, G. 34(2); Daish, S.L. 15(1); Danzey, M.J. 1(1); Dennis, J.A. 12(4); Fensome, A.B. 27(3); Filan, J.R. 6; Fowler, J.A. 2(1); Francis J.A. 15(14); Heathcote, M. 42; Kimble, A.F. 46; Leadbitter, C. 34(4); Lyne, N.G. 5(9); McGlashan, J. (1); Norbury, M.S. 7(5); O'Shea, D.E. 37; Patmore, W.J. 1; Philpott, L. 16; Raynor, P.J. 41; Rowett, G. 17(4); Rush, M.J. 4(6); Sheffield, J. 13; Vaughan, J. 27; White, D.W. 14(6); Wilkins, R.J. 1.
League (48): Claridge 7, Butler 6, Leadbitter 6, Kimble 4 (4 pens), White 4, Clayton 3, Francis 3, Chapple 2, Heathcote 2, Philpott 2, Raynor 2, Rowett 2, Ainsworth 1, Bartlett 1, Dennis 1, Norbury 1, own goal 1.
Coca Cola Cup (10): Clayton 2, Chapple 1, Danzey 1, Fowler 1, Francis 1, Heathcote 1, Philpott 1, Rowett 1, White 1.
FA Cup (1): Heathcote 1.
Ground: Abbey Stadium, Newmarket Rd, Cambridge. Telephone (0223) 566500.
Record attendance: 14,000 v Chelsea, Friendly, 1 May 1970.
Manager: Gary Johnson.
Secretary: Steve Greenall.
Honours – Football League: Division 3 Champions – 1990–91. Division 4 Champions – 1976–77.
Colours: Amber & black striped shirts, black shorts with amber & black trim, black & amber stockings.

CARDIFF CITY   DIV. 2

Baddeley, Lee M.
Blake, Nathan A.
Brazil, Derek M.
Dale, Carl.
Grew, Mark.

Griffith, Cohen.
James, Robert M.
Millar, William P.
Perry, Jason.
Ramsey, Paul.

Richardson, Nicholas J.
Searle, Damon P.
Stant, Philip.
Ward, Gavin J.
Williams, William J.

League Appearances: Baddeley, L.M. 7(1); Bird, A. 3(6); Blake, N.A. 30(4); Brazil, D.M. 33(1); Dale, C. 19(1); Gibbins, R.G. 1(7); Gorman, A.D. 1; Grew, M. 10; Griffith, C. 28(6); James, R.M. 42; Kelly, A.O. 5; Matthews, N.P. 12(2); Millar, W.P. 30(3); Perry, J. 38(1); Pike, C. 20(8); Ramsey, P. 30; Ratcliffe, K. 19; Richardson, N. 36(3); Searle, D.P. 42; Stant, P. 24; Ward, G.J. 32; Williams, W.J. (1).
League (77): Pike 12 (4 pens), Blake 11, Stant 11, Griffith 10, Dale 8, Ramsey 4 (3 pens), Richardson 4, Millar 3, Perry 3, James 2, Bird 1, Gorman 1, Kelly 1, Matthews 1, Ratcliffe 1, Searle 1, own goals 3.
Coca Cola Cup (2): Dale 2.
FA Cup (2): Blake 1, Millar 1.
Ground: Ninian Park, Cardiff CF1 8SX. Telephone Cardiff (0222) 398636.
Record attendance: 61,566, Wales v England, 14 October 1961.
Manager: Eddie May.
Secretary: Jim Finney.
Honours –
Football League: Division 3 (S) Champions – 1946–47.
FA Cup winners 1926–27 (only occasion the Cup has been won by a club outside England).
Welsh Cup winners 21 times.
Colours: All blue.

CARLISLE UNITED   DIV. 3

Craig, Antony.
Davey, Simon.
Edmondson, Darren S.
Holden, Steven A.

McCreery, David.
Oghani, George W.
Ohanlon, Kelham G.
Potts, Craig.

Proudlock, Paul.
Thorpe, Jeffrey R.
Walling, Dean A.
Walsh, Derek.

League Appearances: Arnold, I. 26(3); Barnsley, A. 25(2); Burgess, D.J. 6; Caig, A. 1; Connelly, D. (3); Dalziel, I. 11(1); Davey, S. 38; Delap, R.J. (1); Edmondson, D.S. 33(1); Finley, A.J. 1; Gabbiadini, R. 18(6); Gallimore, A. 8; Hawke, W.R. 8; Holden, S.A. 21; Holliday, J.R. 2; Holmes, M.A. 18(1); Hopper, T. 1; Knight, I.J. 1; McCreery, D. 19(3); Oghani, G.W. 37(2); O'Hanlon, K.G. 41; Potts, C. 6(2); Prins, J. 2(7); Proudlock, P. 24(2); Sendall, R.A. (10); Thorpe, J.R. 28; Walling, D.A. 21(2); Walsh, D. 20(4); Watson, A.A. 21; White, E.W. 6; Williams, N.J. 19.
League (51): Oghani 15, Watson 8, Arnold 6 (2 pens), Davey 5, Gabbiadini 3, Proudlock 3, Barnsley 2 (1 pen), Hawke 2, Gallimore 1, Holden 1, Sendall 1, Walsh 1, Williams 1, own goals 2.

Coca Cola Cup (7): Barnsley 2 (2 pens), Gabbiadini 2, Edmondson 1, Oghani 1, Watson 1.

FA Cup (1): Arnold 1.

Ground: Brunton Park, Carlisle CA1 1LL. Telephone Carlisle (0228) 26237.

Record attendance: 27,500 v Birmingham C, FA Cup 3rd rd, 5 January 1957 and v Middlesbrough, FA Cup 5th rd, 7 February 1970.

Player-coach: David McCreery.

Secretary: Phillip Vine.

Honours – Football League: Division 3 Champions – 1964–65.

Colours: Blue shirts, white shorts, blue stockings.

CHARLTON ATHLETIC   DIV. 1

Balmer, Stuart M.	Gritt, Stephen J.	Primus, Linvoy S.
Bolder, Robert.	Leaburn, Carl W.	Robinson, John R. C.
Curbishley, Llewellyn.	Minto, Scott C.	Salmon, Michael B.
Garland, Peter J.	Nelson, Garry P.	Walsh, Colin D.
Gorman, Paul M.	Pardew, Alan S.	Webster, Simon P.
Grant, Kim T.	Pitcher, Darren, E. J.	

League Appearances: Bacon, P.D. 14(4); Balmer, S.M. 42(3); Barness, A. 5; Bolder, R. 27; Bumstead, J. 18(2); Curbishley, L. 1; Dyer, A.C. 23(7); Garland, P.J. 10(3); Gatting, S.P. 31(1); Gorman, P.M. 5(5); Grant, K.T. 11(10); Gritt, S.J. 4(3); Houghton, S.A. 6; Leaburn, C.W. 28(11); Lee, R.M. 7; Linger, P.H. (2); Minto, S.C. 34(2); Nelson, G.P. 39(5); Newton, S.O. 2; Pardew, A.S. 29(1); Pitcher, D.E. 40(1); Power, L.M. 5; Primus, L.S. 4; Robinson, J.R. 15; Salmon, M.B. 19; Sturgess, P.C. 1(3); Walsh, C.D. 42; Warden, D. 1(2); Webster, S.P. 43.

League (49): Pardew 9 (2 pens), Dyer 6, Nelson 6, Leaburn 5, Bumstead 3, Balmer 2, Gatting 2, Gorman 2, Grant 2, Pitcher 2, Robinson 2, Webster 2, Garland 1, Lee 1, Minto 1, Walsh 1, own goals 2.

Coca Cola Cup (0):

FA Cup (2): Nelson 1, Pitcher 1 (pen).

Ground: The Valley, Floyd Road, Charlton, London SE7 8BL. Telephone 081–859 8888.

Record attendance: 75,031 v Aston Villa, FA Cup 5th rd, 12 February 1938 (at The Valley).

Managers: Steve Gritt and Alan Curbishley.

Secretary: Chris Parkes.

Honours –

Football League: Division 3 (S) Champions – 1928–29, 1934–35.

FA Cup winners 1947.

Colours: Red shirts, white shorts, red stockings.

CHELSEA   FA PREMIER

Barnard, Darren S.	Beasant, David.	Cascarino, Anthony G.
Barness, Anthony.	Burley, Craig W.	Clarke, Stephen.

Colgan, Nicholas V.
Donaghy, Malachy.
Elliott, Paul M.
Fleck, Robert.
Hall, Gareth D.
Hitchcock, Kevin.
Hopkin, David.
Johnsen, Erland.

Kharine, Dmitri V.
Lee, David J.
Livingstone, Stephen.
Matthew, Damian.
Myers, Andrew.
Newton, Edward J. I.
Pearce, Ian A.
Rowe, Ezekiel B.

Shipperley, Neil J.
Sinclair, Frank M.
Spackman, Nigel.
Spencer, John.
Stuart, Graham C.
Townsend, Andrew D.
Wise, Dennis F.

League Appearances: Allon, J.B. 1(2); Barnard, D.S. 8(5); Barness, A. 2; Beasant, D. 17; Burley, C.W. 1(2); Cascarino, A. 8(1); Clarke, S. 18(2); Donaghy, M. 39(1); Elliott, P.M. 7; Fleck, R. 28(3); Hall, G.D. 36(1); Harford, M.G. 27(1); Hitchcock, K. 20; Hopkin, D. 2(2); Johnsen, E. 13; Jones, V. P. 7; Kharine, D.V. 5; Lee, D.J. 23(2); Le Saux, G.P. 10(4); Livingstone, S. (1); Matthew, D. 3(1); Myers, A. 3; Newton, E.J. 32(2); Pearce, I.A. (1); Peyton, G.J. (1); Shipperley, N.J. 2(1); Sinclair, F.M. 32; Spackman, N. 6; Spencer, J. 13(10); Stuart, G.C. 31(8); Townsend, A.D. 41; Wise, D.F. 27.

League (51): Harford 9, Stuart 9, Spencer 7, Newton 5, Townsend 4, Wise 3 (1 pen), Cascarino 2, Donaghy 2, Fleck 2, Hall 2, Lee 2, Barnard 1, Jones 1, Shipperley 1, own goal 1.

Coca Cola Cup (10): Townsend 3, Harford 2, Fleck 1 (pen), Newton 1, Sinclair 1, Stuart 1, Wise 1.

FA Cup (1): own goal 1.

Ground: Stamford Bridge, London SW6. Telephone 071-385 5545.

Record attendance: 82,905 v Arsenal, Division 1, 12 Oct 1935.

Manager: Glenn Hoddle.

Secretary: Yvonne Todd.

Honours –

Football League: Division 1 Champions – 1954–55.

FA Cup winners 1970.

Football League Cup winners 1964–65.

Full Members' Cup winners 1985–86. **Zenith Data Systems Cup winners** 1989–90.

European Cup-Winners' Cup winners 1970–71.

Colours: Royal blue shirts and shorts, white stockings.

CHESTER CITY   DIV. 3

Barrow, Graham.
Bishop, Edward M.
Came, Mark R.
Hinnigan, Joseph P.

Lightfoot, Christopher I.
Preece, Roger.
Pugh, David.
Rimmer, Stuart A.

Stewart, William I.
Wheeler, Paul.
Whelan, Spencer R.

League Appearances: Abel, G. 28(5); Albiston, A.R. 23(1); Barrow, G. 32(1); Bishop, E.M. 25(4); Butler, B.G. 30(1); Came, M.R. 17; Comstive, P.T. 27(2); Garnett, S.M. 9; Goodwin, C. 3(2); Keeley, J.H. 4; Kelly, J. 24(7); Lightfoot, C. 39; Limbert, M. 12(2); Morton, N. 20(7); Preece, R. 23; Pugh, D. 35; Rimmer, S.A. 43(7); Ryan, D.T. 5(12); Stewart, W.I. 42; Thompson, D.S. 30(9); Wheeler, P. 11(3); Whelan, S.R. 24(4).

League (49): Rimmer 20 (3 pens), Bishop 6, Pugh 5, Morton 4, Comstive 3 (1 pen), Thompson 3, Barrow 2, Lightfoot 2, Ryan 2, Abel 1, Kelly 1.

22

Coca Cola Cup (2): Bishop 1, Comstive 1.
FA Cup (1): Ryan 1.
Ground: The Deva Stadium, Bumpers Lane, Chester. Telephone Chester (0244) 371376, 371809.
Record attendance: 20,500 v Chelsea, FA Cup 3rd rd (replay), 16 January, 1952 (at Sealand Road).
Manager: Graham Barrow.
Secretary: R. A. Allan.
Honours –
Welsh Cup winners 1908, 1933, 1947. **Debenhams Cup: Winners** 1977.
Colours: Royal blue shirts, white shorts, blue stockings, white trim.

CHESTERFIELD   DIV. 3

Brien, Anthony J.	Kennedy, Michael F.	Norris, Stephen M.
Carr, Clifford P.	Leonard, Michael C.	Rogers, Lee J.
Cash, Stuart P.	Marples, Christopher.	Turnbull, Lee M.
Dyche, Sean M.	McGugan, Paul J.	Whitehead, Scott A.
Hebberd, Trevor N.	Morris, Andrew D.	Williams, Steven B.

League Appearances: Brien, A.J. 39; Carr, C.P. 42; Cash, S.P. 23; Clarke, N.J. 7; Davidson, J. (1); Dyche, S.M. 18(2); Falana, W.R. 4(1); Fee, G.P. 10; Hebberd, T.N. 31(1); Kennedy, M.F. 19(8); Kopel, S. 1; Lancaster, D. 39(1); Lemon, P.A. 28(3); Leonard, M.C. 17; Marples, C. 25; McGugan, P.J. 13; Morris, A.D. 31(9); Norris, S.M. 28(2); Rogers, L.J. 29(6); Smith, M. 6: Turnbull, L.M. 27(6); Whitehead, S.A. 1(3); Williams, S.B. 24(7).
League (59): Norris 11, Morris 10, Lancaster 9, Turnbull 8 (3 pens), Lemon 6, Williams 5, McGugan 2, Brien 1, Carr 1, Dyche 1, Hebberd 1, Kennedy 1, Rogers 1, Smith 1, own goal 1.
Coca Cola Cup (7): Norris 3, Lancaster 2, Hebberd 1, Morris 1.
FA Cup (2): Turnbull 1, Williams 1 (pen).
Ground: Recreation Ground, Chesterfield S40 4SX. Telephone Chesterfield (0246) 209765.
Record attendance: 30,968 v Newcastle U, Division 2, 7 April 1939.
Manager: John Duncan.
Secretary: Miss N. J. Hodgson.
Honours –
Football League: Division 3 (N) Champions – 1930–31, 1935–36. **Division 4 Champions** – 1969–70, 1984–85.
Anglo-Scottish Cup winners 1980–81.
Colours: Blue shirts, white shorts, blue stockings.

COLCHESTER UNITED   DIV. 3

Ball, Steven J.	Cawley, Peter.	Donald, Warren.
Bennett, Gary.	Cook, Jason P.	English, Anthony K.

Grainger, Martin R.   McDonough, Roy.   Roberts, Paul.
Kinsella, Mark A.   McGavin, Steven J.   Smith, Nicholas L.

League Appearances: Abrahams, P. 9(14); Ball, S.J. 19(5); Barber, F. 10; Bennett, G. 30(8); Betts, S.R. 23; Cawley, P. 22(2); Cook, J.P. 30(4); Devereux, R. 3(3); Donald, W. 8(2); Emberson, C.W. 13; English, A.K. 30(3); Flowers, P.A. 2(1); Grainger, M.R. 28(3); Green, R.R. 4; Hazel, J.E. 2; Hopkins, R.A. 13(1); Kinsella, M.A. 37(1); Martin, D. 8; McDonough, R. 21(4); McGavin, S.J. 35(2); Munson, N.W. 1; Newell, P.C. 14; Oxbrow, D.W. 12(4); Partner, A.N. (1); Phillips, I.A. (1); Roberts, P. 42; Smith, N.L. 42; Sorrell, A.C. 4(1).

League (67): McDonough 9 (3 pens), McGavin 9, Bennett 8, Abrahams 6, Kinsella 6, Ball 4 (1 pen), Oxbrow 4, Smith 4, Cawley 3, Grainger 3 (1 pen), Martin 2, Cook 1, English 1, Hopkins 1, Roberts 1, Sorrell 1, own goals 4.

Coca Cola Cup (1): English 1.

FA Cup (7): Ball 3, Bennett 2, McGavin 1, Sorrell 1.

Ground: Layer Rd Ground, Colchester.

Record attendance: 19,072 v Reading, FA Cup 1st rd, 27 Nov, 1948.

Player-coach: Roy McDonough.

Secretary: Sue Smith.

Honours –

GM Vauxhall Conference winners 1991–92. **FA Trophy winners** 1991–92.

Colours: Blue shirts, white shorts with blue band, blue stockings with white band.

COVENTRY CITY   FA PREMIER

Atherton, Peter.   Gould, Jonathan A.   Rennie, David.
Babb, Phil.   Hurst, Lee J.   Roberts, Brian L.
Billing, Peter G.   Jenkinson, Leigh.   Robson, Stewart I.
Boland, Willie J.   McGrath, Lloyd A.   Sheridan, Anthony, J.
Booty, Martyn J.   Ndlovu, Peter.   Stephenson, Michael J.
Borrows, Brian.   Ogrizovic, Steven.   Wegerle, Roy C.
Busst, David J.   Pearce, Andrew J.   Williams, John N.
Flynn, Sean.   Quinn, Michael.   Woods, Raymond.

League Appearances: Atherton, P. 39; Babb, P. 27(7); Billing, P.G. 3; Boland, W.J. (1); Borrows, B. 36(2); Busst, D.J. 10; Fleming, T.M. 8(3); Flynn, S. 4(3); Gallacher, K.W. 19(1); Gould, J.A. 9; Greenman, C. 1(1); Gynn, M. 18(2); Hurst, L.J. 35; Jenkinson, L. 2(3); McGrath, L.A. 20(5); Middleton, C.D. 1; Ndlovu, P. 27(5); Ogrizovic, S. 33; Pearce, A.J. 21(3); Quinn, M. 26; Rennie, D. 9; Robson, S.I. 14(1); Rosario, R.M. 28; Rowland, K. (2); Sansom, K.G. 21; Sheridan, A.J. 1; Smith, D. 6; Wegerle, R.C. 5(1); Williams, J.N. 38(3); Williams, P.A. 1(1).

League (52): Quinn 17 (1 pen), Williams 8, Ndlovu 7, Gallacher 6, Rosario 4, Borrows 2 (1 pen), Gynn 2, Hurst 2, Pearce 1, Smith 1, own goals 2.

Coca Cola Cup (2): Borrows 1 (pen), Ndlovu.

FA Cup (0):

Ground: Highfield Road Stadium, King Richard Street, Coventry CV2 4FW.

Telephone (General Enquiries): (0203) 2223535.

Record attendance: 51,455 v Wolverhampton W, Division 2, 29 April 1967.

Team manager: Bobby Gould.

Secretary: Graham Hover.
Honours – Football League: Division 2 Champions – 1966–67. Division 3 Champions – 1963–64. Division 3 (S) Champions 1935–36.
FA Cup winners 1986–87.
Colours: All Sky blue.

CREWE ALEXANDRA   DIV. 3

Annon, Richard.
Carr, Darren.
Clark, Martin A.
Clarkson, Philip I.
Edwards, Robert.
Evans, Stewart J.
Gardiner, Mark C.
Garvey, Stephen H.

Hughes, Anthony B.
Jackson, Michael J.
Lennon, Neil F.
Lyons, Andrew.
Macauley, Steven R.
McKearney, David J.
Naylor, Anthony J.
Rushton, Paul.

Smith, Gareth S.
Tierney, Francis.
Walters, Steven P.
Ward, Ashley, S.
Whalley, Gareth.
Wilson, Eugene.
Woodward, Andrew S.

League Appearances: Adebola, D. (6); Annon, R. 8(1); Carr, D. 31(1); Clarkson, P.I. 32(3); Duffield, P. (2); Edwards, R. 17(6); Evans, S.J. 22(4); Gardiner, M.C. 11(2); Garvey, S.H. 3(7); Greygoose, D. 30; Harvey, J. 16(1); Hignett, C. 14; Hughes, A.B. 14(3); Jackson, M.J. 4; Kite, P.D. 5; Lennon, N.F. 23(1); Lyons, A. 6(3); Macauley, S.R. 25; McKearney, D.J. 28(1); Mettioui, A. 1(2); Naylor, A.J. 35; Smith, G.S. 29(7); Smith, M.A. 7; Tierney, F. (1); Vaughan, J.D. 3(4); Walters, S.P. 23; Ward, A.S. 18(2); Whalley, G. 22(3); Wilson, E. 35; Woodward, A.S. (6).
League (75): Naylor 16, Clarkson 13, Hignett 8 (1 pen), Edwards 7, McKearney 6 (2 pens), Smith 4 (1 pen) Ward 4, Macauley 3, Walters 3, Carr 2, Lyons 2, Evans 1, Gardiner 1, Garvey 1, Hughes 1, Whalley 1, own goals 2.
Coca Cola Cup (8): Hignett 3, Naylor 2, Clarkson 1, Garvey 1, Harvey 1.
FA Cup (15): Hignett 4, McKearney 3 (1 pen), Clarkson 2, Naylor 2, Whalley 2, Carr 1, Edwards 1.
Ground: Football Ground, Gresty Rd, Crewe. Telephone Crewe (0270) 213014.
Record attendance: 20,000 v Tottenham H, FA Cup 4th rd, 30 January 1960.
Manager: Dario Gradi.
Secretary: Mrs Gill Palin.
Honours –
Welsh Cup: Winners 1936, 1937.
Colours: Red shirts, white shorts, red stockings.

CRYSTAL PALACE   DIV. 1

Armstrong, Christopher.
Barnes, Andrew J.
Bowry, Robert.
Coleman, Christopher.
Edwards, Russell J.

Glass, James R.
Gordon, Dean D.
Hawthorne, Mark D.
Holman, Mark B.
Humphrey, John.

Martyn, Antony N.
Massey, Stuart A.
McGoldrick, Eddie J. P.
Mortimer, Paul H.
Ndah, George E.

Newman, Richard A.
O'Connor, Martyn J.
Osborn, Simon E.
O'Connor, Martin J.
Patterson, Darren J.
Rodger, Simon L.
Salako, John A.

Shaw, Richard E.
Sinnott, Lee.
Smith, Eric.
Southgate, Gareth.
Thomas, Geoffrey R.
Thompson, Niall J.
Thorn, Andrew C.

Watts, Grant S.
Whyte, David A.
Williams, Paul A.
Woodman, Andrew J.
Young, Eric.

League Appearances: Armstrong, C. 35; Bowry, R. 6(5); Bright, M.A. 5; Coleman, C. 31(7); Collymore, S. (2); Gordon, D.D. 6(4); Humphrey, J. 28(4); Martyn, A.N. 42; Massey, S.A. (1); McGoldrick, E.J. 42; Ndah, G.E. 4(9); Newman, R.A. 1(1); Osborn, S.E. 27(4); Rodger, S.L. 22(1); Salako, J.A. 12(1); Shaw, R.E. 32(1); Sinnott, L. 18(1); Southgate, G. 33; Thomas, G.R. 28(1); Thorn, A.C. 34; Watts, G.S. 2(2); Williams, P.A. 15(3); Young, E. 38.
League (48): Armstrong 15, McGoldrick 8, Young 6, Coleman 5, Southgate 3, Osborn 2, Rodger 2, Thomas 2, Bowry 1, Bright 1, Thorn 1, own goals 2.
Coca Cola Cup (13): Coleman 2, McGoldrick 2, Salako 2, Southgate 2, Watts 2, Ndah 1, Osborn 1 (pen), Thorn 1.
FA Cup (0):
Ground: Selhurst Park, London SE25 6PU. Telephone 081–653 1000.
Record attendance: 51,482 v Burnley, Division 2, 11 May 1979.
Team Manager: Alan Smith.
Club Secretary: Mike Hurst.
Honours –
Football League: Division 2 Champions – 1978–79. **Division 3 (S)** 1920–21.
Zenith Data Systems Cup winners 1991.
Colours: Red and blue shirts, red shorts, red stockings.

DARLINGTON   DIV. 3

Ball, Stephen.
Dobie, Mark W. G.
Dowson, Alan P.
Ellison, Anthony L.
Gaughen, Steven E.

Gregan, Sean M.
Isaacs, Anthony.
Juryeff, Ian M.
Mardenborough,
Stephen A.

O'Shaughnessy, Stephen.
Prudhoe, Mark.
Shaw, Simon R.
Sunley, Mark.
Toman, James A.

League Appearances: Ball, S. 15(7); Dobie, M.W. 35(1); Dobson, P. 4(10); Dowson, A.P. 30(2); Ellison, A.L. 2(1); Fickling, A. 14; Gaughen, S.E. 34(3); Gregan, S.M. 15(2); Hinchley, G. 7; Isaacs, A. 17(5); Juryeff, I.M. 25(8); Maddick, K.A. (1); Mardenborough, S. 41(1); O'Shaughnessy, S. 41; Parkin, T.J. 40; Pickering, N. 28; Prudhoe, M. 42; Reed, J.P. 8(2); Shaw, S.R. 19(4); Smith, K. 13; Sunley, M. 2; Toman, J.A. 22(7); Tupling, S. 8(3).
League (48): Mardenborough 11, Dobie 8 (1 pen), Juryeff 6, Shaw 4, Ball 2, Dobson 2, Parkin 2, Pickering 2, Reed 2, Gaughan 1, Gregan 1, Hinchley 1, Isaacs 1, O'Shaughnessy 1, Toman 1, own goals 3.
Coca Cola Cup (1): Mardenborough 1.
FA Cup (1): Dobie 1.

Ground: Feethams Ground, Darlington. Telephone Darlington (0325) 465097.
Record attendance: 21,023 v Bolton W, League Cup 3rd rd, 14 November 1960.
Manager: Billy McEwan.
Secretary: Brian Anderson.
Honours –
Football League: Division 3 (N) Champions – 1924–25. Division 4 Champions – 1990–91.
Colours: Black and white.

DERBY COUNTY   DIV. 1

Carsley, Lee K.
Chalk, Martyn P. G.
Coleman, Simon.
Comyn, Andrew J.
Forsyth, Michael E.
Gabbiadini, Marco.
Goulooze, Richard.
Hadley, Stewart.
Hayward, Steve L.
Johnson, Thomas.
Kavanagh, Jason C.

Kitson, Paul.
Kuhl, Martin.
McMinn, Kevin C.
Nicholson, Shane M.
Patterson, Mark.
Pembridge, Mark A.
Philips, Justin L.
Ramage, Craig D.
Richardson, Paul A.
Round, Stephen.
Sage, Melvyn.

Short, Craig J.
Simpson, Paul D.
Stallard, Mark.
Sturridge, Dean C.
Sutton, Stephen J.
Sutton, Wayne F.
Taylor, Martin J.
Thomson, Jon M.
Wassall, Darren P.
Williams, Paul D.

League Appearances: Coleman, S. 17(8); Comyn, A.J. 13(4); Forsyth, M.E. 41; Gabbiadini, M. 42(2); Goulooze, R. 7(5); Hayward, S.L. 6(1); Johnson, T. 34(1); Kavanagh, J.C. 10; Kitson, P. 44; Kuhl, M. 32; McMinn, K.C. 6(13); Micklewhite, G. 4(2); Nicholson, S.M. 17; Patterson, M. 17(1); Pembridge, M.A. 42; Ramage, C.D. (1); Round, S. 6; Short, C.J. 38; Simpson, P.D. 32(3); Stallard, M. 1(4); Sturridge, D.C. 8(2); Sutton, S.J. 25; Taylor, M.J. 21; Wassall, D.P. 24; Williams, P.D. 19.
League (68): Kitson 17, Simpson 12 (2 pens), Gabbiadini 9, Johnson 8, Pembridge 8 (3 pens), Williams 4, Short 3, McMinn 2, Forsyth 1, Hayward 1, Kuhl 1, own goals 2.
Coca Cola Cup (9): Simpson 3 (1 pen), Gabbiadini 2, Johnson 1, Kitson 1, Pembridge 1 (pen), own goals 1.
FA Cup (13): Short 4, Pembridge 3, Gabbiadini 2, Kitson 1, Nicholson 1, Williams 1, own goal 1.
Ground: Baseball Ground, Shaftesbury Crescent, Derby DE3 8NB. Telephone Derby (0332) 40105.
Record attendance: 41,826 v Tottenham H, Division 1, 20 September 1969.
Manager: Arthur Cox.
Secretary/General Manager: Michael Dunford.
Honours –
Football League: Division 1 Champions – 1971–72, 1974–75. Division 2 Champions – 1911–12, 1914–15, 1968–69, 1986–87. Division 3 (N) 1956–57.
FA Cup winners 1945–46.
Colours: White shirts, black shorts, white stockings.

DONCASTER ROVERS   DIV. 3

Bennett, Craig.   Heritage, Peter M.   Jeffrey, Michael R.
Crosby, Andrew K.   Hewitt, James R.   Prindiville, Steven A.
Cullen, David J.   Hicks, Stuart J.
Gormley, Edward J.   Hine, Mark.

League Appearances: Bennett, C. 1; Brady, K. 4; Crichton, P.A. 41; Crosby, A.K.
26(3); Douglas, C.F. 12(9); Falana, W.R. 2(2); Gilzean, I.R. 3; Gormley, E.J. 41;
Heritage, P.M. 25(6); Hewitt, J.R. 27; Hicks, S.J. 36; Hine, M. 18(7); Hodder, S.J.
1(1); Hodson, S.P. 15; Jeffrey, M.R. 29(1); Kabia, J. 5; Masefield, P.D. 8(1);
Morrow, G.R. 17(6); Moss, D. 9; Prindiville, S. 42; Quinlan, P.E. 2(7); Reddish, S.
27(4); Reece, P.J. 1; Richards, S.C. 36(2); Roberts, J.S. 1(1); Rowe, B. 21(4); Taylor,
C.D. 2; White, C. 6; White, E.W. 4
League (42): Jeffrey 12 (3 pens), Gormley 6 (1 pen), Morrow 4, Brady 3 (2 pens),
Richards 3, Moss 3, Heritage 2, Prindiville 2, White W 2, Douglas 1, Hine 1,
Reddish 1, Rowe 1, own goal 1.
Coca Cola Cup (1): Hewitt 1.
FA Cup (1): Quinlan 1.
Ground: Belle Vue Ground, Doncaster. Telephone Doncaster (0302) 539441.
Record attendance: 37,149 v Hull C, Division 3 (N), 2 October 1948.
Manager: Steve Beaglehole.
Secretary: Mrs K. J. Oldale.
Honours –
Football League: Division 3 (N) Champions – 1934–35, 1946–47, 1949–50. Division
4 Champions – 1965–66, 1968–69.
Colours: White shirts with red lightning stripes, red shorts, red stockings.

EVERTON   FA PREMIER

Ablett, Gary I.   Holmes, Paul.   Radosavljevic, Predrag.
Barlow, Stuart.   Horne, Barry.   Rideout, Paul.
Beagrie, Peter S.   Jackson, Matthew A.   Snodin, Ian.
Beardsley, Peter A.   Johnston, Maurice.   Southall, Neville.
Cottee, Antony R.   Kearton, Jason B.   Unsworth, avid G.
Doohan, John.   Kenny, William.   Ward, Mark W.
Ebbrell, John K.   Moore, Neil.   Warzycha, Robert.
Hinchcliffe, Andrew G.   Priest, Christopher.   Watson, David.

League Appearances: Ablett, G.I. 40; Barlow, S. 8(18); Beagrie, P.S. 11(11); Beardsley, P.A. 39; Cottee, A.R. 25(1); Ebbrell, J.K. 24; Harper, A. 16(2); Hinchcliffe, A.
25; Holmes, P. 4; Horne, B. 34; Jackson, M.A. 25(2); Jenkins, I. 1; Johnston, M.
7(6); Kearton, J.B. 2(3); Kenny, W. 16(1); Keown, M.R. 13; Moore, Neil. (1);
Radosavljevic, P. 13(10); Rideout, P. 17(7); Sansom, K.G. 6(1); Snodin, I. 19(1);
Southall, N. 40; Unsworth, D.G. 3; Ward, M.W. 19; Warzycha, R. 15(5); Watson,
D. 40.

28

League (53): Cottee 12, Beardsley 10 (4 pens), Barlow 5, Beagrie 3, Jackson 3, Johnston 3, Radosavljevic 3, Rideout 3, Ebbrell 1, Hinchcliffe 1, Horne 1, Kenny 1, Sansom 1, Snodin 1, Ward 1, Warzycha 1, Watson 1, own goals 2.
Coca Cola Cup: (6): Beardsley 2, Rideout 2, Barlow 1, Cottee 1 (pen).
FA Cup (1): Watson 1.
Ground: Goodison Park, Liverpool L4 4EL. Telephone 051–521 2020.
Record attendance: 78,299 v Liverpool, Division 1, 18 September 1948.
Manager: Howard Kendall.
Secretary: Jim Greenwood.
Honours –
Football League: Division 1 Champions – 1890–91, 1914–15, 1927–28, 1931–32, 1938–39, 1962–63, 1969–70, 1984–85, 1986–87. Division 2 Champions – 1930–31.
FA Cup: Winners 1906, 1933, 1966, 1984.
European Competitions:
European Cup-Winners' Cup winners: 1984–85.
Colours: Royal blue shirts with white collar, white shorts, blue stockings.

EXETER CITY   DIV. 2

Bond, Kevin J.	Harris, Andrew.	Taylor, Craig.
Brown, Jonathan.	Hodge, John.	Tonge, Alan J.
Cook, Andrew C.	Jepson, Ronald F.	Whiston, Peter.
Cooper, David B. E.	Miller, Kevin.	White, Christopher J.
Daniels, Scott.	Redwood, Toby R. B.	
Dolan, Eammon J.	Storer, Stuart J.	

League Appearances: Bailey, D.S. 27; Bond, K.J. 17(1); Brown, J. 40; Chapman, G.A. 3(1); Collins, E. 8(3); Cook, A.C. 32; Cooper, D.B. 16(4); Daniels, S. 26; Dolan, E.J. 10(9); Evans, R.W. 5; Gallen, J.M. 6; Harris, A. 23(5); Hiley, S.P. 33; Hodge, J. 41(1); Jepson, R.F. 35(3); Kelly, T.J. 20(2); Loram, M.J. 2(1); McIntyre, J. 12(3); Miller, K. 44; Minett, J. 11(1); Moran, S.J. 19(4); O'Keefe, J.V. 2; Phillips, M.J. (6); Redwood, T.R. 3(3); Storer, S.J. 10; Taylor, C. 2(3); Tonge, A.J. 13(2); Whiston, P. 27; White, C. 11; Williams, S.C. 8(4).
League (54): Hodge 9, Jepson 8, Moran 8, Dolan 4, Storer 4, Hiley 3, McIntyre 3, Whiston 3, Daniels 2, Evans 2, Brown 1, Chapman 1, Cook 1, Harris 1, Kelly 1, Tonge 1, own goals 2.
Coca Cola Cup (4): Dolan 2, Hodge 1, Kelly 1.
FA Cup (3): Moran 2, Cook 1.
Ground: St James Park, Exeter EX4 6PX. Telephone Exeter (0392) 54073.
Record attendance: 20,984 v Sunderland, FA Cup 6th rd (replay), 4 March 1931.
Manager: Alan Ball.
Secretary: Margaret Bond.
Honours – Football League: Division 4 Champions – 1989–90.
Division 3 (S) Cup: Winners 1934.
Colours: Red and white striped shirts, black shorts, red stockings.

FULHAM   DIV. 2

Baah, Peter H.   Gough, Alan T.   Pike, Martin R.
Brazil, Gary N.   Hails, Julian.   Stannard, James.
Cooper, Mark N.   Kelly, Paul L. M.   Thomas, Glen A.
Eckhardt, Jeffrey E.   Marshall, John P.   Tierling, Lee A.
Farrell, Sean P.   Morgan, Simon C.
Ferney, Martin J.   Onwere, Udo A.

League Appearances: Archibald, S. 2; Baah, P.H. 12(4); Bailey, D.S. 2(1); Bedrossian, A. 7(2); Brazil, G.N. 27(3); Cooper, M.N. 8(1); Eckhardt, J.E. 30; Farrell, S.P. 34(1); Ferney, M.J. 10(6); Gough, A.T. 3; Haag, K.J. 5(5); Hails, J. 45(1); Jupp, D.A. 3; Kelly, M.D. 19(6); Lewis, K.J. 4(2); Marshall, J.P. 40(1); McGlashan, J. 5; Morgan, S.C. 38(1); Nebbeling, G.M. 28(2); Newson, M.J. 26(3); Onwere, U.A. 22(7); Pike, M.R. 46; Stannard, J. 43; Thomas, G.A. 43; Tierling, L.A. 2(3); Tucker, M.J. 2.
League (57): Farrell 12, Morgan 8, Brazil 7, Eckhardt 6, Hails 6, Pike 6 (1 pen), Onwere 3, Marshall 2, Nebbeling 2, Ferney 1, Kelly 1, McGlashan 1, own goals 2.
Coca Cola Cup (0):
FA Cup (1): Farrell 1.
Ground: Craven Cottage, Stevenage Rd, Fulham, London SW6. Telephone 071–736 6561.
Record attendance: 49,335 v Millwall, Division 2, 8 October 1938.
Manager: Don Mackay.
Secretary: Mrs Janice O'Doherty.
Honours – Football League: Division 2 Champions – 1948–49. Division 3 (S) Champions – 1931–32.
Colours: White shirts, red and black trim, black shorts, white stockings red and black trim.

GILLINGHAM   DIV. 3

Arnot, Andrew J.   Crown, David I.   Martin, Eliot J.
Baker, DAvid P.   Dempsey, Mark A.   Osborne, Lawrence W.
Barrett, Scott.   Dunne, Joseph J.   Palmer, Lee J.
Breen, Gary.   Eeles, Anthony G.   Reinelt, Robert S.
Butler, Philip A.   Forster, Nicholas M.   Smith, Neil J.
Carpenter, Richard.   Green, Richard E.   Watson, Paul D.
Clark, Paul P.   Hague, Paul.
Crane, Steven J.   Henry, Liburd A.

League Appearances: Arnot, A.J. 13(2); Aylott, T.K. 8(2); Baker, D.P. 21; Barrett, S. 34; Breen, G. 25(4); Butler, P.A. 41; Carpenter, R. 25(3); Clark, P.P. 34(1); Crane, S.J. 2(5); Crown, D.I. 19(1); Dempsey, M.A. 9(7); Dunne, J.J. 3(1); Eeles, A.G. 12(2); Forster, N.M. 19(7); Green, R.E. 39; Hague, P. 1; Henry, L.A. 25(3); Houghton, S.A. 3; Lim, H. 8; Lovell, S.J. 11(2); Martin, E.J. 22; O'Connor, M.A. 16(5); Osborne, L.W. 1; Palmer, L.J. 9(1); Ritchie, P.M. 6; Roeder, G.V. 6; Smith, N.J. 37(2); Stephenson, P. 12; Watson, P.D. 1.

League (48): Arnott 6, Baker 6, Forster 6, Crown 5, Green 3, Lovell 3 (1 pen), Ritchie 3, Smith 3, Aylott 2, Eeles 2, Stephenson 2, Clark 1, Crane 1, Henry 1, Martin 1, O'Connor 1, Osborne 1, own goal 1.
Coca Cola Cup (4): Crown 2, Aylott 1, Lovell 1.
FA Cup (8): Crown 2, Forster 2, Arnott 1, Clark 1, Green 1 (pen), Henry 1 (pen).
Ground: Priestfield Stadium, Gillingham. Telephone Medway (0634) 851854/576828.
Record attendance: 23,002 v QPR, FA Cup 3rd rd 10 January 1948.
Manager: Mike Flanagan.
Company Secretary: Barry Bright.
Honours –
Football League: Division 4 Champions – 1963–64.
Colours: All Royal blue.

GRIMSBY TOWN   DIV. 1

Agnew, Paul.
Childs, Gary P. C.
Croft, Gary.
Daws, Anthony.
Dobbin, James.
Ford, Tony.
Futcher, Paul.

Gilbert, David J.
Groves, Paul.
Handyside, Peter D.
Hargreaves, Christian.
Jobling, Kevin A.
Lever, Mark.
McDermott, John.

Mendonca, Clive P.
Rees, Anthony A.
Rodger, Graham.
Smith, Mark C.
Watson, Thomas R.
Wilmot, Rhys J.
Woods, Neil S.

League Appearances: Agnew, P. 20(3); Baraclough, I.R. 1; Beasant, D. 6; Childs, G.P. 11(6); Croft, G. 28(4); Daws, A. 5(1); Dobbin, J. 39; Ford, A. 15(2); Futcher, P. 35; Gilbert, D.J. 41; Groves, P. 45(1); Handyside, P.D. 11; Hargreaves, C. (4); Jobling, K.A. 11(3); Lever, M. 14; McDermott, J. 38; Mendonca, C.P. 38(4); Rees, A.A. 24(7); Rodger, G. 27(3); Sherwood, S. 7; Smith, M.C. 8(18); Tillson, A. 4; Watson, T.R. 24; Wilmot, R.J. 33; Woods, N.S. 21(9).
League (58): Groves 12, Mendonca 10 (2 pens), Rodger 7, Dobbin 6, Rees 5, Gilbert 4, Watson 4, Woods 4, Ford 2, McDermott 2, Daws 1, Lever 1.
Coca Cola Cup (5): Mendonca 2, Watson 2, Woods 1.
FA Cup (4): Mendonca 2, Dobbin 1, Gilbert 1.
Ground: Blundell Park, Cleethorpes, South Humberside DN35 7PY. Telephone Cleethorpes (0472) 697111.
Record attendance: 31,651 v Wolverhampton W, FA Cup 5th rd, 20 February 1937.
Manager: Alan Buckley.
Secretary: Ian Fleming.
Honours –
Football League: Division 2 Champions – 1900–01, 1933–34. Division 3 (N) Champions – 1925–26, 1955–56. Division 3 Champions – 1979–80. Division 4 Champions – 1971–72.
League Group Cup: Winners 1981–82.
Colours: Black and white vertical striped shirts, black shorts with red triangular panel on side, white stockings with red band on turnover.

Barr, William J.
Bracey, Lee M. I.
Bradley, Russell.
Brown, Nicholas J.
German, David.

Greenwood, Nigle P.
Hardy, Jason P.
Longley, Scott E.
Lucketti, Christopher J.
Megson, Kevin C.

Paterson, Jamie R.
Peake, Jason W.
Ridings, David.

League Appearances: Barr, W.J. 28; Bracey, L.M. 41; Bradley, R. 29(1); Brown, L. 3; Brown, N.J. 1; Case, J.R. 17(4); Christie, D. 6(3); Circuit, S. (1); Craven, P.A. 7; Edmonds, D. (2); Everingham, N. 2; Gayle, H. 2(3); German, D. 28(7); Greenwood, N.P. 21(4); Griffiths, N. 1; Hardy, J.P. 20(2); Hildersley, R. 7(6); Juryeff, I.M. 1; Kamara, A. (1); Lancashire, G. 2; Lewis, D.K. 10(3); Lucketti, C. 42; Matthews, M. 23; Megson, K.C. 24(2); Obebo, G. (3); Paterson, J.R. 18(5); Peake, J.W. 32(1); Peel, N.J. 3; Ridings, D. 21; Thomas, J.W. 10(2); Thompstone, I.P. 31; Williams, M.A. 9; Wilson, P.A. 22; Wright, P.A. 1.

League (45): Thompstone 9, Greenwood 5, Ridings 4, Barr 3 (1 pen), Case 2, German 2, Hardy 2, Hildersley 2, Lucketti 2, Matthews 2, Patterson 2, Wilson 2 (2 pens), Bradley 1, Megson 1, Peake 1, Williams 1, own goals 4.

Coca Cola Cup (3): Lucketti 1, Megson 1, Thomas 1.

FA Cup (1): German 1.

Ground: Shay Ground, Halifax HX1 2YS. Offices: 7 Clare Road, Halifax HX1 2HX. Telephone Halifax (0422) 353423.

Record attendance: 36,885 v Tottenham H, FA Cup 5th rd, 15 February 1953.

Manager: Peter Wragg.

Secretary: Bev Fielding.

Honours – Nil.

Colours: Blue and white vertical striped shirts, black shorts, black stockings.

Cross, Paul.
Cross, Ryan.
Emerson, Dean.
Gallacher, John.
Garrett, Scott.
Gilchrist, Philip A.
Hodge, Martin J.

Honour, Brian.
Johnrose, Leonard.
Jones, Steven.
Macphail, John.
McGuckin, Thomas I.
Nobbs, Alan K.
Olsson, Paul.

Peverell, Nicholas J.
Southall, Leslie N.
Tair, Michael P.
Thompson, Paul D. Z.
Wratten, Paul.

League Appearances: Cross, P. 36(1); Cross, R. 32(1); Ellison, A.L. 3(1); Emerson, D. 32; Gallacher, J. 16(5); Gilchrist, P.A. 24; Hodge, M.J. 29; Honour, B. 36(1); Johnrose, L. 35(3); Johnson, D.A. 3; Jones, S. 3; Lynch, C. (1); MacPhail, J. 27; McGuckin, T.I. 12(2); Nobbs, A.K. 27; Olsson, P. 39; Peverell, N. 8(11); Proudlock, P. 3(3); Saville, A.V. 36; Skedd, A.S. 1; Southall, L.N. 30(9); Tait, M.P. 35; Talia, F. 14; Thompson, P.D. (2); Wratten, P. 10(5).

League (42): Saville 13 (4 pens), Johnrose 6, Southall 6, Honour 3, Cross R 2, Olsson 2, Cross P 1, Ellison 1, Emerson 1, Gallacher 1, McGuckin 1, MacPhail 1, Peverell 1, Tait 1, Thompson 1, Wratten 1.

Coca Cola Cup (7): Johnrose 4, MacPhail 1, Saville 1 (pen), Southall 1.
FA Cup (7): Saville 5 (2 pens), Johnrose 1, Peverell 1.
Ground: The Victoria Ground, Clarence Road, Hartlepool. Telephone Hartlepool (0429) 272584.
Record attendance: 17,426 v Manchester U, FA Cup 3rd rd, 5 January 1957.
Manager: Viv Busby.
Assistant Secretary: Lisa Charlton.
Honours – Nil.
Colours: Navy/sky blue.

HEREFORD UNITED   DIV. 3

Abraham, Gareth J.   Davies, Gareth M.   Judge, Alan G.
Anderson, Colin R.   Dows, Gregory.   Morris, David K.
Armstrong-May, Leroy.   Fry, Christopher D.   Nicholson, Maximillian.
Brain, Simon A. J.   Hall, Derek R.   Pickard, Owen A.

League Appearances: Abraham, G.J. 19; Anderson, C.R. 35; Armstrong-May, L. 11(3); Brain, S.A. 19(2); Browning, M.T. 7; Cousins, A.J. 3; Cross, M. (1); Davies, G.M. 31(1); Devine, S.B. 26(1); Downs, G. 36(2); Fry, C.D. 31(6); Hall, D.R. 41; Heathcock, A.N. 1(1); Jennings, K. 2(3); Jones, R.J. 34(1); Judge, A.G. 42; Langford, C.R. 1; Morris, D.K. 10(1); Nicholson, M. 30(6); Pickard, O.A. 36(1); Rowbotham, D. 8; Rowbotham, J. 3(2); Smith, K. 6; Theodosiou, A. 8(1); Titterton, D.S. 19(7); Wade, P.M. 3(4).
League (47): Hall 9 (1 pen), Pickard 9, Browning 5, Fry 4, Jones 3, Nicholson 3, Brain 2, May 2, Rowbotham D 2, Abraham 1, Davies 1, Rowbotham J 1, Theodosiou 1, own goals 4.
Coca Cola Cup (2): Pickard 2.
FA Cup (3): Pickard 2, own goal 1.
Ground: Edgar Street, Hereford. Telephone Hereford (0432) 276666.
Record attendance: 18,114 v Sheffield W, FA Cup 3rd rd, 4 January 1958.
Manager: Greg Downs.
Secretary: David Vaughan.
Honours –
Football League: Division 3 Champions – 1975–76.
Welsh Cup winners: 1990.
Colours: White shirts, black shorts, white stockings.

HUDDERSFIELD TOWN   DIV. 2

Barnet, Gary L.   Dunn, Iain G. W.   O'Regan, Kieran.
Billy, Christopher A.   Dyson, Jonathan P.   Onuora, Ifem.
Booth, Andrew D.   Jackson, Peter A.   Parsley, Neil.
Brennan, Anthony.   Lampkin, Kevin.   Roberts, Iwan W.
Charlton, Simon T.   Marsden, Christopher.   Robinson, Philip J.
Clarke, Timothy J.   Mitchell, Graham L.   Starbuck, Philip M.
Collins, Simon.   Mooney, Thomas.   Trevitt, Simon.

33

League Appearances: Barnett, G.L. 45(1); Billy, C. 4(9); Booth, A.D. 3(2); Charlton, S.T. 46; Clarke, T.J. 31; Collins, S. (1); Cooper, M.N. 10; Dewhurst, R.M. 7; Donovan, K. 2(1); Dunn, I.G. 25(3); Dyson, J.P. 15; Elliott, A.R. 15; Ireland, S.P. 4; Jackson, P.A. 39; Lampkin, K. 13; Marsden, C. 6(1); Mitchell, G.L. 3(1); Mooney, T. 1; O'Regan, K. 37(4); Onuora, I. 30(9); Parsley, N. 44; Roberts, I.W. 37; Robinson, P.J. 35(1); Smith, M.C. 5; Starbuck, P.M. 29(9); Stuart, M.R. 9(6); Wright, M.A. 11(3).
League (54): Roberts 9 (1 pen), Starbuck 9, Barnett 7, Onuora 6, O'Regan 5 (5 pens), Cooper 4, Robinson 4, Dunn 3, Stuart 3, Booth 2, Charlton 1, Jackson 1.
Coca Cola Cup (7): Roberts 2, Barnett 1, Ireland 1, Onuora 1, Parsley 1, Starbuck 1.
FA Cup (7): Barnett 2, Dunn 2, Mitchell 1, O'Regan 1 (pen), Robinson 1.
Ground: Leeds Rd, Huddersfield HD1 6PE. Telephone (0484) 420335/6.
Record attendance: 67,037 v Arsenal, FA Cup 6th rd, 27 February1932.
Manager: Neil Warnock.
Secretary: Alan D. Sykes.
Honours –
Football League: Division 1 Champions – 1923–24, 1924–25, 1925–26. Division 2 Champions – 1969–70. Division 4 Champions – 1969–70.
FA Cup winners 1922.
Colours: Blue and white striped shirts, white shorts, white stockings.

HULL CITY   DIV. 2

Abbott, Gregory S.   Hobson, Gary.   Warren, Lee A.
Allison, Neil J.   Jones (Quartey), David. Wilcox, Russell.
Atkinson, Graeme,   Mail, David.   Wilson, Stephen L.
Brown, Linton.   Miller, Robert J.   Windass, Dean.
Fettis, Alan.   Norton, David W.

League Appearances: Abbott, G.S. 27; Allison, N.J. 7(4); Atkinson, G. 44(2); Brown, L. 20(3); Calvert, M.R. 5(2); Carruthers, M. 13; Edeson, M.K. (2); Fettis, A. 20; France, D.B. 9(17); Heard, T.P. 3(1); Hobson, G. 17(4); Hockaday, D. 25; Hunter, P. 19(7); Jenkinson, L. 25(1); Jones (Quartey), D. 11(1); Lund, G.J. 11; Mail, D. 38(1); Miller, R.J. 20(5); Mohan, N. 5; Norton, D.W. 45; Stoker, G. 5(1); Stowe, D.D. (1); Warren, L.A. 35(1); Wilcox, R. 28(1); Williams, G.J. 4; Wilson, S.L. 26; Windass, D. 40(1); Young, S.R. 4.
League (46): Windass 7 (1 pen), Atkinson 6, Carruthers 6, Hunter 6, Jenkinson 4, France 3, Lund 3, Wilcox 2, Abbott 1, Brown L 1, Hockaday 1, Jones 1, Mohan 1, Norton 1, own goals 3.
Coca Cola Cup (2): Atkinson 1, Hockaday 1.
FA Cup (2): Atkinson 1, Norton 1.
Ground: Boothferry Park, Hull HU4 6EU. Telephone Hull (0482) 51119.
Record attendance: 55,019 v Manchester U, FA Cup 6th rd, 26 February 1949.
Manager: Terry Dolan.
Secretary: Tom Wilson.
Honours –
Football League: Division 3 (N) Champions – 1932–33, 1948–49. Division 3 Champions – 1965–66.
Colours: Black and amber striped shirts, black shorts, amber stockings.

IPSWICH TOWN   FA PREMIER

Baker, Clive E.
Bernal, Andrew.
Bozinoski, Vlado.
Dozzell, Jason A. W.
Durrant, Lee R.
Fearon, Ronald.
Forrest, Craig L.
Goddard, Paul.
Gregory, David S.

Gregory, Neil R.
Guentchev, Bontcho L.
Honeywood, Lee B.
Johnson, Gavin.
Kiwomya, Christopher M.
Linighan, David.
Milton, Simon C.
Palmer, Stephen L.
Stockwell, Michael T.

Tanner, Adam D.
Thompson, Gary M.
Thompson, Neil.
Wark, John.
Whelan, Philip J.
Whitton, Stephen P.
Williams, David G.
Yallop, Frank W.
Youds, Edward P.

League Appearances: Baker, C.E. 30(1); Bozinoski, V. 3(6); Dozzell, J.A. 41; Forrest, C.L. 11; Goddard, P. 19(6) Gregory, D.S. 1(2); Guentchev, B. 19(2); Johnson, G. 39(1); Kiwomya, C. 38; Linighan, D. 42; Milton, S.C. 7(5); Palmer, S.L. 4(3); Pennyfather, G. 2(2); Petterson, A. 1; Stockwell, M. 38(1); Thompson, N. 31; Wark, J. 36(1); Whelan, P.J. 28(4); Whitton, S.P. 20(4); Williams, D.G. 37; Yallop, F.W. 5(1); Youds, E.P. 10(6).
League (50): Kiwomya 10, Dozzell 7, Wark 6 (2 pens), Johnson 5, Stockwell 4, Goddard 3, Guentchev 3, Thompson 3, Whitton 3 (2 pens), Milton 2, Yallop 2, Gregory 1, Linighan 1.
Coca Cola Cup (11): Kiwomya 6, Johnson 2, Thompson 1, Whitton 1 (pen), own goal 1.
FA Cup (11): Guentchev 5, Dozzell 2, Kiwomya 1, Thompson 1, Wark 1, Whitton 1.
Ground: Portman Road, Ipswich, Suffolk IP1 2DA. Telephone Ipswich (0473) 219211 (4 lines).
Record attendance: 38,010 v Leeds U, FA Cup 6th rd, 8 March 1975.
Team Manager: Mick McGiven.
Secretary: David C. Rose.
Honours –
Football League: Division 1 Champions – 1961–62. Division 2 Champions – 1960–61, 1967–68, 1991–92. Division 3 (S) Champions – 1953–54, 1956–57.
FA Cup: Winners 1977–78.
European Competitions:
UEFA Cup winners: 1980–81, 1982–83.
Colours: Blue shirts, white sleeves, white shorts, blue stockings.

LEEDS UNITED   FA PREMIER

Batty, David.
Beeney, Mark.
Bowman, Robert A.
Chapman, Lee R.
Cousin, Scott.
Couzens, Andrew J.
Dorigo, Anthony R.
Fairclough, Courtney H.

Ford, Mark S.
Forrester, Jamie.
Hodge, Stephen B.
Kelly, Garry.
Kerr, Dylan.
Kerslake, David.
Lukic, Jovan.
McAllister, Gary.

Newsome, Jon.
Nicholls, Ryan R.
O'Hara, Gary J.
Pettinger, Paul A.
Rocastle, David C.
Sharp, Kevin.
Shutt, Carl S.
Smithard, Mathew P.

Speed, Gary A.   Tinkler, Mark R.   Wetherall, David.
Sterland, Melvyn.   Wallace, Raymond G.   Whelan, Noel.
Strachan, Gordon D. Wallace, Rodney S.   Whyte, Christopher A.

League Appearances: Batty, D. 30; Beeney, M. 1; Bowman, R.A. 3(1); Cantona, E. 12(1); Chapman, L.R. 36(4); Day, M.R. 2; Dorigo, A.R. 33; Fairclough, C. 29(1); Forrester, J. 5(1); Hodge, S.B. 9(14); Kerr, D. 3(2); Kerslake, D. 8; Lukic, J. 39; McAllister, G. 32; Newsome, J. 30(7); Rocastle, D.C. 11(7); Sellars, Scott. 6(1); Sharp, K. 4; Shutt, C.S. 6(8); Speed, G.A. 39; Sterland, M. 3; Strachan, G.D. 25(6); Strandli, F. 5(5); Tinkler, M.R. 5(2); Varadi, I. 2(2); Wallace, R.G. 5(1); Wallace, R.S. 31(1); Wetherall, D. 13; Whelan, N. 1; Whyte, C. 34.
League (57): Chapman 14, Speed 7, Rod Wallace 7, Cantona 6, McAllister 5 (2 pens), Strachan 4 (2 pens), Fairclough 3, Hodge 2, Strandli 2, Batty 1, Dorigo 1 (pen), Rocastle 1, Varadi 1, Wetherall 1, Whyte 1, own goal 1.
Coca Cola Cup (7): Chapman 2, McAllister 1, Shutt 1, Speed 1, Strachan 1, Rod Wallace 1.
FA Cup (8): Speed 3, McAllister 2, Chapman 1, Shutt 1, own goal 1.
Ground: Elland Road, Leeds LS11 0ES. Telephone Leeds (0532) 716037 (4 lines).
Record attendance: 57,892 v Sunderland, FA Cup 5th rd (replay), 15 March 1967.
Manager: Howard Wilkinson.
Company Secretary: Nigel Pleasants.
Honours –
Football League: Division 1 Champions – 1968–69, 1973–74, 1991–92. **Division 2 Champions** – 1923–24, 1963–64, 1989–90.
FA Cup: Winners 1972. **Football League Cup:** Winners 1967–68.
European Competitions: European Fairs Cup winners: 1967–68, 1970–71.
Colours: All white.

LEICESTER CITY   DIV. 1

Agnew, Stephen M.   James, Anthony C.   Poole, Kevin.
Blyth, Ian.   Joachim, Julian K.   Smith, Richard G.
Coatsworth, Gary.   Lewis, Neil A.   Thompson, Ian T.
Davison, Robert.   Lowe, David A.   Thompson, Stephen J.
Gee, Phillip.   Mills, Gary R.   Trotter, Michael.
Grayson, Simon N.   Muggleton, Carl D.   Walsh, Steven.
Haughton, Warren A.   Oldfield, David C.   Whitlow, Michael.
Hill, Colin F.   Ormondroyd, Ian.   Willis, James A.
Houtl, Russell.   Philpott, Lee.

League Appearances: Agnew, S.M. 9; Coatsworth, G. 10; Davison, R. 21(4); Fitzpatrick, P.J. (1); Gee, P. 11(7); Gibson, C.J. 5(4); Gordon, C.K. (3); Grayson, S.M. 14(10); Hill, C.F. 46; Hoult, R. 10; James, A.C. 2(14); Joachim, J.K. 25(1); Lewis, N.A. 2(5); Lowe, D.A. 27(5); Mills, G.R. 42(1); Muggleton, C.D. 17; Oldfield, D.C. 44; Ormondroyd, I. 17(9); Philpott, L. 27; Platnauer, N. 6; Poole, K. 19; Smith, R.G. 44; Thompson, S.J. 44; Trotter, M. 1; Walsh, S. 40; Whitlow, M. 23(1).
League (71): Walsh 15, Joachim 10, Lowe 11, Thompson 8 (2 pens), Davison 6,

36

Oldfield 5, Gee 4, Philpott 3, Coatsworth 2, Ormondroyd 2, Agnew 1, Grayson 1, Whitlow 1, own goals 2.
Coca Cola Cup (4): Davison 1, Joachim 1, Lowe 1, Thompson 1.
FA Cup (3): Joachim 1, Oldfield 1, Thompson 1 (pen).
Ground: City Stadium, Filbert St, Leicester LE2 7FL. Telephone Leicester (0533) 555000.
Record attendance: 47,298 v Tottenham H, FA Cup 5th rd, 18 February 1928.
Manager: Brian Little.
General Secretary: Alan Bennett.
Honours –
Football League: Division 2 Champions – 1924–25, 1936–37, 1953–54, 1956–57, 1970–71, 1979–80.
Football League Cup: Winners 1964.
Colours: All blue.

LEYTON ORIENT   DIV. 2

Bellamy, Gary.	Jones, Andrew M.	Otto, Ricky.
Benstock, Danny.	Kitchen, David E.	Ryan, Vaughan W.
Carter, Darren S.	Lakin, Barry.	Taylor, Robert A.
Cooper, Mark D.	Livett, Simon R.	Tomlinson, Michael L.
Hackett, Warren J.	Ludden, Dominic J. R.	Truner, Christopher R.
Heald, Paul A.	Newell, Paul C.	Warren, Mark W.
Howard, Terence.	Okai, Stephen P.	Whitbread, Adrian R.

League Appearances: Achampong, K. 19(6); Bellamy, G. 38(1); Benstock, D. 8(1); Carter, D.S. 26(3); Cooper, M.D. 20(8); Day, K. 7(3); Hackett, W.J. 16(1); Hales, K.P. 29; Harvey, L.D. 19(2); Heald, P.A. 26; Howard, T. 41; Jones, A.M. 24(5); Kitchen, D.E. 28(4); Lakin, B. 8(1); Livett, S.R. 16(7); Ludden, D.J. 21(3); Newell, P.C. 3; Okai, S.P. 5(8); Otto, R. 18(5); Ryan, V.W. 18(2); Taylor, R.A. 36(3); Tomlinson, M. 3(5); Turner, C. 17; Warren, M.W. 14; Whitbread, A.R. 36; Zoricich, C. 10(2).
League (69): Taylor 18, Jones 8, Otto 8, Cooper 7, Howard 5 (1 pen), Bellamy 4, Harvey 4, Carter 3, Lakin 2, Achampong 1, Day 1, Hales 1 (pen), Kitchen 1, Ludden 1, Okai 1, Whitbread 1, Zoricich 1, own goals 2.
Coca Cola Cup (2): Cooper 1, Tomlinson 1.
FA Cup (5): Cooper 2, Howard 1, Jones 1, Whitbread 1.
Ground: Leyton Stadium, Brisbane Road, Leyton, London E10 5NE. Telephone 081–539 2223/4.
Record attendance: 34,345 v West Ham U, FA Cup 4th rd, 25 January 1964.
Team Manager: Peter Eustace.
Secretary: Miss Carol Stokes.
Honours –
Football League: Division 3 Champions – 1969–70. Division 3 (S) Champions – 1955–56.
Colours: Red shirts with white pinstripe, white shorts, red stockings.

Baraclough, Ian R.
Bowling, Ian.
Bressington, Graham.
Brown, Grant A.
Carbon, Matthew P.

Carmichael, Matthew.
Costello, Peter.
Dixon, Ben.
Dunphy, Sean.
Lee, Jason B.

Matthews, Neil.
Pollitt, Michael F.
Puttnam, David P.
Schofield, John D.
Smith, Paul M.

League Appearances: Alexander, K. (7); Baraclough, I.R. 34(2); Bowling, I. 15; Bressington, G. 25(3); Brown, G.A. 40; Carbon, M.P. 1; Carmichael, M. 41; Clarke, D.A. 30(1); Costello, P. 22(5); Dixon, B. 1(1); Dunphy, S. 29(2); Finney, K. 10(4); Kabia, J. 7(6); Lee, J.B. 36(5); Matthews, N. 21(3); McParland, J.I. 3(1); Parkinson, S. (2); Pollitt, M.F. 27; Puttnam, D.P. 37; Schofield, J.D. 32(8); Smith, P.M. 28(5); Ward, P.T. 1; West, D. 12(7); Yates, M.J. 10(4).
League (57): Lee 12, Matthews 11, Costello 7, Baraclough 5 (3 pens), Bressington 4 (3 pens), Carmichael 4, Smith 3, West 3, Clarke 2, Puttnam 2, Brown 1, Dunphy 1, Kabia 1, own goal 1.
Coca Cola Cup: (6): Bressington 2, Carmichael 1, Dunphy 1, Finney 1, Puttnam 1.
FA Cup (1): Costello 1.
Ground: Sincil Bank, Lincoln LN5 8LD. Telephone Lincoln (0522) 522224 and 510263.
Record attendance: 23,196 v Derby Co, League Cup 4th rd, 15 November 1967.
Manager: Keith Alexander.
Secretary: G. R. Davey.
Honours –
Football League: Division 3 (N) Champions – 1931–32, 1947–48, 1951–52. Division 4 Champions – 1975–76.
Colours: Red and white striped shirts, black shorts, red stockings with white trim.

Barnes, John C. B.
Bjornebye, Stig I.
Brydon, Lee.
Burrows, David.
Charnock, Philip A.
Embleton, Daniel C.
Fowler, Robert B.
Frodsham, Ian T.
Grobbelaar, Bruce D.
Harkness, Steven.
Hooper, Michael D.
Hutchinson, Donald.
James, David B.

Johnston, Craig P.
Jones, Philip L.
Jones, Robert.
Kozma, Istvan.
Marsh, Michael A.
Matteo, Dominic.
McAree, Rodney J.
McManaman, Steven.
Molby, Jan.
Neal, Ashley J.
Nestor, Terry.
Nicol, Stephen.
O'Donnell, Paul G.

Paterson, Scott.
Piechnik, Torben.
Redknapp, Jamie F.
Rosenthal, Ronny.
Rush, Ian J.
Scott, John A.
Stalker, Mark E.
Stewart, Paul A.
Tanner, Nicholas.
Thomas, Michael L.
Walters, Mark.
Whelan, Ronald A.
Wright, Mark.

League Appearances: Barnes, J.C. 26(1); Bjornebye, S.I. 11; Burrows, D. 29(1); Grobbelaar, B.D. 5; Harkness, S. 9(1); Hooper, M.D. 8(1); Hutchison, D. 27(4); James, D.B. 29; Jones, R. 30; Kozma, I. (1); Marsh, M.A. 22(6); McManaman, S.

27(4); Molby, J. 8(2); Nicol, S. 32; Piechnik, T. 15(1); Redknapp, J.F. 27(2); Rosenthal, R. 16(11); Rush, I.J. 31(1); Saunders, D.N. 6; Stewart, P.A. 21(3); Tanner, N. 2(2); Thomas, M.L. 6(2); Walters, M. 26(8); Whelan, R.A. 17; Wright, M. 32(1).

League (62): Rush 14, Walters 11 (4 pens), Hutchison 7, Rosenthal 6, Barnes 5 (1 pen), McManaman 4, Molby 3 (3 pens), Burrows 2, Redknapp 2, Wright 2, Harkness 1, Marsh 1, Saunders 1, Stewart 1, Thomas 1, Whelan 1.
Coca Cola Cup (13): Marsh 3 (3 pens), Hutchison 2, McManaman 2, Walters 2, Redknapp 1, Rosenthal 1, Rush 1, Wright 1.
FA Cup (2): Rush 1, own goal 1.
Ground: Anfield Road, Liverpool 4. Telephone 051–263 2361.
Record attendance: 61,905 v Wolverhampton W, FA Cup 4th rd, 2 February 1952.
Honours –
Football League: Division 1 – Champions 1900–01, 1905–06, 1921–22, 1922–23, 1946–47, 1963–64, 1965–66, 1972–73, 1975–76, 1976–77, 1978–79, 1979–80, 1981–82, 1982–83, 1983–84, 1985–86, 1987–88, 1989–90 (Liverpool have a record number of 18 League Championship wins). Division 2 Champions – 1893–94, 1895–96, 1904–05, 1961–62. FA Cup: Winners 1965, 1974, 1986, 1989, 1992.
League Super Cup: Winners 1985–86.
European Competitions: European Cup winners: 1976–77, 1977–78, 1980–81, 1983–84.
UEFA Cup winners: 1972–73, 1975–76.
Super Cup winners: 1977.
Colours: All red with white markings.

LUTON TOWN   DIV. 1

Benjamin, Ian T.   James, Julian C.   Rees, Jason M.
Campbell, Jamie.   Johnson, Marvin A.   Salton, Darren B.
Dreyer, John B.   Kamara, Christopher.   Skelton, Aaron M.
Gray, Philip.   Linton, Desmond M.   Sommer, Juergen P.
Greene, David M.   Oakes, Scott J.   Telfer, Paul N.
Hartson, John.   Peake, Trevor.   Thorpe, Anthony.
Harvey, Richard G.   Petterson, Andrew K.   Williams, Martin K.
Hughes, Ceri M.   Preece, David W.

League Appearances: Benjamin, I.T. 5(5); Campbell, J. 2(7); Chamberlain, A.F. 32; Claridge, S.E. 15(1); Dixon, K.M. 16(1); Dreyer, J.B. 38; Gray, P. 45; Greene, D.M. 1; Harvey, R.G. 1; Hughes, C.M. 26(3); James, J.C. 43; Johnson, M.A. 38(2); Kamara, C. 21; Linton, D.M. 17(3); Matthew, D. 3(2); Oakes, S.J. 25(19); Peake, T. 40; Petterson, A.K. 14; Preece, D.W. 43; Rees, J.M. 29(3); Salton, D.B. 15; Telfer, P.N. 30(2); Williams, M.K. 7(15).
League (48): Gray 19 (2 pens) Oakes 5, Dixon 3, Johnson 3, Preece 3, Claridge 2 (1 pen) Dreyer 2, Hughes 2, James 2, Telfer 2, Benjamin 1, Campbell 1, Linton 1, Williams 1, own goal 1.
Coca Cola Cup (4): Claridge 3, Preece 1.
FA Cup (3): Gray 1, Hughes 1, Telfer 1.
Ground: Kenilworth Road Stadium, 1 Maple Rd, Luton, Beds. LU4 8AW. Telephone, Offices: Luton (0582) 411622; Ticket Office: (0582) 416976.
Record attendance: 30,069 v Blackpool, FA Cup 6th rd replay, 4 March 1959.

Manager: David Pleat.
Secretary: J. K. Smylie.
Honours – Football League: Division 2 Champions – 1981–82. Division 4 Champions – 1967–68. Division 3 (S) Champions – 1936–37.
Football League Cup winners 1987–88.
Colours: White shirts with royal blue and orange stripe on collar, sleeves and waist, royal blue shorts with white and orange trim, white stockings with royal blue and orange turnover.

MANCHESTER CITY   FA PREMIER

Beech, Christopher.
Brightwell, David J.
Brightwell, Ian R.
Coton, Anthony P.
Curle, Keith.
Dibble, Andrew.
Edghill, Richard A.
Finney, Stephen K.
Flitcroft, Gary W.
Foster, John C.
Harkin, Joseph.

Hill, Andrew R.
Holden, Richard W.
Ingebrigsten, Kaare.
Kerr, David W.
Lake, Paul A.
Limber, Nicholas.
Lomas, Stephen M.
Margetson, Martyn W.
McMahon, Stephen.
Mike, Adrian R.
Phelan, Terry.

Quigley, Michael A.
Quinn, Niall J.
Reid, Peter.
Sheron, Michael N.
Simpson, Fitzroy.
Thomas, Scott L.
Thomson, Greg.
Vonk, Michel C.
White, David.

League Appearances: Brightwell, D.J. 4(4); Brightwell, I.R. 21; Coton, A.P. 40; Curle, K. 39; Dibble, A. 1(1); Flitcroft, G.W. 28(4); Hill, A.R. 23(1); Holden, R.W. 40(1); Ingebrigtsen, K. 2(5); Kerr, D.W. (1); Lake, P.A. 2; Margetson, M.W. 1; McMahon, S. 24(3); Mike, A.R. 1(2); Phelan, T. 37; Quigley, M.A.1(4); Quinn, N.J. 39; Ranson, R. 17; Reid, P. 14(6); Sheron, M.N. 33(5); Simpson, F. 27(2); Vonk, M.C. 26; White, D. 42.
League (56): White 16, Sheron 11, Quinn 9, Flitcroft 5, Curle 3 (3 pens), Holden 3, Vonk 3, Brightwell I 1, Hill 1, McMahon 1, Simpson 1, own goals 2.
Coca Cola Cup (2): Holden 1, own goal 1.
FA Cup (11): Sheron 3, White 3, Flitcroft 1, Holden 1, Phelan 1, Quinn 1, Vonk 1.
Ground: Maine Road, Moss Side, Manchester M14 7WN. Telephone 061-226 1191/2.
Record attendance: 84,569 v Stoke C, FA Cup 6th rd, 3 March 1934 (British record for any game outside London or Glasgow).
Player-Manager: Peter Reid.
General Secretary: J. B. Halford.
Honours –
Football League: Division 1 Champions – 1936–37, 1967–68. Division 2 Champions – 1898–99, 1902–03, 1909–10, 1927–28, 1946–47, 1965–66.
FA Cup winners 1904, 1934, 1956, 1969.
Football League Cup winners 1970, 1976.
European Competitions:
European Cup-Winners' Cup winners: 1969–70.
Colours: Sky blue shirts, white shorts, sky blue stockings.

Beckham, David R. J.
Blackmore, Clayton G.
Bruce, Stephen R.
Butt, Nicholas.
Cantona, Eric.
Carey, Brian P.
Casper, Christopher M.
Davies, Simon I.
Dublin, Dion.
Ferguson, Darren.
Giggs, Ryan J.
Gillespie, Keith R.
Hughes, Leslie M.

Ince, Paul E. C.
Irving, Richard J.
Irwin, Dennis J.
Kanchelskis, Andrei.
Lawton, Craig T.
Martin, Lee A.
McClair, Brian J.
McGibbon, Patrick C. G.
McKee, Colin.
Murdock, Colin J.
Neville, Gary A.
O'Kane, John A.
Pallister, Garry A.

Parker, Paul A.
Phelan, Michael C.
Pilkington, Kevin W.
Robson, Bryan.
Schmeichel, Peter B.
Scholes, Paul.
Sealey, Leslie J.
Sharpe, Lee S.
Thornley, Benjamin L.
Wallace, David L.
Walsh, Gary.
Whitworth, Neil A.

League Appearances: Blackmore, C. 12(2); Bruce, S.R. 42; Butt, N. (1); Cantona, E. 21(1); Dublin, D. 3(4); Ferguson, D. 15; Giggs, R.J. 40(1); Hughes, L.M. 41; Ince, P.E. 41; Irwin, D.J. 40; Kanchelskis, A. 14(13); McClair, B.J. 41(1); Pallister, G.A. 42; Parker, P.A. 31; Phelan, M.C. 5(6); Robson, B. 5(9); Schmeichel, P.B. 42; Sharpe, L.S. 27; Wallace, D.L. (2); Webb, N.J. (1).

League (67): Hughes 15, Cantona 9 (1 pen), Giggs 9, McClair 9, Ince 6, Bruce 5 (2 pens), Irwin 5, Kanchelskis 3, Dublin 1, Pallister 1, Parker 1, Robson 1, Sharpe 1, own goal 1.

Coca Cola Cup (2): Hughes 1, Wallace 1.

FA Cup (4): Giggs 2, Gillespie 1, Phelan 1.

Ground: Old Trafford, Manchester M16 0RA. Telephone 061-872 1661.

Record attendance: 76,962 Wolverhampton W v Grimsby T, FA Cup semi-final. 25 March 1939.

Manager: Alex Ferguson.

Secretary: Kenneth Merrett.

Honours –

FA Premier League: Champions – 1992-93. **Football League:** Division 1 Champions – 1907-8, 1910-11, 1951-52, 1955-56, 1956-57, 1964-65, 1966-67. Division 2 Champions – 1935-36, 1974-75.

FA Cup winners 1909, 1948, 1963, 1977, 1983, 1985, 1990.

Football League Cup winners 1991-92.

European Competitions: European Cup winners: 1967-68.

European Cup-Winners' Cup winners: 1990-91. **European Fairs Cup winners:** 1964-65.

Super Cup winners: 1991.

Colours: Red shirts, white shorts, black stockings.

MANSFIELD TOWN   DIV. 3

Castledine, Gary J.
Clarke, Nicholas J.
Davison, Wayne.

Fairclough, Wayne R.
Gray, Kevin J.
Hodson, Simeon P.

Holland, Paul.
McLoughlin, Paul B.
Noteman, Kevin S.

Parkin, Stephen J. Stringfellow, Ian R. Ward, Darren.
Pearcey, Jason. Sykes, Alexander. Wilkinson, Stephen J.
Perkins, Christopher P. Walker, Alan.

League Appearances: Castledine, G.J. 23(5); Charles, S. 22(1); Clarke, N.J. 9(3); Fairclough, W.R. 32(1); Fee, G.P. 7(3); Ford, G. 37; Foster, G.W. 10; Gray, K.J. 31(2); Hodson, S.P. 17; Holland, P. 39; McCord, B.J. 11; McLoughlin, P.B. 20(6); Noteman, K.S. 15(9); Parkin, S.J. 16; Pearcey, J. 33; Peer, D. 10; Perkins, C. 1(4); Rowbotham, D. 4; Spooner, S.A. 12(3); Stant, P. 17; Stringfellow, I.R. 26(4); Walker, A. 22; Ward, D. 13; Wilkinson, S. 35(8); Wilson, L. (4); Withe, C. 44(1).
League (52): Wilkinson 11, Stant 6 (1 pen), Stringfellow 5, McLoughlin 4, Noteman 4 (1 pen), Withe 4, Castledine 3, Charles 3 (2 pens), Fee 3 (1 pen), Holland 3, Clarke 1, Fairclough 1, Ford 1, McCord 1, Spooner 1, Walker 1.
Coca Cola Cup (1): Stant 1.
FA Cup (1): Fairclough 1.
Ground: Field Mill Ground, Quarry Lane, Mansfield.
Record attendance: 24,467 v Nottingham F, FA Cup 3rd rd, 10 January 1953.
Player-Manager: George Foster.
Secretary: J. D. Eaton.
Honours – Football League: Division 3 Champions – 1976–77. Division 4 Champions – 1974–75.
Freight Rover Trophy winners 1986–87.
Colours: Amber shirts with blue trim, blue shorts, amber stockings.

MIDDLESBROUGH   DIV. 1

Barron, Michael J. Kernaghan, Alan N. Pollock, Jamie.
Collett, Andrew A. Liburd, Richard. Roberts, Ben J.
Falconer, William H. Mohan, Nicholas. Stamp, Philip L.
Fleming, Curtis. Moore, Alan. Taylor, Mark S.
Forrester, Paul. Morris, Christopher Barry. Todd, Andrew J. J.
Hendrie, John G. Mustoe, Robbie. Whyte, Derek.
Hignett, Craig. Oliver, Michael. Wilkinson, Paul.
Illman, Neil D. Peake, Andrew M. Wright, Thomas E.
Ironside, Ian. Pears, Stephen.
Kavanagh, Graham A. Phillips, James N.

League Appearances: Collett, A.A. 2; Falconer, W.H. 22(6); Fleming, C. 22(2); Gittens, J. 13; Hendrie, J.G. 31(1); Hignett, C. 18(3); Horne, B. 3(1); Ironside, I. 11(1); Kamara, C. 3(2); Kavanagh, G.A. 6(4); Kernaghan, A.N. 22; Marshall, D. (3); Mohan, N. 18; Moore, A. 22(3); Morris, C. 22(3); Mustoe, R. 21(2); Parkinson, G. 4; Peake, A.M. 33; Pears, S. 26; Phillips, J.N. 40; Pollock, J. 17(5); Proctor, M.G. 6(5); Slaven, B. 13(5); Whyte, D. 34(1); Wilkinson, P. 41; Wright, T.E. 34(2).
League (54): Wilkinson 14, Hendrie 9, Falconer 5, Wright 5, Hignett 4, Slaven 4, Kernaghan 2, Mohan 2, Phillips 2 (1 pen), Morris 1, Mustoe 1, Pollock 1, own goals 4.
Coca Cola Cup (1): Wilkinson 1.
FA Cup (3): Falconer 2, Wright 1.
Ground: Ayresome Park, Middlesbrough, Cleveland TS1 4PB. Telephone Middlesbrough (0642) 819659.

Record attendance: 53,596 v Newcastle U, Division 1, 27 December 1949.
Manager: Lennie Lawrence.
Chief Executive/Secretary: Keith Lamb.
Honours – Football League: Division 2 Champions 1926–27, 1928–29, 1973–74.
Amateur Cup winners 1895, 1898
Anglo-Scottish Cup: Winners 1975–76.
Colours: Red shirts, white shorts, red stockings.

MILLWALL   DIV. 1

Allen, Malcolm.	Dolby, Tony C.	McCarthy, Michael.
Babrer, Phillip A.	Emberson, Carl W.	Middleton, Matthew J.
Beard, Mark.	Foran, Mark J.	Moralee, Jamie D.
Bogie, Ian.	Goodman, Jonathan.	Pitcher, Geoffrey.
Byrne, John F.	Holsgrove, Paul.	Rae, Alex.
Chapman, Daniel G.	Keller, Kasey.	Roberts, Andrew J.
Connor, James R.	Kerr, John.	Stevens, Keith H.
Cooper, Colin T.	Maguire, Gavin T.	Thatcher, Ben D.
Cunningham, Kenneth E.	Manning, Paul J.	Verveer, Etienne.
Davison, Aidan J.	May, Andrew M.	Wright, Jermaine M.
Dawes, Ian R.	McCarthy, Anthony P.	

League Appearances: Allen, M. 30(11); Armstrong, C. 3; Barber, P.A. 46; Bogie, I. 20(2); Byrne, J.F. 11(2); Cooper, C.T. 41; Cunningham, K. 37; Davison, A.J. 1; Dawes, I.R. 46; Dolby, T.C. 4(14); Gaynor, T. (3); Holsgrove, P. 3(8); Keller, K. 45; Kennedy, M. (1); Kerr, J. 1(5); Maguire, G.T. 9; Manning, P.J. 1; May, A.M. 34(1); McCarthy, A.P. 6(1); McGinlay, J. 6(1); McLeary, A.T. 4(2); Moralee, J.D. 31(6); Rae, A. 23(7); Roberts, A.J. 41(4); Stephenson, P. (5); Stevens, K.H. 31; Verveer, E. (1); Wallace, D.L. 3

League (65): Moralee 15, Goodman 12, Allen 10 (2 pens), Barber 8, Rae 6, Cooper 4, McGinlay 2, Stevens 2, Armstrong 1, Byrne 1, Dolby 1, Kerr 1, McCarthy 1, May 1.
Coca Cola Cup (7): Allen 2, Roberts 2, Armstrong 1, Stevens 1, own goal 1.
FA Cup (0):
Ground: The Den, Zampa Road, Bermondsey SE16 3LH. Telephone 071–232 1222.
Player-Manager: Mick McCarthy.
Chief Executive Secretary: Graham Hortop.
Honours –
Football League: Division 2 Champions – 1987–88. Division 3 (S) Champions – 1927–28, 1937–38. Division 4 Champions – 1961–62.
Football League Trophy winners 1982–83.
Colours: Blue shirts, white shorts, blue stockings.

NEWCASTLE UNITED   FA PREMIER

Appleby, Matthew W.	Bracewell, Paul W.	Clark, Lee R.
Beresford, John.	Brock, Kevin S.	Cole, Andrew A.

Cormack, Peter.
Elliot, Robert J.
Galvin, Anthony.
Howey, Stephen N.
Hunt, Andrew.
Kelly, David T.
Kilcline, Brian.
Lee, Robert M.

McDonough, Darron K.
Murray, Nathan A.
Neilson, Alan B.
O'Brien, Liam F.
Peacock, Gavi K.
Robinson, Mark J.
Roche, David.
Scott, Kevin W.

Sellars, Scott.
Srnicek, Pavel.
Stimson, Mark.
Thompson, Alan.
Venison, Barry.
Watson, Stephen C.
Wright, Thomas J.

League Appearances: Beresford, J. 42; Bracewell, P.W. 19(6); Brock, K.S. 4(3); Carr, F.A. 8(2); Clark, L.R. 46; Cole, A.A. 11(1); Howey, S.N. 41; Kelly, D.T. 45; Kilcline, B. 7(12); Lee, R.M. 36; Neilson, A.B. 2(1); O'Brien, L.F. 33; Peacock, G.K. 29(3); Quinn, M. 4(1); Ranson, R. 3; Robinson, M.J. 2(7); Scott, K.W. 45; Sellars, S. 13; Sheedy, K.M. 23(1); Srnicek, P. 32; Stimson, M. 1(1); Thompson, A. 1(1); Venison, B. 44; Watson, S.C. 1(1); Wright, T.J. 14.

League (92): Kelly 24 (2 pens), Cole 12, Peacock 12 (2 pens), Lee 10, Clark 9, O'Brien 6, Sheedy 3, Bracewell 2, Brock 2, Howey 2, Quinn 2, Scott 2, Sellars 2, Beresford 1 (pen), Carr 1, own goals 2.

Coca Cola Cup (6): Kelly 2, Peacock 2, Lee 1, O'Brien 1.

FA Cup (7): Lee 2, Peacock 2, Clark 1, Kelly 1, Sheedy 1.

Ground: St James' Park, Newcastle-upon-Tyne NE1 4ST. Telephone 091–232 8361.

Record attendance: 68,386 v Chelsea, Division 1, 3 Sept 1930.

Manager: Kevin Keegan.

General Manager/Secretary: R. Cushing.

Honours –

Football League: Division 1 – Champions 1904–05, 1906–07, 1908–09, 1926–27, 1992–93. Division 2 Champions – 1964–65.

FA Cup winners 1910, 1924, 1932, 1951, 1952, 1955.

Texaco Cup winners 1973–74, 1974–75.

European Competitions: European Fairs Cup winners: 1968–69.

Anglo-Italian Cup winners: Winners 1973.

Colours: Black and white striped shirts, black shorts, black stockings.

NORTHAMPTON TOWN   DIV. 3

Bell, Michael.
Brown, Stephen.
Burnham, Jason J.
Chard, Phillip J.

Colkin, Lee.
Gillard, Kenneth J.
Harmon, Darren J.
Richardson, Barry.

Terry, Steve G.
Wilkin, Kevin.

League Appearances: Aldridge, M.J. 7(2); Angus, T.N. 36(1); Beavon, M.S. 21(3); Bell, M. 34(5); Benton, J. 2(3); Brown, S. 38; Burnham, J.J. 28(3); Chard, P.J. 29(5); Colkin, L. 12(1); Curtis, P. 22; Fox, M.C. (1); Gavin, P.J. 13(1); Gillard, K.J. 9; Harmon, D.J. 22(3); Hawke, W.R. 7; Holmes, M.A. 6; Lamb, P.D. 2(1); McParland, J.I. 11; Parker, S. 4; Parsons, M.C. 19; Richardson, B. 42; Scott, M.J. 10(7); Terry, S.G. 42; Tisdale, P.R. 5; Wilkin, K. 34(7); Young, S.R. 7(1).

League (48): Brown 9 (1 pen), Chard 6, Bell 5, Terry 5, Gavin 4, Wilkin 4, McParland 3, Aldridge 2, Angus 2, Scott 2, Young 2, Beavon 1 (pen), Curtis 1, Harmon 1, Hawke 1.

Coca Cola Cup (1): Terry 1.

FA Cup (8): Brown 2, Wilkin 2, Bell 1, Chard 1, McParland 1, Terry 1.

Ground: County Ground, Abington Avenue, Northampton NN1 4PS. Telephone Northampton (0604) 234100.

Record attendance: 24,523 v Fulham, Division 1, 23 April 1966.

Player-Manager: Phil Chard.

Secretary: Philip Mark Hough.

Honours –

Football League: Division 3 Champions – 1962–63. Division 4 Champions – 1986–87.

Colours: Maroon shirts, white shorts, maroon stockings.

NORWICH CITY   FA PREMIER

Akinbiyi, Adeola P.
Bowen, Mark R.
Butterworth, Ian S.
Crook, Ian S.
Culverhouse, Ian B.
Cureton, Jamie.
Eadie, Darren M.
Ekoku, Efan.

Fox, Ruel A.
Goss, Jeremy.
Gunn, Bryan J.
Johnson, Andrew J.
Megson, Gary J.
Newman, Robert N.
Phillips, David O.
Polston, John D.

Power, Lee M.
Robins, Mark G.
Smith, David C.
Sutch, Daryl.
Sutton, Christopher R.
Ullathorne, Robert.
Walton, Mark A.
Woodthorpe, Colin J.

League Appearances: Beckford, D.R. 7(1); Bowen, M.R. 42; Butterworth, I.S. 26; Crook, I.S. 32(2); Culverhouse, I.B. 41; Ekoku, E. 1(3); Fox, R.A. 32(2); Goss, J. 25; Gunn, B.J. 42; Johnson, A.J. 1(1); Megson, G.J. 20(3); Minett, J. (1); Newman, R.N. 16(2); Phillips, D.O. 42; Polston, J.D. 34; Power, L.M. 11(7); Robins, M.G. 34(3); Smith, D.C. 5(1); Sutch, D. 14(8); Sutton, C. 32(6); Woodthorpe, C.J. 5(2).

League (61): Robins 15, Phillips 9 (2 pens), Sutton 8, Power 6, Fox 4, Crook 3, Ekoku 3, Newman 2, Sutch 2, Beckford 1, Bowen 1 (pen), Butterworth 1, Goss 1, Johnson 1, Megson 1, Polston 1, own goals 2.

Coca Cola Cup (4): Sutton 2, Goss 1, Robins 1.

FA Cup (1): Beckford 1.

Ground: Carrow Road, Norwich NR1 1JE. Telephone Norwich (0603) 612131.

Record attendance: 43,984 v Leicester C, FA Cup 6th rd, 30 March 1963.

Manager: Mike Walker.

Secretary: A. R. W. Neville.

Honours –

Football League: Division 2 Champions – 1971–72, 1985–86. Division 3 (S) Champions – 1933–34.

Football League Cup: Winners 1962, 1985.

Colours: Yellow shirts, green trim, green shorts, yellow trim, yellow stockings.

NOTTINGHAM FOREST   DIV. 1

Armstrong, Craig.
Black, Kingsley.
Blatherwick, Steven S.

Byrne, Raymond.
Charles, Gary A.
Chettle, Stephen.

Clough, Nigel H.
Crosby, Gary.
Crossley, Mark G.

Drury, Nathan.
Finnigan, John.
Gemmill, Scot.
Glover, Edward L.
Guinan, Stephen.
Haywood, Paul.
Hinshelwood, Danny.
Howe, Stephen.
Hughes, Luke.
Kaminsky, Jason M. G.
Keane, Roy M.

Kilford, Ian A.
Laws, Brian.
Marriott, Andrew.
Marshall, Lee.
McGregor, Paul A.
McKinnon, Raymond.
Perce, Stuart.
Rookyard, Carl.
Rosario, Robert M.
Smith, Richard.
Statham, Mark.

Stone, Stephen B.
Statford, Lee.
Tiler, Carl.
Walker, Justin.
Warner, Vance.
Webb, Neil J.
Williams, Brett.
Woan, Ian S.
Wright, Dale C.

League Appearances: Bannister, G. 27(4); Black, K. 19(5); Charles, G.A. 14; Chettle, S. 30; Clough, N.H. 42; Crosby, G. 20(3); Crossley, M.G. 37; Gemmill, S. 33; Glover, E.L. 9(5); Keane, R.M. 40; Laws, B. 32(1); Marriott, A. 5; McKinnon, R. 5(1); Orlygsson, T. 15(5); Pearce, S. 23; Rosario, R.M. 10; Sheringham, E. 3; Stone, S.B. 11(1); Tiler, C. 37; Webb, N.J. 9; Williams, B. 9; Wilson, T. 5; Woan, I.S. 27(1).

League (41): Clough 10 (3 pens), Bannister 8, Keane 6, Black 5, Woan 3, Pearce 2 (1 pen), Crosby 1, Gemmill 1, McKinnon 1, Orlygsson 1, Rosario 1, Sheringham 1, Stone 1.

Coca Cola Cup (8): Orlygsson 2, Bannister 1, Black 1, Clough 1, Keane 1, Woan 1, own goal 1.

FA Cup (6): Webb 2, Bannister 1, Clough 1, Keane 1, Woan 1.

Ground: City Ground, Nottingham NG2 5FJ. Telephone Nottingham (0602) 822202.

Record attendance: 49,945 v Manchester U, Division 1, 28 October 1967.

Manager: Frank Clark.

Secretary: P. White.

Honours –

Football League: Division 1 – Champions 1977–78. Division 2 Champions – 1906–07, 1921–22. Division 3 (S) Champions – 1950–51.

FA Cup: Winners 1898, 1959. **Football League Cup:** Winners 1977–78, 1978–79, 1988–89, 1989–90.

Anglo-Scottish Cup: Winners 1976–77.

Simod Cup: Winners 1989. **Zenith Data Systems Cup:** Winners 1991–92.

European Competitions:

European Cup winners: 1978–79, 1979–80, 1980–81. **Super Cup winners:** 1979–80.

Colours: Red shirts, white shorts, red stockings.

NOTTS COUNTY   DIV. 1

Agana, Patrick A. O.
Catlin, Robert.
Cherry, Steven R.
Cox, Paul R.
Devlin, Paul J.
Dijkstra, Meindert.
Dolan, Kenneth P.
Draper, Mark A.

Gallagher, Thomas D.
Harding, Paul.
Hill, Philip W.
Johnson, Michael O.
Lund, Gary J.
Matthews, Robert.
Murphy, Shaun P.
Palmer, Charles A.

Paris, Alan D.
Reeves, David.
Robinson, David A.
Sherlock, Paul G.
Short, Christian M.
Simpson, Michael.
Slawson, Stephen M.
Smith, David A.

Smith, Mark C.   Turner, Robert P.   Wilson, Kevin J.
Snook, Edward K.   Walker, Richard N.   Worboys, Gavin.
Thomas, Dean R.   Wells, Mark A.   Yates, Dean R.
Turner, Philip.   Williams, Andrew.

League Appearances: Agana, P.A. 23(6); Bartlett, K.F. 11(5); Catlin, R. 2; Cherry, S.R. 44; Cox, P.R. 21; Devlin, P.J. 28(4); Dijkstra, M. 11; Draper, M.A. 44; Dryden, R.A. 2; Harding, P. (1); Johnson, M.O. 37; Lund, G.J. 26(2); Matthews, R. 5(3); Murphy, S.P. 3(5); O'Riordan, D.J. 15(2); Palmer, C.A. 30(1); Reeves, D. 8(1); Robinson, D.A. 1; Short, C.M. 30(1); Short, C.J. 3; Slawson, S.M. 9(11); Smith, D.A. 37; Smith, M.C. 4(1); Thomas, D.R. 36(1); Turner, P. 17(3); Turner, R.P. 7(1); Walker, R.N. 12; Wells, M.A. (1); Williams, A. 17(5); Wilson, K.J. 23(9).
League (55): Draper 11, Smith D 8 (4 pens), Bartlett 5, Lund 4, Devlin 3, Slawson 3, Thomas 3, Walker 3, Agana 2, Matthews 2, Reeves 2, Cox 1, Murphy 1, O'Riordan 1, Chris Short 1, Craig Short 1, Turner P 1, Turner R 1, Williams 1, Wilson 1.
Coca Cola Cup (6): Lund 2, Agana 1, Draper 1, O'Riordan 1, Robinson 1.
FA Cup (0):
Ground: County Ground, Meadow Lane, Nottingham NG2 3HJ. Telephone Nottingham (0602) 861155.
Record attendance: 47,310 v York C, FA Cup 6th rd, 12 March 1955.
Manager: Mick Walker.
Secretary: N. E. Hook MCIM, AMLD.
Honours –
Football League: Division 2 Champions – 1896–97, 1913–14, 1922–23. Division 3 (S) Champions – 1930–31, 1949–50. Division 4 Champions – 1970–71.
FA Cup: Winners 1893–94.
Colours: Black and white striped shirts, black shorts, white stockings.

OLDHAM ATHLETIC   FA PREMIER

Adams, Neil J.   Halle, Guner.   Milligan, Michael J.
Barlow, Andrew J.   Hallworth, Jonathan G. Olney, Ian D.
Beckford, Darren, R. Henry, Nicholas I.   Pointon, Neil G.
Bernard, Paul R. J.   Holden, Andrew I.   Redmond, Stephen.
Brennan, Mark R.   Jobson, Richard I.   Ritchie, Andrew T.
Donachie, William.   Keeley, John H.   Sharp, Graeme M.
Fleming, Craig.   Makin, Christopher.   Tolson, Neil.
Gerrard, Paul W.   Marshall, Ian P.
Hall, David T.   McDonald, Neil R.

League Appearances: Adams, N.J. 26(6); Barlow, A.J. 6; Beckford, D.R. 6(1); Bernard, P.R. 32(1); Brennan, M.R. 14; Fleming, C. 23(1); Gerrard, P.W. 25; Halle, G. 41; Hallworth, J. 16; Henry, N. I. 32; Jobson, R.I. 40; Keeley, J.H. 1; Keizerweerd, O. (1); Marshall, I.P. 26(1); McDonald, N.R. 2(2); Milligan, M.J. 42; Moulden, P.A. 1(3); Olney, I.D. 32(2); Palmer, R.N. 5(12); Pointon, N.G. 34; Redmond, S. 28(3); Ritchie, A.T. 10(2); Sharp, G.M. 20(1); Tolson, N. (3).
League (63): Olney 12, Adams 9 (1 pen), Sharp 7, Henry 6, Halle 5, Bernard 4, Beckford 3, Brennan 3, Milligan 3, Pointon 3, Ritchie 3, Jobson 2, Marshall 2, own goal 1.

Coca Cola Cup (2): Bernard 1, Henry 1.
FA Cup (2): Bernard 1, Olney 1.
Ground: Boundary Park, Oldham. Telephone 061–624 4972.
Record attendance: 47,671 v Sheffield W, FA Cup 4th rd. 25 January 1930.
Manager: Joe Royle.
Secretary: Terry Cale.
Honours –
Football League: Division 2 Champions – 1990–91, Division 3 (N) Champions –
1952–53. Division 3 Champions – 1973–74.
Colours: All blue with red piping.

OXFORD UNITED   DIV. 1

Allen, Christopher A.	Holmes, Keith N.	Narbett, Jonathan V.
Beauchamp, Joseph D.	Jackson, Darren W.	Penney, David M.
Collins, David D.	Kee, Paul V.	Reece, Paul J.
Cusack, Nicholas J.	Keeble, Matthew E.	Robinson, Leslie.
Didcock, Trista S.	Lewis, Michael.	Smart, Garry J.
Druce, Mark A.	Magilton, James.	Tavinor, Stephen J.
Durnin, John.	McClaren, Stephen.	Wallbridge, Andrew J.
Evans, Ceri L.	Melville, Andrew R.	Wanless, Paul S.
Ford, Michael P.	Murphy, Matthew S.	
Ford, Robert J.	Mutchell, Robert D.	

League Appearances: Allen, C. 18(13); Beauchamp, J.D. 44; Collins, D.D. 12(1);
Cusack, N.J. 30(9); Druce, M.A. 3(1); Durnin, J. 34(3); Evans, C.L. 41; Ford, M.P.
43(1); Jackson, D.W. 1; Keeble, M.E. 1; Kee, P.V. 11; Lewis, Michael, 40(1);
Magilton, J. 40: Melville, A.R. 44; Murphy, M.S. 2; Narbett, J.V. 12(2); Penney,
D.M. 23(10); Phillips, L.M. 9(2); Reece, P.J. 35; Robinson, L. 14(2); Smart, G.J. 41;
Varadi, I. 3(2); Wanless, P.S. 5(2).
League (53): Durnin 11, Magilton 11 (6 pens), Beauchamp 7, Melville 6, Penney 6 (1
pen), Cusack 4, Ford 4, Allen 3, Druce 1.
Coca Cola Cup (5): Allen 2, Cusack 2, Beauchamp 1.
FA Cup (3): Beauchamp 1, Cusack 1, Magilton 1 (pen).
Ground: Manor Ground, Headington, Oxford. Telephone Oxford (0865) 61503.
Record attendance: 22,750 v Preston NE, FA Cup 6th rd, 29 February 1964.
Manager: Brian Horton.
Secretary: Mick Brown.
Honours – Football League: Division 2 Champions – 1984–85. Division 3 Champions
– 1967–68, 1983–84.
Football League Cup: Winners 1985–86.
Colours: Gold shirts with blue sleeves, blue shorts, gold stockings.

PETERBOROUGH UNITED   DIV. 1

Adcock, Anthony C.	Barnes, David O.	Bradshaw, Darren S.
Barber, Frederick.	Bennett, Ian M.	Cooper, Gary.

Ebdon, Marcus.   Iorfa, Dominic.   Spearing, Anthony.
Greenman, Christopher. McGlashan, John.   Sterling, Worrel R.
Halsall, Michael.   Philliskirk, Anthony.   Welsh, Stephen.
Howarth, Lee.   Robinson, Ronald.

League Appearances: Adcock, A.C. 44(1); Barnes, D.O. 22(4); Bennett, I.M. 46;
Bradshaw, D.S. 32(2); Charlery, K. 10; Cooper, G. 35; Costello, P. (2); Curtis, A.
8(3); Ebdon, M. 28; Gavin, P.J. (1); Greenman, C. 8(1); Halsall, M. 25; Howarth, L.
26(4); Ingram, G.P. (1); Iorfa, D. 3(23); Limber, N.E. 22(6); McGlashan,
J. 18; Philliskirk, A. 31(1); Retallick, G.J. 2(3); Robinson, D.A. 1; Robinson, R. 20;
Roche, D. 4; Spearing, A. 21(1); Sterling, W.R. 43(1); Tuttle, D.P. 7; Welsh, S. 45;
White, C. 3(2).

League (55): Adcock 16, Philliskirk 11, Sterling 8, Ebdon 4, Barnes 3, Charlery 3,
Cooper 3 (1 pen), Halsall 2, Curtis 1, Iorfa 1, Welsh 1, own goals 2.

Coca Cola Cup (8): Charlery 3, Adcock 2, Cooper 1 (pen), Costello 1, Halsall 1.

FA Cup (4): Sterling 2, Adcock 1, Philliskirk 1.

Ground: London Road Ground, Peterborough PE2 8AL. Telephone Peterborough
(0733) 63947.

Record attendance: 30,096 v Swansea T, FA Cup 5th rd, 20 February 1965.

Manager: Lil Fuccillo.

Secretary: Miss Caroline Hand.

Honours –

Football League: Division 4 Champions – 1960–61, 1973–74.

Colours: Royal blue shirts, white shorts, white stockings.

PLYMOUTH ARGYLE   DIV. 2

Barlow, Martin D.   Evans, Micahel J.   Morgan, Stephen A.
Boardman, Paul.   Garner, Darren J.   Morrison, Andrew C.
Burrows, Adrian M.   Hill, Keith J.   Newland, Raymond J.
Castle, Stephen C.   Joyce, Warren G.   Nugent, Kevin P.
Dalton, Paul.   Marshall, Dwight W.   Poole, Gary J.
Edworthy, Marc.   McCall, Stephen H.   Skinner, Craig R.

League Appearances: Adcock, P.M. 2(7); Barlow, M.D. 17(7); Boardman, P. 2;
Burrows, A.M. 20; Castle, S.C. 31; Crocker, M.A. 1(3); Dalton, P. 30(2); Dryden,
R.A. 5; Edworthy, M. 14(1); Evans, M.J. 16(7); Fiore, M.J. (1); Garner, D.J. 8(2);
Hill, K.J. 36; Hodges, K. 2(2); Hodges, L.L. 6(1); Joyce, W.G. 28(2); Kite, P.D. 2;
Marker, N.R. 7; Marshall, D.W. 21(3); McCall, S.H. 35; Morgan, J.A. 3; Morgan,
S.A. 35(1); Morrison, A.C. 29; Newland, R.J. 21; Nugent, K.P. 45; Poole, G.J. 39;
Regis, D. 7; Shilton, P.L. 23; Skinner, C.R. 12(1); Spearing, A. 5; Turner, R.P. 2;
Walker, A. 2.

League (59): Castle 11 (1 pen), Nugent 11, Dalton 9, Poole 5 (4 pens), Joyce 3,
Adcock 2, Hodges L 2, Marker 2, Regis 2, Barlow 1, Boardman 1, Burrows 1, Evans
1, McCall 1, Marshall 1, Morgan S 1, Skinner 1, Walker 1, own goals 3.

Coca Cola Cup (11): Regis 3, Dalton 2, Nugent 2, Poole 2 (1 pen), Joyce 1, Marker
1.

FA Cup (7): Marshall 3, Castle 2, Dalton 2.

Ground: Home Park, Plymouth, Devon PL2 3DQ. Telephone Plymouth (0752)
562561-2-3.

Record attendance: 43,596 v Aston Villa, Division 2, 10 October 1936.
Manager: Peter Shilton.
Secretary: Michael Holladay.
Honours –
Football League: Division 3 (S) Champions – 1929–30, 1951–52. Division 3
Champions – 1958–59.
Colours: Green and white striped shirts, black shorts, black stockings.

PORTSMOUTH   DIV. 1

Aspinall, Warren.	Hall, Paul A.	Price, Christopher J.
Awford, Andrew T.	Horne, Brian.	Ross, Michael P.
Burns, Christopher.	Kelly, Mark J.	Russell, Lee.
Butters, Guy.	Knight, Alan E.	Symons, Christopher J.
Chamberlain, Mark V.	Kristensen, Bjorn.	Walsh, Paul A.
Clarke, Colin J.	McLoughlin, Alan F.	Whittingham, Guy.
Daniel, Raymond C.	Murray, Shaun.	Young, Roy E.
Doling, Stuart J.	Neill, Warren A.	
Gale, Shaun M.	Powell, Darryl A.	

League Appearances: Agnew, S.M. 3(2); Aspinall, W. 19(8); Awford, A.T. 44; Burns,
C. 28(4); Butters, G. 13(2); Chamberlain, M.V. 37(4); Clarke, C.J. 11(8); Daniel,
R.C. 40; Doling, S.J. 2(4); Knight, A.E. 46; Kristensen, B. 10; Kuhl, M. 3;
Lawrence, G.R. (12); Maguire, G.T. 18(3); McLoughlin, A.F. 46; Murray, S. 2(5);
Neill, W.A. 28; Powell, D.A. 4(19); Price, C.J. 13; Russell, L. 12(2); Stimson, M.
3(1); Symons, C. 41; Walsh, P.A. 37(6); Whittingham, G. 46.
League (80): Whittingham 42 (1 pen), McLoughlin 9, Walsh 9, Chamberlain 4,
Daniel 4, Aspinall 2 (2 pens), Symons 2, Burns 1, Butters 1, Clarke 1, Kristensen 1,
Kuhl 1, own goals 3.
Coca Cola Cup (6): McLoughlin 2, Whittingham 2, Clarke 1, Murray 1.
FA Cup (0):
Ground: Fratton Park, Frogmore Rd, Portsmouth PO4 8RA. Telephone Portsmouth
(0705) 731204.
Record attendance: 51,385 v Derby Co, FA Cup 6th rd, 26 February 1949.
Team Manager: Jim Smith.
Club Secretary: P. Weld.
Honours –
Football League: Division 1 Champions – 1948–49, 1949–50. Division 3 (S)
Champions – 1923–24. Division 3 Champions – 1961–62, 1982–83.
FA Cup: Winners 1939.
Colours: Blue shirts, white shorts, red stockings.

PORT VALE   DIV. 2

Aspin, Neil.	Glover, Dean V.	Hughes, Darren J.
Cross, Nicholas J. R.	Griffiths, Gareth J.	Jeffers, John J.
Foyle, Martin J.	Harrison, Michael.	Kent, Kevin J.

Kerr, Paul A.
Mills, Simon A.
Musselwhite, Paul S.
Porter, Andrew M.

Sandeman, Bradley R.
Slaven, Bernard.
Stokes, Dean A.
Swan, Peter H.

Taylor, Ian K.
Van Der Laan, Robertus P.
Walker, Raymond.
Wood, Trevor J.

League Appearances: Aspin, N. 35; Bartlett, K.F. 5; Billing, P.G. 10(2); Cross, N.J. 33(5); Foyle, M.J. 10(6); Glover, D.V. 39; Houchen, K.M. 26(2); Jeffers, J.J. 15(11); Kent, K.J. 21(6); Kerr, P.A. 34(4); Mathie, A.M. (3); Mills, S.A. 3; Musselwhite, P.S. 41; Porter, A.M. 12(5); Sandeman, B.R. 20(2); Slaven, B. 9(1); Smith, M.C. 6; Sulley, C. 40; Swan, P.H. 38; Taylor, I.K. 41; Van Der Laan, R. 29(9); Walker, R. 34(1); Wood, T.J. 5.
League (79): Taylor 15, Cross 12, Kerr 11 (2 pens), Walker 9 (3 pens), Houchen 6, Van der Laan 6, Foyle 4, Glover 3, Jeffers 2, Slaven 2, Swan 2, Bartlett 1, Kent 1, Porter 1, Sandeman 1, Sulley 1, own goals 2.
Coca Cola Cup (2): Foyle 1, Taylor 1.
FA Cup (7): Foyle 3, Porter 1, Swan 1, Taylor 1, Van der Laan 1.
Ground: Vale Park, Burslem, Stoke-on-Trent. Telephone Stoke-on-Trent (0782) 814134.
Record attendance: 50,000 v Aston Villa, FA Cup 5th rd, 20 February 1960.
Manager: John Rudge.
Secretary: Eddie Harrison.
Honours –
Football League: Division 3 (N) Champions – 1929–30, 1953–54. Division 4 Champions – 1958–59.
Colours: White shirts, black shorts, black and white stockings.

PRESTON NORTH END   DIV. 3

Ainsworth, Gareth.
Ashcroft, Lee.
Burton, Simon P.
Callaghan, Aaron J.
Cartwright, Lee.
Davidson, Jonathan S.
Ellis, Anthony J.

Farnworth, Simon.
Flitcroft, David J.
Fowler, Lee.
Johnstone, Glenn P.
Kidd, Ryan A.
Leonard, Mark A.
Lucas, Richard.

Magee, Kevin.
Norbury, Michael S.
Tinkler, John.
Watson, Liam.
Whalley, David N.

League Appearances: Ainsworth, G. 26; Allardyce, C.S. (1); Allardyce, S. 1(2); Ashcroft, L. 37(2); Burton, S.P. 17(4); Callaghan, A.J. 33(2); Cartwright, L. 33(1); Christie, D. 1(1); Davidson, J. 18(3); Eaves, D.M. 1(3); Ellis, A.J. 34(1); Farnworth, S. 35; Finney, S.K. 1(3); Flitcroft, D.J. 4(4); Flynn, M.A. 35; Fowler, J.A. 5(1); Fowler, L. 29(3); Garnett, S.M. 10; Graham, D.W. 8; Greenall, C.A. 20; James, M.J. 22(3); Johnstone, G.P. 10; Kidd, R.A. 13(2); Leonard, M.A. 19(3); Lucas, R. 26; Moylon, C.J. (1); Norbury, M.S. 21; Siddall, B. 1; Taylor, C.D. 4; Tinkler, J. 22(2); Watson, L. 6(2); Whalley, D.N. 14.
League (65): Ellis 22, Norbury 8, Ashcroft 7 (2 pens), James 5, Burton 3, Cartwright 3, Watson 3, Callaghan 2, Flitcroft 2, Flynn 2, Fowler L 2, Garnett 2, Tinkler 2, Davidson 1, Leonard 1.
Coca Cola Cup (2): Ellis 1, Tinkler 1.
FA Cup (5): Callaghan 1, Davidson 1, Ellis 1, Fowler L 1, Graham 1.

51

Ground: Deepdale, Preston PR1 6RU. Telephone Preston (0772) 795919 (club).
Record attendance: 42,684 v Arsenal, Division 1, 23 April 1938.
Manager: John Beck.
Chief Executive: Paul Agnew.
Honours –
Football League: Division 1 Champions – 1888–89 (first champions), 1889–90.
Division 2 Champions – 1903–04, 1912–13, 1950–51. Division 3 Champions –
1970–71.
FA Cup winners 1889, 1938.
Colours: White shirts, navy blue shorts, navy blue stockings.

QUEENS PARK RANGERS   FA PREMIER

Allen, bradley J.
Bailey, Dennis L.
Bardsley, David J.
Barker, Simon.
Brevett, Rufus E.
Bryan, Marvin L.
Caldwell, Peter J.
Croft, Brian G.
Doyle, Maurice.
Ferdinand, Leslie.
Finlay, Darren J.

Freedman, Douglas A.
Gallen, Kevin A.
Gallen, Stephen J.
Herrera, Roberto.
Holloway, Ian S.
Impey, Andrew R.
Maddix, Danny S.
McCarthy, Alan J.
McDonald, Alan.
Meaker, Michael J.
Peacock, Darren.

Penrice, Gary K.
Ready, Karl.
Roberts, Anthony M.
Sinton, Andrew.
Stejskal, Jan.
White, Devon W.
Wilkins, Raymond C.
Wilson, Clive.
Witter, Anthony J.

League Appearances: Allen, B.J. 21(4); Bailey, D.L. 13(2); Bardsley, D.J. 40; Barker,
S. 21(4); Brevett, R.E. 14(1); Channing, J.A. 2; Doyle, M. 5; Ferdinand, L. 37;
Holloway, I.S. 23(1); Impey, A.R. 39(1); Maddix, D.S. 9(5); McDonald, A. 39;
Meaker, M.J. 3; Peacock, D. 35(3); Penrice, G.K. 10(5); Ready, K. 2(1); Roberts,
A.M. 28; Sinton, A. 36; Stejskal, J. 14(1); Thompson, G.L. (4); White, D.W. 3(4);
Wilkins, R.C. 27; Wilson, C. 41.
League (63): Ferdinand 20, Allen 10, Sinton 7 (1 pen), Penrice 6, Bardsley 3, Wilson
3 (2 pens), Holloway 2, Impey 2, Peacock 2, White 2, Wilkins 2, Bailey 1, Barker 1,
Channing 1, own goal 1.
Coca Cola Cup (5): Ferdinand 2, Allen 1, Bailey 1, Peacock 1.
FA Cup (4): Ferdinand 2, Holloway 1, Penrice 1.
Ground: South Africa Road, W12 7PA. Telephone 081–743 0262.
Record attendance: 35,353 v Leeds U, Division 1, 27 April 1974.
Manager: Gerry Francis.
Secretary: Miss S. F. Marson.
Honours –
Football League: Division 2 Champions – 1982–83. Division 3 (S) Champions –
1947–48. Division 3 Champions – 1966–67.
Football League Cup winners 1966–67.
Colours: Blue and white hooped shirts, white shorts, white stockings.

READING DIV. 2

Barkus, Lea P.	Gray, Andrew.	McCance, Daren.
Deaner, Andrew J.	Hislop, Neil S.	McPherson, Keith A.
Dillon, Kevin P.	Holzman, Jeffrey.	Parkinson, Philip J.
Francis, Stephen S.	Jones, Tom.	Quinn, James M.
Gilkes, Earl G. M.	Lambert, Christopher J. P.	Taylor, Scott D.
Gooding, Michael C.	Lovell, Stuart A.	Williams, Adrian.

League Appearances: Barkus, L.P. 4(5); Bass, D. 5; Dillon, K.P. 40; Francis, S.S. 34; Gilkes, E.G. 38; Gooding, M.C. 38(2); Gray, A. 8(3); Hislop, N.S. 12; Holzman, M.R. 12(4); Hopkins, N.S. 36; Jackson, D.W. 5; Jones, T. 21; Lambert, C. 9(18); Lovell, S.A. 18(4); MacDonald, D.H. 11; McCance, D. 1; McGhee, M. 9(4); McPherson, K.A. 44; Moody, P. 5; Parkinson, P.J. 38(1); Quinn, J.M. 42; Richardson, S. 11(4); Taylor, S.D. 30(2); Viveash, A.L. 5; Williams, A. 30(1).

League (66): Quinn 17 (2 pens), Gilkes 12, Lovell 8, Taylor 5, Parkinson 4, Williams 4, Gooding 3, Gray 3, Lambert 3, McGhee 2, Dillon 1, Hopkins 1, Jones 1, McPherson 1, Moody 1.

Coca Cola Cup (2): Quinn 1, Williams 1.

FA Cup (5): Quinn 3 (1 pen), Parkinson 1, Taylor 1.

Ground: Elm Park, Norfolk Road, Reading. Telephone Reading (0734) 507878.

Record attendance: 33,042 v Brentford, FA Cup 5th rd, 19 February 1927.

Manager: Mark McGhee.

Secretary: Jayne E. Hill.

Honours –

Football League: Division 3 Champions – 1985–86. Division 3 (S) Champions – 1925–26. Division 4 Champions – 1978–79.

Simod Cup winners 1987–88.

Colours: Navy and white hooped shirts, white shorts, white stockings.

ROCHDALE DIV. 3

Anders, Jason S.	Howard, Andrew P.	Ryan, John B.
Bowden, Jon L.	Jones, Alexander.	Snowdon, Trevor.
Butler, Paul J.	Milner, Andrew J.	Thackeray, Andrew J.
Doyle, Stephen C.	Mulrain, Steven F.	Whitehall, Steven C.
Flounders, Andrew J.	Reeves, Alan.	
Graham, James.	Reid, Shaun.	

League Appearances: Anders, J.S. 2(13); Ashurst, J. 1; Beever, A.M. (1); Bowden, J.L. 31(4); Brown, A.J. 4(1); Butler, P.J. 14(2); Clarke, T.J. 2; Doyle, S.C. 18; Flounders, A.J. 31(1); Graham, J. 37(1); Howard, A.P. 4(11); Jones, A. 28(1); Luke, N.E. 2(1); Milner, A.J. 17(1); Mulrain, S.F. 3(3); Page, D.R. 3(1); Parker, C. 4(6); Payne, M.R. 26(2); Reeves, A. 40(1); Reid, S. 40; Rose, K.P. 40; Ryan, J.B. 25(1); Snowdon, T. 8(5); Thackeray, A.J. 41; Whitehall, S.C. 41(1).

League (70): Flounders 14 (2 pens), Whitehall 14, Bowden 8, Payne 6 (4 pens), Thackeray 6, Milner 4, Reid 4 (1 pen), Reeves 3, Butler 2, Howard 2, Jones 2, Mulrain 2, Anders 1, Page 1, own goal 1.

53

Coca Cola Cup (2): Reeves 1, Ryan 1.

FA Cup (2): Reid 1, Whitehall 1.

Ground: Spotland, Sandy Lane, Rochdale OL11 5DS. Telephone Rochdale (0706) 44648.

Record attendance: 24,231 v Notts Co, FA Cup 2nd rd, 10 December 1949.

Manager: Dave Sutton.

Secretary: Keith Clegg.

Honours – Nil.

Colours: Blue/white trim.

ROTHERHAM UNITED   DIV. 2

Banks, Ian F.	Howard, Jonathan.	Pickering, Albert G.
Barrick, Dean.	Hutchings, Christopher.	Richardson, Neil T.
Buckley, John W.	Johnson, Nigel M.	Russell, William.
Clarke, Matthew J.	Law, Nicholas.	Todd, Mark K.
Curtis, Leonardo S.	Marginson, Karl.	Varadi, Imre.
Goodwin, Shaun L.	Mercer, William.	Wilder, Christopher J.
Hazel, Desmond L.	Page, Donald R.	

League Appearances: Banks, I.F. 45; Barrick, D. 45(1); Buckley, J.W. 2(2); Campbell, D.A. (1); Clarke, M.J. 9; Cunningham, A. 31(2); Currie, D.N. 5; Flounders, A.J. 6; Goater, L.S. 20(3); Goodwin, S.L. 28(2); Gridelet, P.R. 9; Hazel, D.L. 31(5); Howard, J. 12(5); Hutchings, C. 30; Johnson, N.M. 31; Kite, P.D. 1; Law, N. 44; Marginson, K. (1); Mercer, W. 36; Page, D.R. 11(13); Pickering, A.G. 38; Richardson, N.T. 8(6); Taylor, A. 6(1); Todd, M.K. 16; Varadi, I. 11; Wilder, C. 31(1).

League (60): Wilder 8 (5 pens), Goater 7, Hazel 7, Cunningham 6 (1 pen), Banks 5, Barrick 4, Todd 4 (2 pens), Varadi 4 (1 pen) Currie 2, Flounders 2, Howard 2, Johnson 2, Page 2, Goodwin 1, Law 1, Pickering 1, own goals 2.

Coca Cola Cup (4): Todd 2 (1 pen), Banks 1, Goater 1.

FA Cup (7): Cunningham 2, Goodwin 2, Howard 2, Johnson 1.

Ground: Millmoor Ground, Rotherham. Telephone Rotherham (0709) 562434.

Record attendance: 25,000 v Sheffield U, Division 2, 13 December 1952 and v Sheffield W, Division 2, 26 January 1952.

Manager: Phil Henson.

Secretary: N. Darnill.

Honours –

Football League: Division 3 Champions – 1980–81. Division 3 (N) Champions – 1950–51. Division 4 Champions – 1988–89.

Colours: Red shirts, white shorts, red stockings.

SCARBOROUGH   DIV. 3

Ashdjian, John A.	Curran, Christopher P.	Gill, Martin.
Carter, Stephen G.	Evans, Mark.	Horsfield, Geoffrey M.
Charles, Stephen.	Foreman, Darren.	Jules, Mark A.

Lightbourne, Kyle L.   Mooney, Thomas J.   Thompson, Simon L.
McGeee, Owen E.   Mudd, Paul A.
Mockler, Andrew J.   Swales, Stephen C.

League Appearances: Ashdjian, J.A. 20(8); Barrow, L.A. 11; Cawthorn, P.J. 2(1); Charles, S. 16; Curran, C. 32; Edmonds, D. (1); Evans, M. 20; Ford, S.T. 22; Foreman, D. 41(1); Hargreaves, C. 2(1); Himsworth, G.P. 27(6); Hirst, L.W. 35(1); Horsfield, G. 6; James, L. (6); Jules, M.A. 27(9); Lee, C. 26(2); Lightbourne, K.L. 11(8); McGee, O.E. 13(3); McKenzie, R.M. (1); Mockler, A.J. 8(2); Mooney, T.J. 39(1); Mudd, P.A. 38; Murphy, A.J. 7(1); Ormsby, B.T. 15(1); Swales, S.C. 2(1); Thompson, S.L. 34(3); Toman, J.A. 6; Wheeler, P. 2(5).

League (66): Foreman 27 (1 pen), Mooney 9, Jules 8, Ashdjian 5, Charles 3 (3 pens), Lightbourne 3, Curran 2, Hirst 2, Himsworth 1, Horsefield 1, Lee 1, Mockler 1, Mudd 1, Ormsby 1, Wheeler 1.

Coca Cola Cup (16): Mooney 5, Foreman 2, Hirst 2, Lee 2, Ashdjian 1, Curran 1, Jules 1, Mockler 1, own goal 1.

FA Cup (1): Mockler 1.

Ground: The McCain Stadium, Seamer Road, Scarborough YO12 4HF. Telephone (0723) 375094.

Manager: Phil Chambers.

Administrator: Miss H. Crinnion.

Honours –

FA Trophy: Winners 1973, 1976, 1977.

GM Vauxhall Conference: Winners 1987.

Colours: Red shirts, white shorts, red stockings.

SCUNTHORPE UNITED   DIV. 3

Alexander, Graham.   Hill, David M.   Ryan, Tim J.
Ellender, Paul.   Joyce, Joseph P.   Samways, Mark.
Elliott, Matthew S.   Longden, David P.   Thompstone, Ian P.
Foy, David L.   Martin, Dean S.   White, Jason G.
Goodacre, Samuel D.   McCullagh, Paul A.
Helliwell, Ian.   McNeil, James W.

League Appearances: Alexander, G. 41; Broddle, J. 5; Buckley, J.W. 13(2); Charles, S. 4; Constable, S.D. 2(5); Crisp, R.I. 6(2); Daws, A. 21(3); Duffy, D.G. 4; Elliott, M.S. 39; Farrell, D. 4(1); Foy, D.L. 1(2); Goodacre, S.D. 13(8); Greaves, S.R. 9(6); Helliwell, I. 40(1); Hill, D.M. 19; Humphries, G. 29(1); Joyce, J.P. 30; Longden, D.P. 20; Martin, D.S. 38; Maxwell, J.D. (2); McCullagh, P.A. 5; Platnauer, N. 14; Ryan, T.J. 1; Samways, M. 31; Stevenson, A.J. 25; Thompstone, I.P. 10(1); Whitehead, P.M. 8; White, J.G. 27(10); Wilmot, R.G. 3.

League (57): Helliwell 13, Goodacre 9, Elliott 6, Alexander 5, White 5, Daws 4 (2 pens), Martin 3, Stevenson 3, Buckley 2, Platnauer 2, Thompstone 2, Farrell 1, Humphries 1, McCullagh 1.

Coca Cola Cup (6): Helliwell 4, Alexander 1, Daws 1.

FA Cup (1): Buckley 1.

Ground: Glanford Park, Scunthorpe, South Humberside. Telephone Scunthorpe (0724) 848077.

Record attendance: Old Showground: 23,935 v Portsmouth, FA Cup 4th rd, 30 January 1954. Glanford Park: 8775 v Rotherham U, Division 4, 1 May 1989.

Manager: Richard Money.
Secretary: A. D. Rowing.
Honours –
Division 3 (N) Champions – 1957–58.
Colours: Sky blue shirts with two claret rings on sleeves, white collar, white shorts with claret stripe, white stockings with claret and blue bar.

SHEFFIELD UNITED   FA PREMIER

Barnes, David.	Fickling, Ashley.	Peel, Nathan J.
Beesley, Paul.	Gage, Kevin W.	Pemberton, John M.
Bradshaw, Carl.	Gannon, John S.	Reed, John P.
Brocklehurst, David.	Gayle, Brian W.	Rees, Melvyn J.
Bryson, James I. C.	Hartfield, Charles J.	Rogers, Paul A.
Carr, Franz.	Hodges, Glyn P.	Scott, Andrew.
Cork, Alan G.	Hoyland, Jamie W.	Tracey, Simon P.
Cowan, Thomas.	Kelly, Alan T.	Walton, David L.
Deane, Brian C.	Kite, Philip D.	Ward, Mitchum D.
Duffield, Peter.	Littlejohn, Adrian S.	Whitehouse, Dane L.

League Appearances: Barnes, D. 13; Beesley, P. 39; Bradshaw, C. 24(8); Bryson, J.I. 9(7); Carr, F. 8; Cork, A.G. 11(16); Cowan, T. 21; Deane, B.C. 41; Gage, K.W. 31; Hartfield, C. 12(5); Hodges, G.P. 28(3); Hoyland, J.W. 15(7); Kamara, C. 6(2); Kelly, A.T. 32(1); Lake, M.C. 6; Littlejohn, A. 18(9); McLeary, A. 3; Pemberton, J.M. 19; Rogers, P.A. 26(1); Scott, A. 1(1); Tracey, S.P. 10; Ward, M.D. 22(4); Whitehouse, D.L. 14.
League (54): Deane 15 (1 pen), Littlejohn 8, Whitehouse 5, Hodges 4, Bryson 3, Carr 3, Rogers 3, Beesley 2, Cork 2, Gayle 2, Hoyland 2, Bradshaw 1, Gannon 1, Scott 1, own goals 2.
Coca Cola Cup (5): Deane 2, Bradshaw 1, Rogers 1, Whitehouse 1.
FA Cup (12): Deane 3, Cork 2, Hodges 2, Ward 2, Beesley 1, Hoyland 1, Littlejohn 1.
Ground: Bramall Lane Ground, Sheffield S2 4SU. Telephone Sheffield (0742) 738955.
Record attendance: 68,287 v Leeds U, FA Cup 5th rd, 15 February 1936.
Team Manager: Dave Bassett.
Secretary: D. Capper AFA.
Honours –
Football League: Division 1 Champions – 1897–98. Division 2 Champions – 1952–53. Division 4 Champions – 1981–82.
FA Cup: Winners 1899, 1902, 1915, 1925.
Colours: Broad red/white striped shirts, white shorts, red stripe at side, white stockings with red trim.

SHEFFIELD WEDNESDAY   FA PREMIER

Anderson, Vivian A.	Bright, Mark A.	Faulkner, David P.
Bart-Williams, Christopher G.	Chambers, Leroy D.	Harkes, John A.

Hirst, David E.
Hyde, Graham.
Jemson, Nigel B.
Johnson, David A.
Jones, Ryan A.
Key, Lance.
King, Philip G.
Linighan, Brian.
Linighan, John.

Nilsson, Nils L. R.
Palmer, Carlton L.
Pearson, Nigel G.
Pressman, Kevin P.
Rowntree, Michael C.
Sheridan, John J.
Shirtliff, Peter A.
Simpson, Ronald K.
Stewart, Simon A.

Waddle, Christopher R.
Warhurst, Paul.
Watson, Gordon W. G.
Watts, Julian.
Williams, Michael A.
Wilson, Daniel J.
Woods, Christopher C.
Worthington, Nigel.

League Appearances: Anderson, V.A. 24(2); Bart-Williams, C. 21(13); Bright, M.A. 28(2); Francis, T.J. 1(4); Harkes, J.A. 23(6); Hirst, D.E. 22; Hyde, G. 14(6); Jemson, N.B. 5(8); Jones, R.A. 9; King, P.G. 11(1); Nilsson, N.L. 32; Palmer, C.L. 33(1); Pearson, N.G. 13(3); Pressman, K.P. 3; Sheridan, J.J. 25; Shirtliff, P.A. 20; Stewart, S.A. 6; Waddle, C. 32(1); Warhurst, P. 25(4); Watson, G.W. 4(7); Watts, J. 2(2); Williams, M.A. 2(1); Williams, P.A. 7; Wilson, D.J. 21(5); Woods, C. 39; Worthington, N. 40.

League (55): Bright 11, Hirst 11 (1 pen), Bart-Williams 6, Warhurst 6, Anderson 3, Sheridan 3 (2 pens), Harkes 2, Wilson 2, Hyde 1, King 1, Nilsson 1, Palmer 1, Pearson 1, Waddle 1, Watson 1, Williams P 1, Worthington 1, own goals 2.
Coca Cola Cup (25): Bright 6, Warhurst 4, Hirst 3, Watson 3, Harkes 2, Sheridan 2, Bart-Williams 1, Nilsson 1, Palmer 1, Wilson 1, Worthington 1.
FA Cup (13): Warhurst 5, Bright 3, Waddle 2, Harkes 1, Hirst 1, Sheridan 1 (pen).
Ground: Hillsborough, Sheffield, S6 1SW. Telephone Sheffield (0742) 343122.
Record attendance: 72,841 v Manchester C, FA Cup 5th rd, 17 February 1934.
Manager: Trevor Francis.
Secretary: G. H. Mackrell FCCA.
Honours –
Football League: Division 1 Champions – 1902–03, 1903–04, 1928–29, 1929–30. Division 2 Champions – 1899–1900, 1925–26, 1951–52, 1955–56, 1958–59.
FA Cup winners 1896, 1907, 1935.
Football League Cup winners 1990–91.
Colours: Blue and white striped shirts, blue shorts, blue stockings.

SHREWSBURY TOWN   DIV. 3

Blake, Mark C.
Brough, John R.
Brown, Michael A.
Edwards, Paul.
Griffiths, Carl B.

Lynch, Thomas.
Mackenzie, Stephen.
Seabury, Kevin.
Smith, Mark A.
Spink, Dean P.

Summerfield, Kevin.
Taylor, Robert M.
Williams, Mark S.

League Appearances: Barham, M.F. 7(1); Blake, M.C. 32; Brooks, C. 1; Brough, J.R. 6(8); Brown, M.A. 17; Clark, H.W. 30(3); Edwards, P. 42; Evans, J.S. (1); Evans, P.S. 3(1); Griffiths, C.B. 41(1); Harmon, D.J. (1); Haylock, P. 16(2); Hodges, D.T. 1; Kinnaird, P.J. 4; Lynch, T. 39; Lyne, N.G. 18(2); Mackenzie, S. 3(5); O'Toole, C. 2(6); Piggott, G.D. 3(1); Seabury, K. (1); Smith, M.A. 31; Smith, N.P. 2; Spink, D.P. 22(1); Summerfield, K. 34(1); Taylor, R.M. 42; Turner, R.P. 9; Watts, J. 9; Williams, L. 2(1); Williams, M. (2); Williams, M.S. 26(2); Worsley, G. 20(8).

57

League (57): Griffiths 27 (3 pens), Summerfield 7, Taylor 5, Lyne 3, Lynch 2, Worsley 2, Barham 1, Blake 1, Brough 1, Brown 1, Haylock 1, Kinnaird 1, O'Toole 1, Smith 1, Spink 1, Williams MS 1, own goal 1.
Coca Cola Cup (2): Griffiths 1, Smith 1.
FA Cup (5): Griffiths 2, Lyne 1, Summerfield 1, Williams L 1.
Ground: Gay Meadow, Shrewsbury. Telephone Shrewsbury (0743) 360111.
Record attendance: 18,917 v Walsall, Division 3, 26 April 1961.
Manager: John Bond.
Secretary: M. J. Starkey.
Honours –
Football League: Division 3 Champions – 1978–79.
Welsh Cup winners 1891, 1938, 1977, 1979, 1984, 1985.
Colours: Amber/blue trim shirts, blue shorts, amber stockings, blue trim.

SOUTHAMPTON   FA PREMIER

Adams, Michael, R.	Ferguson, Gary.	Moody, Paul.
Allan, Derek T.	Flowers, Timothy D.	Moore, Kevin T.
Andrews, Ian E.	Gray, Stuart.	Powell, Lee.
Banger, Nicholas, L.	Groves, Perry.	Sheerin, Paul.
Benali, Francis V.	Hall, Richard A.	Speedie, David R.
Bennett, Frank.	Hughes, David R.	Thomas, Martin R.
Bound, Matthew T.	Hurlock, Terence A.	Tisdale, Paul R.
Cockerill, Glenn.	Kenna, Jeffrey J.	Widdrington, Thomas.
Dixon, Kerry M.	Le Tissier, Matthew P.	Wood, Stephen A.
Dodd, Jason R.	Maddison, Neil S.	
Dowie, Iain.	Monkou, Kenneth J.	

League Appearances: Adams, M.R. 38; Allan, D.T. (1); Banger, N.L. 10(17); Bartlett, N. (1); Benali, F.V. 31(2); Bound, M.T. 1(2); Cockerill, G. 21(2); Dixon, K.M. 8(1); Dodd, J.R. 27(3); Dowie, I. 34(2); Flowers, T.D. 42; Groves, P. 13(2); Hall, R.A. 28; Hurlock, T.A. 30; Kenna, J.J. 27(2); Lee, D. (1); Le Tissier, M.P. 40; Maddison, N.S. 33(4); Monkou, K.J. 33; Moody, P. 2(1); Moore, K.T. 18; Powell, L. (2); Speedie, D.R. 11; Widdrington, T. 11(1); Wood, S.A. 4.
League (54): Le Tissier 15 (2 pens), Dowie 11, Banger 6, Adams 4, Hall 4, Maddison 4, Dixon 2, Groves 2, Kenna 2, Moore 2, Dodd 1, Monkou 1.
Coca Cola Cup (3): Le Tissier 2 (1 pen), Dowie 1.
FA Cup (1): Le Tissier 1.
Ground: The Dell, Milton Road, Southampton SO9 4XX. Telephone Southampton (0703) 220505.
Record attendance: 31,044 v Manchester U, Division 1, 8 October 1969.
Manager: Ian Branfoot.
Secretary: Brian Truscott.
Honours –
Football League: Division 3 (S) Champions – 1921–22. Division 3 Champions – 1959–60.
FA Cup: Winners 1975–76.
Colours: Red and white striped shirts, black shorts, black stockings.

SOUTHEND UNITED   DIV. 1

Angell, Brett.   Hyslop, Christian T.   Royce, Simon.
Ansah, Andrew.   Jones, Keith A.   Sansome, Paul E.
Collymore, Stanley V.   Locke, Adam S.   Scully, Patrick J.
Cornwell, John A.   Martin, Jae A.   Sussex, Andrew R.
Edwards, Andrew D.   Powell, Christopher G. R. Tilson, Stephen B.
Hall, Mark A.   Prior, Spencer J.

League Appearances: Angell, B. 13; Ansah, A. 28(2); Ashenden, S. 4(1); Benjamin,
I.T. 16; Brown, S.R. 10; Cagigao, F. (1); Collymore, S. 30; Cornwell, J.A. 36(3);
Edwards, A.D. 41; Hall, M.A. 3(6); Hyslop, C.T. 4(2); Jones, K.A. 29; Locke, A.S.
26(1); Martin, D. 26; O'Callaghan, K. 8(5); Parkinson, G. 6; Powell, C. 42; Prior,
S.J. 45; Royce, S. 3; Sansome, P.E. 43; Scully, P.J. 41(1); Smith, P.W. 8; Southon,
J.P. (1); Sussex, A.R. 18(5); Tilson, S.B. 26(5).
League (54): Collymore 15, Ansah 7, Benjamin 7 (2 pens), Angell 5, Sussex 4 (2
pens), Cornwell 3, Scully 3, Tilson 3, Brown 2, Powell 2, Jones 1, Martin 1,
O'Callaghan 1.
Coca Cola Cup (1): Benjamin 1.
FA Cup (3): Collymore 3.
Ground: Roots Hall Football Ground, Victoria Avenue, Southend-on-Sea SS2 6NQ.
Telephone Southend (0702) 340707.
Record attendance: 31,090 v Liverpool FA Cup 3rd rd, 10 January 1979.
Manager: Barry Fry.
Secretary: J. W. Adams.
Honours –
Football League: Division 4 Champions – 1980–81.
Colours: Blue shirts, yellow trim, blue shorts, blue trim, blue stockings.

STOCKPORT COUNTY   DIV. 2

Barras, Anthony.   Frain, David.   Ryan, Darren T.
Beaumont, Christopher P. Francis, Kevin D. M.   Todd, Lee.
Carstairs, James W.   Gannon, James P.   Wallace, Michael.
Connelly, Sean P.   James, Martin J.   Ward, Peter.
Edwards, Neil R.   McCord, Brian J.   Williams, Paul A.
Finley, Alan J.   Miller, David B.   Williams, Paul R. C.
Flynn, Michael A.   Preece, Andrew P.   Williams, William R.

League Appearances: Barras, A. 12(2); Beaumont, C. 44; Carstairs, J.W. 13(1);
Connelly, S.P. 7; Duffield, P. 6(1); Edwards, N.R. 35; Finley, A.J. 22; Flynn, M.A.
9(1); Frain, D. 37(4); Francis, K.D. 41(1); Gannon, J.P. 46; James, M.J. 4(4); Kite,
P.D. 5; Knowles, D.T. 10(1); Masefield, P.D. 7; Matthews, N. 1(4); McCord, B.J.
4(4); Miller, D.B. 36(1); Muir, J.G. 7(2); Preece, A.P. 23(6); Redfern, D. 6; Ryan,
D.T. 3(1); Todd, L. 36(3); Wallace, M. 5(3); Ward, P. 35; Wheeler, P. (1); Williams,
P.A. 6(10); Williams, P.R. 24(2); Williams, W.R. 22.
League (81): Francis 28, Beaumont 14, Gannon 12 (4 pens), Preece 8, Duffield 4,
Muir 3, Ward 3, Williams PA 3, Carstairs 1, Finley 1, Miller 1, Williams B 1,
Williams P 1, own goal 1.

Coca Cola Cup (6): Beaumont 2, Francis 2, Carstairs 1, Gannon 1.
FA Cup (6): Francis 2, McCord 1, Preece 1, Todd 1, Williams B 1.
Ground: Edgeley Park, Hardcastle Road, Stockport, Cheshire SK3 9DD. Telephone 061–480 8888.
Record attendance: 27,833 v Liverpool, FA Cup 5th rd, 11 February 1950.
Manager: Danny Bergara.
Assistant Secretary: Andrea Welborn.
Honours –
Football League: Division 3 (N) Champions – 1921–22, 1936–37. Division 4 Champions – 1966–67.
Colours: Royal blue shirts with red/white pattern, white shorts, white stockings.

STOKE CITY   DIV. 1

Beeston, Carl F.	Kevan, David J.	Sandford, Lee R.
Butler, John E.	Leslie, Steven.	Shaw, Graham P.
Cranson, Ian.	Macari, Michael.	Sinclair, Ronald M.
Devlin, Mark A.	Mulligan, James.	Stein, Earl M. S.
Foley, Steven.	Overson, Vincent D.	Tapai, Ernie.
Gallimore, Anthony.	Pick, Gary.	Ware, Paul D.
Gleghorn, Nigel W.	Regis, David.	Wright, Ian M.
Harbey, Graham K.	Rennie, Paul A.	
Kelly, Anthony O. N.	Russell, Kevin J.	

League Appearances: Beeston, C.F. 25(2); Biggins, W. 8; Butler, J.E. 44; Cranson, I. 45; Devlin, M.A. 3; Foley, S. 44; Fox, P.D. 10; Gleghorn, N.W. 34; Grobbelaar, B.D. 4; Harbey, G.K. 16(1); Hockaday, D. 7; Horne, B. 1; Kelly, A.O. 2(5); Kevan, D.J. 13(2); Overson, V.D. 43; Parks, A. 2; Regis, D. 16(9); Russell, K.J. 30(10); Sandford, L.R. 42; Shaw, G.P. 20(9); Sinclair, R.M. 29; Stein, E.M. 46; Ware, P.D. 21(7); Wright, I.M. 1.
League (73): Stein 26 (5 pens), Foley 7, Gleghorn 7, Regis 5, Russell 5, Shaw 5, Ware 4, Beeston 3, Cranson 3, Biggins 2, Sandford 2, Butler 1, Kevan 1, Overson 1, own goal 1.
Coca Cola Cup (8): Stein 4, Biggins 2, Overson 1, Shaw 1.
FA Cup (1): Sandford 1.
Ground: Victoria Ground, Stoke-on-Trent. Telephone Stoke-on-Trent (0782) 413511.
Record attendance: 51,380 v Arsenal, Division 1, 29 March 1937.
Manager: Lou Macari.
Secretary: M. J. Potts.
Honours – Football League: Division 2 Champions – 1932–33, 1962–63, 1992–93. Division 3 (N) Champions – 1926–27.
Football League Cup: Winners 1971–72.
Autoglass Trophy winners 1992.
Colours: Red and white striped shirts, white shorts, red stockings.

Armstrong, Gordon I.
Atkinson, Brian.
Ball, Kevin A.
Bennett, Gary E.
Brodie, Stephen E.
Butcher, Terence I.
Carter, Timothy D.
Colquhoun, John.
Cronin, Gareth.

Cunnington, Shaun G.
Goodman, Donald R.
Gray, Martin D.
Gray, Michael.
Harford, Michael G.
Howey, Lee M.
Kay, John.
Norman, Anthony J.
Ord, Richard J.

Owers, Gary.
Pascoe, Colin J.
Robinson, Anthony.
Rogan, Anthony G. P.
Rush, David.
Russell, Craig S.
Sampson Ian.
Smith, Anthony.
Smith, Martin.

League Appearances: Armstrong, G.I. 41(4); Atkinson, B. 31(5); Ball, K.A. 43; Bennett, G.E. 14(1); Butcher, T.I. 37(1); Byrne, J.F. 6; Carter, T.D. 13; Colquhoun, J. 12(8); Cunnington, S.G. 38(1); Davenport, P. 20(14); Goodman, D.R. 41; Gray, M.D. 9(3); Gray, M. 23(4); Harford, M.G. 10(1); Hawke, (2); Howey, L.M. (1); Kay, J. 36; Mooney, B.J. 10(2); Norman, A.J. 33; Ord, R.J. 21(3); Owers, G. 33; Rogan, A.G. 12(1); Rush, D. 12(6); Sampson, I. 4(1); Smith, A. 7.

League (50): Goodman 16 (4 pens), Cunnington 7, Rush 6, Davenport 4 (1 pen), Armstrong, Ball 3, Atkinson 2, Michael Gray 2, Harford 2, Byrne 1, Martin Gray 1, Mooney 1, Owers 1, Sampson 1.

Coca Cola Cup (3): Ball 1, Butcher 1, Davenport 1.

FA Cup (2): Cunnington 1, Goodman 1.

Ground: Roker Park Ground, Sunderland. Telephone Sunderland 091–514 0332.

Record attendance: 75,118 v Derby Co, FA Cup 6th rd replay, 8 March 1933.

Manager: Terry Butcher.

Secretary: G. Davidson FCA.

Honours –

Football League: Division 1 Champions – 1891–92, 1892–93, 1894–95, 1901–02, 1912–13, 1935–36. Division 2 Champions – 1975–76. Division 3 Champions – 1987–88.

FA Cup: Winners 1937, 1973.

Colours: Red and white striped shirts, black shorts, red stockings, white turnover.

Bowen, Jason P.
Chappell, Shaun R.
Cornforth, John M.
Coughlin, Russell.
Ford, Jonathan S.

Freestone, Roger.
Harris, Mark A.
Hayes, Martin.
Jenkins, Stephen R.
Legg, Andrew.

Lyttle, Desmond.
McFarlane, Andrew A.
Walker, Keith C.
West, Colin.

League Appearances: Agboola, R.O. 6(1); Bowen, J.P. 23(15); Chappell, S.R. 4; Connor, T.F. 3; Cornforth, J.M. 44; Coughlin, R. 38(1); Cullen, A.S. 20(7); Ford, J.S. 36(7); Freestone, R. 46; Harris, M.A. 42; Hayes, M. 8(7); Jenkins, S.R. 29(4); Legg, A. 46; Lyttle, D. 46; McFarlane, A.A. 17(7); McMahon, S. 2; Pascoe, C.J. 15; Walker, K.C. 42; West, C. 29(4); Wimbledon, P.P. 10(5).

League (65): Legg 12, West 12 (4 pens), Bowen 10, Cornforth 5, Harris 5, McFarlane

5, Pascoe 4, Cullen 3, Ford 3, Walker 2, Coughlin 1, Lyttle 1, Wimbleton 1, own goal 1.
Coca Cola Cup (1): McFarlane 1.
FA Cup (8): Legg 2, West 2, Bowen 1, Cornforth 1, Cullen 1, Wimbleton 1.
Ground: Vetch Field, Swansea SA1 3SU. Telephone Swansea (0792) 474114.
Record attendance: 32,796 v Arsenal, FA Cup 4th rd, 17 February 1968.
Team Manager: Frank Burrows.
Secretary: George Taylor.
Honours –
Football League: Division 3 (S) Champions – 1924–25, 1948–49.
Welsh Cup: Winners 9 times.
Colours: White shirts, white shorts, black stockings.

SWINDON TOWN   FA PREMIER

Berkley, Austin J.
Bodin, Paul J.
Calderwood, Colin.
Digby, Fraser C.
Hammond, Nicholas D.
Hamon, Christopher A.
Hazard, Michael.
Hoddle, Glenn.

Horlock, Kevin.
Ling, Martin.
Maskell, Craig D.
McLaren, Ross.
Middleton, Lee J.
Mitchell, David S.
Moncur, John.
Murray, Edwin J.

O'Sullivan, Wayne S. J.
Phillips, Marcus S.
Summerbee, Nicholas J.
Taylor, Shaun.
Thomson, Andrew J.
Viveash, Adrian L.
White, Stephen J.

League Appearances: Bodin, P.J. 34(1); Calderwood, C. 46; Close, S.C. 1(6); Digby, F.C. 33; Gray, A.A. 3; Hammond, N.D. 13; Hamon, C. 1(1); Hazard, M. 30(2); Hoddle, G. 41(1); Horlock, K. 13(1); Hunt, P.C. 3(2); Kerslake, D. 30(1); Ling, M. 43; Marwood, B. 6(5); Maskell, C.D. 32(1); McLaren, R. 22; Mitchell, D.S. 37(4); Moncur, J. 11(3); Summerbee, N. 36(3); Taylor, S. 46; Viveash, A.L. 5; White, S.J. 20(14).
League (74): Maskell 19 (2 pens), Bodin 11 (4 pens), Mitchell 11, Taylor 11, White 7, Hazard 3, Ling 3, Summerbee 3, Calderwood 2, Hoddle 1, Horlock 1, Marwood 1, Moncur 1.
Coca Cola Cup (9): Mitchell 3, White 2, Hoddle 1, Ling 1, Maskell 1, Taylor 1.
FA Cup (0):
Ground: County Ground, Swindon, Wiltshire SN1 2ED. Telephone Swindon (0793) 430430.
Record attendance: 32,000 v Arsenal, FA Cup 3rd rd, 15 January 1972.
Manager: John Gorman.
Secretary: Jon Pollard.
Honours – Football League: Division 4 Champions – 1985–86.
Football League Cup: Winners 1968–69.
Anglo-Italian Cup: Winners 1970.
Colours: All red.

TORQUAY UNITED   DIV. 3

Barrow, Lee A.
Colcombe, Scott.

Curran, Christopher.
Darby, Duane A.

Foster, Adrian M.
Hancox, Richard.

Hodges, Kevin.   Moore, Darren M.   Sale, Mark D.
Kelly, Thomas J.   Myers, Christopher.   Trollope, Paul J.
Lowe, Matthew I.   O'Riordan, Donald J.

League Appearances: Barrow, L.A. 15; Blackwell, K.P. 18; Chapman, G.A. 6(2);
Colcombe, S. 20(4); Compton, P.D. (2); Curran, C. 33(1); Darby, D.A. 20(14);
Davies, A.J. 1(2); Davis, A. 11(1); Fashanu, J.S. 20; Foster, A.M. 23(13); Gardiner,
M. 5(2); Ginter, A.P. 1; Hall, P.A. 27(1); Hancox, R. 5(2); Hayrettin, H. 3(1); Herd,
S.A. 5(2); Herrera, R. 5; Hodges, K. 7(1); Johnson, I. 9; Joyce, S.W. 26(1); Kelly,
T.J. 18; Lewis, D.K. 9; Lowe, M.I. 13; Moore, D.M. 30(1); Muir, J.G. 7(5); Myers,
C. 28; O'Riordan, D.J. 16; Sale, M.D. 10(1); Salman, D.M. 20; Saunders, W. 6;
Sommer, J.P. 10; Stamps, S. 1(1); Trollope, P.J. 33(3); Walter, W.D. 1.
League (45): Darby 12, Foster 9, Fashanu 5, Joyce 3, Kelly 3 (2 pens), Barrow 2,
Moore 2, Sale 2, Trollope 2, Colcombe 1, Hodges 1, Johnson 1, Myers 1, own goal
1.
Coca Cola Cup (9): Saunders 3 (1 pen), Fashanu 2, Foster 2, Darby 1, Myers 1.
FA Cup (2): Foster 1, Herd 1.
Ground: Plainmoor Ground, Torquay, Devon TQ1 3PS. Telephone Torquay (0803)
328666/7.
Record attendance: 21,908 v Huddersfield T, FA Cup 4th rd, 29 January 1955.
Player-Manager: Don O'Riordan.
Secretary/General Manager: D. F. Turner.
Honours – Nil
Colours: Yellow and navy hooped shirts, navy shorts, yellow stockings.

TOTTENHAM HOTSPUR   FA PREMIER

Allen, Paul K.   Gray, Andrew A.   Ruddock, Neil.
Anderton, Darren R.   Hendon, Ian M.   Samways, Vincent.
Austin, Dean B.   Hendry, John.   Sedgley, Stephen P.
Barmby, Nicholas J.   Hill, Daniel R. L.   Sheringham, Edward P.
Beadle, Peter C.   Hodges, Lee L.   Thompson-Minton, Jeffrey S.
Bergsson, Gudni.   Houghton, Scott A.   Thorstvedt, Erik.
Campbell, Sulzeer J.   Howells, David.   Turner, Andrew P.
Caskey, Darren M.   Mabbutt, Gary V.   Tuttle, David P.
Culverhouse, David P.   Mahorn, Paul G.   Van Denhauwe, Patrick W.
Cundy, Jason V.   McDonald, David H.   Walker, Ian M.
Day, Christopher N.   McMahon, Gerard J.   Watson, Kevin E.
Dearden, Kevin C.   Moran, Paul.   Young, Neil A.
Durie, Gordon.   Nethercott, Stuart.
Edinburgh, Justin C.   Robinson, Stephen.

League Appearances: Allen, P.K. 38; Anderton, D.R. 32(2); Austin, D.B. 33(1);
Barmby, N.J. 17(5); Bergsson, G. (5); Campbell, S.J. (1); Cundy, J.V. 13(2);
Dearden, K.C. (1); Durie, G. 17; Edinburgh, J.C. 31(1); Fenwick, T.W. 3(2); Gray,
A.A. 9(8); Hendry, J. 2(3); Hill, D.R. 2(2); Hodges, L.L. (4); Howells, D. 16(2);
Mabbutt, G.V. 29; McDonald, D.H. 2; Moran, P. (3); Nayim Amar, M.A. 15(3);
Nethercott, S. 3(2); Ruddock, N. 38; Samways, V. 34; Sedgley, S.P. 20(2); Sher-
ingham, E. 38; Thorstvedt, E. 25(2); Turner, A.P. 7(11); Tuttle, D.P. 4(1); Van Den
Hauwe, P. 13(5); Walker, I.M. 17; Watson, K.E. 4(1).

League (60): Sheringham 21 (6 pens), Anderton 6, Barmby 6, Allen 3, Durie 3, Nayim 3, Ruddock 3, Sedgley 3, Turner 3, Hendry 2, Mabbutt 2, Campbell 1, Cundy 1, Gray 1, Howells 1, own goal 1.
Coca Cola Cup (8): Sheringham 3 (1 pen), Anderton 1, Durie 1, Samways 1, Turner 1, Watson 1.
FA Cup (14): Sheringham 4, Barmby 3, Nayim 3, Samways 2, Anderton 1, Sedgley 1.
Ground: 748 High Rd, Tottenham, London N17. Telephone 081–808 6666.
Record attendance: 75,038 v Sunderland, FA Cup 6th rd, 5 March 1938.
Manager: Ossie Ardiles.
Secretary: Peter Barnes.
Honours –
Football League: Division 1 Champions – 1950–51, 1960–61. Division 2 Champions – 1919–20, 1949–50.
FA Cup: Winners 1901 (as non-League club), 1921, 1961, 1962, 1967, 1981, 1982, 1991 (8 wins stands as the record).
Football League Cup: Winners 1970–71, 1972–73.
European Competitions:
European Cup-Winners' Cup winners: 1962–63.
UEFA Cup winners: 1971–72, 1983–84.
Colours: White shirts, navy blue shorts, white stockings.

TRANMERE ROVERS   DIV. 1

Aldridge, John W.
Branch, Graham.
Brannon, Gerald D.
Cooper, Stephen B.
Coyne, Daniel.
Coyne, Thomas.
Garnett, Shaun M.
Higgins, David A.

Hughes, Mark.
Irons, Kenneth.
Malkin, Christopher G.
Martindale, David.
McGreal, David.
McGreal, John.
Morgan, Alan M.
Morrisey, John.

Muir, Ian J.
Mungall, Steven H.
Nevin, Patrick K. F.
Nixon, Eric W.
Nolan, Iain R.
Thomas, Tony.
Vickers, Stephen.

League Appearances: Aldridge, J.W. 29(1); Branch, G. (3); Brannon, G.D. 38; Cooper, S.B. 3(3); Coyne, D. 1; Coyne, T. 9(3); Garnett, S.M. 5; Higgins, D.A. 40; Hughes, M. 7(4); Irons, K. 40(2); Malkin, C. 35(1); Martindale, D. 18(8); McNab, N. 30(1); Morrissey, J. 42(1); Muir, I.J. 7(4); Mungall, S.H. 29(6); Nevin, P.K. 43; Nixon, E.W. 45; Nolan, I.R. 14; Proctor, M.G. 13; Thomas, T. 16; Vickers, S. 42.
League (72): Aldridge 21 (4 pens), Nevin 13, Irons 7, Malkin 7, Morrissey 5, Higgins 4, Mungall 3, McNab 2, Martindale 2, Muir 2, Brannan 1, Coyne T 1, Garnett 1, Proctor 1, own goals 2.
Coca Cola Cup (3): Aldridge 2, Garnett 1.
FA Cup (6): Morrissey 2, Nevin 2, Aldridge 1 (pen), Vickers 1.
Ground: Prenton Park, Prenton Road West, Birkenhead. Telephone 051–608 3677.
Record attendance: 24,424 v Stoke C, FA Cup 4th rd, 5 February 1972.
Manager: John King.
Secretary: Norman Wilson FAAI.
Honours –
Football League Division 3 (N) Champions – 1937–38.
Welsh Cup: Winners 1935.
Leyland Daf Cup: Winners 1990.
Colours: All white.

Cecere, Michele J.
Clarke, Wayne.
Edwards, David J.
Gayle, Mark S. R.
Knight, Richard.

Macdonald, Kevin D.
Marsh, Christopher J.
McDonald, Rodney.
Ntamark, Charles.
O'Hara, Stephen.

Ryder, Stuart H.
Smith, Dean.
Winter, Steven D.

League Appearances: Cecere, M.J. 33(6); Clarke, W. 39; Demetrios, C. 3(4); Edwards, D.J. 3(2); Fearon, R.T. 1; Gayle, M.S. 41; Kelly, J. 7(3); Knight, R. 26(1); MacDonald, K.D. 28(5); Marsh, C. 29(4); McDonald, R. 39; McManus, S. (1); Methven, C.J. 23; Ntamark, C. 40(1); O'Connor, M.J. 10; O'Hara, S. 22(4); Ollerenshaw, S. 8(12); Parker, R.J. (1); Reece, A.J. 9; Ryder, S.H. 20(2); Smith, D. 39(3); Statham, D. 18(3); West, G. 9; Williams, W. 14; Winter, S.D. 1(1).
League (76): Clarke 21 (4 pens), Cecere 16, McDonald 12, Ntamark 4, Ollerenshaw 4, MacDonald 3, Marsh 3, Kelly 2, Demetrios 1, Knight 1, O'Connor 1, O'Hara 1, Reece 1, Smith 1, West 1, Williams 1, own goals 3.
Coca Cola Cup (2): Clarke 1, McDonald 1.
FA Cup (0):
Ground: Bescot Stadium, Bescot Cresent, Walsall WS1 4SA. Telephone Walsall (0922) 22791.
Record attendance: 10,628 B International, England v Switzerland, 20 May 1991.
Manager: Kenny Hibbitt.
Secretary/Commercial Manager: Roy Whalley.
Honours –
Football League: Division 4 Champions – 1959–60.
Colours: Red shirts, red shorts, black stockings.

WATFORD   DIV. 1

Alsford, Julian.
Ashby, Barry J.
Bazeley, Darren S.
Charlery, Kenneth.
Drysdale, Jason.
Dublin, Keith B. L.
Dyer, Bruce A.
Fulong, Paul A.
Gibbs, Nigel J.

Hessenthaler, Andrew.
Holdsworth, David G.
Inglethorpe, Alex M.
Johnson, Richard M.
Lavin, Gerard.
McIntosh, Craig.
Meara, James S.
Nogan, Lee M.
Nwaokolo, Daniel N. P.

Page, Robert J.
Porter, Gary.
Putney, Trevor A.
Sheppard, Simon.
Slinn, Kevin P.
Soloman, Jason R.
Suckling, Perry J.
White, John S.
Willis, Roger C.

League Appearances: Alsford, J. 2(3); Ashby, B.J. 33(2); Bazeley, D.S. 10(12); Butler, S. 2(7); Charlery, K. 30(2); Drysdale, J. 37(2); Dublin, K.B. 46; Dyer, B.A. (2); Furlong, P.A. 41; Gibbs, N.J. 7; Hessenthaler, A. 45; Holdsworth, D.G. 38(1); Johnson, R.M. (1); Lavin, G. 24(4); Meara, J.S. 1(1); Nogan, L.M. 40(2); Porter, G. 25(8); Putney, T.A. 16(8); Sheppard, S. 5; Soloman, J.R. 34(2); Suckling, P.J. 37; Thomas, R.C. 1; Waugh, K. 4; Willis, R.C. 28(4).
League (57): Furlong 19, Charlery 11, Nogan 11, Drysdale 6 (4 pens), Hessenthaler 3, Soloman 2, Willis 2, Bazeley 1, Dublin 1, own goal 1.
Coca Cola Cup (7): Furlong 3, Drysdale 2 (1 pen), Holdsworth 1, Lavin 1.

FA Cup (1): Nogan 1.

Ground: Vicarage Road Stadium, Watford WD1 8ER. Telephone Watford (0923) 230933.

Record attendance: 34,099 v Manchester U, FA Cup 4th rd (replay), 3 February 1969.

Team Manager: Glenn Roeder.

Chief Executive: Eddie Plumley FAAI.

Honours –

Football League: Division 3 Division 1 – 1968–69. Division 4 Champions – 1977–78.

Colours: Yellow shirts, black shorts, black stockings.

WEST BROMWICH ALBION   DIV. 1

Ampadu, Kwame.
Bradley, Darren M.
Burgess, Daryl.
Coldicott, Stacy.
Darton, Scott R.
Donovan, Kevin.
Fereday, Wayne.
Garner, Simon.
Hackett, Gary S.
Hamilton, Ian R.
Heggs, Carl S.
Hunter, Roy I.
Lange, Anthony S.
Lilwall, Stephen.
McCue, James G.
McNally, Bernard A.
Mellon, Michael J.
Naylor, Stuart W.
Raven, Paul.
Reid, Nicholas S.
Shakespeare, Craig R.
Strodder, Gary J.
Taylor, Robert.

League Appearances: Ampadu, K. 1(9); Blissett, L.L. 3; Bradley, D.M. 41(1); Burgess, D. 17(1); Coldicott, S. 10(4); Darton, S.R. 2; Dickens, A.W. 3; Donovan, K. 30(2); Fereday, W. 13(3); Garner, S. 21(4); Hackett, G.S. 4(6); Hamilton, I.R. 46; Heggs, C.S. 17); Hodson, S.P. 1(1); Hunt, A. 9(1); Hunter, R.I. 1; Lange, A.S. 14; Lilwall, S. 44; McNally, B.A. 39(1); Melon, M.J. 15(2); Naylor, S.W. 32; Raven, P. 43(1); Reid, N.S. 10(5); Robson, G. 16(6); Shakespeare, C. 12(2); Speedie, D.R. 7; Strodder, G.J. 26(3); Taylor, R. 46.

League (88): Taylor 30 (3 pens), Hunt 9, Garner 8, Hamilton 7 (1 pen), Raven 7, Donovan 6, McNally 3, Mellon 3, Heggs 2, Robson 2, Shakespeare 2 (1 pen), Speedie 2, Blissett 1, Bradley 1, Burgess 1, Dickens 1, Fereday 1, Hackett 1, Strodder 1.

Coca Cola Cup (1): Taylor 1.

FA Cup (11): Donovan 3, Taylor 3, Bradley 1, Hamilton 1, McNally 1, Raven 1, Robson 1.

Ground: The Hawthorns, West Bromwich B71 4LF. Telephone 021–525 8888 (all Depts).

Record attendance: 64,815 v Arsenal, FA Cup 6th rd, 6 March 1937.

Manager: Keith Burkinshaw.

Secretary: Dr. J. J. Evans BA, PHD. (Wales).

Honours –

Football League: Division 1 Champions – 1919–20. Division 2 Champions – 1901–02, 1910–11.

FA Cup: Winners 1888, 1892, 1931, 1954, 1968. **Football League Cup:** Winners 1965–66.

Colours: Navy blue and white striped shirts, white shorts, blue and white stockings.

WEST HAM UNITED   FA PREMIER

Allen, Clive D.
Allen, Martin J.
Basham, Michael.
Bishop, Ian W.
Breacher, Timothy S.
Brown, Kenneth J.
Bunbury, Alexander.
Butler, Peter J.
Dicks, Julian A.

Foster, Colin J.
Gale, Anthony P.
Holland, Matthew R.
Holmes, Matthew J.
Jones, Stephen G.
Keen, Kevin I.
Marquis, Paul R.
Martin, Alvin E.
Martin, Dean.

Miklosko, Ludek.
Morley, Trevor W.
Potts, Steven J.
Robson, Mark A.
Rush, Matthew J.
Small, Michael A.
Thomasm Mitchell A.
Whitmarsh, Paul.
Williamson, Daniel A.

League Appearances: Allen, C.D. 25(2); Allen, M.J. 33(1); Bishop, I.W. 15(7); Breacker, T.S. 39; Brown, K.J. 13(2); Bunbury, A. 2(2); Butler, P.J. 39; Clarke, S.N. (1); Dicks, J.A. 34; Foster, C.J. 3(3); Gale, A.P. 21(2); Holmes, M.J. 6(12); Jones, S.G. 4(2); Keen, K.I. 46; Martin, A.E. 23; Miklosko, L. 46; Morley, T.W. 41; Parris, G. 10(6); Potts, S.J. 46; Robson, M.A. 41(3); Small, M.A. 5(4); Speedie, D.R. 11; Thomas, M.A. 3.
League (81): Morley 20, Allen C 14, Dicks 11 (6 pens) Robson 8, Keen 7, Allen M 4, Speedie 4, Breacker 2, Brown 2, Butler 2, Jones 2, Bishop 1, Foster 1, Gale 1, Martin 1, own goal 1.
Coca Cola Cup (0):
FA Cup (3): Allen C 1, Morley 1 (pen), Robson 1.
Ground: Boleyn Ground, Green Street, Upton Park, London E13. Telephone 081 472-2740.
Record attendance: 42,322 v Tottenham H, Division 1, 17 October 1970.
Manager: Billy Bonds MBE.
Secretary: Tom Finn
Honours –
Football League: Division 2 Champions – 1957–58, 1980–81. ·
FA Cup: Winners 1964, 1975, 1980. **European Competitions:**
European Cup-Winners' Cup winners: 1964–65.
Colours: Claret shirts, white shorts, white stockings.

WIGAN ATHLETIC   DIV. 3

Connelly, Dean.
Daley, Phillip.
Dooland, John.
Dowe, Julian W. W.
Griffiths, Bryan K.

Johnson, Alan K.
Langley, Kevin J.
Parkinson, Joseph S.
Pennock, Anthony.
Rimmer, Neill.

Robertson, John N.
Skipper, Peter D.
Strong, Greg.
Tankard, Allen J.

League Appearances: Adkins, N.H. 38; Appleton, S. 24(5); Brolly, R. 2; Connelly, D. 7; Cooper, S.B. 4; Daley, P. 31; Doolan, J. 16(1); Garnett, S.M. 13; Griffiths, B.K. 43(1); Johnson, A.K. 36; Jones, P.A. 25(2); Langley, K.J. 40; Makin, C. 14(1); Nugent, S. 5(4); Ogden, N. 1(1); Parkinson, J.S. 13; Pennock, A. 8; Pilling, A.J. 27(4); Powell, G. 22(14); Rimmer, N. 1; Robertson, J.N. 21(3); Sharratt, C. 11(9); Skipper, P.D. 32; Tankard, A.J. 39(2); White, E.W. 10; Wilson, I.W. 5; Woods, R.G. 12(1); Worthington, G.L. 7(3).

League (43): Griffiths 13 (3 pens), Daley 6, Powell 6, Pilling 4, Sharratt 3, Makin 2, White 2, Appleton 1, Brolly 1, Garnett 1, Johnson 1, Robertson 1, Skipper 1, Tankard 1.

Coca Cola Cup (4): Daley 1, Johnson 1, Tankard 1, Worthington 1.

FA Cup (4): Griffiths 1 (pen), Powell 1, own goals 2.

Ground: Springfield Park, Wigan. Telephone Wigan (0942) 44433.

Record attendance: 27,500 v Hereford U, 12 December 1953.

Secretary:

Manager: Kenny Swain.

Honours –

Freight Rover Trophy: Winners 1984–85.

Colours: Black and blue striped shirts, black shorts with blue and white trim, black stockings with blue turnover.

WIMBLEDON   FA PREMIER

Allen, Leighton G.	Elkins, Gary.	Newhouse, Aidan R.
Anthrobus, Stephen A.	Fashanu, John.	Payne, Grant.
Ardley, Neal C.	Fear, Peter S.	Perry, Christopher J.
Barton, Warren D.	Fitzgerald, Scott B.	Sanchez, Lawrence P.
Berry, Gregory J.	Holdsworth, Dean C.	Scales, John R.
Blackwell, Dean R.	Jones, Vincent P.	Segers, Johannes C.
Castledine, Stewart M.	Joseph, Roger.	Skinner, Justin J.
Clarke, Andrew W.	McAllister, Brian.	Sullivan, Neil.
Cotterill, Stephen.	McCarthy, Jamie.	Talboys, Steven.
Dobbs, Gerald F.	McGee, Paul.	
Earle, Robert.	Miller, Paul A.	

League Appearances: Anthrobus, S. 4(1); Ardley, N.C. 24(2); Barton, W.D. 23; Berry, G.J. 2(1); Blackwell, D.R. 19(5); Clarke, A.W. 23(10); Cotterill, S. 4(3); Dobbs, G.F. 16(3); Earle, R. 42; Elkins, G. 17(1); Fashanu, J. 27(2); Fear, P.S. 2(2); Fitzgerald, S.B. 18(2); Gibson, T.B. 6(2); Holdsworth, D.C. 34(2); Jones, V.P. 27; Joseph, R. 31(1); McAllister, B. 26(1); McGee, P. 1(2); McLeary, A. 4; Miller, P.A. 11(8); Newhouse, A.R. (1); Sanchez, L.P. 23(4); Scales, J.R. 32; Segers, J.C. 41; Skinner, J.J. 1; Sullivan, N. 1; Talboys, S. 3(4).

League (56): Holdsworth 19, Earle 7, Fashanu 6 (1 pen), Clarke 5, Ardley 4, Sanchez 4, Cotterill 3, Barton 2, Dobbs 1, Gibson 1, Jones 1 (pen), Miller 1, Newhouse 1, Scales 1.

Coca Cola Cup (3): Ardley 1, Fashanu 1, Jones 1.

FA Cup (5): Cotterill 1, Dobbs 1, Earle 1, Elkins 1, Fashanu 1.

Ground: Selhurst Park, South Norwood, London SE25 6PY. Telephone 081 771 2233.

Record attendance: 30,115 v Manchester U, FA Premier League, 9 May 1993.

Manager: Joe Kinnear.

Secretary: Steve Rooke.

Honours –

Football League: Division 4 Champions – 1982–83.

FA Cup: Winners 1987–88.

Colours: Blue shirts yellow trim, blue shorts yellow trim, blue stockings yellow trim.

WOLVERHAMPTON WANDERERS   DIV. 1

Ashley, Kevin M.
Bennett, Thomas M.
Birch, Paul.
Blades, Paul A.
Bradbury, Shaun D.
Bull, Stephen G.
Burke, Mark S.
Collier, Daniel J.
Cook, Paul A.

De Bont, Andrew C.
Dennison, Robert.
Edwards, Paul R.
Howard, Jonathan M.
Jones, Paul S.
Kelly, James.
Mills, Rowan L.
Mountfield, Derek N.
Mutch, Andrew T.

Rankine, Simon M.
Roberts, Darren A.
Simkin, Darren S.
Stowell, Michael.
Thompson, Andrew R.
Turner, Graham M.
Venus, Mark.

League Appearances: Ashley, K.M. 28; Beasant, D. 4; Bennett, T.M. (1); Birch, P. 27(1); Blades, P.A. 38(2); Bradbury, S.D. 2; Bull, S.G. 36; Burke, M.S. 27(5); Cook, P.A. 44; Dennison, R. 31(6); Downing, K.G. 30(1); Edwards, P.R. 33(2); Jones, P.S. 16; Madden, L.D. 19(5); Mountfield, D.N. 34(2); Mutch, A.T. 34(5); Rankine, S.M. 23(4); Roberts, D.A. 12(9); Simkin, D.S. 7; Steele, T.W. 1(3); Stowell, M. 26; Taylor, C.D. (1); Thompson, A.R. 15(5); Turner, G.M. 1; Venus, M. 12; Westley, S.L. 6(2).
League (57): Bull 16, Mutch 9, Burke 8, Dennison 5, Roberts 5, Birch 3 (1 pen), Bradbury 2, Downing 2, Mountfield 2, Blades 1, Cook 1, own goals 3.
Coca Cola Cup (2): Bull 1, Cook 1 (pen).
FA Cup (4): Bull 1, Downing 1, Mutch 1, own goal 1.
Ground: Molineux Grounds, Wolverhampton WV1 4QR. Telephone Admin office: Wolverhampton (0902) 712181; lottery shop: (0902) 27524.
Record attendance: 61,315 v Liverpool, FA Cup 5th rd, 11 February 1939.
Team Manager: Graham Turner.
Secretary: Keith Pearson ACIS.
Honours –
Football League: Division 1 Champions – 1953–54, 1957–58, 1958–59. Division 2 Champions – 1931–32, 1976–77. Division 3 (N) Champions – 1923–24. Division 3 Champions – 1988–89. Division 4 Champions – 1987–88.
FA Cup: Winners 1893, 1908, 1949, 1960.
Football League Cup: Winners 1973–74, 1979–80.
Sherpa Van Trophy winners 1988.
Colours: Gold shirts, black shorts, gold stockings.

WREXHAM   DIV. 2

Bennett, Gary M.
Connolly, Karl.
Cross, Jonathan N.
Durkan, Kieron J.
Hardy, Philip.
Humes, Anthony.
Jones, Barry.

Jones, Kevin R.
Knight, Craig.
Lake, Michael C.
Morris, Mark.
Myddleton, Phillip J.
Owen, Gareth.
Paskin, William J.

Pejic, Melvyn.
Phillips, Wayne.
Pugh, Stephen.
Sertori, Mark A.
Taylor, Peter M. R.
Watkin, Stephen.

League Appearances: Bennett, G.M. 34(1); Brammer, D. 1(1); Case, J.R. 1(3); Connolly, K. 40(2); Cross, J.N. 34(3); Durkan, K.J. (1); Esdaille, D. 4; Flynn, B.

1(1); Hardy, Philip. 32; Hughes, K.D. 8; Humes, A. 38; Jones, B. 42; Jones, K.R. 3; Lake, M.C. 25(1); Morris, M. 34; Owen, G. 38(3); Paskin, W.J. 10(9); Pejic, M. 39; Phillips, W. 14(1); Pugh, S. 1(2); Sertori, M.A. 10(2); Taylor, P.M. 13(6); Thomas, R.M. 8; Watkin, S. 31(2); Williams, S.J. 1.

League (75): Watkin 18 (1 pen), Bennett 16 (2 pens), Connolly 9, Paskin 8, Cross 7, Lake 5, Owen 3, Jones B 2, Pejic 2, Taylor 2, Thomas 1, own goals 2.

Coca Cola Cup (4): Bennett 2, Pejic 1, own goal 1.

FA Cup (1): Bennett 1.

Ground: Racecourse Ground, Mold Road, Wrexham. Telephone Wrexham (0978) 262129.

Record attendance: 34,445 v Manchester U, FA Cup 4th rd, 26 January 1957.

Manager: Brian Flynn.   **Secretary:** D. L. Rhodes.

Honours – Football League: Division 3 Champions – 1977–78.

Welsh Cup: Winners 21 times.

Colours: Red shirts, white shorts, red stockings.

WYCOMBE WANDERERS   DIV. 3

Ground: Adams Park, Hillbottom Road, Sands, High Wycombe HP12 4HJ. Telephone 0494 472100.

Manager: Martin O'Neill.   **Secretary:** John Goldsworthy.

Honours – GM Vauxhall Conference winners: 1993. **FA Trophy winners:** 1991, 1993.

Colours: Light & dark blue quartered shirts, navy blue shorts, sky blue stockings.

YORK CITY   DIV. 2

Atkin, Paul A.
Barnes, Paul L.
Barratt, Anthony.
Blackstone, Ian K.
Bushell, Stephen.
Canham, Anthony.
Ellis, Robert J.
Hall, Craig.
Hall, Wayne.
Jordan, Scott D.
Kiely, Dean L.
Livingstone, Glen.
McCarthy, Jonathan D.
McMillan, Lyndon A.
Murty, Graeme S.
Naylor, Glenn.
Pepper, Colin N.
Stancliffe, Paul I.
Swann, Gary.
Tutill, Stephen A.
Warburton, Raymond.

League Appearances: Atkin, P.A. 28(3); Barnes, P.L. 40; Barratt, A. 4(6); Blackstone, I.K. 37(2); Borthwick, J.R. 28(5); Bushell, S. 8; Canham, A. 16(13); Hall, W. 42; Jordan, S.D. (1); Kiely, D.L. 40; Marples, C. 2; McCarthy, J. 42; McMillan, L.A. 42; Naylor, G. 1(3); Pepper, C.N. 34; Stancliffe, P.I. 41; Swann, G. 38; Tilley, D.J. 4(2); Tutill, S.A. 6(2); Warburton, R. 9(1).

League (72): Barnes 21, Blackstone 16, Borthwick 8, Pepper 8 (7 pens), McCarthy 7, Canham 4, Warburton 2, Atkin 2, Hall 1, Stancliffe 1, own goal 1.

Coca Cola Cup (0):

FA Cup (1): Canham 1.

Ground: Bootham Crescent, York. Telephone York 0904 624447.

Record attendance: 28,123 v Huddersfield T, FA Cup 6th rd, 5 March 1938.

Manager: Alan Little.   **Secretary:** Keith Usher.

Honours – Football League: Division 4 Champions – 1983–84.

Colours: Red shirts, blue shorts, red stockings.

70

LEAGUE REVIEW

Manchester United achieved their first championship success in 26 years by capturing the initial FA Premier League title. They successfully held off a strong challenge from Aston Villa after Norwich City had appeared likely contenders in the middle of the season. On 5 December, Norwich had been top, eight points clear of their nearest rivals, with Manchester United lying only seventh.

For United Manager Alex Ferguson it was a triumph after several near misses, the most notable being the 1992–92 season when they were edged out in dramatic fashion by Leeds United. He became the first manager to win League titles on either side of the border, having been previously in charge of Aberdeen during their most effective seasons.

There was as much excitement at the other end of the table where Oldham, who had beaten both Manchester United and Villa in the last couple of months of the season, escaped the drop with a 4-3 win over Southampton on the last full Saturday.

It was a disappointing season for defending champions Leeds, who never mounted a serious challenge for their title and failed to win any away games. In fact they were in the danger zone for several weeks.

The three teams relegated from the Premier League were Crystal Palace, Middlesbrough and Nottingham Forest, the latter having a particularly unhappy season which culminated in Brian Clough quitting as manager.

In the Barclays League, Newcastle United began with 11 straight victories and finished as worthy champions of the newly-constituted Football League, First Division. West Ham United won automatic promotion behind them, but Portsmouth missed out despite having the country's most prolific goalscorer in their ranks. Guy Whittingham scored 47 League and Cup goals, including 42 in the League alone to establish a club record, which had existed since 1926–27.

From the play-offs, Swindon Town emerged to take the third promotion place, beating Tranmere Rovers and then Leicester City 4-3 in a thrilling final at Wembley, but immediately lost player-manager Glenn Hoddle, who took up a similar appointment with Chelsea.

Brentford, Cambridge United and Bristol Rovers were relegated; their places being taken by Stoke City, Bolton Wanderers and West Bromwich who also lost their manager when Ossie Ardiles took over at Tottenham Hotspur. Ironically he was replaced by another ex-Spurs manager, Keith Burkinshaw.

The four relegated from Division Two were Preston North End, Mansfield Town, Wigan Athletic and Chester City, while up from Division Three came Cardiff City, Wrexham, Barnet and York City.

Out of the League went Halifax Town, relegated to the GM Vauxhall Conference. Their place in the Third Division will be taken by Wycombe Wanderers, the highly successful non-league team who also achieved the double by winning the FA Trophy.

FA PREMIER LEAGUE

HOME TEAM	Arsenal	Aston Villa	Blackburn R	Chelsea	Coventry C	Crystal Palace	Everton	Ipswich T
Arsenal	—	0–1	0–1	2–1	3–0	3–0	2–0	0–0
Aston Villa	1–0	—	0–0	1–3	0–0	3–0	2–1	2–0
Blackburn R	1–0	3–0	—	2–0	2–5	1–2	2–3	2–1
Chelsea	1–0	0–1	0–0	—	2–1	3–1	2–1	2–1
Coventry C	0–2	3–0	0–2	1–2	—	2–2	0–1	2–2
Crystal Palace	1–2	1–0	3–3	1–1	0–0	—	0–2	3–1
Everton	0–0	1–0	2–1	0–1	1–1	0–2	—	3–0
Ipswich T	1–2	1–1	2–1	1–1	0–0	2–2	1–0	—
Leeds U	3–0	1–1	5–2	1–1	2–2	0–0	2–0	1–0
Liverpool	0–2	1–2	2–1	2–1	4–0	5–0	1–0	0–0
Manchester C	0–1	1–1	3–2	0–1	1–0	0–0	2–5	3–1
Manchester U	0–0	1–1	3–1	3–0	5–0	1–0	0–3	1–1
Middlesbrough	1–0	2–3	3–2	0–0	0–2	0–1	1–2	2–2
Norwich C	1–1	1–0	0–0	2–1	1–1	4–2	1–1	0–2
Nottingham F	0–1	0–1	1–3	3–0	1–1	1–1	0–1	0–1
Oldham Ath	0–1	1–1	0–1	3–1	0–1	1–1	1–0	4–2
QPR	0–0	2–1	0–3	1–1	2–0	1–3	4–2	0–0
Sheffield U	1–1	0–2	1–3	4–2	1–1	0–1	1–0	3–0
Sheffield W	1–0	1–2	0–0	3–3	1–2	2–1	3–1	1–1
Southampton	2–0	2–0	1–1	1–0	2–2	1–0	0–0	4–3
Tottenham H	1–0	0–0	1–2	1–2	2–2	2–2	2–1	0–2
Wimbledon	3–2	2–3	1–1	0–0	1–2	4–0	1–3	0–1

1992–93 RESULTS

	Leeds U	Liverpool	Manchester C	Manchester U	Middlesbrough	Norwich C	Nottingham F	Oldham Athletic	QPR	Sheffield U	Sheffield W	Southampton	Tottenham H	Wimbledon
	0-0	0-1	1-0	0-1	1-1	2-4	1-1	2-0	0-0	1-1	2-1	4-3	1-3	0-1
	1-1	4-2	3-1	1-0	5-1	2-3	2-1	0-1	2-0	3-1	2-0	1-1	0-0	1-0
	3-1	4-1	1-0	0-0	1-1	7-1	4-1	2-0	1-0	1-0	1-0	0-0	0-2	0-0
	1-0	0-0	2-4	1-1	4-0	2-3	0-0	1-1	1-0	1-2	0-2	1-1	1-1	4-2
	3-3	5-1	2-3	0-1	2-1	1-1	0-1	3-0	0-1	1-3	1-0	2-0	1-0	0-2
	1-0	1-1	0-0	0-2	4-1	1-2	1-1	2-2	1-1	2-0	1-1	1-2	1-3	2-0
	2-0	2-1	1-3	0-2	2-2	0-1	3-0	2-2	3-5	0-2	1-1	2-1	1-2	0-0
	4-2	2-2	3-1	2-1	0-1	3-1	2-1	1-2	1-1	0-0	0-0	0-0	1-1	2-1
	—	2-2	1-0	0-0	3-0	0-0	1-4	2-0	1-1	3-1	3-1	2-1	5-0	2-1
	2-0	—	1-1	1-2	4-1	4-1	0-0	1-0	1-0	2-1	1-0	1-1	6-2	2-3
	4-0	1-1	—	1-1	0-1	3-1	2-2	3-3	1-1	2-0	1-2	1-0	0-1	1-1
	2-0	2-2	2-1	—	3-0	1-0	2-0	3-0	0-0	2-1	2-1	2-1	4-1	0-1
	4-1	1-2	2-0	1-1	—	3-3	1-2	2-3	0-1	2-0	1-1	1-2	3-0	2-0
	4-2	1-0	2-1	1-3	1-1	—	3-1	1-0	2-1	2-1	1-0	1-0	0-0	2-1
	1-1	1-0	0-2	0-2	1-0	0-3	—	2-0	1-0	0-2	1-2	1-2	2-1	1-1
	2-2	3-2	0-1	1-0	4-1	2-3	5-3	—	2-2	1-1	1-1	4-3	2-1	6-2
	2-1	0-1	1-1	1-3	3-3	3-1	4-3	3-2	—	3-2	3-1	3-1	4-1	1-2
	2-1	1-0	1-1	2-1	2-0	0-1	0-0	2-0	1-2	—	1-1	2-0	6-0	2-2
	1-1	1-1	0-3	3-3	2-3	1-0	2-0	2-1	1-0	1-1	—	5-2	2-0	1-1
	1-1	2-1	0-1	0-1	1-3	3-0	1-2	1-0	1-2	3-2	1-2	—	0-0	2-2
	4-0	2-0	3-1	1-3	2-2	5-1	2-1	4-1	3-2	2-0	0-0	4-2	—	1-1
	1-0	2-0	0-1	1-2	2-0	3-0	1-0	5-2	0-2	2-0	1-1	1-2	1-1	—

BARCLAYS LEAGUE – DIVISION 1

HOME TEAM	Barnsley	Birmingham C	Brentford	Bristol C	Bristol R	Cambridge U	Charlton Ath	Derby Co	Grimsby T
Barnsley	—	1-0	3-2	2-1	2-1	2-0	1-0	1-1	0-2
Birmingham C	3-0	—	1-3	0-1	2-1	0-2	1-0	1-1	2-1
Brentford	3-1	0-2	—	5-1	0-3	0-1	2-0	2-1	1-3
Bristol C	2-1	3-0	4-1	—	2-1	0-0	2-1	0-0	1-0
Bristol R	1-5	3-3	2-1	4-0	—	1-1	0-2	1-2	0-3
Cambridge U	1-2	0-3	1-0	2-1	0-1	—	0-1	1-3	2-0
Charlton Ath	0-0	0-0	1-0	2-1	4-1	0-0	—	2-1	3-1
Derby Co	3-0	3-1	3-2	3-4	3-1	0-0	4-3	—	2-1
Grimsby T	4-2	1-1	0-1	2-1	2-0	1-1	1-0	0-2	—
Leicester C	2-1	2-1	0-0	0-0	0-1	2-2	3-1	3-2	3-0
Luton T	2-2	1-1	0-0	0-1	1-1	2-0	1-0	1-3	1-4
Millwall	0-4	0-0	6-1	4-1	0-3	2-2	1-0	1-0	2-1
Newcastle U	6-0	2-2	5-1	5-0	0-0	4-1	2-2	1-1	0-1
Notts Co	1-3	3-1	1-1	0-0	3-0	1-0	2-0	0-2	1-0
Oxford U	0-0	0-0	0-2	2-0	2-1	3-0	0-1	0-1	0-1
Peterborough U	1-1	2-1	0-0	1-1	1-1	1-0	1-1	1-0	1-0
Portsmouth	1-0	4-0	1-0	2-3	4-1	3-0	1-0	3-0	2-1
Southend U	3-0	4-0	3-0	1-1	3-0	1-1	0-2	0-0	1-0
Sunderland	2-1	1-2	1-3	0-0	1-1	3-3	0-2	1-0	2-0
Swindon T	1-0	0-0	0-2	2-1	2-2	4-1	2-2	2-4	1-0
Tranmere R	2-1	4-0	3-2	3-0	2-1	2-0	0-0	2-1	1-1
Watford	1-2	1-0	1-0	0-0	4-2	2-2	1-1	0-0	2-3
West Ham U	1-1	3-1	4-0	2-0	2-1	2-0	0-1	1-1	2-1
Wolverhampton W	1-0	2-1	1-2	0-0	5-1	1-2	2-1	0-2	2-1

1992–93 RESULTS

Leicester C	Luton T	Millwall	Newcastle U	Notts Co	Oxford U	Peterborough U	Portsmouth	Southend U	Sunderland	Swindon T	Tranmere R	Watford	West Ham U	Wolverhampton W
2–3	3–0	0–0	1–0	0–0	0–1	1–2	1–1	3–1	2–0	1–0	3–1	0–1	0–1	0–1
0–2	2–1	0–0	2–3	1–0	1–0	2–0	2–3	2–0	1–0	4–6	0–0	2–2	1–2	0–4
1–3	1–2	1–1	1–2	2–2	1–0	0–1	4–1	2–1	1–1	0–0	0–1	1–1	0–0	0–2
2–1	0–0	0–1	1–2	1–0	1–1	0–1	3–3	0–1	0–0	2–2	1–3	2–1	1–5	1–0
0–0	2–0	1–0	1–2	3–3	0–1	3–1	1–2	0–2	2–2	3–4	1–0	0–3	0–4	1–1
1–3	3–3	1–1	0–3	3–0	2–2	2–2	0–1	3–1	2–1	1–0	0–1	1–1	2–1	1–1
2–0	0–0	0–2	1–3	2–1	1–1	0–1	1–0	1–1	0–1	2–0	2–2	3–1	1–0	0–1
2–0	1–1	1–2	1–2	2–0	0–1	2–3	2–4	2–0	0–1	2–1	1–2	1–2	0–2	2–0
1–3	3–1	1–0	0–2	3–3	1–1	1–3	3–0	1–0	1–0	2–1	0–0	3–2	1–1	1–0
—	2–1	3–0	2–1	1–1	2–1	0–2	1–0	4–1	3–2	4–2	0–1	5–2	1–2	0–0
2–0	—	1–1	0–0	0–0	3–1	0–0	1–4	2–2	0–0	0–0	3–3	2–0	2–0	1–1
2–0	1–0	—	1–2	6–0	3–1	4–0	1–1	1–1	0–0	2–1	0–0	5–2	2–1	2–0
7–1	2–0	1–1	—	4–0	2–1	3–0	3–1	3–2	1–0	0–0	1–0	2–0	2–0	2–1
1–1	0–0	1–2	0–2	—	1–1	1–0	0–1	4–0	3–1	1–1	5–1	1–2	1–0	2–2
0–0	4–0	3–0	4–2	1–1	—	2–1	5–5	0–1	0–1	0–1	1–2	1–1	1–0	0–0
3–0	2–3	0–0	0–1	1–3	1–1	—	1–1	1–0	5–2	3–3	1–1	0–0	1–3	2–3
1–1	2–1	1–0	2–0	0–0	3–0	4–0	—	2–0	2–0	3–1	4–0	1–0	0–1	2–0
3–1	2–1	3–3	1–1	3–1	0–3	0–1	0–0	—	0–1	1–1	1–2	1–2	1–0	1–1
1–2	2–2	2–0	1–2	2–2	2–0	3–0	4–1	2–4	—	0–1	1–0	1–2	0–0	2–0
1–1	1–0	3–0	2–1	5–1	2–2	1–0	1–0	3–2	1–0	—	2–0	3–1	1–3	1–0
2–3	0–2	1–1	0–3	3–1	4–0	1–1	0–2	3–0	2–1	3–1	—	2–1	5–2	3–0
0–3	0–0	3–1	1–0	1–3	0–1	1–2	0–0	0–0	2–1	0–4	3–2	—	1–2	3–1
3–0	2–2	2–2	0–0	2–0	5–3	2–1	2–0	2–0	6–0	0–1	2–0	2–1	—	3–1
3–0	1–2	3–1	1–0	3–0	0–1	4–3	1–1	1–1	2–1	2–2	0–2	2–2	0–0	—

BARCLAYS LEAGUE – DIVISION 2

HOME TEAM	Blackpool	Bolton W	Bournemouth	Bradford C	Brighton & HA	Burnley	Chester C	Exeter C	Fulham
Blackpool	—	1-1	2-0	3-3	2-2	1-3	2-0	2-0	1-1
Bolton W	3-0	—	1-1	5-0	0-1	4-0	5-0	4-1	1-0
Bournemouth	5-1	1-2	—	1-1	1-1	1-1	0-0	1-3	2-1
Bradford C	2-0	2-1	0-1	—	1-1	1-0	3-1	3-1	3-2
Brighton & HA	1-1	2-1	1-0	1-1	—	3-0	3-2	3-0	0-2
Burnley	2-2	0-1	1-1	2-2	1-3	—	5-0	3-1	5-2
Chester C	1-2	2-2	1-0	2-5	2-1	3-0	—	0-3	2-3
Exeter C	0-1	1-3	1-1	0-1	2-3	2-2	2-0	—	1-2
Fulham	1-0	1-4	1-1	1-1	2-0	4-0	1-0	1-1	—
Hartlepool U	1-0	0-2	0-1	2-0	2-0	0-0	2-0	1-3	0-3
Huddersfield T	5-2	1-1	0-1	1-2	1-2	1-1	0-2	0-0	1-0
Hull C	3-2	1-2	3-0	0-2	1-0	0-2	1-1	4-0	1-1
Leyton Orient	1-0	1-0	1-0	4-2	3-2	3-2	4-3	5-0	0-0
Mansfield T	2-2	1-1	0-2	5-2	1-3	1-1	2-0	0-0	2-3
Plymouth Arg	2-1	2-1	2-1	3-0	3-2	1-2	2-0	0-3	1-1
Port Vale	2-1	0-0	3-0	1-2	3-1	3-0	2-0	2-2	0-0
Preston NE	3-3	2-2	1-1	3-2	1-0	2-0	4-3	2-2	1-2
Reading	0-0	1-2	3-2	1-1	3-0	1-0	1-0	2-3	3-0
Rotherham U	3-2	2-1	1-2	2-0	1-0	0-1	3-3	1-1	1-1
Stockport Co	0-0	2-0	0-0	2-2	0-0	2-1	2-0	2-2	0-0
Stoke C	0-1	0-0	0-1	0-0	1-1	1-1	2-0	1-1	0-1
Swansea C	3-0	1-2	2-1	1-1	0-1	1-1	4-2	0-0	2-2
WBA	3-1	3-1	2-1	1-1	3-1	2-0	2-0	2-0	4-0
Wigan Ath	2-1	0-2	0-0	1-2	1-2	1-1	1-2	0-1	1-3

1992–93 RESULTS

Hartlepool U	Huddersfield T	Hull C	Leyton Orient	Mansfield T	Plymouth Arg	Port Vale	Preston NE	Reading	Rotherham U	Stockport Co	Stoke C	Swansea C	WBA	Wigan Ath
1–1	2–2	5–1	3–1	1–1	1–1	2–4	2–3	0–1	2–0	2–0	1–3	0–0	2–1	2–1
1–2	2–0	2–0	1–0	2–1	3–1	1–1	1–0	2–1	2–0	2–1	1–0	3–1	0–2	2–1
0–2	1–1	0–0	3–0	4–1	1–3	2–1	2–1	1–1	0–0	1–0	1–1	0–2	0–1	0–0
0–2	0–1	1–2	1–0	0–0	0–0	3–2	4–0	3–0	0–3	2–3	3–1	0–0	2–2	2–1
1–1	2–1	2–0	1–3	3–1	2–1	0–2	2–0	0–1	1–2	2–0	2–2	0–2	3–1	1–0
3–0	2–1	2–0	2–0	1–0	0–0	1–1	2–0	1–1	1–1	1–1	0–2	1–0	2–1	0–1
1–0	0–2	3–0	1–3	1–2	1–2	1–2	2–4	0–3	1–2	0–3	1–1	2–2	1–3	1–2
1–3	0–1	3–3	1–0	0–0	3–1	1–2	2–1	0–0	2–1	0–0	1–1	1–1	1–0	
—	1–0	1–0	0–2	0–1	1–0	1–1	0–0	1–1	0–2	3–2	1–2	0–1	2–2	0–0
3–0	—	3–0	1–1	2–1	2–1	1–2	1–0	0–0	1–1	2–1	1–0	1–2	0–1	2–1
3–2	2–3	—	0–0	1–0	2–0	0–1	2–4	1–1	0–1	0–1	1–0	1–0	1–2	0–0
0–0	4–1	0–0	—	5–1	2–0	0–1	3–1	1–2	1–1	3–0	1–0	4–2	2–0	1–2
2–0	1–2	3–1	3–0	—	0–0	0–1	2–2	1–1	1–3	0–4	3–3	0–3	2–0	
2–2	1–3	0–0	2–0	3–2	—	0–1	4–0	2–2	2–1	3–4	1–1	0–1	0–0	2–0
2–0	1–0	1–1	2–0	3–0	4–0	—	2–2	3–1	4–2	0–0	0–2	2–0	2–1	2–2
0–2	2–1	1–2	1–4	1–5	1–2	2–5	—	2–0	5–2	2–3	1–2	1–3	1–1	2–0
2–0	2–1	1–2	1–1	3–1	3–0	1–0	4–0	—	3–1	2–4	0–1	2–0	1–1	4–0
0–0	1–0	0–1	1–1	2–0	2–2	4–1	1–0	3–2	—	0–2	0–2	0–0	0–2	2–3
4–1	5–0	5–3	1–2	2–0	3–0	2–0	3–0	2–2	2–2	—	1–1	1–1	5–1	3–0
0–1	3–0	3–0	2–1	4–0	1–0	2–1	1–0	2–0	2–0	2–1	—	2–1	4–3	2–1
3–0	3–0	1–0	0–1	4–0	0–0	2–0	2–0	2–1	2–0	2–2	1–2	—	0–0	2–1
3–1	2–2	3–1	2–0	0	2–5	0–1	3–2	3–0	2–3	3–0	1–2	3–0	—	5–1
2–2	1–0	2–0	3–1	2–0	0–2	0–4	2–3	1–1	1–1	1–2	1–1	2–3	1–0	—

BARCLAYS LEAGUE – DIVISION 3

HOME TEAM	Barnet	Bury	Cardiff C	Carlisle U	Chesterfield	Colchester U	Crewe Alex	Darlington
Barnet	—	1-0	2-1	2-0	2-1	3-1	3-2	0-0
Bury	0-0	—	1-0	6-0	3-0	3-2	1-2	1-1
Cardiff C	1-1	3-0	—	2-2	2-1	3-1	1-1	0-0
Carlisle U	0-1	5-1	1-2	—	3-1	0-2	1-3	2-2
Chesterfield	1-2	2-1	2-1	1-0	—	4-0	2-1	2-0
Colchester U	1-2	0-0	2-4	2-1	3-0	—	3-2	0-3
Crewe Alex	4-1	2-1	2-0	4-0	0-2	7-1	—	
Darlington	1-0	0-0	0-2	1-1	1-1	1-0	3-0	—
Doncaster R	2-1	2-3	0-1	1-2	2-1	1-0	1-1	0-1
Gillingham	1-1	1-4	0-1	1-0	0-0	0-1	1-2	3-1
Halifax T	1-2	0-1	0-1	0-2	1-1	2-4	1-2	1-0
Hereford U	1-1	3-1	1-1	1-0	1-3	3-1	0-1	1-1
Lincoln C	4-1	1-2	3-2	2-1	1-1	1-1	1-1	2-0
Northampton T	1-1	1-0	1-2	2-0	0-1	1-0	0-2	1-2
Rochdale	0-1	1-2	1-2	2-2	2-1	5-2	0-1	3-1
Scarborough	2-2	1-3	1-3	2-2	2-2	0-1	1-0	0-3
Scunthorpe U	2-0	2-0	0-3	0-0	0-1	3-1	3-3	1-3
Shrewsbury T	1-0	2-0	3-2	2-3	2-2	4-3	4-1	1-2
Torquay U	0-1	0-1	2-1	0-2	2-2	2-2	1-2	0-2
Walsall	2-0	4-3	2-3	2-1	3-2	1-3	1-0	2-2
Wrexham	2-3	4-2	0-2	3-1	5-4	4-3	2-0	1-1
York C	2-0	1-2	3-1	2-2	0-0	2-0	3-1	0-0

	Doncaster R	Gillingham	Halifax T	Hereford U	Lincoln C	Northampton T	Rochdale	Scarborough	Scunthorpe U	Shrewsbury T	Torquay U	Walsall	Wrexham	York C
	2-0	2-0	0-0	2-0	1-1	3-0	2-0	3-1	3-0	2-2	5-4	3-0	3-1	1-5
	3-0	1-0	1-2	2-0	1-2	3-3	2-2	0-2	0-0	0-0	2-0	2-1	3-1	1-1
	1-1	3-1	2-1	2-1	3-1	2-1	1-1	1-0	3-0	2-1	4-0	2-1	1-2	3-3
	1-1	1-0	1-1	0-0	2-0	2-0	3-0	2-2	0-2	1-0	0-1	3-4	0-2	1-2
	0-0	1-1	2-1	1-0	2-1	1-3	2-3	0-3	1-2	2-4	1-0	2-1	2-3	1-1
	2-0	3-0	2-1	3-1	2-1	2-0	4-4	1-0	1-0	0-2	2-0	3-1	2-4	0-0
	4-0	3-1	2-1	1-1	1-2	3-2	1-1	2-3	1-0	2-2	4-2	0-0	0-1	3-1
	1-2	1-1	0-3	0-1	1-3	3-1	0-4	2-3	2-2	0-2	4-1	1-2	1-1	0-1
	—	1-0	0-1	2-1	0-0	2-2	1-1	4-3	0-1	0-1	2-3	0-3	1-1	0-1
	1-1	—	2-0	3-1	3-1	2-3	4-2	3-1	1-1	1-0	0-2	0-1	4-1	1-4
	2-2	2-0	—	0-1	2-1	2-2	2-3	3-4	0-0	1-1	0-2	0-4	0-1	0-1
	0-2	3-1	3-0	—	0-2	3-2	1-1	1-1	2-2	1-1	3-1	1-3	1-1	1-1
	2-1	1-1	2-1	2-0	—	2-0	1-2	3-0	1-0	0-1	2-2	0-2	0-0	0-1
	0-1	2-2	2-5	1-1	0-2	—	1-0	1-3	1-0	0-0	0-1	0-0	0-2	4-3
	1-1	1-1	2-3	1-3	5-1	0-3	—	3-0	2-0	2-0	1-0	4-3	1-2	1-0
	1-1	1-1	2-0	2-0	0-1	4-2	1-1	—	1-2	1-2	1-0	4-1	1-1	4-2
	0-1	2-2	4-1	3-1	1-1	5-0	5-1	1-2	—	1-1	2-2	2-0	0-0	1-2
	2-1	2-1	1-0	1-1	3-2	2-3	1-2	2-0	2-1	—	0-1	0-3	0-1	1-1
	1-2	2-1	2-0	0-0	1-2	1-0	0-2	1-3	0-1	1-0	—	0-1	1-1	1-0
	3-1	1-1	1-2	1-1	1-2	2-0	3-1	3-2	3-2	1-1	2-2	—	1-1	3-1
	1-1	2-0	1-1	2-0	2-0	0-1	3-1	4-1	0-2	2-0	4-2	3-1	—	3-0
	1-1	1-1	1-1	4-2	2-0	2-1	3-0	1-0	5-1	2-0	2-1	0-1	4-0	—

FA PREMIER LEAGUE

		Home			Goals		Away			Goals			
	P	W	D	L	F	A	W	D	L	F	A	Pts	GD
1 Manchester U	42	14	5	2	39	14	10	7	4	28	17	84	+36
2 Aston Villa	42	13	5	3	36	16	8	6	7	21	24	74	+17
3 Norwich City	42	13	6	2	31	19	8	3	10	30	46	72	−4
4 Blackburn R	42	13	4	4	38	18	7	7	7	30	28	71	+22
5 QPR	42	11	5	5	41	32	6	7	8	22	23	63	+8
6 Liverpool	42	13	4	4	41	18	3	7	11	21	37	59	+7
7 Sheffield W	42	9	8	4	34	26	6	6	9	21	25	59	+4
8 Tottenham H	42	11	5	5	40	25	5	6	10	20	41	59	−6
9 Manchester C	42	7	8	6	30	25	8	4	9	26	26	57	+5
10 Arsenal	42	8	6	7	25	20	7	5	9	15	18	56	+2
11 Chelsea	42	9	7	5	29	22	5	7	9	22	32	56	−3
12 Wimbledon	42	9	4	8	32	23	5	8	8	24	32	54	+1
13 Everton	42	7	6	8	26	27	8	2	11	27	28	53	−2
14 Sheffield U	42	10	6	5	33	19	4	4	13	21	34	52	+1
15 Coventry C	42	7	4	10	29	28	6	9	6	23	29	52	−5
16 Ipswich T	42	8	9	4	29	22	4	7	10	21	33	52	−5
17 Leeds U	42	12	8	1	40	17	0	7	14	17	45	51	−5
18 Southampton	42	10	6	5	30	21	3	5	13	24	40	50	−7
19 Oldham Ath	42	10	6	5	43	30	3	4	14	20	44	49	−11
20 Crystal Palace	42	6	9	6	27	25	5	7	9	21	36	49	−13
21 Middlesbrough	42	8	5	8	33	27	3	6	12	21	48	44	−21
22 Nottingham F	42	6	4	11	17	25	4	6	11	24	37	40	−21

TOP GOALSCORERS 1992–93

FA PREMIER LEAGUE	League	FA Cup	Coca Cola Cup	Other Cups	Total
Teddy Sheringham (Tottenham Hotspur)- (Including 1 for Nottingham Forest)	22	4	3	0	29
Ian Wright (Arsenal)	15	10	6	0	31
Mick Quinn (Coventry City)(Including 2 League and 3 Coca Cola Cup for Newcastle United)	19	0	3	0	22
Les Ferdinand (QPR)	20	2	2	0	24
Alan Shearer (Blackburn Rovers)	16	0	6	0	22
Ian Rush (Liverpool)	14	1	1	5	21
Mike Newell (Blackburn Rvoers)	13	5	3	0	21
Brian Deane (Sheffield United)	15	3	2	0	20
Mark Bright (Sheffield Wednesday)(Including 1 for Crystal Palace)	12	3	6	0	21
David White (Manchester City)	16	3	0	0	19
Lee Chapman (Leeds United)	14	1	2	1	18
Dean Holdsworth (Wimbledon)	19	0	0	0	19
Matthew Le Tissier (Southampton)	15	1	2	0	18
Eric Cantona (Manchester United)(Including 6 League and 2 European Cup for Leeds United)	15	0	0	2	17
Mark Hughes (Manchester United)	15	0	1	0	16
Dean Saunders (Aston Villa)(Including 1 for Liverpool)	14	2	2	0	18

BARCLAYS LEAGUE DIVISION ONE

			Home			Goals			Away			Goals			
		P	W	D	L	F	A	W	D	L	F	A	PTS	GLS
1	Newcastle U	46	16	6	1	58	15	13	3	7	34	23	96	(92)
2	West Ham U	46	16	5	2	50	17	10	5	8	31	24	88	(81)
3	Portsmouth	46	19	2	2	48	9	7	8	8	32	37	88	(80)
4	Tranmere R	46	15	4	4	48	24	8	6	9	24	32	79	(72)
5	Swindon T	46	15	5	3	41	23	6	8	9	33	36	76	(74)
6	Leicester C	46	14	5	4	43	24	8	5	10	28	40	76	(71)
7	Millwall	46	14	6	3	46	21	4	10	9	19	32	70	(65)
8	Derby Co	46	11	2	10	40	33	8	7	8	28	24	66	(68)
9	Grimsby T	46	12	6	5	33	25	7	1	15	25	32	64	(58)
10	Peterborough U	46	7	11	5	30	26	9	3	11	25	37	62	(55)
11	Wolverhampton W	46	11	6	6	37	26	5	7	11	20	30	61	(57)
12	Charlton Ath	46	10	8	5	28	19	6	5	12	21	27	61	(49)
13	Barnsley	46	12	4	7	29	19	5	5	13	27	41	60	(56)
14	Oxford U	46	8	7	8	29	21	6	7	10	24	35	56	(53)
15	Bristol C	46	10	7	6	29	25	4	7	12	20	42	56	(49)
16	Watford	46	8	7	8	27	30	6	6	11	30	41	55	(57)
17	Notts Co	46	10	7	6	33	21	2	9	12	22	49	52	(55)
18	Southend U	46	9	8	6	33	22	4	5	14	21	42	52	(54)
19	Birmingham C	46	10	4	9	30	32	3	8	12	20	40	51	(50)
20	Luton T	46	6	13	4	26	26	4	8	11	22	36	51	(48)
21	Sunderland	46	9	6	8	34	28	4	5	14	16	36	50	(49)
22	Brentford	46	7	6	10	28	30	6	4	13	24	41	49	(52)
23	Cambridge U	46	8	6	9	29	32	3	10	10	19	37	49	(48)
24	Bristol R	46	6	6	11	30	42	4	5	14	25	45	41	(55)

DIVISION 1

Guy Whittingham (Portsmouth)		42	0	2	3	47
Gary Blissett (Brentford)		21	0	4	4	29
Andy Cole (Newcastle United) (Including 12 League, 3 Coca Cola and 1 Anglo-Italian for Bristol City)		24	0	3	1	28
John Aldridge (Tranmere Rovers)		21	1	2	2	26
David Kelly (Newcastle United)		21	1	2	1	25
Craig Maskell (Swindon Town)		19	0	1	4	24
Paul Kitson (Derby County)		17	1	1	4	23
Trevor Morley (West Ham United)		20	1	0	1	22
Paul Furlong (Watford)		19	0	3	0	22
Paul Gray (Luton Town)		19	1	0	0	20
Tony Adcock (Peterborough United)		16	1	2	0	19
Steve Bull (Wolverhampton Wanderers)		16	1	1	1	19
Marco Gabbiadini (Derby County)		9	2	2	6	19
Stan Collymore (Southend United)		15	3	0	0	18

BARCLAYS LEAGUE DIVISION TWO

		Home			Goals		Away			Goals			
	P	W	D	L	F	A	W	D	L	F	A	PTS	GLS
1 Stoke C	46	17	4	2	41	13	10	8	5	32	21	93	(73)
2 Bolton W	46	18	2	3	48	14	9	7	7	32	27	90	(80)
3 Port Vale	46	14	7	2	44	17	12	4	7	35	27	89	(79)
4 WBA	46	17	3	3	56	22	8	7	8	32	32	85	(88)
5 Swansea C	46	12	7	4	38	17	8	6	9	27	30	73	(65)
6 Stockport Co	46	11	11	1	47	18	8	4	11	34	39	72	(81)
7 Leyton Orient	46	16	4	3	49	20	5	5	13	20	33	72	(69)
8 Reading	46	14	4	5	44	20	4	11	8	22	31	69	(66)
9 Brighton & HA	46	13	4	6	36	24	7	5	11	27	35	69	(63)
10 Bradford C	46	12	5	6	36	24	6	9	8	33	43	68	(69)
11 Rotherham U	46	9	7	7	30	27	8	7	8	30	33	65	(60)
12 Fulham	46	9	9	5	28	22	7	8	8	29	33	65	(57)
13 Burnley	46	11	8	4	38	21	4	8	11	19	38	61	(57)
14 Plymouth Arg	46	11	6	6	38	28	5	6	12	21	36	60	(59)
15 Huddersfield T	46	10	6	7	30	22	7	3	13	24	39	60	(54)
16 Hartlepool U	46	8	6	9	19	23	6	6	11	23	37	54	(42)
17 AFC Bournemouth	46	7	10	6	28	24	5	7	11	17	28	53	(45)
18 Blackpool	46	9	9	5	40	30	3	6	14	23	45	51	(63)
19 Exeter C	46	5	8	10	26	30	6	9	8	28	39	50	(54)
20 Hull C	46	9	5	9	28	26	4	6	13	18	43	50	(46)
21 Preston NE	46	8	5	10	41	47	5	3	15	24	47	47	(65)
22 Mansfield T	46	7	8	8	34	34	4	3	16	18	46	44	(52)
23 Wigan Ath	46	6	6	11	26	34	4	5	14	17	38	41	(43)
24 Chester C	46	6	2	15	30	47	2	3	18	19	55	29	(49)

DIVISION 2

Bob Taylor *(West Bromwich Albion)*	30	3	1	3	37
Kevin Francis *(Stockport County)*	28	2	2	6	38
Mark Stein *(Stoke City)*	26	0	4	3	33
Andy Walker *(Bolton Wanderers)*	26	4	1	2	33
Tony Ellis *(Preston North End)*	22	1	1	1	25
Sean McCarthy *(Bradford City)*	17	2	1	5	25
Jimmy Quinn *(Reading)*	17	3	1	2	23
Kurt Nogan *(Brighton & HA)*	20	0	0	2	22
Adrian Heath *(Burnely)*	19	3	0	0	22
John McGinlay *(Bolton Wanderers)*	16	5	0	1	22
Stuart Rimmer *(Chester City)*	20	0	0	0	20
Paul Jewell *(Bradford City)*	16	2	1	0	19
Ian Taylor *(Port Vale)*	15	1	1	2	19
Robert Taylor *(Leyton Orient)*	18	0	0	0	18
David Eyres *(Blackpool)*	16	0	1	2	19

BARCLAYS LEAGUE DIVISION THREE

		Home			Goals		Away			Goals			
	P	W	D	L	F	A	W	D	L	F	A	PTS	GLS
1 Cardiff C	42	13	7	1	42	20	12	1	8	35	27	83	(77)
2 Wrexham	42	14	3	4	48	26	9	8	4	27	26	80	(75)
3 Barnet	42	16	4	1	45	19	7	6	8	21	29	79	(66)
4 York C	42	13	6	2	41	15	8	6	7	31	30	75	(66)
5 Walsall	42	11	6	4	42	31	11	1	9	34	30	73	(76)
6 Crewe Alex	42	13	3	5	47	23	8	4	9	28	33	70	(75)
7 Bury	42	10	7	4	36	19	8	2	11	27	36	63	(63)
8 Lincoln C	42	10	6	5	31	20	8	3	10	26	33	63	(57)
9 Shrewsbury T	42	11	3	7	36	30	6	8	7	21	22	62	(57)
10 Colchester U	42	13	3	5	38	26	5	2	14	29	50	59	(67)
11 Rochdale	42	10	3	8	38	29	6	7	8	32	41	58	(70)
12 Chesterfield	42	11	3	7	32	28	4	8	9	27	35	56	(59)
13 Scarborough	42	7	7	7	32	30	8	2	11	34	41	54	(66)
14 Scunthorpe U	42	8	7	6	38	25	6	5	10	19	29	54	(57)
15 Darlington	42	5	6	10	23	31	7	8	6	25	22	50	(48)
16 Doncaster R	42	6	5	10	22	28	5	9	7	20	29	47	(42)
17 Hereford U	42	7	9	5	31	27	3	6	12	16	33	45	(47)
18 Carlisle U	42	7	5	9	29	27	4	6	11	22	38	44	(51)
19 Torquay U	42	6	4	11	18	26	6	3	12	27	41	43	(45)
20 Northampton T	42	6	5	10	19	28	5	3	13	29	46	41	(48)
21 Gillingham	42	9	4	8	32	28	0	9	12	16	36	40	(48)
22 Halifax T	42	3	5	13	20	35	6	4	11	25	33	36	(45)

DIVISION 3

Darren Foreman *(Scarborough)*	27	0	2	2	31
Carl Griffiths *(Shrewsbury Town)*	27	2	1	1	31
Wayne Clarke *(Walsall)*	21	0	1	2	24
Andy Barnes *(York City)*	21	0	0	0	21
Gary Bennett *(Wrexham)*	16	1	2	2	21
Steve Watkin *(Wrexham)*	18	0	0	2	20
Tony Naylor *(Crewe Alexandra)*	16	2	2	5	25
Gary Bull *(Barnet)*	17	0	2	0	19
Phil Stant *(Cardiff City) (Including 6 League and 1 Coca Cola for Mansfield Town)*	17	0	1	1	19
Michele Cecere *(Walsall)*	16	0	0	2	18
Ian Helliwell *(Scunthorpe United)*	13	0	4	0	17
Ian Blackstone *(York City)*	16	0	0	0	16
George Oghani *(Carlisle United)*	15	0	1	0	16
Phil Clarkson *(Crewe Alexandra)*	13	2	1	1	17
Tommy Mooney *(Scarborough)*	9	0	5	2	16

DIVISION 1 LEAGUE POSITIONS
1967–68 TO 1991–92

	1991-92	1990-91	1989-90	1988-89	1987-88	1986-87	1985-86	1984-85	1983-84	1982-83	1981-82	1980-81	1979-80
Arsenal	4	1	4	1	6	4	7	7	6	10	5	3	4
Aston Villa	7	17	2	17	–	22	16	10	10	6	11	1	7
Birmingham C	–	–	–	–	–	–	21	–	20	17	16	13	–
Blackpool	–	–	–	–	–	–	–	–	–	–	–	–	–
Bolton W	–	–	–	–	–	–	–	–	–	–	–	–	22
Brighton & HA	–	–	–	–	–	–	–	–	–	22	13	19	16
Bristol C	–	–	–	–	–	–	–	–	–	–	–	–	20
Burnley	–	–	–	–	–	–	–	–	–	–	–	–	–
Carlisle U	–	–	–	–	–	–	–	–	–	–	–	–	–
Charlton Ath	–	–	19	14	17	19	–	–	–	–	–	–	–
Chelsea	14	11	5	–	18	14	6	6	–	–	–	–	–
Coventry C	19	16	12	7	10	10	17	18	19	19	14	16	15
Crystal Palace	10	3	15	–	15	–	–	–	–	–	–	22	13
Derby Co	–	20	16	5	15	–	–	–	–	–	–	–	21
Everton	12	9	6	8	4	1	2	1	7	7	8	15	19
Fulham	–	–	–	–	–	–	–	–	–	–	–	–	–
Huddersfield T	–	–	–	–	–	–	–	–	–	–	–	–	–
Ipswich T	–	–	–	–	–	–	20	17	12	9	2	2	3
Leeds U	1	4	–	–	–	–	–	–	–	–	20	9	11
Leicester C	–	–	–	–	–	20	19	15	15	–	–	21	–
Liverpool	6	2	1	2	1	2	1	2	1	1	1	5	1
Luton T	20	18	17	16	9	7	9	13	16	18	–	–	–
Manchester C	5	5	14	–	–	21	15	–	–	20	10	12	17
Manchester U	2	6	13	11	2	11	4	4	4	3	3	8	2
Middlesbrough	–	–	–	18	–	–	–	–	–	–	22	14	9
Millwall	–	–	20	10	–	–	–	–	–	–	–	–	–
Newcastle U	–	–	–	20	8	17	11	14	–	–	–	–	–
Norwich C	18	15	10	4	14	5	–	20	14	14	–	20	12
Nottingham F	8	8	9	3	3	8	8	9	3	5	12	7	5
Notts Co	21	–	–	–	–	–	–	–	21	15	15	–	–
Oldham Ath	17	–	–	–	–	–	–	–	–	–	–	–	–
Oxford U	–	–	–	–	21	18	18	–	–	–	–	–	–
Portsmouth	–	–	–	–	19	–	–	–	–	–	–	–	–
QPR	11	12	11	9	5	16	13	19	5	–	–	–	–
Sheffield U	9	13	–	–	–	–	–	–	–	–	–	–	–
Sheffield W	3	–	18	15	11	13	5	8	–	–	–	–	–
Southampton	16	14	7	13	12	12	14	5	2	12	7	6	8
Stoke C	–	–	–	–	–	–	22	18	13	18	11	18	–
Sunderland	–	19	–	–	–	–	21	13	16	19	17	–	–
Swansea	–	–	–	–	–	–	–	21	6	–	–	–	–
Tottenham H	15	10	3	6	13	3	10	3	8	4	4	10	14
Watford	–	–	–	–	20	9	12	11	11	2	–	–	–
WBA	–	–	–	–	–	–	22	12	17	11	17	4	10
West Ham U	22	–	–	19	16	15	3	16	9	8	9	–	–
Wimbledon	13	7	8	12	7	6	–	–	–	–	–	–	–
Wolv'hampton W	–	–	–	–	–	–	–	–	22	–	21	18	6

	1978-79	1977-78	1976-77	1975-76	1974-75	1973-74	1972-73	1971-72	1970-71	1969-70	1968-69	1967-68
Arsenal	7	5	8	17	16	10	2	5	1	12	4	9
Aston Villa	8	8	4	16	–	–	–	–	–	–	–	–
Birmingham C	21	11	13	19	17	19	10	–	–	–	–	–
Blackpool	–	–	–	–	–	–	–	–	22	–	–	–
Bolton W	17	–	–	–	–	–	–	–	–	–	–	–
Brighton & HA												
Bristol C	13	17	18	–	–	–	–	–	–	–	–	–
Burnley	–	–	–	21	10	6	–	–	21	14	14	14
Carlisle	–	–	–	–	22	–	–	–	–	–	–	–
Charlton Ath												
Chelsea	22	16	–	–	21	17	12	7	6	3	5	6
Coventry C	10	7	19	14	14	16	19	18	10	6	20	20
Crystal Palace	–	–	–	–	–	–	21	20	18	20	–	–
Derby Co	19	12	15	4	1	3	7	1	9	4	–	–
Everton	4	3	9	11	4	7	17	15	14	1	3	5
Fulham	–	–	–	–	–	–	–	–	–	–	–	22
Huddersfield T	–	–	–	–	–	–	–	22	15	–	–	–
Ipswich T	6	18	3	6	3	4	4	13	19	18	12	–
Leeds U	5	9	10	5	9	1	3	2	2	2	1	4
Leicester C	–	22	11	7	18	9	16	12	–	–	21	13
Liverpool	1	2	1	1	2	2	1	3	5	5	2	3
Luton T	–	–	–	–	20	–	–	–	–	–	–	–
Manchester C	15	4	2	8	8	14	11	4	11	10	13	1
Manchester U	9	10	6	3	–	21	18	8	8	8	11	2
Middlesbrough	12	14	12	13	7	–	–	–	–	–	–	–
Millwall												
Newcastle U	–	21	5	15	15	15	9	11	12	7	9	10
Norwich C	16	13	16	10	–	22	20	–	–	–	–	–
Nottingham F	2	1	–	–	–	–	–	21	16	15	18	11
Notts Co												
Oldham Ath												
Oxford U												
Portsmouth												
QPR	20	19	14	2	11	8	–	–	–	–	22	–
Sheffield U	–	–	–	22	6	13	14	10	–	–	–	21
Sheffield W	–	–	–	–	–	–	–	–	–	22	15	19
Southampton	14	–	–	–	–	20	13	19	7	19	7	16
Stoke C	–	–	21	12	5	5	15	17	13	9	19	18
Sunderland	–	–	20	–	–	–	–	–	–	21	17	15
Swansea C												
Tottenham H	11	–	22	9	19	11	8	6	3	11	6	7
Watford												
WBA	3	6	7	–	–	–	22	16	17	16	10	8
West Ham U	–	20	17	18	13	18	6	14	20	17	8	12
Wimbledon												
Wolv'hampton W	18	15	–	20	12	12	5	9	4	13	16	17

DIVISION 2 LEAGUE POSITIONS
1967–68 TO 1991–92

	1991–92	1990–91	1989–90	1988–89	1987–88	1986–87	1985–86	1984–85	1983–84	1982–83	1981–82	1980–81	1979–80
Aston Villa	–	–	–	–	2	–	–	–	–	–	–	–	–
Barnsley	16	8	19	7	14	11	12	11	14	10	6	–	–
Birmingham C	–	–	–	23	19	19	–	2	–	–	–	–	3
Blackburn R	6	19	5	5	5	12	19	5	6	11	10	4	–
Blackpool	–	–	–	–	–	–	–	–	–	–	–	–	–
Bolton W	–	–	–	–	–	–	–	–	–	22	19	18	–
Bournemouth	–	–	22	12	17	–	–	–	–	–	–	–	–
Bradford C	–	–	23	14	4	10	13	–	–	–	–	–	–
Brighton & HA	23	6	18	19	–	22	11	6	9	–	–	–	–
Bristol C	17	9	–	–	–	–	–	–	–	–	–	21	–
Bristol R	13	13	–	–	–	–	–	–	–	–	–	22	19
Burnley	–	–	–	–	–	–	–	–	–	21	–	–	21
Bury	–	–	–	–	–	–	–	–	–	–	–	–	–
Cambridge U	5	–	–	–	–	–	–	–	22	12	14	13	8
Cardiff C	–	–	–	–	–	–	–	21	15	–	20	19	15
Carlisle U	–	–	–	–	–	20	16	7	14	–	–	–	–
Charlton Ath	7	16	–	–	–	–	2	17	13	17	13	–	22
Chelsea	–	–	–	1	–	–	–	–	1	18	12	12	4
Coventry C	–	–	–	–	–	–	–	–	–	–	–	–	–
Crystal Palace	–	–	3	6	6	5	15	18	15	15	–	–	–
Derby Co	3	–	–	–	–	1	–	–	20	13	16	6	–
Fulham	–	–	–	–	–	22	9	11	4	–	–	–	20
Grimsby T	19	–	–	–	–	21	15	10	5	19	17	7	–
Hereford U	–	–	–	–	–	–	–	–	–	–	–	–	–
Huddersfield T	–	–	–	–	23	17	16	13	12	–	–	–	–
Hull C	–	24	14	21	15	14	6	–	–	–	–	–	–
Ipswich T	1	14	9	8	8	5	–	–	–	–	–	–	–
Leeds U	–	–	1	10	7	4	14	7	10	8	–	–	–
Leicester C	4	22	13	15	13	–	–	–	–	3	8	–	1
Leyton Orient	–	–	–	–	–	–	–	–	–	–	22	17	14
Luton T	–	–	–	–	–	–	–	–	–	–	1	5	6
Manchester C	–	–	–	2	9	–	–	3	4	–	–	–	–
Manchester U	–	–	–	–	–	–	–	–	–	–	–	–	–
Mansfield T	–	–	–	–	–	–	–	–	–	–	–	–	–
Middlesbrough	2	7	21	–	3	–	21	19	17	16	–	–	–
Millwall	15	5	–	–	1	16	9	–	–	–	–	–	–
Newcastle U	20	11	3	–	–	–	–	–	3	5	9	11	9
Norwich C	–	–	–	–	–	–	1	–	–	–	3	–	–
Nottingham F	–	–	–	–	–	–	–	–	–	–	–	–	–
Notts Co	–	4	–	–	–	–	–	20	–	–	–	2	17
Oldham Ath	–	1	8	16	10	3	8	14	19	7	11	15	11
Oxford U	21	10	17	17	–	–	–	1	–	–	–	–	–
Plymouth Arg	22	18	16	18	16	7	–	–	–	–	–	–	–
Port Vale	24	15	11	–	–	–	–	–	–	–	–	–	–
Portsmouth	9	17	12	20	–	2	4	16	–	–	–	–	–
Preston NE	–	–	–	–	–	–	–	–	–	–	–	20	10

1978-79	1977-78	1976-77	1975-76	1974-75	1973-74	1972-73	1971-72	1970-71	1969-70	1968-69	1967-68	
-	-	-	-	2	14	3	-	-	21	18	16	Aston Villa
-	-	-	-	-	-	-	-	-	-	-	-	Barnsley
-	-	-	-	-	-	-	2	9	18	7	4	Birmingham C
22	5	12	15	-	-	-	-	21	8	19	8	Blackburn R
-	20	5	10	7	5	7	6	-	2	8	3	Blackpool
-	1	4	4	10	11	-	-	22	16	17	12	Bolton W
-	-	-	-	-	-	-	-	-	-	-	-	Bournemouth
-	-	-	-	-	-	-	-	-	-	-	-	Bradford C
2	4	-	-	-	22	-	-	-	-	-	-	Brighton & HA
-	-	-	2	5	16	5	8	19	14	16	19	Bristol C
16	18	15	18	19	-	-	-	-	-	-	-	Bristol R
13	11	16	-	-	-	1	7	-	-	-	-	Burnley
-	-	-	-	-	-	-	-	-	-	21	-	Bury
12	-	-	-	-	-	-	-	-	-	-	-	Cambridge U
9	19	18	-	21	17	20	19	3	7	5	13	Cardiff C
-	-	20	19	-	3	18	10	4	12	12	10	Carlisle U
19	17	7	9	-	-	-	21	20	20	3	15	Charlton Ath
-	-	2	11	-	-	-	-	-	-	-	-	Chelsea
-	-	-	-	-	-	-	-	-	-	-	-	Coventry C
1	9	-	-	-	20	-	-	-	-	2	11	Crystal Palace
-	-	-	-	-	-	-	-	-	-	1	18	Derby Co
10	10	17	12	9	13	9	20	-	-	22	-	Fulham
-	-	-	-	-	-	-	-	-	-	-	-	Grimsby T
-	-	22	-	-	-	-	-	-	-	-	-	Hereford U
-	-	-	-	-	-	21	-	-	1	6	14	Huddersfield T
-	22	14	14	8	9	13	12	5	13	11	17	Hull C
-	-	-	-	-	-	-	-	-	-	-	1	Ipswich T
-	-	-	-	-	-	-	-	-	-	-	-	Leeds U
17	-	-	-	-	-	-	-	1	3	-	-	Leicester C
11	14	19	13	12	4	15	17	17	-	-	-	Leyton Orient
18	13	6	7	-	2	12	13	6	-	-	-	Luton T
-	-	-	-	-	-	-	-	-	-	-	-	Manchester C
-	-	-	-	1	-	-	-	-	-	-	-	Manchester U
-	21	-	-	-	-	-	-	-	-	-	-	Mansfield T
-	-	-	-	-	1	4	9	7	4	4	6	Middlesbrough
21	16	10	-	20	12	11	3	8	10	10	7	Millwall
8	-	-	-	-	-	-	-	-	-	-	-	Newcastle U
-	-	-	3	-	-	-	1	10	11	13	9	Norwich C
-	3	8	16	7	14	-	-	-	-	-	-	Nottingham F
6	15	8	5	14	10	-	-	-	-	-	-	Notts Co
14	8	13	17	18	-	-	-	-	-	-	-	Oldham Ath
-	-	-	20	11	18	8	15	14	15	20	-	Oxford U
-	21	16	-	-	-	-	-	-	-	-	22	Plymouth Arg
-	-	-	-	-	-	-	-	-	-	-	-	Port Vale
-	-	-	22	17	15	17	16	16	17	15	5	Portsmouth
7	-	-	-	-	21	19	18	-	22	14	20	Preston NE

DIVISION 2 LEAGUE POSITIONS
1967–68 TO 1991–92 (cont.)

	1991-92	1990-91	1989-90	1988-89	1987-88	1986-87	1985-86	1984-85	1983-84	1982-83	1981-82	1980-81	1979-80
QPR	–	–	–	–	–	–	–	–	–	1	5	8	5
Reading	–	–	–	–	22	13	–	–	–	–	–	–	–
Rotherham U	–	–	–	–	–	–	–	–	–	20	7	–	–
Sheffield U	–	–	2	–	21	9	7	18	–	–	–	–	–
Sheffield W	–	3	–	–	–	–	–	–	2	6	4	10	–
Shrewsbury T	–	–	–	22	18	18	17	8	8	9	18	14	13
Southampton	–	–	–	–	–	–	–	–	–	–	–	–	–
Southend U	12	–	–	–	–	–	–	–	–	–	–	–	–
Stoke C	–	–	24	13	11	8	10	–	–	–	–	–	–
Sunderland	18	–	6	11	–	20	18	–	–	–	–	–	2
Swansea C	–	–	–	–	–	–	–	–	21	–	3	12	–
Swindon T	8	21	4	6	12	–	–	–	–	–	–	–	–
Tottenham H	–	–	–	–	–	–	–	–	–	–	–	–	–
Tranmere R	14	–	–	–	–	–	–	–	–	–	–	–	–
Walsall	–	–	–	24	–	–	–	–	–	–	–	–	–
Watford	10	20	15	4	–	–	–	–	–	–	2	9	18
WBA	–	23	20	9	20	15	–	–	–	–	–	–	–
West Ham U	–	2	7	–	–	–	–	–	–	–	–	1	7
Wimbledon	–	–	–	–	–	–	3	12	–	–	–	–	–
Wolv'hampton W	11	12	10	–	–	–	–	22	–	2	–	–	–
Wrexham	–	–	–	–	–	–	–	–	–	–	21	16	16
York C	–	–	–	–	–	–	–	–	–	–	–	–	–

DIVISION 3 LEAGUE POSITIONS
1967–68 TO 1991–92

	1991-92	1990-91	1989-90	1988-89	1987-88	1986-87	1985-86	1984-85	1983-84	1982-83	1981-82	1980-81	1979-80
Aldershot	–	–	–	24	20	–	–	–	–	–	–	–	–
Aston Villa	–	–	–	–	–	–	–	–	–	–	–	–	–
Barnsley	–	–	–	–	–	–	–	–	–	–	–	2	11
Barrow	–	–	–	–	–	–	–	–	–	–	–	–	–
Birmingham C	2	12	7	–	–	–	–	–	–	–	–	–	–
Blackburn R	–	–	–	–	–	–	–	–	–	–	–	–	2
Blackpool	–	–	23	19	10	9	12	–	–	–	–	23	18
Bolton W	13	4	6	10	–	21	18	17	10	–	–	–	–
Bournemouth	8	9	–	–	1	15	10	17	14	–	–	–	–
Bradford C	16	8	–	–	–	–	1	7	12	–	–	–	–
Brentford	1	6	13	7	12	11	10	13	20	9	8	9	19
Brighton & HA	–	–	–	–	2	–	–	–	–	–	–	–	–
Bristol C	–	–	2	11	5	6	9	5	–	–	–	23	–
Bristol R	–	–	1	5	8	19	16	6	5	7	15	–	–

1978-79	1977-78	1976-77	1975-76	1974-75	1973-74	1972-73	1971-72	1970-71	1969-70	1968-69	1967-68	
-	-	-	-	-	-	2	4	11	9	-	2	QPR
-	-	-	-	-	-	-	-	-	-	-	21	Reading
20	12	11	-	-	-	-	-	2	6	9	-	Rotherham U
-	-	-	-	22	19	10	14	15	-	-	-	Sheffield U
-	-	-	-	-	-	-	-	-	-	-	-	Sheffield W
-	-	-	-	-	-	-	-	-	-	-	-	Shrewsbury T
-	2	9	6	13	-	-	-	-	-	-	-	Southampton
-	-	-	-	-	-	-	-	-	-	-	-	Southend U
3	7	-	-	-	-	-	-	-	-	-	-	Stoke C
4	6	-	1	4	6	6	5	13	-	-	-	Sunderland
-	-	-	-	-	-	-	-	-	-	-	-	Swansea C
-	-	-	-	22	16	11	12	5	-	-	-	Swindon T
-	3	-	-	-	-	-	-	-	-	-	-	Tottenham H
-	-	-	-	-	-	-	-	-	-	-	-	Tranmere R
-	-	-	-	-	-	-	-	-	-	-	-	Walsall
-	-	-	-	-	-	-	22	18	19	-	-	Watford
-	-	-	3	6	8	-	-	-	-	-	-	WBA
5	-	-	-	-	-	-	-	-	-	-	-	West Ham U
-	-	-	-	-	-	-	-	-	-	-	-	Wimbledon
-	-	1	-	-	-	-	-	-	-	-	-	Wolv'hampton W
15	-	-	-	-	-	-	-	-	-	-	-	Wrexham
-	-	-	21	15	-	-	-	-	-	-	-	York C

1978-79	1977-78	1976-77	1975-76	1974-75	1973-74	1972-73	1971-72	1970-71	1969-70	1968-69	1967-68	
-	-	-	21	20	8	-	-	-	-	-	-	Aldershot
-	-	-	-	-	-	-	1	4	-	-	-	Aston Villa
-	-	-	-	-	-	22	12	7	10	-	-	Barnsley
-	-	-	-	-	-	-	-	23	19	8	-	Barrow
-	-	-	1	13	3	10	-	-	-	-	-	Birmingham C
12	-	-	-	-	-	-	-	-	-	-	-	Blackburn R
-	-	-	-	-	-	1	7	-	-	-	-	Blackpool
-	-	-	21	11	7	3	-	21	4	12	-	Bolton W
-	22	-	-	-	-	-	-	-	-	-	-	Bournemouth
-	-	-	-	-	-	-	24	19	10	-	-	Bradford C
10	-	-	-	-	22	-	-	-	-	-	-	Brentford
-	-	2	4	19	19	-	2	14	5	12	10	Brighton & HA
-	-	-	-	-	-	-	-	-	-	-	-	Bristol C
-	-	-	-	-	2	5	6	6	3	16	15	Bristol R

DIVISION 3 LEAGUE POSITIONS
1967–68 TO 1991–92 (cont.)

	1991–92	1990–91	1989–90	1988–89	1987–88	1986–87	1985–86	1984–85	1983–84	1982–83	1981–82	1980–81	1979–80
Burnley	–	–	–	–	–	–	–	21	12	–	1	8	–
Bury	21	7	5	13	14	16	20	–	–	–	–	–	21
Cambridge U	–	1	–	–	–	–	–	24	–	–	–	–	–
Cardiff C	–	–	21	16	–	–	22	–	–	2	–	–	–
Carlisle U	–	–	–	–	–	22	–	–	–	2	19	6	–
Charlton Ath	–	–	–	–	–	–	–	–	–	–	–	3	–
Chester C	18	19	16	8	15	15	–	–	–	–	24	18	9
Chesterfield	–	–	–	22	18	17	17	–	–	24	11	5	4
Colchester U	–	–	–	–	–	–	–	–	–	–	–	22	5
Crewe Alex	–	22	12	–	–	–	–	–	–	–	–	–	–
Crystal Palace	–	–	–	–	–	–	–	–	–	–	–	–	–
Darlington	24	–	–	–	–	22	13	–	–	–	–	–	–
Derby Co	–	–	–	–	–	–	3	7	–	–	–	–	–
Doncaster R	–	–	–	24	13	11	–	14	–	23	19	–	–
Exeter C	20	16	–	–	–	–	–	–	24	19	18	11	8
Fulham	9	21	20	4	9	18	–	–	–	–	3	13	–
Gillingham	–	–	–	23	13	5	5	4	8	13	6	15	16
Grimsby T	–	3	–	–	22	–	–	–	–	–	–	–	1
Halifax T	–	–	–	–	–	–	–	–	–	–	–	–	–
Hartlepool U	11	–	–	–	–	–	–	–	–	–	–	–	–
Hereford U	–	–	–	–	–	–	–	–	–	–	–	–	–
Huddersfield T	3	11	8	14	–	–	–	–	–	3	17	4	–
Hull C	14	–	–	–	–	–	–	3	4	–	–	24	20
Leyton Orient	10	13	14	–	–	–	–	22	11	20	–	–	–
Lincoln C	–	–	–	–	–	–	21	19	14	6	4	–	–
Luton T	–	–	–	–	–	–	–	–	–	–	–	–	–
Mansfield T	–	24	15	15	19	10	–	–	–	–	–	–	23
Middlesbrough	–	–	–	–	–	2	–	–	–	–	–	–	–
Millwall	–	–	–	–	–	–	–	2	9	17	9	16	14
Newport Co	–	–	–	–	–	23	19	18	13	4	16	12	–
Northampton T	–	–	22	20	6	–	–	–	–	–	–	–	–
Notts Co	–	–	3	9	4	7	8	–	–	–	–	–	–
Oldham Ath	–	–	–	–	–	–	–	–	–	–	–	–	–
Oxford U	–	–	–	–	–	–	–	–	1	5	5	14	17
Peterborough U	6	–	–	–	–	–	–	–	–	–	–	–	–
Plymouth Arg	–	–	–	–	–	–	2	15	19	8	10	7	15
Portsmouth	–	–	–	–	–	–	–	–	–	1	13	6	–
Port Vale	–	–	–	3	11	12	–	–	23	–	–	–	–
Preston NE	17	17	19	6	16	–	–	23	16	16	14	–	–
Reading	12	15	10	18	–	–	1	9	–	21	12	10	7
Rochdale	–	–	–	–	–	–	–	–	–	–	–	–	–
Rotherham U	–	23	9	–	21	14	14	12	18	–	–	1	13
Scunthorpe U	–	–	–	–	–	–	–	–	21	–	–	–	–
Sheffield U	–	–	–	2	–	–	–	–	3	11	–	21	12
Sheffield W	–	–	–	–	–	–	–	–	–	–	–	–	3
Shrewsbury T	22	18	11	–	–	–	–	–	–	–	–	–	–
Southend U	–	2	–	21	17	–	–	–	22	15	7	–	22

Team	1978-79	1977-78	1976-77	1975-76	1974-75	1973-74	1972-73	1971-72	1970-71	1969-70	1968-69	1967-68
Burnley	–	–	–	–	–	–	–	–	–	–	–	–
Bury	19	15	7	13	14	–	–	–	22	19	–	2
Cambridge U	–	2	–	–	21	–	–	–	–	–	–	–
Cardiff C	–	–	–	2	–	–	–	–	–	–	–	–
Carlisle U	6	13	–	–	–	–	–	–	–	–	–	–
Charlton Ath	–	–	–	–	3	14	11	–	–	–	–	–
Chester C	16	5	13	17	–	–	–	–	–	–	–	–
Chesterfield	20	9	18	15	15	5	16	13	5	–	–	–
Colchester U	7	8	–	22	11	–	–	–	–	–	–	22
Crewe Alex	–	–	–	–	–	–	–	–	–	23	–	–
Crystal Palace	–	–	3	5	5	–	–	–	–	–	–	–
Darlington	–	–	–	–	–	–	–	–	–	–	–	–
Derby C	–	–	–	–	–	–	–	–	–	–	–	–
Doncaster R	–	–	–	–	–	–	–	23	11	–	–	–
Exeter C	9	17	–	–	–	–	–	–	–	–	–	–
Fulham	–	–	–	–	–	–	–	–	2	4	–	–
Gillingham	4	7	12	14	10	–	–	–	24	20	20	11
Grimsby T	–	–	23	18	16	6	9	–	–	–	–	21
Halifax T	–	–	–	24	17	9	20	17	3	18	–	–
Hartlepool U	–	–	–	–	–	–	–	–	–	–	22	–
Hereford U	–	23	–	1	12	18	–	–	–	–	–	–
Huddersfield T	–	–	–	–	24	10	–	–	–	–	–	–
Hull C	8	–	–	–	–	–	–	–	–	–	–	–
Leyton Orient	–	–	–	–	–	–	–	–	–	1	18	18
Lincoln C	24	16	9	–	–	–	–	–	–	–	–	–
Luton T	–	–	–	–	–	–	–	–	–	2	3	–
Mansfield T	18	–	1	11	–	–	–	21	7	6	15	20
Middlesbrough	–	–	–	3	–	–	–	–	–	–	–	–
Millwall	–	–	–	–	–	–	–	–	–	–	–	–
Newport Co	–	–	–	–	–	–	–	–	–	–	–	–
Northampton T	–	–	22	–	–	–	–	–	–	–	21	17
Notts Co	–	–	–	–	–	–	2	4	–	–	–	–
Oldham Ath	–	–	–	–	–	1	4	11	–	–	24	16
Oxford U	11	18	17	–	–	–	–	–	–	–	–	1
Peterborough U	21	4	16	10	7	–	–	–	–	–	–	24
Plymouth Arg	15	19	–	–	2	17	8	8	15	17	5	–
Portsmouth	–	24	20	–	–	–	–	–	–	–	–	–
Port Vale	–	21	19	12	6	20	6	15	17	–	–	–
Preston NE	–	3	6	8	9	–	–	–	1	–	–	–
Reading	–	–	21	–	–	–	–	–	21	8	14	5
Rochdale	–	–	–	–	24	13	18	16	9	–	–	–
Rotherham U	17	20	4	16	–	–	21	5	8	14	11	–
Scunthorpe U	–	–	–	–	–	–	24	–	–	–	–	23
Sheffield U	–	–	–	–	–	–	–	–	–	–	–	–
Sheffield W	14	14	8	20	–	–	–	–	–	–	–	–
Shrewsbury T	1	11	10	9	–	22	15	12	13	15	17	3
Southend U	13	–	–	23	18	12	14	–	–	–	–	–

DIVISION 3 LEAGUE POSITIONS
1967–68 TO 1991–92 (cont.)

	1991-92	1990-91	1989-90	1988-89	1987-88	1986-87	1985-86	1984-85	1983-84	1982-83	1981-82	1980-81	1979-80
Southport	–	–	–	–	–	–	–	–	–	–	–	–	–
Stockport Co	5	–	–	–	–	–	–	–	–	–	–	–	–
Stoke C	4	14	–	–	–	–	–	–	–	–	–	–	–
Sunderland	–	–	–	–	1	–	–	–	–	–	–	–	–
Swansea C	19	20	17	12	–	–	24	20	–	–	–	–	–
Swindon T	–	–	–	–	–	3	–	–	–	–	22	17	10
Torquay U	23	–	–	–	–	–	–	–	–	–	–	–	–
Tranmere R	–	5	4	–	–	–	–	–	–	–	–	–	–
Walsall	–	–	24	–	3	8	6	11	6	10	20	20	–
Watford	–	–	–	–	–	–	–	–	–	–	–	–	–
WBA	7	–	–	–	–	–	–	–	–	–	–	–	–
Wigan Ath	15	10	18	17	7	4	4	16	15	18	–	–	–
Wimbledon	–	–	–	–	–	–	–	–	2	–	21	–	24
Wolv'hampton W	–	–	–	1	–	23	–	–	–	–	–	–	–
Wrexham	–	–	–	–	–	–	–	–	–	22	–	–	–
York City	–	–	–	–	23	20	7	8	–	–	–	–	–

DIVISION 4 LEAGUE POSITIONS
1967–68 TO 1991–92

	1991-92	1990-91	1989-90	1988-89	1987-88	1986-87	1985-86	1984-85	1983-84	1982-83	1981-82	1980-81	1979-80
Aldershot	*	23	22	–	–	6	16	13	5	18	16	6	10
Barnet	7	–	–	–	–	–	–	–	–	–	–	–	–
Barnsley	–	–	–	–	–	–	–	–	–	–	–	–	–
Barrow	–	–	–	–	–	–	–	–	–	–	–	–	–
Blackpool	4	5	–	–	–	–	2	6	21	12	–	–	–
Bolton W	–	–	–	–	3	–	–	–	–	–	–	–	–
Bournemouth	–	–	–	–	–	–	–	–	–	–	4	13	11
Bradford C	–	–	–	–	–	–	–	–	–	–	2	14	5
Bradford PA	–	–	–	–	–	–	–	–	–	–	–	–	–
Brentford	–	–	–	–	–	–	–	–	–	–	–	–	–
Bristol C	–	–	–	–	–	–	–	4	14	–	–	–	–
Burnley	1	6	16	16	10	22	14	–	–	–	–	–	–
Bury	–	–	–	–	–	–	4	15	5	9	12	–	–
Cambridge U	–	–	6	8	15	11	22	–	–	–	–	–	–
Cardiff C	9	13	–	–	2	13	–	–	–	–	–	–	–
Carlisle U	22	20	8	12	23	–	–	–	–	–	–	–	–
Chester C	–	–	–	–	–	2	16	24	13	–	–	–	–
Chesterfield	13	18	7	–	–	–	1	13	–	–	–	–	–

*Record expunged

	1991-92	1990-91	1989-90	1988-89	1987-88	1986-87	1985-86	1984-85	1983-84	1982-83	1981-82	1980-81	1979-80
Colchester U	–	–	24	22	9	5	6	7	8	6	6	–	–
Crewe Alex	6	–	–	3	17	17	12	10	16	23	24	18	23
Darlington	–	1	–	24	13	–	–	3	14	17	13	8	22
Doncaster R	21	11	20	23	–	–	–	–	2	–	–	3	12
Exeter C	–	–	1	13	22	14	21	18	–	–	–	–	–
Gillingham	11	15	14	–	–	–	–	–	–	–	–	–	–
Grimsby T	–	–	2	9	–	–	–	–	–	–	–	–	–
Halifax T	20	22	23	21	18	15	20	21	21	11	19	23	18
Hartlepool U	–	3	19	19	16	18	7	19	23	22	14	9	19
Hereford U	17	17	17	15	19	16	10	5	11	24	10	22	21
Huddersfield T	–	–	–	–	–	–	–	–	–	–	–	–	1
Hull C	–	–	–	–	–	–	–	–	–	2	8	–	–
Leyton Orient	–	–	–	6	8	7	5	–	–	–	–	–	–
Lincoln C	10	14	10	10	–	24	–	–	–	–	–	2	7
Luton T	–	–	–	–	–	–	–	–	–	–	–	–	–
Maidstone U	18	19	5	–	–	–	–	–	–	–	–	–	–
Mansfield T	3	–	–	–	–	–	3	14	19	10	20	7	–
Newport Co	–	–	–	–	24	–	–	–	–	–	–	–	3
Northampton T	16	10	–	–	–	1	8	23	18	15	22	10	13
Notts Co	–	–	–	–	–	–	–	–	–	–	–	–	–
Oldham Ath	–	–	–	–	–	–	–	–	–	–	–	–	–
Peterborough U	–	4	9	17	7	10	17	11	7	9	5	5	8
Portsmouth	–	–	–	–	–	–	–	–	–	–	–	–	4
Port Vale	–	–	–	–	–	4	12	–	–	3	7	19	20
Preston NE	–	–	–	–	2	23	–	–	–	–	–	–	–
Reading	–	–	–	–	–	–	–	3	–	–	–	–	–
Rochdale	8	12	12	18	21	21	18	17	22	20	21	15	24
Rotherham U	2	–	1	–	–	–	–	–	–	–	–	–	–
Scarborough	12	9	18	5	12	–	–	–	–	–	–	–	–
Scunthorpe U	5	8	11	4	4	8	15	9	–	4	23	16	14
Sheffield U	–	–	–	–	–	–	–	–	–	–	1	–	–
Shrewsbury T	–	–	–	–	–	–	–	–	–	–	–	–	–
Southend U	–	–	3	–	–	3	9	20	–	–	–	1	–
Southport	–	–	–	–	–	–	–	–	–	–	–	–	–
Stockport Co	–	2	4	20	20	19	11	22	12	16	18	20	16
Swansea C	–	–	–	–	6	12	–	–	–	–	–	–	–
Swindon T	–	–	–	–	–	–	1	8	17	8	–	–	–
Torquay U	–	7	15	14	5	23	24	24	9	12	15	17	9
Tranmere R	–	–	–	2	14	20	19	6	10	19	11	21	15
Walsall	15	16	–	–	–	–	–	–	–	–	–	–	2
Watford	–	–	–	–	–	–	–	–	–	–	–	–	–
Wigan Ath	–	–	–	–	–	–	–	–	–	–	3	11	6
Wimbledon	–	–	–	–	–	–	–	–	1	–	4	–	–
Wolv'hampton W	–	–	–	–	1	4	–	–	–	–	–	–	–
Workington	–	–	–	–	–	–	–	–	–	–	–	–	–
Wrexham	14	24	21	7	11	9	13	15	20	–	–	–	–
York C	19	21	13	11	–	–	–	–	1	7	17	24	17

1978-79	1977-78	1976-77	1975-76	1974-75	1973-74	1972-73	1971-72	1970-71	1969-70	1968-69	1967-68	
–	–	3	–	–	3	22	11	6	10	6	–	Colchester U
24	15	12	16	18	21	21	24	15	15	–	4	Crewe Alex
21	19	11	20	21	20	24	19	12	22	5	16	Darlington
22	12	8	10	17	22	17	12	–	–	1	10	Doncaster R
–	–	2	7	9	10	8	15	9	18	17	20	Exeter C
–	–	–	–	–	2	9	13	–	–	–	–	Gillingham
2	6	–	–	–	–	–	1	19	16	23	–	Grimsby T
23	20	21	–	–	–	–	–	–	–	2	11	Halifax T
13	21	22	14	13	11	20	18	23	23	–	3	Hartlepool U
14	–	–	–	–	–	2	–	–	–	–	–	Hereford U
9	11	9	5	–	–	–	–	–	–	–	–	Huddersfield T
–	–	–	–	–	–	–	–	–	–	–	–	Hull C
–	–	–	–	–	–	–	–	–	–	–	–	Leyton Orient
–	–	1	5	12	10	5	21	8	8	13	–	Lincoln C
–	–	–	–	–	–	–	–	–	–	–	1	Luton T
–	–	–	–	–	–	–	–	–	–	–	–	Maidstone U
–	–	–	1	17	6	–	–	–	–	–	–	Mansfield T
8	16	19	22	12	9	5	14	22	21	22	12	Newport C
19	10	–	2	16	5	23	21	7	14	–	–	Northampton T
–	–	–	–	–	–	–	–	1	7	19	17	Notts Co
–	–	–	–	–	–	–	3	19	–	–	–	Oldham Ath
–	–	–	–	1	19	8	16	9	18	–	–	Peterborough U
7	–	–	–	–	–	–	–	–	–	–	–	Portsmouth
16	–	–	–	–	–	–	–	4	13	18	–	Port Vale
–	–	–	–	–	–	–	–	–	–	–	–	Preston NE
1	8	–	3	7	6	7	16	–	–	–	–	Reading
20	24	18	15	19	–	–	–	–	–	3	19	Rochdale
–	–	–	3	15	–	–	–	–	–	–	–	Rotherham U
–	–	–	–	–	–	–	–	–	–	–	–	Scarborough
12	14	20	19	24	18	–	4	17	12	16	–	Scunthorpe U
–	–	–	–	–	–	–	–	–	–	–	–	Sheffield U
–	–	–	–	2	–	–	–	–	–	–	–	Shrewsbury T
–	2	10	–	–	–	2	18	17	7	6	–	Southend U
–	23	23	23	11	–	1	7	8	–	–	–	Stockport Co
17	18	14	21	20	24	11	23	11	–	–	–	Swansea C
–	3	5	11	22	14	–	–	–	3	10	15	Swindon T
11	9	16	9	14	16	18	–	–	–	–	–	Torquay U
–	–	–	4	–	–	–	–	–	–	–	–	Tranmere R
–	–	–	–	–	–	–	–	–	–	–	–	Walsall
–	1	7	8	–	–	–	–	–	–	–	–	Watford
6	–	–	–	–	–	–	–	–	–	–	–	Wigan Ath
3	13	–	–	–	–	–	–	–	–	–	–	Wimbledon
–	–	–	–	–	–	–	–	–	–	–	–	Wolv'hampton W
–	–	24	24	23	23	13	6	10	20	12	23	Workington
–	–	–	–	–	–	–	–	–	2	9	8	Wrexham
10	22	–	–	–	–	–	–	4	13	21	21	York C

LEAGUE CHAMPIONSHIP HONOURS

FA PREMIER LEAGUE
Maximum points: 126

	First	*Pts*	*Second*	*Pts*	*Third*	*Pts*
1992–93	Manchester U	84	Aston Villa	74	Norwich C	72

FIRST DIVISION
Maximum points: 138

1992–93	Newcastle U	96	West Ham U	88	Portsmouth††	88

SECOND DIVISION
Maximum points: 138

1992–93	Stoke C	93	Bolton W	90	Port Vale††	89

THIRD DIVISION
Maximum points: 126

1992–93	Cardiff C	83	Wrexham	80	Barnet	79

†† *Not promoted after play-offs.*

FOOTBALL LEAGUE

	First	*Pts*	*Second*	*Pts*	*Third*	*Pts*
1888–89a	Preston NE	40	Aston Villa	29	Wolverhampton W	28
1889–90a	Preston NE	33	Everton	31	Blackburn R	27
1890–91a	Preston NE	29	Everton	27	Notts Co	26
1891–92b	Sunderland	42	Preston NE	37	Bolton W	36

FIRST DIVISION to 1991–92
Maximum points: a 44; b 52; c 60; d 68; e 76; f 84; g 126; h 120; k 114.

	First	*Pts*	*Second*	*Pts*	*Third*	*Pts*
1892–93c	Sunderland	48	Preston NE	37	Everton	36
1893–94c	Aston Villa	44	Sunderland	38	Derby Co	36
1894–95c	Sunderland	47	Everton	42	Aston Villa	39
1895–96c	Aston Villa	45	Derby Co	41	Everton	39
1896–97c	Aston Villa	47	Sheffield U*	36	Derby Co	36
1897–98c	Sheffield U	42	Sunderland	37	Wolverhampton W*	35
1898–99d	Aston Villa	45	Liverpool	43	Burnley	39
1899–1900d	Aston Villa	50	Sheffield U	48	Sunderland	41
1900–01d	Liverpool	45	Sunderland	43	Notts Co	40
1901–02d	Sunderland	44	Everton	41	Newcastle U	37
1902–03d	The Wednesday	42	Aston Villa*	41	Sunderland	41
1903–04d	The Wednesday	47	Manchester C	44	Everton	43
1904–05d	Newcastle U	48	Everton	47	Manchester C	46
1905–06e	Liverpool	51	Preston NE	47	The Wednesday	44
1906–07e	Newcastle U	51	Bristol C	48	Everton*	45
1907–08e	Manchester U	52	Aston Villa*	43	Manchester C	43
1908–09e	Newcastle U	53	Everton	46	Sunderland	44
1909–10e	Aston Villa	53	Liverpool	48	Blackburn R*	45
1910–11e	Manchester U	52	Aston Villa	51	Sunderland*	45
1911–12e	Blackburn R	49	Everton	46	Newcastle U	44
1912–13e	Sunderland	54	Aston Villa	50	Sheffield W	49
1913–14e	Blackburn R	51	Aston Villa	44	Middlesbrough*	43

	First	Pts	Second	Pts	Third	Pts
1914–15e	Everton	46	Oldham Ath	45	Blackburn R*	43
1919–20f	WBA	60	Burnley	51	Chelsea	49
1920–21f	Burnley	59	Manchester C	54	Bolton W	52
1921–22f	Liverpool	57	Tottenham H	51	Burnley	49
1922–23f	Liverpool	60	Sunderland	54	Huddersfield T	53
1923–24f	Huddersfield T*	57	Cardiff C	57	Sunderland	53
1924–25f	Huddersfield T	58	WBA	56	Bolton W	55
1925–26f	Huddersfield T	57	Arsenal	52	Sunderland	48
1926–27f	Newcastle U	56	Huddersfield T	51	Sunderland	49
1927–28f	Everton	53	Huddersfield T	51	Leicester C	48
1928–29f	Sheffield W	52	Leicester C	51	Aston Villa	50
1929–30f	Sheffield W	60	Derby Co	50	Manchester C*	47
1930–31f	Arsenal	66	Aston Villa	59	Sheffield W	52
1931–32f	Everton	56	Arsenal	54	Sheffield W	50
1932–33f	Arsenal	58	Aston Villa	54	Sheffield W	51
1933–34f	Arsenal	59	Huddersfield T	56	Tottenham H	49
1934–35f	Arsenal	58	Sunderland	54	Sheffield W	49
1935–36f	Sunderland	56	Derby Co*	48	Huddersfield T	48
1936–37f	Manchester C	57	Charlton Ath	54	Arsenal	52
1937–38f	Arsenal	52	Wolverhampton W	51	Preston NE	49
1938–39f	Everton	59	Wolverhampton W	55	Charlton Ath	50
1946–47f	Liverpool	57	Manchester U*	56	Wolverhampton W	56
1947–48f	Arsenal	59	Manchester U*	52	Burnley	52
1948–49f	Portsmouth	58	Manchester U*	53	Derby Co	53
1949–50f	Portsmouth*	53	Wolverhampton W	53	Sunderland	52
1950–51f	Tottenham H	60	Manchester U	56	Blackpool	50
1951–52f	Manchester U	57	Tottenham H*	53	Arsenal	53
1952–53f	Arsenal*	54	Preston NE	54	Wolverhampton W	51
1953–54f	Wolverhampton W	57	WBA	53	Huddersfield T	51
1954–55f	Chelsea	52	Wolverhampton W*	48	Portsmouth*	48
1955–56f	Manchester U	60	Blackpool*	49	Wolverhampton W	49
1956–57f	Manchester U	64	Tottenham H*	56	Preston NE	56
1957–58f	Wolverhampton W	64	Preston NE	59	Tottenham H	51
1958–59f	Wolverhampton W	61	Manchester U	55	Arsenal*	50
1959–60f	Burnley	55	Wolverhampton W	54	Tottenham H	53
1960–61f	Tottenham H	66	Sheffield W	58	Wolverhampton W	57
1961–62f	Ipswich T	56	Burnley	53	Tottenham H	52
1962–63f	Everton	61	Tottenham H	55	Burnley	54
1963–64f	Liverpool	57	Manchester U	53	Everton	52
1964–65f	Manchester U*	61	Leeds U	61	Chelsea	56
1965–66f	Liverpool	61	Leeds U*	55	Burnley	55
1966–67f	Manchester U	60	Nottingham F*	56	Tottenham H	56
1967–68f	Manchester C	58	Manchester U	56	Liverpool	55
1968–69f	Leeds U	67	Liverpool	61	Everton	57
1969–70f	Everton	66	Leeds U	57	Chelsea	55
1970–71f	Arsenal	65	Leeds U	64	Tottenham H*	52
1971–72f	Derby Co	58	Leeds U*	57	Liverpool*	57
1972–73f	Liverpool	60	Arsenal	57	Leeds U	53
1973–74f	Leeds U	62	Liverpool	57	Derby Co	48
1974–75f	Derby Co	53	Liverpool*	51	Ipswich T	57
1975–76f	Liverpool	60	QPR	59	Manchester U	56
1976–77f	Liverpool	57	Manchester C	56	Ipswich T	52
1977–78f	Nottingham F	64	Liverpool	57	Everton	55
1978–79f	Liverpool	68	Nottingham F	60	WBA	59
1979–80f	Liverpool	60	Manchester U	58	Ipswich T	53

* *Won or placed on goal average.*

	First	Pts	Second	Pts	Third	Pts
1980–81f	Aston Villa	60	Ipswich T	56	Arsenal	53
1981–82g	Liverpool	87	Ipswich T	83	Manchester U	78
1982–83g	Liverpool	82	Watford	71	Manchester U	70
1983–84g	Liverpool	80	Southampton	77	Nottingham F*	74
1984–85g	Everton	90	Liverpool*	77	Tottenham H	77
1985–86g	Liverpool	88	Everton	86	West Ham U	84
1986–87g	Everton	86	Liverpool	77	Tottenham H	71
1987–88h	Liverpool	90	Manchester U	81	Nottingham F	73
1988–89k	Arsenal*	76	Liverpool	76	Nottingham F	64
1989–90k	Liverpool	79	Aston Villa	70	Tottenham H	63
1990–91k	Arsenal†	83	Liverpool	76	Crystal Palace	69
1991–92g	Leeds U	82	Manchester U	78	Sheffield W	75

No official competition during 1915–19 and 1939–46.
† 2 pts deducted

SECOND DIVISION to 1991–92

Maximum points: a 44; b 56; c 60; d 68; e 76; f 84; g 126; h 132; k 138.

	First	Pts	Second	Pts	Third	Pts
1892–93a	Small Heath	36	Sheffield U	35	Darwen	30
1893–94b	Liverpool	50	Small Heath	42	Notts Co	39
1894–95c	Bury	48	Notts Co	39	Newton Heath*	38
1895–96c	Liverpool*	46	Manchester C	46	Grimsby T*	42
1896–97c	Notts Co	42	Newton Heath	39	Grimsby T	38
1897–98c	Burnley	48	Newcastle U	45	Manchester C	39
1898–99d	Manchester C	52	Glossop NE	46	Leicester Fosse	45
1899–1900d	The Wednesday	54	Bolton W	52	Small Heath	46
1900–01d	Grimsby T	49	Small Heath	48	Burnley	44
1901–02d	WBA	55	Middlesbrough	51	Preston NE*	42
1902–03d	Manchester C	54	Small Heath	51	Woolwich A	48
1903–04d	Preston NE	50	Woolwich A	49	Manchester U	48
1904–05d	Liverpool	58	Bolton W	56	Manchester U	53
1905–06e	Bristol C	66	Manchester U	62	Chelsea	53
1906–07e	Nottingham F	60	Chelsea	57	Leicester Fosse	48
1907–08e	Bradford C	54	Leicester Fosse	52	Oldham Ath	50
1908–09e	Bolton W	52	Tottenham H*	51	WBA	51
1909–10e	Manchester C	54	Oldham Ath*	53	Hull C*	53
1910–11e	WBA	53	Bolton W	51	Chelsea	49
1911–12e	Derby Co*	54	Chelsea	54	Burnley	52
1912–13e	Preston NE	53	Burnley	50	Birmingham	46
1913–14e	Notts Co	53	Bradford PA*	49	Woolwich A	49
1914–15e	Derby Co	53	Preston NE	50	Barnsley	47
1919–20f	Tottenham H	70	Huddersfield T	64	Birmingham	56
1920–21f	Birmingham*	58	Cardiff C	58	Bristol C	51
1921–22f	Nottingham F	56	Stoke C*	52	Barnsley	52
1922–23f	Notts Co	53	West Ham U*	51	Leicester C	51
1923–24f	Leeds U	54	Bury*	51	Derby Co	51
1924–25f	Leicester C	59	Manchester U	57	Derby Co	55
1925–26f	Sheffield W	60	Derby Co	57	Chelsea	52
1926–27f	Middlesbrough	62	Portsmouth*	54	Manchester C	54
1927–28f	Manchester C	59	Leeds U	57	Chelsea	54
1928–29f	Middlesbrough	55	Grimsby T	53	Bradford*	48
1929–30f	Blackpool	58	Chelsea	55	Oldham Ath	53
1930–31f	Everton	61	WBA	54	Tottenham H	51
1931–32f	Wolverhampton W	56	Leeds U	54	Stoke C	52
1932–33f	Stoke C	56	Tottenham H	55	Fulham	50

	First	Pts	Second	Pts	Third	Pts
1933–34f	Grimsby T	59	Preston NE	52	Bolton W*	51
1934–35f	Brentford	61	Bolton W*	56	West Ham U	56
1935–36f	Manchester U	56	Charlton Ath	55	Sheffield U*	52
1936–37f	Leicester C	56	Blackpool	55	Bury	52
1937–38f	Aston Villa	57	Manchester U*	53	Sheffield U	53
1938–39f	Blackburn R	55	Sheffield U	54	Sheffield W	53
1946–47f	Manchester C	62	Burnley	58	Birmingham C	55
1947–48f	Birmingham C	59	Newcastle U	56	Southampton	52
1948–49f	Fulham	57	WBA	56	Southampton	55
1949–50f	Tottenham H	61	Sheffield W*	52	Sheffield U*	52
1950–51f	Preston NE	57	Manchester C	52	Cardiff C	50
1951–52f	Sheffield W	53	Cardiff C*	51	Birmingham C	51
1952–53f	Sheffield U	60	Huddersfield T	58	Luton T	52
1953–54f	Leicester C*	56	Everton	56	Blackburn R	55
1954–55f	Birmingham C*	54	Luton T*	54	Rotherham U	54
1955–56f	Sheffield W	55	Leeds U	52	Liverpool*	48
1956–57f	Leicester C	61	Nottingham F	54	Liverpool	53
1957–58f	West Ham U	57	Blackburn R	56	Charlton Ath	55
1958–59f	Sheffield W	62	Fulham	60	Sheffield U*	53
1959–60f	Aston Villa	59	Cardiff C	58	Liverpool*	50
1960–61f	Ipswich T	59	Sheffield U	58	Liverpool	52
1961–62f	Liverpool	62	Leyton O	54	Sunderland	53
1962–63f	Stoke C	53	Chelsea*	52	Sunderland	52
1963–64f	Leeds U	63	Sunderland	61	Preston NE	56
1964–65f	Newcastle U	57	Northampton T	56	Bolton W	50
1965–66f	Manchester C	59	Southampton	54	Coventry C	53
1966–67f	Coventry C	59	Wolverhampton W	58	Carlisle U	52
1967–68f	Ipswich T	59	QPR*	58	Blackpool	58
1968–69f	Derby Co	63	Crystal Palace	56	Charlton Ath	50
1969–70f	Huddersfield T	60	Blackpool	53	Leicester C	51
1970–71f	Leicester C	59	Sheffield U	56	Cardiff C*	53
1971–72f	Norwich C	57	Birmingham C	56	Millwall	55
1972–73f	Burnley	62	QPR	61	Aston Villa	50
1973–74f	Middlesbrough	65	Luton T	50	Carlisle U	49
1974–75f	Manchester U	61	Aston Villa	58	Norwich C	53
1975–76f	Sunderland	56	Bristol C*	53	WBA	53
1976–77f	Wolverhampton W	57	Chelsea	55	Nottingham F	52
1977–78f	Bolton W	58	Southampton	57	Tottenham H*	56
1978–79f	Crystal Palace	57	Brighton*	56	Stoke C	56
1979–80f	Leicester C	55	Sunderland	54	Birmingham C*	53
1980–81f	West Ham U	66	Notts Co	53	Swansea C*	50
1981–82g	Luton T	88	Watford	80	Norwich C	71
1982–83g	QPR	85	Wolverhampton W	75	Leicester C	70
1983–84g	Chelsea*	88	Sheffield W	88	Newcastle U	80
1984–85g	Oxford U	84	Birmingham C	82	Manchester C	74
1985–86g	Norwich C	84	Charlton Ath	77	Wimbledon	76
1986–87g	Derby Co	84	Portsmouth	78	Oldham Ath††	75
1987–88h	Millwall	82	Aston Villa*	78	Middlesbrough	78
1988–89k	Chelsea	99	Manchester C	82	Crystal Palace	81
1989–90k	Leeds U*	85	Sheffield U	85	Newcastle U††	80
1990–91k	Oldham Ath	88	West Ham U	87	Sheffield W	82
1991–92k	Ipswich T	84	Middlesbrough	80	Derby Co	78

No competition during 1915–19 and 1939–46.
* Won or placed on goal average/goal difference.
††Not promoted after play-offs.

THIRD DIVISION to 1991–92

Maximum points: 92; 138 from 1981–82.

	First	Pts	Second	Pts	Third	Pts
1958–59	Plymouth Arg	62	Hull C	61	Brentford*	57
1959–60	Southampton	61	Norwich C	59	Shrewsbury T*	52
1960–61	Bury	68	Walsall	62	QPR	60
1961–62	Portsmouth	65	Grimsby T	62	Bournemouth*	59
1962–63	Northampton T	62	Swindon T	58	Port Vale	54
1963–64	Coventry C*	60	Crystal Palace	60	Watford	58
1964–65	Carlisle U	60	Bristol C*	59	Mansfield T	59
1965–66	Hull C	69	Millwall	65	QPR	57
1966–67	QPR	67	Middlesbrough	55	Watford	54
1967–68	Oxford U	57	Bury	56	Shrewsbury T	55
1968–69	Watford*	64	Swindon T	64	Luton T	61
1969–70	Orient	62	Luton T	60	Bristol R	56
1970–71	Preston NE	61	Fulham	60	Halifax T	56
1971–72	Aston Villa	70	Brighton	65	Bournemouth*	62
1972–73	Bolton W	61	Notts Co	57	Blackburn R	55
1973–74	Oldham Ath	62	Bristol R*	61	York C	61
1974–75	Blackburn R	60	Plymouth Arg	59	Charlton Ath	55
1975–76	Hereford U	63	Cardiff C	57	Millwall	56
1976–77	Mansfield T	64	Brighton & HA	61	Crystal Palace*	59
1977–78	Wrexham	61	Cambridge U	58	Preston NE*	56
1978–79	Shrewsbury T	61	Watford*	60	Swansea C	60
1979–80	Grimsby T	62	Blackburn R	59	Sheffield W	58
1980–81	Rotherham U	61	Barnsley*	59	Charlton Ath	59
1981–82	Burnley*	80	Carlisle U	80	Fulham	78
1982–83	Portsmouth	91	Cardiff C	86	Huddersfield T	82
1983–84	Oxford U	95	Wimbledon	87	Sheffield U*	83
1984–85	Bradford C	94	Millwall	90	Hull C	87
1985–86	Reading	94	Plymouth Arg	87	Derby Co	84
1986–87	Bournemouth	97	Middlesbrough	94	Swindon T	87
1987–88	Sunderland	93	Brighton & HA	84	Walsall	82
1988–89	Wolverhampton W	92	Sheffield U	84	Port Vale	84
1989–90	Bristol R	93	Bristol C	91	Notts Co	87
1990–91	Cambridge U	86	Southend U	85	Grimsby T*	83
1991–92	Brentford	82	Birmingham C	81	Huddersfield T	78

* Won or placed on goal average/goal difference.

FOURTH DIVISION (1958–1992)

Maximum points: 92; 138 from 1981–82.

	First	Pts	Second	Pts	Third	Pts
1958–59	Port Vale	64	Coventry C*	60	York C	60
1959–60	Walsall	65	Notts Co*	60	Torquay U	60
1960–61	Peterborough U	66	Crystal Palace	64	Northampton T*	60
1961–62†	Millwall	56	Colchester U	55	Wrexham	53
1962–63	Brentford	62	Oldham Ath*	59	Crewe Alex	59
1963–64	Gillingham*	60	Carlisle U	60	Workington U	59
1964–65	Brighton	63	Millwall*	62	York C	62
1965–66	Doncaster R*	59	Darlington	59	Torquay U	58
1966–67	Stockport Co	64	Southport*	59	Barrow	59
1967–68	Luton T	66	Barnsley	61	Hartlepools U	60
1968–69	Doncaster R	59	Halifax T	57	Rochdale*	56
1969–70	Chesterfield	64	Wrexham	61	Swansea C	60
1970–71	Notts Co	69	Bournemouth	60	Oldham Ath	59

100

	First	Pts	Second	Pts	Third	Pts
1971–72	Grimsby T	63	Southend U	60	Brentford	59
1972–73	Southport	62	Hereford U	58	Cambridge U	57
1973–74	Peterborough U	65	Gillingham	62	Colchester U	60
1974–75	Mansfield T	68	Shrewsbury T	62	Rotherham U	59
1975–76	Lincoln C	74	Northampton T	68	Reading	60
1976–77	Cambridge U	65	Exeter C	62	Colchester U*	59
1977–78	Watford	71	Southend U	60	Swansea C*	56
1978–79	Reading	65	Grimsby T*	61	Wimbledon*	61
1979–80	Huddersfield T	66	Walsall	64	Newport Co	61
1980–81	Southend U	67	Lincoln C	65	Doncaster R	56
1981–82	Sheffield U	96	Bradford C*	91	Wigan Ath	91
1982–83	Wimbledon	98	Hull C	90	Port Vale	88
1983–84	York C	101	Doncaster R	85	Reading*	82
1984–85	Chesterfield	91	Blackpool	86	Darlington	85
1985–86	Swindon T	102	Chester C.	84	Mansfield T	81
1986–87	Northampton T	99	Preston NE	90	Soqthend U	80
1987–88	Wolverhampton W	90	Cardiff C	85	Bolton W	78
1988–89	Rotherham U	82	Tranmere R	80	Crewe Alex	78
1989–90	Exeter C	89	Grimsby T	79	Southend U	75
1990–91	Darlington	83	Stockport Co*	82	Hartlepool U	82
1991–92††	Burnley	80	Rotherham U*	77	Mansfield T	77

†*Maximum points:* 88 owing to Accrington Stanley's resignation.   ††*Not promoted after play-offs.*
†*Maximum points:* 126 owing to Aldershot being expelled.

THIRD DIVISION—SOUTH (1920–1958)
Maximum points: a 84; b 92.

	First	Pts	Second	Pts	Third	Pts
1920–21a	Crystal Palace	59	Southampton	54	QPR	53
1921–22a	Southampton*	61	Plymouth Arg	61	Portsmouth	53
1922–23a	Bristol C	59	Plymouth Arg*	53	Swansea T	53
1923–24a	Portsmouth	59	Plymouth Arg	55	Millwall	54
1924–25a	Swansea T	57	Plymouth Arg	56	Bristol C	53
1925–26a	Reading	57	Plymouth Arg	56	Millwall	53
1926–27a	Bristol C	62	Plymouth Arg	60	Millwall	56
1927–28a	Millwall	65	Northampton T	55	Plymouth Arg	53
1928–29a	Charlton Ath*	54	Crystal Palace	54	Northampton T*	52
1929–30a	Plymouth Arg	68	Brentford	61	QPR	51
1930–31a	Notts Co	59	Crystal Palace	51	Brentford	50
1931–32a	Fulham	57	Reading	55	Southend U	53
1932–33a	Brentford	62	Exeter C	58	Norwich C	57
1933–34a	Norwich C	61	Coventry C*	54	Reading*	54
1934–35a	Charlton Ath	61	Reading	53	Coventry C	51
1935–36a	Coventry C	57	Luton T	56	Reading	54
1936–37a	Luton T	58	Notts Co	56	Brighton	53
1937–38a	Millwall	56	Bristol C	55	QPR*	53
1938–39a	Newport Co	55	Crystal Palace	52	Brighton	49
1939–46	Competition cancelled owing to war.					
1946–47a	Cardiff C	66	QPR	57	Bristol C	51
1947–48a	QPR	61	Bournemouth	57	Walsall	51
1948–49a	Swansea T	62	Reading	55	Bournemouth	52
1949–50a	Notts Co	58	Northampton T*	51	Southend U	51
1950–51b	Nottingham F	70	Norwich C	64	Reading*	57
1951–52b	Plymouth Arg	66	Reading*	61	Norwich C	61

	First	Pts	Second	Pts	Third	Pts
1952–53b	Bristol R	64	Millwall*	62	Northampton T	62
1953–54b	Ipswich T	64	Brighton	61	Bristol C	56
1954–55b	Bristol C	70	Leyton O	61	Southampton	59
1955–56b	Leyton O	66	Brighton	65	Ipswich T	64
1956–57b	Ipswich T*	59	Torquay U	59	Colchester U	58
1957–58b	Brighton	60	Brentford*	58	Plymouth Arg	58

* Won or placed on goal average.

THIRD DIVISION—NORTH (1921–1958)

Maximum points: a 76; b 84; c 80; d 92.

	First	Pts	Second	Pts	Third	Pts
1921–22a	Stockport Co	56	Darlington*	50	Grimsby T	50
1922–23a	Nelson	51	Bradford PA	47	Walsall	46
1923–24b	Wolverhampton W	63	Rochdale	62	Chesterfield	54
1924–25b	Darlington	58	Nelson*	53	New Brighton	53
1925–26b	Grimsby T	61	Bradford PA	60	Rochdale	59
1926–27b	Stoke C	63	Rochdale	58	Bradford PA	55
1927–28b	Bradford PA	63	Lincoln C	55	Stockport Co	54
1928–29g	Bradford C	63	Stockport Co	62	Wrexham	52
1929–30b	Port Vale	67	Stockport Co	63	Darlington*	50
1930–31b	Chesterfield	58	Lincoln C	57	Wrexham*	54
1931–32c	Lincoln C*	57	Gateshead	57	Chester	50
1932–33b	Hull C	59	Wrexham	57	Stockport Co	54
1933–34b	Barnsley	62	Chesterfield	61	Stockport Co	59
1934–35b	Doncaster R	57	Halifax T	55	Chester	54
1935–36b	Chesterfield	60	Chester*	55	Tranmere R	55
1936–37b	Stockport Co	60	Lincoln C	57	Chester	53
1937–38b	Tranmere R	56	Doncaster R	54	Hull C	53
1938–39b	Barnsley	67	Doncaster R	56	Bradford C	53
1939–46	Competition cancelled owing to war.					
1946–47b	Doncaster R	72	Rotherham U	60	Chester	56
1947–48b	Lincoln C	60	Rotherham U	59	Wrexham	50
1948–49b	Hull C	65	Rotherham U	62	Doncaster R	50
1949–50b	Doncaster R	55	Gateshead	53	Rochdale*	51
1950–51d	Rotherham U	71	Mansfield T	64	Carlisle U	62
1951–52d	Lincoln C	69	Grimsby T	66	Stockport Co	59
1952–53d	Oldham Ath	59	Port Vale	58	Wrexham	56
1953–54d	Port Vale	69	Barnsley	58	Scunthorpe U	57
1954–55d	Barnsley	65	Accrington S	61	Scunthorpe U*	58
1955–56d	Grimsby T	68	Derby Co	63	Accrington S	59
1956–57d	Derby Co	63	Hartlepool U	59	Accrington S*	58
1957–58d	Scunthorpe U	66	Accrington S	59	Bradford C	57

* Won or placed on goal average.

PROMOTED AFTER PLAY-OFFS
(Not accounted for in previous section)

1986–87	Aldershot to Division 3.
1987–88	Swansea C to Divison 3.
1988–89	Leyton O to Division 3.
1989–90	Cambridge U to Division 3; Notts Co to Division 2; Sunderland to Division 1.
1990–91	Notts Co to Division 1; Tranmere R to Division 2; Torquay U to Division 3.
1991–92	Blackburn R to Premier League; Peterborough U to Division 1.
1992–93	Swindon T to Premier League; WBA to Division 1; York C to Division 2.

RELEGATED CLUBS

FA PREMIER LEAGUE TO DIVISION 1

1992–93 Crystal Palace, Middlesbrough, Nottingham Forest

DIVISION 1 TO DIVISION 2

1898–99 Bolton W and Sheffield W
1899–1900 Burnley and Glossop
1900–01 Preston NE and WBA
1901–02 Small Heath and Manchester C
1902–03 Grimsby T and Bolton W
1903–04 Liverpool and WBA
1904–05 League extended. Bury and Notts Co, two bottom clubs in First Division, re-elected.
1905–06 Nottingham F and Wolverhampton W
1906–07 Derby Co and Stoke C
1907–08 Bolton W and Birmingham C
1908–09 Manchester C and Leicester Fosse
1909–10 Bolton W and Chelsea
1910–11 Bristol C and Nottingham F
1911–12 Preston NE and Bury
1912–13 Notts Co and Woolwich Arsenal
1913–14 Preston NE and Derby Co
1914–15 Tottenham H and Chelsea*
1919–20 Notts Co and Sheffield W
1920–21 Derby Co and Bradford PA
1921–22 Bradford C and Manchester U
1922–23 Stoke C and Oldham Ath
1923–24 Chelsea and Middlesbrough
1924–25 Preston NE and Nottingham F
1925–26 Manchester C and Notts Co
1926–27 Leeds U and WBA
1927–28 Tottenham H and Middlesbrough
1928–29 Bury and Cardiff C
1929–30 Burnley and Everton
1930–31 Leeds U and Manchester U
1931–32 Grimsby T and West Ham U
1932–33 Bolton W and Blackpool
1933–34 Newcastle U and Sheffield U
1934–35 Leicester C and Tottenham H
1935–36 Aston Villa and Blackburn R
1936–37 Manchester U and Sheffield W
1937–38 Manchester C and WBA
1938–39 Birmingham C and Leicester C

1946–47 Brentford and Leeds U
1947–48 Blackburn R and Grimsby T
1948–49 Preston NE and Sheffield U
1949–50 Manchester C and Birmingham C
1950–51 Sheffield W and Everton
1951–52 Huddersfield and Fulham
1952–53 Stoke C and Derby Co
1953–54 Middlesbrough and Liverpool
1954–55 Leicester C and Sheffield W
1955–56 Huddersfield and Sheffield U
1956–57 Charlton Ath and Cardiff C
1957–58 Sheffield W and Sunderland
1958–59 Portsmouth and Aston Villa
1959–60 Luton T and Leeds U
1960–61 Preston NE and Newcastle U
1961–62 Chelsea and Cardiff C
1962–63 Majchester C and Leyton O
1963–64 Bolton W and Ipswich T
1964–65 Wolverhampton W and Birmingham C
1965–66 Northampton T and Blackburn R
1966–67 Aston Villa and Blackpool
1967–68 Fulham and Sheffield U
1968–69 Leicester C and QPR
1969–70 Sunderland and Sheffield W
1970–71 Burnley and Blackpool
1971–72 Huddersfield T and Nottingham F
1972–73 Crystal Palace and WBA
1973–74 Southampton, Manchester U, Norwich C
1974–75 Luton T, Chelsea, Carlisle U
1975–76 Wolverhampton W, Burnley, Sheffield U
1976–77 Sunderland, Stoke C, Tottenham H
1977–78 West Ham U, Newcastle U, Leicester C
1978–79 QPR, Birmingham C, Chelsea
1979–80 Bristol C, Derby Co, Bolton W
1980–81 Norwich C, Leicester C, Crystal Palace
1981–82 Leeds U, Wolverhampton W, Middlesbrough

103

1982–83 Manchester C, Swansea C, Brighton & HA
1983–84 Birmingham C, Notts Co, Wolverhampton W
1984–85 Norwich C, Sunderland, Stoke C
1985–86 Ipswich T, Birmingham C, WBA
1986–87 Leicester C, Manchester C, Aston Villa
1987–88 Chelsea**, Portsmouth, Watford, Oxford U

1988–89 Middlesbrough, West Ham U, Newcastle U
1989–90 Sheffield W, Charlton Ath, Millwall
1990–91 Sunderland and Derby Co
1991–92 Luton T, Notts Co, West Ham U
1992–93 Brentford, Cambridge U, Bristol R

**Relegated after play-offs.*
Subsequently re-elected to Division 1 when League was extended after the War.

DIVISION 2 TO DIVISION 3

1920–21 Stockport Co
1921–22 Bradford and Bristol C
1922–23 Rotherham C and Wolverhampton W
1923–24 Nelson and Bristol C
1924–25 Crystal Palace and Coventry C
1925–26 Stoke C and Stockport Co
1926–27 Darlington and Bradford C
1927–28 Fulham and South Shields
1928–29 Port Vale and Clapton O
1929–30 Hull C and Notts Co
1930–31 Reading and Cardiff C
1931–32 Barnsley and Bristol C
1932–33 Chesterfield and Charlton Ath
1933–34 Millwall and Lincoln C
1934–35 Oldham Ath and Notts Co
1935–36 Port Vale and Hull C
1936–37 Doncaster R and Bradford C
1937–38 Barnsley and Stockport Co
1938–39 Norwich C and Tranmere R
1946–47 Swansea T and Newport Co
1947–48 Doncaster R and Millwall
1948–49 Nottingham F and Lincoln C
1949–50 Plymouth Arg and Bradford
1950–51 Grimsby T and Chesterfield
1951–52 Coventry C and QPR
1952–53 Southampton and Barnsley
1953–54 Brentford and Oldham Ath
1954–55 Ipswich T and Derby Co
1955–56 Plymouth Arg and Hull C
1956–57 Port Vale and Bury
1957–58 Doncaster R and Notts Co
1958–59 Barnsley and Grimsby T
1959–60 Bristol C and Hull C
1960–61 Lincoln C and Portsmouth
1961–62 Brighton & HA and Bristol R

1962–63 Walsall and Luton T
1963–64 Grimsby T and Scunthorpe U
1964–65 Swindon T and Swansea T
1965–66 Middlesbrough and Leyton O
1966–67 Northampton T and Bury
1967–68 Plymouth Arg and Rotherham U
1968–69 Fulham and Bury
1969–70 Preston NE and Aston Villa
1970–71 Blackburn R and Bolton W
1971–72 Charlton Ath and Watford
1972–73 Huddersfield T and Brighton & HA
1973–74 Crystal Palace, Preston NE, Swindon T
1974–75 Millwall, Cardiff C, Sheffield W
1975–76 Oxford U, York C, Portsmouth
1976–77 Carlisle U, Plymouth Arg, Hereford U
1977–78 Blackpool, Mansfield T, Hull C
1978–79 Sheffield U, Millwall, Blackburn R
1979–80 Fulham, Burnley, Charlton Ath
1980–81 Preston NE, Bristol C, Bristol R
1981–82 Cardiff C, Wrexham, Orient
1982–83 Rotherham U, Burnley, Bolton W
1983–84 Derby Co, Swansea C, Cambridge U
1984–85 Notts Co, Cardiff C, Wolverhampton W
1985–86 Carlisle U, Middlesbrough, Fulham

1986–87 Sunderland**, Grimsby T,
Brighton & HA
1987–88 Huddersfield T, Reading,
Sheffield U**
1988–89 Shrewsbury T, Birmingham
C, Walsall
1989–90 Bournemouth, Bradford,
Stoke C

1990–91 WBA and Hull C
1991–92 Plymouth Arg, Brighton &
HA, Port Vale
1992–93 Preston NE, Mansfield T,
Wigan Ath, Chester C

DIVISION 3 TO DIVISION 4

1958–59 Rochdale, Notts Co,
Doncaster R and Stockport
1959–60 Accrington S, Wrexham,
Mansfield T and York C
1960–61 Chesterfield, Colchester U,
Bradford C and Tranmere R
1961–62 Newport Co, Brentford,
Lincoln C and Torquay U
1962–63 Bradford PA, Brighton,
Carlisle U and Halifax T
1963–64 Millwall, Crewe Alex,
Wrexham and Notts Co
1964–65 Luton T, Port Vale,
Colchester U and Barnsley
1965–66 Southend U, Exeter C,
Brentford and York C
1966–67 Doncaster R, Workington,
Darlington and Swansea T
1967–68 Scunthorpe U, Colchester U,
Grimsby T and
Peterborough U (demoted)
1968–69 Oldham Ath, Crewe Alex,
Hartlepool and
Northampton
1969–70 Bournemouth, Southport,
Barrow, Stockport Co
1970–71 Reading, Bury, Doncaster R,
Gillingham
1971–72 Mansfield T, Barnsley,
Torquay U, Bradford C
1972–73 Rotherham U, Brentford,
Swansea C, Scunthorpe U
1973–74 Cambridge U, Shrewsbury T,
Southport, Rochdale
1974–75 AFC Bournemouth,
Tranmere R, Watford,
Huddersfield T

1975–76 Aldershot, Colchester U,
Southend U, Halifax T
1976–77 Reading, Northampton T,
Grimsby T, York C
1977–78 Port Vale, Bradford C,
Hereford U, Portsmouth
1978–79 Peterborough U, Walsall,
Tranmere R, Lincoln C
1979–80 Bury, Southend U, Mansfield
T, Wimbledon
1980–81 Sheffield U, Colchester U,
Blackpool, Hull C
1981–82 Wimbledon, Swindon T,
Bristol C, Chester
1982–83 Reading, Wrexham,
Doncaster R, Chesterfield
1983–84 Scunthorpe U, Southend U,
Port Vale, Exeter C
1984–85 Burnley, Orient, Preston NE,
Cambridge U
1985–86 Lincoln C, Cardiff C,
Wolverhampton W,
Swansea C
11986–87 Bolton W**, Carlisle U,
Darlington, Newport Co
1987–88 Doncaster R, York C,
Grimsby T, Rotherham U**
1988–89 Southend U, Chesterfield,
Gillingham, Aldershot
1989–90 Cardiff C, Northampton T,
Blackpool, Walsall
1990–91 Crewe Alex, Rotherham U,
Mansfield T
1991–92 Bury, Shrewsbury T,
Torquay U, Darlington

*** Relegated after play-offs.*

105

TRANSFERS TRAIL 1992–93

(from May 1992 to May 1993)

	From	To
May 1992		
27 Gray, Andrew. A	Crystal Palace	Tottenham Hotspur
21 Hobson, Paul J.	St Albans City	Enfield
20 Holmes P	Torquay United	Birmingham City
28 Jeffrey, Michael A.	Bolton Wdrs.	Doncaster Rovers
20 Joyce, Warren G.	Preston North End	Plymouth Argyle
27 Olney, Ian D.	Aston Villa	Oldham Athletic
27 Pembridge, Mark	Luton Town	Derby County
20 Taylor, Ian	Moor Green	Port Vale
Temporary transfers		
1 Day, Mervyn R.	Leeds United	Sheffield United
4 Day, Mervyn R.	Sheffield United	Leeds United (Tr. back)
1 Sullivan, Neil	Wimbledon	Crystal Palace
6 Varadi, Imre	Luton Town	Leeds United (Tr. back)
20 Arnott, Andrew J.	Gillingham	Manchester United
20 Swan, Adrian	Darlington	Leicester City
June 1992		
3 Anderton, Darren R.	Portsmouth	Tottenham Hotspur
3 Austin, Dean B.	Southend United	Tottenham Hotspur
22 Barrows, Nigel J.	Stourbridge	Hednesford Town
3 Beadle, Peter C.	Gillingham	Tottenham Hotspur
16 Bracewell, Paul W.	Sunderland	Newcastle United
4 Castle, Stephen C.	Leyton Orient	Plymouth Argyle
4 Cross, Ryan	Plymouth Argyle	Hartlepool United
5 Dalton, Paul	Hartlepool United	Plymouth Argyle
19 Elliott, Matthew S.	Torquay United	Scunthorpe United
19 Fishenden, Paul	Wokingham Town	Crawley Town
2 Golley, Mark A.	Welling United	Sutton United
15 Hackett, Brendan	Telford United	Halesowen Town
30 Hallam, Mark	Leicester United	Boston United
10 Hamilton, Ian R.	Scunthorpe United	West Bromwich Albion
10 Hine, Mark	Scunthorpe United	Doncaster Rovers
10 Lilwall, Stephen	Kidderminster Harriers	West Bromwich Albion
25 McCarthy, Anthony P.	Shelbourne	Millwall
8 May, Andrew M.	Bristol City	Millwall
26 O'Connor, Martin J.	Bromsgrove Rovers	Crystal Palace
11 O'Neill, Daren S.	Wokingham Town	Crawley Town
25 Patterson, Darren J.	Wigan Athletic	Crystal Palace
2 Rouse, Shaun	Rangers	Bristol City
17 Samways, Mark	Doncaster Rovers	Scunthorpe United
8 Thomas, Paul D.	Newport (IOW)	Waterlooville
13 Thompson, David	Millwall	Bristol City
11 Thompson, David J.	Wokingham Town	Crawley Town
5 Walsh, Paul A.	Tottenham Hotspur	Portsmouth
17 Wassall, Darren P	Nottingham Forest	Derby County
July 1992		
21 Babb, Philip A.	Bradford City	Coventry City
15 Barnes, Paul L.	Stoke City	York City
2 Beresford, John	Portsmouth	Newcastle United

		From	To
3	Brooks, Christopher	Ilkeston Town	Luton Town
3	Carroll, Mathew P.	Kidderminster Harriers	Sutton Coldfield Town
17	Carty, Paul	Nuneaton Borough	VS Rugby
29	Claridge, Stephen E.	Cambridge United	Luton Town
17	Clark, Martin J.	Mansfield Town	Partick Thistle
22	Coates, Neil R.	Dorchester Town	Yeovil Town
21	Cole, Andrew	Arsenal	Bristol City
10	Colquhoun, John	Millwall	Sunderland
25	Coombe, Mark A.	Salisbury	Dorchester Town
2	Cundy, Jason V.	Chelsea	Tottenham Hotspur
20	Cunnington, Shaun G.	Grimsby Town	Sunderland
16	Cusack, Nicholas J.	Darlington	Oxford United
17	Davidson, Jonathan S	Derby County	Preston North End
22	Dixon, Kerry M.	Chelsea	Southampton
22	Furlong, Paul A.	Coventry City	Watford
27	Gittens, Jon	Southampton	Middlesbrough
30	Gosney, Andrew	Portsmouth	Birmingham City
29	Gould, Jonathan A.	West Bromwich Albion	Coventry City
6	Harbey, Graham K.	West Bromwich Albion	Stoke City
14	Hardyman, Paul G. T.	Sunderland	Bristol Rovers
31	Hill, Colin F.	Sheffield United	Leicester City
29	Horne, Barry	Southampton	Everton
28	Houghton, Raymond J.	Liverpool	Aston Villa
13	Hurst, Mark D.	Grantham Town	Leicester United
6	James, David	Watford	Liverpool
22	Jones, Murray L.	Grimsby Town	Brentford
3	Jones, Tom	Swindon Town	Reading
10	Kerr, Paul A.	Millwall	Port Vale
28	Lowe, David A.	Ipswich Town	Leicester City
20	Makel, Lee	Newcastle United	Blackburn Rovers
3	Maskell, Craig D.	Reading	Swindon Town
17	Massey, Stuart A.	Sutton United	Crystal Palace
7	McKenna, John	Boston United	Dagenham & Redbridge
13	Morrell Peter A.	Dorchester Town	Wimborne Town
22	Musselwhite, Paul S.	Scunthorpe United	Port Vale
1	Narbett, Jonathan V.	Hereford United	Oxford United
10	Parkinson, Philip J.	Bury	Reading
2	Quinn, James M.	AFC Bournemouth	Reading
21	Reid, Paul R.	Leicester City	Bradford City
9	Ripley, Stuart E	Middlesbrough	Blackburn Rovers
20	Rosegreen Mark A.	VS Rugby	Nuneaton Borough
22	Ruddock, Neil	Southampton	Tottenham Hotspur
3	Russell, Andrew	Woking	Kingstonian
16	Russell, Kevin J.	Leicester City	Stoke City
29	Sellars, Scott	Blackburn Rovers	Leeds United
27	Shearer, Alan	Southampton	Blackburn Rovers
10	Smith, David A.	Plymouth Argyle	Notts County
27	Speedie, David R.	Blackburn Rovers	Southampton
29	Stewart, Paul A.	Tottenham Hotspur	Liverpool
31	Sulley, Christopher S.	Blackburn Rovers	Port Vale
15	Thackeray, Andrew J.	Wrexham	Rochdale
31	Venison, Barry	Liverpool	Newcastle United
29	Wilmot, Rhys J.	Plymouth Argyle	Grimsby Town
15	Williams,David G.	Derby County	Ipswich Town
9	Williams, John	Swansea City	Coventry City
22	Wright, Thomas E.	Leicester City	Middlesbrough

		From	To
Temporary transfers			
29	Bailey, Danny S.	Reading	Fulham
14	Bennett, Michael R.	Wimbledon	Brentford
23	Duffield, Peter	Sheffield United	Blackpool
13	Holdsworth, Dean C.	Brentford	Wimbledon
24	Kelly, Alan T.	Preston North End	Sheffield United
14	Kruszynski, Zbigniew	Wimbledon	Brentford
23	McLeary, Alan T.	Millwall	Sheffield United
30	Morah, Olisa H.	Tottenham Hotspur	Swindon Town
24	Pascoe, Colin J.	Sunderland	Swansea City
30	Wilder, Christopher J.	Sheffield United	Rotherham United
August 1992			
20	Alleyne Xavier J.	Leatherhead	Crawley Town
10	Bennett, Michael R.	Wimbledon	Brentford
28	Beresford, Marlon	Sheffield Wednesday	Burnley
14	Berry, Gregory J.	Leyton Orient	Wimbledon
26	Brazil, Derek M.	Manchester United	Cardiff City
20	Brindley, Christopher P.	Telford United	Kidderminster Harriers
19	Burnett, Wayne	Leyton Orient	Blackburn Rovers
7	Butler, Peter J. F.	Southend United	West Ham United
14	Callaghan, Aaron J.	Crewe Alexandra	Preston North End
11	Campbell, Stephen A.	Redditch United	Atherstone United
17	Carroll, Robert	Yeovil Town	Woking
13	Collins, Paul	Fisher Athletic	Welling United
11	Cormack, Lee D.	Basingstoke Town	Waterlooville
21	Crawley, Ian S.	VS Rugby	Tamworth
20	Croft, Brian	Chester City	Queens Park Rangers
2	Davison, Robert	Leeds United	Leicester City
14	Daws, Nicholas J.	Altrincham	Bury
7	Dear, Andrew M.	Kingstonian	Hayes
17	Dent, Nicholas W.	Poole Town	Dover Athletic
13	Donaghy, Malachy M.	Manchester United	Chelsea
7	Dublin, Dion	Cambridge United	Manchester United
14	Ellis, Anthony	Stoke City	Preston North End
8	Elmes, Richard M.	Havant Town	Newport (IOW)
13	Fleck, Robert	Norwich City	Chelsea
3	Fletcher, Steven M.	Hartlepool United	AFC Bournemouth
12	Francis, John A.	Burnley	Cambridge United
6	Garner, Simon	Blackburn Rovers	West Bromwich Albion
5	Graham, Jon	Kettering Town	Boston United
12	Groves, Paul	Blackpool	Grimsby Town
24	Groves, Perry	Arsenal	Southampton
13	Harford, Michael G.	Luton Town	Chelsea
6	Holden, Richard W.	Oldham Athletic	Manchester City
10	Holdsworth, Dean C.	Brentford	Wimbledon
19	Holmes, Matthew J. E.	AFC Bournemouth	West Ham United
14	Horlock, Kevin	West Ham United	Swindon Town
28	Hulme, Timothy J.	Crawley Town	Sittingbourne
8	Huxford, Richard	Kettering Town	Barnet
14	James, Robert M.	Bradford City	Cardiff City
6	Jepson, Ronald F.	Preston North End	Exeter City
20	Kelly, Alan T.	Preston North End	Sheffield United
27	Kelly, Anthony J.	Unattached	Hayes
11	Kitchen, David E.	Frickley Athletic	Leyton Orient
10	Kruszynski, Zbigniew	Wimbledon	Brentford

	From	To
14 Leonard, Mark A.	Rochdale	Preston North End
6 McFarlane, Andrew A.	Portsmouth	Swansea City
4 Megson, Gary J.	Manchester City	Norwich City
13 Mendonca, Clive P.	Sheffield United	Grimsby Town
21 Monkou, Kenneth J.	Chelsea	Southampton
21 Nevin, Patrick K. F.	Everton	Tranmere Rovers
6 Nuttell, Michael J.	Boston United	Kettering Town
14 Pennock, Adrian	Norwich City	AFC Bournemouth
25 Phelan, Terry	Wimbledon	Manchester City
7 Pointon, Neil G.	Manchester City	Oldham Athletic
7 Redmond, Stephen	Manchester City	Oldham Athletic
21 Reid, Andrew M.	Altrincham	Bury
24 Richardson, Nicholas J.	Halifax Town	Cardiff City
14 Robins, Mark G.	Manchester United	Norwich City
4 Rocastle, David C.	Arsenal	Leeds United
28 Rogers, Anthony K.	Dover Athletic	Chelmsford City
4 Ryan, Vaughan W.	Wimbledon	Leyton Orient
12 Shaw, Graham P.	Preston North End	Stoke City
28 Sheringham, Teddy	Nottingham Forest	Tottenham Hotspur
14 Slater, Stuart	West Ham United	Celtic
28 Wilder, Christopher J.	Sheffield United	Rotherham United

Temporary transfers

	From	To
21 Baraclough, Ian R.	Grimsby Town	Lincoln City
10 Bennett, Michael R.	Brentford	Wimbledon (Tr. back)
8 Blades, Paul A.	Norwich City	Wolverhampton Wdrs.
10 Brazil, Derek M.	Manchester United	Cardiff City
27 Connelly, Dean	Barnsley	Carlisle United
13 Cotterill, Stephen	Wimbledon	Brighton & Hove Albion
6 Dearden, Kevin C.	Tottenham Hotspur	Portsmouth
28 Dobson, Paul	Lincoln City	Darlington
21 Duffield, Peter	Sheffield United	Blackpool
8 Edwards, Paul R.	Coventry City	Wolverhampton Wdrs.
10 Hicks, Stuart J.	Scunthorpe United	Doncaster Rovers
28 Horne, Brian	Millwall	Middlesbrough
28 Hoyle, Colin R.	Barnsley	Bradford City
27 Juryeff, Ian M.	Halifax Town	Darlington
28 Keeley, John H.	Oldham Athletic	Chester City
10 Kruszynski, Zbigniew	Brentford	Wimbledon (Tr. back)
4 Lund, Gary J.	Notts County	Hull City
28 Makin, Christopher	Oldham Athletic	Wigan Athletic
13 McCord, Brian J.	Barnsley	Mansfield Town
28 McDonald, David H.	Tottenham Hotspur	Bradford City
14 Moulden, Paul A.	Oldham Athletic	Brighton & Hove Albion
6 Newell, Paul C.	Leyton Orient	Colchester United
13 Regis, David	Plymouth Argyle	AFC Bournemouth
3 Richardson, Nicholas J.	Halifax Town	Cardiff City
21 Skinner, Craig R.	Blackburn Rovers	Plymouth Argyle

September 1992

	From	To
1 Armstrong, Christopher	Millwall	Crystal Palace
7 Barness, Anthony	Charlton Athletic	Chelsea
11 Bright, Mark A.	Crystal Palace	Sheffield Wednesday
19 Coe, John Ryan	VS Rugby	Rushden & Diamonds
23 Costello, Peter	Peterborough United	Lincoln City
29 Dobson, Paul	Lincoln City	Darlington

		From	*To*
1	Friel, George P.	Woking	Slough Town
22	Hill, Keith J.	Blackburn Rovers	Plymouth Argyle
5	James, Simon	Havant Town	Waterlooville
10	Jones, Vincent P.	Chelsea	Wimbledon
29	Juryeff, Ian M.	Halifax Town	Darlington
22	Kennedy, Andrew J.	Watford	Brighton & Hove Albion
25	Kuhl, Martin	Portsmouth	Derby County
2	Lee, Robert M.	Charlton Athletic	Newcastle United
24	Marker, Nicholas R.	Plymouth Argyle	Falkirk
1	McLaughlin, Joseph	Watford	Blackburn Rovers
22	Massey, Andrew D.	Redditch United	Shepshed Albion
30	McGinlay, John	Millwall	Bolton Wdrs.
1	Moralee, Jamie D.	Crystal Palace	Millwall
18	Olner, Paul	Atherstone United	VS Rugby
15	Robinson, David A.	Peterborough United	Notts County
15	Robinson, John R. C.	Brighton & Hove Albion	Charlton Athletic
6	Saunders, Dean N.	Liverpool	Aston Villa
16	Short, Craig J.	Notts County	Derby County
2	Skinner, Craig R.	Blackburn Rovers	Plymouth Argyle
11	Williams, Paul A.	Sheffield Wednesday	Crystal Palace

Temporary transfers

		From	*To*
3	Bartlett, Kevin F.	Notts County	Port Vale
10	Bellamy, Gary	Wolverhampton Wdrs.	Leyton Orient
18	Broddle, Julian	St Mirren	Scunthorpe United
18	Browning, Marcus T.	Bristol Rovers	Hereford United
11	Cairns, Darren	Hull City	Ards
21	Chamberlain, Alec F.R.	Luton Town	Chelsea
25	Evans, Michael J.	Plymouth Argyle	Blackburn Rovers
4	Fox, Peter D.	Stoke City	Linfield
12	Heald, Paul A.	Leyton Orient	Crystal Palace
17	Houghton, Scott A.	Tottenham Hotspur	Cambridge United
4	Jones, Alexander	Motherwell	Rochdale
9	Keeley, John H.	Chester City	Plymouth Argyle
9	Kite, Philip D.	Sheffield United	Plymouth Argyle
18	Kite, Philip D.	Plymouth Argyle	Sheffield United (Tr. back)
1	Loram, Mark J.	Torquay United	Exeter City
28	Makin, Christopher	Oldham Athletic	Wigan Athletic
25	Matthew, Damian	Chelsea	Luton Town
2	Mohan, Nicholas	Middlesbrough	Hull City
11	Mooney, Brian J.	Sunderland	Burnley
17	Moran, Paul	Tottenham Hotspur	Cambridge United
17	Peyton, Gerald J.	Everton	Brentford
24	Pollitt, Michael F.	Bury	Lincoln City
3	Proudlock, Paul	Carlisle United	Hartlepool United
17	Reid, Nicholas S.	Blackburn Rovers	Bristol City
1	Robinson, Philip J.	Notts County	Huddersfield Town
17	Stringfellow, Ian R.	Mansfield Town	Grimsby Town
5	Tillson, Andrew	Queens Park Rangers	Grimsby Town
30	Wallace, Michael	Manchester City	Stockport County
4	West, Gary	Lincoln City	Walsall
4	Whitehead, Philip M.	Barnsley	Scunthorpe United
17	Williams, Gareth J.	Barnsley	Hull City

October 1992

		From	*To*
23	Baraclough, Ian R.	Grimsby Town	Lincoln City
1	Biggins, Wayne	Stoke City	Barnsley

		From	To
2	Blades, Paul A.	Norwich City	Wolverhampton Wdrs.
26	Byrne, John F.	Sunderland	Millwall
15	Charley, Kenneth L.	Peterborough United	Watford
1	Donovan, Kevin	Huddersfield Town	West Bromwich Albion
21	Danzey, Michael J.	St Albans City	Cambridge United
22	Eaton, Jason	Gloucester City	Cheltenham Town
13	Edwards, Paul R.	Coventry City	Wolverhampton Wdrs.
23	Gleghorn, Nigel W.	Birmingham City	Stoke City
23	Harmon, Darren J.	Shrewsbury Town	Northampton Town
9	Hicks, Stuart J.	Scunthorpe United	Doncaster Rovers
2	Hoyle, Colin R.	Barnsley	Bradford City
16	Joseph, Antone E.	Kidderminster Harriers	Hednesford Town
30	Millar, Robert J.	Oldham Athletic	Hull City
1	Niblett, Nigel	VS Rugby	Telford United
19	Philliskirk, Anthony	Bolton Wdrs.	Peterborough United
23	Regis, David	Plymouth Argyle	Stoke City
2	Smith, Mark C.	Barnsley	Notts County
28	Walker, Gary	Radcliffe Borough	Buxton
30	Westley, Shane L. M.	Wolverhampton Wdrs.	Brentford
5	Willis, Roger C.	Barnet	Watford

Temporary transfers

24	Beasant, David	Chelsea	Grimsby Town
23	Blissett, Luther L.	Watford	West Bromwich Albion
23	Brady, Kieron	Sunderland	Doncaster Rovers
5	Burns, Philip	Airdrieonians	Portsmouth
31	Carruthers, Martin G.	Aston Villa	Hull City
24	Channing, Justin A.	Queens Park Rangers	Bristol Rovers
15	Currie, David N.	Barnsley	Rotherham United
2	Dewhurst, Robert M.	Blackburn Rovers	Huddersfield Town
14	Emberson, Carl W.	Millwall	Rotherham United
25	Evans, Michael	Plymouth Argyle	Blackburn Rovers
2	Evans, Richard W.	Bristol Rovers	Exeter City
1	Garnett, Shaun M.	Tranmere Rovers	Chester City
24	Graham, Deniol W. T.	Barnsley	Preston North End
30	Harvey, Richard G.	Luton Town	Blackpool
9	Hawke, Warren R.	Sunderland	Carlisle United
24	Herrera, Roberto	Queens Park Rangers	Torquay United
17	Holden, Steven A.	Leicester City	Carlisle United
2	Horne, Brian	Millwall	Stoke City
30	Kelly, Anthony O. N.	Stoke City	Cardiff City
2	Kite, Philip D.	Sheffield United	Rotherham United
29	Kite, Philip D.	Rotherham United	Sheffield United (Tr. back)
9	Limber, Nicholas	Manchester City	Peterborough United
6	McLeary, Alan	Millwall	Wimbledon
17	Moore, Kevin T.	Southampton	Bristol Rovers
32	Morgan, Nicholas	Bristol City	AFC Bournemouth
10	Parkinson, Gary	Middlesbrough	Southend United
7	Philliskirk, Tony	Bolton Wdrs.	Peterborough United
2	Sealey, Leslie J.	Aston Villa	Birmingham City
17	Smith, Kevan	Darlington	Hereford United
31	Sommer, Jurgen P.	Luton Town	Torquay United
23	Speedie, David R.	Southampton	Birmingham City
31	Taylor, Colin D.	Wolverhampton Wdrs.	Preston North End
2	Wheeler, Paul	Stockport County	Scarborough
23	Williams, Paul A.	West Bromwich Albion	Coventry City

111

	From	To
November 1992		
19 Allon, Joseph B.	Chelsea	Brentford
17 Bellamy, Gary	Wolverhampton Wdrs.	Leyton Orient
20 Benjamin, Ian T.	Southend United	Luton Town
24 Brennan, Mark R.	Manchester City	Oldham Athletic
27 Cantona, Eric	Leeds United	Manchester United
20 Claridge, Stephen E.	Luton Town	Cambridge United
20 Cooper, Mark N.	Birmingham City	Fulham
20 Hallam, Mark	Boston United	Hednesford Town
27 Hignett, Craig J.	Crewe Alexandra	Middlesbrough
3 Ireland, Simon P.	Huddersfield Town	Blackburn Rovers
24 Jenkins, Michael G.	Havant Town	Waterlooville
16 Jones, Stephen G.	Billericay Town	West Ham United
3 Morah, Olisa H.	Tottenham Hotspur	Swindon Town
5 Nelson, Stephen E.	Telford United	Burton Albion
24 Philpott, Lee	Cambridge United	Leicester City
7 Reid, Nicholas S.	Blackburn Rovers	West Bromwich Albion
3 Robinson, Philip J.	Notts County	Huddersfield Town
13 Smart, Erskine	Enfield	St Albans City
5 Tillson, Andrew	Queens Park Rangers	Bristol Rovers
5 Waddock, Gary P.	Queens Park Rangers	Bristol Rovers
23 Webb, Neil J.	Manchester United	Nottingham Forest
Temporary transfers		
21 Agnew, Stephen M.	Blackburn Rovers	Portsmouth
11 Bellamy, Gary	Wolverhampton Wdrs.	Leyton Orient
20 Branch, Graham	Tranmere Rovers	Bury
5 Browning, Marcus T.	Hereford United	Bristol Rovers (Tr. back)
23 Charles, Stephen	Mansfield Town	Scunthorpe United
20 Collymore, Stanley V.	Crystal Palace	Southend United
20 Connor, Terence F.	Bristol City	Swansea City
27 Cousins, Anthony J.	Liverpool	Hereford United
27 Dewhurst, Robert M.	Huddersfield Town	Blackburn Rovers (Tr. back)
4 Digby, Fraser G.	Swindon Town	Manchester United
18 Dryden, Richard A.	Notts County	Plymouth Argyle
26 Fee, Gregory P.	Mansfield Town	Chesterfield
26 Fickling, Ashley	Sheffield United	Darlington
29 Horne, Brian	Millwall	Sunderland
20 Johnson, David A.	Sheffield Wednesday	Hartlepool United
13 Kamara, Christopher	Luton Town	Sheffield United
21 Keeley, John H.	Oldham Athletic	Chester City
26 Keeley, John H.	Chester City	Oldham Athletic (Tr. back)
21 Kite, Philip D.	Sheffield United	Crewe Alexandra
20 Kristensen, Bjorn	Newcastle United	Bristol City
26 Lake, Michael C.	Sheffield United	Wrexham
20 Lancashire, Graham	Burnley	Halifax Town
2 Lee, David	Southampton	Bolton Wdrs.
21 Livingstone, Glen	Aston Villa	York City
25 Makin, Christopher	Wigan Athletic	Oldham Athletic (Tr. back)
5 O'Hanlon, George T.	Leyton Orient	Swindon Town
19 Quinn, Michael	Newcastle United	Coventry City
20 Reece, Andrew J.	Bristol Rovers	Walsall
21 Sonner, Daniel J.	Burnley	Bury
21 Stephenson, Paul	Millwall	Gillingham
21 Turner, Robert P.	Plymouth Argyle	Notts County
21 Ward, Ashley S.	Leicester City	Blackpool

	From	To
19 Whitehead, Philip M.	Barnsley	Bradford City
8 Williams, Lee	Aston Villa	Shrewsbury Town

December 1992

	From	To
23 Ainsworth, Gareth	Cambridge United	Preston North End
24 Benstock, Danny	Barking	Leyton Orient
23 Butler, Stephen	Watford	Cambridge United
4 Came, Mark R.	Bolton Wdrs.	Chester City
21 Collymore, Stanley V.	Crystal Palace	Southend United
18 Garland, Peter J.	Newcastle United	Charlton Athletic
7 Hodges, Kevin	Plymouth Argyle	Torquay United
24 Horne, Brian S.	Millwall	Portsmouth
1 Jones, Alexander	Motherwell	Rochdale
30 Lee, David M.	Southampton	Bolton Wdrs.
15 Livingstone, Glen	Aston Villa	York City
23 Norbury, Michael S.	Cambridge United	Preston North End
22 Quinn, Michael	Newcastle United	Coventry City
1 Scott, Andrew	Sutton United	Sheffield United
8 Stant, Philip	Mansfield Town	Cardiff City
11 Taylor, Justin S.	Tamworth	Redditch United
23 Turner, Robert P.	Plymouth Argyle	Notts County
23 Wallace, Michael	Manchester City	Stockport County
1 Ward, Ashley S.	Leicester City	Crewe Alexandra

Temporary transfers

	From	To
21 Brooks, Shaun	AFC Bournemouth	Stockport County
23 Brown, Michael A.	Bolton Wdrs.	Shrewsbury Town
18 Butler, Stephen	Watford	AFC Bournemouth
23 Butler, Stephen	AFC Bournemouth	Watford (Tr. back)
24 Cooper, Stephen B.	Tranmere Rovers	Wigan Athletic
30 Dickens, Alan W.	Chelsea	West Bromwich Albion
30 Digby, Fraser	Manchester United	Swindon Town (Tr. back)
17 Emberson, Carl W.	Millwall	Colchester United
17 Finley, Alan J.	Stockport County	Carlisle United
17 Gallen, Joseph M.	Watford	Exeter City
11 Garnett, Shaun M.	Tranmere Rovers	Preston North End
23 Gray, Andrew A.	Tottenham Hotspur	Swindon Town
18 Harrison, Lee D.	Charlton Athletic	Fulham
17 Houghton, Scott A.	Tottenham Hotspur	Gillingham
31 Jenkins, Iain	Everton	Bradford City
24 Lucas, Richard	Sheffield United	Preston North End
17 Marples, Christopher	York City	Chesterfield
31 Martin, Dean	West Ham United	Colchester United
17 Matthews, Neil	Stockport County	Lincoln City
11 McGlashan, John	Millwall	Fulham
9 Moody, Paul	Southampton	Reading
18 Peer, Dean	Birmingham City	Mansfield Town
4 Power, Lee M.	Norwich City	Charlton Athletic
18 Rowbotham, Darren	Birmingham City	Mansfield Town
30 Stimson, Mark	Newcastle United	Portsmouth
29 Talia, Frank	Blackburn Rovers	Hartlepool United
30 Veysey, Kenneth J.	Oxford United	Sheffield United
1 Ward, Ashley S.	Blackpool	Leicester City (Tr. back)
18 Watts, Julian	Sheffield Wednesday	Shrewsbury Town
23 Williams, Lee	Shrewsbury Town	Aston Villa (Tr. back)
18 Williams, Michael A.	Sheffield Wednesday	Halifax Town

	From	To
January 1993		
7 Baker, David P.	Motherwell	Gillingham
15 Blackwell, Kevin P.	Notts County	Torquay United
7 Channing, Justin A.	Queens Park Rangers	Bristol Rovers
6 Hayes, Martin	Celtic	Swansea City
14 Kelly, Thomas J.	Exeter City	Torquay United
15 Lyne, Neil G.	Shrewsbury Town	Cambridge United
8 May, Leroy A.	Tividale	Hereford United
27 McGlashan, John	Millwall	Peterborough United
15 Murray, Paul G.	Burnley	Berwick Rangers
29 Price, Christopher J.	Blackburn Rovers	Portsmouth
25 Ryan, Darren T.	Chester City	Stockport County
9 Watkins, Dale A.	Grantham Town	Rushden & Diamonds
25 Wheeler, Paul	Stockport County	Chester City
26 White, Devon W.	Cambridge United	Queens Park Rangers
11 Williams, Paul A.	West Bromwich Albion	Stockport County
Temporary transfers		
22 Allpress, Timothy J.	Luton Town	Boston United
12 Beasant, David	Chelsea	Wolverhampton Wdrs.
12 Carr, Franz A.	Newcastle United	Sheffield United
12 Dickins, Matthew J.	Blackburn Rovers	Blackpool
15 Donowa, Brian L.	Birmingham City	Burnley
12 Dryden, Richard A.	Plymouth Argyle	Notts County (Tr. back)
1 Duffield, Peter	Sheffield United	Crewe Alexandra
25 Farrell, David	Aston Villa	Scunthorpe United
28 Gallen, Joseph M.	Watford	Shamrock Rovers
15 Hayrettin, Hakan	Barnet	Torquay United
2 Kabia, Jason	Lincoln City	Doncaster Rovers
13 Kite, Philip D.	Crewe Alexandra	Sheffield United (Tr. back)
25 Lund, Gary J.	Notts County	Hull City
1 McGlashan, John	Millwall	Cambridge United
26 McGlashan, John	Cambridge United	Millwall (Tr. back)
8 McKee, Colin	Manchester United	Bury
15 Maddison, Lee	Bristol Rovers	Bath City
22 Mortimer, Paul H.	Crystal Palace	Brentford
6 Ranson, Raymond	Newcastle United	Manchester City
8 Roche, David	Newcastle United	Peterborough United
8 Rowland, Keith	AFC Bournemouth	Coventry City
8 Smith, David	Coventry City	AFC Bournemouth
25 Smith, Mark C.	Notts County	Port Vale
21 Speedie, David R.	Birmingham City	Southampton (Tr. back)
21 Speedie, David R.	Southampton	West Bromwich Albion
29 Thomas, Martin R.	Birmingham City	Aston Villa
21 Tuttle, David P.	Tottenham Hotspur	Peterborough United
21 Varadi, Imre	Leeds United	Oxford United
13 Veysey, Kenneth J.	Sheffield United	Oxford United (Tr. back)
4 Viveash, Adrian L.	Swindon Town	Reading
15 White, Christopher	Peterborough United	Doncaster Rovers
15 Williams, David P.	Burnley	Crewe Alexandra
8 Woods, Raymond G.	Coventry City	Wigan Athletic
February 1993		
9 Agnew Stephen M.	Blackburn Rovers	Leicester City
24 Bennett, Frank	Halesowen Town	Southampton
5 Bradder, Gary V.	VS Rugby	Nuneaton Borough

		From	To
25	Buckley, John W.	Scunthorpe United	Rotherham United
19	Chapman, Gary A.	Exeter City	Torquay United
26	Charles, Stephen	Mansfield Town	Scarborough
5	Fashanu, Justin	Torquay United	Airdrieonians
19	Greeno, Michael P.	Fareham Town	Havant Town
25	Harriman, Lee J.	Hinckley Town	VS Rugby
24	Holden, Steven A.	Leicester City	Carlisle United
11	Jordan, David	Ashford Town	Margate
4	Keown, Martin R.	Everton	Arsenal
25	Lucas, Richard	Sheffield United	Preston North End
1	Marples, Christopher	York City	Chesterfield
26	Masefield, Paul D.	Stockport County	Doncaster Rovers
17	Matthews, Neil	Stockport County	Lincoln City
11	Mellon, Michael J.	Bristol City	West Bromwich Albion
12	Murphy, Matthew S.	Corby Town	Oxford United
4	Sansom, Kenneth	Coventry City	Everton
5	Watson, Andrew	Carlisle United	Blackpool
1	Wilson, Paul A.	Halifax Town	Burnley
26	Young, Stuart R.	Hull City	Northampton Town

Temporary transfers

25	Alexander, Timothy M.	Barnet	Woking
1	Barber, Frederick	Peterborough United	Chesterfield
9	Beasant, David	Wolverhampton Wdrs.	Chelsea (Tr. back)
26	Billing, Peter G.	Coventry City	Port Vale
9	Brooks, Christopher	Luton Town	Shrewsbury Town
26	Burgess, David J.	Blackpool	Carlisle United
25	Clarke, Nicholas J.	Mansfield Town	Chesterfield
12	Clarke, Timothy J.	Huddersfield Town	Rochdale
26	Clarke, Timothy J.	Rochdale	Huddersfield Town (Tr. back)
2	Cooper, Geoffrey	Barnet	Welling United
5	Dobson, Paul	Darlington	Gateshead
19	Dixon, Kerry M.	Southampton	Luton Town
5	Fee, Gregory P.	Chesterfield	Mansfield Town (Tr. back)
17	Flounders, Andrew J.	Rochdale	Rotherham United
9	Fowler, John A.	Cambridge United	Preston North End
26	Garnett, Shaun M.	Tranmere Rovers	Wigan Athletic
19	Gilzean, Ian R.	Dundee	Doncaster Rovers
26	Hodges, Lee L.	Tottenham Hotspur	Plymouth Argyle
26	Houghton, Scott A.	Tottenham Hotspur	Charlton Athletic
4	Jackson, Darren W.	Oxford United	Reading
19	Kamara, Christopher	Luton Town	Middlesbrough
24	Lake, Michael	Wrexham	Sheffield United (Tr. back)
11	McIntyre, James	Bristol City	Exeter City
11	Manning, Paul J.	Millwall	Farnborough Town
8	Muir, Johnny G.	Stockport County	Torquay United
19	Mulligan, James	Stoke City	Macclesfield Town
17	Page, Donald R.	Rotherham United	Rochdale
3	Peel, Nathan J.	Sheffield United	Halifax Town
6	Pennyfather, Glenn J.	Ipswich Town	Bristol City
5	Ritchie, Paul M.	Dundee	Gillingham
12	Slawson, Stephen M.	Notts County	Burnley
25	Smark, Mark C.	Notts County	Huddersfield Town
1	Sommer, Jurgen P.	Luton Town	Kettering Town
26	Taylor, Colin D.	Wolverhampton Wdrs.	Doncaster Rovers
12	Thompson, Leslie A.	Burnley	Wycombe Wdrs.

	From	To
12 Tisdale, Paul R.	Southampton	Northampton Town
25 Toman, James A.	Darlington	Scarborough
16 Watts, Julian	Shrewsbury Town	Sheffield Wednesday (Tr. back)
4 Williamson, Daniel A.	West Ham United	Farnborough Town
26 Wilson, Darren A.	Bury	Cliftonville
19 Yates, Mark J.	Burnley	Lincoln City
5 Young, Stuart R.	Hull City	Northampton Town

March 1993

	From	To
25 Bartlett, Kevin F.	Notts County	Cambridge United
25 Beckford, Darren R.	Norwich City	Oldham Athletic
8 Brown, Michael A.	Bolton Wdrs.	Shrewsbury Town
19 Buzaglo, Timothy J.	Woking	Marlow
30 Byrne, Alan	Solihull Borough	Nuneaton Borough
12 Cole, Andrew	Bristol City	Newcastle United
12 Coyne, Thomas	Celtic	Tranmere Rovers
26 Daws, Anthony	Scunthorpe United	Grimsby Town
5 Dobson, Paul	Darlington	Gateshead
19 Dryden, Richard A.	Notts County	Birmingham City
25 Ekoku, Efangwu	AFC Bournemouth	Norwich City
25 Flynn, Michael A.	Preston North End	Stockport County
19 Foy, David L.	Birmingham City	Scunthorpe United
8 Francis, John A.	Cambridge United	Burnley
23 Gallacher, Kevin W.	Coventry City	Blackburn Rovers
25 Greenman, Christopher	Coventry City	Peterborough United
25 Hall, Paul A.	Torquay United	Portsmouth
19 Harford, Michael G.	Chelsea	Sunderland
12 Hiley, Scott	Exeter City	Birmingham City
18 Holmes, Paul	Birmingham City	Everton
12 Hurst, Mark D.	Leicester United	Gresley Rovers
16 James, Martin J.	Preston North End	Stockport County
2 Jenkinson, Leigh	Hull City	Coventry City
11 Kerslake, David	Swindon Town	Leeds United
26 Kristensen, Bjorn	Newcastle United	Portsmouth
3 Lake, Michael C.	Sheffield United	Wrexham
25 Le Saux, Graeme P.	Chelsea	Blackburn Rovers
23 Liburn, Richard	Eastwood Town	Middlesbrough
23 Livingstone, Stephen	Blackburn Rovers	Chelsea
25 Maguire, Gavin T.	Portsmouth	Millwall
12 Moulden, Paul A.	Oldham Athletic	Birmingham City
11 Parris, George M.	West Ham United	Birmingham City
12 Pennyfather, Glenn J.	Ipswich Town	Bristol City
24 Pickering, Nicholas	Darlington	Burnley
8 Platnauer, Nicholas R.	Leicester City	Scunthorpe United
25 Reeves, David	Bolton Wdrs.	Notts County
11 Rennie, David	Birmingham City	Coventry City
9 Robinson, Mark J.	Barnsley	Newcastle United
2 Rosario, Robert M.	Coventry City	Nottingham Forest
25 Sale, Mark D.	Birmingham City	Torquay United
22 Saville, Andrew V.	Hartlepool United	Birmingham City
9 Sellars, Scott	Leeds United	Newcastle United
25 Shail, Mark E. D.	Yeovil Town	Bristol City
19 Slaven, Bernard	Middlesbrough	Port Vale
11 Smith, David	Coventry City	Birmingham City
19 Smith, Gary J.	Sutton Coldfield Town	Worcester City

		From	*To*
4	Stephenson, Paul	Millwall	Brentford
24	Storer, Stuart J.	Bolton Wdrs.	Exeter City
25	Thompstone, Ian P.	Halifax Town	Scunthorpe United
22	Tinnion, Brian	Bradford City	Bristol City
5	Varadi, Imre	Leeds United	Rotherham United
23	Vircavs, Anton	Cheltenham Town	Wycombe Wdrs.
23	Wegerle, Roy C.	Blackburn Rovers	Coventry City

Temporary transfers

25	Aylott, Trevor	Gillingham	Wycombe Wdrs.
25	Banks, Steven	West Ham United	Gillingham
19	Barber, Frederick	Peterborough United	Colchester United
25	Bartlett, Kevin F.	Notts County	Peterborough United
25	Bartlett, Kevin F.	Peterborough United	Notts County (Tr. back)
25	Beadle, Peter C.	Tottenham Hotspur	AFC Bournemouth
25	Beasley, Andrew	Mansfield Town	Bristol Rovers
25	Bowling, Ian	Lincoln City	Bradford City
5	Brain, Simon	Hereford United	Bromsgrove Rovers
25	Byrne, John F.	Millwall	Brighton & Hove Albion
5	Catlin, Robert	Notts County	Birmingham City
25	Cooper, Mark N.	Fulham	Huddersfield Town
3	Crisp, Richard I.	Aston Villa	Scunthorpe United
25	Davidson, Jonathan S.	Preston North End	Chesterfield
18	Digweed, Perry M.	Brighton & Hove Albion	Wimbledon
24	Donowa, Brian L.	Birmingham City	Crystal Palace
19	Duffield, Peter	Sheffield United	Stockport County
25	Ellison, Anthony L.	Darlington	Hartlepool United
18	Emberson, Carl W.	Millwall	Slough Town
19	Emmett, Darren	Bury	Altrincham
11	Farrell, David	Scunthorpe United	Aston Villa (Tr. back)
23	Fitzpatrick, Paul J.	Birmingham City	Bury
25	Fox, Peter D.	Stoke City	Wrexham
25	Gallimore, Anthony	Stoke City	Carlisle United
19	Gardner, Stephen G.	Bury	Witton Albion
19	Gillard, Kenneth J.	Luton Town	Northampton Town
25	Gorton, Andrew	Bury	Altrincham
17	Greenhalgh, Lawrence	Bury	Cliftonville
5	Gridelet, Philip R.	Barnsley	Rotherham United
17	Grobbelaar, Bruce D.	Liverpool	Stoke City
4	Hargreaves, Christian	Grimsby Town	Scarborough
19	Hawke, Warren R.	Sunderland	Northampton Town
17	Hendon, Ian M.	Tottenham Hotspur	Barnsley
23	Hitchcock, Kevin	Chelsea	West Ham United
8	Hockaday, David	Hull City	Stoke City
25	Hunt, Andrew	Newcastle United	West Bromwich Albion
25	Kamara, Christopher	Middlesbrough	Luton Town (Tr. back)
25	Kelly, James	Wolverhampton Wdrs.	Walsall
25	Kelly, Paul	Fulham	Woking
25	Kite, Philip D.	Sheffield United	Stockport County
19	Kristensen, Bjorn	Newcastle United	Portsmouth
19	Lambert, Matthew R.	Bury	Witton Albion
25	Lim, Harvey C.	Gillingham	Kettering Town
6	McDonald, David H.	Tottenham Hotspur	Reading
25	Marshall, Dwight W.	Plymouth Argyle	Middlesbrough
30	Mathie, Alexander M.	Morton	Port Vale
25	Mike, Adrian R.	Manchester City	Bury

		From	To
19	Minett, Jason	Norwich City	Exeter City
19	Mulligan, James	Macclesfield Town	Stoke City (Tr. back)
19	Mulligan, James	Stoke City	Telford United
24	O'Connor, Martin J.	Crystal Palace	Walsall
25	Peters, Robert	Brentford	Woking
22	Pickering, Nicholas	Darlington	Burnley
15	Proctor, Mark G.	Middlesbrough	Tranmere Rovers
19	Reed, John P.	Sheffield United	Darlington
25	Rowbotham, Darren	Birmingham City	Hereford United
12	Rush, Matthew J.	West Ham United	Cambridge United
5	Sale, Mark D.	Birmingham City	Torquay United
25	Smith, Mark C.	Notts County	Chesterfield
25	Sommer, Jurgen P.	Kettering Town	Luton Town (Tr. back)
19	Speedie, David R.	West Bromwich Albion	Southampton (Tr. back)
19	Speedie, David R.	Southampton	West Ham United
24	Thomas, Martin R.	Birmingham City	Crystal Palace
25	Turner, Robert P.	Notts County	Shrewsbury Town
25	Wallace, David L.	Manchester United	Millwall
25	Williams, Wayne	Walsall	Kidderminster Harriers
25	Williams, William J.	Cardiff City	Yeovil Town
15	Williamson, Daniel A.	Farnborough Town	West Ham United (Tr. back)

April 1993

22	Beeney, Mark R.	Brighton & Hove Albion	Leeds United
8	Carr, Franz A.	Newcastle United	Sheffield United
20	Gillard, Kenneth J.	Luton Town	Northampton Town

Temporary transfers

20	Broddle, Julian	Partick Thistle	Preston North End
24	Digweed, Perry M.	Wimbledon	Brighton & Hove Albion (Tr. back)
13	Fowler, John A.	Preston North End	Cambridge United (Tr. back)
2	Fox, Peter D.	Wrexham	Stoke City (Tr. back)
8	Gridelet, Philip R.	Rotherham United	Barnsley (Tr. back)
2	Grobbelaar, Bruce D.	Stoke City	Liverpool (Tr. back)
29	Kee, Paul	Oxford United	Wimbledon
13	Thomas, Martin R.	Crystal Palace	Birmingham City (Tr. back)

May 1993

17	Brown, Ian	Chelmsford City	Bristol City
21	Jules, Mark A.	Scarborough	Chesterfield
14	Miller, Kevin	Exeter City	Birmingham City

FA CUP REVIEW

Arsenal completed a unique cup double when they beat Sheffield Wednesday at the second attempt in the FA Cup final, having earlier defeated the Owls in the Coca-Cola Cup. Manager George Graham became the first to lead a team to both domestic trophies in one season.

The history of the occasion will survive the memory of the two matches involved, which both needed extra time before reaching a conclusion. The original game was fast, furious and flawed. Wednesday had the territorial advantage but trailed after 21 minutes to a headed goal from Ian Wright.

Despite forcing a stream of corners, Wednesday were unable to break through a solid Arsenal defence behind which goalkeeper David Seaman was in safe-handling form.

But their pressure rather than any guile eventually led to an equaliser from David Hirst after 61 minutes. Extra time produced more of the same, though with both teams tiring, neither wanted to risk too much adventure.

The teams reappeared on the following Thursday in front of a smaller crowd, many Wednesday patrons understandably being unable to finance yet another trip to Wembley.

There was no noticeable improvement in the standard of play, which was developed on a background of heavy rain. Arsenal again took the lead through Wright who outwitted a hesitant Chris Woods following Alan Smith's finely-judged opening in the 34th minute.

But Wednesday again hauled themselves back into contention after 68 minutes when Chris Waddle, the Football Writers' Player of the Year, hit an angled shot which was deflected past Seaman.

There were several unpleasant incidents, not all of which were punished or acknowledged by the referee. However the worst confrontation involved Mark Bright elbowing Andy Linighan in an aerial clash. Bright was booked and Linighan received a broken nose and dislocated finger.

Play did brighten up despite the weather as both teams became conscious that at the end of extra time penalty kicks would be required to separate the contestants. And it was Linighan who had the last laugh, heading in Paul Merson's in-swinging corner in the last minute, to put the few uncommitted out of their misery, Wednesday into it and Arsenal to ecstasy.

FINAL at Wembley
15 MAY
Arsenal (1) 1 *(Wright)*
Sheffield W (0) 1 (Hirst) aet 79,347
Arsenal: Seaman; Dixon, Winterburn, Davis, Linighan, Adams, Jensen, Wright (O'Leary), Campbell, Merson, Parlour (Smith).
Sheffield W: Woods; Nilsson, Worthington, Palmer, Anderson (Hyde), Warhurst, Harkes, Waddle (Bart-Williams), Hirst, Bright, Sheridan.
Referee: K. Barratt (Coventry).
FINAL REPLAY at Wembley
20 MAY
Arsenal (1) 2 *(Wright, Linighan)*
Sheffield W (0) 1 *(Waddle) aet* 62,267
Arsenal: Seaman; Dixon, Winterburn, Davis, Linighan, Adams, Jensen, Wright (O'Leary), Smith, Merson, Campbell.
Sheffield W: Woods; Nilsson (Bart-Williams), Worthington, Harkes, Palmer, Warhurst, Wilson (Hyde), Waddle, Hirst, Bright, Sheridan.
Referee: K. Barratt (Coventry).

FA CUP 1992–93

First Round

Accrington S	(1) 3	Gateshead	(1) 2
Blackpool	(1) 1	Rochdale	(1) 1
Blyth S	(1) 1	Southport	(1) 1
Bolton W	(1) 2	Sutton Cd	(0) 1
Bournemouth	(0) 0	Barnet	(0) 0
Bradford C	(0) 1	Preston NE	(0) 1
Brighton & HA	(1) 2	Hayes	(0) 0
Burnley	(1) 2	Scarborough	(0) 1
Bury	(1) 2	Witton Alb	(0) 0
Cardiff C	(2) 2	Bath C	(1) 3
Chester C	(1) 1	Altrincham	(0) 1
Colchester U	(2) 4	Slough	(0) 0
Crewe Alex	(2) 6	Wrexham	(0) 1
Dagenham & Redbge	(3) 4	Leyton Orient	(2) 5
Darlington	(0) 1	Hull C	(0) 2
Doncaster R	(1) 1	Hartlepool U	(0) 2
Exeter C	(1) 1	Kidderminster H	(0) 0
Gillingham	(2) 3	Kettering T	(1) 2
Kingstonian	(1) 1	Peterborough U	(0) 1
Lincoln C	(0) 0	Stafford R	(0) 0
Macclesfield	(0) 0	Chesterfield	(0) 0
Marine	(3) 4	Halifax T	(0) 1
Marlow	(1) 3	Salisbury	(2) 3
Northampton T	(2) 3	Fulham	(0) 1
Rotherham U	(2) 4	Walsall	(0) 0
Scunthorpe U	(0) 0	Huddersfield T	(0) 0
Shrewsbury T	(2) 3	Mansfield T	(1) 1
Solihull	(2) 2	VS Rugby	(1) 2
St Albans	(0) 1	Cheltenham T	(0) 2
Sutton U	(1) 1	Hereford U	(1) 2
Torquay U	(0) 2	Yeovil	(1) 5
WBA	(4) 8	Aylesbury	(0) 0
Wigan Ath	(3) 3	Carlisle U	(1) 1
Woking	(1) 3	Nuneaton	(1) 1
Wycombe W	(2) 3	Merthyr T	(1) 1
York C	(0) 1	Stockport Co	(0) 3
Dorking	(1) 2	Plymouth Arg	(1) 3
Reading	(1) 1	Birmingham C	(0) 0
Stoke C	(0) 0	Port Vale	(0) 0

First Round Replays

Port Vale	(2) 3	Stoke C	(1) 1
Altrincham	(0) 2	Chester C	(0) 0
Barnet	(0) 1	Bournemouth	(2) 2
Chesterfield	(1) 2	Macclesfield*	(1) 2
Huddersfield T	(1) 2	Scunthorpe U	(0) 1
Peterborough U	(3) 9	Kingstonian	(0) 1

Replay ordered after missile from crowd hit Kingstonian goalkeeper

120

Preston NE	(1) 4	Bradford C	(3) 5
Rochdale	(0) 1	Blackpool	(0) 0
VS Rugby	(0) 2	Solihull	(1) 1
Stafford R	(1) 2	Lincoln C	(0) 1
Peterborough U	(0) 1	Kingstonian	(0) 0
Salisbury	(1) 2	Marlow*	(0) 2

Second Round

Accrington S	(0) 1	Crewe Alex	(2) 6
Altrincham	(0) 1	Port Vale	(2) 4
Bolton W	(1) 4	Rochdale	(0) 0
Brighton & HA	(1) 1	Woking	(0) 1
Burnley	(0) 1	Shrewsbury T	(0) 1
Cheltenham T	(0) 1	Bournemouth	(1) 1
Gillingham	(1) 1	Colchester U	(0) 1
Macclesfield	(0) 0	Stockport Co	(1) 2
Marine	(2) 3	Stafford R	(0) 0
Reading	(2) 3	Leyton Orient	(0) 0
Rotherham U	(0) 1	Hull C	(0) 0
Yeovil	(0) 0	Hereford U	(0) 0
Bath C	(0) 2	Northampton T	(0) 2
Bradford C	(0) 0	Huddersfield T	(1) 2
Hartlepool U	(0) 4	Southport	(0) 0
Wycombe W	(0) 2	WBA	(2) 2
Plymouth Arg	(2) 3	Peterborough U	(0) 2
VS Rugby	(0) 0	Marlow	(0) 0
Exeter C	(1) 2	Swansea C	(2) 5
Wigan Ath	(0) 1	Bury	(1) 1

Second Round Replays

Northampton T	(0) 3	Bath C	(0) 0
Shrewsbury T	(0) 1	Burnley	(0) 2
WBA	(0) 1	Wycombe W	(0) 0
Bournemouth	(1) 3	Cheltenham T	(0) 0
Colchester U	(0) 2	Gillingham	(3) 3
Hereford U	(0) 1	Yeovil	(1) 2
Marlow	(0) 2	VS Rugby	(0) 0
Woking	(1) 1	Brighton & HA	(1) 2
Bury	(0) 1	Wigan Ath	(0) 0

Third Round

Aston Villa	(1) 1	Bristol R	(0) 1
Blackburn R	(0) 3	Bournemouth	(1) 1
Brentford	(0) 0	Grimsby T	(1) 2
Brighton & HA	(1) 1	Portsmouth	(0) 0
Derby Co	(1) 2	Stockport Co	(0) 1
Gillingham	(0) 0	Huddersfield T	(0) 0
Hartlepool U	(0) 1	Crystal Palace	(0) 0
Leeds U	(0) 1	Charlton Ath	(0) 1
Manchester C	(0) 1	Reading	(1) 1

Marlow	(0) 1	Tottenham H	(2) 5
Newcastle U	(0) 4	Port Vale	(0) 0
Oldham Ath	(0) 2	Tranmere R	(2) 2
Sheffield U	(0) 2	Burnley	(2) 2
Swansea C	(0) 1	Oxford U	(0) 1
Watford	(1) 1	Wolverhampton W	(1) 4
WBA	(0) 0	West Ham U	(2) 2
Wimbledon	(0) 0	Everton	(0) 0
Yeovil	(0) 1	Arsenal	(2) 3
Bolton W	(2) 2	Liverpool	(0) 2
Nottingham F	(2) 2	Southampton	(1) 1
QPR	(3) 3	Swindon T	(0) 0
Manchester U	(1) 2	Bury	(0) 0
Crewe Alex	(3) 3	Marine	(0) 1
Ipswich T	(1) 3	Plymouth Arg	(1) 1
Northampton T	(0) 0	Rotherham U	(0) 1
Notts Co	(0) 0	Sunderland	(1) 2
Cambridge U	(0) 1	Sheffield W	(0) 2
Leicester C	(0) 2	Barnsley	(1) 2
Middlesbrough	(0) 2	Chelsea	(0) 1
Norwich C	(0) 1	Coventry C	(0) 0
Southend U	(1) 1	Millwall	(0) 0
Luton T	(1) 2	Bristol C	(0) 0

Third Round Replays

Burnley	(1) 2	Sheffield U	(3) 4
Everton	(0) 1	Wimbledon	(1) 2
Oxford U	(0) 2	Swansea C*	(0) 2
Tranmere R	(1) 3	Oldham Ath	(0) 0
Charlton Ath	(0) 1	Leeds U	(1) 3
Huddersfield T	(1) 2	Gillingham	(0) 1
Liverpool	(0) 0	Bolton W	(1) 2
Reading	(0) 0	Manchester C	(2) 4
Barnsley*	(0) 1	Leicester C	(1) 1
Bristol R	(0) 0	Aston Villa	(1) 3

Fourth Round

Aston Villa	(1) 1	Wimbledon	(1) 1
Crewe Alex	(0) 0	Blackburn R	(1) 3
Huddersfield T	(1) 1	Southend U	(1) 2
Luton T	(1) 1	Derby Co	(3) 5
Manchester U	(0) 1	Brighton & HA	(0) 0
Nottingham F	(0) 1	Middlesbrough	(1) 1
QPR	(0) 1	Manchester C	(0) 2
Rotherham U	(0) 1	Newcastle U	(1) 1
Sheffield U	(0) 1	Hartlepool U	(0) 0
Tranmere R	(1) 1	Ipswich T	(0) 2
Barnsley	(2) 4	West Ham U	(0) 1
Norwich C	(0) 0	Tottenham H	(1) 2
Sheffield W	(0) 1	Sunderland	(0) 0
Wolverhampton W	(0) 0	Bolton W	(2) 2

Arsenal	(0) 2	Leeds U	(2) 2
Swansea C	(0) 0	Grimsby T	(0) 0

Fourth Round Replays

Leeds U	(0) 2	Arsenal	(0) 3
Middlesbrough	(0) 0	Nottingham F	(2) 3
Newcastle U	(0) 2	Rotherham	(0) 0
Wimbledon*	(0) 0	Aston Villa	(0) 0
Grimsby T	(1) 2	Swansea C	(0) 0

Fifth Round

Arsenal	(2) 2	Nottingham F	(0) 0
Blackburn R	(0) 1	Newcastle U	(0) 0
Derby Co	(1) 3	Bolton W	(1) 1
Ipswich T	(1) 4	Grimsby T	(0) 0
Manchester C	(1) 2	Barnsley	(0) 0
Sheffield W	(1) 2	Southend U	(0) 0
Sheffield U	(2) 2	Manchester U	(1) 1
Tottenham H	(3) 3	Wimbledon	(0) 2

Sixth Round

Sheffield W	(0) 0	Blackburn R	(0) 0
Ipswich T	(1) 2	Arsenal	(1) 4
Manchester C	(1) 2	Tottenham H	(2) 4
Derby Co	(1) 3	Sheffield W	(2) 3

Sixth Round Replays

Sheffield W	(1) 1	Derby Co	(0) 0
Blackburn R	(0) 0	Sheffield U*	(0) 0

Semi-finals

Sheffield U	(1) 1	Sheffield W	(1) 2
Arsenal	(0) 1	Tottenham H	(0) 0

Final

Arsenal	(1) 1	Sheffield W	(0) 1

Replay

Arsenal	(1) 2	Sheffield W	(0) 1

*Won on penalties

PAST FA CUP FINALS

Details of some goalscorers are not available for the early years

1872	The Wanderers .... 1 *Betts*	Royal Engineers........................0		
1873	The Wanderers .... 2 *Kinnaird, Wollaston*	Oxford University 0		
1874	Oxford University .... 2 *Mackarness, Patton*	Royal Engineers........................0		
1875	Royal Engineers............ 1 *Renny-Tailyour*	Old Etonians ....1* *Bonsor*		
Replay	Royal Engineers............ 2 *Renny-Tailyour, Stafford*	Old Etonians 0		
1876	The Wanderers .... 1 *Edwards*	Old Etonians ....1* *Bonsor*		
Replay	The Wanderers .... 3 *Wollaston, Hughes 2*	Old Etonians 0		
1877	The Wanderers .... 2 *Kenrick, Heron*	Oxford University ....1* *Kinnaird (og)*		
1878	The Wanderers .... 3 *Kenrick 2, unknown*	Royal Engineers........................1 *Unknown*		
1879	Old Etonians .... 1 *Clerke*	Clapham Rovers 0		
1880	Clapham Rovers .... 1 *Lloyd-Jones*	Oxford University 0		
1881	Old Carthusians .... 3 *Wyngard, Parry, Todd*	Old Etonians 0		
1882	Old Etonians .... 1 *Anderson*	Blackburn Rovers....................0		
1883	Blackburn Olympic....... 2 *Costley, Matthews*	Old Etonians ....1* *Goodhart*		
1884	Blackburn Rovers.......... 2 *Brown, Forrest*	Queen's Park, Glasgow ....1 *Christie*		
1885	Blackburn Rovers.......... 2 *Forrest, Brown*	Queen's Park, Glasgow 0		
1886	Blackburn Rovers.......... 0	West Bromwich Albion 0		
Replay	Blackburn Rovers.......... 2 *Brown, Sowerbutts*	West Bromwich Albion 0		
1887	Aston Villa .... 2 *Hunter, Hodgetts*	West Bromwich Albion 0		
1888	West Bromwich Albion . 2 *Woodhall, Bayliss*	Preston NE ....1 *Goodall*		
1889	Preston NE .... 3 *Dewhurst, Ross, Thompson*	Wolverhampton W 0		
1890	Blackburn Rovers.......... 6 *Dewar, John, Southworth, Lofthouse, Townley 3*	Sheffield W ....1 *Bennett*		

1891	Blackburn Rovers.........3	Notts Co............................1	
	Dewar, John Southworth, Townley	*Oswald*	
1892	West Bromwich Albion . 3	Aston Villa 0	
	Geddes, Nicholls, Reynolds		
1893	Wolverhampton W 1	Everton 0	
	Allen		
1894	Notts Co......................4	Bolton W..............................1	
	Watson, Logan 3	*Cassidy*	
1895	Aston Villa 1	West Bromwich Albion 0	
	Devey		
1896	Sheffield W 2	Wolverhampton W 1	
	Spiksley 2	*Black*	
1897	Aston Villa 3	Everton 2	
	Campbell, Wheldon, Crabtree	*Boyle, Bell*	
1898	Nottingham F 3	Derby Co 1	
	Capes 2, McPherson	*Bloomer*	
1899	Sheffield U..................4	Derby Co 1	
	Bennett, Beers, Almond, Priest	*Boag*	
1900	Bury 4	Southampton 0	
	McLuckie 2, Wood, Plant		
1901	Tottenham H 2	Sheffield U............................2	
	Brown 2	*Bennett, Priest*	
Replay	Tottenham H 3	Sheffield U............................1	
	Cameron, Smith, Brown	*Priest*	
1902	Sheffield U..................1	Southampton 1	
	Common	*Wood*	
Replay	Sheffield U..................2	Southampton 1	
	Hedley, Barnes	*Brown*	
1903	Bury 6	Derby Co 0	
	Ross, Sagar, Leeming 2, Wood, Plant		
1904	Manchester C 1	Bolton W..............................0	
	Meredith		
1905	Aston Villa 2	Newcastle U...........................0	
	Hampton 2		
1906	Everton 1	Newcastle U...........................0	
	Young		
1907	Sheffield W 2	Everton 1	
	Stewart, Simpson	*Sharp*	
1908	Wolverhampton W 3	Newcastle U...........................1	
	Hunt, Hedley, Harrison	*Howie*	
1909	Manchester U 1	Bristol C..............................0	
	A. Turnbull		
1910	Newcastle U.................1	Barnsley 1	
	Rutherford	*Tuffnell*	
Replay	Newcastle U.................2	Barnsley 0	
	Shepherd 2 (1 pen)		

125

1911	Bradford C 0	Newcastle U 0
Replay	Bradford C 1	Newcastle U 0
	Spiers	
1912	Barnsley 0	West Bromwich Albion 0
Replay	Barnsley 1	West Bromwich Albion 0*
	Tuffnell	
1913	Aston Villa 1	Sunderland........................0
	Barber	
1914	Burnley 1	Liverpool..........................0
	Freeman	
1915	Sheffield U 3	Chelsea 0
	Simmons, Fazackerley, Kitchen	
1920	Aston Villa 1	Huddersfield T....................0*
	Kirton	
1921	Tottenham H............... 1	Wolverhampton W 0
	Dimmock	
1922	Huddersfield T.............. 1	Preston NE 0
	Smith (pen)	
1923	Bolton W..................... 2	West Ham U 0
	Jack, J.R. Smith	
1924	Newcastle U 2	Aston Villa 0
	Harris, Seymour	
1925	Sheffield U 1	Cardiff C 0
	Tunstall	
1926	Bolton W..................... 1	Manchester C 0
	Jack	
1927	Cardiff C 1	Arsenal 0
	Ferguson	
1928	Blackburn Rovers..........3	Huddersfield T.....................1
	Roscamp 2, McLean	*A. Jackson*
1929	Bolton W..................... 2	Portsmouth 0
	Butler, Blackmore	
1930	Arsenal 2	Huddersfield T....................0
	James, Lambert	
1931	West Bromwich Albion . 2	Birmingham 1
	W.G. Richardson 2	*Bradford*
1932	Newcastle U 2	Arsenal 1
	Allen 2	*John*
1933	Everton 3	Manchester C 0
	Stein, Dean, Dunn	
1934	Manchester C 2	Portsmouth 1
	Tilson 2	*Rutherford*
1935	Sheffield W 4	West Bromwich Albion 2
	Rimmer 2, Palethorpe, Hooper	*Boyes, Sandford*
1936	Arsenal 1	Sheffield U........................0
	Drake	
1937	Sunderland.................. 3	Preston NE 1
	Gurney, Carter, Burbanks	*F. O'Donnell*

1938	Preston NE 1	Huddersfield T 0*
	Mutch (pen)	
1939	Portsmouth 4	Wolverhampton W 1
	Parker 2, Barlow,	*Dorsett*
	Anderson	
1946	Derby Co 4	Charlton Ath 1*
	H. Turner (og), Doherty,	*H. Turner*
	Stamps 2	
1947	Charlton Ath 1	Burnley 0*
	Duffy	
1948	Manchester U 4	Blackpool 2
	Rowley 2, Pearson,	*Shimwell (pen), Mortensen*
	Anderson	
1949	Wolverhampton W 3	Leicester C 1
	Pye 2, Smyth,	*Griffiths*
1950	Arsenal 2	Liverpool 0
	Lewis 2	
1951	Newcastle U 2	Blackpool 0
	Milburn 2	
1952	Newcastle U 1	Arsenal 0
	G. Robledo	
1953	Blackpool 4	Bolton W 3
	Mortensen 3, Perry	*Lofthouse, Moir, Bell*
1954	West Bromwich Albion ...	Preston NE 2
	Allen 2 (1 pen), Griffin	*Morrison, Wayman*
1955	Newcastle U 3	Manchester C 1
	Milburn, Mitchell,	*Johnstone*
	Hannah	
1956	Manchester C 3	Birmingham C 1
	Hayes, Dyson, Johnstone	*Kinsey*
1957	Aston Villa 2	Manchester U 1
	McParland 2	*T. Taylor*
1958	Bolton W 2	Manchester U 0
	Lofthouse 2	
1959	Nottingham F 2	Luton T 1
	Dwight, Wilson	*Pacey*
1960	Wolverhampton W 3	Blackburn Rovers 0
	McGrath (og), Deeley 2	
1961	Tottenham H 2	Leicester C 0
	Smith, Dyson	
1962	Tottenham H 3	Burnley 1
	Greaves, Smith,	*Robson*
	Blanchflower (pen)	
1963	Manchester U 3	Leicester C 1
	Herd 2, Law	*Keyworth*
1964	West Ham U 3	Preston NE 2
	Sissons, Hurst, Boyce	*Holden, Dawson*
1965	Liverpool 2	Leeds U 1*
	Hunt, St John	*Bremner*

1966	Everton 3	Sheffield W 2	
	Trebilcock 2, Temple	*McCalliog, Ford*	
1967	Tottenham H.............2	Chelsea 1	
	Robertson, Saul	*Tambling*	
1968	West Bromwich Albion .1	Everton 0*	
	Astle		
1969	Manchester C 1	Leicester C 0	
	Young		
1970	Chelsea 2	Leeds U 2*	
	Houseman, Hutchinson	*Charlton, Jones*	
Replay	Chelsea 2	Leeds U 1*	
	Osgood, Webb	*Jones*	
1971	Arsenal 2	Liverpool.............1*	
	Kelly, George	*Heighway*	
1972	Leeds U 1	Arsenal 0	
	Clarke		
1973	Sunderland 1	Leeds U 0	
	Porterfield		
1974	Liverpool.............3	Newcastle 0	
	Keegan 2, Heighway		
1975	West Ham U 2	Fulham.............0	
	A. Taylor 2		
1976	Southampton 1	Manchester U.............0	
	Stokes		
1977	Manchester U 2	Liverpool.............1	
	Pearson, J. Greenhoff	*Case*	
1978	Ipswich T.............1	Arsenal 0	
	Osborne		
1979	Arsenal 3	Manchester U.............2	
	Talbot, Stapleton,	*McQueen, McIlroy*	
	Sunderland		
1980	West Ham U 1	Arsenal 0	
	Brooking		
1981	Tottenham H.............1	Manchester C.............1*	
	Hutchison (og)	*Hutchison*	
Replay	Tottenham H.............3	Manchester C.............2	
	Villa 2, Crooks	*Mackenzie, Reeves (pen)*	
1982	Tottenham H.............1	QPR.............1*	
	Hoddle	*Fenwick*	
Replay	Tottenham H.............1	QPR.............0	
	Hoddle (pen)		
1983	Manchester U 2	Brighton & HA 2*	
	Stapleton, Wilkins	*Smith, Stevens*	
Replay	Manchester U 4	Brighton & HA 0	
	Robson 2, Whiteside, Muhren (pen)		
1984	Everton 2	Watford.............0	
	Sharp, Gray		
1985	Manchester U 1	Everton 0*	
	Whiteside		

1986	Liverpool 3	Everton 1
	Rush 2, Johnston	*Lineker*
1987	Coventry C 3	Tottenham H.............................2*
	Bennett, Houchen,	*C. Allen, Kilcline (og)*
	Mabbutt (og)	
1988	Wimbledon 1	Liverpool 0
	Sanchez	
1989	Liverpool 3	Everton 2*
	Aldridge, Rush 2	*McCall 2*
1990	Manchester U 3	Crystal Palace 3*
	Robson, Hughes 2	*O'Reilly, Wright 2*
Replay	Manchester U 1	Crystal P 0
	Martin	
1991	Tottenham H................ 2	Nottingham F 1*
	Stewart, Walker (og)	*Pearce*
1992	Liverpool 2	Sunderland.................................0
	Thomas, Rush	
1993	Arsenal 1	Sheffield W 1
	Wright	*Hirst*
Replay	Arsenal 2	Sheffield W 1
	Wright Linighan	*Waddle*

*After extra-time

FA CUP WINNERS SINCE 1871

Tottenham Hotspur 8	Barnsley 1
Aston Villa 7	Blackburn Olympic 1
Manchester United 7	Blackpool 1
Blackburn Rovers 6	Bradford City 1
Newcastle United 6	Burnley 1
Arsenal 6	Cardiff City 1
Liverpool 5	Charlton Athletic 1
The Wanderers 5	Chelsea 1
West Bromwich Albion 5	Clapham Rovers 1
Bolton Wanderers 4	Coventry City 1
Everton 4	Derby County 1
Manchester City 4	Huddersfield Town 1
Sheffield United 4	Ipswich Town 1
Wolverhampton Wanderers 4	Leeds United 1
Sheffield Wednesday 3	Notts County 1
West Ham United 3	Old Carthusians 1
Bury 2	Oxford University 1
Nottingham Forest..................... 2	Portsmouth 1
Old Etonians 2	Royal Engineers 1
Preston North End 2	Southampton 1
Sunderland............................... 2	Wimbledon 1

APPEARANCES IN FA CUP FINAL

Arsenal	12	Burnley	3
Everton	11	Chelsea	3
Manchester United	11	Nottingham Forest	3
Newcastle United	11	Portsmouth	3
Liverpool	10	Southampton	3
West Bromwich Albion	10	Barnsley	2
Aston Villa	9	Birmingham City	2
Tottenham Hotspur	9	Bury	2
Blackburn Rovers	8	Cardiff City	2
Manchester City	8	Charlton Athletic	2
Wolverhampton Wanderers	8	Clapham Rovers	2
Bolton Wanderers	7	Notts County	2
Preston North End	7	Queen's Park (Glasgow)	2
Old Etonians	6	Blackburn Olympic	1
Sheffield United	6	Bradford City	1
Huddersfield Town	5	Brighton & Hove Albion	1
Sheffield Wednesday	6	Bristol City	1
The Wanderers	5	Coventry City	1
Derby County	4	Crystal Palace	1
Leeds United	4	Fulham	1
Leicester City	4	Ipswich Town	1
Oxford University	4	Luton Town	1
Royal Engineers	4	Old Carthusians	1
Sunderland	4	Queen's Park Rangers	1
West Ham United	4	Watford	1
Blackpool	3	Wimbledon	1

COCA-COLA CUP REVIEW

Coca-Cola took over the sponsorship of the League Cup when Rumbelows decided to discontinue their involvement at the start of the season. It was also the first time clubs from outside the Football League had taken part, the Premier League being under the auspices of the Football Association. But the winners again qualify for a place in the UEFA Cup.

The holders of the Rumbelows Cup, Manchester United were knocked out in the third round, losing 1-0 to Aston Villa. They in turn were beaten by the same scoreline in a replay at Ipswich in round four. By the arrival of the fifth round, Cambridge United were the sole representatives from the Football League and they were edged out 3-2 at Blackburn.

However, the near shock of the second round happened at Anfield where Liverpool found themselves 3-0 and then 4-2 down to Chesterfield before recovering to draw 4-4. Then Liverpool easily won at Saltergate 4-1.

Two teams managed seven goals in a game, Derby County beating Southend United 7-0 in the second leg of their second round tie and Sheffield Wednesday having a 7-1 success over Leicester City in the next round.

Wednesday eventually reached the final, their other victims being Hartlepool United, QPR, Ipswich after a replay and Blackburn Rovers in the semi-final. They scored freely at times, 24 goals in all before the final.

In contrast their opponents Arsenal only survived the second round on penalty kicks against Millwall after both games ended 1-1. They also drew 1-1 at Derby in the third round before winning the replay 2-1. After a 1-0 win at Scarborough and it was not until the fifth round that they managed a win of more than one goal. Then they beat Nottingham Forest 2-0. But in the semi-final they won 3-1 at Crystal Palace and 2-0 in the second leg at Highbury.

At Wembley, Sheffield Wednesday made the first serious goal attempt when Paul Warhurst hit a post and they took the lead in the ninth minute when John Harkes drove in from the edge of the area following a free-kick which was not properly cleared. Arsenal equalised when a free-kick was headed out and fell to Paul Merson who scored with a swerving shot from 20 yards after 18 minutes. Kevin Campbell hit a post for Arsenal and the Gunners began to look the more composed team.

The second half was a much duller affair with Wednesday unable to complete a final pass of any consequence and Arsenal content to threaten them on the break. In the 68th minute a cross by Merson was not cleared by Carlton Palmer and Steve Morrow pounced to score his first goal for the club. Ian Wright had a goal disallowed for a foul and despite making desperate substitutions Wednesday were unable to fashion a goal. But there was drama after the final whistle when Arsenal captain Tony Adams hoisted hero Morrow and dropped him, breaking his arm in the process.

FINAL at Wembley
18 APR
Arsenal (1) 2 *(Merson, Morrow)*

Sheffield W (1) 1 *(Harkes)*   74,007

Arsenal: Seaman; O'Leary, Winterburn, Parlour, Adams, Linighan, Morrow, Merson, Wright, Campbell, Davis.
Sheffield W: Woods; Nilsson, King (Hyde), Palmer, Anderson, Harkes, Wilson (Hirst), Waddle, Warhurst, Bright, Sheridan.
Referee: A. Gunn (Sussex).

COCA-COLA CUP 1992–93

First Round, First Leg

Bolton W	(2) 2	Port Vale	(0) 1
Cardiff C	(1) 1	Bristol C	(0) 0
Carlisle U	(2) 4	Burnley	(0) 1
Chesterfield	(0) 2	York C	(0) 0
Colchester U	(0) 1	Brighton & HA	(0) 1
Crewe Alex	(3) 4	Rochdale	(0) 1
Darlington	(0) 1	Scunthorpe U	(0) 0
Doncaster R	(0) 0	Lincoln C	(2) 3
Exeter C	(0) 0	Birmingham C	(0) 0
Fulham	(0) 0	Brentford	(1) 2
Gillingham	(1) 2	Northampton T	(0) 1
Halifax T	(0) 1	Hartlepool U	(1) 2
Hereford U	(2) 2	Torquay U	(0) 2
Hull C	(1) 2	Rotherham U	(1) 2
Leyton Orient	(1) 2	Millwall	(0) 2
Oxford U	(1) 3	Swansea C	(0) 0
Peterborough U	(2) 4	Barnet	(0) 1
Preston NE	(1) 2	Stoke C	(1) 1
Shrewsbury T	(0) 1	Wigan Ath	(1) 2
Stockport Co	(1) 1	Chester C	(0) 0
Sunderland	(0) 2	Huddersfield T	(2) 3
Wrexham	(0) 1	Bury	(0) 0
Grimsby T	(1) 1	Barnsley	(1) 1
Newcastle U	(1) 2	Mansfield T	(0) 1
Scarborough	(2) 3	Bradford C	(0) 0
Tranmere R	(0) 3	Blackpool	(0) 0
Walsall	(1) 1	Bournemouth	(0) 1
WBA	(1) 1	Plymouth Arg	(0) 0

First Round, Second Leg

Barnet	(1) 2	Peterborough U	(1) 2
Barnsley	(0) 1	Grimsby T	†(1) 1*
Birmingham C	(0) 1	Exeter C	(2) 4
Blackpool	(0) 4	Tranmere R	(0) 0
Bournemouth	(0) 0	Walsall	(0) 1
Brentford	(0) 2	Fulham	(0) 0
Bristol C	(3) 5	Cardiff C	(0) 1
Burnley	(0) 1	Carlisle U	(1) 1
Bury	(1) 4	Wrexham	(1) 3
Chester C	(0) 1	Stockport Co	(1) 2
Hartlepool U	(2) 3	Halifax T	(2) 2
Lincoln C	(0) 1	Doncaster R	(1) 1
Mansfield T	(0) 0	Newcastle U	(0) 0
Plymouth Arg	(1) 2	WBA	(0) 0
Port Vale	(1) 1	Bolton W	(1) 1
Rochdale	(1) 1	Crewe Alex	(0) 2
Rotherham U	(1) 1	Hull C	(0) 0
Scunthorpe U	(2) 2	Darlington	(0) 0

Swansea C	(1) 1	Oxford U	(0) 0
Torquay U	(2) 5	Hereford U	(0) 0
Wigan Ath	††(0) 0	Shrewsbury T	(1) 1*
York C	(0) 0	Chesterfield	(0) 0
Bradford C	(2) 3	Scarborough	(3) 5
Brighton & HA	(0) 1	Colchester U	(0) 0
Huddersfield T	††(0) 0	Sunderland	(0) 1*
Millwall	(2) 3	Leyton Orient	(0) 0
Stoke C	(0) 4	Preston NE	(0) 0*
Northampton T	(0) 0	Gillingham	(0) 2

Second Round, First Leg

Tottenham H	(1) 3	Brentford	(0) 1
Arsenal	(0) 1	Millwall	(0) 1
Bolton W	(0) 1	Wimbledon	(2) 3
Bristol C	(2) 2	Sheffield U	(1) 1
Bury	(0) 0	Charlton Ath	(0) 0
Cambridge U	(1) 2	Stoke C	(1) 2
Carlisle U	(1) 2	Norwich C	(0) 2
Crystal Palace	(1) 3	Lincoln C	(0) 1
Exeter C	(0) 0	Oldham Ath	(0) 1
Leeds U	(2) 4	Scunthorpe U	(0) 1
Liverpool	(0) 4	Chesterfield	(2) 4
Notts Co	(3) 3	Wolverhampton W	(1) 2
Watford	(1) 2	Reading	(1) 2
Wigan Ath	(0) 2	Ipswich T	(1) 2
Blackpool	(0) 0	Portsmouth	(0) 4
Brighton & HA	(0) 1	Manchester U	(1) 1
Coventry C	(0) 2	Scarborough	(0) 0
Gillingham	(0) 0	Southampton	(0) 0
Huddersfield T	(0) 1	Blackburn R	(0) 1
Leicester C	(0) 2	Peterborough U	(0) 0
Luton T	(1) 2	Plymouth Arg	(0) 2
Manchester C	(0) 0	Bristol R	(0) 0
Newcastle U	(0) 0	Middlesbrough	(0) 0
Oxford U	(0) 1	Aston Villa	(0) 2
QPR	(1) 2	Grimsby T	(0) 1
Rotherham U	(1) 1	Everton	(0) 0
Sheffield W	(0) 3	Hartlepool U	(0) 0
Southend U	(0) 0	Derby Co	(0) 0
Stockport Co	(1) 2	Nottingham F	(1) 3
Torquay U	(0) 0	Swindon T	(3) 6
Walsall	(0) 0	Chelsea	(2) 3
West Ham U	(0) 0	Crewe Alex	(0) 0

Second Round, Second Leg

Blackburn R	(1) 4	Huddersfield T	(0) 3*
Chesterfield	(1) 1	Liverpool	(3) 4
Grimsby T	(0) 2	QPR	†(0) 1*
Hartlepool U	(0) 2	Sheffield W	(1) 2
Ipswich T	(2) 4	Wigan Ath	(0) 0
Lincoln C	(1) 1	Crystal Palace	(1) 1

133

Peterborough U	(2) 2	Leicester C	(1) 1
Plymouth Arg	(1) 3	Luton T	(0) 2
Portsmouth	(1) 2	Blackpool	(0) 0
Swindon T	(3) 3	Torquay U	(0) 2
Wimbledon	(0) 0	Bolton W	(0) 1
Aston Villa	(1) 2	Oxford U	(0) 1
Brentford	(1) 2	Tottenham H	(2) 4
Bristol R	(0) 1	Manchester C	(0) 2*
Charlton Ath	(0) 0	Bury	(0) 1
Chelsea	(0) 1	Walsall	(0) 0
Crewe Alex	(0) 2	West Ham U	(0) 0
Derby Co	(3) 7	Southend U	(0) 0
Everton	(2) 3	Rotherham U	(0) 0
Manchester U	(1) 1	Brighton & HA	(0) 0
Middlesbrough	(0) 1	Newcastle U	(1) 3
Millwall	(1) 1	Arsenal	†(1) 1*
Norwich C	(0) 2	Carlisle	(0) 0
Nottingham F	(1) 2	Stockport Co	(1) 1
Oldham Ath	(0) 0	Exeter C	(0) 0
Reading	(0) 0	Watford	(1) 2
Scarborough	(0) 3	Coventry C	(0) 0
Sheffield U	(2) 4	Bristol C	(1) 1
Southampton	(1) 3	Gillingham	(0) 0
Stoke C	(0) 1	Cambridge U	(1) 2
Wolverhampton W	(0) 0	Notts Co	(0) 1
Scunthorpe U	(2) 2	Leeds U	(1) 2

Third Round

Bury	(0) 0	QPR	(0) 2
Notts Co	(0) 2	Cambridge U	(1) 3
Plymouth Arg	(0) 3	Scarborough	(1) 3
Portsmouth	(0) 0	Ipswich T	(1) 1
Sheffield W	(2) 7	Leicester C	(0) 1
Swindon T	(0) 0	Oldham Ath	(0) 1
Aston Villa	(0) 1	Manchester U	(0) 0
Blackburn R	(1) 2	Norwich C	(0) 0
Chelsea	(0) 2	Newcastle U	(0) 1
Crewe Alex	(0) 0	Nottingham F	(0) 1
Derby Co	(0) 1	Arsenal	(0) 1
Everton	(0) 0	Wimbledon	(0) 0
Manchester C	(0) 0	Tottenham H	(1) 1
Sheffield U	(0) 0	Liverpool	(0) 0
Southampton	(0) 0	Crystal Palace	(2) 2
Watford	(0) 2	Leeds U	(0) 1

Third Round Replays

Wimbledon	(0) 0	Everton	(0) 1
Liverpool	(2) 3	Sheffield U	(0) 0
Scarborough	(0) 2	Plymouth Arg	(1) 1
Arsenal	(2) 2	Derby Co	(1) 1

Fourth Round

Cambridge U	(1) 1	Oldham Ath	(0) 0
Liverpool	(0) 1	Crystal Palace	(0) 1
Aston Villa	(0) 2	Ipswich T	(0) 2
Everton	(2) 2	Chelsea	(1) 2
Nottingham F	(1) 2	Tottenham H	(0) 0
Sheffield W	(2) 4	QPR	(0) 0
Blackburn R	(2) 6	Watford	(0) 1
Scarborough	(0) 0	Arsenal	(0) 1

Fourth Round Replays

Ipswich T	(0) 1	Aston Villa	(0) 0
Chelsea	(1) 1	Everton	(0) 0
Crystal Palace	(1) 2	Liverpool	(1) 1*

Fifth Round

Blackburn R	(0) 3	Cambridge U	(0) 2
Crystal Palace	(2) 3	Chelsea	(1) 1
Arsenal	(0) 2	Nottingham F	(0) 0
Ipswich T	(0) 1	Sheffield W	(0) 1

Fifth Round Replay

Sheffield W	(0) 1	Ipswich T	(0) 0

Semi-final First Leg

Crystal Palace	(0) 1	Arsenal	(2) 3
Blackburn R	(2) 2	Sheffield W	(4) 4

Semi-final Second Leg

Arsenal	(2) 2	Crystal Palace	(0) 0
Sheffield W	(0) 2	Blackburn R	(1) 1

Final at Wembley

Arsenal	(1) 2	Sheffield W	(1) 1

*after extra time †won on penalties ††won on away goals

PAST LEAGUE CUP FINALS

Played as two legs up to 1966

1961	Rotherham U 2	Aston Villa 0	
	Webster, Kirkman		
	Aston Villa 3	Rotherham U 0*	
	O'Neill, Burrows, McParland		
1962	Rochdale 0	Norwich C 3	
		Lythgoe 2, Punton	
	Norwich C 1	Rochdale 0	
	Hill		
1963	Birmingham C 3	Aston Villa 1	
	Leek 2, Bloomfield	*Thomson*	
	Aston Villa 0	Birmingham C 0	
1964	Stoke C 1	Leicester C 1	
	Bebbington	*Gibson*	
	Leicester C 3	Stoke C 2	
	Stringfellow, Gibson, Riley	*Viollet, Kinnell*	
1965	Chelsea 3	Leicester C 2	
	Tambling, Venables (pen), McCreadie	*Appleton, Goodfellow*	
	Leicester C 0	Chelsea 0	
1966	West Ham U 2	WBA 1	
	Moore, Byrne	*Astle*	
	WBA 4	West Ham U 1	
	Kaye, Brown, Clark, Williams	*Peters*	
1967	QPR 3	WBA 2	
	Morgan R, Marsh, Lazarus	*Clark C 2*	
1968	Leeds U 1	Arsenal 0	
	Cooper		
1969	Swindon T 3	Arsenal 1	
	Smart, Rogers 2	*Gould*	
1970	Manchester C 2	WBA 1	
	Doyle, Pardoe	*Astle*	
1971	Tottenham H 2	Aston Villa 0	
	Chivers 2		
1972	Chelsea 1	Stoke C 2	
	Osgood	*Conroy, Eastham*	
1973	Tottenham H 1	Norwich C 0	
	Coates		
1974	Wolverhampton W 2	Manchester C 1	
	Hibbitt, Richards	*Bell*	
1975	Aston Villa 1	Norwich C 0	
	Graydon		
1976	Manchester C 2	Newcastle U 1	
	Barnes, Tueart	*Gowling*	
1977	Aston Villa 0	Everton 0	
Replay	Aston Villa 1	Everton 1*	
	Kenyon (og)	*Latchford*	

Replay	Aston Villa............3	Everton 2*	
	Little 2, Nicholl	*Latchford, Lyons*	
1978	Nottingham F............0	Liverpool............0*	
Replay	Nottingham F............1	Liverpool............0	
	Robertson (pen)		
1979	Nottingham F............3	Southampton 2	
	Birtles 2, Woodcock	*Peach, Holmes*	
1980	Wolverhampton W............1	Nottingham F............0	
	Gray		
1981	Liverpool............1	West Ham U............1*	
	Kennedy, A	*Stewart (pen)*	
Replay	Liverpool............2	West Ham U............1	
	Dalglish, Hansen	*Goddard*	
1982	Liverpool............3	Tottenham H............1*	
	Whelan 2, Rush	*Archibald*	
1983	Liverpool............2	Manchester U............1*	
	Kennedy, Whelan	*Whiteside*	
1984	Liverpool............0	Everton 0*	
Replay	Liverpool............1	Everton 0	
	Souness		
1985	Norwich C............1	Sunderland............0	
	Chisholm (og)		
1986	Oxford U............3	QPR............0	
	Hebberd, Houghton, Charles		
1987	Arsenal............2	Liverpool............1	
	Nicholas 2	*Rush*	
1988	Luton T............3	Arsenal............2	
	Stein B 2, Wilson	*Hayes, Smith*	
1989	Nottingham F............3	Luton T............1	
	Clough 2, Webb	*Harford*	
1990	Nottingham F............1	Oldham Ath............0	
	Jemson		
1991	Sheffield W............1	Manchester U............0	
	Sheridan		
1992	Manchester U............1	Nottingham F............0	
	McClair		

*After extra time

ANGLO-ITALIAN CUP 1992–93

Preliminary Round

Bristol C	(0) 1	Watford	(0) 0
Cambridge U	(0) 1	Sunderland	(1) 1
Oxford U	(0) 1	Swindon	(2) 3
Peterborough U	(0) 0	Tranmere R	(0) 0
Derby Co	(2) 4	Notts Co	(2) 2
Leicester C	(3) 4	Grimsby T	(0) 0
Millwall	(1) 1	Charlton Ath	(0) 2
West Ham U	(1) 2	Bristol R	(0) 2
Charlton Ath	(0) 1	Portsmouth	(2) 3
Notts Co	(0) 1	Barnsley	(0) 1
Sunderland	(0) 0	Birmingham C	(1) 1
Tranmere R	(0) 2	Wolverhampton W	(1) 1
Watford	(0) 0	Luton T	(0) 0
Bristol R	(1) 3	Southend U	(0) 0
Grimsby T	(1) 2	Newcastle U	(2) 2
Swindon T	(0) 1	Brentford	(1) 2
Barnsley	(1) 1	Derby Co	(1) 2
Birmingham C	(1) 3	Cambridge U	(2) 3
Brentford	(0) 2	Oxford U	(0) 0
Luton T	(0) 1	Bristol C	(0) 1
Portsmouth	(0) 1	Millwall	(1) 1
Newcastle U	(2) 4	Leicester C	(0) 0
Southend U	(0) 0	West Ham U	(2) 3
Wolverhampton W	(1) 2	Peterborough U	(0) 0

International Stage

Ascoli	(0) 1	Brentford	(2) 3
Birmingham C	(0) 1	Bari	(0) 0
Lucchese	(1) 1	Newcastle U	(0) 1
Portsmouth	(1) 2	Cesena	(0) 0
Bristol C	(0) 0	Cosenza	(0) 2
Cremonese	(0) 2	West Ham U	(0) 0
Derby Co	(2) 3	Pisa	(0) 0
Reggiana	(0) 0	Tranmere R	(0) 0
Bari	(0) 3	Portsmouth	(0) 0
Brentford	(0) 1	Lucchese	(0) 0
Newcastle U	(0) 0	Ascoli	(0) 1
Cosenza	(0) 0	Derby Co	(3) 3
Pisa	(4) 4	Bristol C	(2) 3
Tranmere R	(1) 1	Cremonese	(1) 2
West Ham U	(0) 2	Reggiana	(0) 0
Cesena	(0) 1	Birmingham C	(0) 0
Bari	(2) 3	Newcastle U	(0) 0
Birmingham C	(1) 1	Ascoli	(1) 1
Cesena	(0) 0	Brentford	(0) 1
Portsmouth	(0) 2	Lucchese	(1) 1
Bristol C	(1) 1	Reggiana	(1) 2
Cosenza	(0) 0	West Ham U	(1) 1

Derby Co	(1) 1	Cremonese	(3) 3
Pisa	(0) 0	Tranmere R	(0) 1
Ascoli	(1) 1	Portsmouth	(0) 2
Brentford	(1) 2	Bari	(0) 1
Lucchese	(2) 3	Birmingham C	(0) 1
Newcastle U	(1) 2	Cesena	(1) 2
Cremonese	(0) 2	Bristol C	(0) 2
Reggiana	(0) 0	Derby Co	(3) 3
Tranmere R	(2) 2	Cosenza	(0) 1
West Ham U	(0) 0	Pisa	(0) 0

Semi-final, First Leg

| Brentford | (2) 3 | Derby Co | (3) 4 |
| Cremonese | (2) 4 | Bari | (1) 1 |

Semi-final, Second Leg

| Derby Co | (1) 1 | Brentford | (0) 2 |
| Bari | (2) 2 | Cremonese | (1) 2 |

FINAL (at Wembley)
27 MAR
Cremonese (1) 3 *(Verdelli, Maspero (pen), Tentoni)*
Derby Co (1) 1 *(Gabbiadini)* 37,024
Cremonese: Turci; Gualco, Pedroni, Cristiani, Colonnese, Verdelli, Giandebiaggi, Nicolini, Tentoni (Montorfano), Maspero, Florjancic (Dezotti).
Derby Co: Taylor; Patterson, Forsyth, Nicholson, Coleman, Pembridge, Micklewhite, Goulooze (Hayward), Kitson, Gabbiadini, Johnson (Simpson).
Referee: J.Velasquez (Spain).

AUTOGLASS TROPHY 1992–93

First Round

Colchester U	(1) 1	Northampton T	(1) 2
Doncaster R	(0) 2	York C	(0) 1
Halifax T	(0) 0	Bradford C	(2) 4
Leyton Orient	(3) 4	Gillingham	(1) 1
Lincoln C	(0) 0	Rotherham U	(1) 1
Preston NE	(0) 1	Blackpool	(1) 1
Reading	(0) 1	Brighton & HA	(1) 1
Rochdale	(0) 0	Bolton W	(0) 0
Shrewsbury T	(0) 1	Cardiff C	(1) 3
Chester C	(0) 0	Chesterfield	(1) 1
Scarborough	(1) 4	Carlisle U	(0) 0
Blackpool	(2) 3	Wigan Ath	(1) 2
Bolton W	(0) 1	Bury	(1) 1
Cardiff C	(1) 3	Hereford U	(1) 2

Chesterfield	(0) 0	Stockport Co	(1) 3
Crewe Alex	(0) 0	Wrexham	(0) 3
Exeter C	(2) 5	Torquay U	(0) 0
Gillingham	(1) 3	Fulham	(1) 3
Hartlepool U	(3) 4	Scarborough	(0) 1
Rotherham U	(1) 3	Scunthorpe U	(0) 1
Walsall	(1) 2	Mansfield T	(0) 0
York C	(0) 0	Hull C	(0) 0
Bradford C	(0) 0	Huddersfield T	(0) 0
Brighton & HA	(3) 3	Bournemouth	(2) 2
Northampton T	(0) 2	Barnet	(0) 1
Scunthorpe U	(1) 2	Lincoln C	(0) 2
Carlisle U	(0) 2	Hartlepool U	(0) 0
Fulham	(0) 2	Leyton Orient	(1) 2
Huddersfield T	(1) 5	Halifax T	(0) 0
Hull C	(0) 2	Doncaster R	(1) 1
Stockport Co	(0) 2	Chester C	(0) 0
Wrexham	(0) 0	Stoke C	(2) 2
Barnet	(3) 4	Colchester U	(0) 2
Hereford U	(2) 2	Shrewsbury T	(0) 1
Bournemouth	(0) 1	Reading	(1) 1
Plymouth Arg	(0) 1	Exeter C	(1) 2
WBA	(1) 4	Walsall	(0) 0
Stoke C	(2) 2	Crewe Alex	(0) 2
Wigan Ath	(1) 2	Preston NE	(1) 1
Bury	(1) 1	Rochdale	(0) 2
Mansfield T	(0) 0	WBA	(0) 1
Torquay U	(0) 2	Plymouth Arg	(1) 1

Second Round

Hull C	(0) 0	Chesterfield	(0) 1
Port Vale	(1) 4	Fulham	(1) 3
Scarborough	(1) 3	Bradford C	(3) 4
Stockport Co	(1) 1	Hartlepool U	(0) 0
Leyton Orient	(1) 4	Wrexham	(1) 1
Brighton & HA	(1) 4	Walsall	(0) 2
Blackpool	(1) 1	Burnley	(0) 3
Cardiff C	(1) 1	Swansea C	(0) 2
Darlington	(1) 3	Bolton W	(3) 4
Northampton T	(0) 4	Hereford U	(0) 0
Rotherham U	(3) 3	Wigan Ath*	(2) 3
Huddersfield T	(2) 3	Doncaster R	(0) 0
Stoke C	(1) 4	Barnet	(0) 1
Rochdale	(1) 1	Scunthorpe U	(1) 2
Exeter C*	(0) 2	Reading	(0) 2
WBA	(0) 2	Torquay U	(1) 1

Area Quarter-finals

Bradford C	(1) 3	Stockport Co	(3) 4
Chesterfield	(2) 3	Burnley	(0) 0
Huddersfield T	(2) 3	Bolton W	(0) 0

Port Vale	(2) 4	Northampton T	(1) 2
Wigan Ath	(1) 2	Scunthorpe U	(0) 1
Swansea C	(0) 1	Leyton Orient	(0) 0
Stoke C	(0) 2	WBA	(0) 1
Brighton & HA	(0) 0	Exeter C	(0) 1

South Semi-finals

| Swansea C | (1) 2 | Exeter C | (2) 3 |
| Stoke C | (0) 0 | Port Vale | (0) 1 |

North Semi-finals

| Stockport Co | (1) 2 | Chesterfield | (1) 1 |
| Wigan Ath | (2) 5 | Huddersfield T | (0) 2 |

Area Finals, First Leg

| Port Vale | (1) 2 | Exeter C | (1) 1 |
| Wigan Ath | (1) 2 | Stockport Co | (0) 1 |

Area Finals, Second Leg

| Stockport Co | (1) 2 | Wigan Ath | (0) 0 |
| Exeter C | (0) 1 | Port Vale | (0) 1 |

FINAL at Wembley
22 MAY
Port Vale (2) 2 *(Kerr, Slaven)*
Stockport Co (0) 1 *(Francis)* 35,885
Port Vale: Musselwhite; Aspin, Kent, Porter, Swan, Glover, Slaven, Van der Laan (Billing), Foyle, Kerr, Taylor.
Stockport Co: Edwards; Todd, Wallace, Finley, Miller, Williams B, Gannon, Ward, Francis, Beaumont (Preece), Duffield.
Referee: D. Elleray (Harrow).

* after extra time

1908	Manchester U v QPR	
	4-0 after 1-1 draw	
1909	Newcastle U v Northampton T	2-0
1910	Brighton v Aston Villa	1-0
1911	Manchester U v Swindon T	8-4
1912	Blackburn R v QPR	2-1
1913	Professionals v Amateurs	7-2
1919	WBA v Tottenham H	2-0
1920	Tottenham H v Burnley	2-0
1921	Huddersfield T v Liverpool	1-0
1922	Not played	
1923	Professionals v Amateurs	2-0
1924	Professionals v Amateurs	3-1
1925	Amateurs v Professionals	6-1
1926	Amateurs v Professionals	6-3
1927	Cardiff C v Corinthians	2-1
1928	Everton v Blackburn R	2-1
1929	Professionals v Amateurs	3-0
1930	Arsenal v Sheffield W	2-1
1931	Arsenal v WBA	1-0
1932	Everton v Newcastle U	5-3
1933	Arsenal v Everton	3-0
1934	Arsenal v Manchester C	4-0
1935	Sheffield W v Arsenal	1-0
1936	Sunderland v Arsenal	2-1
1937	Manchester C v Sunderland	2-0
1938	Arsenal v Preston NE	2-1
1948	Arsenal v Manchester U	4-3
1949	Portsmouth v Wolverhampton W	1-1*
1950	World Cup Team v Canadian	
	Touring Team	4-2
1951	Tottenham H v Newcastle U	2-1
1952	Manchester U v Newcastle U	4-2
1953	Arsenal v Blackpool	3-1
1954	Wolverhampton W v WBA	4-4*
1955	Chelsea v Newcastle U	3-0
1956	Manchester U v Manchester C	1-0

1957	Manchester U v Aston Villa	4-0
1958	Bolton W v Wolverhampton W	4-1
1959	Wolverhampton W v	
	Nottingham F	3-1
1960	Burnley v Wolverhampton W	2-2*
1961	Tottenham H v FA XI	3-2
1962	Tottenham H v Ipswich T	5-1
1963	Everton v Manchester U	4-0
1964	Liverpool v West Ham U	2-2*
1965	Manchester U v Liverpool	2-2*
1966	Liverpool v Everton	1-0
1967	Manchester U v Tottenham H	3-3*
1968	Manchester C v WBA	6-1
1969	Leeds U v Manchester C	2-1
1970	Everton v Chelsea	2-1
1971	Leicester C v Liverpool	1-0
1972	Manchester C v Aston Villa	1-0
1973	Burnley v Manchester C	1-0
1974	Liverpool† v Leeds U	1-1
1975	Derby Co v West Ham U	2-0
1976	Liverpool v Southampton	1-0
1977	Liverpool v Manchester U	0-0*
1978	Nottingham F v Ipswich T	5-0
1979	Liverpool v Arsenal	3-1
1980	Liverpool v West Ham U	1-0
1981	Aston Villa v Tottenham H	2-2*
1982	Liverpool v Tottenham H	1-0
1983	Manchester U v Liverpool	2-0
1984	Everton v Liverpool	1-0
1985	Everton v Manchester U	2-0
1986	Everton v Liverpool	1-1*
1987	Everton v Coventry C	1-0
1988	Liverpool v Wimbledon	2-1
1989	Liverpool v Arsenal	1-0
1990	Liverpool v Manchester U	1-1*
1991	Arsenal v Tottenham H	0-0*

*Each club retained shield for six months. †Won on penalties.

FA CHARITY SHIELD 1992

Leeds U (2) 4, Liverpool (1) 3

at Wembley, 8 August 1992, attendance 61,291

Leeds U: Lukic; Newsome (Strachan), Dorigo, Batty, Fairclough, Whyte, Cantona, Wallace, Chapman (Hodge), McAllister, Speed. *Scorers:* Cantona 3, Dorigo.

Liverpool: Grobbelaar; Tanner, Burrows, March (Hutchison), Whelan, Wright, Saunders, Stewart, Rush, Rosenthal (Kozma), Walters. *Scorers:* Rush, Saunders, Strachan (og).

Referee: D. Elleray (Harrow).

SCOTTISH CLUBS

ABERDEEN   PREM. DIV.

Ground: Pittodrie Stadium, Aberdeen AB2 1QH (0224 632328)
Colours: All red with white trim.
Manager: Willie Miller.
League Appearances: Aitken R 18(8); Bett J 17; Booth S 21(8); Connor R 5(1); Ferguson G (1); Gibson A 1; Grant B 29; Irvine B 39; Jess E 28(3); Kane P 13(14); McKimmie S 14; McLeish A 27; Mason P 31(8); Paatelainen M 33; Richardson L 28(1); Roddie A 1(10); Shearer D 32(2); Smith G 40; Snelders T 41; Ten Caat T 11(4); Thomson S (2); Watt M 3; Winnie D 18(3); Wright S 34(2).
Goals–League (87): Shearer 22, Paatelainen 16, Booth 13, Jess 12, Irvine 5, Kane 4, Mason 4, Grant 3, Aitken 2, Richardson 2, Roddie 2, Gibson 1, own goal 1.
Scottish Cup (13): Booth 6, Irvine 2, Jess 2, Paatelainen 1, Richardson 1, Shearer 1 (pen).
Skol Cup (11): Shearer 5, Paatelainen 3, Jess 2, Irvine 1.

AIRDRIEONIANS   DIV. 1

Ground: Broomfield Park, Gartlea Road, Airdrie ML6 9JL (0236 62067)
Colours: White shirts with red diamond, white shorts.
Manager: Alex MacDonald.
League Appearances: Balfour E 26(1); Black K 33; Boyle J 36(4); Caesar G 29; Conn S 4(10); Coyle O 42; Dempsey S (1); Dick J (1); Fashanu J 16; Honor C 28(1); Jack P 32(1); Kidd W 30(1); Kirkwood D 17(10); Lawrence A 23(12); McCulloch W 1; Martin J 43; Reid W 18(7); Sandison J 37(1); Smith A 20(14); Stewart A 43; Watson J 4(4); Wilson M 2(2)
Goals–League (35): Coyle 9, Fashanu 5, Boyle 4 (1 pen), Smith 4, Honor 3 (1 pen), Jack 3 (2 pens), Kirkwood 2 (2 pens), Lawrence 2, Balfour 1, Black 1, Stewart 1.
Scottish Cup (0).
Skol Cup (2): Conn 1, Kirkwood 1.

ALBION ROVERS   DIV. 2

Ground: Cliffhill Stadium, Main Street, Coatbridge ML5 3RB (0236 432350)
Colours: Yellow shirts with red trim, red shorts with yellow stripes.
Manager: Tommy Gemmell.
League Appearances: Andrews G 2; Archer S 9(2); Armour N 11(1); Brown R 2(1); Cadden S 30; Conway M 3; Ferguson W 13(2); Fraser A 1; Gallagher J 11(2); Gaughan M 10(4); Gray W 7(5); Guidi M 18; Hendry A 9(5); Houston J 11(1); Jackson S 7(3); Kelly J 22; Kerrigan S 24(5); Kiernan D 3(2); McAulay I 3; McBride M 31(7); McCaffrey J 29; McConnachie R 10; McCoy G 7(4); McDonald D 1; McGuigan R 1; McKeown D 37(1); McQuade A 3(4); Millar G 13(1); Mirner E 8; Moore S 19(2); Pathak J 1; Pryde A 4(3); Riley D 17(1); Scott M 37(2); Seggie S 5(5); Walsh R 10(4)
Goals–League (36): Scott 16 (4 pens), Kerrigan 8, Ferguson 3, Kelly 2, Archer 1, Cadden 1, Gallagher 1, McCaffrey 1, McKeown 1, Moore 1, Riley 1.
Scottish Cup (0).
Skol Cup (1): Ferguson 1.
B & Q Cup (0)

ALLOA   DIV. 2

Ground: Recreation Park, Alloa FK10 1RR (0259 722695)
Colours: Gold shirts with black trim, black shorts.
Manager: Billy Lamont.
League Appearances: Bennett N 30(3); Binnie N 2; Butter J 37; Campbell C 33; Campbell K (2); Conroy J 1(2); Crombie L 18(1); Gibson J 9(9); Hendry M 24(5); Herd W 3; Lee R 6; McAvoy N 34(3); McCormick S 9(9); McCulloch K 25(1); McNiven J 31(1); Moffat B 35(2); Newbigging W 27(3); Ramsay S 6(3); Romaines S 4(1); Russell G 5(19); Sheerin P 7(2); Smith S 32(2); Tait G 18(2); Thomson J 2; Wilcox D 31(1)

Goals–League (63): Moffat 19 (1 pen), Smith 9, McAvoy 6, Hendry 5, McCormick 5, Tait 5, Newbigging 4 (4 pens), McNiven 2, Russell 2, Wilcox 2, Bennett 1, Crombie 1, Lee 1, own goal 1.
Scottish Cup (2): McAvoy 1, Moffat 1.
Skol Cup (2): McAvoy 1, Moffat 1.
B & Q Cup (2): McNiven 1, Wilcox 1.

ARBROATH   DIV. 2

Ground: Gayfield Park, Arbroath DD11 1QB (0241 72157)
Colours: Maroon shirts, white shorts.
Manager: Danny McGrain MBE.
League Appearances: ; Adam C 28(1); Balfour D 5; Boyd W 34(1); Buckley G 14; Farnan C 36; Florence S 28; Godfrey P 11; Hamilton J 21(4); Harkness M 34; Holmes W (8); Macdonald K 28(1); McNaughton B 12(6); Martin C 32(2); Mitchell B 36; Sneddon H (2); Sorbie S 39; Strachan J 7(1); Tindal K 29(4); Tosh P 26(8); Will B 9(5)

Goals–League (59): Sorbie 19, Tosh 12, Buckley 6 (1 pen), Tindal 5, Adam 4, Macdonald 4 (1 pen), McNaughton 3 (1 pen), Godfrey 2, Martin 2, Strachan 1, own goal 1.
Scottish Cup (10): Sorbie 3, Martin 2, Tosh 2, Macdonald 1, McNaughton 1, Tindal 1.
Skol Cup (3): Adam 1, Macdonald 1, Tindal 1.
B & Q Cup (3): Macdonald 1, Sorbie 1, Tosh 1.

AYR UNITED   DIV. 1

Ground: Somerset Park, Ayr KA8 9NB (0292 263435)
Colours: White shirts with black trim, black shorts.
Manager: George Burley.
League Appearances: Agnew G 18; Allan D 5; Bryce S 14; Burke P 4(2); Burley G 33; Carse J 1(5); Crews B 1(3); Duncan C 41; Furphy W 6; Gardner L 2; George D 37; Graham A 30; Hood G 12; Howard N 24; Kennedy D 29(3); McGivern S 9; McGuigan R 3(2); McLean P 2; McTurk A 12(11); McVie G 6(2); Mair G 20(2); Robertson G 43(1); Robertson S 4(2); Russell R 4; Scott B 12(1); Shaw G (5); Shotton M 35; Spence W 3; Traynor J 36; Walker T 38(3)

Goals–League (49): Graham 9, Mair 7, Traynor 7, Walker 7, Bryce 5 (2 pens), Scott 3, Agnew 2, Kennedy 2, McTurk 2, Hood 1, Robertson G 1, Russell 1, Shotton 1, own goal 1.
Scottish Cup (2): Mair 1 (pen), Walker 1.
Skol Cup (0).
B & Q Cup (2): Walker 2

BERWICK RANGERS DIV. 2

Ground: Shielfield Park, Berwick-on-Tweed TD15 2EF (0289 307424)
Colours: Black and gold striped shirts, black shorts.
Manager: Jim Crease.
League Appearances: Anderson P 8; Bickmore S 2(1); Brownlee P 1; Cass M 13; Cunningham C 28(1); Davidson G 31; Egan J 4; Fisher W 10(2); Gibson K 5; Graham T 38; Hall A 37; Hendrie T 26(4); Hutchinson I 12(8); Irvine W 28(1); Kane K 11; Kerr D 1(3); McGovern P 2; Malone L 1(4); Massie K 13; Muir S 3(2); Murray P 8(4); Neil M 6; Neilson D 9; O'Connor G 13; O'Donnell J 5; Richardson S 22; Robertson J 10(4); Scott D 22(5); Shell K 1; Thomson G 1; Thorpe B 5(2); Valentine C 38; Waldie I 3(11); Wilson M 12(4)
Goals–League (56): Scott 11, Cunningham 9, Graham 9 (3 pens), Irvine 9, Davidson 4, Fisher 2, Richardson 2, Wilson 2, Cass 1, Hall 1, Hutchinson 1, Kane 1, McGovern 1, Neil 1, Robertson 1, Waldie 1.
Scottish Cup (3): Anderson 1, Hall 1, Richardson 1.
Skol Cup (0).
B & Q Cup (5): Davidson 2, Cunningham 1, Irvine 1, Scott 1.

BRECHIN CITY DIV. 1

Ground: Glebe Park, Brechin DD9 6BJ (0356 622856)
Colours: All red.
Manager: Ian Redford.
League Appearances: Allan R 39; Baillie R 11(6); Brand R 23(8); Brown R 37; Cairney H 38; Conway F 4(3); Fisher D 1; Heggie A 11(8); Hutt G 23(4); Lees G 17(9); Lorimer R 29(3); McKillop A 36; McLaren P 29(3); McNeill W 11; Miller M 30(1); O'Brien P 20(3); Paterson I G (2); Ross A 36(2); Scott D 30; Sexton P (1); Thomson N 4(8)
Goals–League (62): Ross 23 (3 pens), Miller 11 (2 pens), Brand 9, McNeill 4, Heggie 3, O'Brien 3, Scott 3, Lees 2, Lorimer 2, Hutt 1, McKillop 1.
Scottish Cup (1): Lees 1.
Skol Cup (7): Brown 2, Miller 2, Hutt 1, Lees 1, Ross 1.
B & Q Cup (1): Lorimer 1.

CELTIC PREM. DIV.

Ground: Celtic Park, Glasgow G40 3RE (041-556 2611)
Colours: Green and white hooped shirts, white shorts.
Manager: Liam Brady.
League Appearances: Bonner P 33; Boyd T 42; Collins J 43; Coyne T 5(5); Creaney G 23(3); Fulton S 3(3); Galloway M 29(1); Gillespie G 18; Grant P 27(4); Gray S 1; McAvennie F 19; McCarrison D (1); McNally M 25(2); McQuilken J 1; McStay P 43; Marshall G 11; Miller J 10(13); Morris C 3; Mowbray A 26; Nicholas C 12(4); O'Neil R 11(6); Payton A 19(10); Slater S 37(2); Smith B 4(2); Vata R 15(7); Wdowczyk D 24(1); Whyte D (1)
Goals–League (68): Payton 13, Creaney 9, McAvennie 9 (1 pen), Collins 8, McStay 4, Coyne 3 (2 pens), Galloway 3 (1 pen), O'Neil 3, Wdowczyk 3 (1 pen), Grant 2, Miller 2, Mowbray 2, Nicholas 2, Slater 2, Vata 2, own goal 1.
Scottish Cup (1): Coyne 1.
Skol Cup (6): Creaney 3, Payton 2, Coyne 1.

CLYDE   DIV. 1

Ground: Douglas Park, Hamilton ML3 0DF (Mon-Fri: 041-248 7953) (Match days: 0698 286103)
Colours: White shirts with red and black trim, black shorts.
Manager: Alex Smith.
League Appearances: Clarke S 26(3); Dickson J 13(14); Howie S 39; Knox K 37; McAulay J 20(8); McCarron J 24(8); McCheyne G 19(2); McFarlane R 31; McGarvey F 33(1); McGill D 7(2); Mallan S 1(1); Mitchell J 9(7); Morrison S 15(9); Neill A 1; Quinn K 6(9); Ronald P 15; Speirs C 1(2); Strain B 24(1); Tennant S 35; Thompson D 19(4); Thomson J 36; Watson E 1(5); Wylde G 17(1)
Goals–League (77): McGarvey 16, Clarke 10, Thompson D 8 (1 pen), Morrison 7 (1 pen), McCarron 6, Strain 6, Quinn 4, Tennant 4 (2 pens), Knox 3, McAulay 3, Thomson J 3, Dickson 2, Ronald 2, McGill 1, Mitchell 1, Wylde 1.
Scottish Cup (4): McCarron 2, Dickson 1, Thomson J 1.
Skol Cup (5): Clarke 2, Thompson D 2, Speirs 1.
B & Q Cup (1): McCheyne 1.

CLYDEBANK   DIV. 1

Ground: Kilbowie Park, Clydebank G81 2PB (041-952 2887)
Colours: White, black and red trim, white shorts.
Manager: John Steedman.
League Appearances: Barron D 23(4); Bowman G 1; Brown T 1; Bryce T 16(8); Crawford J 15(13); Currie T 5; Eadie K 36; Flannigan C 37(1); Flannigan M 1(2); Goldie P 3(3); Harvey P 37(2); Hay G 30; Henderson D 2(3); Henry J 32; Jack S 42(1); Lansdowne A 14(14); McIntosh M 32(1); Maher J 33(1); Murdoch S 16; Murray M 6; Sludden J 1; Smith B 2; Smith L 5(5); Spence W 2; Sweeney S 36; Wilson K 14(7); Woods S 42
Goals–League (71): Flannigan C 21, Eadie 20 (4 pens), Henry 12, Harvey 5, McIntosh 4, Wilson 3, Sweeney 2, Bryce 1, Crawford 1, Hay 1, Henderson 1.
Scottish Cup (8): Eadie 4, Flannigan C 1, Henry 1, McIntosh 1, Maher 1.
Skol Cup (0).
B & Q Cup (1): Flannigan C 1.

COWDENBEATH   DIV. 2

Ground: Central Park, Cowdenbeath KY4 9EY (0383 511205)
Colours: Royal blue shirts with white stripes, white shorts.
Manager: Andy Harrow.
League Appearances: Archibald A 6(1); Archibald E 33; Bennett W 1; Bowmaker K 1(1); Buckley G 12(7); Callaghan W 29(1); Combe A 20; Condie T 25(5); Dixon A 3(14); Douglas H 28(3); Ferguson S 2(1); Harris C 5; Henderson N 30(2); Herd W 33(2); Irvine N 7; Johnston P 3(1); Kelso M 1; Lamont P 2(3); Lamont W 23; Lee I 18(1); McGovern D 27; McMahon B 12; Malone G 16; Maratea D 4(6); O'Hanlon S 1; Petrie E 32(1); Robertson A 30; Scott C 14(5); Stout D 2(1); Syme W 5(2); Watt D 32(2); Wright J 28(9)
Goals–League (33): Callaghan 9, Robertson 6, Henderson 5 (3 pens), Condie 3, Wright 3, Malone 2, Buckley 1, Douglas 1, Herd 1, Syme 1, Watt 1.
Scottish Cup (1): Henderson 1 (pen).
Skol Cup (0).
B & Q Cup (4): Buckley 1, Callaghan 1, Lee 1, Malone 1.

DUMBARTON   DIV. 1

Ground: Boghead Park, Dumbarton G82 2JA (0389 62569 and 67864)
Colours: All Gold.
Manager: Murdo MacLeod.
League Appearances: Boag J 6(1); Boyd J 35(2); Cowell J (7); Dempsey J 3; Docherty
R 26(6); Foster A 15(5); Furphy W 1; Gibson C 36(6); Gilmour J 5; Gow S 38;
McAnenay M 27(11); McConville R 17(6); McDonald D 3; MacFarlane I 40;
McGarvey M 1(3); McQuade J 38(2); Marsland J 37(1); Martin P 40; Meechan J
27(7); Melvin M 42; Monaghan M 4; Mooney M 27(7); Nelson M 9(9); Speirs A 1;
Willock A 1(7); Wishart F 2; Young J 3
Goals–League (56): McQuade 15, Mooney 12 (1 pen), Gibson 7, McAnenay 6, Boyd
5, Foster 2, Martin 2, Meechan 2, Boag 1, Docherty 1, Gilmour 1, Gow 1, Nelson 1.
Scottish Cup (0).
Skol Cup (0).
B & Q Cup (0).

DUNDEE   PREM. DIV.

Ground: Dens Park, Dundee DD3 7JY (0382 826104)
Colours: Dark blue shirts with red and white trim, white shorts.
Manager: Simon Stainrod.
League Appearances: Armstrong L 1; Bain K 24; Beedie S 8(6); Campbell D 2(2);
Campbell S 20; Christie M 1(2); David L 8; Den Bieman I 23(1); Dinnie A 26;
Dodds W 41; Dow A 8(6); Duffy J 39; Frail S 7; Gallagher E 2(2); Gilzean I 17(7);
Kiwomya A 11(10); Leighton J 8; McCann N 2(1); McGowan J 21; McKeown G 20;
McMartin G 2(1); McQuillan J 27(2); Mathers P 36; Paterson G 11(9); Pittman S 20;
Ratcliffe K 4; Ritchie P 17(2); Rix G 12(2); Stainrod S 10(10); Vrto D 32; West C
2(5); Wieghorst M 22(1)
Goals–League (48): Dodds 16 (2 pens), Stainrod 7, Gilzean 5, Den Bieman 3, Ritchie
3, Paterson 2, Rix 2, Wieghorst 2, Dinnie 1, Dow 1, Kiwomya 1, McGowan 1,
McKeown 1, Pittman 1, Vrto 1, own goal 1.
Scottish Cup (2): Dodds 1 (pen), Wieghorst.
Skol Cup (3): Campbell D 1, Dodds 1, McGowan 1.

DUNDEE UNITED   PREM. DIV.

Ground: Tannadice Park, Dundee DD3 7JW (0382 833166)
Colours: Tangerine shirts with black trim, black shorts.
Manager: Ivan Golac.
League Appearances: Bollan G 12(3); Bowman D 18(6); Clark J 35(2); Cleland A
21(3); Connolly P 32(10); Crabbe S 22(5); Dailly C 8(6); Ferguson D 30; Ferreyra V
3(4); Hannah D (5); Johnson G 15(2); Krivokapic M 8; McInally J 26(6); McKinlay
W 36(1); McLaren A 4(1); Main A 43; Malpas M 37; Narey D 27(1); O'Neil J 21(7);
O'Neill M 22(3); Perry M 17(1); Van De Kamp G 1; Van Der Hoorn F 31(1); Welsh
F 15
Goals–League 56: Connolly 16, Ferguson 12, McInally 5, Crabbe 4 (1 pen), Dailly 4,
Bollan 3, O'Neil J 3, Clark 2, O'Neill M 2, Johnson 1, McKinlay 1, Perry 1, Welsh 1,
own goal 1.
Scottish Cup (3): Ferguson 1, McKinlay 1, Welsh 1.
Skol Cup (11): Connolly 3, Ferguson 2, Ferreyra 2, Johnson 2, McKinlay 1, O'Neil J
1.

DUNFERMLINE ATHLETIC   DIV. 1

Ground: East End Park, Dunfermline KY12 7RB (0383 724295)
Colours: Black and white striped shirts, black shorts.
Manager: Bert Paton.
League Appearances: Bowes M 4; Chalmers P 23(9); Cooper N 33; Cunnington E 26(8); Davies W 39(2); French H 36(2); Grant R 18(14); Hamilton L 39; Haro M 2; Hillcoat J 5; Kelly N 4; Laing D 11(2); Leitch S 34(8); McAllister P (1); McCathie N 30(2); McNamara J 1(2); McWilliams D 22(3); Moyes D 30; O'Boyle G 3; Reilly J (1); Robertson C 34; Shannon R 42; Sharp R 27; Sinclair C 1(5); Smith P 16; Williamson A 4(1)
Goals–League (64): French 12, Davies 10, Chalmers 9, Leitch 9, Grant 4, Laing 3, McWilliams 3, Robertson 3, Cooper 2, McCathie 2, O'Boyle 2, Moyes 1, Smith 1, Williamson 1, own goals 2.
Scottish Cup (1): Chalmers 1.
Skol Cup (6): O'Boyle 2, Davies 1, Grant 1, Leitch 1, McWilliams 1.
B & Q Cup (0).

EAST FIFE   DIV. 2

Ground: Bayview Park, Methil, Fife KY8 3AG (0333 426323)
Colours: Amber shirts with black trim, amber shorts.
Manager: Alex Totten.
League Appearances: Allan G 18(8); Andrew B 9(12); Barron D 5; Beaton D 35; Bell G 19(6); Blyth A (1); Brown W 32(2); Burgess S 21; Burns W 34(3); Charles R 32; Elliott D 9(13); Fraser A 3(3); Gibson J 1; Hope D 33(4); Lennox S 8(1); Long D 1(1); McBride J 33(1); McCracken D 10(2); Moffat J 4; Scott R 26(2); Skelligan R 14(6); Sludden J 31(1); Speirs A (1); Spence T 24(1); Taylor P H 24(2); Wilson E 3
Goals–League (70): Scott 16, Sludden 13, McBride 9, Hope 7, Beaton 5 (3 pens), Skelligan 5, Brown 4, Burns 4, Elliott 3, Allan 2, Andrew 2.
Scottish Cup (5): Skelligan 2, Brown 1, Hope 1, Sludden 1.
Skol Cup (0).
B & Q Cup (0).

EAST STIRLING   DIV. 2

Ground: Firs Park, Falkirk FK2 7AY (0324 23583)
Colours: Black and white hoops, black shorts.
Manager: Bobby McCulley.
League Appearances: Auld A 2(2); Barclay S 13(6); Clark R 3; Craig D 16; Friar P 30(1); Geraghty M 29; Houston P 16(3); Imrie P 15; Kemp B 36; Lawson O 2; McAulay I 3(2); McCarter S (1); McFadyen I 2; Mackie P (1); McKinnon C 36; McMillan C 6(7); O'Sullivan D 10(1); Roberts P 20(10); Ross B 34; Russell G 22(2); Thomson S 32(2); Tierney S 15(5); Walker D 25(1); Watson G 22; Woods T 19(5); Yates D 21
Goals–League (50): Roberts 9, Geraghty 7, Walker 6 (3 pens), McKinnon 5, Friar 4, Tierney 4, Houston 3, Kemp 3, Craig 2, Thomson 2, Woods 2, Barclay 1, Ross 1, Russell 1.
Scottish Cup (10): Geraghty 2, McKinnon 2, Roberts 2, Barclay 1, Thomson 1, Walker 1, own goal 1.
Skol Cup (0).
B & Q Cup (2): Geraghty 2.

FALKIRK
DIV. 1

Ground: Brockville Park, Falkirk FK1 5AX (0324 24121 and 32487)
Colours: Dark blue shirts with white trim, white shorts.
Manager: Jim Jefferies.
League Appearances: Baptie C 8(1); Cadette R 24(7); Drinkell K 33(2); Duffy C 33(1); Hughes J 15; Johnston F 17(5); Lennox G 17(3); McAllister K 40(1); McCall I 27(8); McDougall G 5; McGivern S 1; MacKenzie S 2(1); McLaughlin J 8; McQueen T 30; May E 40(2); Oliver N 24(1); Parks A 15; Rice B 15(2); Shaw G 4(2); Sloan S 21(8); Smith P 19; Taggart C 3(2); Taylor A 3(5); Treanor M 3; Weir D 30; Westwater I 24; Wishart F 23(1); Young K (1)
Goals—League (60): Cadette 8, Drinkell 7, McCall 6, May 6 (1 pen), McQueen 4 (3 pens), McAllister 3, Baptie 2, Lennox 2, Rice 2, Shaw 2, Wishart 2, Johnston 1, McLaughlin 1, Smith 1, Taylor 1, Weir 1.
Scottish Cup (7): May 2, Sloan 2, Cadette 1, Duffy 1, McCall 1.
Skol Cup (6): Drinkell 2, McAllister 1, McQueen 1, May 1, Smith 1.

FORFAR ATHLETIC
DIV. 2

Ground: Station Park, Forfar, Angus DD8 3BT (0307 463576)
Colours: Sky blue shirts, white shorts.
Manager: Tommy Campbell.
League Appearances: Bingham D 20; Byrne J 1; Cameron D 2(1); Donaldson G 11; Glass S 1; Hall A 2; Hamill A 39; Heddle I 37(1); McAulay A 1(6); McCafferty A 6(12); McIntyre S 27(3); McKenna I 24(12); McPhee I 36; Mann R 35; Mearns G 28(3); Morris R 23; Perry J (3); Petrie S 37; Price G (2); Pryde I 1; Sheridan J 7(7); Smith R 15(10); Thomson S 39; Winter G 37
Goals—League (74): Petrie 21, McKenna 10, Smith 8, Winter 8 (3 pens), Bingham 6, Heddle 6, Donaldson 4, McPhee 3, Hamill 1, McCafferty 1, McIntyre 1, Mann 1, Mearns 1, Morris 1, Sheridan 1, own goal 1.
Scottish Cup (8): Heddle 3, McIntyre 1, McKenna 1, Mearns 1, Petrie 1, own goal 1.
Skol Cup (1): Heddle 1.
B & Q Cup (2): Mearns 1, Winter 1.

HAMILTON ACADEMICAL
DIV. 1

Ground: Douglas Park, Hamilton ML3 0DF (0698 286103)
Colours: Red and white hooped shirts, white shorts.
Manager: Iain Munro.
League Appearances: Clark G 34(3); Cramb C 25(8); Doyle P 1; Ferguson A 37; Harris C 14(13); Hillcoat C 33; Lorimer D 1(5); McCulloch R 7; McDonald P 44; McEntegart S 12(3); McInulty S 8(1); McKee K 19(1); McKenzie P 15(6); McLean C 4(2); Millen A 41; Miller C 30; Napier C 27(2); Rae G 9; Reid W 35(2); Smith T 22(6); Ward K 25(9); Waters M 4(7); Weir J 37
Goals—League (65): McDonald 11 (3 pens), Ward 10, Clark 8, Smith 8, Cramb 7, Harris 6, Millen 3, Miller 3, Reid 3, Lorimer 1, McKee 1, McLean 1, Napier 1, Weir 1, own goal 1.
Scottish Cup (1): Reid 1.
Skol Cup (2): Clark 1, Smith 1.
B & Q Cup (14): Clark 5, McDonald 3 (1 pen), Smith 2, Hillcoat 1, Reid 1, Ward 1, Weir 1.

HEART OF MIDLOTHIAN   PREM. DIV.

Ground: Tynecastle Park, Gorgie Road, Edinburgh EH11 2NL (031-337 6132)
Colours: Maroon shirts, white shorts.
Manager: Sandy Clark.
League Appearances: Baird I 34; Bannon E 8(11); Berry N 16(1); Boothroyd A (4);
Crabbe S 4(4); Ferguson D 37; Ferguson I 9(15); Foster W 7(4); Harrison T 3(1);
Hogg G 20(2); Johnston A 2; Levein C 37; Locke G (1); Mackay G 36(1); McKinlay
T 32(2); McLaren A 34; Mauchlen A 16(2); Millar J 23(1); Preston A 19(2);
Robertson J 41(1); Smith H 25; Snodin G 16(11); Thomas K 2(2); Van De Ven P 37;
Walker N 18; Wright G 8(4)
Goals—League (46): Robertson 11 (2 pens), Baird 9, Ferguson I 4, Levein 3, Hogg 2,
Mackay 2, Preston 2, Thomas 2, Bannon 1, Berry 1, Crabbe 1, Ferguson D 1,
Harrison 1, Johnston 1, McKinlay 1, McLaren 1, Millar 1, own goals 2.
Scottish Cup (11): Robertson 3 (1 pen), Baird 2, Boothroyd 2, Preston 2, Ferguson D
1, Snodin 1.
Skol Cup (4): Mackay 1, McKinlay 1, McLaren 1, Robertson 1.

HIBERNIAN   PREM. DIV.

Ground: Easter Road Stadium, Edinburgh EH7 5QG (031-661 2159)
Colours: Green shirts with white sleeves and collar, white shorts.
Manager: Alex Miller.
League Appearances: Beaumont D 16; Burridge J 30; Donald G 1(3); Evans G
22(17); Farrell D 9(3); Fellenger D 1(4); Findlay W 3(4); Hamilton B 39(2); Hunter
G 23; Jackson C (1); Jackson D 35(1); Lennon D 7(6); Love G 1; McGinlay P 40;
McGraw M 1(1); McIntyre T 12; MacLeod M 26(5); Miller G 1; Miller W 29(5);
Milne C 10(5); Mitchell G 41; Orr N 20(1); Raynes S 2; Reid C 14; Tortolano J
16(5); Tweed S 13(1); Weir M 30(3); Wright K 42
Goals—League (54): Jackson D 13 (4 pens), Wright 11, McGinlay 10 (1 pen), Evans
6, Weir 5, Tortolano 3, Fellenger 2, Hamilton 1, McIntyre 1, own goals 2.
Scottish Cup (8): McGinlay 2, Weir 2, Wright 2, Jackson D 1, Tweed 1.
Skol Cup (5): Evans 2, Hamilton 1, McGinlay 1, Wright 1.

KILMARNOCK   PREM. DIV.

Ground: Rugby Park, Kilmarnock KA1 2DP (0563 25184)
Colours: Blue and white striped shirts, blue shorts.
Manager: Tommy Burns.
League Appearances: Black T 10; Burns H 9(1); Burns T 39; Campbell C 13(11);
Crainie D 3(6); Furphy W 1; Geddes R 44; Jack R 11(7); McCarrison D 6(2);
McCluskey G 29(2); MacPherson A 39(1); McSkimming S 35; McStay W (1);
Mitchell A 26(6); Montgomerie R 42; Paterson C 21; Porteous I 17(3); Reilly M
18(1); Roberts M 4(1); Skilling M 40; Stark W 28; Tait T 5; Williamson R 26(7);
Wilson T 18(1)
Goals—League (67): McCluskey 11, Mitchell 6, Porteous 6, Williamson 6 (1 pen),
Jack 5, MacPherson 5, McSkimming 5, Campbell 4, Skilling 4, Reilly 3 (2 pens),
Stark 3, Burns T 2, Black 1 (pen), Crainie 1, McCarrison 1, Paterson 1, Tait 1, own
goals 2.
Scottish Cup (5): Williamson 3, McCluskey 1, MacPherson 1.
Skol Cup (7): Burns T 2, Campbell 1, Jack 1, McCluskey 1, McSkimming 1, Skilling
1.
B & Q Cup (4): McCluskey 2, Burns T 1, Mitchell 1.

MEADOWBANK THISTLE   DIV. 2

Ground: Meadowbank Stadium, Edinburgh EH7 6AE (031-661 5351)
Colours: Amber with black trim, black shorts.
Manager: Donald Park.
League Appearances: Armstrong G 14; Bailey L 29(1); Banks A 24(4); Coughlin J 35(2); Coyle M 4(3); Duthie M 5(13); Elder S 21(6); Ellison S 26; Fleming D 3(1); Graham T 2; Grant D 7; Hutchison M 13(3); Irvine W 6(3); Kane K 3(7); Little I 26(13); Logan S (3); McLeod G 28; McNeill W 2; McQueen J 18; Murray M 31; Neil C 1(1); Nicol A 11; Rae G 21; Roseburgh D 35(2); Rutherford P 27; Ryrie B 7(4); Scott S 1; Williamson S 35; Wilson S 39; Young J 10(1)
Goals–League (51): Rutherford 9, Roseburgh 8 (1 pen), Bailey 7, Little 7, Irvine 4, Wilson 4, McLeod 3, Coughlin 2, Rae 2, Banks 1, Coyle 1, Duthie 1, Hutchison 1, own goal 1.
Scottish Cup (1): Rutherford 1.
Skol Cup (0).

B & Q Cup (5): Wilson 2, Kane 1, Logan 1, Roseburgh 1.

MONTROSE   DIV. 2

Ground: Links Park, Montrose DD10 8QD (0674 73200)
Colours: Blue with white trim, white shorts.
Manager: John Holt.
League Appearances: Allan M 20(5); Burnett C 8; Callaghan W 4; Christie G 13(7); Craib M 38; Craib S 16(5); Davidson G 1; Dolan A 1(1); Fleming J 22; Forbes G 12; Forsyth S 14; Fotheringham J (1); Fraser C 18; Furphy W 1; Garden M 2; Grant D 28; Houghton G 10(2); Irvine N 25; Jack R 6; Kasule V 1; Kelly M 3(5); Larter D 27; Lavelle M 6(2); Logan A 17(4); McGovern P 2; Masson P (3); Maver C 18(5); Moffat J 12; Morrison B 10(2); Nelson M 5; Ritchie M 5; Robertson I 36; Smith J 28; Smith L (1); Yeats C 20(7)
Goals–League (46): Grant 10, Fraser 5, Logan 4, Maver 4, Yeats 4, Allan 3 (1 pen), Craib S 3 (1 pen), Craib M 2, Jack 2, Callaghan 1, Christie 1, Fleming 1, Forsyth 1, Kelly 1, Nelson 1, Robertson 1, own goals 2.
Scottish Cup (0).
Skol Cup (0).
B & Q Cup (9): Grant 3, Fraser 2, Allan 1, Forsyth 1, Kelly 1, Logan 1.

GREENOCK MORTON   DIV. 1

Ground: Cappielow Park, Greenock PA15 2TY (0475 23511)
Colours: Royal blue tartan shirts, royal blue shorts.
Manager: Allan McGraw.
League Appearances: Alexander R 30(1); Boag J 5; Collins D 41; Doak M 27(4); Fowler J 13(6); Gahagan J 16(3); Hopkin D 9; Johnstone D 32; Lilley D 16(6); McArthur J 39; MacCabe D 10(3); McCahill S 23(1); McDonald I 14(11); McEwan A 1(1); McGhee D 3; McInnes D 40; Mahood A 17; Mathie A 31(1); Pickering M 25(3); Rafferty S 31(7); Sanders G (1); Shearer N 1; Thomson R 2(6); Tolmie J 14(7); Wylie D 44
Goals–League (65): Mathie 13 (1 pen), Alexander 10, Johnstone 6, McArthur 6, MacCabe 6, Mahood 6, Lilley 4, Gahagan 2, McEwan 2, McInnes 2, Rafferty 2, Tolmie 2, Doak 1, Hopkin 1, McDonald 1, own goal 1.
Scottish Cup (0).
Skol Cup (2): Alexander 1, Mathie 1.
B & Q Cup (14): Mathie 7, Alexander 4, Lilley 1, Mahood 1, Tolmie 1.

151

MOTHERWELL
PREM. DIV.

Ground: Fir Park, Motherwell ML1 2QN (0698 261437/8/9)
Colours: Amber shirts with claret band, claret shorts.
Manager: Tommy McLean.
League Appearances: Angus I 25(6); Arnott D 28(5); Baker P 5(4); Bryce S 1; Cooper D 42(1); Dolan J 15(10); Dykstra S 35; Ferguson I 11(4); Gardner J (2); Gourlay A (2); Graham A 4; Griffin J 24(1); Kirk S 26(14); Kromheer E 11(1); McCart C 28(1); McGrillen P 12(10); McKinnon R 35; McLeod J 4(6); Martin B 43(1); Nijholt L 31(3); O'Donnell P 32; Philliben J 31; Shepherd A 2(3); Shepstone P 1; Simpson N 12; Sneddon A 16; Thomson W 9; Verheul B (1)
Goals–League (46): Kirk 10, Arnott 6, McGrillen 6, O'Donnell 4, Angus 3, McCart 3, Martin 3, Cooper 2 (1 pen), Dolan 2, Ferguson 2, Baker 1, Graham 1, Griffin 1, Simpson 1, own goal 1.
Scottish Cup (0).
Skol Cup (4): Ferguson 3, Angus 1.

PARTICK THISTLE
PREM. DIV.

Ground: Firhill Park, Glasgow G20 7AL (041-945 4811)
Colours: Red and yellow striped shirts, black shorts.
Manager: John Lambie.
League Appearances: Britton G 39(1); Broddle J 6; Cameron I 38(3); Chisholm G 8(1); Clark M 8; Craig A 26(3); Docherty S (1); English I 3(10); Farningham R 35(2); Irons D 43; Jamieson W 26(2); Johnston S 11(4); Kinnaird P 14(6); Law R 34; McGlashan C 12(10); McKilligan N 3(2); McLaughlin P 22(1); McVicar D 38; McWalter M 7(5); Magee K (5); Murdoch A 17; Nelson C 27; Palin L 5; Peebles G 8(1); Shaw G 28(3); Smith T 2; Taylor A 8; Tierney G 16
Goals–League (50): Britton 12 (1 pen), Shaw 10 (1 pen), Farningham 8, Cameron 5 (2 pens), Jamieson 3, Irons 2, McGlashan 2, Tierney 2, Craig 1, Johnston 1, Kinnaird 1, Taylor 1, own goals 2.
Scottish Cup (0).
Skol Cup (4): Britton 1, Farningham 1, Kinnaird 1, Shaw 1

QUEEN OF THE SOUTH
DIV. 2

Ground: Palmerston Park, Dumfries DG2 9BA (0387 54853)
Colours: Royal blue shirts, white shorts.
Manager: William McLaren.
League Appearances: Bell A 20(4); Davidson A 8; Dickson J 27(2); Fraser G 6(4); Frye J F (1); Gillespie A 1; Gordon S 16(6); Hair P 3; Henderson D 25(1); Hetherington K 1; Hoy D 28; McCulloch D 1; McFarlane A 37; McGhie W 31(3); McGuire D 19(7); McGuire J 15(1); McKeown B 12(1); Mills D 19; Robertson J 15(8); Rowe G 36; Sermanni P 27(1); Sharp K (2); Sim W 18(2); Templeton H 1(7); Thomson A 38; Wright B 25
Goals–League (57): Thomson 21 (1 pen), Henderson 9, McGuire D 5, McFarlane 4, McGhie 4, Robertson 4 (1 pen), McGuire J 3, Sermanni 3, Rowe 2, Templeton 1, own goal 1.
Scottish Cup (4): Henderson 2, Rowe 2.
Skol Cup (3): Templeton 3.
B & Q Cup (4): Rowe 2, Templeton 1, Thomson 1.

QUEEN'S PARK   DIV. 2

Ground: Hampden Park, Glasgow G42 9BA (041-632 1275)
Colours: Black and white hooped shirts, white shorts.
Coach: Eddie Hunter.
League Appearances: Black S 4(5); Bradley R 3(2); Bryers C (1); Callan D 12(1); Caven R 34; Chalmers J 28; Crooks G 3(5); Devlin W 6; Elder G 27; Ferguson P 1; Graham D 29(3); Greig D 5(3); Henrici R 2(2); Jackson D 35; Kavanagh J 9; Kerr G 26; McCormick S 30(2); McIntyre D (1); Mackay M 33; Mackenzie K 2; Millar G 5(15); Moonie D 11; Morris S 4(1); O'Brien J (1); O'Neill J 19(8); Orr G 33(2); Orr J 11; Rodden J 22(4); Sneddon S 11; Stevenson C 24(2)
Goals–League (51): Caven 11, Rodden 9, O'Neill 6, McCormick 5, Black 3, Elder 3, Mackay 3, Stevenson 2, Crooks 1, Graham 1, Greig 1, Jackson 1, Kerr 1, Millar 1, Orr G 1, own goals 2.
Scottish Cup (0).
Skol Cup (1): McCormick 1.
B & Q Cup (2): Jackson 1, McCormick 1.

RAITH ROVERS   PREM. DIV.

Ground: Stark's Park, Pratt Street, Kirkcaldy KY1 1SA (0592 263514)
Colours: Navy blue shirts, white shorts.
Manager: Jimmy Nicholl.
League Appearances: ; Arthur G 17; Brewster C 44; Cameron C 13(3); Carson T 27; Coyle R 35; Crawford S 10(10); Cusick J 1(1); Dair J 10(5); Dalziel G 44; Dennis S 31; Hetherston P 44; McGeachie G 29(1); MacKenzie A 5(18); MacLeod I 34(2); McStay J 41; Nicholl J 38; Raeside R 10; Sinclair D 25(7); Thomson I 26(8); Williamson T (2)
Goals–League (85): Dalziel 32 (1 pen), Brewster 22, McStay 5, Nicholl 5, Hetherston 4, Thomson 4, Crawford 3, MacKenzie 3, MacLeod 2, Cameron 1, Coyle 1, Dair 1, Dennis 1, own goal 1.
Scottish Cup (0).
Skol Cup (1): McStay 1.
B & Q Cup (0).

RANGERS   PREM. DIV.

Ground: Ibrox Stadium, Glasgow G51 2XD (041-427 8500)
Colours: Royal blue shirts, white shorts.
Manager: Walter Smith.
League Appearances: Brown J 39; Durrant I 19(11); Ferguson I 29(1); Goram A 34; Gordon D 18(4); Gough R 25; Hagen D 5(3); Hateley M 36(1); Huistra P 27(3); Kouznetsov O 8(1); McCall S 35(1); McCoist A 32(2); McPherson D 34; McSwegan G 8(1); Maxwell A 10; Mikhailichenko A 16(13); Murray N 11(5); Nisbet S 10; Pressley S 8; Reid B 2; Rideout P (1); Robertson A (2); Robertson D 39; Robertson L 1; Spackman N 2; Steven T 24; Stevens G 9; Watson S 3
Goals–League (97): McCoist 34 (2 pens), Hateley 19, McCall 5, Mikhailichenko 5, Steven 5, Brown 4, Ferguson 4, Huistra 4, McSwegan 4, Durrant 3, Robertson D 3, Gough 2, Hagen 2, McPherson 2, Gordon 1.
Scottish Cup (11): McCoist 5 (1 pen), Hateley 2, Murray 2, Gordon 1, McPherson 1.
Skol Cup (18): McCoist 8, Hateley 3, Durrant 1, Gordon 1, Gough 1, Huistra 1, McCall 1, Mikhailichenko 1, own goal 1.

ST JOHNSTONE   PREM. DIV.

Ground: McDiarmid Park, Crieff Road, Perth PH1 2SJ (0738 26961)
Colours: Royal blue shirts with white trim, white shorts.
Manager: John McClelland.
League Appearances: Arkins V 24(2); Baltacha S 25; Buglione M 6(1); Byrne D 12; Cherry P 12(4); Cole A 7; Curran H 32(2); Davies J 33(5); Deas P 25; Dunne L 4(4); Inglis J 39; Kinnaird P 2(6); McAuley S 24(2); McClelland J 25(1); McGinnis G 26(1); McGowne K 25(1); Maskrey S 3(16); Moore A 17(9); Redford I 12(4); Rhodes A 44; Scott P 2(1); Sweeney P 2; Torfason G 9(1); Treanor M 7(2); Turner T 25(3); Wright P 42
Goals–League (52): Wright 14 (1 pen), Curran 8, Arkins 6, Davies 4, Torfason 4 (1 pen), Moore 3, Buglione 2, Dunne 2, Maskrey 2, Redford 2, Cherry 1, Deas 1, McGowne 1, Treanor 1, Turner 1.
Scottish Cup (7): Arkins 2, Wright 2, Cherry 1, Davies 1, Maskrey 1.
Skol Cup (9): Wright 5 (1 pen), Curran 1, McAuley 1, Maskrey 1, Torfason 1.

ST MIRREN   DIV. 1

Ground: St Mirren Park, Paisley PA3 2EJ (041-889 2558 and 041-840 1337)
Colours: White shirts with black vertical stripes, white shorts.
Manager: Jimmy Bone.
League Appearances: Baillie A 38; Baker M 29; Beattie J 2; Bone A 2(7); Broddle J 13(1); Charnley J 14; Cummings P 1(3); Dawson R 34; Elliot D 38(2); Fabiani R (6); Farrell S 15(4); Fridge L 18; Fullarton J 25(1); Gallagher E 18(1); Gillies K 8(11); Gillies R 2(6); Hetherston B (1); Hewitt J 24(3); Lambert P 38(1); Lavety B 32(10); McDowall K 12(1); McGill D 6(3); McGrotty G (2); McIntyre P 14(6); McLaughlin B 2; McVie G 3(3); McWhirter N 34; Manley R 20; Money C 25; Paterson A 1; Peacock J 7(1); Reid M 5; Taylor S 2; Torfason G 1; Watson D 1
Goals–League (62): Lavety 18, Gallagher 12 (2 pens), Elliot 5, Hewitt 5, Baillie 4, McDowall 3, Farrell 2, Money 2 (2 pens), Charnley 1 (pen), Gillies K 1, Gillies R 1, Lambert 1, McIntyre 1, McVie 1, McWhirter 1, own goals 2.
Scottish Cup (2): Gallagher 1, Lavety 1.
Skol Cup (1): Lavety 1.
B & Q Cup (1): Charnley 1.

STENHOUSEMUIR   DIV. 2

Ground: Ochilview Park, Stenhousemuir FK5 5QL (0324 562992)
Colours: Maroon shirts with silver trim, white shorts.
Manager: Terry Christie.
League Appearances: Aitken N 23(1); Anderson P 9(1); Armstrong G 28; Barnstaple K 23; Barr R 4(5); Bell D 15(10); Black K 2; Clarke J 26(2); Clouston B 27(3); Dickov S 10(7); Fisher J 36; Godfrey P 19; Haddow L 24(4); Hallford E 38(1); Irvine J 8(5); Kelly C 16; Kemp R 2; Logan S 22(1); Lytwyn C 13(4); Mackie P 8(5); McLafferty W 4(4); Mathieson M 39; Prior S 6(1); Reid J 1; Steel T 22(5); Tracey K 4(1)
Goals–League (59): Mathieson 26, Steel 6, Bell 3, Dickov 3, Haddow 3, Irvine 3, Lytwyn 3, Aitken 2, Fisher 2, McLafferty 2, Armstrong 1, Hallford 1, Kemp 1 (pen), Mackie 1, own goals 2.
Scottish Cup (2): Hallford 1 (pen), Lytwyn 1.
Skol Cup (2): Irvine 1, Steel 1.
B & Q Cup (2): Bell 1, Mathieson 1.

STIRLING ALBION   DIV. 1

Ground: Forthbank Stadium, Springkerse Industrial Estate, Stirling FK7 7UW (0786 450399)
Colours: Red shirts with white sleeves, white shorts.
Manager: John Brogan.
League Appearances: Armstrong P 42; Brogan J (1); Brown I 1(3); Callaghan T 18(8); Clark R 7; Dempsey J 4; Docherty A 7(17); Docherty R 3(4); Kerr J 26; Lawrie D 28; McCallum M 9(10); McCormack J T 18; McGeown M 44; McInnes I 34(9); McKenna A 17(2); Mitchell C 39; Moore V 28(3); Pew D 17(3); Reilly R 24(9); Robertson S 9; Ross B 2; Shanks D 21(3); Tait T 26(1); Taylor G 4; Watson P 31; Watters W 25(9)
Goals–League (44): Watters 11 (2 pens), McCallum 4, McInnes 4, Moore 4, Mitchell 3 (1 pen), Pew 3, Reilly 3, Armstrong 2 (2 pens), Callaghan 2, Lawrie 2, Tait 2, McKenna 1, Shanks 1, Watson 1, own goal 1.
Scottish Cup (1): McInnes.
Skol Cup (0).
B & Q Cup (2): Moore 1, Watters 1.

STRANRAER   DIV. 2

Ground: Stair Park, Stranraer DG9 8BS (0776 3271)
Colours: Royal blue shirts with amber band, blue shorts.
Manager: Alex McAnespie.
League Appearances: Brannigan K 38; Butler J 2; Cody S 20(9); Diver D 21(4); Duffy B 15; Duncan G 35(4); Evans S 6(4); Ferguson W 4(7); Fraser A 1(2); Gallagher A 23(2); Geraghty M (1); Grant A 36(2); Hughes J 37; Kelly P 9(14); Love J 11(9); McCann J 35; McIntyre S 26(1); McLean P 22(1); Millar G 11; Ross S 24; Sloan T 38; Smith A (2); Spittal I 15
Goals–League (69): Sloan 19, Diver 11, Grant 11, Duncan 8 (5 pens), Gallagher 5, McLean 5, McIntyre 3, Ferguson 2, Brannigan 1, Cody 1, Hughes 1, Millar 1, own goal 1.
Scottish Cup (2): Cody 1, Duncan 1.
Skol Cup (3): Cody 1, Grant 1, Sloan 1.
B & Q Cup (3): Diver 1, McIntyre 1, Sloan 1.

SCOTTISH REVIEW

Rangers again completely dominated the Scottish scene and recorded their 43rd championship in the process of winning League, Scottish Cup and Skol Cup for a splendid treble.

In addition to this domestic success, they had a fine season in Europe and were unfortunate to be eliminated under the new format which saw them retire though unbeaten in the latter stages, now known as The Champions League.

Ally McCoist was again the leading marksman in Europe, finishing with exactly the same number of League goals he scored in 1991–92 – 34. But he missed the last seven League games with injury, otherwise he might well have gone on to break Sam English's long-standing record of 44 goals achieved way back in 1931–32.

He was given fine support up front by target man Mark Hateley who scored 19 goals himself of a total of 97 in the League. No Rangers player managed to appear in all games among the 28 called upon, but John Brown and Dave Robertson with 39 outings came nearest to being an ever present members of the staff.

Highlight of the campaign was undoubtedly the run of 29 League games without defeat from losing 4-3 at Dundee on 15 August, until being beaten 2-1 at Celtic on 20 February. Rangers suffered only two more reverses, losing 3-0 at Partick and 1-0 at Aberdeen. Aberdeen found themselves runners-up to Rangers in all three competitions! Celtic finished third, but they were a long way in front of Dundee United in fourth place. At Tannadice, Jim McLean finally retired as manager and was replaced in the summer by Ivan Golac, whose previous experience in the role had been briefly with Torquay United.

Relegated teams from the Premier League were Falkirk and Airdrie, while their places were taken by Raith Rovers and Kilmarnock, who overhauled Dunfermline Athletic in the closing matches.

Down from the First Division went Meadowbank and Cowdenbeath, who had a wretched season, failing to win at home at all and conceding 109 goals overall in the process. They will be replaced by Clyde and Brechin, though Stranraer, who enjoyed their best season in the League, came close to snatching second place. On the last day of the season, only a penalty two minutes from time enabled Brechin to make it in a 2-1 win at already promoted Clyde.

As far as the 1993–94 season is concerned, it is hard to imagine Rangers being challenged for the title. They may find it harder in the cup competitions, but it will be interesting to see how Ferguson fits in at Ibrox.

With the prospect of four divisions being fashioned in the future, there will be a keen edge to play in all three divisions this season.

At international level, the disappointment of a poor showing so far in the World Cup qualifying matches can be put aside if there is a genuine realisation that Scotland's youth has a role to play at the highest level.

SCOTTISH LEAGUE – PREMIER DIVISION RESULTS 1992–93

	Aberdeen	Airdrie	Celtic	Dundee	Dundee U	Falkirk	Hearts	Hibernian	Motherwell	Partick	Rangers	St Johnstone
Aberdeen	—	1-2	1-1	2-0	0-0	1-1	6-2	3-0	2-0	2-0	1-0	3-1
Airdrie	0-0	—	0-1	4-0	2-0	3-1	3-2	1-1	2-2	1-0	1-0	0-2
Celtic	2-2	2-0	—	2-1	1-2	0-1	1-0	1-3	2-0	2-2	0-1	3-1
Dundee	0-2	4-0	1-0	—	1-4	1-2	0-1	3-0	1-1	0-2	3-0	3-1
Dundee U	2-2	2-1	1-1	2-0	—	1-1	2-2	3-1	2-0	0-1	3-2	5-1
Falkirk	0-1	3-0	2-3	2-0	0-3	—	2-1	3-1	4-0	2-1	5-0	1-0
Hearts	0-4	5-1	4-3	2-2	6-0	1-1	—	0-0	1-2	2-2	2-1	3-1
Hibernian	1-1	2-0	0-1	3-0	3-1	3-1	2-0	—	1-2	2-3	3-0	2-0
Motherwell	1-2	0-2	0-0	1-1	0-0	1-1	0-0	1-0	—	2-2	4-1	2-2
Partick	2-1	2-0	2-3	0-3	1-1	0-2	0-1	2-3	0-2	—	0-2	2-0
Rangers	2-0	2-2	1-0	3-1	4-0	5-0	2-1	3-0	4-1	3-0	—	1-1
St Johnstone	0-2	1-0	1-1	3-1	0-4	2-0	1-1	2-0	0-0	0-0	1-1	—

157

SCOTTISH LEAGUE – DIVISION I RESULTS 1992–93

	Ayr U	Clydebank	Cowdenbeath	Dumbarton	Dunfermline Ath	Hamilton A	Kilmarnock	Meadowbank T	Morton	Raith R	St Mirren	Stirling Alb
Ayr U	—	2-0	0-1	5-2	1-0	0-0	2-0	1-1	2-1	1-0	3-3	2-2
Clydebank	1-1	—	3-1	3-0	1-0	1-1	0-1	1-2	0-3	5-0	3-0	2-4
Cowdenbeath	1-2	3-3	—	3-3	0-0	3-1	2-0	3-1	2-2	4-3	0-3	1-1
Dumbarton	0-3	0-2	5-0	—	2-5	0-4	2-3	0-2	2-2	2-0	1-2	1-1
Dunfermline Ath	2-0	1-3	1-2	1-2	—	2-2	0-1	2-2	0-1	1-1	4-2	4-3
Hamilton A	1-1	0-3	4-2	0-1	0-1	—	2-1	3-0	1-0	0-2	2-2	1-0
Kilmarnock	1-1	2-1	3-0	2-1	2-2	2-1	—	1-0	3-1	0-2	2-2	1-0
Meadowbank T	1-3	3-0	4-0	1-0	0-3	0-4	2-2	—	2-1	1-2	0-0	2-1
Morton	3-0	6-0	3-0	3-3	1-2	1-2	0-1	4-0	—	2-3	1-2	1-0
Raith R	1-0	2-2	2-4	1-2	0-1	2-1	2-0	5-2	2-0	—	1-1	2-0
St Mirren	2-0	4-2	1-2	4-1	1-0	1-2	0-2	1-1	2-0	0-1	—	2-0
Stirling Alb	1-1	2-3	2-1	1-2	0-5	2-0	2-0	2-2	1-2	2-1	1-2	—

SCOTTISH LEAGUE – DIVISION II RESULTS 1992-93

	Albion R	Alloa	Arbroath	Berwick R	Brechin C	Clyde	East Fife	East Stirling	Forfar Ath	Montrose	Queen of South	Queen's Park	Stenhousemuir	Stranraer
Albion R	—	0-1	1-2	1-1	1-4	1-2	0-2	2-2	2-1	2-2	2-1	3-2	0-0	1-2
Alloa	1-0	—	1-2	0-2	1-3	1-1	4-2	1-0	1-1	3-1	1-3	0-1	2-1	1-2
Arbroath	2-0	0-0	—	2-1	0-0	0-1	1-3	4-5	2-3	1-1	0-0	1-0	0-2	1-1
Berwick R	1-1	2-2	6-0	—	0-2	0-1	1-0	2-2	3-1	1-0	1-3	1-1	2-1	0-0
Brechin C	2-0	4-2	2-0	5-1	—	2-1	2-2	2-1	1-2	3-1	1-1	4-1	2-2	0-0
Clyde	4-0	0-1	0-1	0-1	1-2	—	2-2	5-2	2-3	2-0	2-5	1-1	0-0	0-1
East Fife	5-0	2-0	1-3	1-0	1-2	2-3	—	5-1	0-2	1-2	1-1	1-1	1-1	1-1
East Stirling	1-1	2-2	1-2	2-0	1-0	1-3	1-3	—	0-3	2-0	1-2	2-1	2-2	2-1
Forfar Ath	3-2	4-2	2-0	5-3	0-1	2-4	2-2	5-1	—	4-3	5-1	4-0	3-0	4-1
Montrose	2-1	1-1	0-2	2-0	2-1	1-6	1-1	1-2	4-3	—	0-1	2-2	0-1	0-2
Queen of South	0-3	0-7	0-1	1-0	0-2	3-1	0-1	1-2	0-2	5-1	—	0-2	0-1	0-3
Queen's Park	1-0	0-3	1-1	4-0	2-4	3-0	0-2	4-2	2-4	0-1	1-1	—	2-2	1-2
Stenhousemuir	2-0	2-1	1-3	1-0	3-0	3-1	3-1	1-2	2-0	3-1	1-1	0-1	—	2-5
Stranraer	1-1	1-2	1-0	3-1	0-0	1-1	2-1	1-0	2-0	3-1	2-2	4-2	0-0	—

159

SCOTTISH LEAGUE FINAL TABLES 1992–93

Premier Divison	P	Home W	D	L	Goals F	A	Away W	D	L	Goals F	A	Pt	GD
Rangers	44	20	2	0	52	11	13	5	4	45	24	73	+62
Aberdeen	44	13	7	2	41	13	14	3	5	46	23	64	+51
Celtic	44	13	5	4	37	18	11	7	4	31	23	60	+27
Dundee U	44	8	7	7	25	27	11	2	9	31	22	47	+7
Hearts	44	12	6	4	26	15	3	8	11	11	20	44	−5
St Johnstone	44	8	10	4	29	27	2	10	10	23	39	40	−14
Hibernian	44	8	8	6	32	28	4	5	13	22	36	37	−10
Partick T	44	5	6	11	26	41	7	6	9	24	30	36	−21
Motherwell	44	7	4	11	27	37	4	9	9	19	25	35	−16
Dundee	44	7	4	11	25	34	4	8	10	23	34	34	−20
Falkirk	44	7	5	10	40	39	4	2	16	20	47	29	−26
Airdrieonians	44	4	9	9	22	27	2	8	12	13	43	29	−35

First Division	P	Home W	D	L	Goals F	A	Away W	D	L	Goals F	A	Pt	GD
Raith R	44	17	5	0	54	14	8	10	4	31	27	65	+44
Kilmarnock	44	13	6	3	43	14	8	6	8	24	26	54	+27
Dunfermline Ath	44	10	5	7	33	27	12	3	7	31	20	52	+17
St Mirren	44	11	5	6	33	20	10	4	8	29	32	51	+10
Hamilton A	44	11	7	4	36	23	8	5	9	29	22	50	+20
Morton	44	11	3	8	36	27	8	7	7	29	29	48	+9
Ayr U	44	9	9	4	27	19	5	9	8	22	25	46	+5
Clydebank	44	10	8	4	42	22	6	5	11	29	44	45	+5
Dumbarton	44	10	3	9	30	30	5	4	13	26	41	37	−15
Stirling Albion	44	7	5	10	23	31	4	8	10	21	30	35	−17
Meadowbank T	44	6	6	10	23	32	5	4	13	28	48	32	−29
Cowdenbeath	44	0	5	17	18	55	3	2	17	15	54	13	−76

Second Division	P	Home W	D	L	Goals F	A	Away W	D	L	Goals F	A	Pt	GD
Clyde	39	11	5	4	37	18	11	5	3	40	24	54	+35
Brechin C	39	13	3	3	37	13	10	4	6	25	19	53	+30
Stranraer	39	8	9	2	33	21	11	6	3	36	23	53	+25
Forfar Ath	39	10	5	4	47	30	8	5	7	27	24	46	+20
Alloa	39	8	4	7	25	28	8	8	4	38	26	44	+9
Arbroath	39	8	6	6	34	26	10	2	7	25	24	44	+9
Stenhousemuir	39	9	3	8	30	25	6	7	6	29	23	40	+11
Berwick R	39	8	5	6	30	25	8	2	10	26	39	39	−8
East Fife	39	6	6	8	32	33	8	4	7	38	31	38	+6
Queen of the S	39	5	4	11	27	37	7	5	7	30	35	33	−15
Queen's Park	39	6	6	7	29	32	2	6	12	22	41	28	−22
Montrose	39	5	3	12	24	35	5	4	10	22	36	27	−25
East Stirling	39	4	4	12	24	39	4	5	10	26	46	25	−35
Albion R	39	4	5	10	22	36	2	5	13	14	40	22	−40

SCOTTISH LEAGUE HONOURS LIST

PREMIER DIVISION
Maximum points: 72

	First	Pts	Second	Pts	Third	Pts
1975–76	Rangers	54	Celtic	48	Hibernian	43
1976–77	Celtic	55	Rangers	46	Aberdeen	43
1977–78	Rangers	55	Aberdeen	53	Dundee U	40
1978–79	Celtic	48	Rangers	45	Dundee U	44
1979–80	Aberdeen	48	Celtic	47	St Mirren	42
1980–81	Celtic	56	Aberdeen	49	Rangers*	44
1981–82	Celtic	55	Aberdeen	53	Rangers	43
1982–83	Dundee U	56	Celtic*	55	Aberdeen	55
1983–84	Aberdeen	57	Celtic	50	Dundee U	47
1984–85	Aberdeen	59	Celtic	52	Dundee U	47
1985–86	Celtic*	50	Hearts	50	Dundee U	47

Maximum points: 88

	First	Pts	Second	Pts	Third	Pts
1986–87	Rangers	69	Celtic	63	Dundee U	60
1987–88	Celtic	72	Hearts	62	Rangers	60

Maximum points: 72

	First	Pts	Second	Pts	Third	Pts
1988–89	Rangers	56	Aberdeen	50	Celtic	46
1989–90	Rangers	51	Aberdeen*	44	Hearts	44
1990–91	Rangers	55	Aberdeen	53	Celtic*	41

Maximum points: 88

	First	Pts	Second	Pts	Third	Pts
1991–92	Rangers	72	Hearts	63	Celtic	62
1992–93	Rangers	73	Aberdeen	64	Celtic	60

FIRST DIVISION
Maximum points: 52

	First	Pts	Second	Pts	Third	Pts
1975–76	Partick T	41	Kilmarnock	35	Montrose	30

Maximum points: 78

	First	Pts	Second	Pts	Third	Pts
1976–77	St Mirren	62	Clydebank	58	Dundee	51
1977–78	Morton*	58	Hearts	58	Dundee	57
1978–79	Dundee	55	Kilmarnock*	54	Clydebank	54
1979–80	Hearts	53	Airdrieonians	51	Ayr U	44
1980–81	Hibernian	57	Dundee	52	St Johnstone	51
1981–82	Motherwell	61	Kilmarnock	51	Hearts	50
1982–83	St Johnstone	55	Hearts	54	Clydebank	50
1983–84	Morton	54	Dumbarton	51	Partick T	46
1984–85	Motherwell	50	Clydebank	48	Falkirk	45
1985–86	Hamilton A	56	Falkirk	45	Kilmarnock	44

Maximum points: 88

	First	Pts	Second	Pts	Third	Pts
1986–87	Morton	57	Dunfermline Ath	56	Dumbarton	53
1987–88	Hamilton A	56	Meadowbank T	52	Clydebank	49

		Maximum points: 78			
1988–89	Dunfermline Ath	54	Falkirk	52	Clydebank	48
1989–90	St Johnstone	58	Airdrieonians	54	Clydebank	44
1990–91	Falkirk	54	Airdrieonians	53	Dundee	52

		Maximum points: 88			
1991–92	Dundee	58	Partick T*	57	Hamilton A	57
1992–93	Raith R	65	Kilmarnock	54	Dunfermline Ath	52

SECOND DIVISION

		Maximum points: 52			
1975–77	Clydebank*	40	Raith R	40	Alloa	35

		Maximum points: 78			
1976–77	Stirling A	55	Alloa	51	Dunfermline Ath	50
1977–78	Clyde*	53	Raith R	53	Dunfermline Ath	48
1978–79	Berwick R	54	Dunfermline Ath	52	Falkirk	50
1979–80	Falkirk	50	East Stirling	49	Forfar Ath	46
1980–81	Queen's Park	50	Queen of the S	46	Cowdenbeath	45
1981–82	Clyde	59	Alloa*	50	Arbroath	50
1982–83	Brechin C	55	Meadowbank T	54	Arbroath	49
1983–84	Forfar Ath	63	East Fife	47	Berwick R	43
1984–85	Montrose	53	Alloa	50	Dunfermline Ath	49
1985–86	Dunfermline Ath	57	Queen of the S	55	Meadowbank T	49
1986–87	Meadowbank T	55	Raith R*	52	Stirling A	52
1987–88	Ayr U	61	St Johnstone	59	Queen's Park	51
1988–89	Albion R	50	Alloa	45	Brechin C	43
1989–90	Brechin C	49	Kilmarnock	48	Stirling A	47
1990–91	Stirling A	54	Montrose	46	Cowdenbeath	45

		Maximum points: 78			
1991–92	Dumbarton	52	Cowdenbeath	51	Alloa	50
1992–93	Clyde	54	Brechin C*	53	Stranraer	53

FIRST DIVISION to 1974–75

Maximum points: *a* 36; *b* 44; *c* 40; *d* 52; *e* 60; *f* 68; *g* 76; *h* 84.

	First	Pts	Second	Pts	Third	Pts
1890–91*a*††	Dumbarton	29	Rangers	29	Celtic	24
1891–92*b*	Dumbarton	37	Celtic	35	Hearts	30
1892–93*a*	Celtic	29	Rangers	28	St Mirren	23
1893–94*a*	Celtic	29	Hearts	26	St Bernard's	22
1894–95*a*	Hearts	31	Celtic	26	Rangers	21
1895–96*a*	Celtic	30	Rangers	26	Hibernian	24
1896–97*a*	Hearts	28	Hibernian	26	Rangers	25

1897–98a	Celtic	33	Rangers	29	Hibernian	22
1898–99a	Rangers	36	Hearts	26	Celtic	24
1899–						
1900a	Rangers	32	Celtic	25	Hibernian	24
1900–01c	Rangers	35	Celtic	29	Hibernian	25
1901–02a	Rangers	28	Celtic	26	Hearts	22
1902–03b	Hibernian	37	Dundee	31	Rangers	29
1903–04d	Third Lanark	43	Hearts	39	Rangers*	38
1904–05d	Celtic‡	41	Rangers	41	Third Lanark	35
1905–06e	Celtic	49	Hearts	43	Airdrieonians	38
1906–07f	Celtic	55	Dundee	48	Rangers	45
1907–08f	Celtic	55	Falkirk	51	Rangers	50
1908–09f	Celtic	51	Dundee	50	Clyde	48
1909–10f	Celtic	54	Falkirk	52	Rangers	46
1910–11f	Rangers	52	Aberdeen	48	Falkirk	44
1911–12f	Rangers	51	Celtic	45	Clyde	42
1912–13f	Rangers	53	Celtic	49	Hearts*	41
1913–14g	Celtic	65	Rangers	59	Hearts*	54
1914–15g	Celtic	65	Hearts	61	Rangers	50
1915–16g	Celtic	67	Rangers	56	Morton	51
1916–17g	Celtic	64	Morton	54	Rangers	53
1917–18f	Rangers	56	Celtic	55	Kilmarnock	43
1918–19f	Celtic	58	Rangers	57	Morton	47
1919–20h	Rangers	71	Celtic	68	Motherwell	57
1920–21h	Rangers	76	Celtic	66	Hearts	56
1921–22h	Celtic	67	Rangers	66	Raith R	56
1922–23g	Rangers	55	Airdrieonians	50	Celtic	46
1923–24g	Rangers	59	Airdrieonians	50	Celtic	41
1924–25g	Rangers	60	Airdrieonians	57	Hibernian	52
1925–26g	Celtic	58	Airdrieonians*	50	Hearts	50
1926–27g	Rangers	56	Motherwell	51	Celtic	49
1927–28g	Rangers	60	Celtic*	55	Motherwell	55
1928–29g	Rangers	67	Celtic	51	Motherwell	50
1929–30g	Rangers	60	Motherwell	55	Aberdeen	53
1930–31g	Rangers	60	Celtic	58	Motherwell	56
1931–32g	Motherwell	66	Rangers	61	Celtic	48
1932–33g	Rangers	62	Motherwell	59	Hearts	50
1933–34g	Rangers	66	Motherwell	62	Celtic	47
1934–35g	Rangers	55	Celtic	52	Hearts	50
1935–36g	Celtic	66	Rangers*	61	Aberdeen	61
1936–37g	Rangers	61	Aberdeen	54	Celtic	52
1937–38g	Celtic	61	Hearts	58	Rangers	49
1938–39g	Rangers	59	Celtic	48	Aberdeen	46
1946–47e	Rangers	46	Hibernian	44	Aberdeen	39
1947–48e	Hibernian	48	Rangers	46	Partick T	36
1948–49e	Rangers	46	Dundee	45	Hibernian	39
1949–50e	Rangers	50	Hibernian	49	Hearts	43
1950–51e	Hibernian	48	Rangers*	38	Dundee	38
1951–52e	Hibernian	45	Rangers	41	East Fife	37

163

1952–53e	Rangers*	43	Hibernian	43	East Fife	39
1953–54e	Celtic	43	Hearts	38	Partick T	35
1954–55e	Aberdeen	49	Celtic	46	Rangers	41
1955–56f	Rangers	52	Aberdeen	46	Hearts*	45
1956–57f	Rangers	55	Hearts	53	Kilmarnock	42
1957–58f	Hearts	62	Rangers	49	Celtic	46
1958–59f	Rangers	50	Hearts	48	Motherwell	44
1959–60f	Hearts	54	Kilmarnock	50	Rangers*	42
1960–61f	Rangers	51	Kilmarnock	50	Third Lanark	42
1961–62f	Dundee	54	Rangers	51	Celtic	46
1962–63f	Rangers	57	Kilmarnock	48	Partick T	46
1963–64f	Rangers	55	Kilmarnock	49	Celtic*	47
1964–65f	Kilmarnock*	50	Hearts	50	Dunfermline Ath	49
1965–66f	Celtic	57	Rangers	55	Kilmarnock	45
1966–67f	Celtic	58	Rangers	55	Clyde	46
1967–68f	Celtic	63	Rangers	61	Hibernian	45
1968–69f	Celtic	54	Rangers	49	Dunfermline Ath	45
1969–70f	Celtic	57	Rangers	45	Hibernian	44
1970–71f	Celtic	56	Aberdeen	54	St Johnstone	44
1971–72f	Celtic	60	Aberdeen	50	Rangers	44
1972–73f	Celtic	57	Rangers	56	Hibernian	45
1973–74f	Celtic	53	Hibernian	49	Rangers	48
1974–75f	Rangers	56	Hibernian	49	Celtic	45

SECOND DIVISION to 1974–75

Maximum points: a 76; b 72; c 68; d 52; e 60; f 36; g 44; h 52.

1893–94f	Hibernian	29	Cowlairs	27	Clyde	24
1894–95f	Hibernian	30	Motherwell	22	Port Glasgow	20
1895–96f	Abercorn	27	Leith Ath	23	Renton	21
1896–97f	Partick T	31	Leith Ath	27	Kilmarnock	21
1897–98f	Kilmarnock	29	Port Glasgow	25	Morton	22
1898–99f	Kilmarnock	32	Leith Ath	27	Port Glasgow	25
1899–1900f	Partick T	29	Morton	26	Port Glasgow	20
1900–01f	St Bernard's	26	Airdrieonians	23	Abercorn	21
1901–02g	Port Glasgow	32	Partick T	31	Motherwell	26
1902–03g	Airdrieonians	35	Motherwell	28	Ayr U	28
1903–04g	Hamilton A	37	Clyde	29	Ayr U	28
1904–05g	Clyde	32	Falkirk	28	Hamilton A	27
1905–06g	Leith Ath	34	Clyde	31	Albion R	27
1906–07g	St Bernard's	32	Vale of Leven*	27	Arthurlie	27
1907–08g	Raith R	30	Dumbarton	‡‡27	Ayr U	27
1908–09g	Abercorn	31	Raith R*	28	Vale of Leven	27
1909–10g‡‡	Leith Ath	33	Raith R	33	St Bernard's	27
1910–11g	Dumbarton	31	Ayr U	27	Albion R	25
1911–12g	Ayr U	35	Abercorn	30	Dumbarton	27

1912–13*h*	Ayr U	34	Dunfarmline Ath	33	East Stirling	32
1913–14*g*	Cowdenbeath	31	Albion R	27	Dunfermline Ath	26
1914–15*h*	Cowdenbeath*	37	St Bernard's*	37	Leith Ath	37
1921–22*a*	Alloa	60	Cowdenbeath	47	Armadale	45
1922–23*a*	Queen's Park	57	Clydebank	¶50	St Johnstone	¶45
1923–24*a*	St Johnstone	56	Cowdenbeath	55	Bathgate	44
1924–25*a*	Dundee U	50	Clydebank	48	Clyde	47
1925–26*a*	Dunfermline Ath	59	Clyde	53	Ayr U	52
1926–27*a*	Bo'ness	56	Raith R	49	Clydebank	45
1927–28*a*	Ayr U	54	Third Lanark	50	King's Park	44
1928–29*b*	Dundee U	51	Morton	50	Arbroath	47
1929–30*a*	Leith Ath*	57	East Fife	57	Albion R	54
1930–31*a*	Third Lanark	61	Dundee U	50	Dunfermline Ath	47
1931–32*a*	East Stirling*	55	St Johnstone	55	Raith Rovers*	46
1932–33*c*	Hibernian	54	Queen of the S	49	Dunfermline Ath	47
1933–34*c*	Albion R	45	Dunfermline Ath*	44	Arbroath	44
1934–35*c*	Third Lanark	52	Arbroath	50	St Bernard's	47
1935–36*c*	Falkirk	59	St Mirren	52	Morton	48
1936–37*c*	Ayr U	54	Morton	51	St Bernard's	48
1937–38*c*	Raith R	59	Albion R	48	Airdrieonians	47
1938–39*c*	Cowdenbeath	60	Alloa*	48	East Fife	48
1946–47*d*	Dundee	45	Airdrieonians	42	East Fife	31
1947–48*e*	East Fife	53	Albion R	42	Hamilton A	40
1948–49*e*	Raith R*	42	Stirling Albion	42	Airdrieonians*	41
1949–50*e*	Morton	47	Airdrieonians	44	St Johnstone*	36
1950–51*e*	Queen of the S*	45	Stirling Albion	45	Ayr U	36
1951–52*e*	Clyde	44	Falkirk	43	Ayr U	39
1952–53*e*	Stirling Albion	44	Hamilton A	43	Queen's Park	37
1953–54*e*	Motherwell	45	Kilmarnock	42	Third Lanark*	36
1954–55*e*	Airdrieonians	46	Dunfermline Ath	42	Hamilton A	39
1955–56*b*	Queen's Park	54	Ayr U	51	St Johnstone	49
1956–57*b*	Clyde	64	Third Lanark	51	Cowdenbeath	45
1957–58*b*	Stirling Albion	55	Dunfermline Ath	53	Arbroath	47
1958–59*b*	Ayr U	60	Arbroath	51	Stenhousemuir	40
1959–60*b*	St Johnstone	53	Dundee U	50	Queen of the S	49
1960–61*b*	Stirling Albion	55	Falkirk	54	Stenhousemuir	50
1961–62*b*	Clyde	54	Queen of the S	53	Morton	441
1962–63*b*	St Johnstone	55	East Stirling	49	Morton	48
1963–64*b*	Morton	67	Clyde	53	Arbroath	46
1964–65*b*	Stirling Albion	59	Hamilton A	50	Queen of the S	45
1965–66*b*	Ayr U	53	Airdrieonians	50	Queen of the S	49
1966–67*b*	Morton	69	Raith R	58	Arbroath	57

1967–68b	St Mirren	62	Arbroath	53	East Fife	40
1968–69b	Motherwell	64	Ayr U	53	East Fife*	47
1969–70b	Falkirk	56	Cowdenbeath	55	Queen of the S	50
1970–71b	Partick T	56	East Fife	51	Arbroath	46
1971–72b	Dumbarton*	52	Arbroath	52	Stirling Albion	50
1972–73b	Clyde	56	Dumferline Ath	52	Raith R*	47
1973–74b	Airdrieonians	60	Kilmarnock	59	Hamilton A	55
1974–75a	Falkirk	54	Queen of the S	53	Montrose	53

Elected to First Division: 1894 Clyde; 1897 Partick T; 1899 Kilmarnock; 1900 Partick T; 1902 Partick T; 1903 Airdrieonians; 1905 Falkirk, Aberdeen and Hamilton A; 1906 Clyde; 1910 Raith R; 1913 Ayr U.

RELEGATED CLUBS

From Premier Divsion

1975–76 Dundee, St Johnstone
1976–77 Hearts, Kilmarnock
1977–78 Ayr U, Clydebank
1978–79 Hearts, Motherwell
1979–80 Dundee, Hibernian
1980–81 Kilmarnock, Hearts
1981–82 Partick T, Airdrieonians
1982–83 Morton, Kilmarnock
1983–84 St Johnstone, Motherwell
1984–85 Dumbarton, Morton
1985–86 *No relegation due to League
reorganization*
1986–87 Clydebank, Hamilton A
1987–88 Falkirk, Dunfermline Ath,
Morton
1988–89 Hamilton A
1989–90 Dundee
1990–91 None
1991–92 St Mirren, Dunfermline Ath
1992–93 Falkirk, Airdrieonians

From First Division

1975–76 Dunfermline Ath, Clyde
1976–77 Raith R, Falkirk
1977–78 Alloa Ath, East Fife
1978–79 Montrose, Queen of the S
1979–80 Arbroath, Clyde
1980–81 Stirling A, Berwick R
1981–82 East Stirling, Queen of the S
1982–83 Dunfermline Ath, Queen's Park
1983–84 Raith R, Alloa
1984–85 Meadowbank T, St Johnstone

1985–86 Ayr U, Alloa
1986–87 Brechin C, Montrose

1987–88 East Fife, Dumbarton

1988–89 Kilmarnock, Queen of the S
1989–90 Albion R, Alloa
1990–91 Clyde, Brechin C
1991–92 Montrose, Forfar Ath
1992–93 Meadowbank T, Cowdenbeath

Relegated from First Division 1973–74

1921–22 *Queen's Park, Dumbarton,
Clydebank
1922–23 Albion R, Alloa Ath
1923–24 Clyde, Clydebank
1924–25 Third Lanark, Ayr U
1925–26 Raith R, Clydebank
1926–27 Morton, Dundee U
1927–28 Dunfermline Ath, Bo'ness
1928–29 Third Lanark, Raith R

1951–52 Morton, Stirling Albion
1952–53 Motherwell, Third Lanark
1953–54 Airdrieonians, Hamilton A
1954–55 No clubs relegated
1955–56 Stirling Albion, Clyde
1956–57 Dunfermline Ath, Ayr U
1957–58 East Fife, Queen's Park
1958–59 Queen of the S, Falkirk
1959–60 Arbroath, Stirling Albion

Continued on Page 171

166

SKOL CUP 1992–93

First Round

E Stirling	(0) 0	Alloa	(1) 1
Stranraer	(0) 0	East Fife	(0) 0

(Stranraer won 5-4 on penalties)

Stenhousemuir	(2) 2	Arbroath	(1) 3
Brechin C	(1) 2	Albion R	(1) 1
Queen's Park	(0) 1	Clyde	(3) 3
Queen of the S	(1) 3	Berwick R	(0) 0

Second Round

Alloa	(1) 1	St Johnstone	(1) 3
Airdrieonians	(2) 2	Stranraer	(1) 3*
Brechin C	(1) 4	Hamilton A	(1) 2
Dumbarton	(0) 0	Rangers	(2) 5
Dundee U	(4) 6	Queen of the S	(0) 0
Morton	(1) 2	Kilmarnock	(0) 3*
Motherwell	(1) 4	Clyde	(1) 2
Partick T	(0) 2	Ayr U	(0) 0
Meadowbank T	(0) 0	Dundee	(1) 3
Falkirk	(0) 4	Forfar Ath	(0) 1
Hearts	(0) 1	Clydebank	(0) 0
Hibernian	(2) 4	Raith R	(0) 1
Montrose	(0) 0	Dunfermline Ath	(4) 6
St Mirren	(1) 1	Cowdenbeath	(0) 0
Arbroath	(0) 0	Aberdeen	(1) 4
Stirling Alb	(0) 0	Celtic	(0) 3

Third Round

Dundee U	(1) 3	St Mirren	(0) 0
Kilmarnock	(1) 3	Hibernian	(0) 1*
Aberdeen	(0) 1	Dunfermline Ath	(0) 0*
Brechin C	(0) 1	Hearts	(0) 2*
Celtic	(1) 1	Dundee	(0) 0
Motherwell	(0) 0	Falkirk	(1) 1
St Johnstone	(2) 2	Partick T	(2) 2*

(St Johnstone won 4-3 on penalties)

Stranraer	(0) 0	Rangers	(3) 5

Quarter-finals

Kilmarnock	(0) 1	St Johnstone	(0) 3
Dundee U	(0) 2	Rangers	(0) 3*
Falkirk	(1) 1	Aberdeen	(2) 4
Hearts	(1) 1	Celtic	(1) 2

Semi-finals

St Johnstone	(0) 1	Rangers	(2) 3
Celtic	(0) 0	Aberdeen	(1) 1

Final—at Hampden Park, 45,298

Aberdeen	(0) 1	Rangers	(1) 2*
Shearer		*McCall, Smith (og)*	

*after extra time

PAST SCOTTISH LEAGUE CUP FINALS

1946–47	Rangers	4	Aberdeen	0
1947–48	East Fife	0 4	Falkirk	0 1
1948–49	Rangers	2	Raith Rovers	0
1949–50	East Fife	3	Dunfermline	0
1950–51	Motherwell	3	Hibernian	0
1951–52	Dundee	3	Rangers	2
1952–53	Dundee	2	Kilmarnock	0
1953–54	East Fife	3	Partick Thistle	2
1954–55	Hearts	4	Motherwell	2
1955–56	Aberdeen	2	St Mirren	1
1956–57	Celtic	0 3	Partick Thistle	0 0
1957–58	Celtic	7	Rangers	1
1958–59	Hearts	5	Partick Thistle	1
1959–60	Hearts	2	Third Lanark	1
1960–61	Rangers	2	Kilmarnock	0
1961–62	Rangers	1 3	Hearts	1 1
1962–63	Hearts	1	Kilmarnock	0
1963–64	Rangers	5	Morton	0
1964–65	Rangers	2	Celtic	1
1965–66	Celtic	2	Rangers	1
1966–67	Celtic	1	Rangers	0
1967–68	Celtic	5	Dundee	3
1968–69	Celtic	6	Hibernian	2
1969–70	Celtic	1	St Johnstone	0
1970–71	Rangers	1	Celtic	0
1971–72	Partick Thistle	4	Celtic	1
1972–73	Hibernian	2	Celtic	1
1973–74	Dundee	1	Celtic	0
1974–75	Celtic	6	Hibernian	3
1975–76	Rangers	1	Celtic	0
1976–77	Aberdeen	2	Celtic	1
1977–78	Rangers	2	Celtic	1
1978–79	Rangers	2	Aberdeen	1
1979–80	Aberdeen	0 0	Dundee U	0 3
1980–81	Dundee	0	Dundee U	3
1981–82	Rangers	2	Dundee U	1
1982–83	Celtic	2	Rangers	1
1983–84	Rangers	3	Celtic	2
1984–85	Rangers	1	Dundee U	0
1985–86	Aberdeen	3	Hibernian	0
1986–87	Rangers	2	Celtic	1
1987–88	Rangers†	3	Aberdeen	3
1988–89	Aberdeen	2	Rangers	3
1989–90	Aberdeen	2	Rangers	1
1990–91	Rangers	2	Celtic	1
1991–92	Rangers	2	Aberdeen	1

†Won on penalties

B & Q CUP 1992–93

First Round

Ayr U	(1) 2	St Mirren	(0) 1
Berwick R	(1) 2	E Stirling	(0) 2*
(Berwick R won 5-4 on penalties)			
Dumbarton	(0) 0	Hamilton A	(1) 3
Forfar Ath	(0) 2	Morton	(4) 5
Kilmarnock	(2) 2	Clyde	(0) 1
Queen's Park	(2) 2	Montrose	(2) 3*
Stenhousemuir	(0) 2	Cowdenbeath	(3) 4
Stranraer	(2) 3	Alloa	(1) 2
Meadowbank T	(0) 1	East Fife	(0) 0*
Arbroath	(2) 3	Dunfermline Ath	(0) 0

Second Round

Albion R	(0) 0	Hamilton A	(1) 2
Berwick R	(1) 1	Arbroath	(0) 0
Brechin C	(1) 1	Morton	(2) 2
Cowdenbeath	(0) 0	Montrose	(2) 4
Kilmarnock	(1) 1	Ayr U	(0) 0
Raith R	(0) 0	Meadowbank T	(0) 0*
(Meadowbank T won 4-2 on penalties)			
Stirling Alb	(1) 2	Clydebank	(0) 1
Stranraer	(0) 0	Queen of the S	(1) 2

Quarter-finals

Stirling Alb	(0) 0	Montrose	(0) 1
Hamilton A	(3) 5	Berwick R	(1) 2
Kilmarnock	(0) 1	Morton	(0) 2
Meadowbank T	(2) 3	Queen of the S	(1) 2

Semi-finals

Morton	(1) 3	Montrose	(1) 1*
Hamilton A	(0) 1	Meadowbank T	(1) 1*
(Hamilton A won 2-1 on penalties)			

Final—at St Mirren, 7391

Hamilton A	(2) 3	Morton	(1) 2
Clark 2, Hillcoat		*Alexander 2*	

*after extra time

169

SCOTTISH CUP 1992–93

FIRST ROUND

Huntly	(2) 4	Stranraer	(0) 2
Inverness T	(1) 3	Civil Service Strollers	(0) 1
Queen of the S	(1) 3	Spartans	(0) 0
Queen's Park	(0) 0	Clyde	(1) 1
Cove R	(1) 2	Peterhead	(0) 0
Forfar Ath	(0) 5	Albion R	(0) 0

SECOND ROUND

Clyde	(0) 3	Brechin C	(1) 1
Cove R	(1) 2	Montrose	(0) 0
East Fife	(1) 1	Alloa	(0) 1
Gala Fairydean	(1) 1	Arbroath	(1) 1
Vale of Leithen	(0) 2	East Stirling	(1) 2
Inverness T	(0) 0	Berwick R	(0) 1
Stenhousemuir	(0) 2	Forfar Ath	(0) 3
Huntly	(2) 2	Queen of the S	

SECOND ROUND REPLAYS

Alloa	(0) 1	East Fife	(0) 1

aet; East Fife won 6–5 on penalties

Arbroath	(0) 2	Gala Fairydean	(0) 0
East Stirling	(1) 3	Vale of Leithen	(0) 2

THIRD ROUND

Aberdeen	(1) 4	Hamilton A	(1) 1
Airdrieonians	(0) 0	Clydebank	(0) 0
Arbroath	(0) 3	Morton	(0) 0
Clyde	(0) 0	Celtic	(0) 0
Cove R	(0) 2	East Stirling	(1) 2
Dundee U	(1) 3	Meadowbank T	(1) 1
Dunfermline Ath	(0) 1	Ayr U	(2) 2
Hearts	(4) 6	Huntly	(0) 0
Hibernian	(3) 5	St Mirren	(0) 2
Kilmarnock	(2) 5	Raith R	(0) 0
Motherwell	(0) 0	Rangers	(1) 2
Partick T	(0) 0	Cowdenbeath	(0) 1
St Johnstone	(3) 6	Forfar Ath	(0) 0
Stirling Albion	(0) 1	East Fife	(2) 2
Dundee	(0) 2	Dumbarton	(0) 0
Falkirk	(2) 5	Berwick R	(1) 2

THIRD ROUND REPLAYS

Clydebank	(1) 2	Airdrieonians	(0) 0
Celtic	(1) 1	Clyde	(0) 0
East Stirling	(2) 2	Cove R	(0) 1

FOURTH ROUND

Arbroath	(0) 0	East Fife	(0) 0
Ayr U	(0) 0	Rangers	(1) 2
Cowdenbeath	(0) 0	Hibernian	(0) 2
Falkirk	(1) 2	Celtic	(0) 0
Hearts	(1) 2	Dundee	(0) 0
Kilmarnock	(0) 0	St Johnstone	(0) 0

| Aberdeen | (0) 2 | Dundee U | (0) 0 |
| East Stirling | (1) 1 | Clydebank | (1) 2 |

FOURTH ROUND REPLAYS

Hibernian	(1) 1	Cowdenbeath	(0) 0
St Johnstone	(0) 1	Kilmarnock	(0) 0
East Fife	(1) 1	Arbroath	(1) 4

QUARTER-FINALS

Aberdeen	(1) 1	Clydebank	(0) 1
Arbroath	(0) 0	Rangers	(2) 3
Hearts	(1) 2	Falkirk	(0) 0
Hibernian	(1) 2	St Johnstone	(0) 0

QUARTER-FINAL REPLAY

| Clydebank | (1) 3 | Aberdeen | (2) 4 |

SEMI-FINALS

| Hibernian | (0) 0 | Aberdeen | (0) 1 |
| Rangers | (0) 2 | Hearts | (0) 1 |

FINAL at Celtic Park

| Rangers | (2) 2 | Aberdeen | (0) 1 |

FINAL

29 MAY

Rangers (2) 2 *(Murray, Hateley)*
Aberdeen (0) 1 *(Richardson)* 50715
Rangers: Goram; McCall, Robertson D, Gough, McPherson, Brown, Murray,
Ferguson, Durrant, Hateley, Huistra (Pressley) *Aberdeen:* Snelders; McKimmie,
Wright (Smith), Grant, Irvine, McLeish, Richardson, Mason, Booth, Shearer (Jess),
Paatelainen
Referee: J McCluskey (Stewarton)

Continued from Page 166

1929–30 St Johnstone, Dundee U	1960–61 Ayr U, Clyde
1930–31 Hibernian, East Fife	1961–62 St Johnstone, Stirling Albion
1931–32 Dundee U, Leith Ath	1962–63 Clyde, Raith R
1932–33 Morton, East Stirling	1963–64 Queen of the S, East Stirling
1933–34 Third Lanark, Cowdenbeath	1964–65 Airdrieonians, Third Lanark
1934–35 St Mirren, East Fife	1965–66 Morton, Hamilton A
1935–36 Airdrieonians, Ayr U	1966–67 St Mirren, Ayr U
1936–37 Dunfermline Ath, Albion R	1967–68 Motherwell, Stirling Albion
1937–38 Dundee, Morton	1968–69 Falkirk, Arbroath
1938–39 Queen's Park, Raith R	1969–70 Raith R, Partick T
1946–47 Kilmarnock, Hamilton A	1970–71 St Mirren, Cowdenbeath
1947–48 Airdrieonians, Queen's Park	1971–72 Clyde, Dunfermline Ath
1948–49 Morton, Albion R	1972–73 Kilmarnock, Airdrieonians
1949–50 Queen of the S, Stirling Albion	1973–74 East Fife, Falkirk
1950–51 Clyde, Falkirk	

*Season 1921–22 – only 1 club promoted, 3 clubs relegated.

Scottish League championship wins: Rangers 43, Celtic 35, Aberdeen 4, Hearts 4,
Hibernian 4, Dumbarton 2, Dundee 1, Dundee United 1, Kilmarnock 1, Motherwell
1, Third Lanark 1.

PAST SCOTTISH CUP FINALS

1874	Queens Park	2	Clydesdale	0
1875	Queen's Park	3	Renton	0
1876	Queen's Park	1 2	Third Lanark	1 0
1877	Vale of Leven	0 1 3	Rangers	0 1 2
1878	Vale of Leven	1	Third Lanark	0
1879	Vale of Leven	1	Rangers	1

Vale of Leven awarded, Rangers did not appear for replay

1880	Queen's Park	3	Thornlibank	0
1881	Queen's Park	2 3	Dumbarton	1 1

Replayed because of protest

1882	Queen's Park	2 4	Dumbarton	2 1
1883	Dumbarton	2 2	Vale of Leven	2 1
1884				

Queen's Park awarded cup when Vale of Leven did not appear for the final

1885	Renton	0 3	Vale of Leven	0 1
1886	Queen's Park	3	Renton	1
1887	Hibernian	2	Dumbarton	1
1888	Renton	6	Cambuslang	1
1889	Third Lanark	3 2	Celtic	0 1

Replayed because of protest

1890	Queen's Park	1 2	Vale of Leven	1 1
1891	Hearts	1	Dumbarton	0
1892	Celtic	1 5	Queen's Park	0 1

Replayed because of protest

1893	Queen's Park	2	Celtic	1
1894	Rangers	3	Celtic	1
1895	St Bernards	3	Renton	1
1896	Hearts	3	Hibernian	1
1897	Rangers	5	Dumbarton	1
1898	Rangers	2	Kilmarnock	0
1899	Celtic	2	Rangers	0
1900	Celtic	4	Queen's Park	3
1901	Hearts	4	Celtic	3
1902	Hibernian	1	Celtic	0
1903	Rangers	1 0 2	Hearts	1 0 0
1904	Celtic	3	Rangers	2
1905	Third Lanark	0 3	Rangers	0 1
1906	Hearts	1	Third Lanark	0
1907	Celtic	3	Hearts	0
1908	Celtic	5	St Mirren	1
1909				

After two drawn games between Celtic and Rangers, 2.2, 1.1, there was a riot and the cup was withheld

1910	Dundee	2 0 2	Clyde	2 0 1
1911	Celtic	0 2	Hamilton Acad	0 0
1912	Celtic	2	Clyde	0
1913	Falkirk	2	Raith Albion R	2
1921	Partick Th	1	Rangers	0
1922	Morton	1	Rangers	0
1923	Celtic	1	Hibernian	0
1924	Airdrieonians	2	Hibernian	0
1925	Celtic	2	Dundee	1
1926	St Mirren	2	Celtic	0
1927	Celtic	3	East Fife	1
1928	Rangers	4	Celtic	0
1929	Kilmarnock	2	Rangers	0

Year		Score		Score
1930	Rangers	0 2	Partick Th	0 1
1931	Celtic	2 4	Motherwell	2 2
1932	Rangers	1 3	Kilmarnock	1 0
1933	Celtic	1	Motherwell	0
1934	Rangers	5	St Mirren	0
1935	Rangers	2	Hamilton Acad	1
1936	Rangers	1	Third Lanark	0
1937	Celtic	2	Aberdeen	1
1938	East Fife	1 4	Kilmarnock	1 2
1939	Clyde	4	Motherwell	0
1947	Aberdeen	2	Hibernian	1
1948	Rangers	1 1	Morton	1 0
1949	Rangers	4	Clyde	1
1950	Rangers	3	East Fife	0
1951	Celtic	1	Motherwell	0
1952	Motherwell	4	Dundee	0
1953	Rangers	1 1	Aberdeen	1 0
1954	Celtic	2	Aberdeen	1
1955	Clyde	1 1	Celtic	1 0
1956	Hearts	3	Celtic	1
1957	Falkirk	1 2	Kilmarnock	1 1
1958	Clyde	1	Hibernian	0
1959	St Mirren	3	Aberdeen	1
1960	Rangers	2	Kilmarnock	0
1961	Dunfermline Ath	0 2	Celtic	0 0
1962	Rangers	2	St Mirren	0
1963	Rangers	1 3	Celtic	1 0
1964	Rangers	3	Dundee	1
1965	Celtic	3	Dunfermline Ath	2
1966	Rangers	0 1	Celtic	0 0
1967	Celtic	2	Aberdeen	0
1968	Dunfermline Ath	3	Hearts	1
1969	Celtic	4	Rangers	0
1970	Aberdeen	3	Celtic	1
1971	Celtic	1 2	Rangers	1 1
1972	Celtic	6	Hibernian	1
1973	Rangers	3	Celtic	2
1974	Celtic	3	Dundee U	0
1975	Celtic	3	Airdrieonians	1
1976	Rangers	3	Hearts	1
1977	Celtic	1	Rangers	0
1978	Rangers	2	Aberdeen	1
1979	Rangers	0 0 3	Hibernian	0 0 2
1980	Celtic	1	Rangers	0
1981	Rangers	0 4	Dundee U	0 1
1982	Aberdeen	4	Rangers	1 (aet)
1983	Aberdeen	1	Rangers	0 (aet)
1984	Aberdeen	2	Celtic	1 (aet)
1985	Celtic	2	DundeeU	1
1986	Aberdeen	3	Hearts	0
1987	St Mirren	1	Dundee U	0 (aet)
1988	Celtic	2	Dundee U	1
1989	Celtic	1	Rangers	0
1990	Aberdeen†	0	Celtic	0
1991	Rangers	2	Airdrieonians	1

†won on penalties

173

WELSH FOOTBALL 1992-93

KONICA LEAGUE OF WALES 1992-93

	P	W	D	L	F	A	Pts
Cwmbran	38	26	9	3	69	22	87
Inter Cardiff	38	26	5	7	79	36	83
Aberystwyth Town	38	25	3	10	85	49	78
Ebbw Vale	38	19	9	10	76	61	66
Bangor City	38	19	7	12	77	58	64
Holywell Town	38	17	8	13	65	48	59
Conwy United	38	16	9	13	51	51	57
Connah's Quay Nomads	38	17	4	17	66	67	55
Porthmadog	38	14	11	13	61	49	53
Haverfordwest County	38	16	5	17	66	66	53
Caersws	38	14	10	14	64	60	52
Afan Lido	38	14	10	14	64	65	52
Mold Alexandra	38	16	4	18	63	69	48*
Llanelli	38	11	8	19	49	64	41
Maesteg Park Athletic	38	9	13	16	52	59	40
Flint Town United	38	11	6	21	47	67	39
Briton Ferry Athletic	38	10	9	19	61	87	39
Newtown	38	9	9	20	55	87	36
Llanidloes Town	38	7	9	22	48	93	30
Abergavenny Thursdays	38	7	7	24	36	76	28

*3 points deducted

KONICA LEAGUE CUP

Group One

	P	W	D	L	F	A	Pts
Caersws	8	6	1	1	22	11	19
Bangor City	8	5	1	2	18	14	16
Porthmadog	8	4	0	4	14	13	12
Conwy United	8	3	1	4	14	16	10
Llanidloes Town	8	0	1	7	12	26	1

Group Two

	P	W	D	L	F	A	Pts
Newtown	8	5	2	1	17	7	17
Flint Town United	8	4	1	3	13	13	13
Connah's Quay Nomads	8	3	3	2	15	14	12
Holywell Town	8	2	1	5	12	17	7
Mold Alexandra	8	2	1	5	10	15	7

Group Three

	P	W	D	L	F	A	Pts
Maesteg Park Athletic	8	3	4	1	19	11	13
Ebbw Vale	8	3	4	1	20	14	13
Cwmbran Town	8	3	2	3	14	17	11
Inter Cardiff	8	3	1	4	11	14	10
Abergavenny Thursdays	8	1	3	4	8	16	6

	P	W	D	L	F	A	Pts
Afan Lido	8	5	2	1	15	7	17
Haverfordwest County	8	4	1	3	15	10	13
Llanelli	8	3	2	3	10	14	11
Aberystwyth Town	8	2	3	3	13	10	9
Briton Ferry Athletic	8	1	2	5	10	22	5

SEMI-FINALS: Newtown 0 Caersws 1 (*at Newtown*)
Afan Lido 2 Maesteg Park Athletic 0 (*at Afan Lido*)
FINAL: Afan Lido 1, Caersws 1 (*at Aberystwyth*) (*Caersws won on penalties aet*)

NORTHERN IRISH FOOTBALL 1992–93

SMIRNOFF IRISH LEAGUE CHAMPIONSHIP

FINAL TABLE

	P	W	D	L	F	A	Pts
Linfield	30	20	6	4	49	15	66
Crusaders	30	21	3	6	53	27	66
Bangor	30	20	4	6	61	32	64
Portadown	30	18	9	3	70	26	63
Distillery	30	20	2	8	61	36	62
Glenavon	30	14	6	10	48	36	48
Glentoran	30	13	8	9	70	40	47
Ards	30	12	9	9	45	45	45
Carrick	30	12	2	16	50	73	38
Ballymena	30	10	6	14	41	51	36
Cliftonville	30	10	3	17	42	48	33
Omagh	30	9	5	16	38	57	32
Larne	30	9	3	18	41	59	30
Newry	30	5	5	20	30	72	20
Coleraine	30	5	3	22	28	63	18
Ballyclare	30	2	6	22	28	75	12

EUROPEAN CUPS REVIEW

Italian hopes of a clean sweep of European trophies failed at the final hurdle when Marseille beat AC Milan 1-0 in the European Cup. Parma had earlier defeated Antwerp 3-1 in the Cup-Winners' final and Juventus overcame Borussia Dortmund 6-1 on aggregate in the UEFA Cup.

Wembley Stadium was the stage for the Cup-Winners' Cup and Parma gave a fine display to underline their emergence as a force in the game. Even without the injured Faustino Asprilla, who sat on the substitutes bench throughout, they were by far the more inventive team.

Lorenzo Minotti put them ahead in the tenth minute, but Belgian spirits were raised three minutes later when Francis Severeyns equalised. However Alessandro Melli restored Parma's lead after 31 minutes.

There was no further scoring until four minutes from the final whistle when Stefano Cuoghi made the score more of a realistic margin between the two sides.

Juventus were already half-way towards taking the UEFA Cup title. They had recovered well from going down as early as the second minute in Dortmund to a goal from Borussia's Michael Rummenigge. Dino Baggio levelled the scores after 26 minutes and his unrelated namesake Roberto made it 2-1 five minutes later. The Juventus captain scored his second and the team's third in the 74th minute.

Cushioned with a 3-1 lead from the away leg, Juventus put the tie beyond the Germans when the younger Baggio scored after five minutes. Dino added another three minutes before the interval and in the second half their German midfield player Andreas Moller finished the scoring at 3-0 in the 65th minute.

With two trophies safely tucked away, AC Milan were generally expected to make it a hat-trick for Italy. Although their form on the domestic front had been disappointing after a splendid first half of the season, they had managed to give better displays in Europe. They had finished the new-style Champions League six points clear of their nearest rivals in Group B.

In contrast Marseille had been chased all the way by Rangers who had the galling experience of being eliminated without losing a match in Group A.

According to UEFA, the Champions League which took over from the European Cup two-legged system at the semi-final stage, was an outstanding success. Attendances for the 24 games before the final totalled 799,851. But though they had witnessed just one goalless draw between Rangers and CSKA Moscow, only 55 goals had been scored overall.

Thus the background to the final in Munich's Olympic Stadium provided the respective owners of the clubs involved, Silvio Berlusconi (Milan) and Bernard Tapie (Marseille), with the platform they had sought. Both were keen to develop a European League and this was the closest UEFA had come to launching one. Alas the match was an anti-climax, Basile Boli's glancing header from six yards after 43 minutes giving the French the prize.

EUROPEAN CUP 1992–93

Preliminary Round, First Leg

KI Klaksvikar	(1) 1	Olimpija Ljubljana	(0) 3
Shelbourne	(0) 0	Tavria Simferopol	(0) 0
Valletta	(0) 1	Maccabi Tel Aviv	(0) 2

Preliminary Round, Second Leg

Maccabi Tel Aviv	(1) 1	Valletta	(0) 0
Norma Tallinn	(0) 0	Olimpija Ljubljana	(1) 2
Skonto Riga	(2) 3	KI Klaksvikar	(0) 0
Tavria Simferopol	(2) 2	Shelbourne	(1) 1

First Round, First leg

AEK Athens	(1) 3	Apoel	(0) 1
FK Austria	(1) 3	CSKA Sofia	(0) 1
Barcelona	(0) 1	Viking Stavanger	(0) 0
Glentoran	(0) 0	Marseille	(4) 5
IFK Gothenburg	(0) 2	Besiktas	(0) 0
Kuusysi	(1) 1	Dinamo Bucharest	(0) 0
Lech Poznan	(2) 2	Skonto Riga	(0) 0
Maccabi Tel Aviv	(0) 0	FC Brugge	(1) 1
AC Milan	(2) 4	Olimpija Ljubljana	(0) 0
PSV Eindhoven	(2) 6	Zalgiris Vilnius	(0) 0
Rangers	(1) 2	Lyngby	(0) 0
Sion	(2) 4	Tavria Simferopol	(0) 1
Slovan Bratislava	(1) 4	Ferencvaros	(0) 1
Stuttgart	(0) 3	Leeds U	(0) 0
Union Luxembourg	(0) 1	FC Porto	(1) 4
Vikingur	(0) 0	CSKA Moscow	(0) 1

First Round, Second leg

Apoel	(0) 2	AEK Athens	(1) 2
Besiktas	(1) 2	IFK Gothenburg	(1) 1
FC Brugge	(0) 3	Maccabi Tel Aviv	(0) 0
CSKA Moscow	(3) 4	Vikingur	(0) 0
CSKA Sofia	(1) 3	FK Austria	(1) 2
Dinamo Bucharest	(0) 2	Kuusysi	(0) 0
Ferencvaros	(0) 0	Slovan Bratislava	(0) 0
Leeds U	(2) 4	Stuttgart	(1) 1

Leeds U awarded match 3-0 on forfeit as Stuttgart included fourth foreign player

Replay: Leeds U	(1) 2	Stuttgart	(1) 1
Lyngby	(0) 0	Rangers	(0) 1
Marseille	(2) 3	Glentoran	(0) 0
Olimpija Ljubljana	(0) 0	AC Milan	(1) 3
FC Porto	(3) 5	Union Luxembourg	(0) 0
Skonto Riga	(0) 0	Lech Poznan	(0) 0
Tavria Simferopol	(0) 1	Sion	(0) 3
Viking Stavanger	(0) 0	Barcelona	(0) 0
Zalgiris Vilnius	(0) 0	PSV Eindhoven	(2) 2

Second Round, First Leg

AEK Athens	(0) 1	PSV Eindhoven	(0) 0
FC Brugge	(2) 2	FK Austria	(0) 0
CSKA Moscow	(1) 1	Barcelona	(0) 1
Dinamo Bucharest	(0) 0	Marseille	(0) 0
IFK Gothenburg	(0) 1	Lech Poznan	(0) 0
Rangers	(2) 2	Leeds U	(1) 1
Sion	(0) 2	FC Porto	(0) 2
Slovan Bratislava	(0) 0	AC Milan	(0) 1

Second Round, Second Leg

FK Austria	(0) 3	FC Brugge	(0) 1
Barcelona	(2) 2	CSKA Moscow	(1) 3
Lech Poznan	(0) 0	IFK Gothenburg	(1) 3
Leeds U	(0) 1	Rangers	(1) 2
Marseille	(1) 2	Dinamo Bucharest	(0) 0
AC Milan	(2) 4	Slovan Bratislava	(0) 0
FC Porto	(0) 4	Sion	(0) 0
PSV Eindhoven	(1) 3	AEK Athens	(0) 0

Champions League

Group A

FC Brugge	(1) 1	CSKA Moscow	(0) 0
Rangers	(0) 2	Marseille	(1) 2
CSKA Moscow	(0) 0	Rangers	(1) 1
Marseille	(3) 3	FC Brugge	(0) 0
FC Brugge	(1) 1	Rangers	(0) 1
CSKA Moscow	(0) 1	Marseille	(1) 1
Marseille	(3) 6	CSKA Moscow	(0) 0
Rangers	(1) 2	FC Brugge	(0) 1
CSKA Moscow	(1) 1	FC Brugge	(1) 2
Marseille	(1) 1	Rangers	(0) 1
FC Brugge	(0) 0	Marseille	(1) 1
Rangers	(0) 0	CSKA Moscow	(0) 0

Group B

AC Milan	(1) 4	IFK Gothenburg	(0) 0
FC Porto	(1) 2	PSV Eindhoven	(1) 2
IFK Gothenburg	(0) 1	FC Porto	(0) 0
PSV Eindhoven	(0) 1	AC Milan	(1) 2
PSV Eindhoven	(1) 1	IFK Gothenburg	(3) 3
FC Porto	(0) 0	AC Milan	(0) 1
IFK Gothenburg	(2) 3	PSV Eindhoven	(0) 0
AC Milan	(1) 1	FC Porto	(0) 0
IFK Gothenburg	(0) 0	AC Milan	(0) 1
PSV Eindhoven	(0) 0	FC Porto	(0) 1
AC Milan	(2) 2	PSV Eindhoven	(0) 0
FC Porto	(1) 2	IFK Gothenburg	(0) 0

Final: Marseille (1) 1, AC Milan (0) 0

(in Munich, 26 May 1993, 64,400)

Marseille: Barthez; Angloma (Durand 64), Boli, Desailly, Pele, Eydelie, Sauzee, Deschamps, Di Meco, Boksic, Voller (Thomas 78). *Scorer:* Boli 43.

AC Milan: Rossi; Tassotti, Costacurta, Baresi, Maldini, Donadoni (Papin 56), Albertini, Rijkaard, Lentini, Van Basten (Eranio), Massaro.

Referee: Rothlisberger (Switzerland)

EUROPEAN CUP-WINNERS' CUP 1992–93

Preliminary Round, First Leg

Avenir Beggen	(1) 1	B36 Torshavn	(0) 0
Branik Maribor	(2) 4	Hamrun Spartans	(0) 0
Stromsgodset	(0) 0	Hapoel Petah Tikva	(0) 2
Vaduz	(0) 0	Chernomoretz Odessa	(1) 5

Preliminary Round, Second Leg

Chernomoretz Odessa	(3) 7	Vaduz	(0) 1
Hamrun Spartans	(1) 2	Branik Maribor	(1) 1
Hapoel Petah Tikva	(1) 2	Stromsgodset	(0) 0
B36 Torshavn	(1) 1	Avenir Beggen	(1) 1

First Round, First Leg

AIK Stockholm	(0) 3	Aarhus	(2) 3
Airdrieonians	(0) 0	Sparta Prague	(0) 1
Bohemians	(0) 0	Steaua Bucharest	(0) 0
Branik Maribor	(0) 0	Atletico Madrid	(2) 3
Cardiff C	(0) 1	Admira Wacker	(3) 1
Feyenoord	(0) 1	Hapoel Petah Tikva	(0) 0
Glenavon	(1) 1	Antwerp	(0) 1
Levski Sofia	(0) 2	Lucerne	(1) 1
Liverpool	(3) 6	Apollon Limassol	(0) 1
Miedz Legnica	(0) 0	Monaco	(1) 1
Moscow Spartak	(0) 0	Avenir Beggen	(0) 0
Olympiakos	(0) 0	Chernomoretz Odessa	(1) 1
Parma	(0) 1	Ujpest	(0) 0
Trabzonspor	(0) 2	TPS Turku	(0) 0
Valur	(0) 0	Boavista	(0) 0
Werder Bremen	(3) 3	Hannover	(1) 1

First Round, Second Leg

Aarhus	(0) 1	AIK Stockholm	(1) 1
Admira Wacker	(0) 2	Cardiff C	(0) 0
Apollon Limassol	(0) 1	Liverpool	(0) 2
Antwerp	(0) 1	Glenavon	(0) 1

Antwerp won 3-1 on penalties

Atletico Madrid	(2) 6	Branik Maribor	(1) 1
Avenir Beggen	(0) 1	Moscow Spartak	(2) 5
Boavista	(2) 3	Valur	(0) 0
Chernomoretz Odessa	(0) 0	Olympiakos	(2) 3
Hannover	(2) 2	Werder Bremen	(1) 1
Hapoel Tel Aviv	(1) 2	Feyenoord	(0) 1
Lucerne	(1) 1	Levski Sofia	(0) 0
Monaco	(0) 0	Miedz Legnica	(0) 0
Sparta Prague	(2) 2	Airdrieonians	(0) 1
Steaua Bucharest	(3) 4	Bohemians	(0) 0
TPS Turku	(1) 2	Trabzonspor	(1) 2
Ujpest	(0) 1	Parma	(0) 1

Second Round, First Leg

Aarhus	(2) 3	Steaua Bucharest	(0) 2
Admira Wacker	(2) 2	Antwerp	(1) 4
Lucerne	(0) 1	Feyenoord	(0) 0
Monaco	(0) 0	Olympiakos	(0) 1
Parma	(0) 0	Boavista	(0) 0
Spartak Moscow	(1) 4	Liverpool	(0) 2
Trabzonspor	(0) 0	Atletico Madrid	(1) 2
Werder Bremen	(0) 2	Sparta Prague	(2) 3

Second Round, Second Leg

Antwerp	(2) 3	Admira Wacker	(0) 4
Atletico Madrid	(0) 0	Trabzonspor	(0) 0
Boavista	(0) 0	Parma	(0) 2
Feyenoord	(2) 4	Lucerne	(1) 1
Liverpool	(0) 0	Moscow Spartak	(0) 2
Olympiakos	(0) 0	Monaco	(0) 0
Sparta Prague	(1) 1	Werder Bremen	(0) 0
Steaua Bucharest	(0) 2	Aarhus	(1) 1

Quarter-finals, First Leg

Antwerp	(0) 0	Steaua Bucharest	(0) 0
Feyenoord	(0) 0	Moscow Spartak	(1) 1
Olympiakos	(0) 1	Atletico Madrid	(1) 1
Sparta Prague	(0) 0	Parma	(0) 0

Quarter-finals, Second Leg

Atletico Madrid	(1) 3	Olympiakos	(0) 1
Moscow Spartak	(1) 3	Feyenoord	(1) 1
Parma	(2) 2	Sparta Prague	(0) 0
Steaua Bucharest	(1) 1	Antwerp	(0) 1

Semi-finals, First Leg

| Atletico Madrid | (1) 1 | Parma | (0) 2 |
| Moscow Spartak | (1) 1 | Antwerp | (0) 0 |

Semi-finals, Second Leg

| Antwerp | (1) 3 | Moscow Spartak | (1) 1 |
| Parma | (0) 0 | Atletico Madrid | (0) 1 |

Final: Parma (2) 3, Antwerp (1) 1

(at Wembley, 12 May 1993, 37,393)

Parma: Ballotta; Benarrivo, Di Chiara, Minotti, Apolloni, Grun, Melli, Zoratto (Pin 27), Osio (Pizzi 65), Cuoghi, Brolin. *Scorers:* Minotti 10, Melli 31, Cuoghi 86.
Antwerp: Stojanovic; Kiekens, Broeckaert, Taeymans, Smidts, Jakovljevic (Van Veirdeghem), Van Rethy, Segers (Moukrim 84), Severeyns, Lehnhoff, Czerniatynski.
Scorer: Severeyns 13.
Referee: Assenmacher (Germany).

UEFA CUP 1992-93

First Round, First Leg

Benfica	(2) 3	Belvedur Izola	(0) 0
Caen	(3) 3	Zaragoza	(1) 2
Cologne	(1) 2	Celtic	(0) 0
FC Copenhagen	(2) 5	MP Mikkeli	(0) 0
Electroputere Craiova	(0) 0	Panathinaikos	(2) 6
Fenerbahce	(2) 3	Botev Plovdiv	(0) 1
Floriana	(0) 0	Borussia Dortmund	(0) 1
Fram	(0) 0	Kaiserslautern	(1) 3
Grasshoppers	(1) 1	Sporting Lisbon	(1) 2
Hibernian	(1) 2	Anderlecht	(1) 2
Juventus	(4) 6	Anorthosis	(0) 1
GKS Katowice	(0) 0	Galatasaray	(0) 0
Kiev Dynamo	(0) 1	Rapid	(0) 0
Lokomotiv Plovdiv	(1) 2	Auxerre	(1) 2
Manchester U	(0) 0	Moscow Torpedo	(0) 0
Mechelen	(1) 2	Orebro	(0) 1
Moscow Dynamo	(1) 5	Rosenborg	(0) 1
Neuchatel Xamax	(0) 2	Frem	(2) 2
Norrkoping	(0) 1	Torino	(0) 0
Paris St Germain	(2) 2	PAOK Salonika	(0) 0
Politehnica Timisoara	(0) 1	Real Madrid	(1) 1
Salzburg	(0) 0	Ajax	(0) 3
Sheffield W	(4) 8	Spora Luxembourg	(0) 1
Sigma Olomouc	(0) 1	Uni Craiova	(0) 0
Slavia Prague	(0) 1	Hearts	(0) 0
Standard Liege	(2) 5	Portadown	(0) 0
Vac Izzo	(1) 1	Groningen	(0) 0
Valencia	(0) 1	Napoli	(1) 5
Vitesse	(1) 3	Derry City	(0) 0
Wacker Innsbruck	(1) 1	Roma	(3) 4
Widzew Lodz	(2) 2	Eintracht Frankfurt	(0) 2
Vitoria Guimaraes	(2) 3	Real Sociedad	(0) 0

First Round, Second Leg

Ajax	(1) 3	Salzburg	(0) 1
Anderlecht	(1) 1	Hibernian	(1) 1
Anorthosis	(0) 0	Juventus	(2) 4
Auxerre	(4) 7	Botev Plovdiv	(1) 1
Belvedur Izola	(0) 0	Benfica	(1) 5
Borussia Dortmund	(2) 7	Floriana	(2) 2
Botev Plovdiv	(2) 2	Fenerbahce	(1) 2
Celtic	(2) 3	Cologne	(0) 0
Derry City	(0) 1	Vitesse	(1) 2
Eintracht Frankfurt	(6) 9	Widzew Lodz	(0) 0
Frem	(3) 4	Neuchatel Xamax	(1) 1
Galatasaray	(1) 2	GKS Katowice	(1) 1
Groningen	(0) 1	Vac Izzo	(1) 1

Second Round, First Leg

Anderlecht	(2) 4	Kiev Dynamo	(1) 2
Auxerre	(2) 5	FC Copenhagen	(0) 0
Benfica	(1) 5	Vac Izzo	(0) 1
Borussia Dortmund	(0) 1	Celtic	(0) 0
Eintracht Frankfurt	(0) 0	Galatasaray	(0) 0
Fenerbahce	(1) 1	Sigma Olomouc	(0) 0
Frem	(0) 0	Zaragoza	(1) 1
Hearts	(0) 0	Standard Liege	(1) 1
Kaiserslautern	(1) 3	Sheffield W	(1) 1
Napoli	(0) 0	Paris St Germain	(2) 2
Panathinaikos	(0) 0	Juventus	(0) 1
Real Madrid	(3) 5	Moscow Torpedo	(2) 2
Roma	(3) 3	Grasshoppers	(0) 0
Torino	(0) 1	Moscow Dynamo	(1) 2
Vitesse	(1) 1	Mechelen	(0) 0
Vitoria Guimaraes	(0) 0	Ajax	(2) 3
Hearts	(3) 4	Slavia Prague	(1) 2
Kaiserslautern	(1) 4	Fram	(0) 0
Moscow Torpedo	(0) 0	Manchester U	(0) 0

Moscow Torpedo won 4-3 on penalties

MP Mikkeli	(0) 1	FC Copenhagen	(2) 5
Napoli	(1) 1	Valencia	(0) 0
Orebro	(0) 0	Mechelen	(0) 0
Panathinaikos	(1) 4	Electroputere Craiova	(0) 0
PAOK Salonika	(0) 0	Paris St Germain	(2) 2

Abandoned 46 minutes; crowd trouble

Portadown	(0) 0	Standard Liege	(0) 0
Rapid	(3) 3	Kiev Dynamo	(1) 2
Real Madrid	(1) 4	Politehnica Timisoara	(0) 0
Real Sociedad	(2) 2	Vitoria Guimaraes	(0) 0
Roma	(0) 1	Wacker Innsbruck	(0) 0
Rosenborg	(1) 2	Moscow Dynamo	(0) 0
Spora Luxembourg	(1) 1	Sheffield W	(2) 2
Sporting Lisbon	(0) 1	Grasshoppers	(1) 3
Torino	(1) 3	Norrkoping	(0) 0
Uni Craiova	(1) 1	Sigma Olomouc	(2) 2
Zaragoza	(1) 2	Caen	(0) 0

Second Round, Second Leg

Ajax	(1) 2	Vitoria Guimaraes	(0) 1
Celtic	(1) 1	Borussia Dortmund	(0) 2
FC Copenhagen	(0) 0	Auxerre	(0) 2
Galatasaray	(1) 1	Eintracht Frankfurt	(0) 0
Grasshoppers	(1) 4	Roma	(2) 3
Juventus	(0) 0	Panathinaikos	(0) 0
Kiev Dynamo	(0) 0	Anderlecht	(1) 3
Mechelen	(0) 0	Vitesse	(0) 0
Moscow Dynamo	(0) 0	Torino	(0) 0
Moscow Torpedo	(1) 3	Real Madrid	(1) 2
Paris St Germain	(0) 0	Napoli	(0) 0
Sheffield W	(1) 2	Kaiserslautern	(0) 2

Sigma Olomouc	(3) 7	Fenerbahçe	(1) 1
Standard Liege	(0) 1	Hearts	(0) 0
Vac Izzo	(0) 0	Benfica	(1) 1
Zaragoza	(3) 5	Frem	(0) 1

Third Round, First Leg

Ajax	(1) 2	Kaiserslautern	(0) 0
Borussia Dortmund	(3) 3	Zaragoza	(0) 1
Moscow Dynamo	(0) 2	Benfica	(1) 2
Paris St Germain	(0) 0	Anderlecht	(0) 0
Roma	(0) 3	Galatasaray	(0) 1
Sigma Olomouc	(0) 1	Juventus	(1) 2
Standard Liege	(1) 2	Auxerre	(0) 2
Vitesse	(0) 0	Real Madrid	(0) 1

Third Round, Second Leg

Anderlecht	(0) 1	Paris St Germain	(0) 1
Auxerre	(0) 2	Standard Liege	(0) 1
Benfica	(0) 2	Moscow Dynamo	(0) 0
Galatasaray	(1) 3	Roma	(1) 2
Juventus	(2) 5	Sigma Olomouc	(0) 0
Kaiserslautern	(0) 0	Ajax	(0) 1
Real Madrid	(0) 2	Vitesse	(0) 0
Zaragoza	(1) 2	Borussia Dortmund	(0) 1

Quarter-finals, First Leg

Auxerre	(2) 4	Ajax	(2) 2
Benfica	(1) 2	Juventus	(0) 1
Real Madrid	(2) 3	Paris St Germain	(0) 1
Roma	(0) 1	Borussia Dortmund	(0) 0

Quarter-finals, Second Leg

Ajax	(0) 1	Auxerre	(0) 0
Borussia Dortmund	(1) 2	Roma	(0) 0
Juventus	(2) 3	Benfica	(0) 0
Paris St Germain	(1) 4	Real Madrid	(0) 1

Semi-finals, First Leg

Borussia Dortmund	(0) 2	Auxerre	(0) 0
Juventus	(0) 2	Paris St Germain	(1) 1

Semi-finals, Second Leg

Auxerre	(1) 2	Borussia Dortmund	(0) 0

Borussia Dortmund won 6-5 on penalties

| Paris St Germain | (0) 0 | Juventus | (0) 1 |

Final, First Leg: Borussia Dortmund (1) 1, Juventus (2) 3

(in Dortmund, 5 May 1993, 37,000)

Borussia Dortmund: Klos; Reinhardt, Franck (Mill 46), Schmidt, Grauer, Lusch, Reuter, Zorc (Karl 70), Chapuisat, Rummenigge, Poscher. *Scorer:* Rummenigge.
Juventus: Peruzzi; Carrera, De Marchi, Dino Baggio, Kohler, Julio Cesar, Conte, Marocchi, Vialli, Roberto Baggio (Di Canio 76), Moller (Galia 88). *Scorers:* Dino Baggio 26, Roberto Baggio 31,74.
Rfereee: Puhl (Hungary).

Final, Second Leg: Juventus (2) 3, Borussia Dortmund (0) 0

(in Turin, 19 May 1993, 62,781)

Juventus: Peruzzi; Carrera, Torricelli (Di Canio 66), De Marchi, Kohler, Julio Cesar, Galia, Dino Baggio, Vialli (Ravanelli 80), Roberto Baggio, Moller. *Scorers:* Dino Baggio 5, 42, Moller 65.
Borussia Dortmund: Klos; Reinhardt, Schmidt (Lusch 66), Schultz, Zelic, Poscher, Reuter, Karl, Sippel, Rummenigge (Franck 43), Mill.
Referee: Blankenstein (Holland).

EUROPEAN CUPS DRAW 1993–94

EUROPEAN CUP

Preliminary Round
HJK Helsinki v Norma Tallinn; Ekranas v Floriana; Tofta B68 v Croatia Zagreb; Skonto Riga v Olimpija Ljubljana; Cwmbran Town v Cork City; Dynamo Tbilisi v Linfield; Avenir Beggen v Rosenborg; Partizani Tirana v Akranes; Omonia v Aarau; Zimbru Kishinev v Beitar Jerusalem.

First Round
Galatasaray v Cwmbran Town or Cork City; Werder Bremen v Dynamo Minsk; Dynamo Kiev v Barcelona; Marseille v AEK Athens; Kispest Honved v Manchester United; Rangers v Levski; AIK Stockholm v Sparta Prague; Dynamo Tbilisi or Linfield v FC Copenhagen; HJK Helsinki or Norma Tallinn v Anderlecht; Partizani Tirana or Akranes v Feyenoord; Steaua Bucharest v Tofta B68 or Croatia Zagreb; Avenir Beggen or Rosenborg v FK Austria; Porto v Ekranas or Floriana; Skonto Riga or Olimpija Ljubljana v Spartak Moscow; Omonia or Aarau v AC Milan; Lech Poznan v Zimbru Kishinev or Beitar Jerusalem.

EUROPEAN CUP-WINNERS' CUP

Preliminary Round
Karpaty Lvov v Shelbourne; RAF Jelgava v Havnar HB; Sliema Wanderers v Degerfors; Bangor v Apoel; Maccabi Haifa v Dudelange; Valur v Anjalankoski; Balzers v Albpetrol; Nikol Tallinn v Lillestrom; Kosice v Vilnius; Lugano v Neman Grodno; Odense v Publikum.

First Round
CSKA Sofia v Balzers or Albpetrol; Real Madrid v Lugano or Neman Grodno; Torpedo Moscow v Dudelange or Maccabi Haifa; Besiktas v Kosice or Vilnius; Panathinaikos v Karpaty Lvov or Shelbourne; Odense or Publikum v Arsenal; Uni Craiova v RAF Jelgava or Havnar HB; Innsbruck Tirol v Ferencvaros; Standard Liege v Cardiff City; Bangor or Apoel v Paris St Germain; Hajduk Split v Ajax; Nikol Tallinn or Lillestrom v Torino; Benfica v Katowice; Bayer Leverkusen v Zbrovjovka Brno; Sliema Wanderers or Degerfors v Parma; Valur or Anjalankoski v Aberdeen.

UEFA CUP

First Round
Twente v Bayern Munich; Bohemians v Bordeaux; Young Boys v Celtic; Aalborg v La Coruna; Norwich City v Vitesse; Hearts v Atletico Madrid; Slavia Prague v Ofi Crete; Union Luxembourg v Boavista; Norrkoping v Mechelen; Nantes v Valencia; Karlsruhe v PSV Eindhoven; FC Reykjavik v MTK Budapest; Dynamo Moscow v Eintracht Frankfurt; Kuusysi v Waregem; Crusaders v Servette; Brondby v Dundee United; Slovan Bratislava v Aston Villa; Borussia Dortmund v Spartak Vladikavkaz; Lazio v Lokomotiv Plovdiv; Osters v Kongsvinger; Admira Wacker v Dnepr; Internazionale v Rapid Bucharest; Botev Plovdiv v Olympiakos; VAC Samsung v Apollon; Kocaelispor v Sporting Lisbon; Juventus v Lokomotiv Moscow; Salzburg v Dunajska Streda; Gloria Bistrita v Maribor Branik; Tenerife v Monaco; Antwerp v Maritimo; Trabzonspor v Valetta; Dinamo Bucharest v Cagliari.

UEFA CUP PAST FINALS

Year	Team	Score		Opponent	Score	
1972	Tottenham H	2	1	Wolverhampton W	1	1
1973	Liverpool	3	0	Borussia Moenchengladbach	0	2
1974	Feyenoord	2	2	Tottenham H	2	0
1975	Borussia Moenchengladbach	0	5	Twente Enschede	0	1
1976	Liverpool	3	1	FC Bruges	2	1
1977	Juventus**	1	1	Athletic Bilbao	0	2
1978	PSV Eindhoven	0	3	SEC Bastia	0	0
1979	Borussia Moenchengladbach	1	1	Red Star Belgrade	1	0
1980	Borussia Moenchengladbach	3	0	Eintracht Frankfurt**	2	1
1981	Ipswich T	3	2	AZ 67 Alkmaar	0	4
1982	IFK Gothenburg	1	3	SV Hamburg	0	0
1983	Anderlecht	1	1	Benfica	0	1
1984	Tottenham H†	1	1	RSC Anderlecht	1	1
1985	Real Madrid	3	0	Videoton	0	1
1986	Real Madrid	5	0	Cologne	1	2
1987	IFK Gothenburg	1	1	Dundee U	0	1
1988	Bayer Leverkusen†	0	3	Espanol	3	0
1989	Napoli	2	3	Stuttgart	1	3
1990	Juventus	3	0	Fiorentina	1	0
1991	Internazionale	2	0	AS Roma	0	1
1992	Ajax**	0	2	Torino	0	2

*After extra time ** Won on away goals †Won on penalties ‡Aggregate score*

EUROPEAN CUP PAST FINALS

Year	Team	Score	Opponent	Score
1956	Real Madrid	4	Stade de Rheims	3
1957	Real Madrid	2	Fiorentina	0
1958	Real Madrid	3	AC Milan	2*
1959	Real Madrid	2	Stade de Rheims	0
1960	Real Madrid	7	Eintracht Frankfurt	3
1961	Benfica	3	Barcelona	2
1962	Benfica	5	Real Madrid	3
1963	AC Milan	2	Benfica	1
1964	Internazionale	3	Real Madrid	1
1965	Internazionale	1	SL Benfica	0
1966	Real Madrid	2	Partizan Belgrade	1
1967	Celtic	2	Internazionale	1
1968	Manchester U	4	Benfica	1*
1969	AC Milan	4	Ajax	1
1970	Feyenoord	2	Celtic	1*
1971	Ajax	2	Panathinaikos	0
1972	Ajax	2	Internazionale	0
1973	Ajax	1	Juventus	0
1974	Bayern Munich	1 4	Atletico Madrid	1 0
1975	Bayern Munich	2	Leeds U	0
1976	Bayern Munich	1	St Etienne	0
1977	Liverpool	3	Borussia Moenchengladbach	1
1978	Liverpool	1	FC Brugge	0
1979	Nottingham F	1	Malmö	0

1980	Nottingham F	1	Hamburg	0
1981	Liverpool	1	Real Madrid	0
1982	Aston Villa	1	Bayern Munich	0
1983	Hamburg	1	Juventus	0
1984	Liverpool†	1	Roma	1
1985	Juventus	1	Liverpool	0
1986	Steaua Bucharest†	0	Barcelona	0
1987	Porto	2	Bayern Munich	1
1988	PSV Eindhoven†	0	Benfica	0
1989	AC Milan	4	Steaua Bucharest	0
1990	AC Milan	1	Benfica	0
1991	Red Star Belgrade†	0	Marseille	0
1992	Barcelona	1	Sampdoria	0

EUROPEAN CUP-WINNERS' CUP PAST FINALS

1961	Fiorentina	4	Rangers	1‡
1962	Atletico Madrid	1 3	Fiorentina	1 0
1963	Tottenham H	5	Atletico Madrid	1
1964	Sporting Lisbon	3 1	MTK Budapest	3* 0
1965	West Ham U	2	Munich 1860	0
1966	Borussia Dortmund	2	Liverpool	1*
1967	Bayern Munich	1	Rangers	0*
1968	AC Milan	2	Hamburg	0
1969	Slovan Bratislava	3	Barcelona	2
1970	Manchester C	2	Gornik Zabrze	1
1971	Chelsea	1 2	Real Madrid	1* 1*
1972	Rangers	3	Dynamo Moscow	2
1973	AC Milan	1	Leeds U	0
1974	Magdeburg	2	AC Milan	0
1975	Dynamo Kiev	3	Ferencvaros	0
1976	Anderlecht	4	West Ham U	2
1977	Hamburg	2	Anderlecht	0
1978	Anderlecht	4	Austria Vienna	0
1979	Barcelona	4	Fortuna Dusseldorf	3*
1980	Valencia†	0	Arsenal	0
1981	Dynamo Tbilisi	2	Carl Zeiss Jena	1
1982	Barcelona	2	Standard Liege	1
1983	Aberdeen	2	Real Madrid	1*
1984	Juventus	2	Porto	1
1985	Everton	3	Rapid Vienna	1
1986	Dynamo Kiev	3	Atletico Madrid	0
1987	Ajax	1	Lokomotiv Leipzig	0
1988	Mechelen	1	Ajax	0
1989	Barcelona	2	Sampdoria	0
1990	Sampdoria	2	Anderlecht	0
1991	Manchester U	2	Barcelona	1
1992	Werder Bremen	2	Monaco	0

FAIRS CUP FINALS

1958	Barcelona	8	London	2‡
1960	Barcelona	4	Birmingham C	1‡
1961	Roma	4	Birmingham C	2‡
1962	Valencia	7	Barcelona	3‡
1963	Valencia	4	Dynamo Zagreb	1‡
1964	Real Zaragoza	2	Valencia	1
1965	Ferencvaros	1	Juventus	0
1966	Barcelona	4	Real Zaragoza	3‡
1967	Dynamo Zagreb	2	Leeds U	0‡
1968	Leeds U	1	Ferencvaros	0‡
1969	Newcastle U	6	Ujpest Dozsa	2‡
1970	Arsenal	4	Anderlecht	3‡
1971	Leeds U	3**	Juventus	3‡

SOUTH AMERICAN CHAMPIONSHIP

(Copa America)

1916 Uruguay	1935 Uruguay	1957 Argentina
1917 Uruguay	1937 Argentina	1959 Argentina
1919 Brazil	1939 Peru	1959 Uruguay
1920 Uruguay	1941 Argentina	1963 Bolivia
1921 Argentina	1942 Uruguay	1967 Uruguay
1922 Brazil	1945 Argentina	1975 Peru
1923 Uruguay	1946 Argentina	1979 Paraguay
1924 Uruguay	1947 Argentina	1983 Uruguay
1925 Argentina	1949 Brazil	1987 Uruguay
1926 Uruguay	1953 Paraguay	1989 Brazil
1927 Argentina	1955 Argentina	1991 Argentina
1929 Argentina	1956 Uruguay	1993 Argentina

SOUTH AMERICAN CUP

(Copa Libertadores)

1960 Penarol (Uruguay)	1977 Boca Juniors (Argentina)
1961 Penarol	1978 Boca Juniors
1962 Santos (Brazil)	1979 Olimpia (Paraguay)
1963 Santos	1980 Nacional
1964 Independiente (Argentina)	1981 Flamengo (Brazil)
1965 Independiente	1982 Penarol
1966 Penarol	1983 Gremio Porto Alegre (Brazil)
1967 Racing Club (Argentina)	1984 Independiente
1968 Estudiantes (Argentina)	1985 Argentinos Juniors (Argentina)
1969 Estudiantes	1986 River Plate (Argentina)
1970 Estudiantes	1987 Penarol
1971 Nacional (Uruguay)	1988 Nacional (Uruguay)
1972 Independiente	1989 Nacional (Colombia)
1973 Independiente	1990 Olimpia
1974 Independiente	1991 Colo Colo (Chile)
1975 Independiente	1992 Sao Paulo (Brazil)
1976 Cruzeiro (Brazil)	1993 Sao Paulo

PAST EUROPEAN CHAMPIONSHIP FINALS

Paris, 10 July 1960 USSR 2, YUGOSLAVIA 1*
USSR: Yachin; Tchekeli, Kroutikov, Voinov, Maslenkin, Netto, Metreveli, Ivanov, Ponedelnik, Bubukin, Meshki. **Scorers:** Metreveli, Ponedelnik.
Yugoslavia: Vidinic; Durkovic, Jusufi, Zanetic, Miladinovic, Perusic, Sekularac, Jerkovic, Galic, Matus, Kostic. **Scorer:** Netto (og).

Madrid, 21 June 1964 SPAIN 2, USSR 1
Spain: Iribar; Rivilla, Calleja, Fuste, Olivella, Zoco, Amancio, Pereda, Marcellino, Suarez, Lapetra. **Scorers:** Perede, Marcellino.
USSR: Yachin; Chustikov, Mudrik, Voronin, Shesternjev, Anitchkin, Chislenko, Ivanov, Ponedelnik, Kornaev, Khusainov. **Scorer:** Khusainov.

Rome, 8 June 1968 ITALY 1, YUGOSLAVIA 1
Italy: Zoff; Burgnich, Facchetti, Ferrini, Guarneri, Castano, Domenghini, Juliano, Anastasi, Lodetti, Prati. **Scorer:** Domenghini.
Yugoslavia: Pandelic; Fazlagic, Damjanovic, Pavlovic, Paunovic, Holcer, Petkovic, Acimovic, Musemic, Trivic, Dzajic. **Scorer:** Dzajic.

Replay: Rome, 10 June 1968 ITALY 2, YUGLOSLAVIA 0
Italy: Zoff; Burgnich, Facchetti, Rosato, Guarneri, Salvadore, Domenghini, Mazzola, Anastasi, De Sista, Riva. **Scorers:** Riva, Anastasi.
Yugoslavia: Pantelic; Fazlagic, Damjanovic, Pavlovic, Paunovic, Holcer, Hosic, Acimovic, Musemic, Trivic, Dzajic.

Brussels, 18 June 1972 WEST GERMANY 3, USSR 0
West Germany: Maier; Hottges, Schwarzenbeck, Beckenbauer, Breitner, Hoeness, Wimmer, Netzer, Heynckes, Müller, Kremers. **Scorers:** Müller 2, Wimmer.
USSR: Rudakov; Dzodzuashvili, Khurtsilava, Kaplichny, Istomin, Troshkin, Kolotov, Baidachni, Konkov (Dolmatov), Banishevski (Konzinkievits), Onishenko.

Belgrade, 20 June 1976 CZECHOSLOVAKIA 2, WEST GERMANY 2*
Czechoslovakia: Viktor; Dobias (Vesely F), Pivarnik, Ondrus, Capkovic, Gogh, Moder, Panenka, Svehlik (Jurkemik), Masny, Nehoda. **Scorers:** Svehlik, Dobias.
West Germany: Maier; Vogts, Beckenbauer, Schwarzenbeck, Dietz, Bonhof, Wimmer (Flohe), Müller D, Beer (Bongartz), Hoeness, Holzenbein. **Scorers:** Müller, Holzenbein.
Czechoslovakia won 5-3 on penalties.

Rome, 22 June 1980 WEST GERMANY 2, BELGIUM 1
West Germany: Schumacher; Briegel, Forster K, Dietz, Schuster, Rummenigge, Hrubesch, Müller, Allofs, Stielike, Kalz. **Scorers:** Hrubesch 2.
Belgium: Pfaff; Gerets, Millecamps, Meeuws, Renquin, Cools, Van der Eycken, Van Moer, Mommens, Van der Elst, Ceulemans. **Scorer:** Van der Eycken.

Paris, 27 June 1984 FRANCE 2, SPAIN 0
France: Bats; Battiston (Amoros), Le Roux, Bossis, Domergue, Giresse, Platini, Tigana, Fernandez, Lacombe (Genghini), Bellone. **Scorers:** Platini, Bellone.
Spain: Arconada; Urquiaga, Salva (Roberto), Gallego, Camacho, Francisco, Julio Alberto (Sarabia), Senor, Victor, Carrasco, Santilana.

Munich, 25 June 1988 HOLLAND 2, USSR 0
Holland: Van Breukelen; Van Aerle, Van Tiggelen, Wouters, Koeman R, Rijkaard, Vanenburg, Gullit, Van Basten, Muhren, Koeman E. **Scorers:** Gullit, Van Basten.
USSR: Dassayev; Khidiatulin, Aleinikov, Mikhailichenko, Litovchenko, Demianenko, Belanov, Gotsmanov (Baltacha), Protasov (Pasulko), Zavarov, Rats.

Gothenburg, 26 June 1992 DENMARK 2, GERMANY 0
Denmark: Schmeichel; Sivebaek (Christiansen), Nielsen, K, Olsen, L, Christofte, Jensen, Povlsen, Laudrup, Piechnik, Larsen, Vilfort. **Scorers:** Jensen, Vilfort.
Germany: Illgner; Reuter, Brehme, Kohler, Buchwald, Hässler, Riedle, Helmer, Sammer (Doll), Effenberg (Thon), Klinsmann.

* After extra time

THE WORLD CUP FINALS

Uruguay 1930
URUGUAY 4, ARGENTINA 2 (1–2) *Montevideo*
Uruguay: Ballesteros; Nasazzi (capt), Mascheroni, Andrade, Fernandez, Gestido, Dorado, Scarone, Castro, Cea, Iriarte. **Scorers:** Dorado, Cea, Iriarte, Castro.
Argentina: Botasso; Della, Torre, Paternoster, Evaristo, J., Monti, Suarez, Peucelle, Varallo, Stabile, Ferreira (capt), Evaristo, M. **Scorers:** Peucelle, Stabile.
Leading scorer: Stabile (Argentina) 8.

Italy 1934
ITALY 2, CZECHOSLOVAKIA 1 (0–0) (1–1)* *Rome*
Italy: Combi (capt); Monseglio, Allemandi, Ferraris IV, Monti, Bertolini, Guaita, Meazza, Schiavio, Ferrari, Orsi. **Scorers:** Orsi, Schiavio.
Czechoslovakia: Planicka (capt); Zenisek, Ctyroky, Kostalek, Cambal, Krcil, Junek, Svoboda, Sobotka, Nejedly, Puc. **Scorer:** Puc.
Leading scorers: Schiavio (Italy), Nejedly (Czechoslovakia), Conen (Germany) each 4.

France 1938
ITALY 4, HUNGARY 2 (3–1) *Paris*
Italy: Olivieri; Foni, Rava, Serantoni, Andreolo, Locatelli, Biavati, Meassa (capt), Piola, Ferrari, Colaussi. **Scorers:** Colaussi 2, Piola 2.
Hungary: Szabo; Polgar, Biro, Szalay, Szucs, Lazar, Vincze, Sarosi (capt), Szengeller, Titkos. **Scorers:** Titkos, Sarosi.
Leading scorer: Leonidas (Brazil) 8.

Brazil 1950
Final pool (replaced knock-out system)

Uruguay 2, Spain 2	Brazil 6, Spain 1
Brazil 7, Sweden 1	Sweden 3, Spain 1
Uruguay 3, Sweden 2	Uruguay 2, Brazil 1

Final positions	P	W	D	L	F	A	Pts
Uruguay	3	2	1	0	7	5	5
Brazil	3	2	0	1	14	4	4
Sweden	3	1	0	2	6	11	2
Spain	3	0	1	2	4	11	1

Leading scorers: Ademir (Brazil) 7, Schiaffino (Uruguay), Basora (Spain) 5.

Switzerland 1954
WEST GERMANY 3, HUNGARY 2 (2–2) *Berne*
West Germany: Turek; Posipal, Kohlmeyer, Eckel, Liebrich, Rahn, Morlock, Walter, O., Walter, F. (capt), Schaefer. **Scorers:** Morlock, Rahn 2.
Hungary: Grosics; Buzansky, Lantos, Bozsik, Lorant, Zakarias, Czibor, Kocsis, Hidegkuti, Puskas (capt), Toth, J. **Scorers:** Puskas, Czibor.
Leading scorer: Kocsis (Hungary) 11.

Sweden 1958
BRAZIL 5, SWEDEN 2 (2–1) *Stockholm*
Brazil: Gilmar; Santos, D., Santos, N., Zito, Bellini, Orlando, Garrincha, Didi, Vavà, Pelé, Zagalo **Scorers:** Vavà 2, Pelé 2, Zagalo.
Sweden: Svensson; Bergmark, Axbom, Boerjesson, Gustavsson, Parling, Hamrin, Gren, Simonsson, Liedholm, Skoglund. **Scorers:** Liedholm, Simonsson.
Leading scorer: Fontaine (France) 13 (present record total).

Chile 1962
BRAZIL 3, CZECHOSLOVAKIA 1 (1–1) *Santiago*
Brazil: Gilmar; Santos, D., Mauro, Zozimo, Santos, N., Zito, Didi, Garrincha, Vavà, Amarildo, Zagalo. **Scorers:** Amarildo, Zito, Vavà.
Czechoslovakia: Schroiff; Tichy, Novak, Pluskal, Popluhar, Masopust, Pospichal, Scherer, Kvasniak, Kadraba, Jelinek. **Scorer:** Masopust.
Leading scorer: Jerkovic (Yugoslavia) 5.

England 1966
ENGLAND 4, WEST GERMANY 2 (1–1) (2–2)* *Wembley*
England: Banks; Cohen, Wilson, Stiles, Charlton, J., Moore, Ball, Hurst, Hunt, Charlton, R., Peters. **Scorers:** Hurst 3, Peters.
West Germany: Tilkowski; Hottges, Schulz, Weber, Schnellinger, Haller, Beckenbauer, Overath, Seeler, Held, Emmerich. **Scorers:** Haller, Weber.
Leading scorer: Eusebio (Portugal) 9.

Mexico 1970
BRAZIL 4, ITALY 1 (1–1) *Mexico City*
Brazil: Felix; Carlos Alberto, Piazza, Everaldo, Gerson, Clodoaldo, Jairzinho, Pelé, Tostão, Rivelino. **Scorers:** Pelé, Gerson, Jairzinho, Carlos Alberto.
Italy: Albertosi; Burgnich, Cera, Rosato, Fachetti, Bertini (Juliano), Riva, Domenghini, Mazzola, De Sista, Boninsegna (Rivera). **Scorer:** Boninsegna.
Leading scorer: Müller (West Germany) 10.

West Germany 1974
WEST GERMANY 2, HOLLAND 1 (2–1) *Munich*
West Germany: Maier; Vogts, Schwarzenbeck, Beckenbauer, Breitner, Bonhof, Hoeness, Overath, Grabowski, Müller, Holzenbein. **Scorers:** Breitner (pen), Müller.
Holland: Jongbloed; Suurbier, Rijsbergen (De Jong), Haan, Krol, Jansen, Van Hanegem, Neeskens, Rep (Nanninga), Cruyff, Rensenbrink (Van der Kerkhof, R.) **Scorer:** Nanninga (pen).
Leading scorer: Lato (Poland) 7.

Argentina 1978
ARGENTINA 3, HOLLAND 1 (1–1)* *Buenos Aires*
Argentina: Fillol; Olguin, Passarella, Galvan, Tarantini, Ardiles (Larrosa), Gallego,Ortiz (Houseman), Bertoni, Luque, Kempes. **Scorers:** Kempes 2, Bertoni.
Holland: Jongbloed; Poortvliet, Brandts, Krol, Jansen (Suurbier), Neeskens, Van der Kerkhof, W., Van der Kerkhof, R., Haan, Rep (Nanninga), Rensenbrink. **Scorer:** Nanninga.
Leading scorer: Kempes (Argentina) 6.

Spain 1982
ITALY 3 WEST GERMANY 1 (0–0) *Madrid*
Italy: Zoff; Bergomi, Cabrini, Collovati, Scirea, Gentile, Oriali, Tardelli, Conti, Graziani (Altobelli), Rossi (Causio). **Scorers:** Rossi, Tardelli, Altobelli.
West Germany: Schumacher; Kaltz, Forster, K-H., Stielike, Forster, B. Breitner, Dremmler (Hrubesch), Littbarski, Briegel, Fischer, Rummenigge (Müller). **Scorer:** Breitner.
Leading scorer: Rossi (Italy) 6.

Mexico 1986
ARGENTINA 3, WEST GERMANY 2 (1–0) *Mexico City*
Argentina: Pumpido; Cuciuffo, Olarticoechea, Ruggeri, Brown, Giusti, Burruchaga (Trobbiani), Batista, Valdano, Maradona, Enrique. **Scorers:** Brown, Valdano, Burruchaga.

193

West Germany: Schumacher; Berthold, Briegel, Jakobs, Forster, Eder, Brehme, Matthaus, Allofs (Voller), Magath (Hoeness), Rummenigge. **Scorers:** Rummenigge, Voller.
Leading scorer: Lineker (England) 6.

Italy 1990
WEST GERMANY 1, ARGENTINA 0 (0–0) *Rome*
West Germany: Illgner; Berthold (Reuter 73), Kohler, Augenthaler, Buchwald, Brehme, Littbarski, Hässler, Matthäus, Völler, Klinsmann. **Scorer:** Brehme (pen).
Argentina: Goycochea; Lorenzo, Serrizuela, Sensini, Ruggeri (Monzon 46), Simon, Basualdo, Burruchaga (Calderon 53), Maradona, Troglio, Dezotti.
Referee: Codesal (Mexico). Monzon and Dezotti sent off.
Leading scorer: Schillaci (Italy) 6.

*After extra time

OLYMPIC FOOTBALL

Previous winners

1896	Athens*	1.	Denmark	1956	Melbourne	1. USSR
		2.	Greece			2. Yugoslavia
1900	Paris*	1.	England			3. Bulgaria
		2.	France	1960	Rome	1. Yugoslavia
1904	St Louis**	1.	Canada			2. Denmark
		2.	USA			3. Hungary
1908	London	1.	England	1964	Tokyo	1. Hungary
		2.	Denmark			2. Czechoslovakia
		3.	Holland			3. East Germany
1912	Stockholm	1.	England	1968	Mexico City	1. Hungary
		2.	Denmark			2. Bulgaria
		3.	Holland			3. Japan
1920	Antwerp	1.	Belgium	1972	Munich	1. Poland
		2.	Spain			2. Hungary
		3.	Holland			3. East Germany/
1924	Paris	1.	Uruguay			USSR joint bronze
		2.	Switzerland	1976	Montreal	1. East Germany
		3.	Sweden			2. Poland
1928	Amsterdam	1.	Uruguay			3. USSR
		2.	Argentina	1980	Moscow	1. Czechoslovakia
		3.	Italy			2. East Germany
1932	Los Angeles no competition					3. USSR
1936	Berlin	1.	Italy	1984	Los Angeles	1. France
		2.	Austria			2. Brazil
		3.	Norway			3. Yugoslavia
1948	London	1.	Sweden	1988	Seoul	1. USSR
		2.	Yugoslavia			2. Brazil
		3.	Denmark			3. West Germany
1952	Helsinki	1.	Hungary	1992	Barcelona	1. Spain
		2.	Yugoslavia			2. Poland
		3.	Sweden			3. Ghana

*No official tournament
**No official tournament but gold medal later awarded by IOC

WORLD CUP 1994

Europe
Group 1
Tallinn, 16 August 1992, 3000
Estonia (0) 0

Switzerland (2) 6 *(Chapuisat 23, 68, Bregy 29, Knup 46, Ohrel 66, Sforza 84)*

Estonia: Poom; Hepner, Kaljend, Kallaste T, Lindmaa (Veensalu 78), Kristal, Olumets, Linnunae, Kallaste R, Reim, Pustov (Kirs 64).
Switzerland: Pascolo; Egli, Geiger, Hottiger, Rothenbuhler, Bregy, Sutter B (Bonvin 79), Ohrel, Sforza, Chapuisat, Knup.

Berne, 9 September 1992, 10,000
Switzerland (1) 3 *(Knup 2, 71, Bregy 81)*

Scotland (1) 1 *(McCoist)*

Switzerland: Pascolo; Hottiger, Quentin, Egli, Geiger, Bregy (Piffaretti 89), Sutter A, Ohrel, Knup (Sutter B 86), Sforza, Chapuisat.
Scotland: Goram; Gough, Malpas, McCall, Boyd (Gallacher 75), McPherson, Durie, McAllister, McCoist, McStay, McClair (Durrant 57).

Cagliari, 14 October 1992, 34,000
Italy (0) 2 *(Roberto Baggio 83, Eranio 89)*

Switzerland (2) 2 *(Ohrel 17, Chapuisat 21)*

Italy: Marchegiani; Tassotti, Di Chiara, Eranio, Costacurta, Lanna, Lentini, Donadoni (Albertini 71), Vialli, Roberto Baggio, Evani (Bianchi 48).
Switzerland: Pascolo; Hottiger, Quentin, Egli, Geiger, Bregy, Sutter A, Ohrel (Piffaretti 56), Knup (Sutter B 89), Sforza, Chapuisat.

Ibrox, 14 October 1992, 22,583
Scotland (0) 0

Portugal (0) 0

Scotland: Goram; Malpas, Boyd, McCall, Whyte, Levein, Gallacher (McClair 33), McStay, McCoist, McAllister, Collins (Durrant 71).
Portugal: Vitor Baia; Joao Pinto I, Helder, Veloso, Fernando Couto, Oceano, Vitor Paneira, Semedo (Figo 53), Domingos, Futre, Andre.

Valletta, 25 October 1992, 8000
Malta (0) 0

Estonia (0) 0

Malta: Cluett; Gregory (Suda 78), Vella S, Galea, Brincat, Buttigieg, Busuttil, Vella R, Zerafa (Saliba 78), Laferla, Sultana.
Estonia: Poom; Kaljend, Hepner, Prins, Kallaste T, Ratnikov, Olumets, Pustov (Rayala 75), Kirs, Reim, Kallaste R.

Ibrox, 18 November 1992, 33,029
Scotland (0) 0

Italy (0) 0

Scotland: Goram; McPherson, Malpas, McStay, McLaren, Whyte, Durie (Jess 71), McAllister, McCoist, Durrant (Robertson 88), Boyd.
Italy: Pagliuca; Mannini, Di Chiara (Costacurta 7), Maldini, Baresi, Lentini, Albertini, Eranio, Bianchi, Signori (Donadoni 46), Roberto Baggio.

Berne, 18 November 1992, 14,200
Switzerland (2) 3 *(Bickel 2, Sforza 42, Chapuisat 89)*

Malta (0) 0

Switzerland: Pascolo; Hottiger, Geiger, Egli, Rothenbuhler, Bickel (Bonvin 82), Bregy, Sforza, Sutter A, Knup (Turkyilmaz 75), Chapuisat.
Malta: Cluett; Buttigieg, Buhagiar, Galea (Camilleri E 17), Vella S, Brincat, Gregory, Camilleri J, Saliba, Vella R (Scerri 75), Busuttil.

Valletta, 19 December 1992, 15,000
Malta (0) 1 *(Gregory 85)*

Italy (0) 2 *(Vialli 59, Signori 62)*

Malta: Cluett; Vella S, Buhagiar (Camilleri J 46), Galea, Brincat, Buttigieg, Busuttil, Saliba (Vella R 73), Gregory, Laferla, Scerri.
Italy: Pagliuca; Maldini, Di Chiara (Bianchi 46), Baresi, Costacurta, Eranio, Albertini, Donadoni (Simone 58), Evani, Vialli, Signori.

Valletta, 24 January 1993, 10,000
Malta (0) 0

Portugal (0) 1 *(Rui Aguas 56)*

Malta: Cluett; Vella S, Galea, Brincat, Buhagiar, Buttigieg, Vella R (Suda 75), Busuttil, Gregory, Laferla, Scerri (Degiorgio 65).
Portugal: Vitor Baia; Joao Pinto I, Veloso, Fernando Couto, Cristovao, Cruz, Vitor Paneira (Joao Pinto II 56), Samedo (Jaime Magalhaes 75), Oliveira, Rui Aguas, Figo.

Ibrox, 17 February 1993, 35,490
Scotland (1) 3 *(McCoist 15, 68, Nevin 84)*

Malta (0) 0

Scotland: Goram; McPherson (Robertson 64), Boyd, McStay, McLeich, McLaren, Nevin, McAllister (Ferguson 73), McCoist, Collins, Jess.
Malta: Cluett; Vella S, Buhagiar (Camilleri E 83), Galea, Brincat, Buttigieg, Busuttil, Saliba, Camilleri J, Laferla, Sultana (Vella R 74).

Oporto, 24 February 1993, 70,000
Portugal (0) 1 *(Couto 57)*

Italy (2) 3 *(Roberto Baggio 2, Casiraghi 24, Dino Baggio 75)*

Portugal: Vitor Baia; Joao Pinto I, Helder (Rui Barros 35), Mendes, Fernando Couto, Oceano, Semedo, Figo, Domingos, Futre, Carlos Xavier (Rui Aguas 46).
Italy: Pagliuca; Tassotti, Maldini, Di Chiara, Costacurta, Vierchowod, Fuser, Albertini, Casiraghi (Lentini 26), Roberto Baggio (Mancini 85), Signori.

Palermo, 24 March 1993, 35,000
Italy (2) 6 *(Dino Baggio 19, Signori 38, Vierchowod 48, Mancini 59, 89, Maldini 73)*

Malta (0) 1 *(Busuttil 68 (pen))*

Italy: Pagliuca (Marchegiani 80); Porrini, Maldini, Dino Baggio, Vierchowod, Baresi, Fuser, Albertini, Melli, Mancini, Signori.
Malta: Cluett; Vella S, Zerafa, Galea, Saliba, Laferla, Busuttil, Vella R, Gregory (Delia 57), Degiorgio (Suda 73), Scerri.

Berne, 31 March 1993, 31,200
Switzerland (1) 1 *(Chapuisat 39)*

Portugal (1) 1 *(Semedo 44)*

Switzerland: Pascolo; Hottiger, Herr, Geiger, Rothenbuhler, Ohrel, Bregy, Sforza, Sutter A, Knup (Bonvin 46), Chapuisat.
Portugal: Vitor Baia; Peixe, Oceano, Jorge Costa, Semedo (Mendes 50), Abel Xavier, Rui Costa, Sousa, Figo (Rui Barros 68), Futre, Rui Aguas.

Trieste, 14 April 1993, 33,000
Italy (1) 2 *(Roberto Baggio 21, Signori 86)*

Estonia (0) 0

Italy: Pagliuca; Porrini (Mannini 46), Di Chiara, Dino Baggio (Di Mauro 68), Vierchowod, Baresi, Fuser, Albertini, Melli, Roberto Baggio, Signori.
Estonia: Poom; Kallaste R, Lensalu, Prins, Kaljend, Kallaste T, Borisov, Kristal, Reim (Olumets 89), Ratnikov, Pustov (Rajala 83).

Valletta, 17 April 1993, 8000
Malta (0) 0

Switzerland (1) 2 *(Ohrel 31, Turkyilmaz 89)*

Malta: Cluett; Vella S, Brincat, Galea, Buhagiar, Busuttil, Buttigieg, Camilleri J (Delia 46), Saliba (Carabott 46), Laferla, Scerri.
Switzerland: Pascolo; Hottiger, Herr, Geiger, Rothenbuhler (Sylvestre 50), Henchoz, Sforza, Sutter A, Ohreil, Grassi, Bonvin (Turkyilmaz 60).

Lisbon, 28 April 1993, 28,000
Portugal (2) 5 *(Rui Barros 5, 70, Cadete 45, 72, Futre 67)*

Scotland (0) 0

Portugal: Vitor Baia; Abel Xavier, Jorge Costa, Rui Costa (Veloso 53), Fernando Couto, Oceano, Rui Barros, Sousa, Semedo, Futre, Cadete (Domingos 81).
Scotland: Goram; Gough, McInally, McPherson, McKimmie, Levein (Nevin 60), McStay, McCall, McCoist, Collins (Durrant 75), Gallacher.

Berne, 1 May 1993, 31,000
Switzerland (0) 1 *(Hottiger 55)*

Italy (0) 0

Switzerland: Pascolo; Hottiger, Geiger, Herr, Quentin, Bregy, Ohrel, Sforza, Sutter A, Knup (Grassi 76), Chapuisat.
Italy: Pagliuca; Mannini, Baresi, Vierchowod, Maldini, Fuser, Zoratto (Lentini 64), Dino Baggio, Signori, Mancini (Di Mauro 46), Roberto Baggio.

Tallinn, 12 May 1993, 14,000
Estonia (0) 0

Malta (1) 1 *(Laferla 16)*

Estonia: Poom; Kallaste R (Bragin 75), Hepner, Prins, Kaljend, Kallaste T, Borisov, Kristal, Reim, Ratnikov (Olumets 20), Pustov.
Malta: Cluett; Vella S, Buhagiar, Saliba, Brincat, Buttigieg, Gregory (Delia 77), Vella R, Carabott (Sultana 46), Laferla, Camilleri J.

Tallinn, 19 May 1993, 5100
Estonia (0) 0

Scotland (1) 3 *(Gallacher 43, Collins 59, Booth 73)*

Estonia: Poom; Kallaste R, Lensalu, Prins, Kaljend, Kallaste T, Borisov, Kristal (Hepner 46), Reim, Veensalu (Pustov 76), Bragin.
Scotland: Gunn; Wright (McLaren 80), Boyd, McStay, Hendry, Irvine, Gallacher, Bowman, Robertson (Booth 61), McClair, Collins.

Aberdeen, 2 June 1993, 14,309
Scotland (2) 3 *(McClair 16, Nevin 27, 72 (pen))*

Estonia (0) 1 *(Bragin 57)*

Scotland: Gunn; McLaren (Robertson 72), Boyd, McStay, Hendry, Irvine, Gallacher, Ferguson (Booth 55), McClair, Collins, Nevin.
Estonia: Poom; Kallaste R, Lensalu (Bragin 46), Prins, Kaljend, Kallaste T, Borisov, Kristal, Reim, Olumets (Veensalu 73), Rajala.

Oporto, 19 June 1993, 7000
Portugal (3) 4 *(Nogueira 2, Rui Costa 9, Joao Pinto II 23, Cadete 87)*

Malta (0) 0

Portugal: Vitor Baia; Nogueira (Figo 70), Fernando Couto, Oceano, Abel Xavier, Semedo, Sousa, Rui Costa, Joao Pinto II, Cadete, Domingos (Rui Aguas 46).
Malta: Cluett; Vella S, Buhagiar, Delia, Cauchi, Buttigieg, Saliba, Gregory, Camilleri J (Scerri 66), Laferla, Zerafa (Vella R 41).

	P	W	D	L	F	A	Pts
Switzerland	7	5	2	0	18	4	12
Italy	7	4	2	1	15	6	10
Portugal	6	3	2	1	12	6	8
Scotland	7	3	2	2	10	9	8
Malta	9	1	1	7	3	21	3
Estonia	6	0	1	5	1	15	1

Group 2
Oslo, 9 September 1992, 6511
Norway (4) 10 *(Rekdal 5, 79, Halle 6, 51, 69, Sorloth 15, 21, Nilsen 46, 67, Mykland 74)*

San Marino (0) 0

Norway: Thorstvedt; Pedersen T, Bratseth, Nilsen R, Halle, Mykland, Rekdal, Leonhardsen (Ingebritsen 57), Jakobsen JI, Sorloth (Fjortoft 75), Flo.
San Marino: Benedettini; Guerra, Gobbi, Canti, Gennari, Mazza M, Bonini, Francini (Matteoni 70), Manzaroli P, Mazza P, Pasolini W (Muccioli B 46).

Oslo, 23 September 1992, 19,998
Norway (1) 2 *(Rekdal 9 (pen), Sorloth 78)*

Holland (1) 1 *(Bergkamp 10)*

Norway: Thorstvedt; Nilsen R, Pedersen T, Bratseth, Bjornebye, Halle (Strandli 60), Mykland, Ingebritsen, Rekdal, Sorloth (Flo 81), Jakobsen JI.
Holland: Menzo; Koeman, Blind, Silooy, De Boer F, Van't Schip (Taument 81), Wouters (Kieft 85), Rijkaard, Rob Witschge, Bergkamp, Van Basten.

198

Poznan, 23 September 1992, 11,000
Poland (1) 1 *(Waldoch 33)*

Turkey (0) 0

Poland: Bako; Rzepa, Szewczyk, Lesiak, Waldoch, Czachowski, Brzeczek, Warzycha R, Araszkiewicz (Kowalczyk 61), Kosecki (Fedoruk 64), Juskowiak.
Turkey: Hayrettin; Recep (Aykut 74), Bulent, Gokhan, Ogun, Tugay, Hami, Riza, Hakan, Oguz (Mehmet 64), Orhan.

Serravalle, 7 October 1992, 1187
San Marino (0) 0

Norway (2) 2 *(Jakobsen JI 7, Flo 19)*

San Marino: Benedettini; Guerra, Gobbi, Gennari, Bonini, Francini (Muccioli B 84), Manzaroli, Mazza M, Matteoni, Zanotti, Mazza P (Bacciocchi 25).
Norway: Thorstvedt; Bratseth, Nilsen R, Pedersen T, Halle (Bjornebye 46), Jakobsen JI, Leonhardsen (Ingebritsen 68), Mykland, Rekdal, Flo, Sorloth.

Wembley, 14 October 1992, 51,441
England (0) 1 *(Platt 55)*

Norway (0) 1 *(Rekdal 76)*

England: Woods; Dixon (Palmer 89), Walker, Adams, Pearce, Batty, Ince, Platt, Gascoigne, Wright (Merson 69), Shearer.
Norway: Thorstvedt; Nilsen R, Bratseth, Pedersen T (Berg 19), Bjornebye, Halle, Jakobsen JI, Ingebritsen, Mykland (Flo 78), Rekdal, Sorloth.

Rotterdam, 14 October 1992, 13,000
Holland (1) 2 *(Van Vossen 43, 46)*

Poland (2) 2 *(Kosecki 18, Kowalczyk 20)*

Holland: Menzo; Van Aerle, Koeman, Rijkaard (Fraser 80), Jonk, Wouters, Numan (Vanenburg 39), Rob Witschge, Bergkamp, Van Basten, Van Vossen.
Poland: Bako; Lesiak, Szewczyk, Kozminski, Adamczuk, Czachowski (Rzepa 39), Brzeczek, Kowalczyk (Smolarek 67) Warzycha R, Kosecki, Ziober.

Ankara, 28 October 1992, 35,000
Turkey (1) 4 *(Hakan 37, 89, Orhan 87, Hami 90)*

San Marino (0) 0

Turkey: Hayrettin; Riza (Mehmet 73), Bulent, Gokhan, Ogun, Orhan, Okan, Ridvan, Hakan, Oguz, Aykut (Hami 46).
San Marino: Benedettini; Gobbi, Gennari, Della Valle (Bizocchi 60), Matteoni, Guerra, Manzaroli, Mazza P, Bacciocchi, Bonini, Francini (Zanotti 80).

Wembley, 18 November 1992, 42,984
England (2) 4 *(Gascoigne 16, 61, Shearer 28, Pearce 60)*

Turkey (0) 0

England: Woods; Dixon, Pearce, Palmer, Walker, Adams, Platt, Gascoigne, Shearer, Wright I, Ince.
Turkey: Hayrettin; Recep, Bulent, Gokhan, Ogun, Orhan, Hami (Riza 69), Unal, Mehmet (Ugur 46), Oguz, Hakan.

Istanbul, 16 December 1992, 15,000
Turkey (0) 1 *(Feyyaz 60)*

Holland (0) 3 *(Van Vossen 57, 87, Gullit 59)*

Turkey: Hayrettin; Recep, Bulent, Gokhan, Ogun, Unal (Hami 77), Oguz, Tugay, Orhan, Saffet (Feyyaz 46), Hakan.
Holland: De Goey; Silooy, Koeman, Jonk (De Boer F 65), Rijkaard, Wouters, Rob Witschge, Gullit, Viscaal, Winter (Numan 76), Van Vossen.

Wembley, 17 February 1993, 51,154
England (2) 6 *(Platt 13, 24, 67, 83, Palmer 76, Ferdinand 86)*

San Marino (0) 0

England: Woods; Dixon, Walker, Adams, Dorigo, Gascoigne, Batty, Platt, Palmer, Ferdinand, Barnes.
San Marino: Benedettini; Muccioli B, Zanotti, Mazza M, Gennari, Canti, Guerra, Manzaroli, Bacciocchi (Mazza P 63), Bonini, Francini (Matteoni 80).

Utrecht, 24 February 1993, 14,000
Holland (2) 3 *(Overmars 4, Rob Witschge 37, 57)*

Turkey (1) 1 *(Feyyaz 36 (pen))*

Holland: De Goey; Silooy, De Kock, Koeman, Rob Witschge, Wouters (Winter 74), Jonk, Bergkamp, Van Vossen (De Boer F 46), Gullit, Overmars.
Turkey: Engin; Recep, Bulent, Gokhan, Ali, Tugay (Serhat 78), Feyyaz (Saffet 61), Unal, Hakan, Oguz, Orhan.

Serravalle, 10 March 1993, 957
San Marino (0) 0

Turkey (0) 0

San Marino: Benedettini (Muccioli S 9); Canti, Gennari, Zanotti, Valentini, Guerra, Manzaroli, Mazza M (Matteoni 61), Mazza P, Bacciocchi, Francini.
Turkey: Engin; Serhat (Hami 62), Bulent, Ali, Ogun, Tugay, Aykut, Unal, Mehmet, Saffet, Orhan.

Utrecht, 24 March 1993, 17,000
Holland (2) 6 *(Van den Brom 2, Canti (og) 29, De Wolf 52, 85, De Boer R 68 (pen), Van Vossen 78)*

San Marino (0) 0

Holland: De Goey; De Wolf, De Boer F, Winter, Rob Witschge, Wouters, Overmars, Meyer, Eykelkamp (De Boer R 46), Van den Brom, Blinker (Van Vossen 67).
San Marino: Muccioli S; Canti, Gennari, Matteoni (Zanotti 22), Valentini, Guerra, Manzaroli, Mazza M, Bacciocchi, Bonini, Francini.

Izmir, 31 March 1993, 60,000
Turkey (0) 0

England (2) 2 *(Platt 6, Gascoigne 44)*

Turkey: Engin (Hayrettin 42); Recep (Hami 69), Ogun, Ali, Tugay, Bulent, Feyyaz, Unal, Mehmet, Oguz, Orhan.
England: Woods; Dixon (Clough 46), Sinton, Palmer, Walker, Adams, Platt, Gascoigne, Barnes, Wright I (Sharpe 84), Ince.

Wembley, 28 April 1993, 73,163
England (2) 2 *(Barnes 2, Platt 23)*
Holland (1) 2 *(Bergkamp 34, Van Vossen 85 (pen))*

England: Woods; Dixon, Walker, Adams, Keown, Ince, Gascoigne (Merson 46), Palmer, Barnes, Platt, Ferdinand.
Holland: De Goey; Blind, De Boer F, Rijkaard, Winter, Wouters, Rob Witschge, Gullit (Van Vossen 69), Bergkamp, Bosman (De Wolf 46), Overmars.

Oslo, 28 April 1993, 21,530
Norway (2) 3 *(Rekdal 14, Fjortoft 17, Jakobsen JI 55)*
Turkey (0) 1 *(Feyyaz 57)*

Norway: Rossbach; Halle, Pedersen T, Bratseth, Bjornebye, Flo, Mykland (Nilsen R 82), Rekdal, Leonhardsen (Ingebritsen 30), Jakobsen JI, Fjortoft.
Turkey: Hayrettin; Recep, Ogun, Sedat, Serhat, Bulent, Feyyaz, Unal, Mehmet (Hamza 81), Hakan (Hami 66), Orhan.

Lodz, 28 April 1993, 10,000
Poland (0) 1 *(Furtok 68)*
San Marino (0) 0

Poland: Klak; Czachowski, Szewczyk, Kozminski, Waldoch, Brzeczek, Pisz, Juskowiak (Staniek 66), Furtok, Kosecki, Ziober.
San Marino: Benedettini; Canti, Gennari, Zanotti (Francini 79), Gobbi, Valentini, Manzaroli, Della Valle, Mazza M, Bonini (Mazza P 70), Bacciocchi.

Serravalle, 19 May 1993, 1500
San Marino (0) 0
Poland (0) 3 *(Lesniak 52, 80, Warzycha K 56)*

San Marino: Benedettini; Canti, Gennari, Zanotti, Gobbi, Valentini, Manzaroli, Francini (Muccioli B 60), Mazza M, Bonini, Bacciocchi (Mazza P 72).
Poland: Matysek; Czachowski, Brzeczek, Szewczyk, Rudy, Lesniak, Szierczewski, Warzycha K; Furtok (Staniek 82), Kosecki, Ziober.

Chorzow, 29 May 1993, 60,000
Poland (1) 1 *(Adamczuk 34)*
England (0) 1 *(Wright I 84)*

Poland: Bako; Czachowski, Szewczyk, Kozminski, Lesiak, Brzeczek (Jalocha 84), Szierczewski, Adamczuk, Furtok, Kosecki, Lesniak (Wegrzyn 75).
England: Woods; Bardsley, Dorigo, Palmer (Wright I 72), Walker, Adams, Platt, Gascoigne (Clough 79), Sheringham, Barnes, Ince.

Oslo, 2 June 1993, 22,250
Norway (1) 2 *(Leonhardsen 42, Bohinen 48)*
England (0) 0

Norway: Thorstvedt; Halle, Pedersen T, Bratseth (Nilsen R 82), Bjornebye, Flo, Mykland, Leonhardsen, Fjortoft (Sorloth 57), Rekdal, Bohinen.
England: Woods; Dixon, Pallister, Palmer, Walker (Clough 63), Adams, Platt, Gascoigne, Ferdinand, Sheringham (Wright I 46), Sharpe.

Rotterdam, 9 June 1993, 40,000
Holland (0) 0

Norway (0) 0

Hollnd: De Goey; Van Gobbel (Winter 81), Rijkaard, Koeman, De Boer F,
Wouters, Overmars, Jonk, Bosman (Van Vossen 46), Bergkamp, Blinker.
Norway: Thorstvedt; Johnsen (Brendesaether 85), Pedersen T, Bratseth, Bjornebye
(Nilsen R 46), Flo, Mykland, Leonhardsen, Fjortoft, Rekdal, Bohinen.

	P	W	D	L	F	A	Pts
Norway	7	5	2	0	20	3	12
England	7	3	3	1	16	6	9
Holland	7	3	3	1	17	8	9
Poland	5	3	2	0	8	3	8
Turkey	8	1	1	6	7	17	3
San Marino	8	0	1	7	1	32	1

Group 3
Seville, 22 April 1992, 10,000
Spain (1) 3 *(Michel 2, 66 (pen), Hierro 87)*

Albania (0) 0

Spain: Zubizarreta; Abelardo, Nando, Giner, Michel (Eusebio 85), Amor, Hierro,
Vizcaino, Manolo (Bakero 53), Butragueno, Goicoechea.
Albania: Strakosha (Dani 69); Josa (Peqini 55), Kola B, Lekbello, Aya, Abazi,
Kushta, Barballushi, Millo, Kola A, Demollari.

Windsor Park, 28 April 1992, 4500
Northern Ireland (2) 2 *(Wilson 13, Taggart 16)*

Lithuania (1) 2 *Narberkovas 41, Fridrikas 48)*

Northern Ireland: Fettis; Donaghy (Fleming 46), Taggart, McDonald, Worthington,
Black, Magilton, Wilson, Hughes, Quinn, Dowie (Rogan 80).
Lithuania: Martinkenas; Buzmakovas, Mika, Janonis, Mazeikis, Tautkas, Urbonas,
Fridrikas (Zhuta 90), Narbekovas, Baranauskas, Ivanauskas (Danisevicius 89).

Dublin, 26 May 1992, 29,727
Republic of Ireland (0) 2 *(Aldridge 60, McGrath 80)*

Albania (0) 0

Republic of Ireland: Bonner; Irwin, Staunton, O'Leary, McGrath, Townsend,
Keane, Houghton, Quinn, Aldridge (Coyne 83), Sheedy (McCarthy 52).
Albania: Dani; Zmijani, Qendro (Pali 71), Peqini, Vata, Abazi, Kushta, Vasi,
Rraklli, Zola A (Sokoll 80), Demollari.

Tirana, 3 June 1992, 15,000
Albania (0) 1 *(Abazi 77)*

Lithuania (0) 0

Albania: Dani; Zmijani, Peqini, Lekbello, Vatɛ, Abazi, Kushta, Milori (Rrafi 46),
Millo (Fortuzi 89), Vasi, Demollari.
Lithuania: Martinkenas; Buzmakovas, Sukristovas, Mazeikis, Tomas, Danisevicius,
Baranauskas, Tautkas (Zhuta 82), Urbonas, Ramelis (Zdanicius 52), Kvitkauskas.

Riga, 12 August 1992, 2000
Latvia (1) 1 *(Linards 15)*
Lithuania (0) 2 *(Poderis 65, Tereskinas 86)*

Latvia: Karavayev; Ivanovs, Sprogis (Zeminskis 65), Gnedois, Glazovs (Teplovs 46), Popkovs, Shevljakovs, Alexeyenko, Semionovs, Linards, Stradins.
Lithuania: Martinkenas; Buzmakovas, Janonis, Sukristovas (Poderis 56), Vainoras, Mazeikis, Baltusnikas, Baranauskas, Narbekovas (Tereskinas 2), Fridrikas, Ivanauskas.

Riga, 26 August 1992, 10,000
Latvia (0) 0
Denmark (0) 0

Latvia: Karavayev; Shevljakovs, Alexeyenko, Ivanovs, Gnedois, Popkovs (Astafjevs 65), Sprogis, Stradins, Yeliseyevs, Linards (Bulders 86), Glazovs.
Denmark: Schmeichel; Sivebaek (Elstrup 46), Olsen, Piechnik, Christofte, Heintze, Vilfort, Jensen, Laudrup B, Povlsen, Christensen.

Dublin, 9 September 1992, 32,000
Republic of Ireland (1) 4 *(Sheedy 30, Aldridge 59, 82 (pen), 86)*
Latvia (0) 0

Republic of Ireland: Bonner; Irwin, Staunton, Kernaghan, McGrath, Townsend, Keane, Whelan, Quinn (Coyne 61), Aldridge, Sheedy (Phelan 76).
Latvia: Igochine; Astafjevs, Alexeyenko, Bulders, Gnedois, Popkovs (Semionovs 63), Sprogis, Abzinovs (Sidorovs 36), Yeliseyevs, Linards, Glazovs.

Windsor Park, 9 September 1992, 8000
Northern Ireland (3) 3 *(Clarke, Wilson, Magilton)*
Albania (0) 0

Northern Ireland: Wright; Fleming, Worthington, Taggart, McDonald, Donaghy, Wilson, Magilton, Clarke (O'Neill M 77), Dowie, Hughes.
Albania: Strakosha; Zmijani, Peqini, Lekbello, Vata, Abazi, Kushta, Milori (Bilali 69), Millo, Kepa, Rraklli.

Riga, 23 September 1992, 60,000
Latvia (0) 0
Spain (0) 0

Latvia: Karavayev; Shevljakovs, Alexeyenko, Ivanovs, Gnedois, Popkovs (Astafjevs 70), Sprogis, Stradins, Bulders (Gilis 81), Linards, Glazovs.
Spain: Zubizarreta; Ferrer, Toni, Solozabal, Lopez, Vizcaino, Goicoechea, Fonseca (Alfonso 72), Bakero, Martin Vazquez, Alvaro (Amor 59).

Vilnius, 23 September 1992, 9500
Lithuania (0) 0
Denmark (0) 0

Lithuania: Martinkenas; Mazeikis, Sukristovas, Baltusnikas, Buzmakovas, Pankratjevas, Zhuta (Poderis 87), Zdanicius, Tereskinas, Baranauskas, Olshanskis.
Denmark: Schmeichel; Olsen, Piechnik, Sivebaek, Christofte, Larsen, Jensen, Vilfort, Laudrup B, Elstrup, Christensen (Moller 80).

Copenhagen, 14 October 1992, 40,100
Denmark (0) 0

Republic of Ireland (0) 0

Denmark: Schmeichel; Olsen, Piechnik, Sivebaek, Heintze, Rieper, Jensen, Vilfort, Larsen, Laudrup B, Povlsen (Christensen 77).
Republic of Ireland: Bonner; Irwin, Phelan, Moran, Kernaghan, Keane, Townsend, Houghton (Kelly 73), Quinn, Aldridge, McGoldrick.

Windsor Park, 14 October 1992, 9500
Northern Ireland (0) 0

Spain (0) 0

Northern Ireland: Wright; Fleming, Worthington, Taggart, McDonald, Donaghy, Black (Morrow 61), Wilson, Clarke, Quinn, Hughes.
Spain: Zubizarreta; Ferrer, Toni, Solozabal, Lopez, Hierro, Amor, Michel, Claudio (Guardiola 63), Martin Vazquez, Manolo (Alfonso 60).

Vilnius, 28 October 1992, 5000
Lithuania (0) 1 *(Fridrikas 85)*

Latvia (1) 1 *(Linards 44)*

Lithuania: Martinkenas; Buzmakovas, Baltusnikas, Tumasonis (Zhuta 61), Tereskinas, Sukristovas, Baranauskas, Ivanauskas, Pankratjevas, Fridrikas, Zdanicius (Vainoras 68).
Latvia: Karavayev; Astafjevs, Alexeyenko, Ivanovs, Gnedois, Popkovs (Jemeljanovs 74), Sprogis, Stradins, Bulders, Linards, Glazovs.

Tirana, 11 Novembr 1992, 3500
Albania (0) 1 *(Kepa 67)*

Latvia (1) 1 *(Alexeyenko 3)*

Albania: Strakosha; Zmijani, Lekbello, Vata, Peqini, Demollari, Fortuzi, Kacaj, Rraklli, Kushta (Prenja 67) (Bisha 74), Kepa.
Latvia: Karavayev; Gnedois, Sprogis, Bulders, Ivanovs, Glazovs (Popkovs 46), Shevljakovs, Alexeyenko, Stradins, Linards, Astafjevs.

Windsor Park, 18 November 1992, 11,000
Northern Ireland (0) 0

Denmark (0) 1 *(Larsen 51)*

Northern Ireland: Fettis; Fleming, Taggart, McDonald, Worthington, Donaghy, Magilton, Wilson (Black), Hughes, Clarke (Gray), Quinn.
Denmark: Schmeichel; Sivebaek (Kjeldberg 46), Rieper, Olsen, Heintze, Vilfort, Jensen, Larsen (Goldbaek 73), Povlsen, Laudrup B, Elstrup.

Seville, 18 November 1992, 33,000
Spain (0) 0

Republic of Ireland (0) 0

Spain: Zubizarreta; Ferrer, Goicoechea, Solozabal, Lopez, Hierro, Salinas (Bakero 52), Michel, Butragueno (Beguiristain 60), Martin Vazquez, Amor.
Republic of Ireland: Bonner; Irwin, Phelan, Moran, Keane, Townsend, McGrath, Houghton, Staunton, Aldridge, Quinn.

Seville, 16 December 1992, 24,500
Spain (0) 5 *(Bakero 49, Guardiola 51, Alfonso 79, Beguiristain 81, 82)*
Latvia (0) 0

Spain: Zubizarreta; Ferrer, Toni, Solozabal, Vizcaino, Amor, Claudio (Alfonso 55), Guardiola, Bakero (Martin Vazquez 62), Kiki, Beguiristain.
Latvia: Karavayev; Erglis, Alexeyendo, Ivanovs, Astafjevs, Popkovs, Gilis, Stradins, Bulders, Linards, Glazovs.

Tirana, 17 February 1993, 12,000
Albania (0) 1 *(Rrakli 89)*
Northern Ireland (0) 2 *(Magilton 14, McDonald 38)*

Albania: Kapliani; Zmijani (Peqini 46), Kacaj, Bano, Vata, Bazgo, Lekbello (Shulku 46), Fortuzi, Abazi, Rraklli, Demollari.
Northern Ireland: Wright; Fleming, Morrow, Taggart, Magilton, McDonald, Donaghy, Gray, Dowie (Quinn 73), O'Neill, Black.

Seville, 24 February 1993, 21,000
Spain (3) 5 *(Cristobal 5, Bakero 13, Beguiristain 18, Christiansen 86, Aldana 89)*
Lithuania (0) 0

Spain: Zubizarreta; Ferrer, Lasa, Alkorta, Giner, Cristobal, Guardiola, Guerrero (Aldana 59), Salinas (Christiansen 69), Bakero, Beguiristain.
Lithuania: Martinkenas; Buzmakovas, Vainoras, Mazeikis, Janonis, Sukristovas, Baranauskas, Ivanauskas, Tereskinas (Zhuta 69), Fridrikas, Zdanicius.

Copenhagen, 31 March 1993, 40,272
Denmark (1) 1 *(Povlsen 20)*
Spain (0) 0

Denmark: Schmeichel; Olsen, Rieper, Kjeldbjerg, Vilfort, Jensen, Larsen (Hansen 76), Nielsen B, Laudrup B (Tofting 86), Elstrup, Povlsen.
Spain: Zubizarreta; Cristobal, Ferrer, Fernando, Alkorta, Toni (Goicoechea 55), Amor, Guardiola (Nadal 46), Beguiristain, Aldana, Salinas.

Dublin, 31 March 1993, 33,000
Republic of Ireland (3) 3 *(Townsend 20, Quinn 22, Staunton 28)*
Northern Ireland (0) 0

Republic of Ireland: Bonner; Irwin, Phelan, McGrath, Moran, Keane, Townsend, Houghton, Quinn (McGoldrick 84), Coyne (Cascarino 78), Staunton.
Northern Ireland: Wright; Donaghy, Worthington, Taggart, McDonald, Morrow, Magilton (Quinn 51), O'Neill M (Black 74), Dowie, Gray, Hughes.

Copenhagen, 14 April 1993, 29,088
Denmark (1) 2 *(Vilfort 23, Strudal 76)*
Latvia (0) 0

Denmark: Schmeichel; Nielsen S, Rieper, Olsen, Kjeldbjerg, Goldbaek, Jensen (Larsen 61), Vilfort, Pingel (Strudal 70), Elstrup, Laudrup B.
Latvia: Karavayev; Gnedois, Shevljakovs, Ivanovs, Zemlinskis, Erglis, Glazovs, Astafjevs, Zelberlins (Gilis 46), Linards, Stradins (Bulders 64).

Vilnius, 14 April 1993, 12,000
Lithuania (2) 3 *(Baltusnikas 20, Sukristovas 25, Baranauskas 63)*

Albania (0) 1 *(Demollari 86)*

Lithuania: Martinkenas (Stauce 60); Ziukas, Baltusnikas, Mazeikis, Kalvaitis, Apanavicius (Slekys 63), Baranauskas, Sukristovas, Poderis, Kirilovas, Zdanicius.
Albania: Kapilani; Dema, Shulku, Bano, Taho, Ocelli, Kushta, Peqini, Dalipi (Dosti 46), Fortuzi, Demollari.

Dublin, 28 April 1993, 33,000
Republic of Ireland (0) 1 *(Quinn 75)*

Denmark (1) 1 *(Vilfort 27)*

Republic of Ireland: Bonner; Irwin, McGoldrick, McGrath, Kernaghan, Keane, Townsend, Houghton, Quinn, Aldridge (Cascarino 62), Staunton.
Denmark: Schmeichel; Nielsen S, Rieper, Olsen, Kjeldbjerg, Hansen F, Jensen, Vilfort, Pingel (Kristensen 60), Elstrup, Laudrup B.

Seville, 28 April 1993, 20,000
Spain (3) 3 *(Salinas 21, 26, Hierro 41)*

Northern Ireland (1) 1 *(Wilson 11)*

Spain: Zubizarreta; Ferrer, Fernando, Toni, Alkorta, Hierro, Guerrero, Adolfo, Beguiristain (Bakero 76), Salinas, Claudio (Kiki 59).
Northern Ireland: Wright, Fleming, Worthington, Donaghy, Taggart, McDonald, Black (Dennison 73), Wilson, O'Neill M (Dowie 73), Gray, Hughes.

Riga, 15 May 1993, 1810
Latvia (0) 0

Albania (0) 0

Latvia: Lajzans; Ergils, Shevljakovs, Ivanovs, Gnedois, Popkovs, Troickis, Astafjevs (Semionovs 46), Zelberlins (Sharando 62), Linards, Gorjacilovs.
Albania: Nailbani; Ocelli, Bano, Shala, Vata, Skulkju, Kushta, Zalla (Kapedani 88), Pequini, Milori, Fortuzi (Daliji 77).

Vilnius, 25 May 1993, 4000
Lithuania (0) 0

Northern Ireland (1) 1 *(Dowie 8)*

Lithuania: Martinkenas; Baltusnikas, Buzmakovas (Vichka 68), Mazeikis, Zhukas, Lushanskis (Shlenskis 46), Baranauskas, Sukristovas, Kirilovas, Fridrikas, Zdanicius.
Northern Ireland: Wright; Fleming, Taggart, McDonald, Worthington, Donaghy, Magilton, O'Neill, Wilson, Hughes, Dowie.

Tirana, 26 May 1993, 10,000
Albania (1) 1 *(Kushta 7)*

Republic of Ireland (1) 2 *(Staunton 13, Cascarino 77)*

Albania: Musta; Zmijani (Fortuzi 58), Shulku, Shala, Vata, Lekbello, Kushta, Pequini, Rraklli (Bozgo 76), Milori, Demollari.
Republic of Ireland: Bonner, Irwin, Phelan, Kernaghan, Moran, Keane, Townsend, Houghton, Quinn, Aldridge (Cascarino 76), Staunton.

Vilnius, 2 June 1993, 7000
Lithuania (0) 0

Spain (0) 2 *(Guerrero 73, 77)*

Lithuania: Martinkenas; Zhutkas, Baltusnikas, Mazeikis, Buzmakovas, Olsanskis, Baranauskas, Sukristovas, Kirilovas, Fridrikas (Zdanicius 54), Skarbalius.
Spain: Zubizarreta; Ferrer, Lasa (Beguiristain 62), Alkorta, Fernando, Hierro, Salinas (Quique Estebaranz 54), Nadal, Claudio, Guerrero, Amor.

Copenhagen, 2 June 1993, 39,504
Denmark (4) 4 *(Jensen 11, Pingel 20, 40, Moller 28)*

Albania (0) 0

Denmark: Schmeichel; Nielsen S, Rieper, Olsen, Kjeldberg, Larsen M, Jensen (Goldbaek 83), Vilfort, Pingel, Moller (Johansen 64), Laudrup B.
Albania: Musta; Fortuzi (Zala 83), Zmijani, Shulku, Ocelli, Pequini, Bano, Demollari (Bozgo 17), Kushta, Vata, Rraklli.

Riga, 2 June 1993, 2000
Latvia (0) 1 *(Linards 55)*

Northern Ireland (2) 2 *(Magilton 4, Taggart 15)*

Latvia: Karavayev; Erglis, Shevljakovs, Ivanovs, Gnedois, Popkovs, Sarando (Yeliseyevs 46), Astafjevs, Zelberlins (Babicevs 63), Linards, Gorjacilovs.
Northern Ireland: Wright; Fleming, McDonald, Taggart, Worthington, O'Neill (Quinn 85), Magilton, Donaghy, Wilson, Hughes, Dowie.

Riga, 9 June 1993, 7000
Latvia (0) 0

Republic of Ireland (2) 2 *(Aldridge 14, McGrath 42)*

Latvia: Karavayev; Erglis, Shevljakovs, Astafjevs, Ivanovs, Gnedois, Popkovs, Bulders, Babicevs (Yeliseyevs 46), Sharando (Gorjacilovs 54), Linards.
Republic of Ireland: Bonner; Irwin, Kernaghan, McGrath, Phelan, Houghton, Townsend, Keane, Staunton, Aldridge (Sheridan 80), Quinn (Cascarino 74).

Vilnius, 16 June 1993, 6000
Lithuania (0) 0

Republic of Ireland (1) 1 *(Staunton 38)*

Lithuania: Martinkenas; Zhukas, Baltusnikas, Mazeikis, Buzmakovas, Skarbalius (Zdanicius 46), Baranauskas, Urbonas (Ramelis 67), Stumprys, Kirilovas, Slekys.
Republic of Ireland: Bonner; Irwin, Phelan, McGrath, Kernaghan, Keane, Townsend, Houghton, Quinn, Aldridge (Whelan 76), Staunton.

	P	W	D	L	F	A	Pts
Republic of Ireland	9	6	3	0	14	2	15
Spain	9	5	3	1	18	2	13
Denmark	8	4	4	0	9	1	12
Northern Ireland	9	4	2	3	11	10	10
Lithuania	10	2	3	5	8	15	7
Latvia	11	0	5	6	4	19	5
Albania	10	1	2	7	5	20	4

Group 4
Brussels, 22 April 1992, 18,000
Belgium (1) 1 *(Wilmots 24)*

Cyprus (0) 0

Belgium: Preud'homme; Albert, Grun, Van der Elst, Emmers, Scifo, Walem, Boffin (Borkelmans 82), Wilmots (Hofmans 75), Degryse, Oliveira.
Cyprus: Christofi; Costa, Pittas, Constantinou C, Nicolau, Yiangudakis, Ioannou, Larku (Constantinou G 88), Sotiriou, Papavasiliou, Hadjilukas (Panayi 70).

Bucharest, 6 May 1992, 10,000
Romania (5) 7 *(Balint 4, 40, 78, Hagi 14, Lacatus 28 (pen), Lupescu 44, Pana 55)*

Faeroes (0) 0

Romania: Stelea; Petrescu, Mihali, Popescu, Munteanu, Pana, Balint, Lupescu (Cheregi 78), Hagi, Lacatus (Gane 63), Rotariu.
Faeroes: Knudsen; Jakobsen, Hansen T, Danielsen, Justinussen, Morkore A, Jarnskor (Nielsen T 50), Dam (Jonsson 60), Hansen A, Reynheim, Muller.

Bucharest, 20 May 1992, 23,000
Romania (5) 5 *(Hagi 5, 35, Lupescu 7, 24, Balint 31)*

Wales (0) 1 *(Rush 50)*

Romania: Stelea; Petrescu, Mihali, Belodedici, Munteanu, Sabau (Timofte I 80), Popescu, Lupescu, Hagi (Gerstenmaier 71), Lacatus, Balint.
Wales: Southall; Phillips, Bowen (Blackmore 71), Aizlewood, Melville, Horne, Speed, Pembridge (Giggs 59), Hughes, Rush, Saunders.

Toftir, 3 June 1992, 5156
Faeroes (0) 0

Belgium (1) 3 *(Albert 30, Wilmots 65,71)*

Faeroes: Johannesen; Jakobsen, Hansen T, Danielsen, Jonsson T (Jensen 71), Morkore A (Justinussen 83), Nielsen T, Dam, Hansen A, Reynheim, Muller.
Belgium: Preud'homme: Staelens, Grun, Albert, Emmers, Boffin (Versavel 75), Van der Elst, Denil, Degryse, Scifo, Oliveira (Wilmots 65).

Toftir, 16 June 1992, 4500
Faeroes (0) 0

Cyprus (1) 2 *(Sotiriu 30, Papavasiliu 58)*

Faeroes: Johannesen; Jakobsen, Hansen T, Danielsen, Jonsson, Morkore A, Hansen A, Nielsen (Jarnskor 62), Rasmussen, Reynheim, Muller (Jensen 66).
Cyprus: Christofi; Costa (Larku 46), Pittas, Constantinou C, Nicolau, Yiangudakis, Ioannou, Charalambous, Savidis, Sotiriou (Panayi 84), Papavasiliou.

Prague, 2 September 1992, 9000
Czechoslovakia (0) 1 *(Kadlec 77)*

Belgium (1) 2 *(Chovanec (og) 44, Czerniatynski 83)*

Czechoslovakia: Stejskal; Chovanec, Glonek, Kadlec, Mistr, Nemecek, Kubik (Hapal 65), Nemec, Kula K (Dubovsky 77), Skuhravy, Moravcik.
Belgium: Preud'homme; Emmers, Medved, Albert, Smidts, Grum, Scifo, Van der Elst, Staelens (Dauwen 87), Czerniatynski, Degryse (Wilmots 66).

Cardiff, 9 September 1992, 7000
Wales (3) 6 *(Rush 5, 64, 89, Saunders 28, Bowen 37, Blackmore 71)*
Faeroes (0) 0

Wales: Southall; Phillips, Bowen (Giggs 66), Symons, Young, Blackmore, Horne, Saunders, Rush, Hughes, Speed.
Faeroes: Knudsen; Jakobsen, Hansen T, Danielsen, Hansen O, Morkore A, Simonsen, Dam (Justinussen 56), Jonsson, Reynheim, Muller.

Kosice, 23 September 1992, 17,000
Czechoslovakia (1) 4 *(Nemecek 24, Kuka 85, 87, Dubovsky 89 (pen))*
Faeroes (0) 0

Czechoslovakia: Stejskal; Glonek, Suchoparek, Novotny, Mistr (Latal 82), Moravcik, Nemecek, Dubovsky, Nemec, Hapal (Timko 68), Kuka.
Faeroes: Knudsen; Jakobsen, Johannesen, Hansen T, Justinussen, Simonsen, Dam, Hansen O (Morkore A 58), Jonsson, Reynheim, Muller (Arge 81).

Brussels, 14 October 1992, 21,000
Belgium (1) 1 *(Smidts 27)*
Romania (0) 0

Belgium: Preud'homme; Medved, Albert, Grun, Smidts, Boffin, Staelens, Van der Elst, Scifo, Degryse, Czerniatynski (Wilmots 69).
Romania: Stelea; Petrescu, Selymes, Mihali, Lupescu, Belodedici, Nunteanu, Sabau, Dumitrescu (Badea 78), Lacatus, Hagi.

Nicosia, 14 October 1992, 15,000
Cyprus (0) 0
Wales (0) 1 *(Hughes 51)*

Cyprus: Christofi M; Costa, Pittas (Hadjilukas 71), Constantinou, Nicolau, Yiangudakis, Ioannou D, Charalambous, Sotiriou (Ioannou Y 59), Papavasiliou, Savidis.
Wales: Southall; Phillips, Bowen, Blackmore, Young, Symons, Horne, Saunders, Rush, Hughes, Speed.

Bucharest, 14 November 1992, 30,000
Romania (0) 1 *(Dumitrescu 48)*
Czechoslovakia (0) 1 *(Nemecek 79 (pen))*

Romania: Stelea; Petrescu, Belodedici, Mihali, Munteanu, Sabau, Lupescu (Timofte D 78), Hagi, Dumitrescu, Lacatus, Hanganu (Vladoiu 66).
Czechoslovakia: Kouba; Novotny, Glonek, Suchoparek, Hapal, Latal, Nemecek, Moravcik, Nemec (Frydek 15), Siegl, Skuhravy (Kuka P 37).

Brussels, 18 November 1992, 21,000
Belgium (0) 2 *(Staelens 53, Degryse 58)*
Wales (0) 0

Belgium: Preud'homme; Medved, Grun, Albert, Smidts, Staelens (Wilmots 82), Van der Elst, Boffin, Degryse, Scifo, Czerniatynski (Nilis 46).
Wales: Southall; Phillips, Bowen (Giggs 60), Blackmore, Young, Symons, Horne, Saunders, Rush, Hughes, Speed (Pembridge 80).

Larnaca, 29 November 1992, 3000
Cyprus (1) 1 *(Pittas 39 (pen))*

Romania (2) 4 *(Popescu 4, Raducioiu 36, Hagi 73, Hanganu 86)*

Cyprus: Christofi M; Kalotheu, Pittas, Constantinou C, Ioannou D, Yiangudakis, Andreou (Hadjilukas 25), Christofi P, Ioannou Y (Sotiriou 62), Papavasiliou, Savidis.
Romania: Stelea; Petrescu, Belodedici, Mihali, Lupescu, Popescu, Lacatus, Dumitrescu, Raducioiu (Hanganu 58), Hagi, Munteanu.

Nicosia, 13 February 1993, 3000
Cyprus (0) 0

Belgium (2) 3 *(Scifo 2, 4, Albert 87)*

Cyprus: Oniferu; Costa, Ioannou Y, Constantinou, Kalotheu (Sotiriou 70), Pittas, Savidis, Yiangudakis (Charalambous 60), Papavasiliou, Christofi, Ioannou D.
Belgium: Preud'homme; Medved, Grun, Albert, Smidts, Staelens, Scifo (Goossens 87), Van der Elst, Boffin, Degryse, Nilis (Czerniatynski 75).

Limassol, 24 March 1993, 3000
Cyprus (0) 1 *(Sotiriou 47)*

Czechoslovakia (1) 1 *(Moravcik 33)*

Cyprus: Ioannou Y; Costa, Pittas, Ioannou D, Christofi E, Yiangudakis, Xiuruppas (Panayi 86), Charalambous, Sotiriou, Papavasiliou (Larku 71), Savidis.
Czechoslovakia: Kouba; Novotny, Suchoparek (Berger 74), Vrabec, Glonek, Nemecek, Nemec, Hapal (Latal 46), Kuka P, Skuhravy, Moravcik.

Cardiff, 31 March 1993, 27,002
Wales (2) 2 *(Giggs 18, Rush 39)*

Belgium (0) 0

Wales: Southall; Horne, Bodin, Aizlewood, Young, Ratcliffe, Saunders, Speed (Phillips 88), Rush, Hughes, Giggs (Bowen 89).
Belgium: Preud'homme; Medved (Oliveira 46), Grun, Albert, Smidts, Staelens, Van der Elst, Boffin, Degryse, Scifo, Czerniatynski (Severeyns 67).

Bucharest, 14 April 1993, 30,000
Romania (1) 2 *(Dumitrescu 33, 55)*

Cyprus (1) 1 *(Sotiriu 23)*

Romania: Stelea; Petrescu, Selymes, Sandoi, Belodedici, Munteanu, Lacatus (Stinga 78), Sabau, Ceausila (Predatu 64), Hagi, Dumitrescu.
Cyprus: Petridis; Kalotheu, Pittas, Constantinou, Christofi, Yiangudakis, Charalambous (Xiuruppas 78), Larku, Sotiriou, Papavasiliou, Savidis (Panayi 89).

Limassol, 25 April 1993, 4000
Cyprus (2) 3 *(Xiuruppas 7, Sotiriou 43, Ioannou Y 75)*

Faeroes (0) 1 *(Arge 82)*

Cyprus: Petridis; Charalambous, Christofi, Pittas, Constantinou C, Yiangudakis, Larku, Xiurruppas (Ioannou 65), Papavasiliou, Sotiriou (Hadjilukas 76), Savidis.
Faeroes: Knudsen; Jakobsen, Johannesen, Morkore K, Justinussen, Morkore A, Faero (Nielsen 46), Olsen, Reynheim (Arge 54), Hansen, Jonsson.

Ostrava, 28 April 1993, 16,000
Czechoslovakia (1) 1 *(Latal 41)*

Wales (1) 1 *(Hughes 31)*

Czechoslovakia: Kouba; Glonek (Bejbl 66), Kadlec, Novotny, Vrabec, Latal, Nemec (Dubovsky 79), Kubik, Nemecek, Kuka P, Luhovy.
Wales: Southall; Phillips, Bodin (Bowen 52), Melville, Symons, Blackmore, Horne, Saunders, Rush, Hughes, Giggs.

Brussels, 22 May 1993, 20,641
Belgium (1) 3 *(Wilmots 32, 75, Scifo 50 (pen))*

Faeroes (0) 0

Belgium: Preud'homme; Smidts (Oliveira 76), Emmers, Grun, Staelens, Boffin, Van der Elst, Degryse, Wilmots, Scifo, Nilis.
Faeroes: Knudsen; Jakobsen, Olsen, Morkore K (Reynatugvu 89), Justinussen, Morkore A, Dam, Hansen A, Nielsen T, Arge (Rasmussen 87), Reynheim.

Kosice, 2 June 1993, 15,000
Czechoslovakia (2) 5 *(Vrabec 13, Latal 37, Dubovsky 58, 83, 89)*

Romania (1) 2 *(Raducioiu 26, 55)*

Czechoslovakia: Kouba; Suchoparek, Novotny, Vrabec, Latal, Moravcik, Nemecek, Kubik (Nemec 46), Dubovsky, Kuka P (Glonek 81), Skuhravy.
Romania: Lung; Belodedici, Prodan (Hanganu 77), Popescu, Munteanu, Sabau, Hagi, Lupescu, Dumitrescu, Lacatus (Pandaru 65), Raducioiu.

Toftir, 6 June 1993, 4209
Faeroes (0) 0

Wales (2) 3 *(Saunders 22, Young 31, Rush 69)*

Faeroes: Knudsen; Jakobsen, Hansen T, Johannesen, Justinussen, Reynatugvu (Ramussen 49), Nielsen T, Dam, Hansen A, Reynheim (Mohr 59), Arge.
Wales: Southall; Phillips, Bodin, Aizlewood, Young (Melville 49), Symons, Horne, Saunders, Rush, Hughes (Speed 75), Giggs.

Toftir, 16 June 1993, 1000
Faeroes (0) 0

Czechoslovakia (3) 3 *(Hasek 3, Postulka 38,44)*

Faeroes: Knudsen; Justinussen R (Rasmussen 68), Johannesen, Jakobsen (Hansen T 70), Morkore K, Justinussen A, Morkore A, Reynatugvu, Hansen A, Dam, Nielsen.
Czechoslovakia: Kouba; Suchoparek, Hasek, Repka, Latal, Nemecek, Dubovsky, Postulka, Berger, Kuka P (Kinder 54), Moravcik (Kubik 81).

	P	W	D	L	F	A	Pts
Belgium	8	7	0	1	15	3	14
Romania	7	4	1	2	21	10	9
Czechoslovakia	7	3	3	1	16	7	9
Wales	7	4	1	2	14	8	9
Cyprus	8	2	1	5	8	13	5
Faeroes	9	0	0	9	1	34	0

Group 5

Yugoslavia excluded due to UN sanctions.

Athens, 13 May 1992, 10,000

Greece (1) 1 *(Sofanidis 28)*

Iceland (0) 0

Greece: Papadopoulos; Apostolakis, Kalitzakis, Manolas, Nsibonas, Tsaluhidis Y, Tsaluhidis G, Sofiandis, Tursunidis (Noblias 77), Alexandria, Tsiantakis (Borbokis 60).

Iceland: Kristinsson B; Jonsson Kr, Marteinsson (Magnusson 74), Vaisson, Bergsson, Jonsson K, Gudjohnsen, Bjarnasson, Gretarsson, Sverrisson, Kristinsson R.

Budapest, 3 June 1992, 10,000

Hungary (1) 1 *(Kiprich 3)*

Iceland (0) 2 *(Orlygsson 51, Magnusson 73)*

Hungary: Petry; Telek, Kovacs E, Lorincz, Simon, Limperger, Pisont (Balog 78), Vincze (Eszenyi 54), Keller, Kiprich, Kovacs K.

Iceland: Kristinsson B; Gretarsson S (Magnusson 64), Bergsson, Orlygsson, Kristinsson R, Gretarsson A, Valsson, Jonsson Kr, Jonsson K (Bragason 80), Bjarnasson, Marteinsson.

Luxembourg, 9 September 1992, 3000

Luxembourg (0) 0

Hungary (1) 3 *(Detari 16, Kovacs K 52, 79)*

Luxembourg: Van Rijswijck; Bossi, Wolf, Petry, Birsens, Girres, Hellers, Weis, Salbene (Holtz 58), Langers, Malget (Thill 80).

Hungary: Petry; Nagy T, Disztl L, Keller, Lorincz, Limperger (Telek 65), Kiprich, Balog, Pisont (Bognar G 81), Detari, Kovacs K.

Reykjavik, 7 October 1992, 6350

Iceland (0) 0

Greece (0) 1 *(Tsaluhidis 61)*

Iceland: Kristinsson B; Bergsson, Jonsson Kr, Gudjohnsen, Marteinsson (Margeirsson 29), Kristinsson R, Bjarnasson (Hakonarsson 71), Gretarsson A, Orlygsson, Gretarsson S, Sverrisson.

Greece: Mirtsos; Apostolakis, Kalitsodakis, Manolas, Kalitzakis, Papaioannou (Mitropoulos 55), Tsiantakis, Tsaluhidis, Dimitriadis (Francheskos 69), Noblias, Donis.

Moscow, 14 October 1992, 13,000

Russia (0) 1 *(Yuran 64)*

Iceland (0) 0

Russia: Cherchesov; Khlestov, Onopko, Kolotovkin, Shalimov, Dobrovolski, Karpin, Lediakhov (Tatarchuk 46), Yuran (Kolivanov 76), Kiriakov.

Iceland: Kristinsson B; Marteinsson, Jonsson Kr, Valsson, Gretarsson A, Kristinsson R (Hakonarsson 88), Bergsson, Orlygsson, Margeirsson, Gudjohnsen (Bjarnasson 76), Gretarsson S.

28 October 1992, 1750
Russia (2) 2 *(Yuran 4, Radchenko 23)*
Luxembourg (0) 0

Russia: Cherchesov; Khlestov, Onopko, Kulkov, Karpin, Shalimov, Dobrovolski, Mostovoi, Radchenko (Tatarchuk 80), Kiriakov (Borodyuk 63), Yuran.
Luxembourg: Van Rijswijck; Birsens, Bossi, Wolf, Hellers, Girres, Salbene (Thill 77), Weis, Holtz (Groff 53), Langers, Malget.

Salonika, 11 November 1992, 40,000
Greece (0) 0
Hungary (0) 0

Greece: Mirtsos; Apostolakis, Pahaturidis, Manolas, Kolitsidakis, Tsaluhidis, Mitropoulos, Nioblias, Dimitriadis (Valtsis 46), Tursunidis, Tsiantakis (Franceskos 63).
Hungary: Petry; Disztl L, Limperger, Lorincz, Nagy, Urban, Lipcsei, Kiprich (Salloi 32), Meszaros (Paling 78), Balog, Kovacs K.

Athens, 17 February 1993, 40,000
Greece (1) 4 *(Dimitriadis 30 (pen), Mitropoulos 65)*
Luxembourg (0) 0

Greece: Minou; Manolas, Apostolakis, Kalitzakis, Tsaluhidis, Nioblias, Tsiantakis, Dimitriadis, Donis (Mitropoulos 58), Franceskos (Karapialis 56), Karataidis.
Luxembourg: Koch; Petry, Wolf, Bossi, Birsens, Salbene, Hellers, Weis, Groff (Scuto 67), Malget, Langers.

Budapest, 31 March 1993, 30,000
Hungary (0) 0
Greece (0) 1 *(Apostolakis 70)*

Hungary: Petry; Telek, Csabo, Disztl L (Nagy T 36), Pisont (Balog 71), Urban, Detari, Eszenyi, Duro, Kiprich, Kovacs K.
Greece: Minou; Manolas, Kalitzakis, Kolitsidakis, Tsiantakis, Apostolakis, Mitropoulos, Nioblias, Tsaluhidis, Maragos (Antoniou 63), Mahias (Franceskos 82).

Luxembourg, 14 April 1993, 3000
Luxembourg (0) 0
Russia (1) 4 *(Kiriakov 12, 46, Shalimov 57, Kulkov 90)*

Luxembourg: Koch; Petry, Bossi, Birsens, Wolf, Salbene (Scuto 80), Hellers, Weis, Groff, Malget, Morocutti (Thill 60).
Russia: Cherchesov; Onopko, Gorlukovich, Ivanov, Shalimov, Kolivanov, Dobrovolski, Korneyev (Kulkov 60), Kanchelskis, Yuran, Kiriakov (Popov 75).

Moscow, 28 April 1993, 30,000
Russia (0) 3 *(Kanchelskis 55, Kolivanov 60, Yuran 86)*
Hungary (0) 0

Russia: Kharine; Gorlukovich, Ivanov A, Onopko, Kanchelskis, Shalimov, Dobrovolski, Korneyev (Kulkov 57), Kolivanov, Yuran, Kiriakov (Mostovoi 72).
Hungary: Petry; Telek, Nagy T, Lorincz, Pisont, Marton, Detari, Balog (Vincze 64), Duro (Banfi 64), Kovacs K, Csabi.

213

Luxembourg, 20 May 1993, 2000
Luxembourg (0) 1 *(Birgisson (og) 70)*
Iceland (1) 1 *(Gudjohnsen 40)*

Luxembourg: Van Rijswijck; Ferron (Carboni 64), Petry, Birsens, Wolf, Holtz, Salbene, Hellers, Groff (Scuto 50), Langers, Malget.
Iceland: Kristinsson B; Birgisson, Bergsson, Jonsson Kr, Orlygsson, Kristinsson R, Gretarsson A, Ingolfsson (Martinsson 82), Gudjohnsen, Gunnlaugsson (Thordarsson 56), Sverrisson.

Moscow, 23 May 1993, 40,000
Russia (0) 1 *(Dobrovolski 75 (pen))*
Greece (1) 1 *(Mitropoulos 45)*

Russia: Kharine; Gorlukovich, Onopko, Ivanov A, Kanchelskis, Shalimov, Dobrovolski, Kulkov (Tatarchuk 62), Kolivanov, Yuran, Kiriakov.
Greece: Minou; Apostolakis, Kolitsidakis, Manolas, Kalitzakis, Tsaluhidis, Marangos, Nioblias, Mahias (Antoniou 82), Mitropoulos (Karapialis 64), Tsiantakis.

Reykjavik, 2 June 1993, 3096
Iceland (1) 1 *(Sverrisson 26)*
Russia (1) 1 *(Kiriakov 38)*

Iceland: Kristinsson B; Bergsson, Birgisson, Jonsson Kr, Dervic, Stefansson, Thordarsson, Kristinsson R (Gretarsson A 78), Gudjohnsen, Sverrisson (Ingolfsson 83), Gunnlaugsson.
Russia: Kharine; Gorlukovich, Onopko, Kulkov, Ivanov, Kanchelskis, Dobrovolski, Tatarchuk (Korneyev 63), Kolivanov, Yuran (Lediakhov 75), Kiriakov.

Reykjavik, 16 June 1993, 5000
Iceland (1) 2 *(Sverrisson 13, Gudjohnsen 77)*
Hungary (0) 0

Iceland: Kristinsson B; Bjarnsson, Bergsson, Jonsson Kr, Dervic, Thordarsson, Kristinsson R, Stefansson (Gretarsson A 64), Gudlaugsson, Gudjohnsen, Sverrisson.
Hungary: Petry; Simon, Telek, Lorincz, Urban, Pisont, Marton, Balog, Kerezturi, Orosz (Hamon 64), Mamar (Salloi 80).

Greece qualified for finals in USA

	P	W	D	L	F	A	Pts
Russia	6	4	2	0	12	2	10
Greece	6	4	2	0	6	1	10
Iceland	7	2	2	3	6	6	6
Hungary	6	1	1	4	4	8	3
Luxembourg	5	0	1	4	1	12	1

Group 6
Helsinki, 14 May 1992, 10,000
Finland (0) 0
Bulgaria (2) 3 *(Balakov 16, Kostadinov 25, 85)*

Finland: Huttunen; Petaja, Holmgren, Heikkinen, Eriksson, Rinne (Huhtamaki 76), Litmanen, Myyry, Jarvinen, Vanhala (Tegelberg 60), Tarkkio.
Bulgaria: Mikhailov; Ivanov, Tzvetanov, Illiev, Hubchev, Sirakov, Yankov, Stoichkov (Yordanov 69), Penev, Balakov, Kostadinov.

Sofia, 9 September 1992, 45,000
Bulgaria (2) 2 *(Stoichkov 21 (pen), Balakov 29)*
France (0) 0

Bulgaria: Mikhailov; Kiriakov, Ivanov T, Tzvetanov, Iliev N, Yankov, Kostadinov E (Yordanov 75), Stoichkov, Penev (Stoilov 76), Sirakov, Balakov.
France: Martini; Fournier, Petit, Boli, Roche, Casoni, Deschamps, Sauzee, Papin, Ginola, Vahirua (Durand 61).

Helsinki, 9 September 1992, 13,617
Finland (0) 0
Sweden (0) 1 *(Ingesson 77 (pen))*

Finland: Laukkanen; Hjelm, Tarkkio (Tauriainen 72), Ukkonen, Litmanen, Myyry (Vanhala 85), Paatelainen, Jarvinen, Holmgren, Kanerva, Remes.
Sweden: Ravelli (Eriksson L 88); Andersson P, Bjorklund, Erlingmark, Ljung, Ingesson, Limpar, Pettersson (Ekstrom 62), Schwarz, Thern, Dahlin.

Stockholm, 7 October 1992, 20,625
Sweden (0) 2 *(Dahlin 56, Pettersson 76)*
Bulgaria (0) 0

Sweden: Eriksson L; Erlingmark, Andersson P, Bjorklund, Ljung, Limpar, Thern, Schwarz, Pettersson, Ingesson, Dahlin (Andersson K 87).
Bulgaria: Mikhailov; Mladenov D, Kiriakov, Ivanov T, Tzvetanov, Kostadinov E (Yordanov 83), Sirakov, Stoilov, Yankov, Balakov, Penev.

Paris, 14 October 1992, 39,186
France (1) 2 *(Papin 3, Cantona 77)*
Austria (0) 0

France: Martini; Sauzee, Boli, Casoni, Deschamps, Sassus, Fournier (Gnako 63), Durand, Gravelaine (Vahirua 73), Papin, Cantona.
Austria: Wohlfahrt; Feiersinger, Streiter, Zsak, Wazinger, Stoger (Pfeifenberger 84), Artner, Herzog, Baur, Schinkels (Ogris 46), Polster.

Vienna, 28 October 1992, 20,000
Austria (2) 6 *(Herzog 41, 46, Polster 49, Stoger 56, Ogris 87)*
Israel (0) 2 *(Zohar 57, 77)*

Austria: Wohlfahrt; Zsak, Streiter (Baur 71), Wazinger, Prosenik, Stoger, Artner, Herzog, Schinkels (Flogel 76), Ogris, Polster.
Israel: Ginzburg; Ben-Shimon, Yeuda, Harazi, Cohen Av (Berkovich 52), Zohar, Klinger, Hazan, Nimny, Rosenthal, Tikva (Drieks 78).

215

Tel Aviv, 11 November 1992, 40,000
Israel (1) 1 *(Banin 42)*

Sweden (1) 3 *(Limpar 37, Dahlin 58, Ingesson 74)*

Israel: Ginzburg; Cohen Avi, Harazi (Berkovich 61), Hazan, Ben-Shimon, Klinger, Banin, Nimny, Revivo (Tikva 70), Zohar, Rosenthal.
Sweden: Ravelli; Nilsson R, Andersson P, Bjorklund, Ljung, Limpar, Rehn, Ingesson, Thern, Dahlin (Ekstrom 82), Brolin (Landberg 87).

Paris, 14 November 1992, 30,000
France (2) 2 *(Papin 17, Cantona 31)*

Finland (0) 1 *(Jarvinen 54)*

France: Martini; Roche, Boli, Casoni, Durand (Karembeu 71), Sauzee, Deschamps, Lizarazu, Papin, Cantona, Gravelaine (Vahirua 78).
Finland: Laukkanen; Holmgren, Kanerva, Ukkonen, Petaja (Kinnunen 85), Hjelm, Litmanen, Myyry, Jarvinen, Tarkkio, Paatelainen (Tauriainen 23).

Tel Aviv, 2 December 1992, 15,000
Israel (0) 0

Bulgaria (0) 2 *(Sirakov 55, Penev 83)*

Israel: Ginzburg; Halfon, Hillel, Shelach, Ben-Shimon, Klinger, Banin, Mizrachi (Hazan 80), Berkovich (Harazi 84), Revivo, Rosenthal.
Bulgaria: Mikhailov; Kiriakov, Ivanov, Bezinski, Iliev N, Yankov, Kostadinov E, Stoichkov, Penev, Sirakov, Yordanov (Iskrenov 89).

Tel Aviv, 17 February 1993, 29,000
Israel (0) 0

France (1) 4 *(Cantona 28, Blanc 62, 84, Roche 89)*

Israel: Ginzburg; Klinger, Halfon, Hazan, Herazi A, Hillel, Atar (Drieks 56), Banin, Nimny, Herazi R, Rosenthal.
France: Lama; Boli, Roche, Blanc, Lizarazu (Loko 82), Deschamps, Sauzee, Le Guen, Ginoli (Petit 63), Papin, Cantona.

Vienna, 27 March 1993, 37,500
Austria (0) 0

France (0) 1 *(Papin 58)*

Austria: Wohlfahrt; Pecl, Zsak, Artner, Feiersinger, Cerny, Kuhbauer, Schinkels (Ogris 71), Herzog, Polster, Pfeifenberger.
France: Lama; Angloma, Roche, Blanc, Petit, Lizarazu, Deschamps, Le Guen, Sauzee (Martins 87), Papin, Gravelaine (Loko 71).

Vienna, 14 April 1993, 19,500
Austria (2) 3 *(Pfeifenberger 11, Kuhbauer 25, Polster 89)*

Bulgaria (0) 1 *(Ivanov 54)*

Austria: Wohlfahrt; Streiter, Pecl, Zsak, Feiersinger, Kuhbauer (Cerny 86), Lainer, Baur, Polster, Herzog, Pfeifenberger (Ogris 68).
Bulgaria: Mikhailov; Dochev (Lechkov 73), Ivanov, Iliev N, Bezinski (Iskrenov 82), Yankov, Kostadinov E, Kiriakov, Balakov, Stoichkov, Penev.

Paris, 28 April 1993, 43,000
France (1) 2 *(Cantona 42 (pen), 82)*

Sweden (1) 1 *(Dahlin 14)*

France: Lama; Angloma, Petit, Boli, Blanc, Le Guen, Deschamps, Sauzee, Ginola (Vahirua 46), Martins (Lizarazu 89), Cantona.
Sweden: Ravelli; Nilsson R, Andersson P, Bjorklund, Ljung, Rehn, Thern (Kamark 27), Brolin, Schwarz, Ingesson, Dahlin (Pettersson 65).

Sofia, 28 April 1993, 35,000
Bulgaria (2) 2 *(Stoichkov 14, Yankov 43)*

Finland (0) 0

Bulgaria: Mikhailov; Kiriakov, Rakov, Markov (Besinski 89), Yankov, Lechkov, Kostadinov E (Iskrenov 56), Stoichkov, Penev, Sirakov, Balakov.
Finland: Jakonen; Kinnunen, Kanerva, Heikkinen, Holmgren, Suominen, Litmanen, Lindberg, Hjelm, Paatelainen, Petaja (Rajamaki 62).

Sofia, 12 May 1993, 25,000
Bulgaria (1) 2 *(Stoichkov 35 (pen), Sirakov 60)*

Israel (0) 2 *(Harazi R 52, Rosenthal 53)*

Bulgaria: Mikhailov; Kiriakov, Ratkov, Markov, Ivanov, Lechkov (Borimirov 65), Balakov, Sirakov, Iskrenov (Yankov 37), Penev, Stoichkov.
Israel: Ginzburg; Halfon, Hillel, Hazan, Shelach, Klinger, Banin, Schwarz, Rosenthal, Harazi R (Atar 88), Ohana (Harazi A 89).

Pori, 13 May 1993, 13,682
Finland (2) 3 *(Paatelainen 17, Rajamaki 20, Hjelm 50)*

Austria (0) 1 *(Zisser 89)*

Finland: Jakonen; Heikkinen, Kanerva, Holmgren (Lindberg 60), Kinnunen, Petaja, Rajamaki, Hjelm, Suominen, Litmanen, Paatelainen (Grunholm 76).
Austria: Wohlfahrt; Streiter, Zsak (Cerny 60), Zisser, Baur, Kuhbauer, Herzog, Artner, Lainer, Ogris, Polster (Stoger 58).

Stockholm, 19 May 1993, 27,800
Sweden (0) 1 *(Eriksson 50)*

Austria (0) 0

Sweden: Ravelli; Nilsson R, Eriksson J, Bjorklund, Ljung, Rehn, Schwarz, Brolin, Ingesson, Ekstrom (Zetterberg 80), Dahlin (Eklund 87).
Austria: Wohlfahrt; Streiter, Pecl, Lainer, Stoger, Baur, Herzog (Janeschitz 62), Artner, Feiersinger, Ogris, Pfeifenberger.

Stockholm, 2 June 1993, 22,000
Sweden (2) 5 *(Brolin 17, 41, 65, Zetterberg 55, Landberg 89)*

Israel (0) 0

Sweden: Ravelli; Nilsson R, Eriksson J, Bjorklund, Ljung, Rehn (Landberg 74), Andersson P, Zetterberg, Ingesson, Brolin, Dahlin.
Israel: Ginzburg; Halfon, Hillel, Klinger, Shelach, Bruomer, Ohana (Revivo 65), Hazan, Schwarz, Harazi R, Rosenthal (Harazi A 46).

Lahti, 16 June 1993, 4620
Finland (0) 0
Israel (0) 0

Finland: Jakonen; Kinnunen (Lindberg 84), Holmgren, Kanerva, Heikkinen, Petaja, Suominen, Litmanen, Rajamaki, Paatelainen, Gronholm (Ruhanan 75).
Israel: Ginzburg; Klinger, Halfon, Bruomer, Shelach, Asalem, Hazan, Schwarz, Banin, Harazi R (Atar 89), Ohana.

	P	W	D	L	F	A	Pts
Sweden	6	5	0	1	13	3	10
France	6	5	0	1	11	4	10
Bulgaria	7	4	1	2	12	7	9
Austria	6	2	0	4	9	10	4
Finland	6	1	1	4	4	9	3
Israel	7	0	2	5	5	21	2

Concacaf

Pre-preliminary round
Dominican Republic 1, Puerto Rico 2
Puerto Rico 1, Dominican Republic 1
St Lucia 1, St Vincent 0
St Vincent 3, St Lucia 1

Preliminary round
Bermuda 1, Haiti 0
Haiti 2, Bermuda 1
Jamaica 2, Puerto Rico 1
Puerto Rico 0, Jamaica 3
Cuba withdrew, St Vicent w.o
Netherlands Antilles 1, Antigua 1
Antigua 3, Netherlands Antilles 0
Guyana 1, Surinam 2
Surinam 1, Guyana 1
Barbados 1, Trinidad & Tobago 2
Trinidad & Tobago 3, Barbados 0

First round

Central Region
Guatemala 0, Honduras 0
Honduras 2, Guatemala 0
Panama 1, Costa Rica 0
Costa Rica 5, Panama 1
Nicaragua 0, El Salvador 5
El Salvador 5, Nicaragua 1

Caribbean Region
Surinam 0, St Vincent 0
St Vincent 2, Surinam 1
Antigua 0, Bermuda 3
Bermuda 2, Antigua 1
Trinidad & Tobago 1, Jamaica 2
Jamaica 1, Trinidad & Tobago 1

Second round

Group A
Costa Rica 2, Honduras 3
St Vincent 0, Mexico 4
Mexico 2, Honduras 0
St Vincent 0, Costa Rica 1
Mexico 4, Costa Rica 0
St Vincent 0, Honduras 4
Honduras 4, St Vincent 0
Costa Rica 2, Mexico 0
Honduras 2, Costa Rica 1
Mexico 11, St Vincent 0
Costa Rica 5, St Vincent 0
Honduras 1, Mexico 1

Group B
Bermuda 1, El Salvador 0
Jamaica 1, Canada 1
Bermuda 1, Jamaica 1
El Salvador 1, Canada 1
Canada 1, Jamaica 0
El Salvador 4, Bermuda 1
Canada 2, El Salvador 3
Jamaica 3, Bermuda 2
Canada 4, Bermuda 2
Jamaica 0, El Salvador 2
Bermuda 0, Canada 0
El Salvador 2, Jamaica 1

Third Round
Honduras 2, Canada 2
El Salvador 2, Mexico 1
Canada 2, El Salvador 0
Mexico 3, Honduras 0
Canada 3, Honduras 1
Mexico 3, El Salvador 1

218

Honduras 2, El Salvador 0
Mexico 4, Canada 0
Honduras 1, Mexico 4
El Salvador 1, Canada 2
Canada 1, Mexico 2
El Salvador 2, Honduras 1

Mexico qualified for finals in USA

Oceania
Group 1
Solomon Islands 1, Tahiti 1
Solomon Islands 1, Australia 2
Tahiti 0, Australia 3
Australia 2, Tahiti 0
Australia 1, Solomon Islands 1
Tahiti 4, Solomon Islands 2

Group 2
New Zealand 3, Fiji 0
Vanuatu 1, New Zealand 4
New Zealand 8, Vanuatu 0
Fiji 3, Vanuatu 0
Fiji 0, New Zealand 0
Vanuatu 0, Fiji 3

Second Round
New Zealand 0, Australia 1
Australia 3, New Zealand 0

Africa
First Round
Group A
Algeria 3, Burundi 1
Burundi 1, Ghana 0
Ghana 2, Algeria 0
Burundi 0, Algeria 0
Ghana 1, Burundi 0
Algeria 2, Ghana 1
Uganda withdrew

Group B
Zaire 4, Liberia 2
Cameroon 5, Swaziland 0
Swaziland 1, Zaire 0
Zaire 1, Cameroon 2
Swaziland 0, Cameroon 0
Zaire v Swaziland not played
Cameroon 0, Zaire 0
Liberia withdrew

Group C
Zimbabwe 1, Togo 0
Egypt 1, Angola 0
Togo 1, Egypt 4
Zimbabwe 2, Egypt 1
Angola 1, Zimbabwe 1
Togo 1, Zimbabwe 2
Angola 0, Egypt 0
Egypt 3, Togo 0
Zimbabwe 2, Angola 1
Angola v Togo not played
Egypt 0, Zimbabwe 0
Togo 0, Angola 1

Group D
Nigeria 4, South Africa 0
South Africa 1, Congo 0
Congo 0, Nigeria 1
South Africa 0, Nigeria 0
Congo 0, South Africa 1
Nigeria 2, Congo 0
Libya withdrew

Group E
Ivory Coast 6, Botswana 0
Niger 0, Ivory Coast 0
Botswana 0, Niger 1
Botswana 0, Ivory Coast 0
Ivory Coast 1, Niger 0
Niger 2, Botswana 1
Sudan withdrew

Group F
Morocco 5, Ethiopia 0
Tunisia 5, Benin 1
Benin 0, Morocco 1
Ethiopia 0, Tunisia 0
Ethiopia 3, Benin 1
Tunisia 1, Morocco 1
Benin 0, Tunisia 5
Ethiopia 0, Morocco 1
Morocco 5, Benin 0
Tunisia 3, Ethiopia 0
Benin 1, Ethiopia 0
Morocco 0, Tunisia 0

Group G
Gabon 3, Mozambique 1
Mozambique 0, Senegal 1
Gabon 3, Senegal 2
Mozambique 0, Gabon 1
Senegal 6, Mozambique 1
Senegal 1, Gabon 0
Mauritania withdrew

Group H
Madagascar 3, Namibia 0
Zambia 2, Tanzania 0
Tanzania 0, Madagascar 0
Namibia 0, Zambia 4
Tanzania 2, Namibia 0
Madagascar 2, Zambia 0
Tanzania 1, Zambia 3
Namibia 0, Madagascar 1
Zambia 4, Namibia 0
Zambia 3, Madagascar 1
Tanzania withdrew

Group I
Guinea 4, Kenya 0
Kenya 2, Guinea 0
Mali and Gambia withdrew

Second round

Group A
Algeria 1, Ivory Coast 1
Ivory Coast 2, Nigeria 1
Group B
Morocco 1, Senegal 0
Group C
Cameroon 3, Guinea 1
Guinea 3, Zimbabwe 0

Asia
First round
Group A
China, Iraq, Jordan, Yemen, Pakistan
Jordan 1, Yemen 1
Pakistan 0, China 5
Jordan 1, Iraq 1
Yeman 5, Pakistan 1
Iraq 6, Yemen 1
Jordan 0, China 3
Iraq 8, Pakistan 0
Yemen 1, China 0
Iraq 1, China 0
Jordan 3, Pakistan 1
China 3, Pakistan 0
Yemen 1, Jordan 1
Iraq 4, Jordan 0
Yemen 3, Pakistan 0
China 4, Jordan 1
Iraq 3, Yemen 0
Iraq 4, Pakistan 0
China 1, Yemen 0
Pakistan 5, Jordan 0
China 2, Iraq 1

Group B
Iran, Syria, Oman, Taiwan, Myanmar (withdrew)
Syria 2, Taiwan 0
Iran 0, Oman 0

Group C
Korea DPR 3, Vietnam 0
Qatar 3, Indonesia 0
Korea DPR 2, Singapore 1
Qatar 4, Vietnam 0
Korea DPR 4, Indonesia 0
Vietnam 2, Singapore 3
Qatar 4, Singapore 1
Vietnam 1, Indonesia 0
Indonesia 0, Singapore 2
Qatar 1, Korea DPR 2
Indonesia 1, Qatar 4
Vietnam 0, Korea DPR 1
Singapore 1, Korea DPR 3
Vietnam 0, Qatar 4
Indonesia 1, Korea DPR 2
Singapore 1, Vietnam 0
Indonesia 2, Vietnam 1
Singapore 1, Qatar 0
Korea DPR 2, Qatar 2
Singapore 2, Indonesia 1

Group D
Hong Kong 2, Bahrain 1
Lebanon 2, India 2
Bahrain 0, Korea Rep 0
Lebanon 2, Hong Kong 2
India 1, Hong Kong 2
Lebanon 0, Korea Rep 1
India 0, Korea Rep 3
Lebanon 0, Bahrain 0
Bahrain 2, India 1
Hong Kong 0, Korea Rep 3
Bahrain 0, Lebanon 0
Korea Rep 4, Hong Kong 1
Bahrain 3, India 0
Korea Rep 2, Lebanon 0
Korea Rep 7, India 0
Lebanon 2, Hong Kong 1
Lebanon 2, India 1
Bahrain 3, Hong Kong 0
Korea Rep 3, Bahrain 0
India 3, Hong Kong 1

Group E
Macao 0, Saudi Arabia 6
Malaysia 1, Kuwait 1
Macao 1, Kuwait 10
Malaysia 1, Saudi Arabia 1
Kuwait 0, Saudi Arabia 0

Malaysia 9, Macao 0
Kuwait 2, Malaysia 0
Saudi Arabia 8, Macao 0
Kuwait 8, Macao 0
Saudi Arabia 3, Malaysia 0
Macao 0, Malaysia 5
Saudi Arabia 2, Kuwait 0

Group F
Japan 1, Thailand 0
Sri Lanka 0, UAE 4
Japan 8, Bangladesh 0
Thailand 1, Sri Lanka 0
Sri Lanka 0, Bangladesh 1

UAE 1, Thailand 0
Japan 5, Sri Lanka 0
UAE 1, Bangladesh 0
Japan 2, UAE 0
Thailand 4, Bangladesh 1
Thailand 0, Japan 1
UAE 3, Sri Lanka 0
Bangladesh 1, Japan 4
Thailand 1, UAE 2
Bangladesh 0, UAE 7
Sri Lanka 0, Thailand 3
Bangladesh 1, Thailand 4
Sri Lanka 0, Japan 6
Bangladesh 3, Sri Lanka 0
UAE 1, Japan 1

REMAINING 1994 FIFA WORLD CUP FIXTURES

Group 1
5. 9.93 Estonia v Portugal
8. 9.93 Scotland v Switzerland
22. 9.93 Estonia v Italy
13.10.93 Italy v Scotland
13.10.93 Portugal v Switzerland
10.11.93 Portugal v Estonia
17.11.93 Italy v Portugal
17.11.93 Malta v Scotland
17.11.93 Switzerland v Estonia

Group 2
8. 9.93 England v Poland
22. 9.93 Norway v Poland
22. 9.93 San Marino v Holland
13.10.93 Holland v England
13.10.93 Poland v Norway
27.10.93 Turkey v Poland
10.11.93 Turkey v Norway
16.11.93 San Marino v England
17.11.93 Poland v Holland

Group 3
25. 8.93 Denmark v Lithuania
8. 9.93 Albania v Denmark
8. 9.93 Northern Ireland v Latvia
8. 9.93 Republic of Ireland v Lithuania
22. 9.93 Albania v Spain
13.10.93 Denmark v Northern Ireland
13.10.93 Republic of Ireland v Spain
17.11.93 Northern Ireland v Republic of Ireland
17.11.93 Spain v Denmark

Group 4
8. 9.93 Wales v Czechoslovakia
8. 9.93 Faeroes v Romania
13.10.93 Romania v Belgium
13.10.93 Wales v Cyprus
27.10.93 Czechoslovakia v Cyprus
17.11.93 Belgium v Czechoslovakia
17.11.93 Wales v Romania

Group 5
22. 8.93 Yugoslavia v Iceland
8. 9.93 Hungary v CIS
8. 9.93 Iceland v Luxembourg
6.10.93 CIS v Yugoslavia
12.10.93 Luxembourg v Greece
27.10.93 Greece v Yugoslavia
27.10.93 Hungary v Luxembourg
17.11.93 Greece v CIS
17.11.93 Yugoslavia v Hungary

Group 6
22. 8.93 Sweden v France
25. 8.93 Austria v Finland
8. 9.93 Bulgaria v Sweden
8. 9.93 Finland v France
13.10.93 Bulgaria v Austria
13.10.93 France v Israel
13.10.93 Sweden v Finland
27.10.93 Israel v Austria
10.11.93 Austria v Sweden
10.11.93 Israel v Finland
17.11.93 France v Bulgaria

Group A (Argentina, Colombia, Paraguay, Peru)
1. 8.93 Colombia v Paraguay
1. 8.93 Peru v Argentina
8. 8.93 Paraguay v Argentina
8. 8.93 Peru v Colombia
15. 8.93 Colombia v Argentina
15. 8.93 Paraguay v Peru
22. 8.93 Argentina v Peru
22. 8.93 Paraguay v Colombia
29. 8.93 Argentina v Paraguay
29. 8.93 Colombia v Peru
5. 9.93 Argentina v Colombia
5. 9.93 Peru v Paraguay

Group B (Brazil, Uruguay, Ecuador, Bolivia, Venezuela)
18. 7.93 Ecuador v Brazil
18. 7.93 Venezuela v Bolivia
25. 7.93 Bolivia v Brazil
25. 7.93 Venezuela v Uruguay
1. 8.93 Uruguay v Ecuador
1. 8.93 Venezuela v Brazil
8. 8.93 Bolivia v Uruguay
8. 8.93 Ecuador v Venezuela
15. 8.93 Bolivia v Ecuador
15. 8.93 Uruguay v Brazil
22. 8.93 Bolivia v Venezuela
22. 8.93 Brazil v Ecuador
29. 8.93 Brazil v Bolivia
29. 8.93 Uruguay v Venezuela
5. 9.93 Brazil v Venezuela
5. 9.93 Ecuador v Uruguay
12. 9.93 Uruguay v Bolivia
12. 9.93 Venezuela v Ecuador
19. 9.93 Brazil v Uruguay
19. 9.93 Ecuador v Bolivia

WORLD CLUB CHAMPIONSHIP

Played annually up to 1974 and intermittently until 1979 between the winners of the European Cup and the winners of the South American Champions Cup— known as the Copa Libertadores. In 1980 the winners were decided by one match arranged in Tokyo in February 1981 and the venue has been the same since.

1960	Real Madrid beat Penarol 0-0, 5-1
1961	Penarol beat Benfica 0-1, 5-0, 2-1
1962	Santos beat Benfica 3-2, 5-2
1963	Santos beat AC Milan 2-4, 4-2, 1-0
1964	Inter-Milan beat Independiente 0-1, 2-0, 1-0
1965	Inter-Milan beat Independiente 3-0, 0-0
1966	Penarol beat Real Madrid 2-0, 2-0
1967	Racing Club beat Celtic 0-1, 2-1, 1-0
1968	Estudiantes beat Manchester United 1-0, 1-1
1969	AC Milan beat Estudiantes 3-0, 1-2
1970	Feyenoord beat Estudiantes 2-2, 1-0
1971	Nacional beat Panathinaikos* 1-1, 2-1
1972	Ajax beat Independiente 1-1, 3-0
1973	Independiente beat Juventus* 1-0
1974	Atletico Madrid* beat Independiente 0-1, 2-0
1975	Independiente and Bayern Munich could not agree dates; no matches.
1976	Bayern Munich beat Cruzeiro 2-0, 0-0
1977	Boca Juniors beat Borussia Moenchengladbach* 2-2, 3-0
1978	Not played
1979	Olimpia beat Malmo* 1-0, 2-1
1980	Nacional beat Nottingham Forest 1-0
1981	Flamengo beat Liverpool 3-0
1982	Penarol beat Aston Villa 2-0
1983	Gremio Porto Alegre beat SV Hamburg 2-1
1984	Independiente beat Liverpool 1-0
1985	Juventus beat Argentinos Juniors 4-2 on penalties after a 2-2 draw
1986	River Plate beat Steaua Bucharest 1-0
1987	FC Porto beat Penarol 2-1 after extra time
1988	Nacional (Uru) beat PSV Eindhoven 7-6 on penalties after 1-1 draw
1989	AC Milan beat Atletico Nacional (Col) 1-0 after extra time
1990	AC Milan beat Olimpia 3-0
1991	Red Star Belgrade beat Colo Colo 3-0

*European Cup runners-up; winners declined to take part.

1992

12 December in Tokyo

Sao Paulo (1) 2 (*Rai 26, 79*)

Barcelona (1) 1 (*Stoichkov 13*) 80,000

Sao Paulo: Zetti; Victor, Adilson, Ronaldo, Pintado, Ronaldo Luiz, Muller, Toninho Cerezo (Dinho 83), Palinha, Rai, Cafu.
Barcelona: Zubizarreta; Ferrer, Guardiola, Koeman, Eusebio, Bakero (Goicoechea 51), Amor, Stoichkov, Laudrup, Witschge, Beguiristain (Nadal 79).
Referee: Loustau (Argentina).

OTHER BRITISH AND IRISH
INTERNATIONAL MATCHES 1992–93

Santander, 9 September 1992, 22,000

Spain (1) 1 *(Fonseca)*

England (0) 0

Spain: Zubizarreta; Ferrer, Toni (Cristobal), Solozabal, Lopez, Vizcaino, Fonseca (Fernandio) Michel (Goicoechea), Bakero (Alfonso), Martin Vazquez (Alvaro), Amor.
England: Woods; Dixon (Bardsley) (Palmer), Pearce, Ince, Walker, Wright M, White (Merson), Platt, Clough, Shearer, Sinton (Deane).

Foxboro, 9 June 1993, 37,652

USA (1) 2 *(Dooley, Lalas)*

England (0) 0

USA: Meola; Armstrong, Lapper, Doyle, Agoos, Clavijo, Dooley (Lalas), Harkes, Ramos (Jones), Wegerle, Wynalda (Stewart).
England: Woods; Dixon, Pallister, Palmer (Walker), Dorigo, Batty, Ince, Sharpe, Clough, Barnes, Ferdinand (Wright I).

Washington, 13 June 1993, 54,118

Brazil (0) 1 *(Marcio Santos 76)*

England (0) 1 *(Platt)*

Brazil: Taffarel; Jorginho, Valber, Marcio Santos, Nonato (Cafu), Luisinho (Palhinha), Dunga, Valdeir (Almir), Rai, Careca, Elivelton.
England: Flowers; Barrett, Pallister, Walker, Dorigo, Sinton Batty (Platt), Ince (Palmer), Sharpe, Wright I, Clough (Merson).

Detroit, 19 June 1993, 62,126

Germany (1) 2 *(Effenberg, Klinsmann)*

England (1) 1 *(Platt)*

Germany: Illgner; Effenberg (Zorc), Helmer, Buchwald, Moller (Sammer), Matthaus, Schulz, Ziege, Strunz, Riedle, Klinsmann.
England: Martyn; Barrett, Pallister (Keown), Walker, Sinton, Platt, Clough (Wright I), Ince, Sharpe (Winterburn), Merson, Barnes.

Dublin, 17 February 1993, 9500

Republic of Ireland: (0) 2 *(Sheedy, Coyne)*

Wales (1) 1 *(Hughes)*

Republic of Ireland: Bonner (Kelly), Morris, McGoldrick, Carey, O'Leary (Whelan) (Sheedy), Keane, O'Brien, Byrne, Cascarino (Slaven), Kelly D, McLoughlin.
Wales: Southall (Roberts), Phillips, Bodin, Aizlewood, Young (Coleman), Symons, Williams (Allen), Horne, Speed, Hughes, Pembridge.

Ibrox, 24 March 1993, 36,400

Scotland (0) 0

Germany (1) 1 *(Riedle)*

Scotland: Walker; Wright (Booth), Boyd, Levein, Irvine, McLaren, Bowman, Ferguson, Collins, McInally, Robertson.
Germany: Kopke; Zorc, Helmer, Kohler, Thon, Buchwald, Klinsmann, Hassler, Riedle, Matthaus, Doll (Effenberg).

Bristol, 21 October, 3360

Barclays League (2) 3 *(Maskell 2, Allen)*

Italy Serie B (0) 1 *(Maini)*

Barclays League: Wright; Kerslake, Drysdale, Futcher, Calderwood, Awford, Magilton, Allen M, Maskell (Cole), Peacock, Goodman (Stewart).
Serie B: Bucci; Tarozzi, Francesconi, Corrado, Verga, Lamacchi (Grossi), Olivares, Piubelli, Carbone (Gennari), Cristallini (Maini), Del Vecchio.

ENGLISH UNDER-21 TEAMS 1992—93

England Under-21 Internationals
8 Sept
Spain (0) 0
England (0) 1 *(Anderton)*   12,000
England: Walker; Hendon, Wright, Awford, Ehiogu, Whelan (Watson S), Anderton, Parlour, Bart-Williams, Clark (Sutton), Froggatt.

13 Oct
England (0) 0
Norway (1) 2 *(Strandli, Haland)*   4918
England: Walker; Hendon, Wright, Watson S (Sheron), Ehiogu, Awford, Parlour, Bart-Williams, McManaman, Clark, Heaney (Allen).

17 Nov
England (0) 0
Turkey (0) 1 *(Aydin)*   7879
England: Walker; Hendon, Minto, Imprey (Sutton), Ehiogu, Awford, Parlour (Sheron), Bart-Williams, McManaman, Allen, Heaney.

16 Feb

England (4) 6 *(Hall, Flitcroft, Anderton, Sheron, Redknapp, McManaman)*
San Marino (0) 0   7660

England: Walker; Jones (Jackson), Small, Flitcroft, Hall, Ehiogu, Anderton, Sheron (Froggatt), Cole, Redknapp, McManaman.

30 Mar

Turkey (0) 0
England (0) 0   20,000

England: Gerrard; Jackson (Whelan), Small, Sutch, Hall, Ehiogu, Kenny (Newton), Clark, Sutton, Cox, McManaman.

28 Apr

England (3) 3 *(Sheron 2, Anderton)*
Holland (0) 0   6752

England: Gerrard; Jones, Small, Jackson, Hall, Ehiogu, Flitcroft, Sheron, Sutton, Cox (Clark), Anderton.

28 May

Poland (1) 1 *(Dabrowski)*
England (2) 4 *(Hall, Cole 2, Anderton)*   4000

England: Gerrard; Ardley, Small, Jackson, Hall (Clark), Ehiogu, Cox, Sheron, Cole, Redknapp, Anderton.

1 June

Norway (0) 1 *(Ostenstad)*
England (0) 1 *(Cole)*   6840

England: Gerrard; Ardley, Small, Jackson, Cox, Ehiogu, Flitcroft, Sheron, Cole, Redknapp, Anderton.

Tournament in France
7 June

England (0) 2 *(Luis (og), Whelan)*
Portugal (0) 0

England: Gerrard; Ardley, Hall, Whelan (Sutton), Small, Flitcroft, Awford (Summerbee), Redknapp, Anderton, Allen, Sheron.

9 June

England (1) 1 *(Sheron)*
Czechoslovakia (0) 1 *(Novotny)*

England: Gerrard; Ardley, Sutton, Hall, Small, Awford, Flitcroft, Sheron, Clark (Allen), Redknapp, Anderton.

11 June

England (0) 0

Brazil (0) 0

England: Gerrard; Ardley, Awford, Hall, Small, Clark, Redknapp, Flitcroft, Anderton, Sutton, Sheron (Oakes).

14 June

England (1) 1 *(Summerbee)*

Scotland (0) 0

England: Gerrard; Ardley, Hall, Awford, Small, Clark (Summerbee), Redknapp, Flitcroft, Anderton, Sheron, Sutton.

15 June (Final)

England (0) 1 *(Flitcroft)*

France (0) 0

England: Gerrard; Ardley, Small, Awford, Hall, Sutton, Flitcroft, Sheron, Summerbee, Redknapp, Anderton.

EUROPEAN SUPER CUP

Played annually between the winners of the European Champions' Cup and the European Cup-Winners' Cup.

Previous Matches
1972 Ajax beat Rangers 3-1, 3-2
1973 Ajax beat AC Milan 0-1, 6-0
1974 Not contested
1975 Dynamo Kiev beat Bayern Munich 1-0, 2-0
1976 Anderlecht beat Bayern Munich 4-1, 1-2
1977 Liverpool beat Hamburg 1-1, 6-0
1978 Anderlecht beat Liverpool 3-1, 1-2
1979 Nottingham F beat Barcelona 1-0, 1-1
1980 Valencia beat Nottingham F 1-0, 1-2
1981 Not contested
1982 Aston Villa beat Barcelona 0-1, 3-0
1983 Aberdeen beat Hamburg 0-0, 2-0
1984 Juventus beat Liverpool 2-0
1985 Juventus v Everton not contested due to UEFA ban on English clubs
1986 Steaua Bucharest beat Dynamo Kiev 1-0
1987 FC Porto beat Ajax 1-0, 1-0
1988 KV Mechelen beat PSV Eindhoven 3-0, 0-1
1989 AC Milan beat Barcelona 1-1, 1-0
1990 AC Milan beat Sampdoria 1-1, 2-0
1991 Manchester U beat Red Star Belgrade 1-0

1992-93 First Leg

Bremen, 10 February 1993, 22,098

Werder Bremen (0) 1 (Allofs 88)

Barcelona (1) 1 (Salinas 38)

Werder Bremen: Reck; Borowka, Bratseth, Legat, Bockenfeld, Neubarth, Votava, Herzog, Eilts, Bode (Kohn 69), Hobsch (Allofs 77).
Barcelona: Zubizarreta; Ferrer, Koeman, Eusebio, Nadal, Goicoechea, Bakero (Beguiristain 67), Amor, Salinas (Christiansen 83), Witschge, Stoichkov.
Referee: Nielsen (Denmark).

Second Leg

Barcelona, 10 March 1993, 75,000

Barcelona (1) 2 (Stoichkov 32, Goicoechea 48)

Werder Bremen (1) 1 (Rufer 41 (pen))

Barcelona: Zubizarreta; Ferrer, Koeman, Eusebio, Nadal, Guardiola (Salinas 79), Bakero (Beguiristain 50), Amor, Goicoechea, Laudrup, Stoichkov.
Werder Bremen: Reck; Wolter, Borowka, Bratseth, Legat (Allofs 77), Schaaf (Gundelach 30), Eilts, Bode, Herzog, Hobsch, Rufer.
Referee: Karlsson (Sweden).

228

POST-WAR INTERNATIONAL APPEARANCES

As at June 1993

ENGLAND

A'Court, A. (5) (Liverpool) 1957/8, 1958/9.
Adams, T.A. (26) (Arsenal) 1986/7, 1987/8, 1988/9, 1990/91, 1992/93.
Allen, C. (5) (QPR) 1983/4, 1986/7 (Tottenham Hotspur) 1987/8.
Allen, R. (5) (West Bromwich Albion) 1951/2, 1953/4, 1954/5.
Allen, T. (3) (Stoke City) 1959/60.
Anderson, S. (2) (Sunderland) 1961/2.
Anderson, V. (30) (Nottingham Forest) 1978/9, 1979/80, 1980/1, 1981/2, 1983/84, (Arsenal) 1984/5, 1985/6, 1986/7, (Manchester United).
Angus, J. (1) (Burnley) 1960/1.
Armfield, J. (43) (Blackpool) 1958/9, 1959/60, 1960/1, 1961/2, 1962/3, 1963/4, 1965/6.
Armstrong, D. (3) (Middlesbrough) 1979/80, (Southampton) 1982/3, 1983/4.
Armstrong, K. (1) (Chelsea) 1954/5.
Astall, G. (2) (Birmingham) 1955/6.
Astle, J. (5) (West Bromwich Albion) 1968/9, 1969/70.
Aston, J. (17) (Manchester United) 1948/9, 1949/50, 1950/1.
Atyeo, J. (6) (Bristol City) 1955/6, 1956/7.

Bailey, G.R. (2) Manchester United) 1984/5.
Bailey, M. (2) (Charlton) 1963/4, 1964/5.
Baily, E. (9) (Tottenham Hotspur) 1949/50, 1950/1, 1951/2, 1952/3.
Baker, J. (8) (Hibernian) 1959/60, 1965/6, (Arsenal).
Ball, A. (72) (Blackpool) 1964/5, 1965/6, 1966/7, (Everton) 1967/8, 1968/9, 1969/70, 1970/1, 1971/2 (Arsenal) 1972/3, 1973/4, 1974/5.
Banks, G. (73) (Leicester) 1962/3, 1963/4, 1964/5, 1965/6, 1966/7, 1967/8, (Stoke) 1968/9, 1969/70, 1970/1, 1971/2.
Banks, T. (6) (Bolton Wanderers) 1957/8, 1958/9.
Bardsley, D. (2) (QPR) 1992/93.
Barham, M. (2) (Norwich City) 1982/3.
Barlow, R. (1) (West Bromwich Albion) 1954/5.
Barnes, J. (73) (Watford) 1982/3, 1983/4, 1984/5, 1985/6, 1986/7, (Liverpool) 1987/8, 1988/9, 1989/90, 1990/91, 1991/2, 1992/93.
Barnes, P. (22) (Manchester City) 1977/8, 1978/9, 1979/80 (West Bromwich Albion) 1980/1, 1981/2 (Leeds United).
Barrass, M. (3) (Bolton Wanderers) 1951/2, 1952/3.
Barrett, E.D. (3) (Oldham Athletic) 1990/91 (Aston Villa) 1992/93.
Batty, D. (14) (Leeds United) 1990/91, 1991/2, 1992/93.
Baynham, R. (3) (Luton Town) 1955/6.
Beardsley P.A. (49) (Newcastle United) 1985/6, 1986/7 (Liverpool) 1987/8, 1988/9, 1989/90, 1990/1.
Beasant, D.J. (2) (Chelsea), 1989/90.
Beattie, T.K. (9) (Ipswich Town) 1974/5, 1975/6, 1976/7, 1977/8.
Bell, C. (48) (Manchester City) 1967/8, 1968/9, 1969/70, 1971/2, 1972/3, 1973/4, 1974/5, 1975/6.
Bentley, R. (12) (Chelsea) 1948/9, 1949/50, 1952/3, 1954/5.
Berry, J. (4) (Manchester United) 1952/3, 1955/6.

229

Birtles, G. (3) (Nottingham Forest) 1979/80, 1980/1 (Manchester United).
Blissett, L. (14) (Watford) 1982/3, 1983/4 (AC Milan).
Blockley, J. (1) (Arsenal) 1972/3.
Blunstone, F. (5) (Chelsea) 1954/5, 1956/7.
Bonetti, P. (7) (Chelsea) 1965/6, 1966/7, 1967/8, 1969/70.
Bowles, S. (5) (QPR) 1973/4, 1976/7.
Boyer, P. (1) (Norwich City) 1975/6.
Brabrook, P. (3) (Chelsea) 1957/8, 1959/60.
Bracewell, P.W. (3) (Everton) 1984/5, 1985/6.
Bradford, G. (1) (Bristol Rovers) 1955/6.
Bradley, W. (3) (Manchester United) 1958/9.
Bridges, B. (4) (Chelsea) 1964/5, 1965/6.
Broadbent, P. (7) (Wolverhampton Wanderers) 1957/8, 1958/9, 1959/60.
Broadis, I. (14) (Manchester City) 1951/2, 1952/3 (Newcastle United) 1953/4.
Brooking, T. (47) (West Ham United) 1973/4, 1974/5, 1975/6, 1976/7, 1977/8, 1978/9, 1979/80, 1980/1, 1981/2.
Brooks, J. (3) (Tottenham Hotspur) 1956/7.
Brown, A. (1) (West Bromwich Albion) 1970/1.
Brown, K. (1) (West Ham United) 1959/60.
Bull, S.G. (13) (Wolverhampton Wanderers) 1988/9, 1989/90, 1990/1
Butcher, T. (77) (Ipswich Town) 1979/80, 1980/1, 1981/2, 1982/3, 1983/4, 1984/5, 1985/6, 1986/7 (Rangers) 1987/8, 1988/9, 1989/90.
Byrne, G. (2) (Liverpool) 1962/3, 1965/6.
Byrne, J. (11) (Crystal Palace) 1961/2, 1962/3, (West Ham United) 1963/4, 1964/5.
Byrne, R. (33) (Manchester United) 1953/4, 1954/5, 1955/6, 1956/7, 1957/8.

Callaghan, I. (4) (Liverpool) 1965/6, 1977/8.
Carter, H. (7) (Derby County) 1946/7.
Chamberlain, M. (8) (Stoke City) 1982/3, 1983/4, 1984/5.
Channon, M. (46) (Southampton) 1972/3, 1973/4, 1974/5, 1975/6, 1976/7, (Manchester City) 1977/8.
Charles, G.A. (2) (Nottingham Forest) 1990/1.
Charlton, J. (35) (Leeds United) 1964/5, 1965/6, 1966/7, 1967/8, 1968/9, 1969/70.
Charlton, R. (106) (Manchester United) 1957/8, 1958/9, 1959/60, 1960/1, 1961/2, 1962/3, 1963/4, 1964/5, 1965/6, 1966/7, 1967/8, 1968/9, 1969/70.
Charnley, R. (1) (Blackpool) 1961/2.
Cherry, T. (27) (Leeds United) 1975/6, 1976/7, 1977/8, 1978/9, 1979/80.
Chilton, A. (2) (Manchester United) 1950/1, 1951/2.
Chivers, M. (24) (Tottenham Hotspur) 1970/1, 1971/2, 1972/3, 1973/4.
Clamp, E. (4) (Wolverhampton Wanderers) 1957/8.
Clapton, D. (1) (Arsenal) 1958/9.
Clarke, A. (19) (Leeds United) 1969/70, 1970/1, 1972/3, 1973/4, 1974/5, 1975/6.
Clarke, H. (1) (Tottenham Hotspur) 1953/4.
Clayton, R. (35) (Blackburn Rovers) 1955/6, 1956/7, 1957/8, 1958/9, 1959/60.
Clemence, R (61) (Liverpool) 1972/3, 1973/4, 1974/5, 1975/6, 1976/7, 1977/8, 1978/9, 1979/80, 1980/1, 1981/2, (Tottenham Hotspur) 1982/3, 1983/4.
Clement, D. (5) (QPR) 1975/6, 1976/7.
Clough, B. (2) (Middlesbrough) 1959/60.
Clough, N.H. (14) (Nottingham Forest) 1988/9, 1990/91, 1991/2, 1992/93.
Coates, R. (4) (Burnley) 1969/70, 1970/1, (Tottenham Hotspur).
Cockburn, H. (13) (Manchester United) 1946/7, 1947/8, 1948/9, 1950/1, 1951/2.
Cohen, G. (37) (Fulham) 1963/4, 1964/5, 1965/6, 1966/7, 1967/8.
Compton, L. (2) (Arsenal) 1950/1.

Connelly J. (20) (Burnley) 1959/60, 1961/2, 1962/3, 1964/5 (Manchester United) 1965/6.
Cooper, T. (20) (Leeds United) 1968/9, 1969/70, 1970/1, 1971/2, 1974/5.
Coppell, S. (42) (Manchester United) 1977/8, 1978/9, 1979/80, 1980/1, 1981/2, 1982/3.
Corrigan J. (9) (Manchester City) 1975/6, 1977/8, 1978/9, 1979/80, 1980/1, 1981/2.
Cottee, A.R. (7) (West Ham United) 1986/7, 1987/8, (Everton) 1988/9.
Cowans, G. (10) (Aston Villa) 1982/3, 1985/6 (Bari) 1990/1 (Aston Villa).
Crawford, R. (2) (Ipswich Town) 1961/2.
Crowe, C. (1) (Wolverhampton Wanderers) 1962/3.
Cunningham, L. (6) (West Bromwich Albion) 1978/9 (Real Madrid) 1979/80, 1980/1.
Curle, K. (3) (Manchester City) 1991/2.
Currie, A. (17) (Sheffield United) 1971/2, 1972/3, 1973/4, 1975/6 (Leeds United) 1977/8, 1978/9.

Daley, A.M. (7) (Aston Villa) 1991/2.
Davenport, P. (1) (Nottingham Forest) 1984/5.
Deane, B.C. (3) (Sheffield United) 1990/91, 1992/93.
Deeley, N. (2) (Wolverhampton Wanderers) 1958/9.
Devonshire, A. (8) (West Ham United) 1979/80, 1981/2, 1982/3, 1983/4
Dickinson, J. (48) (Portsmouth) 1948/9, 1949/50, 1950/1, 1951/2, 1952/3, 1953/4, 1954/5, 1955/6, 1956/7.
Ditchburn, E. (6) (Tottenham Hotspur) 1948/9, 1952/3, 1956/7.
Dixon, K.M. (8) (Chelsea) 1984/5, 1985/6, 1986/7.
Dixon, L.M. (20) (Arsenal) 1989/90, 1990/1, 1991/2, 1992/93.
Dobson, M. (5) (Burnley) 1973/4, 1974/5 (Everton).
Dorigo, A.R. (14) (Chelsea) 1989/90, 1990/1, (Leeds United) 1991/2, 1992/93.
Douglas, B. (36) (Blackburn Rovers) 1957/8, 1958/9, 1959/60, 1960/1, 1961/2, 1962/3.
Doyle, M. (5) (Manchester City) 1975/6, 1976/7
Duxbury, M. (10) (Manchester United) 1983/4, 1984/5.

Eastham, G. (19) (Arsenal) 1962/3, 1963/4, 1964/5, 1965/6.
Eckersley, W. (17) (Blackburn Rovers) 1949/50, 1950/1, 1951/2, 1952/3, 1953/4.
Edwards, D. (18) (Manchester United) 1954/5, 1955/6, 1956/7, 1957/8.
Ellerington, W. (2) (Southampton) 1948/9.
Elliott, W. H. (5) (Burnley) 1951/2, 1952/3.

Fantham, J. (1) (Sheffield Wednesday) 1961/2.
Fashanu, J. (2) (Wimbledon) 1988/9.
Fenwick, T. (20) (QPR) 1983/4, 1984/5, 1985/6 (Tottenham Hotspur) 1987/8.
Ferdinand, L. (4) (QPR) 1992/93.
Finney, T. (76) (Preston) 1946/7, 1947/8, 1948/9, 1949/50, 1950/1, 1951/2, 1952/3, 1953/4, 1954/5, 1955/6, 1956/7, 1957/8, 1958/9.
Flowers R. (49) (Wolverhampton Wanderers) 1954/5, 1958/9, 1959/60, 1960/1, 1961/2, 1962/3, 1963/4, 1964/5, 1965/6.
Flowers T. (1) (Southampton) 1992/93.
Foster, S. (3) (Brighton) 1981/2.
Foulkes, W. (1) (Manchester United) 1954/5.
Francis, G. (12) (QPR) 1974/5, 1975/6.

231

Francis, T. (52) (Birmingham City) 1976/7, 1977/8 (Nottingham Forest) 1978/9, 1979/80, 1980/1, 1981/2 (Manchester City) 1982/3, (Sampdoria) 1983/4, 1984/5, 1985/6.
Franklin, N. (27) (Stoke City) 1946/7, 1947/8, 1948/9, 1949/50.
Froggatt, J. (13) (Portsmouth) 1949/50, 1950/1, 1951/2, 1952/3.
Froggatt, R. (4) (Sheffield Wednesday) 1952/3.

Garrett, T. (3) (Blackpool) 1951/2, 1953/4.
Gascoigne, P.J. (27) (Tottenham Hotspur) 1988/9, 1989/90, 1990/1 (Lazio) 1992/93.
Gates, E. (2) (Ipswich Town) 1980/1.
George, F.C. (1) (Derby County) 1976/7.
Gidman, J. (1) (Aston Villa) 1976/7.
Gillard, I. (3) (QPR) 1974/5, 1975/6.
Goddard, P. (1) (West Ham United) 1981/2.
Grainger, C. (7) (Sheffield United) 1955/6, 1956/7 (Sunderland).
Gray, A.A. (1) (Crystal Palace) 1991/2.
Greaves, J. (57) (Chelsea) 1958/9, 1959/60, 1960/1, 1961/2 (Tottenham Hotspur) 1962/3, 1963/4, 1964/5, 1965/6, 1966/7.
Greenhoff, B. (18) (Manchester United) 1975/6, 1976/7, 1977/8, 1979/80.
Gregory, J. (6) (QPR) 1982/3, 1983/4.

Hagan, J. (1) (Sheffield United) 1948/9.
Haines, J. (1) (West Bromwich Albion) 1948/9.
Hall, J. (17) (Birmingham City) 1955/6, 1956/7.
Hancocks, J. (3) (Wolverhampton Wanderers) 1948/9, 1949/50, 1950/1.
Hardwick, G. (13) (Middlesbrough) 1946/7, 1947/8.
Harford, M.G. (2) (Luton Town) 1987/8, 1988/9.
Harris, G. (1) (Burnley) 1965/6.
Harris, P. (2) (Portsmouth) 1949/50, 1953/4.
Harvey, C. (1) (Everton) 1970/1.
Hassall, H. (5) (Huddersfield Town) 1950/1, 1951/2 (Bolton Wanderers) 1953/4.
Hateley, M. (32) (Portsmouth) 1983/4, 1984/5, (AC Milan) 1985/6, 1986/7, (Monaco) 1987/8, (Rangers) 1991/2.
Haynes, J. (56) (Fulham) 1954/5, 1955/6, 1956/7, 1957/8, 1958/9, 1959/60, 1960/1, 1961/2.
Hector, K. (2) (Derby County) 1973/4.
Hellawell, M. (2) (Birmingham City) 1962/3.
Henry, R. (1) (Tottenham Hotspur) 1962/3.
Hill, F. (2) (Bolton Wanderers) 1962/3.
Hill, G. (6) (Manchester United) 1975/6, 1976/7, 1977/8.
Hill, R. (3) (Luton Town) 1982/3, 1985/6.
Hinton A. (3) (Wolverhampton Wanderers) 1962/3, 1964/5 (Nottingham Forest).
Hirst, D.E. (3) (Sheffield Wednesday) 1990/91, 1991/2.
Hitchens, G. (7) (Aston Villa) 1960/1, (Inter Milan) 1961/2.
Hoddle, G. (53) (Tottenham Hotspur) 1979/80, 1980/1, 1981/2, 1982/3, 1983/4, 1984/5, 1985/6, 1986/7 (Monaco) 1987/8.
Hodge, S.B. (24) (Aston Villa) 1985/6, 1986/7, (Tottenham Hotspur), (Nottingham Forest) 1988/9, 1989/90, 1990/1.
Hodgkinson, A. (5) (Sheffield United) 1956/7, 1960/1.
Holden, D. (5) (Bolton Wanderers) 1958/9.
Holliday, E. (3) (Middlesbrough) 1959/60.
Hollins, J. (1) (Chelsea) 1966/7.
Hopkinson, E. (14) (Bolton Wanderers) 1957/8, 1958/9, 1959/60.

Howe, D. (23) (West Bromwich Albion) 1957/8, 1958/9, 1959/60.
Howe, J. (3) (Derby County) 1947/8, 1948/9.
Hudson, A. (2) (Stoke City) 1974/5.
Hughes, E. (62) (Liverpool) 1969/70, 1970/1, 1971/2, 1972/3, 1973/4, 1974/5, 1976/7, 1977/8, 1978/9 (Wolverhampton Wanderers) 1979/80.
Hughes, L. (3) (Liverpool) 1949/50.
Hunt, R. (34) (Liverpool) 1961/2, 1962/3, 1963/4, 1964/5, 1965/6, 1966/7, 1967/8, 1968/9.
Hunt, S. (2) (West Bromwich Albion) 1983/4.
Hunter, N. (28) (Leeds United) 1965/6, 1966/7, 1967/8, 1968/9, 1969/70, 1970/1, 1971/2, 1972/3, 1973/4, 1974/5.
Hurst, G. (49) (West Ham United) 1965/6, 1966/7, 1967/8, 1968/9, 1969/70, 1970/1, 1971/2.

Ince, P. (9) (Manchester United) 1992/93.

Jezzard, B. (2) (Fulham) 1953/4, 1955/6.
Johnson, D. (8) (Ipswich Town) 1974/5, 1975/6, (Liverpool) 1979/80.
Johnston, H. (10) (Blackpool) 1946/7, 1950/1, 1952/3, 1953/4.
Jones, M. (3) (Sheffield United) 1964/5 (Leeds United) 1969/70.
Jones, R. (1) (Liverpool) 1991/2.
Jones, W.H. (2) (Liverpool) 1949/50.

Kay, A. (1) (Everton) 1962/3.
Keegan, K. (63) (Liverpool) 1972/3, 1973/4, 1974/5, 1975/6, 1976/7 (SV Hamburg) 1977/8, 1978/9, 1979/80 (Southampton) 1980/1, 1981/2.
Kennedy, A. (2) (Liverpool) 1983/4.
Kennedy, R. (17) (Liverpool) 1975/6, 1977/8, 1979/80.
Keown, M.R. (11) (Everton) 1991/2 (Arsenal) 1992/93.
Kevan, D. (14) (West Bromwich Albion) 1956/7, 1957/8, 1958/9, 1960/1.
Kidd, B. (2) (Manchester United) 1969/70.
Knowles, C. (4) (Tottenham Hotspur) 1967/8.

Labone, B. (26) (Everton) 1962/3, 1966/7, 1967/8, 1968/9, 1969/70.
Lampard, F. (2) (West Ham United) 1972/3, 1979/80.
Langley, J. (3) (Fulham) 1957/8.
Langton, R. (11) (Blackburn Rovers) 1946/7, 1947/8, 1948/9, (Preston North End) 1949/50, (Bolton Wanderers) 1950/1.
Latchford, R. (12) (Everton) 1977/8, 1978/9.
Lawler, C. (4) (Liverpool) 1970/1, 1971/2.
Lawton, T. (15) (Chelsea) 1946/7, 1947/8, (Notts County) 1948/9.
Lee, F. (27) (Manchester City) 1968/9, 1969/70, 1970/1, 1971/2.
Lee, J. (1) (Derby County) 1950/1.
Lee, S. (14) (Liverpool) 1982/3, 1983/4.
Lindsay, A. (4) (Liverpool) 1973/4.
Lineker, G. (80) (Leicester City) 1983/4, 1984/5 (Everton) 1985/6, 1986/7, (Barcelona) 1987/8, 1988/9 (Tottenham H) 1989/90, 1990/1, 1991/2.
Little, B. (1) (Aston Villa) 1974/5.
Lloyd, L. (4) (Liverpool) 1970/1, 1971/2, (Nottingham Forest) 1979/80.
Lofthouse, N. (33) (Bolton Wanderers) 1950/1, 1951/2, 1952/3, 1953/4, 1954/5, 1955/6, 1958/9.
Lowe, E. (3) (Aston Villa) 1946/7.

Mabbutt, G. (16) (Tottenham Hotspur) 1982/3, 1983/4, 1986/7, 1987/8, 1991/2.
Macdonald, M. (14) (Newcastle United) 1971/2, 1972/3, 1973/4, 1974/5, (Arsenal) 1975/6.
Madeley, P. (24) (Leeds United) 1970/1, 1971/2, 1972/3, 1973/4, 1974/5, 1975/6, 1976/7.
Mannion, W. (26) (Middlesbrough) 1946/7, 1947/8, 1948/9, 1949/50, 1950/1, 1951/2.
Mariner, P. (35) (Ipswich Town) 1976/7, 1977/8, 1979/80, 1980/1, 1981/2, 1982/3, 1983/4, 1984/5 (Arsenal)
Marsh, R. (9) (QPR) 1971/2 (Manchester City) 1972/3.
Martin, A. (17) (West Ham United) 1980/1, 1981/2, 1982/3, 1983/4, 1984/5, 1985/6, 1986/7.
Marwood, B. (1) (Arsenal) 1988/9.
Matthews, R. (5) (Coventry City) 1955/6, 1956/7.
Matthews, S. (37) (Stoke City) 1946/7, (Blackpool) 1947/8, 1948/9, 1949/50, 1950/1, 1953/4, 1954/5, 1955/6, 1956/7.
McDermott, T. (25) (Liverpool) 1977/8, 1978/9, 1979/80, 1980/1, 1981/2.
McDonald, C. (8) (Burnley) 1957/8, 1958/9.
McFarland, R. (28) (Derby County) 1970/1, 1971/2, 1972/3, 1973/4, 1975/6, 1976/7.
McGarry, W. (4) (Huddersfield Town) 1953/4, 1955/6.
McGuinness, W. (2) (Manchester United) 1958/9.
McMahon, S. (17) (Liverpool) 1987/8, 1988/9, 1989/90, 1990/1.
McNab, R. (4) (Arsenal) 1968/9.
McNeil, M. (9) (Middlesbrough) 1960/1, 1961/2.
Martyn, A.N. (3) (Crystal Palace) 1991/2, 1992/93.
Meadows, J. (1) (Manchester City) 1954/5.
Medley, L. (Tottenham Hotspur) 1950/1, 1951/2.
Melia, J. (2) (Liverpool) 1962/3.
Merrick, G. (23) (Birmingham City) 1951/2, 1952/3, 1953/4.
Merson, P.C. (12) (Arsenal) 1991/2, 1992/93.
Metcalfe, V. (2) (Huddersfield Town) 1950/1.
Milburn, J. (13) (Newcastle United) 1948/9, 1949/50, 1950/1, 1951/2, 1955/6.
Miller, B. (1) (Burnley) 1960/1.
Mills, M. (42) (Ipswich Town) 1972/3, 1975/6, 1976/7, 1977/8, 1978/9, 1979/80, 1980/1, 1981/2.
Milne, G. (14) (Liverpool) 1962/3, 1963/4, 1964/5.
Milton, C.A. (1) (Arsenal) 1951/2.
Moore, R. (108) (West Ham United) 1961/2, 1962/3, 1963/4, 1964/5, 1965/6, 1966/7, 1967/8, 1968/9, 1969/70, 1970/1, 1971/2, 1972/3, 1973/4.
Morley, A. (6) (Aston Villa) 1981/2, 1982/3.
Morris, J. (3) (Derby County) 1948/9, 1949/50.
Mortensen, S. (25) (Blackpool) 1946/7, 1947/8, 1948/9, 1949/50, 1950/1, 1953/4.
Mozley, B. (3) (Derby County) 1949/50.
Mullen, J. (12) (Wolverhampton Wanderers) 1946/7, 1948/9, 1949/50, 1953/4.
Mullery, A. (35) (Tottenham Hotspur) 1964/5, 1966/7, 1967/8, 1968/9, 1969/70, 1970/1, 1971/2.

Neal, P. (50) (Liverpool) 1975/6, 1976/7, 1977/8, 1978/9, 1979/80, 1980/1, 1981/2, 1982/3, 1983/4.
Newton, K. (27) (Blackburn Rovers) 1965/6, 1966/7, 1967/8, 1968/9, 1969/70, (Everton).
Nicholls, J. (2) (West Bromwich Albion) 1953/4.
Nicholson W. (1) (Tottenham Hotspur) 1950/1.

Nish, D. (5) (Derby County) 1972/3, 1973/4.
Norman, M. (23) (Tottenham Hotspur) 1961/2, 1962/3, 1963/4, 1964/5.

O'Grady, M. (2) (Huddersfield Town) 1962/3, 1968/9 (Leeds United).
Osgood, P. (4) (Chelsea) 1969/70, 1973/4.
Osman, R. (11) (Ipswich Town) 1979/80, 1980/1, 1981/2, 1982/3, 1983/4.
Owen, S. (3) (Luton Town) 1953/4.

Paine, T. (19) (Southampton) 1962/3, 1963/4, 1964/5, 1965/6.
Pallister, G. (9) (Middlesbrough) 1987/8, 1990/91 (Manchester United), 1991/2,
1992/93.
Palmer, C.L. (17) (Sheffield Wednesday) 1991/2, 1992/93.
Parker, P.A. (17) (QPR) 1988/9, 1989/90, 1990/1, (Manchester United) 1991/2.
Parkes, P. (1) (QPR) 1973/4.
Parry, R. (2) (Bolton Wanderers) 1959/60.
Peacock, A. (6) (Middlesbrough) 1961/2, 1962/3, 1965/6 (Leeds United).
Pearce, S. (53) (Nottingham Forest) 1986/7, 1987/8, 1988/9, 1989/90, 1990/1,
1991/2, 1992/93.
Person, Stan (8) (Manchester United) 1947/8, 1948/9, 1949/50, 1950/1, 1951/2.
Pearson, Stuart (15) (Manchester United) 1975/6, 1976/7, 1977/8.
Pegg, D. (1) (Manchester United) 1956/7.
Pejic, M. (4) (Stoke City) 1973/4.
Perry, W. (3) (Blackpool) 1955/6.
Perryman, S. (1) (Tottenham Hotspur) 1981/2.
Peters, M. (67) (West Ham United) 1965/6, 1966/7, 1967/8, 1968/9, 1969/70,
(Tottenham Hotspur) 1970/1, 1971/2, 1972/3, 1973/4.
Phelan, M.C. (1) (Manchester United) 1989/90.
Phillips, L. (3) (Portsmouth) 1951/2, 1954/5.
Pickering, F. (3) (Everton) 1963/4, 1964/5.
Pickering, N. (1) (Sunderland) 1982/3.
Pilkington, B. (1) (Burnley) 1954/5.
Platt, D. (42) (Aston Villa) 1989/90, 1990/1, (Bari) 1991/2 (Juventus), 1992/93.
Pointer, R. (3) (Burnley) 1961/2.
Pye, J. (1) (Wolverhampton Wanderers) 1949/50.

Quixall, A. (5) (Sheffield Wednesday) 1953/4, 1954/5.

Radford, J. (2) (Arsenal) 1968/9, 1971/2.
Ramsey, A. (32) (Southampton) 1948/9, 1949/50, (Tottenham Hotspur) 1950/1,
1951/2, 1952/3, 1953/4.
Reaney, P. (3) (Leeds United) 1968/9, 1969/70, 1970/1.
Reeves, K. (2) (Norwich City) 1979/80.
Regis, C. (5) (West Bromwich Albion) 1981/2, 1982/3, (Coventry City).
Reid, P. (13) (Everton) 1984/5, 1985/6, 1986/7.
Revie, D. (6) (Manchester City) 1954/5, 1955/6, 1956/7.
Richards, J. (1) (Wolverhampton Wanderers) 1972/3.
Rickaby, S. (1) (West Bromwich Albion) 1953/4.
Rimmer, J. (1) (Arsenal) 1975/6.
Rix, G. (17) (Arsenal) 1980/1, 1981/2, 1982/3, 1983/4.
Robb, G. (1) (Tottenham Hotspur) 1953/4.
Roberts, G. (6) (Tottenham Hotspur) 1982/3, 1983/4.

235

Robson, B.(90) (West Bromwich Albion) 1979/80, 1980/1, 1981/2, (Manchester United) 1982/3, 1983/4, 1984/5, 1985/6, 1986/7, 1987/8, 1988/9, 1989/90, 1990/1, 1991/2.
Robson, R. (20) (West Bromwich Albion) 1957/8, 1959/60, 1960/1, 1961/2.
Rocastle, D. (14) (Arsenal) 1988/9, 1989/90, 1991/2.
Rowley, J. (6) (Manchester United) 1948/9, 1949/50, 1951/2.
Royle, J. (6) (Everton) 1970/1, 1972/3, (Manchester City) 1975/6, 1976/7.

Sadler, D. (4) (Manchester United) 1967/8, 1969/70, 1970/1.
Salako, J.A. (5) (Crystal Palace) 1990/91, 1991/2.
Sansom, K. (86) (Crystal Palace) 1978/9, 1979/80, 1980/1, (Arsenal) 1981/2, 1982/3, 1983/4, 1984/5, 1985/6, 1986/7, 1987/8.
Scott, L. (17) (Arsenal) 1946/7, 1947/8. 1948/9.
Seaman, D.A. (9) (QPR) 1988/9, 1989/90, 1990/1 (Arsenal), 1991/2.
Sewell, J. (6) (Sheffield Wednesday) 1951/2, 1952/3, 1953/4.
Shackleton, L. (5) (Sunderland) 1948/9, 1949/50, 1954/5.
Sharpe, L.S. (6) (Manchester United) 1990/1, 1992/93.
Shaw, G. (5) (Sheffield United) 1958/9, 1962/3.
Shearer, A. (6) (Southampton) 1991/2 (Blackburn Rovers), 1992/93.
Shellito, K. (1) (Chelsea) 1962/3.
Sheringham, E. (2) (Tottenham Hotspur) 1992/93.
Shilton, P. (125) (Leicester City) 1970/1, 1971/2, 1972/3, 1973/4, 1974/5, (Stoke City) 1976/7, (Nottingham Forest) 1977/8, 1978/9, 1979/80, 1980/1, 1981/2, (Southampton) 1982/3, 1983/4, 1984/5, 1985/6, 1986/7, (Derby County) 1987/8, 1988/9, 1989/90.
Shimwell, E. (1) (Blackpool) 1948/9.
Sillett, P. (3) (Chelsea) 1954/5.
Sinton, A. (10) (QPR) 1991/2, 1992/93.
Slater, W. (12) (Wolverhampton Wanderers) 1954/5, 1957/8, 1958/9, 1959/60.
Smith, A.M. (13) (Arsenal) 1988/9, 1990/1, 1991/2.
Smith, L. (6) (Arsenal) 1950/1, 1951/2, 1952/3.
Smith, R. (15) (Tottenham Hotspur) 1960/1, 1961/2, 1962/3, 1963/4.
Smith, Tom (1) (Liverpool) 1970/1.
Smith, Trevor (2) (Birmingham City) 1959/60.
Spink, N. (1) (Aston Villa) 1982/3.
Springett, R. (33) (Sheffield Wednesday) 1959/60, 1960/1, 1961/2, 1962/3, 1965/6.
Staniforth, R. (8) (Huddersfield Town) 1953/4, 1954/5.
Statham, D. (3) (West Bromwich Albion) 1982/3.
Stein, B. (1) (Luton Town) 1983/4.
Stepney, A. (1) (Manchester United) 1967/8.
Sterland, M. (1) (Sheffield Wednesday) 1988/9.
Steven, T.M. (36) (Everton) 1984/5, 1985/6, 1986/7, 1987/8, 1988/9 (Glasgow Rangers) 1989/90, 1990/1, (Marseille) 1991/2.
Stevens, G.A. (7) (Tottenham Hotspur) 1984/5, 1985/6.
Stevens, M.G. (46) (Everton) 1984/5, 1985/6, 1986/7, 1987/8 (Rangers) 1988/9, 1989/90, 1990/1, 1991/2.
Stewart, P.A. (3) (Tottenham Hotspur) 1991/2.
Stiles, N. (28) (Manchester United) 1964/5, 1965/6, 1966/7, 1967/8, 1968/9, 1969/70.
Storey-Moore, I. (1) (Nottingham Forest) 1969/70.
Storey, P. (19) (Arsenal) 1970/1, 1971/2, 1972/3.
Streten, B. (1) (Luton Town) 1949/50.
Summerbee, M. (8) (Manchester City) 1967/8, 1971/2, 1972/3.
Sunderland, A. (1) (Arsenal) 1979/80.

Swan, P. (19) (Sheffield Wednesday) 1959/60, 1960/1, 1961/2.
Swift, F. (19) (Manchester City) 1946/7, 1947/8, 1948/9.

Talbot, B. (6) (Ipswich Town) 1976/7, 1979/80.
Tambling, R. (3) (Chelsea) 1962/3, 1965/6.
Taylor, E. (1) (Blackpool) 1953/4.
Taylor, J. (2) (Fulham) 1950/1.
Taylor, P.H. (3) (Liverpool) 1947/8.
Taylor, P.J. (4) (Crystal Palace) 1975/6.
Taylor, T. (19) (Manchester United) 1952/3, 1953/4, 1955/6, 1956/7, 1958/9.
Temple, D. (1) (Everton) 1964/5.
Thomas, Danny (2) (Coventry City) 1982/3.
Thomas, Dave (8) (QPR) 1974/5, 1975/6.
Thomas, G.R. (9) (Crystal Palace) 1990/1, 1991/2.
Thomas, M.L. (2) (Arsenal) 1988/9, 1989/90.
Thompson, P. (16) (Liverpool) 1963/4, 1964/5, 1965/6, 1967/8, 1969/70.
Thompson, P.B. (42) (Liverpool) 1975/6, 1976/7, 1978/9, 1979/80, 1980/1, 1981/2, 1982/3.
Thompson, T. (2) (Aston Villa) 1951/2, (Preston North End) 1956/7.
Thomson, R. (8) (Wolverhampton Wanderers) 1963/4, 1964/5.
Todd, C. (27) (Derby County) 1971/2, 1973/4, 1974/5, 1975/6, 1976/7.
Towers, T. (3) (Sunderland) 1975/6.
Tueart, D. (6) (Manchester City) 1974/5, 1976/7.

Ufton, D. (1) (Charlton Athletic) 1953/4.

Venables, T. (2) (Chelsea) 1964/5.
Viljoen, C. (2) (Ipswich Town) 1974/5.
Viollet, D. (2) (Manchester United) 1959/60, 1961/2.

Waddle, C.R. (62) (Newcastle United) 1984/5, (Tottenham Hotspur) 1985/6, 1986/7, 1987/8, 1988/9, (Marseille) 1989/90, 1990/1, 1991/2.
Waiters, A. (5) (Blackpool) 1963/4, 1964/5.
Walker, D.S. (58) (Nottingham Forest) 1988/9, 1989/90, 1990/1, 1991/2 (Sampdoria) 1992/93.
Wallace, D.L. (1) (Southampton) 1985/6.
Walsh, P. (5) (Luton Town) 1982/3, 1983/4.
Walters, K.M. (1) (Rangers) 1990/91.
Ward, P. (1) (Brighton) 1979/80.
Ward, T. (2) (Derby County) 1947/8, 1948/9.
Watson, D. (12) (Norwich City) 1983/4, 1984/5, 1985/6, 1986/7 (Everton) 1987/8.
Watson D.V. (65) (Sunderland) 1973/4, 1974/5, 1975/6 (Manchester City) 1976/7, 1977/8, (Southampton) 1978/9 (Werder Bremen) 1979/80, (Southampton) 1980/1 , 1981/2, (Stoke City).
Watson, W. (4) (Sunderland) 1949/50, 1950/1.
Webb, N. (26) (Nottingham Forest) 1987/8, 1988/9 (Manchester United) 1989/90, 1991/2.
Weller, K. (4) (Leicester City) 1973/4.
West, G. (3) (Everton) 1968/9.
Wheeler, J. (1) (Bolton Wanderers) 1954/5.
White, D. (1) (Manchester City) 1992/93.
Whitworth, S. (7) (Leicester City) 1974/5, 1975/6.
Whymark, T. (1) (Ipswich Town) 1977/8.

Wignall, F. (2) (Nottingham Forest) 1964/5.
Wilkins, R. (84) (Chelsea) 1975/6, 1976/7, 1977/8, 1978/9, (Manchester United) 1979/80, 1980/1, 1981/2, 1982/3, 1983/4, 1984/5, (AC Milan) 1985/6, 1986/7.
Williams, B. (24) (Wolverhampton Wanderers) 1948/9, 1949/50, 1950/1, 1951/2, 1954/5, 1955/6.
Williams, S. (6) (Southampton) 1982/3, 1983/4, 1984/5.
Willis, A. (1) (Tottenham Hotspur) 1951/2.
Wilshaw, D. (12) (Wolverhampton Wanderers) 1953/4, 1954/5, 1955/6, 1956/7.
Wilson, R. (63) (Huddersfield Town) 1959/60, 1961/2, 1962/3, 1963/4, 1964/5, (Everton) 1965/6, 1966/7, 1967/8.
Winterburn, N. (2) (Arsenal) 1989/90, 1992/93.
Wise, D.F. (5) (Chelsea) 1990/91.
Withe, P. (11) (Aston Villa) 1980/1, 1981/2, 1982/3, 1983/4, 1984/5.
Wood, R. (3) (Manchester United) 1954/5, 1955/6.
Woodcock, A. (42) (Nottingham Forest) 1977/8, 1978/9, 1979/80 (FC Cologne) 1980/1, 1981/2, (Arsenal) 1982/3, 1983/4, 1984/5, 1985/6.
Woods, C.C.E. (43) (Norwich City) 1984/5, 1985/6, 1986/7, (Rangers) 1987/8, 1988/9, 1989/90, 1990/1, (Sheffield Wednesday) 1991/2. 1992/93.
Worthington, F. (8) (Leicester City) 1973/4, 1974/5.
Wright, I.E. (13) (Crystal Palace) 1990/1, 1991/2 (Arsenal) 1992/93.
Wright M. (43) (Southampton) 1983/4, 1984/5, 1985/6, 1986/7, (Derby County) 1987/8, 1988/9, 1989/90, 1990/1, (Liverpool) 1991/2, 1992/93.
Wright, T. (11) (Everton) 1967/8, 1968/9, 1969/70.
Wright, W. (105) (Wolverhampton Wanderers) 1946/7, 1947/8, 1948/9, 1949/50, 1950/1, 1951/2, 1952/3, 1953/4, 1954/5, 1955/6, 1956/7, 1957/8, 1958/9.

Young, G. (1) (Sheffield Wednesday) 1964/5.

NORTHERN IRELAND

Aherne, T. (4) (Belfast Celtic) 1946/7, 1947/8, 1948/9, 1949/50 (Luton Town).
Anderson, T. (22) (Manchester United) 1972/3, 1973/4, 1974/5, (Swindon Town) 1975/6, 1976/7, 1977/8, (Peterborough United) 1978/9.
Armstrong, G. (63) (Tottenham Hotspur) 1976/7, 1977/8, 1978/9, 1979/80, 1980/1, (Watford) 1981/2, 1982/3, (Real Mallorca) 1983/4, 1984/5, (West Bromwich Albion) 1985/6 (Chesterfield).

Barr, H. (3) (Linfield) 1961/2, 1962/3, (Coventry City).
Best, G. (37) (Manchester United) 1963/4, 1964/5, 1965/6, 1966/7, 1967/8, 1968/9, 1969/70, 1970/1 , 1971/2, 1972/3, 1973/4 (Fulham) 1976/7, 1977/8.
Bingham, W. (56) (Sunderland) 1950/1, 1951/2, 1952/3, 1953/4, 1954/5, 1955/6, 1956/7, 1957/8, 1958/9 (Luton Town) 1959/60, 1960/1 (Everton) 1961/2, 1962/3, 1963/4 (Port Vale).
Black, K. (27) (Luton Town) 1987/8, 1988/9, 1989/90, 1990/1, (Nottingham Forest) 1991/2, 1992/93.
Blair, R. (5) (Oldham Athletic) 1974/5, 1975/6.
Blanchflower, D. (54) (Barnsley) 1949/50, 1950/1 (Aston Villa) 1951/2, 1952/3, 1953/4, 1954/5, (Tottenham Hotspur) 1955/6, 1956/7, 1957/8, 1958/9, 1959/60, 1960/1, 1961/2, 1962/3.
Blanchflower, J. (12) (Manchester United) 1953/4, 1954/5, 1955/6, 1956/7, 1957/8.
Bowler, G. (3) (Hull City) 1949/50.
Braithwaite, R. (10) (Linfield) 1961/2, 1962/3 (Middlesbrough) 1963/4, 1964/5.

Brennan, R. (5) (Luton Town) 1948/9, 1949/50 (Birmingham City) (Fulham), 1950/1.
Briggs, R. (2) (Manchester United) 1961/2, 1964/5 (Swansea).
Brotherston, N. (27) (Blackburn Rovers) 1979/80, 1980/1, 1981/2, 1982/3, 1983/4, 1984/5.
Bruce, W. (2) (Glentoran) 1960/1, 1966/7.

Campbell, A. (2) (Crusaders) 1962/3, 1964/5.
Campbell, D.A. (10) (Nottingham Forest) 1985/6, 1986/7, 1987/8 (Charlton Athletic).
Campbell, J. (2) (Fulham) 1950/1.
Campbell, R.M. (2) (Bradford City) 1981/2.
Campbell, W. (6) (Dundee) 1967/8, 1968/9, 1969/70.
Carey, J. (7) (Manchester United) 1946/7, 1947/8, 1948/9.
Casey, T. (12) (Newcastle United) 1954/5, 1955/6, 1956/7, 1957/8, 1958/9, (Portsmouth).
Caskey, A. (7) (Derby County) 1978/9, 1979/80, 1981/2 (Tulsa Roughnecks).
Cassidy, T. (24) (Newcastle United) 1970/1, 1971/2, 1973/4, 1974/5, 1975/6, 1976/7, 1979/80 (Burnley) 1980/1, 1981/2.
Caughey, M. (2) (Linfield) 1985/6.
Clarke, C.J. (38) (Bournemouth) 1985/6, 1986/7 (Southampton) 1987/8, 1988/9, 1989/90, 1990/1 (Portsmouth), 1991/2, 1992/93.
Cleary, J. (5) (Glentoran) 1981/2, 1982/3, 1983/4, 1984/5.
Clements, D. (48) (Coventry City) 1964/5, 1965/6, 1966/7, 1967/8, 1968/9, 1969/70, 1970/1, 1971/2 (Sheffield Wednesday) 1972/3 (Everton) 1973/4, 1974/5, 1975/6 (New York Cosmos).
Cochrane, D. (10) (Leeds United) 1946/7, 1947/8, 1948/9, 1949/50.
Cochrane, T. (26) (Coleraine) 1975/6, (Burnley) 1977/8, 1978/9, (Middlesbrough) 1979/80, 1980/1, 1981/2, (Gillingham) 1983/4.
Cowan, J. (1) (Newcastle United) 1969/70.
Coyle, F. (4) (Coleraine) 1955/6, 1956/7, 1957/8 (Nottingham Forest).
Coyle, L. (1) (Derry C) 1988/9.
Coyle, R. (5) (Sheffield Wednesday) 1972/3, 1973/4.
Craig, D. (25) (Newcastle United) 1966/7, 1967/8, 1968/9, 1969/70, 1970/1, 1971/2, 1972/3, 1973/4, 1974/5.
Crossan, E. (3) (Blackburn Rovers) 1949/50, 1950/1, 1954/5.
Crossan, J. (23) (Rotterdam Sparta) 1959/60, 1962/3 (Sunderland), 1963/4, 1964/5, (Manchester City) 1965/6, 1966/7, 1967/8 (Middlesbrough).
Cunningham, W. (30) (St Mirren) 1950/1, 1952/3, 1953/4, 1954/5, 1955/6, 1956/7, (Leicester City) 1957/8, 1958/9, 1959/60, 1960/1 (Dunfermline Athletic) 1961/2.
Cush, W. (26) (Glentoran) 1950/1, 1953/4, 1956/7, 1957/8 (Leeds United) 1958/9, 1959/60, 1960/1 (Portadown) 1961/2.

D'Arcy, S. (5) (Chelsea) 1951/2, 1952/3 (Brentford).
Dennison, R. (16) (Wolverhampton Wanderers) 1987/8, 1988/9, 1989/90, 1990/1, 1991/2, 1992/93.
Devine, J. (1) (Glentoran) 1989/90.
Dickson, D. (4) (Coleraine) 1969/70, 1972/3.
Dickson, T. (1) (Linfield) 1956/7.
Dickson, W. (12) (Chelsea) 1950/1, 1951/2, 1952/3 (Arsenal) 1953/4, 1954/5.
Doherty, L. (2) (Linfield) 1984/5, 1987/8.
Doherty P. (6) (Derby County) 1946/7, (Huddersfield Town) 1947/8, 1948/9, (Doncaster Rovers) 1950/1.

239

Donaghy, M. (84) (Luton Town) 1979/80, 1980/1, 1981/2, 1982/3, 1983/4, 1984/5, 1985/6, 1986/7, 1987/8, (Manchester United) 1988/9, 1989/90, 1990/1, 1991/2 (Chelsea) 1992/93.

Dougan D. (43) (Portsmouth) 1957/8, 1959/60, (Blackburn Rovers), 1960/1, 1962/3 (Aston Villa) 1965/6 (Leicester City), 1966/7 (Wolverhampton Wanderers) 1967/8, 1968/9, 1969/70, 1970/1, 1971/2, 1972/3.

Douglas, J.P. (1) (Belfast Celtic) 1946/7.

Dowd, H. (3) (Glentoran) 1972/3, 1974/5 (Sheffield Wednesday).

Dowie, I. (18) (Luton Town) 1989/90, 1990/1, (Southampton) 1991/2, 1992/93.

Dunlop, G. (4) (Linfield) 1984/5, 1986/7.

Eglington T. (6) (Everton) 1946/7, 1947/8, 1948/9.

Elder, A. (40) (Burnley) 1959/60, 1960/1, 1961/2, 1962/3, 1963/4, 1964/5, 1965/6, 1966/7, (Stoke City) 1967/8, 1968/9, 1969/70.

Farrell, P. (7) (Everton) 1946/7, 1947/8, 1948/9.

Feeney, J. (2) (Linfield) 1946/7 (Swansea City) 1949/50.

Feeney, W. (1) (Glentoran) 1975/6.

Ferguson, W. (2) (Linfield) 1965/6, 1966/7.

Ferris, R. (3) (Birmingham City) 1949/50, 1950/1, 1951/2.

Fettis, A. (3) (Hull City) 1991/2, 1992/93.

Finney, T. (14) (Sunderland) 1974/5, 1975/6 (Cambridge United), 1979/80.

Fleming, J.G. (21) (Nottingham Forest) 1986/7, 1987/8, 1988/9 (Manchester City) 1989/90, 1990/1 (Barnsley), 1991/2, 1992/93.

Forde, T. (4) (Ards) 1958/9, 1960/1.

Gallogly, C. (2) (Huddersfield Town) 1950/1.

Garton, R. (1) (Oxford United) 1968/9.

Gorman, W. (4) (Brentford) 1946/7, 1947/8.

Graham, W. (14) (Doncaster Rovers) 1950/1, 1951/2, 1952/3, 1953/4, 1954/5, 1955/6, 1958/9.

Gray, P. (4) (Luton Town) 1992/93.

Gregg, H. (25) (Doncaster Rovers) 1953/4, 1956/7, 1957/8, (Manchester United) 1958/9, 1959/60, 1960/1, 1961/2, 1963/4.

Hamilton, B. (50) (Linfield) 1968/9, 1970/1, 1971/2 (Ipswich Town), 1972/3, 1973/4, 1974/5, 1975/6 (Everton) 1976/7, 1977/8, (Millwall) 1978/9, (Swindon Town).

Hamilton, W. (41) (QPR) 1977/8, 1979/80 (Burnley) 1980/1, 1981/2, 1982/3, 1983/4, 1984/5, (Oxford United) 1985/6.

Harkin, T. (5) (Southport) 1967/8, 1968/9 (Shrewsbury Town), 1969/70, 1970/1.

Harvey, M. (34) (Sunderland) 1960/1, 1961/2, 1962/3, 1963/4, 1964/5, 1965/6, 1966/7, 1967/8, 1968/9, 1969/70, 1970/1.

Hatton, S. (2) (Linfield) 1962/3.

Healy, F. (4) (Coleraine) 1981/2 (Glentoran) 1982/3.

Hegan, D. (7) (West Bromwich Albion) 1969/70, 1971/2 (Wolverhampton Wanderers) 1972/3.

Hill, C.F. (6) (Sheffield U), 1989/90, 1990/1, 1991/2.

Hill, J. (7) (Norwich City) 1958/9, 1959/60, 1960/1, (Everton) 1961/2, 1963/4.

Hinton, E. (7) (Fulham) 1946/7, 1947/8 (Millwall) 1950/1.

Hughes, M.E. (11) (Manchester City) 1991/2 (Strasbourg) 1992/93.

Hughes, P. (3) (Bury) 1986/7.

Hughes, W. (1) (Bolton Wanderers) 1950/1.

Humphries, W. (14) (Ards) 1961/2 (Coventry City) 1962/3, 1963/4, 1964/5 (Swansea Town).
Hunter, A. (53) (Blackburn Rovers) 1969/70, 1970/1, 1971/2 (Ipswich Town) 1972/3, 1973/4, 1974/5, 1975/6, 1976/7, 1977/8, 1978/9, 1979/80.

Irvine, R. (8) (Linfield) 1961/2, 1962/3 (Stoke City) 1964/5.
Irvine, W. (23) (Burnley) 1962/3, 1964/5, 1965/6, 1966/7, 1967/8, 1968/9 (Preston North End) (Brighton & Hove Albion) 1971/2.

Jackson, T. (35) (Everton) 1968/9, 1969/70, 1970/1 (Nottingham Forest) 1971/2, 1972/3, 1973/4, 1974/5 (Manchester United) 1975/6, 1976/7.
Jamison, A. (1) (Glentoran) 1975/6.
Jennings, P. (119) (Watford) 1963/4, 1964/5, (Tottenham Hotspur), 1965/6, 1966/7, 1967/8, 1968/9, 1969/70, 1970/1, 1971/2, 1972/3, 1973/4, 1974/5, 1975/6, 1976/7, (Arsenal) 1977/8, 1978/9, 1979/80, 1980/1, 1981/2, 1982/3, 1983/4, 1984/5, (Tottenham Hotspur) 1985/6.
Johnston, W. (1) (Glentoran) 1961/2, (Oldham Athletic) 1965/6.
Jones, J. (3) (Glenavon) 1955/6, 1956/7.

Keane, T. (1) (Swansea Town) 1948/9.
Kee, P.V. (7) (Oxford United), 1989/90, 1990/91.
Keith, R. (23) (Newcastle United) 1957/8, 1958/9, 1959/60, 1960/1, 1961/2.
Kelly, H. (4) (Fulham) 1949/50 (Southampton) 1950/1.
Kelly, P. (1) (Barnsley) 1949/50.

Lawther, I. (4) (Sunderland) 1959/60, 1960/1, 1961/2 (Blackburn Rovers).
Lockhart, N. (8) (Linfield) 1946/7, 1949/50, (Coventry City) 1950/1, 1951/2, 1953/4, (Aston Villa) 1954/5, 1955/6.
Lutton, B. (6) (Wolverhampton Wanderers) 1969/70, 1972/3 (West Ham United) 1973/4.

Magill, E. (26) (Arsenal) 1961/2, 1962/3, 1963/4, 1964/5, 1965/6 (Brighton & Hove Albion).
Magilton, J. (15) (Oxford United) 1990/1, 1991/2, 1992/93.
Martin, C. (6) (Glentoran) 1946/7, 1947/8 (Leeds United) 1948/9 (Aston Villa) 1949/50.
McAdams, W. (15) (Manchester City) 1953/4, 1954/5, 1956/7, 1957/8, 1960/1 (Bolton Wanderers) 1961/2 (Leeds United).
McAlinden, J. (2) (Portsmouth) 1946/7, 1948/9, (Southend United).
McBride, S. (4) (Glenavon) 1990/1, 1991/2.
McCabe, J. (6) (Leeds United) 1948/9, 1949/50, 1950/1, 1952/3, 1953/4.
McCavana, T. (3) (Coleraine) 1954/5, 1955/6.
McCleary, J.W. (1) (Cliftonville) 1954/5.
McClelland, J. (6) (Arsenal) 1960/1, 1965/6 (Fulham).
McClelland, J. (53) (Mansfield Town) 1979/80, 1980/1, 1981/2 (Rangers) 1982/3, 1983/4, 1984/5 (Watford) 1985/6, 1986/7, 1987/8, 1988/9 (Leeds U) 1989/90.
McCourt, F. (6) (Manchester City) 1951/2, 1952/3.
McCoy, R. (1) (Coleraine) 1986/7.
McCreery, D. (67) (Manchester United) 1975/6, 1976/7, 1977/8, 1978/9, 1979/80 (QPR) 1980/1 (Tulsa Roughnecks) 1981/2, 1982/3 (Newcastle United), 1983/4, 1984/5, 1985/6, 1986/7, 1987/8, 1988/9 (Hearts) 1989/90.
McCrory, S. (1) (Southend United) 1957/8.
McCullough, W. (10) (Arsenal) 1960/1, 1962/3, 1963/4, 1964/5, 1966/7, (Millwall).

McCurdy, C. (1) (Linfield) 1979/80.
McDonald, A. (41) (QPR) 1985/6, 1986/7, 1987/8, 1988/9, 1990/1, 1991/2, 1992/93.
McElhinney, G. (6) (Bolton Wanderers) 1983/4, 1984/5.
McFaul, I. (6) (Linfield) 1966/7, 1969/70 (Newcastle United) 1970/1, 1971/2, 1972/3, 1973/4.
McGarry, J.K. (3) (Cliftonville) 1950/1.
McGaughey, M. (1) (Linfield) 1984/5.
McGrath, R. (21) (Tottenham Hotspur) 1973/4, 1974/5, 1975/6 (Manchester United) 1976/7, 1977/8, 1978/9.
McIlroy, J. (55) (Burnley) 1951/2, 1952/3, 1953/4, 1954/5, 1955/6, 1956/7, 1957/8, 1958/9, 1959/60, 1960/1, 1961/2, 1962/3, 1965/6 (Stoke City).
McIlroy, S.B. (88) (Manchester United) 1971/2, 1973/4, 1974/5, 1975/6, 1976/7, 1977/8, 1978/9, 1979/80, 1980/1, 1981/2, (Stoke City), 1982/3, 1983/4, 1984/5 (Manchester City) 1985/6, 1986/7.
McKeag, W. (2) (Glentoran) 1967/8.
McKenna, J. (7) (Huddersfield Town) 1949/50, 1950/1, 1951/2.
McKenzie, R. (1) (Airdrieonians) 1966/7.
McKinney, W. (1) (Falkirk) 1965/6.
McKnight, A. (10) (Celtic) 1987/8, (West Ham United) 1988/9.
McLaughlin, J. (12) (Shrewsbury Town) 1961/2, 1962/3 (Swansea City), 1963/4, 1964/5, 1965/6.
McMichael, A. (39) (Newcastle United) 1949/50, 1950/1, 1951/2, 1952/3, 1953/4, 1954/5, 1955/6, 1956/7, 1957/8, 1958/9, 1959/60.
McMillan, S. (2) (Manchester United) 1962/3.
McMordie, E. (21) (Middlesbrough) 1968/9, 1969/70, 1970/1, 1971/2, 1972/3.
McMorran, E. (15) (Belfast Celtic) 1946/7 (Barnsley) 1950/1, 1951/2, 1952/3, (Doncaster Rovers) 1953/4, 1955/6, 1956/7.
McNally, B.A. (5) (Shrewsbury Town) 1985/6, 1986/7, 1987/8.
McParland, P. (34) (Aston Villa) 1953/4, 1954/5, 1955/6, 1956/7, 1957/8, 1958/9, 1959/60, 1960/1, 1961/2 (Wolverhampton Wanderers).
Montgomery, F.J. (1) (Coleraine) 1954/5.
Moore, C. (1) (Glentoran) 1948/9.
Moreland, V. (6) (Derby County) 1978/9, 1979/80.
Morgan, S. (18) (Port Vale) 1971/2, 1972/3, 1973/4 (Aston Villa), 1974/5, 1975/6 (Brighton & Hove Albion) (Sparta Rotterdam) 1978/9.
Morrow, S.J. (10) (Arsenal) 1989/90, 1990/1, 1991/2, 1992/93.
Mullan, G. (4) (Glentoran) 1982/3.

Napier, R. (1) (Bolton Wanderers) 1965/6.
Neill, T. (59) (Arsenal) 1960/1, 1961/2, 1962/3, 1963/4, 1964/5, 1965/6, 1966/7, 1967/8, 1968/9, 1969/70 (Hull City) 1970/1, 1971/2, 1972/3.
Nelson, S. (51) (Arsenal) 1969/70, 1970/1, 1971/2, 1972/3, 1973/4, 1974/5, 1975/6, 1976/7, 1977/8, 1978/9, 1979/80, 1980/1, 1981/2 (Brighton & Hove Albion).
Nicholl, C. (51) (Aston Villa) 1974/5, 1975/6, 1976/7 (Southampton), 1977/8, 1978/9, 1979/80, 1980/1, 1981/2, 1982/3 (Grimsby Town) 1983/4.
Nicholl, J.M. (73) (Manchester United) 1975/6, 1976/7, 1977/8, 1978/9, 1979/80, 1980/1, 1981/2 (Toronto Blizzard) 1982/3 (Sunderland) (Toronto Blizzard) (Rangers) 1983/4 (Toronto Blizzard) 1984/5 (West Bromwich Albion) 1985/6.
Nicholson, J. (41) (Manchester United) 1960/1, 1961/2, 1962/3, 1964/5, (Huddersfield Town) 1965/6, 1966/7, 1967/8, 1968/9, 1969/70, 1970/1, 1971/2.

O'Doherty, A. (2) (Coleraine) 1969/70.
O'Driscoll, J. (3) (Swansea City) 1948/9.

242

O'Kane, L. (20) (Nottingham Forest) 1969/70, 1970/1, 1971/2, 1972/3, 1973/4, 1974/5.

O'Neill, C. (3) (Motherwell) 1988/9, 1989/90, 1990/91.

O'Neill, H.M. (64) (Distillery) 1971/2 (Nottingham Forest) 1972/3, 1973/4, 1974/5, 1975/6, 1976/7, 1977/8, 1978/9, 1979/80, 1980/1 (Norwich City) 1981/2 (Manchester City) (Norwich City) 1982/3 (Notts County) 1983/4, 1984/5.

O'Neill, J. (1) (Sunderland) 1961/2.

O'Neill, J. (39) (Leicester City) 1979/80, 1980/1, 1981/2, 1982/3, 1983/4, 1984/5, 1985/6.

O'Neill, M.A. (22) (Newcastle United) 1987/8, 1988/9 (Dundee United) 1989/90, 1990/1, 1991/2, 1992/93.

Parke, J. (13) (Linfield) 1963/4 (Hibernian), 1964/5 (Sunderland), 1965/6, 1966/7, 1967/8.

Peacock, R. (31) (Celtic) 1951/2, 1952/3, 1953/4, 1954/5, 1955/6, 1956/7, 1957/8, 1958/9, 1959/60, 1960/1 (Coleraine) 1961/2.

Penney, S. (17) (Brighton & Hove Albion) 1984/5, 1985/6, 1986/7, 1987/8, 1988/9.

Platt, J.A. (23) (Middlesbrough) 1975/6, 1977/8, 1979/80, 1980/1, 1981/2, 1982/3, (Ballymena United) 1983/4 (Coleraine) 1985/6.

Quinn, J.M. (34) (Blackburn Rovers) 1984/5, 1985/6, 1986/7, 1987/8 (Leicester) 1988/9 (Bradford City) 1989/90 (West Ham United), 1990/1, (Bournemouth) 1991/2 (Reading) 1992/93.

Rafferty, P. (1) (Linfield) 1979/80.

Ramsey, P. (14) (Leicester City) 1983/4, 1984/5, 1985/6, 1986/7, 1987/8, 1988/9.

Rice, P. (49) (Arsenal) 1968/9, 1969/70, 1970/1, 1971/2, 1972/3, 1973/4, 1974/5, 1975/6, 1976/7, 1977/8, 1978/9, 1979/80.

Rogan, A. (17) (Celtic) 1987/8, 1988/9, 1989/90, 1990/1, 1991/2.

Ross, E. (1) (Newcastle United) 1968/9.

Russell, A. (1) (Linfield) 1946/7.

Ryan, R. (1) (West Bromwich Albion) 1949/50.

Sanchez, L.P. (3) (Wimbledon) 1986/7, 1988/9.

Scott, J. (2) (Grimsby Town) 1957/8.

Scott, P. (10) (Everton) 1974/5, 1975/6, (York City) 1977/8, (Aldershot) 1978/9.

Sharkey, P. (1) (Ipswich Town) 1975/6.

Shields, J. (1) (Southampton) 1956/7.

Simpson, W. (12) (Rangers) 1950/1, 1953/4, 1954/5, 1956/7, 1957/8, 1958/9.

Sloan, D. (2) (Oxford) 1968/9, 1970/1.

Sloan, T. (3) (Manchester United) 1978/9.

Sloan, W. (1) (Arsenal) 1946/7.

Smyth, S. (9) (Wolverhampton Wanderers) 1947/8, 1948/9, 1949/50 (Stoke City) 1951/2.

Smyth, W. (4) (Distillery) 1948/9, 1953/4.

Spence, D. (29) (Bury) 1974/5, 1975/6, (Blackpool) 1976/7, 1978/9, 1979/80, (Southend United) 1980/1, 1981/2.

Stevenson, A. (3) (Everton) 1946/7, 1947/8.

Sfewart, A. (7) (Glentoran) 1966/7, 1967/8 (Derby) 1968/9.

Stewart, D. (1) (Hull City) 1977/8.

Stewart, I. (31) (QPR) 1981/2, 1982/3, 1983/4, 1984/5, (Newcastle United) 1985/6, 1986/7.

Stewart, T. (1) (Linfield) 1960/1.

243

Taggart, G.P. (21) (Barnsley) 1989/90, 1990/1, 1991/2, 1992/93.
Todd, S. (11) (Burnley) 1965/6, 1966/7, 1967/8, 1968/9, 1969/70 (Sheffield Wednesday) 1970/1.
Trainor, D. (1) (Crusaders) 1966/7.
Tully, C. (10) (Celtic) 1948/9, 1949/50, 1951/2, 1952/3, 1953/4, 1955/6, 1958/9.

Uprichard, N. (18) (Swindon Town) 1951/2, 1952/3 (Portsmouth) 1954/5, 1955/6, 1957/8, 1958/9.

Vernon, J. (17) (Belfast Celtic) 1946/7 (West Bromwich Albion) 1947/8, 1948/9, 1949/50, 1950/1 , 1951/2.

Walker, J. (1) (Doncaster Rovers) 1954/5.
Walsh, D. (9) (West Bromwich Albion) 1946/7, 1947/8, 1948/9, 1949/50.
Walsh, W. (5) (Manchester City) 1947/8, 1948/9.
Watson, P. (1) (Distillery) 1970/1.
Welsh, S. (4) (Carlisle United) 1965/6, 1966/7.
Whiteside, N. (38) (Manchester United) 1981/2, 1982/3, 1983/4, 1984/5, 1985/6, 1986/7, 1987/8, (Everton) 1989/90.
Williams, P. (1) (WBA) 1990/1.
Wilson, D.J. (24) (Brighton & Hove Albion) 1986/7 (Luton) 1987/8, 1988/9, 1989/90, 1990/1, (Sheffield Wednesday) 1991/2.
Wilson, K.J. (33) (Ipswich Town) 1986/7 (Chelsea) 1987/8, 1988/9, 1989/90, 1990/1, 1991/2 (Notts County) 1992/93.
Wilson, S. (12) (Glenavon) 1961/2, 1963/4, (Falkirk) 1964/5 (Dundee), 1965/6, 1966/7, 1967/8.
Worthington, N. (44) (Sheffield Wednesday) 1983/4, 1984/5, 1985/6, 1986/7, 1987/8, 1988/9, 1989/90, 1990/1, 1991/2, 1992/93.
Wright, T.J. (15) (Newcastle United) 1988/9, 1989/90, 1991/2, 1992/93.

SCOTLAND

Aird, J. (4) (Burnley) 1953/4.
Aitken, G.G. (8) (East Fife) 1948/9, 1949/50, 1952/3 (Sunderland) 1953/4.
Aitken, R. (57) (Celtic) 1979/80, 1982/3, 1983/4, 1984/5, 1985/6, 1986/7, 1987/8, (Newcastle United) 1989/90, (St Mirren) 1991/2.
Albiston, A. (14) (Manchester United) 1981/2, 1983/4, 1984/5, 1985/6.
Allan, T. (2) (Dundee) 1973/4.
Anderson, J. (1) (Leicester City) 1953/4.
Archibald, S. (27) (Aberdeen) 1979/80 (Tottenham Hotspur) 1980/1, 1981/2, 1982/3, 1983/4, 1984/5, (Barcelona) 1985/6.
Auld, B. (3) (Celtic) 1958/9, 1959/60.

Baird, H. (1) (Airdrieonians) 1955/6.
Baird, S. (7) (Rangers) 1956/7, 1957/8.
Bannon, E. (11) (Dundee United) 1979/80, 1982/3, 1983/4, 1985/6.
Bauld, W. (3) (Heart of Midlothian) 1949/50.
Baxter, J. (34) (Rangers) 1960/1, 1961/2, 1962/3, 1963/4, 1964/5 (Sunderland) 1965/6, 1966/7, 1967/8.
Bell, W. (2) (Leeds United) 1965/6.
Bett, J. (25) (Rangers) 1981/2, 1982/3 (Lokeren) 1983/4, 1984/5 (Aberdeen) 1985/6, 1986/7, 1987/8, 1988/9, 1989/90.
Black, E. (2) (Metz) 1987/8.

Black, I. (1) (Southampton) 1947/8.
Blacklaw, A. (3) (Burnley) 1962/3, 1965/6.
Blackley, J. (7) (Hibernian) 1973/4, 1975/6, 1976/7.
Blair, J. (1) (Blackpool) 1946/7.
Blyth, J. (2) (Coventry City) 1977/8.
Bone, J. (2) (Norwich City) 1971/2, 1972/3.
Booth, S. (3) (Aberdeen) 1992/93.
Bowman, D. (4) (Dundee United) 1991/2, 1992/93.
Boyd, T. (17) (Motherwell) 1990/1 (Chelsea) 1991/2 (Celtic) 1992/93.
Brand, R. (8) (Rangers) 1960/1, 1961/2.
Brazil, A. (13) (Ipswich Town) 1979/80, 1981/2, 1982/3 (Tottenham Hotspur).
Bremner, D. (1) (Hibernian) 1975/6.
Bremner, W. (54) (Leeds United) 1964/5, 1965/6, 1966/7, 1967/8, 1968/9, 1969/70,
1970/1, 1971/2, 1972/3, 1973/4, 1974/5, 1975/6.
Brennan, F. (7) (Newcastle United) 1946/7, 1952/3, 1963/4.
Brogan, J. (4) (Celtic) 1970/1.
Brown, A. (14) (East Fife) 1949/50 (Blackpool) 1951/2, 1952/3, 1953/4.
Brown, H. (3) (Partick Thistle) 1946/7.
Brown, J. (1) (Sheffield United) 1974/5.
Brown, R. (3) (Rangers) 1946/7, 1948/9, 1951/2.
Brown, W. (28) (Dundee) 1957/8, 1958/9, 1959/60 (Tottenham Hotspur) 1961/2, '
1962/3, 1963/4, 1964/5, 1965/6.
Brownlie, J. (7) (Hibernian) 1970/1, 1971/2, 1972/3, 1975/6.
Buchan, M. (34) (Aberdeen) 1971/2 (Manchester United), 1972/3, 1973/4, 1974/5,
1975/6, 1976/7, 1977/8, 1978/9.
Buckley, P. (3) (Aberdeen) 1953/4, 1954/5.
Burley, G. (11) (Ipswich Town) 1978/9, 1979/80, 1981/2.
Burns, F. (1) (Manchester United) 1969/70.
Burns, K. (20) (Birmingham City) 1973/4, 1974/5, 1976/7 (Nottingham Forest)
1977/8, 1978/9, 1979/80, 1980/1.
Burns, T. (8) (Celtic) 1980/1, 1981/2, 1982/3, 1987/8.

Caldow, E. (40) (Rangers) 1956/7, 1957/8, 1958/9, 1959/60, 1960/1, 1961/2, 1962/3.
Callaghan, W. (2) (Dunfermline) 1969/70.
Campbell, R. (5) (Falkirk) 1946/7 (Chelsea) 1949/50.
Campbell, W. (5) (Morton) 1946/7, 1947/8.
Carr, W. (6) (Coventry City) 1969/70, 1970/1, 1971/2, 1972/3.
Chalmers, S. (5) (Celtic) 1964/5, 1965/6, 1966/7.
Clark, J. (4) (Celtic) 1965/6, 1966/7.
Clark, R. (17) (Aberdeen) 1967/8, 1969/70, 1970/1, 1971/2, 1972/3.
Clarke, S. (5) (Chelsea) 1987/8.
Collins, J. (14) (Hibernian) 1987/8, 1989/90, 1990/1 (Celtic) 1991/2, 1992/93.
Collins, R. (31) (Celtic) 1950/1, 1954/5, 1955/6, 1956/7, 1957/8, 1958/9, (Everton)
1964/5, (Leeds United).
Colquhoun, E. (9) (Sheffield United) 1971/2, 1972/3.
Colquhoun, J. (1) (Hearts) 1987/8.
Combe, R. (3) (Hibernian) 1947/8.
Conn, A. (1) (Heart of Midlothian) 1955/6.
Conn, A. (2) (Tottenham Hotspur) 1974/5.
Connachan, E. (2) (Dunfermline Athletic) 1961/2.
Connelly, G. (2) (Celtic) 1973/4.
Connolly, J. (1) (Everton) 1972/3.
Connor, R. (4) (Dundee) 1985/6 (Aberdeen) 1987/8, 1988/9, 1990/91.
Cooke, C. (16) (Dundee) 1965/6 (Chelsea) 1967/8, 1968/9, 1969/70, 1970/1, 1974/5.

245

Cooper, D. (22) (Rangers) 1979/80, 1983/4, 1984/5, 1985/6, 1986/7 (Motherwell) 1989/90.
Cormack, P. (9) (Hibernian) 1965/6, 1969/70 (Nottingham Forest) 1970/1, 1971/2.
Cowan, J. (25) (Morton) 1947/8, 1948/9, 1949/50, 1950/1, 1951/2 (Motherwell).
Cowie, D. (20) (Dundee) 1952/3, 1953/4, 1954/5, 1955/6, 1956/7, 1957/8.
Cox, C. (1) (Hearts) 1947/8.
Cox, S. (24) (Rangers) 1947/8, 1948/9, 1949/50, 1950/1, 1951/2, 1952/3, 1953/4.
Craig, J. (1) (Celtic) 1976/7.
Craig, J.P. (1) (Celtic) 1967/8.
Craig, T. (1) (Newcastle United) 1975/6.
Crerand, P. (16) (Celtic) 1960/1, 1961/2, 1962/3 (Manchester United) 1963/4, 1964/5, 1965/6.
Cropley, A. (2) (Hibernian) 1971/2.
Cruickshank, J. (6) (Heart of Midlothian) 1963/4, 1969/70, 1970/1, 1975/6.
Cullen, M. (1) (Luton Town) 1955/6.
Cumming, J. (9) (Heart of Midlothian) 1954/5, 1959/60.
Cunningham, W. (8) (Preston North End) 1953/4, 1954/5.
Curran, H. (5) (Wolverhampton Wanderers) 1969/70, 1970/1.

Dalglish, K. (102) (Celtic) 1971/2, 1972/3, 1973/4, 1974/5, 1975/6, 1976/7, (Liverpool) 1977/8, 1978/9, 1979/80, 1980/1, 1981/2, 1982/3, 1983/4, 1984/5, 1985/6, 1986/7.
Davidson, J. (8) (Partick Thistle) 1953/4, 1954/5.
Dawson, A. (5) (Rangers) 1979/80, 1982/3.
Deans, D. (2) (Celtic) 1974/5.
Delaney, J. (4) (Manchester United) 1946/7, 1947/8.
Dick, J. (1) (West Ham United) 1958/9.
Dickson, W. (5) (Kilmarnock) 1969/70, 1970/1.
Docherty, T. (25) (Preston North End) 1951/2, 1952/3, 1953/4, 1954/5, 1956/7, 1957/8, 1958/9 (Arsenal).
Dodds, D. (2) (Dundee United) 1983/4.
Donachie, W. (35) (Manchester City) 1971/2, 1972/3, 1973/4, 1975/6, 1976/7, 1977/8, 1978/9.
Dougall, C. (1) (Birmingham City) 1946/7.
Dougan, R. (1) (Heart of Midlothian) 1949/50.
Doyle, J. (1) (Ayr United) 1975/6.
Duncan, A. (6) (Hibernian) 1974/5, 1975/6.
Duncan, D. (3) (East Fife) 1947/8.
Duncanson, J. (1) (Rangers) 1946/7.
Durie, G.S. (23) (Chelsea) 1987/8, 1988/9, 1989/90, 1990/1, (Tottenham Hotspur) 1991/2, 1992/93.
Durrant, I. (9) (Rangers) 1987/8, 1988/9, 1992/93.

Evans, A. (4) (Aston Villa) 1981/2.
Evans, R. (48) (Celtic) 1948/9, 1949/50, 1950/1, 1951/2, 1952/3, 1953/4, 1954/5, 1955/6, 1956/7, 1957/8, 1958/9, 1959/60 (Chelsea).
Ewing, T. (2) (Partick Thistle) 1957/8.

Farm, G. (10) (Blackpool) 1952/3, 1953/4, 1958/9.
Ferguson, D. (2) (Rangers) 1987/8.
Ferguson, D. (6) (Dundee United) 1991/2, 1992/93.
Ferguson, I. (3) (Rangers) 1988/9.
Ferguson, R. (7) (Kilmarnock) 1965/6, 1966/7.

Fernie, W. (12) (Celtic) 1953/4, 1954/5, 1956/7, 1957/8.
Flavell, R. (2) (Airdrieonians) 1946/7.
Fleck, R. (4) (Norwich City) 1989/90, 1990/1.
Fleming, C. (1) (East Fife) 1953/4.
Forbes, A. (14) (Sheffield United) 1946/7, 1947/8 (Arsenal) 1949/50, 1950/1, 1951/2.
Ford, D. (3) (Heart of Midlothian) 1973/4.
Forrest, J. (1) (Motherwell) 1957/8.
Forrest, J. (5) (Rangers) 1965/6 (Aberdeen) 1970/1.
Forsyth, A. (10) (Partick Thistle) 1971/2, 1972/3 (Manchester United) 1974/5, 1975/6.
Forsyth, C. (4) (Kilmarnock) 1963/4, 1964/5.
Forsyth, T. (22) (Motherwell) 1970/1 (Rangers) 1973/4, 1975/6, 1976/7, 1977/8.
Fraser, D. (2) (West Bromwich Albion) 1967/8, 1968/9.
Fraser, W. (2) (Sunderland) 1954/5.

Gabriel, J. (2) (Everton) 1960/1, 1961/2.
Gallacher, K.W. (17) (Dundee United) 1987/8, 1988/9, 1990/91 (Coventry City), 1991/2 (Blackburn Rovers) 1992/93.
Galloway, M. (1) (Celtic) 1991/2.
Gardiner, W. (1) (Motherwell) 1957/8.
Gemmell, T. (2) (St Mirren) 1954/5.
Gemmell, T. (18) (Celtic) 1965/6, 1966/7, 1967/8, 1968/9, 1969/70, 1970/1.
Gemmill, A. (43) (Derby County) 1970/1, 1971/2, 1975/6, 1976/7, 1977/8 (Nottingham Forest) 1978/9 (Birmingham City) 1979/80, 1980/1.
Gibson, D. (7) (Leicester City) 1962/3, 1963/4, 1964/5.
Gillespie, G.T. (13) (Liverpool) 1987/8, 1988/9, 1989/90, (Celtic) 1990/91.
Gilzean, A. (22) (Dundee) 1963/4, 1964/5 (Tottenham Hotspur) 1965/6, 1967/8, 1968/9, 1969/70, 1970/1.
Glavin, R. (1) (Celtic) 1976/7.
Glen, A. (2) (Aberdeen) 1955/6.
Goram, A.L. (28) (Oldham Athletic) 1985/6, 1986/7, (Hibernian) 1988/9, 1989/90, 1990/1, (Rangers) 1991/2, 1992/93.
Gough, C.R. (61) (Dundee United) 1982/3, 1983/4, 1984/5, 1985/6, 1986/7 (Tottenham Hotspur) 1987/8 (Rangers) 1988/9, 1989/90, 1990/1, 1991/2, 1992/93.
Govan, J. (6) (Hibernian) 1947/8, 1948/9.
Graham, A. (10) (Leeds United) 1977/8, 1978/9, 1979/80, 1980/1.
Graham, G. (12) (Arsenal) 1971/2, 1972/3 (Manchester United).
Grant, J. (2) (Hibernian) 1958/9.
Grant, P. (2) (Celtic) 1988/9.
Gray, A. (20) (Aston Villa) 1975/6, 1976/7, 1978/9 (Wolverhampton Wanderers) 1979/80, 1980/1, 1981/2, 1982/3, 1984/5 (Everton).
Gray, E. (12) (Leeds United) 1968/9, 1969/70, 1970/71, 1971/2, 1975/6, 1976/7.
Gray F. (32) (Leeds United) 1975/6, 1978/9, 1979/80 (Nottingham Forest) 1980/1, (Leeds United) 1981/2, 1982/3.
Green, A. (6) (Blackpool) 1970/1 (Newcastle United) 1971/2.
Greig, J. (44) (Rangers) 1963/4, 1964/5, 1965/6, 1966/7, 1967/8, 1968/9, 1969/70, 1970/1, 1975/6.
Gunn, B. (3) (Norwich C) 1989/90, 1992/93.

Haddock, H. (6) (Clyde) 1954/5, 1957/8.
Haffey, F. (2) (Celtic) 1959/60, 1960/1.
Hamilton, A. (24) (Dundee) 1961/2, 1962/3, 1963/4, 1964/5, 1965/6.
Hamilton, G. (5) (Aberdeen) 1946/7, 1950/1, 1953/4.

Hamilton, W. (1) (Hibernian) 1964/5.

Hansen, A. (26) (Liverpool) 1978/9, 1979/80, 1980/1, 1981/2, 1982/3, 1984/5, 1985/6, 1986/7.

Hansen J. (2) (Partick Thistle) 1971/2.

Harper, J. (4) (Aberdeen) 1972/3, 1975/6, 1978/9.

Hartford, A. (50) (West Bromwich Albion) 1971/2, 1975/6 (Manchester City) 1976/7, 1977/8, 1978/9, 1979/80 (Everton) 1980/1, 1981/2 (Manchester City).

Harvey, D. (16) (Leeds United) 1972/3, 1973/4, 1974/5, 1975/6, 1976/7.

Haughney, M. (1) (Celtic) 1953/4.

Hay, D. (27) (Celtic) 1969/70, 1970/1, 1971/2, 1972/3, 1973/4.

Hegarty, P. (8) (Dundee United) 1978/9, 1979/80, 1982/3.

Henderson, J. (7) (Portsmouth) 1952/3, 1953/4, 1955/6, 1958/9 (Arsenal).

Henderson, W. (29) (Rangers) 1962/3, 1963/4, 1964/5, 1965/6, 1966/7, 1967/8, 1968/9, 1969/70.

Hendry, E. C. J. (2) (Blackburn Rovers) 1992/93.

Herd, D. (5) (Arsenal) 1958/9, 1960/1.

Herd, G. (5) (Clyde) 1957/8, 1959/60, 1960/1.

Herriot, J. (8) (Birmingham City) 1968/9, 1969/70.

Hewie, J. (19) (Charlton Athletic) 1955/6, 1956/7, 1957/8, 1958/9, 1959/60.

Holt, D. (5) (Heart of Midlothian) 1962/3, 1963/4.

Holton, J. (15) (Manchester United) 1972/3, 1973/4, 1974/5.

Hope, R. (2) (West Bromwich Albion) 1967/8, 1968/9.

Houliston, W. (3) (Queen of the South) 1948/9.

Houston, S. (1) (Manchester United) 1975/6.

Howie, H. (1) (Hibernian) 1948/9.

Hughes, J. (8) (Celtic) 1964/5, 1965/6, 1967/8, 1968/9, 1969/70.

Hughes, W. (1) (Sunderland) 1974/5.

Humphries, W. (1) (Motherwell) 1951/2.

Hunter, A. (4) (Kilmarnock) 1971/2, 1972/3, (Celtic) 1973/4.

Hunter, W. (3) (Motherwell) 1959/60, 1960/1.

Husband, J. (1) (Partick Thistle) 1946/7.

Hutchison, T. (17) (Coventry City) 1973/4, 1974/5, 1975/6.

Imlach, S. (4) (Nottingham Forest) 1957/8.

Irvine, B. (4) (Aberdeen) 1990/1, 1992/93.

Jackson, C. (8) (Rangers) 1974/5, 1975/6.

Jardine, A. (38) (Rangers) 1970/1, 1971/2, 1972/3, 1973/4, 1974/5, 1976/7, 1977/8, 1978/9, 1979/80.

Jarvie, A. (3) (Airdrieonians) 1970/1.

Jess, E. (2) (Aberdeen) 1992/93.

Johnston, M. (38) (Watford) 1983/4, 1984/5 (Celtic) 1985/6, 1986/7, (Nantes) 1987/8, 1988/9 (Rangers) 1989/90, 1991/2.

Johnston, W. (22) (Rangers) 1965/6, 1967/8, 1968/9, 1969/70, 1970/1 (West Bromwich Albion) 1976/7, 1977/8.

Johnstone, D. (14) (Rangers) 1972/3, 1974/5, 1975/6, 1977/8, 1979/80.

Johnstone, J. (23) (Celtic) 1964/5, 1965/6, 1966/7, 1967/8, 1968/9, 1969/70, 1970/1, 1971/2, 1973/4, 1974/5.

Johnstone, L. (2) (Clyde) 1947/8.

Johnstone, R. (17) (Hibernian) 1950/1, 1951/2, 1952/3, 1953/4, 1954/5, (Manchester City) 1955/6.

Jordan, J. (52) (Leeds United) 1972/3, 1973/4, 1974/5, 1975/6, 1976/7, 1977/8, (Manchester United) 1978/9, 1979/80, 1980/1, 1981/2 (AC Milan).

Kelly, H. (1) (Blackpool) 1951/2.
Kelly, J. (2) (Barnsley) 1948/9.
Kennedy, J. (6) (Celtic) 1963/4, 1964/5.
Kennedy, S. (8) (Aberdeen) 1977/8, 1978/9, 1981/2.
Kennedy, S. (5) (Rangers) 1974/5.
Kerr, A. (2) (Partick Thistle) 1954/5.

Law, D. (55) (Huddersfield Town) 1958/9, 1959/60 (Manchester City) 1960/1, 1961/2 (Torino) 1962/3 (Manchester United) 1963/4, 1964/5, 1965/6, 1966/7, 1967/8, 1968/9, 1971/2, 1973/4 (Manchester City).
Lawrence, T. (3) (Liverpool) 1962/3, 1968/9.
Leggat, G. (18) (Aberdeen) 1955/6, 1956/7, 1957/8, 1958/9 (Fulham) 1959/60.
Leighton, J. (58) (Aberdeen) 1982/3, 1983/4, 1984/5, 1985/6, 1986/7, 1987/8, (Manchester United) 1988/9, 1989/90.
Lennox, R. (10) (Celtic) 1966/7, 1967/8, 1968/9.
Leslie, L. (5) Airdrieonians) 1960/1.
Levein, C. (11) (Hearts) 1989/90, 1991/2, 1992/93.
Liddell, W. (28) (Liverpool) 1946/7, 1947/8, 1949/50, 1950/1, 195/2, 1952/3, 1953/4, 1954/5, 1955/6.
Linwood, A. (1) (Clyde) 1949/50.
Little, A. (1) (Rangers) 1952/3.
Logie, J. (1) (Arsenal) 1952/3.
Long, H. (1) (Clyde) 1946/7.
Lorimer, P. (21) (Leeds United) 1969/70, 1970/1, 1971/2, 1972/3, 1973/4, 1974/5, 1975/6.

Macari, L. (24) (Celtic) 1971/2, 1972/3 (Manchester United) 1974/5, 1976/7, 1977/8, 1978/9.
Macaulay, A. (7) (Brentford) 1946/7 (Arsenal) 1947/8.
MacDougall, E. (7) (Norwich City) 1974/5, 1975/6.
Mackay, D. (22) (Heart of Midlothian) 1956/7, 1957/8, 1958/9 (Tottenham Hotspur) 1959/60, 1960/1, 1962/3, 1963/4, 1965/6.
Mackay, G. (4) (Heart of Midlothian) 1987/8.
Malpas, M. (55) (Dundee United) 1983/4, 1984/5, 1985/6, 1986/7, 1987/8, 1988/9, 1989/90, 1990/1, 1991/2, 1992/93.
Marshall, G. (1) (Celtic) 1991/2.
Martin, F. (6) (Aberdeen) 1953/4, 1954/5.
Martin, N. (3) (Hibernian) 1964/5, 1965/6 (Sunderland).
Martis, J. (1) (Motherwell) 1960/1.
Mason, J. (7) (Third Lanark) 1948/9, 1949/50, 1950/1.
Masson, D. (17) (QPR) 1975/6, 1976/7, 1977/8 (Derby County) 1978/9.
Mathers, D. (1) (Partick Thistle) 1953/4.
McAllister, G. (22) (Leicester City) 1989/90, 1990/1 (Leeds United), 1991/2, 1992/93.
McAvennie, F. (5) (West Ham United) 1985/6 (Celtic) 1987/8.
McBride, J. (2) (Celtic) 1966/7.
McCall, S.M. (23) (Everton) 1989/90, 1990/1, (Rangers) 1991/2, 1992/93.
McCalliog, J. (5) (Sheffield Wednesday) 1966/7, 1967/8, 1968/9, 1970/1 (Wolverhampton Wanderers).
McCann, R. (5) (Motherwell) 1958/9, 1959/60, 1960/1.
McClair, B. (30) (Celtic) 1986/7 (Manchester United) 1987/8, 1988/9, 1989/90, 1990/1, 1991/2, 1992/93.
McCloy, P. (4) (Rangers) 1972/3.

McCoist, A. (46) (Rangers) 1985/6, 1986/7, 1987/8, 1988/9, 1989/90, 1990/1, 1991/2, 1992/93.
McColl, I. (14) (Rangers) 1949/50, 1950/1, 1956/7, 1957/8.
McCreadie, E. (23) (Chelsea) 1964/5, 1965/6, 1966/7, 1967/8, 1968/9.
MacDonald, A. (1) (Rangers) 1975/6.
MacDonald, J. (2) (Sunderland) 1955/6.
McFarlane, W. (1) (Heart of Midlothian) 1946/7.
McGarr, E. (2) (Aberdeen) 1969/70.
McGarvey, F. (7) (Liverpool) 1978/9 (Celtic) 1983/4.
McGhee, M. (4) (Aberdeen) 1982/3, 1983/4.
McGrain, D. (62) (Celtic) 1972/3, 1973/4, 1974/5, 1975/6, 1976/7, 1977/8, 1979/80, 1980/1, 1981/2.
McGrory, J. (3) (Kilmarnock) 1964/5, 1965/6.
McInally, A. (8) (Aston Villa) 1988/9 (Bayern Munich) 1989/90.
McInally, J. (10) (Dundee United) 1986/7, 1987/8, 1990/1, 1991/2, 1992/93.
McKay, D. (14) (Celtic) 1958/9, 1959/60, 1960/1, 1961/2.
McKean, R. (1) (Rangers) 1975/6.
McKenzie, J. (9) (Partick Thistle) 1953/4, 1954/5, 1955/6.
McKimmie, S. (21) (Aberdeen) 1988/9, 1989/90, 1990/1, 1991/2, 1992/93.
McKinnon, R. (28) (Rangers) 1965/6, 1966/7, 1967/8, 1968/9, 1969/70, 1970/1.
McLaren, A. (4) (Preston North End) 1946/7, 1947/8.
McLaren, A. (8) (Heart of Midlothian) 1991/2, 1992/93.
McLean, G. (1) (Dundee) 1967/8.
McLean, T. (6) (Kilmarnock) 1968/9, 1969/70, 1970/1.
McLeish, A. (77) (Aberdeen) 1979/80, 1980/1, 1981/2, 1982/3, 1983/4, 1984/5, 1985/6, 1986/7, 1987/8, 1988/9, 1989/90, 1990/1, 1992/93.
McLeod, J. (4) (Hibernian) 1960/1.
MacLeod, M. (20) (Celtic) 1984/5, 1986/7 (Borussia Dortmund) 1987/8, 1988/9, 1989/90, 1990/1 (Hibernian).
McLintock, F. (9) (Leicester City) 1962/3, 1964/5 (Arsenal) 1966/7, 1969/70, 1970/1.
McMillan, I. (6) (Airdrieonians) 1951/2, 1954/5, 1955/6 (Rangers) 1960/1.
McNaught, W. (5) (Raith Rovers) 1950/1, 1951/2, 1954/5.
McNeill, W. (29) (Celtic) 1960/1, 1961/2, 1962/3, 1963/4, 1964/5, 1965/6, 1966/7, 1967/8, 1968/9, 1969/70, 1971/2.
McPhail, J. (5) (Celtic) 1949/50, 1950/1, 1953/4.
McPherson, D. (27) (Hearts) 1988/9, 1989/90, 1990/1, 1991/2 (Rangers) 1992/93.
McQueen, G. (30) (Leeds United) 1973/4, 1974/5, 1975/6, 1976/7, 1977/8, (Manchester United) 1978/9, 1979/80, 1980/1.
McStay, P. (67) (Celtic) 1983/4, 1984/5, 1985/6, 1986/7, 1987/8, 1988/9, 1989/90, 1990/1, 1991/2, 1992/93.
Millar, J. (2) (Rangers) 1962/3.
Miller, W. (6) (Celtic) 1946/7, 1947/8.
Miller, W. (65) (Aberdeen) 1974/5, 1977/8, 1979/80, 1980/1, 1981/2, 1982/3, 1983/4, 1984/5, 1985/6, 1986/7, 1987/8, 1988/9, 1989/90.
Mitchell, R. (2) (Newcastle United) 1950/1.
Mochan, N. (3) (Celtic) 1953/4.
Moir, W. (1) (Bolton Wanderers) 1949/50.
Moncur, R. (16) (Newcastle United) 1967/8, 1969/70, 1970/1, 1971/2.
Morgan, W. (21) (Burnley) 1967/8 (Manchester United) 1971/2, 1972/3, 1973/4.
Morris, H. (1) (East Fife) 1949/50.
Mudie, J. (17) (Blackpool) 1956/7, 1957/8.
Mulhall, G. (3) (Aberdeen) 1959/60, 1962/3 (Sunderland) 1963/4.
Munro, F. (9) (Wolverhampton Wanderers) 1970/1, 1974/5.

Munro, I. (7) (St Mirren) 1978/9, 1979/80.
Murdoch, R. (12) (Celtic) 1965/6, 1966/7, 1967/8, 1968/9, 1969/70.
Murray, J. (5) (Heart of Midlothian) 1957/8.
Murray, S. (1) (Aberdeen) 1971/2.

Narey, D. (35) (Dundee United) 1976/7, 1978/9, 1979/80, 1980/1, 1981/2, 1982/3, 1985/6, 1986/7, 1988/9.
Nevin, P.K.F. (17) (Chelsea) 1985/6, 1986/7, 1987/8 (Everton) 1988/9, 1990/1, 1991/2 (Tranmere Rovers) 1992/93.
Nicholas, C. (20) (Celtic) 1982/3, (Arsenal) 1983/4, 1984/5, 1985/6, 1986/7, (Aberdeen) 1988/9.
Nicol, S. (27) (Liverpool) 1984/5, 1985/6, 1987/8, 1988/9, 1989/90, 1990/1, 1991/2.

O'Hare, J. (13) (Derby County) 1969/70, 1970/1, 1971/2.
Ormond, W. (6) (Hibernian) 1953/4, 1958/9.
Orr, T. (2) (Morton) 1951/2.

Parker, A. (15) (Falkirk) 1954/5, 1955/6, 1956/7, 1957/8.
Parlane, D. (12) (Rangers) 1972/3, 1974/5, 1975/6, 1976/7.
Paton, A. (2) (Motherwell) 1951/2.
Pearson, T. (2) (Newcastle United) 1946/7.
Penman, A. (1) (Dundee) 1965/6.
Pettigrew, W. (5) (Motherwell) 1975/6, 1976/7.
Plenderleith, J. (1) (Manchester City) 1960/1.
Provan, D. (5) (Rangers) 1963/4, 1965/6.
Provan, D. (10) (Celtic) 1979/80, 1980/1, 1981/2.

Quinn, P. (4) (Motherwell) 1960/1, 1961/2.

Redpath, W. (9) (Motherwell) 1948/9, 1950/1, 1951/2.
Reilly, L. (38) (Hibernian) 1948/9, 1949/50, 1950/1, 1951/2, 1952/3, 1953/4, 1954/5, 1955/6, 1956/7.
Ring, T. (12) (Clydebank) 1952/3, 1954/5, 1956/7, 1957/8.
Rioch, B. (24) (Derby County) 1974/5, 1975/6, 1976/7, (Everton) 1977/8, (Derby County) 1978/9.
Robb, D. (5) (Aberdeen) 1970/1.
Robertson, A. (5) (Clyde) 1954/5, 1957/8.
Robertson, D. (1) (Rangers) 1991/2.
Robertson, H. (1) (Dundee) 1961/2.
Robertson, J. (1) (Tottenham Hotspur) 1964/5.
Robertson, J. (12) (Heart of Midlothian) 1990/1, 1991/2, 1992/93.
Robertson, J.N. (28) (Nottingham Forest) 1977/8, 1978/9, 1979/80, 1980/1, 1981/2, 1982/3 (Derby County) 1983/4.
Robinson, B. (4) (Dundee) 1973/4, 1974/5.
Rough, A. (53) (Partick Thistle) 1975/6, 1976/7, 1977/8, 1978/9, 1979/80, 1980/1, 1981/2, (Hibernian) 1985/6.
Rougvie, D. (1) (Aberdeen) 1983/4.
Rutherford, E. (1) (Rangers) 1947/8.

St John, I. (21) (Motherwell) 1958/9, 1959/60, 1960/1, 1961/2 (Liverpool) 1962/3, 1963/4, 1964/5.
Schaedler, E. (1) (Hibernian) 1973/4.

Scott, A. (16) (Rangers) 1956/7, 1957/8, 1958/9, 1961/2 (Everton) 1963/4, 1964/5, 1965/6.
Scott, J. (1) (Hibernian) 1965/6.
Scott, J. (2) (Dundee) 1970/1.
Scoular, J. (9) (Portsmouth) 1950/1, 1951/2, 1952/3.
Sharp, G.M. (12) (Everton) 1984/5, 1985/6, 1986/7, 1987/8.
Shaw, D. (8) (Hibernian) 1946/7, 1947/8, 1948/9.
Shaw, J. (4) (Rangers) 1946/7, 1947/8.
Shearer, R. (4) (Rangers) 1960/1.
Simpson, N. (4) (Aberdeen) 1982/3, 1983/4, 1986/7, 1987/8.
Simpson, R. (5) (Celtic) 1966/7, 1967/8, 1968/9.
Sinclair, J. (1) (Leicester City) 1965/6.
Smith, D. (2) (Aberdeen) 1965/6, 1967/8 (Rangers).
Smith, E. (2) (Celtic) 1958/9.
Smith, G. (18) (Hibernian) 1946/7, 1947/8, 1951/2, 1954/5, 1955/6, 1956/7.
Smith, H.G. (3) (Heart of Midlothian) 1987/8, 1991/2.
Smith, J. (4) (Aberdeen) 1967/8, 1973/4 (Newcastle United).
Souness, G. (54) (Middlesbrough) 1974/5 (Liverpool) 1977/8, 1978/9, 1979/80, 1980/1, 1981/2, 1982/3, 1983/4, (Sampdoria)K1984/5, 1985/6.
Speedie, D.R. (10) (Chelsea) 1984/5, 1985/6, (Coventry City) 1988/9.
Stanton, P. (16) (Hibernian) 1965/6, 1968/9, 1969/70, 1970/1, 1971/2, 1972/3, 1973/4.
Steel, W. (30) (Morton) 1946/7, 1947/8 (Derby County) 1948/9, 1949/50, (Dundee) 1950/1, 1951/2, 1952/3.
Stein, C. (21) (Rangers) 1968/9, 1969/70, 1970/1, 1971/2 (Coventry City).
Stephen, J. (2) (Bradford City) 1946/7, 1947/8.
Stewart, D. (1) (Leeds United) 1977/8.
Stewart, J. (2) (Kilmarnock) 1976/7 (Middlesbrough) 1978/9.
Stewart, R. (10) (West Ham United) 1980/1, 1981/2, 1983/4, 1986/7.
Strachan, G. (50) (Aberdeen) 1979/80, 1980/1, 1981/2, 1982/3, 1983/4 (Manchester United) 1984/5, 1985/6, 1986/7, 1987/8, 1988/9 (Leeds United) 1989/90, 1990/1, 1991/2.
Sturrock, P. (20) (Dundee United) 1980/1, 1981/2, 1982/3, 1983/4, 1984/5, 1985/6, 1986/7.

Telfer, W. (1) (St Mirren) 1953/4.
Thomson, W. (7) (St Mirren) 1979/80, 1980/1, 1981/2, 1982/3, 1983/4.
Thornton, W. (7) (Rangers) 1946/7, 1947/8, 1948/9, 1951/2.
Toner, W. (2) (Kilmarnock) 1958/9.
Turnbull, E. (8) (Hibernian) 1947/8, 1950/1, 1957/8.

Ure, I. (11) (Dundee) 1961/2, 1962/3 (Arsenal) 1963/4, 1967/8.

Waddell, W. (17) (Rangers) 1946/7, 1948/9, 1949/50, 1950/1, 1951/2, 1953/4, 1954/5.
Walker, A. (1) (Celtic) 1987/8.
Walker, N. (1) (Heart of Midlothian) 1992/93.
Wallace, L.A. (3) (Coventry City) 1977/8, 1978/9.
Wallace, W.S.B. (7) (Heart of Midlothian) 1964/5, 1965/6, 1966/7 (Celtic) 1967/8, 1968/9.
Wardhaugh, J. (2) (Heart of Midlothian) 1954/5, 1956/7.
Wark, J. (29) (Ipswich Town) 1978/9, 1979/80, 1980/1, 1981/2, 1982/3, 1983/4 (Liverpool) 1984/5.

Watson, J. (2) (Motherwell) 1947/8 (Huddersfield Town) 1953/4.
Watson, R. (1) (Motherwell) 1970/1.
Weir, A. (6) (Motherwell) 1958/9, 1959/60.
Weir, P. (6) (St Mirren) 1979/80, 1982/3, (Aberdeen) 1983/4.
White, J. (22) (Falkirk) 1958/9, 1959/60 (Tottenham Hotspur) 1960/1, 1961/2, 1962/3, 1963/4.
Whyte, D. (6) (Celtic) 1987/8, 1988/9, 1991/2 (Middlesbrough) 1992/93.
Wilson, A. (1) (Portsmouth) 1953/4.
Wilson, D. (22) (Rangers) 1960/1, 1961/2, 1962/3, 1963/4, 1964/5.
Wilson, I.A. (5) (Leicester City) 1986/7, (Everton) 1987/8.
Wilson, P. (1) (Celtic) 1974/5.
Wilson, R. (2) (Arsenal) 1971/2.
Wood, G. (4) (Everton) 1978/9, 1981/2 (Arsenal).
Woodburn, W. (24) (Rangers) 1946/7, 1947/8, 1948/9, 1949/50, 1950/1, 1951/2.
Wright, K. (1) (Hibernian) 1991/2.
Wright, S. (2) (Aberdeen) 1992/93.
Wright, T. (3) (Sunderland) 1952/3.

Yeats, R. (2) (Liverpool) 1964/5, 1965/6.
Yorston, H. (1) (Aberdeen) 1954/5.
Young, A. (9) (Heart of Midlothian) 1959/60. 1960/1 (Everton) 1965/6.
Young, G. (53) (Rangers) 1946/7, 1947/8, 1948/9, 1949/50, 1950/1, 1951/2, 1952/3, 1953/4, 1954/5, 1955/6, 1956/7.
Younger, T. (24) (Hibernian) 1954/5, 1955/6, 1956/7 (Liverpool) 1957/8.

WALES

Aizlewood, M. (36) (Charlton Athletic) 1985/6, 1986/7 (Leeds United) 1987/8, 1988/9 (Bradford City) 1989/90, 1990/1 (Bristol City), 1991/2, 1992/93.
Allchurch, I. (68) (Swansea Town) 1950/1, 1951/2, 1952/3, 1953/4, 1954/5, 1955/6, 1956/7, 1957/8, 1958/9 (Newcastle United) 1959/60, 1960/1, 1961/2, 1962/3 (Cardiff City) 1963/4, 1964/5, 1965/6 (Swansea Town).
Allchurch L. (11) (Swansea Town) 1954/5, 1955/6, 1957/8, 1958/9, 1961/2, (Sheffield United) 1963/4.
Allen, B. (2) (Coventry City) 1950/1.
Allen, M. (13) (Watford) 1985/6, (Norwich City) 1988/9 (Millwall) 1989/90, 1990/1, 1991/2, 1992/93.

Baker, C. (7) (Cardiff City) 1957/8, 1959/60. 1960/1, 1961/2.
Baker, W. (1) (Cardiff City) 1947/8.
Barnes, W. (22) (Arsenal) 1947/8, 1948/9, 1949/50, 1950/1, 1951/2, 1953/4, 1954/5.
Berry, G. (5) (Wolverhampton Wanderers) 1978/9, 1979/80, 1982/3 (Stoke City).
Blackmore, C.G. (37) (Manchester United) 1984/5, 1985/6, 1986/7, 1987/8, 1988/9, 1989/90, 1990/1, 1991/2, 1992/93.
Bowen, D. (19) (Arsenal) 1954/5, 1956/7, 1957/8, 1958/9.
Bowen, M.R. (24) (Tottenham Hotspur) 1985/6 (Norwich City) 1987/8, 1988/9, 1989/90, 1991/2, 1992/93.
Bodin, P.J. (19) (Swindon Town) 1989/90, 1990/1 (Crystal Palace), 1991/2 (Swindon Town) 1992/93.
Boyle, T. (2) (Crystal Palace) 1980/1.
Burgess, R. (32) (Tottenham Hotspur) 1946/7, 1947/8, 1948/9, 1949/50, 1950/1, 1951/2, 1952/3, 1953/4.
Burton, O. (9) (Norwich City) 1962/3 (Newcastle United) 1963/4, 1968/9, 1971/2.

Cartwright, L. (7) (Coventry City) 1973/4, 1975/6, 1976/7 (Wrexham) 1977/8, 1978/9.

Charles, J. (38) (Leeds United) 1949/50, 1950/1, 1952/3, 1953/4, 1954/5, 1955/6, 1956/7 (Juventus) 1957/8, 1959/60, 1961/2, 1962/3, (Leeds United) (Cardiff City) 1963/4, 1964/5.

Charles, J.M. (19) (Swansea Town) 1980/1, 1981/2, 1982/3, 1983/4 (QPR), (Oxford United) 1984/5, 1985/6, 1986/7.

Charles, M. (31) (Swansea Town) 1954/5, 1955/6, 1956/7, 1957/8, 1958/9 (Arsenal) 1960/1, 1961/2 (Cardiff City) 1962/3.

Clarke, R. (22) (Manchester City) 1948/9, 1949/50, 1950/1, 1951/2, 952/3, 1953/4, 1954/5, 1955/6.

Coleman, C. (2) (Crystal Palace) 1991/2, 1992/93.

Crowe, V. (16) (Aston Villa) 1958/9, 1959/60, 1960/1, 1961/2, 1962/3.

Curtis, A. (35) (Swansea City) 1975/6, 1976/7, 1977/8, 1978/9, 1979/80, 1981/2, 1982/3, 1983/4 (Southampton) 1984/5, 1985/6, 1986/7 (Cardiff City).

Daniel, R. (21) (Arsenal) 1950/1, 1951/2, 1952/3, 1953/4 (Sunderland) 1954/5, 1956/7.

Davies, A. (13) (Manchester United) 1982/3, 1983/4, 1984/5, (Newcastle United) 1985/6 (Swansea City) 1987/8, 1988/9 (Bradford City) 1989/90.

Davies, D. (52) (Everton) 1974/5, 1975/6, 1976/7, 1977/8, (Wrexham) 1978/9, 1979/80, 1980/1 (Swansea City) 1981/2, 1982/3.

Davies, G. (16) (Fulham) 1979/80, 1981/2, 1982/3, 1983/4, 1984/5 (Chelsea), (Manchester City) 1985/6.

Davies, R. Wyn (34) (Bolton Wanderers) 1963/4, 1964/5, 1965/6, 1966/7 (Newcastle United) 1967/8, 1968/9, 1969/70, 1970/1, 1971/2 (Manchester City), (Blackpool) 1972/3 (Manchester United) 1973/4.

Davies, Reg (6) (Newcastle United) 1952/3, 1953/4, 1957/8.

Davies, Ron (29) (Norwich City) 1963/4, 1964/5, 1965/6, 1966/7, (Southampton) 1967/8, 1968/9, 1969/70, 1970/1, 1971/2, 1973/4 (Portsmouth).

Davis, C. (1) (Charlton Athletic) 1971/2.

Davis, G. (4) (Wrexham) 1977/8.

Deacy, N. (11) (PSV Eindhoven) 1976/7, 1977/8 (Beringen) 1978/9.

Derrett, S. (4) (Cardiff City) 1968/9, 1969/70, 1970/1.

Dibble, A. (3) (Luton Town) 1985/6, (Manchester City) 1988/9.

Durban, A. (27) (Derby County) 1965/6, 1966/7, 1967/8, 1968/9, 1969/70, 1970/1, 1971/2.

Dwyer, P. (10) (Cardiff City) 1977/8, 1978/9, 1979/80.

Edwards, I. (4) (Chester) 1977/8, 1978/9, 1979/80.

Edwards, G. (12) (Birmingham City) 1946/7, 1947/8 (Cardiff City) 1948/9, 1949/50.

Edwards, T. (2) (Charlton Athletic) 1956/7.

Emanuel, J. (2) (Bristol City) 1972/3.

England, M. (44) (Blackburn Rovers) 1961/2, 1962/3, 1963/4, 1964/5, 1965/6, 1966/7 (Tottenham Hotspur) 1967/8, 1968/9, 1969/70, 1970/1, 1971/2, 1972/3, 1973/4, 1974/5.

Evans, B. (7) (Swansea City) 1971/2, 1972/3 (Hereford United) 1973/4.

Evans, I. (13) (Crystal Palace) 1975/6, 1976/7, 1977/8.

Evans, R. (1) (Swansea Town) 1963/4.

Felgate, D. (1) (Lincoln City) 1983/4.

Flynn, B. (66) (Burnley) 1974/5, 1975/6, 1976/7, 1977/8 (Leeds United) 1978/9, 1979/80, 1980/1, 1981/2, 1982/3 (Burnley) 1983/4.
Ford, T. (38) (Swansea City) 1946/7 (Aston Villa) 1947/8, 1948/9, 1949/50, 1950/1 (Sunderland) 1951/2, 1952/3 (Cardiff City) 1953/4, 1954/5, 1955/6, 1956/7.
Foulkes, W. (11) (Newcastle United) 1951/2, 1952/3, 1953/4.

Giggs, R.J. (8) (Manchester United) 1991/2, 1992/93.
Giles, D. (12) (Swansea City) 1979/80, 1980/1, 1981/2 (Crystal Palace) 1982/3.
Godfrey, B. (3) (Preston North End) 1963/4, 1964/5.
Goss, J. (3) (Norwich City) 1990/1, 1991/2.
Green, C. (15) (Birmingham City) 1964/5, 1965/6, 1966/7, 1967/8, 1968/9.
Griffiths, A. (17) (Wrexham) 1970/1, 1974/5, 1975/6, 1976/7.
Griffiths, H. (1) (Swansea Town) 1952/3.
Griffiths, M. (11) (Leicester City) 1946/7, 1948/9, 1949/50, 1950/1, 1953/4.

Hall, G.D. (9) (Chelsea) 1987/8, 1988/9, 1990/91, 1991/2.
Harrington, A. (11) (Cardiff City) 1955/6, 1956/7, 1957/8, 1960/1, 1961/2.
Harris, C. (24) (Leeds United) 1975/6, 1977/8, 1978/9, 1979/80, 1980/1, 1981/2.
Harris, W. (6) (Middlesbrough) 1953/4, 1956/7, 1957/8.
Hennessey, T. (39) (Birmingham City) 1961/2, 1962/3, 1963/4, 1964/5, 1965/6, (Nottingham Forest) 1966/7, 1967/8, 1968/9, 1969/70 (Derby County) 1971/2, 1972/3.
Hewitt, R. (5) (Cardiff City) 1957/8.
Hill, M. (2) (Ipswich Town) 1971/2.
Hockey, T. (9) (Sheffield United) 1971/2, 1972/3 (Norwich City) 1973/4, (Aston Villa).
Hodges, G. (16) (Wimbledon) 1983/4, 1986/7 (Newcastle United) 1987/8, (Watford) 1989/90, (Sheffield United) 1991/2.
Holden, A. (1) (Chester City) 1983/4.
Hole, B. (30) (Cardiff City) 1962/3, 1963/4, 1964/5, 1965/6, 1966/7, (Blackburn Rovers) 1967/8, 1968/9 (Aston Villa) 1969/70 (Swansea Town) 1970/71.
Hollins, D. (11) (Newcastle United) 1961/2, 1962/3, 1963/4, 1964/5, 1965/6.
Hopkins, J. (16) (Fulham) 1982/3, 1983/4, 1984/5 (Crystal P) 1989/90.
Hopkins, M. (34) (Tottenham Hotspur) 1955/6, 1956/7, 1957/8, 1958/9, 1959/60, 1960/1, 1961/2, 1962/3.
Horne, B. (38) (Portsmouth) 1987/8, (Southampton) 1988/9, 1989/90, 1990/1, 1991/2 (Everton) 1992/93.
Howells, R. (2) (Cardiff City) 1953/4.
Hughes, C.M. (1) (Luton Town) 1991/2.
Hughes, I. (4) (Luton Town) 1950/1.
Hughes, L.M. (50) (Manchester United) 1983/4, 1984/5, 1985/6, 1986/7 (Barcelona) 1987/8, 1988/9 (Manchester United) 1989/90, 1990/1, 1991/2, 1992/93.
Hughes, W. (3) (Birmingham City) 1946/7.
Hughes, W.A. (5) (Blackburn Rovers) 1948/9.
Humphreys, J. (1) (Everton) 1946/7.

Jackett, K. (31) (Watford) 1982/3, 1983/4, 1984/5, 1985/6, 1986/7, 1987/8.
James, G. (9) (Blackpool) 1965/6, 1966/7, 1967/8, 1970/1.
James, L. (54) (Burnley) 1971/2, 1972/3, 1973/4, 1974/5, 1975/6 (Derby County) 1976/7, 1977/8 (QPR) (Burnley) 1978/9, 1979/80 (Swansea City) 1980/1, 1981/2 (Sunderland) 1982/3.
James, R.M. (47) (Swansea City) 1978/9, 1979/80, 1981/2, 1982/3 (Stoke City) 1983/4, 1984/5 (QPR) 1985/6, 1986/7 (Leicester City) 1987/8 (Swansea City).

255

Jarvis, A. (3) (Hull City) 1966/7.

Johnson, M. (1) (Swansea City) 1963/4.

Jones, A. (6) (Port Vale) 1986/7, 1987/8 (Charlton Athletic) 1989/90.

Jones, Barrie (15) (Swansea Town) 1962/3, 1963/4, 1964/5 (Plymouth Argyle) 1968/9 (Cardiff City).

Jones, Bryn. (4) (Arsenal) 1946/7, 1947/8, 1948/9.

Jones, C. (59) (Swansea Town) 1953/4, 1955/6, 1956/7, 1957/8 (Tottenham Hotspur) 1958/9, 1959/60, 1960/1, 1961/2, 1962/3, 1963/4, 1964/5, 1966/7, 1967/8, 1968/9 (Fulham) 1969/70.

Jones, D. (8) (Norwich City) 1975/6, 1977/8, 1979/80.

Jones, E. (4) (Swansea Town) 1947/8 (Tottenham Hotspur) 1948/9.

Jones, J. (72) (Liverpool) 1975/6, 1976/7, 1977/8 (Wrexham) 1978/9, 1979/80, 1980/1, 1981/2, 1982/3 (Chelsea) 1983/4, 1984/5 (Huddersfield Town) 1985/6.

Jones, K. (1) (Aston Villa) 1949/50.

Jones, T.G. (13) (Everton) 1946/7, 1947/8, 1948/9, 1949/50.

Jones W. (1) (Bristol City) 1970/1.

Kelsey, J. (41) (Arsenal) 1953/4, 1954/5, 1955/6, 1956/7, 1957/8, 1958/9, 1959/60, 1960/1, 1961/2.

King, J. (1) (Swansea Town) 1954/5.

Kinsey, N. (7) (Norwich City) 1950/1, 1951/2, 1953/4 (Birmingham City) 1955/6.

Knill, A.R. (1) (Swansea City) 1988/9.

Krzywicki, R. (West Bromwich Albion) 1969/70 (Huddersfield Town) 1970/1, 1971/2.

Lambert, R. (5) (Liverpool) 1946/7, 1947/8, 1948/9.

Law, B.J. (1) (QPR) 1989/90.

Lea, C. (2) (Ipswich Town) 1964/5.

Leek, K. (13) (Leicester City) 1960/1, 1961/2 (Newcastle United) (Birmingham City) 1962/3, 1964/5.

Lever, A. (1) (Leicester City) 1952/3.

Lewis, D. (1) (Swansea City) 1982/3.

Lloyd, B. (3) (Wrexham) 1975/6.

Lovell, S. (6) (Crystal Palace) 1981/2 (Millwall) 1984/5, 1985/6.

Lowndes, S. (10) (Newport County) 1982/3 (Millwall) 1984/5, 1985/6, 1986/7, (Barnsley) 1987/8.

Lowrie, G. (4) (Coventry City) 1947/8, 1948/9 (Newcastle United).

Lucas, M. (4) (Leyton Orient) 1961/2, 1962/3.

Lucas, W. (7) (Swansea Town) 1948/9, 1949/50, 1950/1.

Maguire, G.T. (7) (Portsmouth) 1989/90, 1991/2.

Mahoney, J. (51) (Stoke City) 1967/8, 1968/9, 1970/1, 1972/3, 1973/4, 1974/5, 1975/6, 1976/7 (Middlesbrough) 1977/8, 1978/9 (Swansea City) 1979/80, 1981/2, 1982/3.

Marustik, C. (6) (Swansea City) 1981/2, 1982/3.

Medwin, T. (30) (Swansea Town) 1952/3, 1956/7 (Tottenham Hotspur) 1957/8, 1958/9, 1959/60, 1960/1, 1962/3.

Melville, A.K. (15) (Swansea C) 1989/90, 1990/1 (Oxford United), 1991/2, 1992/93.

Mielczarek, R. (1) (Rotherham United) 1970/1.

Millington, A. (21) (West Bromwich Albion) 1962/3, 1964/5 (Crystal Palace) 1965/6 (Peterborough United) 1966/7, 1967/8, 1968/9, 1969/70 (Swansea City) 1970/1, 1971/2.

256

Moore, G. (21) (Cardiff City) 1959/60, 1960/1, 1961/2 (Chelsea) 1962/3, (Manchester United) 1963/4 (Northampton Town) 1965/6, 1968/9 (Charlton Athletic) 1969/70, 1970/1.
Morris, W. (5) (Burnley) 1946/7, 1948/9, 1951/2.

Nardiello, D. (2) (Coventry City) 1977/8.
Neilson, A.B. (1) (Newcastle United) 1991/2.
Nicholas, P. (73) (Crystal Palace) 1978/9, 1979/80, 1980/1 (Arsenal) 1981/2, 1982/3, 1983/4 (Crystal Palace) 1984/5, (Luton Town) 1985/6, 1986/7, 1987/8 (Aberdeen), (Chelsea) 1988/9, 1989/90, 1990/1 (Watford), 1991/2.
Niedzwiecki, E.A. (2) (Chelsea) 1984/5, 1987/8.
Nogan, L.M. (1) (Watford) 1991/2.
Nurse, E.A. (2) (Chelsea) 1984/5, 1987/8.
Norman, A.J. (5) (Hull City) 1985/6, 1987/8.
Nurse, M. (12) (Swansea Town) 1959/60, 1960/1, 1962/3 (Middlesbrough) 1963/4.

O'Sullivan, P. (3) (Brighton & Hove Albion) 1972/3, 1975/6, 1978/9.

Page, M. (28) (Birmingham City) 1970/1, 1971/2, 1972/3, 1973/4, 1974/5, 1975/6, 1976/7, 1977/8, 1978/9.
Palmer, D. (3) (Swansea Town) 1956/7, 1957/8.
Parry, J. (1) (Swansea Town) 1950/1.
Pascoe, C. (10) (Swansea Town) 1983/4, (Sunderland) 1988/9, 1989/90 1990/91, 1991/2.
Paul, R. (33) (Swansea Town) 1948/9, 1949/50 (Manchester City) 1950/1, 1951/2, 1952/3, 1953/4, 1954/5, 1955/6.
Pembridge, M.A. (7) (Luton Town) 1991/2 (Derby County) 1992/93.
Phillips, D. (46) (Plymouth Argyle) 1983/4 (Manchester City) 1984/5, 1985/6, 1986/7 (Coventry City) 1987/8, 1988/9 (Norwich City) 1989/90, 1990/1, 1991/2, 1992/93.
Phillips, J. (4) (Chelsea) 1972/3, 1973/4, 1974/5, 1977/8.
Phillips, L. (58) (Cardiff City) 1970/1, 1971/2, 1972/3, 1973/4,H1974/5, (Aston Villa) 1975/6, 1976/7, 1977/8, 1978/9 (Swansea City) 1979/80, 1980/1, 1981/2 (Charlton Athletic).
Pontin, K. (2) (Cardiff City) 1979/80.
Powell, A. (8) (Leeds United) 1946/7, 1947/8, 1948/9 (Everton) 1949/50, 1950/1 (Birmingham City).
Powell, D. (11) (Wrexham) 1967/8, 1968/9 (Sheffield United) 1969/70, 1970/1.
Powell, I. (8) (QPR) 1946/7, 1947/8, 1948/9 (Aston Villa) 1949/50, 1950/1.
Price, P. (25) (Luton Town) 1979/80, 1980/1, 1981/2 (Tottenham Hotspur) 1982/3, 1983/4.
Pring, K. (3) (Rotherham United) 1965/6, 1966/7.
Pritchard, H.K. (1) (Bristol City) 1984/5.

Rankmore, F. (l (Peterborough United) 1965/6.
Ratcliffe, K. (59) (Everton) 1980/1, 1981/2, 1982/3, 1983/4, 1984/5, 1985/6, 1986/7, 1987/8, 1988/9, 1989/90, 1990/1, 1991/2 (Cardiff City) 1992/93.
Reece, G. (29) (Sheffield United) 1965/6, 1966/7, 1969/70, 1970/1, 1971/2, (Cardiff City) 1972/3, 1973/4, 1974/5.
Reed, W. (2) (Ipswich Town) 1954/5.
Rees, A. (1) (Birmingham City) 1983/4.
Rees, J.M. (1) (Luton Town) 1991/2.

257

Rees, R. (39) (Coventry City) 1964/5, 1965/6, 1966/7, 1967/8 (West Bromwich Albion) 1968/9 (Nottingham Forest) 1969/70, 1970/1, 1971/2.
Rees, W. (4) (Cardiff City) 1948/9 (Tottenham Hotspur) 1949/50.
Richards, S. (1) (Cardiff City) 1946/7.
Roberts, A. M. (1) (QPR) 1992/93.
Roberts, D. (17) (Oxford United) 1972/3, 1973/4, 1974/5 (Hull City) 1975/6, 1976/7, 1977/8.
Roberts, I.W. (4) (Watford) 1989/90, (Huddersfield Town) 1991/2.
Roberts, J.G. (22) (Arsenal) 1970/1, 1971/2, 1972/3, (Birmingham City) 1973/4, 1974/5, 1975/6..
Roberts, J.H. (1) (Bolton Wanderers) 1948/9.
Roberts, P. (4) (Portsmouth) 1973/4, 1974/5.
Rodrigues, P. (40) (Cardiff City) 1964/5, 1965/6 (Leicester City) 1966/7, 1967/8, 1968/9, 1969/70 (Sheffield Wednesday) 1970/1, 1971/2, 1972/3, 1973/4.
Rouse, V. (1) (Crystal Palace) 1958/9.
Rowley, T. (1) (Tranmere Rovers) 1958/9.
Rush, I. (60) (Liverpool) 1979/80, 1980/1, 1981/2, 1982/3, 1983/4, 1984/5, 1985/6, 1986/7 (Juventus) 1987/8, (Liverpool) 1988/9, 1989/90, 1990/1, 1991/2, 1992/93.

Saunders, D. (40) (Brighton & Hove Albion) 1985/6, 1986/7 (Oxford United) 1987/8, (Derby County) 1988/9, 1989/90, 1990/91, (Liverpool) 1991/2 (Aston Villa) 1992/93.
Sayer, P. (7) (Cardiff City) 1976/7, 1977/8.
Scrine, F. (2) (Swansea Town) 1949/50.
Sear, C. (1) (Manchester City) 1962/3.
Sherwood, A. (41) (Cardiff City) 1946/7, 1947/8, 1948/9, 1949/50, 1950/1, 1951/2, 1952/3, 1953/4, 1954/5, 1955/6, 1956/7 (Newport County).
Shortt, W. (12) (Plymouth Argyle) 1946/7, 1949/50, 1951/2, 1952/3.
Showers, D. (2) (Cardiff City) 1974/5.
Sidlow, C. (7) (Liverpool) 1946/7, 1947/8, 1948/9, 1949/50.
Slatter, N. (22) (Bristol Rovers) 1982/3, 1983/4, 1984/5 (Oxford United) 1985/6, 1986/7, 1987/8, 1988/9.
Smallman, D. (7 (Wrexham) 1973/4 (Everton) 1974/5, 1975/6.
Southall, N. (68) (Everton) 1981/2, 1982/3, 1983/4, 1984/5, 1985/6, 1986/7, 1987/8, 1988/9, 1989/90, 1990/1, 1991/2, 1992/93.
Speed, G.A. (20) (Leeds U), 1989/90, 1990/91, 1991/2, 1992/93.
Sprake, G. (37) (Leeds United) 1963/4, 1964/5, 1965/6, 1966/7, 1967/8, 1968/9, 1969/70, 1970/1, 1971/2, 1972/3, 1973/4 (Birmingham City) 1974/5.
Stansfield, F. (1) (Cardiff City) 1948/9.
Stevenson, B. (15) (Leeds United) 1977/8, 1978/9, 1979/80, 1981/2 (Birmingham City).
Stevenson, N. (4) (Swansea City) 1981/2, 1982/3.
Stitfall, R. (2) (Cardiff City) 1952/3, 1956/7.
Sullivan, D. (17) (Cardiff City) 1952/3, 1953/4, 1954/5, 1956/7, 1957/8, 1958/9, 1959/60.
Symons, C.J. (10) (Portsmouth) 1991/2, 1992/93.

Tapscott, D. (14) (Arsenal) 1953/4, 1954/5, 1955/6, 1956/7, 1958/9 (Cardiff City).
Thomas, D. (2) (Swansea Town) 1956/7, 1957/8.
Thomas, M. (51) (Wrexham) 1976/7, 1977/8, 1978/9 (Manchester United) 1979/80, 1980/1, 1981/2 (Everton) (Brighton) 1982/3 (Stoke City) 1983/4, (Chelsea) 1984/5, 1985/6 (West Bromwich Albion).
Thomas, M.R. (1) (Newcastle United) 1986/7.

Thomas, R. (50) (Swindon Town) 1966/7, 1967/8, 1968/9, 1969/70, 1970/1, 1971/2, 1972/3, 1973/4 (Derby County) 1974/5, 1975/6, 1976/7, 1977/8 (Cardiff City).
Thomas, S. (4) (Fulham) 1947/8, 1948/9.
Toshack, J. (40) (Cardiff City) 1968/9, 1969/70 (Liverpool) 1970/1, 1971/2, 1972/3, 1974/5, 1975/6, 1976/7, 1977/8 (Swansea City) 1978/9, 1979/80.

Van Den Hauwe, P.W.R. (13) (Everton) 1984/5, 1985/6, 1986/7, 1987/8, 1988/9.
Vaughan, N. (10) (Newport County) 1982/3, 1983/4 (Cardiff City) 1984/5.
Vearncombe, G. (2) (Cardiff City) 1957/8, 1960/1.
Vernon, R. (32) (Blackburn Rovers) 1956/7, 1957/8, 1958/9, 1959/60 (Everton) 1960/1, 1961/2, 1962/3, 1963/4, 1964/5 (Stoke City) 1965/6, 1966/7, 1967/8.
Villars, A. (3) (Cardiff City) 1973/4.

Walley, T. (1) (Watford) 1970/1.
Walsh, I. (18) (Crystal Palace) 1979/80, 1980/1, 1981/2 (Swansea City).
Ward, D. (2) (Bristol Rovers) 1958/9, 1961/2 (Cardiff City).
Webster, C. (4) (Manchester United) 1956/7, 1957/8.
Williams, D.G. (12) 1987/8 (Derby County) 1988/9, 1989/90 (Ipswich Town) 1992/93.
Williams, D.M. (5) (Norwich City) 1985/6, 1986/7.
Williams, G. (1) (Cardiff City) 1950/1.
Williams, G.E. (26) (West Bromwich Albion) 1959/60, 1960/1, 1962/3, 1963/4, 1964/5, 1965/6, 1966/7, 1967/8, 1968/9.
Williams, G.G. (5) (Swansea Town) 1960/1, 1961/2.
Williams, H. (4) (Newport County) 1948/9 (Leeds United) 1949/50, 1950/1.
Williams, Herbert (3) (Swansea Town) 1964/5, 1970/1.
Williams, S. (43) (West Bromwich Albion) 1953/4, 1954/5, 1955/6, 1957/8, 1958/9, 1959/60, 1960/1, 1961/2, 1962/3 (Southampton) 1963/4, 1964/5, 1965/6.
Witcomb, D. (3) (West Bromwich Albion) 1946/7 (Sheffield Wednesday).
Woosnam, P. (17) (Leyton Orient) 1958/9 (West Ham United) 1959/60, 1960/1, 1961/2, 1962/3 (Aston Villa).

Yorath, T. (59) (Leeds United) 1969/70, 1970/1, 1971/2, 1972/3, 1973/4, 1974/5, 1975/6 (Coventry City) 1976/7, 1977/8, 1978/9 (Tottenham Hotspur) 1979/80, 1980/1.
Young, E. (16) (Wimbledon) 1989/90, 1990/1 (Crystal Palace), 1991/2, 1992/93.

EIRE

Aherne, T. (16) (Belfast Celtic) 1945/6 (Luton Town) 1949/50, 1950/1, 1951/2, 1952/3, 1953/4.
Aldridge, J.W. (54) (Oxford United) 1985/6, 1986/7 (Liverpool) 1987/8, 1988/9 (Real Sociedad) 1989/90, 1990/1, (Tranmere Rovers) 1991/2, 1992/93.
Ambrose, P. (5) (Shamrock Rovers) 1954/5, 1963/4.
Anderson, J. (16) (Preston North End) 1979/80, 1981/2 (Newcastle United) 1983/4, 1985/6, 1986/7, 1987/8, 1988/9.

Bailham, E. (1) (Shamrock Rovers) 1963/4.
Barber, E. (2) (Shelbourne) 1965/6 (Birmingham City) 1965/6.
Beglin, J. (15) (Liverpool) 1983/4, 1984/5, 1985/6, 1986/7.
Bonner, P. (66) (Celtic) 1980/1, 1981/2, 1983/4, 1984/5, 1985/6, 1986/7, 1987/8, 1988/9, 1989/90, 1990/1, 1991/2, 1992/93.
Braddish, S. (1) (Dundalk) 1977/8.

Brady T.R. (6) (QPR) 1963/4.
Brady, W. L. (72) (Arsenal) 1974/5, 1975/6, 1976/7, 1977/8, 1978/9, 1979/80 (Juventus) 1980/1, 1981/2 (Sampdoria) 1982/3, 1983/4 (Internazionale) 1984/5, 1985/6 (Ascoli) 1986/7 (West Ham United) 1987/8, 1988/9, 1989/90.
Breen, T. (3) (Shamrock Rovers) 1946/7.
Brennan, F. (1) (Drumcondra) 1964/5.
Brennan, S.A. (19) (Manchester United) 1964/5, 1965/6, 1966/7, 1968/9, 1969/70 (Waterford) 1970/1.
Browne, W. (3) (Bohemians) 1963/4.
Buckley, L. (2) (Shamrock Rovers) 1983/4 (Waregem) 1984/5.
Burke, F. (1) (Cork Athletic) 1951/2.
Byrne, A.B. (14) (Southampton) 1969/70, 1970/1, 1972/3, 1973/4.
Byrne, J. (23) (QPR) 1984/5, 1986/7, 1987/8 (Le Havre) 1989/90, 1990/1 (Brighton & Hove Albion), 1991/2 (Sunderland) 1992/93 (Millwall).
Byrne, P. (8) (Shamrock Rovers) 1983/4, 1984/5, 1985/6.

Campbell, A. (3) (Santander) 1984/5.
Campbell, N. (11) (St Patrick's Athletic) 1970/1 (Fortuna Cologne) 1971/2, 1972/3, 1974/5, 1975/6.
Cantwell, N. (36) (West Ham United) 1953/4, 1955/6, 1956/7, 1957/8, 1958/9, 1959/60, 1960/1 (Manchester United) 1960/1,K1961/2, 1962/3, 1963/4, 1964/5, 1965/6, 1966/7.
Carey, B.P. (2) (Manchester United) 1991/2, 1992/93.
Carey, J.J. (21) (Manchester United) 1945/6, 1946/7, 1947/8, 1948/9, 1949/50, 1950/1, 1952/3.
Carolan, J. (2) (Manchester United) 1959/60.
Carroll, B. (2) (Shelbourne) 1948/9, 1949/50.
Carroll, T.R. (17) (Ipswich Town) 1967/8, 1968/9, 1969/70, 1970/1 (Birmingham City) 1971/2, 1972/3.
Cascarino, A.G. (43) (Gillingham) 1985/6 (Millwall) 1987/8, 1988/9, 1989/90 (Aston Villa), 1990/9 (Celtic) 1991/2 (Chelsea) 1992/93.
Chandler, J. (2) (Leeds United) 1979/80.
Clarke, J. (1) (Drogheda United) 1977/8.
Clarke, K. (2) (Drumcondra) 1947/8.
Clarke, M. (1) (Shamrock Rovers) 1949/50.
Clinton, T.J. (3) (Everton) 1950/1, 1953/4.
Coad, P. (11) (Shamrock Rovers) 1946/7, 1947/8, 1948/9, 1950/1, 1951/2.
Coffey, T. (1) (Drumcondra) 1949/50.
Colfer, M.D. (2) (Shelbourne) 1949/50, 1950/1.
Conny, O.M. (5) (Peterborough United) 1964/5, 1966/7, 1967/8, 1969/70.
Conroy, G.A. (27) (Stoke City) 1969/70, 1970/1, 1972/3, 1973/4, 1974/5, 1975/6, 1976/7.
Conway, J.P. (20) (Fulham) 1966/7, 1967/8, 1968/9, 1969/70, 1970/1, 1973/4, 1974/5, 1975/6 (Manchester City) 1976/7.
Corr, P.J. (4) (Everton) 1948/9.
Courtney, E. (1) (Cork United) 1945/6.
Coyne, T. (8) (Celtic) 1991/2, 1992/93.
Cummins, G.P. (19) (Luton Town) 1953/4, 1954/5, 1955/6, 1957/8, 1958/9, 1959/60, 1960/1.
Cuneen, T. (1) (Limerick) 1950/1.
Curtis, D.P. (17) (Shelbourne) 1956/7 (Bristol City) 1956/7, 1957/8, (Ipswich Town) 1958/9, 1959/60, 1960/1, 1961/2, 1962/3 (Exeter City) 1963/4.
Cusack, S. (1) (Limerick) 1952/3.

Daish, L.S. (1) (Cambridge United) 1991/2.
Daly, G.A. (48) (Manchester United) 1972/3, 1973/4, 1974/5, 1976/7 (Derby County) 1977/8, 1978/9, 1979/80 (Coventry City) 1980/1, 1981/2, 1982/3, 1983/4 (Birmingham City) 1984/5, 1985/6 (Shrewsbury Town) 1986/7.
Daly, M. (2) (Wolverhampton Wanderers) 1977/8.
Daly, P. (1) (Shamrock Rovers) 1949/50.
De Mange, K.J.P.P. (2) (Liverpool) 1986/7, (Hull City) 1988/9.
Deacy, E. (4) (Aston Villa) 1981/2.
Dempsey, J.T. (19) (Fulham) 1966/7, 1967/8, 1968/9 (Chelsea) 1968/9, 1969/70, 1970/1, 1971/2.
Dennehy, J. (11) (Cork Hibernian) 1971/2 (Nottingham Forest) 1972/3, 1973/4, 1974/5 (Walsall) 1975/6, 1976/7.
Desmond, P. (4) (Middlesbrough) 1949/50.
Devine, J. (12) (Arsenal) 1979/80, 1980/1, 1981/2, 1982/3 (Norwich City) 1983/4, 1984/5.
Donovan, D.C. (5) (Everton) 1954/5, 1956/7.
Donovan, T. (1) (Aston Villa) 1979/80.
Doyle, C. (1) (Shelbourne) 1958/9.
Duffy, B. (1) (Shamrock Rovers) 1949/50.
Dunne, A.P. (33) (Manchester United) 1961/2, 1962/3, 1963/4, 1964/5, 1965/6, 1966/7, 1968/9, 1969/70, 1970/1 (Bolton Wanderers) 1973/4, 1974/5, 1975/6.
Dunne, J.C. (1) (Fulham) 1970/1.
Dunne, P.A.J. (5) (Manchester United) 1964/5, 1965/6, 1966/7.
Dunne, S. (15) (Luton Town) 1952/3, 1953/4, 1955/6, 1956/7, 1957/8, 1958/9, 1959/60.
Dunne, T. (3) (St Patrick's Athletic) 1955/6, 1956/7.
Dunning, P. (2) (Shelbourne) 1970/1.
Dunphy, E.M. (23) (York City) 1965/6 (Millwall) 1965/6, 1966/7, 1967/8, 1968/9, 1969/70, 1970/1.
Dwyer, N.M. (14) (West Ham United) 1959/60 (Swansea Town) 1960/1, 1961/2, 1963/4, 1964/5.

Eccles, P. (1) (Shamrock Rovers) 1985/6.
Eglington, T.J. (24) (Shamrock Rovers) 1945/6 (Everton) 1946/7, 1947/8, 1948/9, 1950/1, 1951/2, 1952/3, 1953/4, 1954/5, 1955/6.

Fagan, E. (1) (Shamrock Rovers) 1972/3.
Fagan, F. (8) (Manchester City) 1954/5, 1959/60 (Derby County) 1959/60, 1960/1.
Fairclough, M. (2) (Dundalk) 1981/2.
Fallon, S. (8) (Celtic) 1950/1, 1951/2, 1952/3, 1954/5.
Farrell, P.D. (28) (Shamrock Rovers) 1945/6 (Everton) 1946/7, 1947/8, 1948/9, 1949/50, 1950/1, 1951/2, 1952/3, 1953/4, 1954/5, 1955/6, 1956/7.
Finucane, A. (11) (Limerick) 1966/7, 1968/9, 1969/70, 1970/1, 1971/2.
Fitzgerald, F.J. (2) (Waterford) 1954/5, 1955/6.
Fitzgerald, P.J. (5) (Leeds United) 1960/1 (Chester) 1961/2.
Fitzpatrick, K. (1) (Limerick) 1969/70.
Fitzsimons, A.G. (26) (Middlesbrough) 1949/50, 1951/2, 1952/3, 1953/4, 1954/5, 1955/6, 1956/7, 1957/8, 1958/9 (Lincoln City) 1958/9.
Fogarty, A. (11) (Sunderland) 1959/60, 1960/1, 1961/2, 1962/3, 1963/4, (Hartlepool United) 1963/4.
Foley, T.C. (9) (Northampton Town) 1963/4, 1964/5, 1965/6, 1966/7.
Fullam, J. (Preston North End) 1960/1 (Shamrock Rovers) 1963/4, 1965/6, 1967/8, 1968/9, 1969/70.

Gallagher, C. (2) (Celtic) 1966/7.
Gallagher, M. (1) (Hibernian) 1953/4.
Galvin, A. (29) (Tottenham Hotspur) 1982/3, 1983/4, 1984/5, 1985/6, 1986/7 (Sheffield Wednesday) 1987/8, 1988/9, 1989/90.
Gannon, E. (14) (Notts County) 1948/9 (Sheffield Wednesday) 1948/9, 1949/50, 1950/1, 1951/2, 1953/4, 1954/5 (ShelbourneK1954/5.
Gannon, M. (1) (Shelbourne) 1971/2.
Gavin, J.T. (7) (Norwich City) 1949/50, 1952/3, 1953/4 (Tottenham Hotspur) 1954/5 (Norwich City) 1956/7.
Gibbons, A. (4) (St Patrick's Athletic) 1951/2, 1953/4, 1955/6.
Gilbert, R. (1) (Shamrock Rovers) 1965/6.
Giles, C. (1) (Doncaster Rovers) 1950/1.
Giles, M.J. (59) (Manchester United) 1959/60, 1960/1, 1961/2, 1962/3 (Leeds United) 1963/4, 1964/5, 1965/6, 1966/7, 1968/9, 1969/70, 1970/1, 1972/3, 1973/4, 1974/5 (West Bromwich Albion) 1975/6, 1976/7 (Shamrock Rovers) 1977/8, 1978/9.
Givens, D.J. (56) (Manchester United) 1968/9, 1969/70 (Luton Town) 1969/70, 1970/1, 1971/2 (QPR) 1972/3, 1973/4, 1974/5, 1975/6, 1976/7, 1977/8 (Birmingham City) 1978/9, 1979/80, 1980/1 (Neuchatel Xamax) 1981/2.
Glynn, D. (2) (Drumcondra) 1951/2, 1954/5.
Godwin, T.F. (13) (Shamrock Rovers) 1948/9, 1949/50 (Leicester City) 1949/50, 1950/1 (Bournemouth) 1955/6, 1956/7, 1957/8.
Gorman, W.C. (2) (Brentford) 1946/7.
Grealish, A. (44) (Orient) 1975/6, 1978/9 (Luton Town) 1979/80, 1980/1, (Brighton & Hove Albion) 1981/2, 1982/3, 1983/4 (West Bromwich Albion) 1984/5, 1985/6.
Gregg, E. (8) (Bohemians) 1977/8, 1978/9, 1979/80.
Grimes, A.A. (17) (Manchester United) 1977/8, 1979/80, 1980/1, 1981/2, 1982/3 (Coventry City) 1983/4 (Luton Town) 1987/8.

Hale, A. (13) (Aston Villa) 1961/2 (Doncaster Rovers) 1962/3, 1963/4, (Waterford) 1966/7, 1967/8, 1968/9, 1969/70, 1970/1, 1971/2.
Hamilton, T. (2) (Shamrock Rovers) 1958/9.
Hand, E.K. (20) (Portsmouth) 1968/9, 1969/70, 1970/1, 1972/3, 1973/4, 1974/5, 1975/6.
Hartnett, J.B. (2) (Middlesbrough) 1948/9, 1953/4.
Haverty, J. (32) (Arsenal) 1955/6, 1956/7, 1957/8, 1958/9, 1959/60, 1960/1, (Blackburn Rovers) 1961/2 (Millwall) 1962/3, 1963/4 (Celtic) 1964/5 (Bristol Rovers) 1964/5 (Shelbourne) 1965/6, 1966/7.
Hayes, A.W.P. (1) (Southampton) 1978/9.
Hayes, W.E. (2) (Huddersfield Town) 1946/7.
Hayes, W.J. (1) (Limerick) 1948/9.
Healey, R. (2) (Cardiff City) 1976/7, 1979/80.
Heighway, S.D. (34) (Liverpool) 1970/1, 1972/3, 1974/5, 1975/6, 1976/7, 1977/8, 1978/9, 1979/80, 1980/1 (Minnesota Kicks) 1981/2.
Henderson, B. (2) (Drumcondra) 1947/8.
Hennessy, J. (5) (Shelbourne) 1955/6, 1965/6 (St Patrick's Athletic) 1968/9.
Herrick, J. (3) (Cork Hibernians) 1971/2 (Shamrock Rovers) 1972/3.
Higgins, J. (1) (Birmingham City) 1950/1.
Holmes, J. (Coventry City) 1970/1, 1972/3, 1973/4, 1974/5, 1975/6, 1976/7 (Tottenham Hotspur) 1977/8, 1978/9, 1980/1 (Vancouver Whitecaps) 1980/1.
Houghton, R.J. (53) (Oxford United) 1985/6, 1986/7, 1987/8 (Liverpool) 1987/8, 1988/9, 1989/90, 1990/1, 1991/2 (Aston Villa) 1992/93.
Howlett, G. (1) (Brighton & Hove Albion) 1983/4.

Hughton, C. (53) (Tottenham Hotspur) 1979/80, 1980/1, 1981/2, 1982/3, 1983/4, 1984/5, 1985/6, 1986/7, 1987/8, 1988/9, 1989/90, 1990/1 (West Ham United), 1991/2.

Hurley, C.J. (40) (Millwall) 1956/7, 1957/8 (Sunderland) 1958/9, 1959/60, 1960/1, 1961/2, 1962/3, 1963/4, 1964/5, 1965/6, 1966/7, 1967/8 (Bolton Wanderers) 1968/9.

Irwin, D.J. (21) (Manchester United) 1990/1, 1991/2, 1992/93.

Keane, R.M. (16) (Nottingham Forest) 1990/1, 1991/2, 1992/93.
Keane, T.R. (4) (Swansea Town) 1948/9.
Kearin, M. (1) (Shamrock Rovers) 1971/2.
Kearns, F.T. (1) (West Ham United) 1953/4.
Kearns, M. (18) (Oxford United) 1969/70 (Walsall) 1973/4, 1975/6, 1976/7, 1977/8, 1978/9 (Wolverhampton Wanderers) 1979/80.
Kelly, A.T. (1) (Sheffield United) 1992/93.
Kelly, D.T. (15) (Walsall) 1987/8 (West Ham) 1988/9 (Leicester City) 1989/90, 1990/1 (Newcastle United) 1991/2, 1992/93.
Kelly J.A. (48) (Drumcondra) 1956/7 (Preston North End) 1961/2, 1962/3, 1963/4, 1964/5, 1965/6, 1966/7, 1967/8, 1969/70, 1970/1, 1971/2, 1972/3.
Kelly, J.P.V. (5) (Wolverhampton Wanderers) 1960/1, 1961/2.
Kelly, M.J. (4) (Portsmouth) 1987/8, 1988/9, 1990/1.
Kelly, N. (1) (Nottingham Forest) 1953/4.
Kennedy, M.F. (2) (Portsmouth) 1985/6.
Keogh, J. (1) (Shamrock Rovers) 1965/6.
Keogh, S. (1) (Shamrock Rovers) 1958/9.
Kernaghan, A. N. (6) (Middlesbrough) 1992/93.
Kiernan, F.W. (5) (Shamrock Rovers) 1950/1 (Southampton) 1951/2.
Kinnear, J.P. (26) (Tottenham Hotspur) 1966/7, 1967/8, 1968/9, 1969/70, 1970/1, 1971/2, 1972/3, 1973/4, 1974/5 (Brighton & Hove Albion) 1975/6.

Langan, D. (25) (Derby County) 1977/8, 1979/80 (Birmingham City) 1980/1, 1981/2 (Oxford United) 1984/5, 1985/6, 1986/7, 1987/8.
Lawler, J.F. (8) (Fulham) 1952/3, 1953/4, 1954/5, 1955/6.
Lawlor, J.C. (3) (Drumcondra) 1948/9 (Doncaster Rovers) 1950/1.
Lawlor, M. (5) (Shamrock Rovers) 1970/1, 1972/3.
Lawrenson, M. (38) (Preston North End) 1976/7 (Brighton & Hove Albion) 1977/8, 1978/9, 1979/80, 1980/1 (Liverpool) 1981/2, 1982/3, 1983/4, 1984/5, 1985/6, 1986/7, 1987/8.
Leech, M. (8) (Shamrock Rovers) 1968/9, 1971/2, 1972/3.
Lowry, D. (1) (St Patrick's Athletic) 1961/2.

McAlindert, J. (2) (Portsmouth) 1945/6.
McCann, J. (1) (Shamrock Rovers) 1956/7.
McCarthy, M. (57) (Manchester City) 1983/4, 1984/5, 1985/6, 1986/7 (Celtic) 1987/8, 1988/9 (Lyon) 1989/90, 1990/1 (Millwall), 1991/2.
McConville, T. (6) (Dundalk) 1971/2 (Waterford) 1972/3.
McDonagh, J. (24) (Everton) 1980/1 (Bolton Wanderers) 1981/2, 1982/3, (Notts County) 1983/4, 1984/5, 1985/6.
McDonagh, Joe (3) (Shamrock Rovers) 1983/4, 1984/5.
McEvoy, M.A. (17) (Blackburn Rovers) 1960/1, 1962/3, 1963/4, 1964/5, 1965/6, 1966/7.
McGee, P. (15) (QPR) 1977/8, 1978/9, 1979/80 (Preston North End) 1980/1.
McGoldrick, E.J. (8) (Crystal Palace) 1991/2, 1992/93.

McGowan, D. (3) (West Ham United) 1948/9.
McGowan, J. (1) (Cork United) 1946/7.
McGrath, M. (22) (Blackburn Rovers) 1957/8, 1958/9, 1959/60, 1960/1, 1961/2, 1962/3, 1963/4, 1964/5, 1965/6 (Bradford Park Avenue) 1965/6, 1966/7.
McGrath, P. (61) (Manchester United) 1984/5, 1985/6, 1986/7, 1987/8, 1988/9 (Aston Villa) 1989/90, 1990/1, 1991/2, 1992/93.
Macken, A. (1) (Derby County) 1976/7.
Mackey, G. (3) (Shamrock Rovers) 1956/7.
McLoughlin, A.F. (13) (Swindon T) 1989/90, 1990/1 (Southampton) 1991/2 (Portsmouth) 1992/93.
McMillan, W. (2) (Belfast Celtic) 1945/6. McNally, J.B. (3) (Luton Town) 1958/9, 1960/1, 1962/3.
Malone, G. (1) (Shelbourne) 1948/9.
Mancini, T.J. (5) (QPR) 1973/4 (Arsenal) 1974/5.
Martin, C.J. (30) (Glentoran) 1945/6, 1946/7 (Leeds United) 1946/7, 1947/8, (Aston Villa) 1948/9, 1949/50 1950/1, 1951/2,K1953/4, 1954/5, 1955/6.
Martin, M.P. (51) (Bohemians) 1971/2, 1972/3 (Manchester United) 1972/3, 1973/4, 1974/5 (West Bromwich Albion) 1975/6, 1976/7 (Newcastle United) 1978/9, 1979/80, 1981/2, 1982/3.
Meagan, M.K. (17) (Everton) 1960/1, 1961/2, 1962/3, 1963/4 (Huddersfield Town) 1964/5, 1965/6, 1966/7, 1967/8 (Drogheda) 1969/70.
Milligan, M.J. (1) (Oldham Athletic) 1991/2.
Mooney, J. (2) (Shamrock Rovers) 1964/5.
Moran, K. (66) (Manchester United) 1979/80, 1980/1, 1981/2, 1982/3, 1983/4, 1984/5, 1985/6, 1986/7, 1987/8 (Sporting Gijon) 1988/9 (Blackburn Rovers) 1989/90, 1990/1, 1991/2, 1992/93.
Moroney, T. (12) (West Ham United) 1947/8, 1948/9, 1949/50, 1950/1, 1951/2, 1953/4.
Morris, C.B. (35) (Celtic) 1987/8, 1988/9, 1989/90, 1990/1, 1991/2 (Middlesbrough) 1992/93.
Moulson, G.B. (3) (Lincoln City) 1947/8, 1948/9.
Mucklan, C. (1) (Drogheda) 1977/8.
Mulligan, P.M. (50) (Shamrock Rovers) 1968/9, 1969/70 (Chelsea) 1969/70, 1970/1, 1971/2 (Crystal Palace) 1972/3, 1973/4, 1974/5 (West Bromwich Albion) 1975/6, 1976/7, 1977/8, 1978/9 (Shamrock Rovers) 1979/80.
Munroe, L. (1) (Shamrock Rovers) 1953/4.
Murphy, A. (1) (Clyde) 1955/6.
Murphy, B. (1) (Bohemians) 1985/6.
Murphy, J. (1) (Crystal Palace) 1979/80.
Murray, T. (1) (Dundalk) 1949/50.

Newman, W. (1) (Shelbourne) 1968/9.
Nolan, R. (10) (Shamrock Rovers) 1956/7, 1957/8, 1959/60, 1961/2, 1962/3.

O'Brien, F. (4) (Philadelphia Fury) 1979/80.
O'Brien, L. (10) (Shamrock Rovers) 1985/6 (Manchester United) 1986/7, 1987/8, (Newcastle United) 1988/9, 1991/2, 1992/93.
O'Brien R. (4) (Notts County) 1975/6, 1976/7.
O'Byrne, L.B. (1) (Shamrock Rovers) 1948/9.
O'Callaghan, B.R. (6) (Stoke City) 1978/9, 1979/80, 1980/1, 1981/2.
O'Callaghan, K. (20) (Ipswich Town) 1980/1, 1981/2, 1982/3, 1983/4, 1984/5, (Portsmouth) 1985/6, 1986/7.
O'Connnell, A. (2) (Dundalk) 1966/7 (Bohemians) 1970/1.
O'Connor, T. (4) (Shamrock Rovers) 1949/50.

O'Connor, T. (7) (Fulham) 1967/8 (Dundalk) 1971/2 (Bohemians) 1972/3.
O'Driscoll, J.F. (3) (Swansea Town) 1948/9.
O'Driscoll, S. (3) (Fulham) 1981/2.
O'Farrell, F. (9) (West Ham United) 1951/2, 1952/3, 1953/4, 1954/5, 1955/6 (Preston North End) 1957/8, 1958/9.
O'Flanagan, K.P. (3) (Arsenal) 1946/7.
O'Flanagan, M. (1) (Bohemians) 1946/7.
O'Hanlon, K.G. (1) (Rotherham United) 1987/8.
O'Keefe, E. (5) (Everton) 1980/1 (Port Vale) 1983/4.
O'Leary, D. (67) Arsenal 1976/7, 1977/8, 1978/9, 1979/80, 1980/1, 1981/2, 1982/3, 1983/4, 1984/5, 1985/6, 1988/9, 1989/90, 1990/1, 1991/2, 1992/93.
O'Leary, P. (7) (Shamrock Rovers) 1979/80, 1980/1.
O'Neill, F.S. (20) (Shamrock Rovers) 1961/2, 1964/5, 1965/6, 1966/7, 1968/9, 1971/2.
O'Neill, J. (17) (Everton) 1951/2, 1952/3, 1953/4, 1954/5, 1955/6, 1956/7, 1957/8, 1958/9.
O'Neill, J. (1) (Preston North End) 1960/1.
O'Regan, K. (4) (Brighton & Hove Albion) 1983/4, 1984/5.
O'Reilly, J. (2) (Cork United) 1945/6.

Peyton, G. (33) (Fulham) 1976/7, 1977/8, 1978/9, 1979/80, 1980/1, 1981/2, 1984/5, 1985/6 (Bournemouth) 1987/8, 1988/9, 1989/90, 1990/1 (Everton) 1991/2.
Peyton, N. (6) (Shamrock Rovers) 1956/7 (Leeds United) 1959/60, 1960/1, 1962/3.
Phelan, T. (15) (Wimbledon) 1991/2 (Manchester City) 1992/93.

Quinn, N.J. (39) (Arsenal) 1985/6, 1986/7, 1987/8, 1988/9 (Manchester City) 1989/90, 1990/1, 1991/2, 1992/93.

Richardson, D.J. (3) (Shamrock Rovers) 1971/2 (Gillingham) 1972/3, 1979/80.
Ringstead, A. (20) (Sheffield United) 1950/1, 1951/2, 1952/3, 1953/4, 1954/5, 1955/6, 1956/7, 1957/8, 1958/9.
Robinson, M. (23) (Brighton & Hove Albion) 1980/1, 1981/2, 1982/3, (Liverpool) 1983/4, 1984/5 (QPR) 1985/6.
Roche, P.J. (8) (Shelbourne) 1971/2 (Manchester United) 1974/5, 1975/6.
Rogers, E. (19) (Blackburn Rovers) 1967/8, 1968/9, 1969/70, 1970/1, (Charlton Athletic) 1971/2, 1972/3.
Ryan, G. (16) (Derby County) 1977/8 (Brighton & Hove Albion) 1978/9, 1979/80, 1980/1, 1981/2, 1983/4, 1984/5.
Ryan, R.A. (16) (West Bromwich Albion) 1949/50, 1950/1, 1951/2, 1952/3, 1953/4, 1954/5 (Derby County) 1955/6.

Saward, P. (18) (Millwall) 1953/4 (Aston Villa) 1956/7, 1957/8, 1958/9, 1959/60, 1960/1 (Huddersfield Town) 1960/1, 1961/2, 1962/3.
Scannell, T. (1) (Southend United) 1953/4.
Scully, P.J. (1) (Arsenal) 1988/9.
Sheedy, K. (45) (Everton) 1983/4, 1984/5, 1985/6, 1986/7, 1987/8, 1988/9, 1989/90, 1990/1 (Newcastle United) 1991/2, 1992/93.
Sheridan, J.J. (15) (Leeds United) 1987/8, 1988/9 (Sheffield Wed) 1989/90, 1990/1, 1991/2, 1992/93.
Slaven, B. (7) (Middlesbrough) 1989/90, 1990/91, 1992/93.
Sloan, J.W. (2) (Arsenal) 1945/6.
Smyth, M. (1) (Shamrock Rovers) 1968/9.

Stapleton, F. (70) (Arsenal) 1976/7, 1977/8, 1978/9, 1979/80, 1980/1 (Manchester United) 1981/2, 1982/3, 1983/4, 1984/5, 1985/6, 1986/7 (Ajax) 1987/8 (Derby County) 1987/8 (Le Havre) 1988/9 (Blackburn Rovers) 1989/90.
Staunton, S. (41) (Liverpool) 1988/9, 1989/90, 1990/1 (Aston Villa) 1991/2, 1992/93.
Stevenson, A.E. (6) (Everton) 1946/7, 1947/8, 1948/9.
Strahan, F. (5) (Shelbourne) 1963/4, 1964/5, 1965/6.
Swan, M.M.G. (1) (Drumcondra) 1959/60.
Synott, N. (3) (Shamrock Rovers) 1977/8, 1978/9.

Thomas, P. (2) (Waterford) 1973/4.
Townsend, A.D. (39) (Norwich City) 1988/9, 1989/90, 1990/1 (Chelsea) 1991/2, 1992/93.
Traynor, T.J. (8) (Southampton) 1953/4, 1961/2, 1962/3, 1963/4.
Treacy, R.C.P. (42) (West Bromwich Albion) 1965/6, 1966/7, 1967/8 (Charlton Athletic) 1967/8, 1968/9, 1969/70, 1970/1 (Swindon Town) 1971/2, 1972/3, 1973/4 (Preston North End)K1973/4, 1974/5, 1975/6 (West Bromwich Albion) 1976/7, 1977/8 (Shamrock Rovers) 1979/80.
Tuohy, L. (8) (Shamrock Rovers) 1955/6, 1958/9 (Newcastle United) 1961/2, 1962/3 (Shamrock Rovers) 1963/4, 1964/5.
Turner, A. (2) (Celtic) 1962/3, 1963/4.

Vernon, J. (2) (Belfast Celtic) 1945/6.

Waddock, G. (20) (QPR) 1979/80, 1980/1, 1981/2, 1982/3, 1983/4, 1984/5, 1985/6 (Millwall) 1989/90.
Walsh, D.J. (20) (West Bromwich Albion) 1945/6, 1946/7, 1947/8, 1948/9, 1949/50, 1950/1 (Aston Villa) 1951/2, 1952/3, 1953/4.
Walsh, J. (1) (Limerick) 1981/2.
Walsh, M. (21) (Blackpool) 1975/6, 1976/7 (Everton) 1978/9 (QPR) 1978/9 (Porto) 1980/1, 1981/2, 1982/3, 1983/4, 1984/5.
Walsh, M. (4) (Everton) 1981/2, 1982/3 (Norwich City) 1982/3.
Walsh, W. (9) (Manchester City) 1946/7, 1947/8, 1948/9, 1949/50.
Waters, J. (2) (Grimsby Town) 1976/7, 1979/80.
Whelan, R. (2) (St Patrick's Athletic) 1963/4.
Whelan, R. (45) (Liverpool) 1980/1, 1981/2, 1982/3, 1983/4, 1984/5, 1985/6, 1986/7, 1987/8, 1988/9, 1989/90, 1990/1, 1991/2, 1992/93.
Whelan, W. (4) (Manchester United) 1955/6, 1956/7.
Whittaker, R. (1) (Chelsea) 1958/9.

BRITISH ISLES INTERNATIONAL GOALSCORERS SINCE 1946

ENGLAND

A'Court, A.	1	Eastham, G.	2	Lineker, G.	48
Adams, T.A.	4	Edwards, D.	5	Lofthouse, N.	30
Allen, R.	2	Elliott, W.H.	3		
Anderson, V.	2			Mabbutt, G.	1
Astall, G.	1	Ferdinand, L.	1	McDermott, T.	3
Atyeo, P.J.W.	5	Finney, T.	30	Macdonald, M.	6
		Flowers, R.	10	Mannion, W.J.	11
Baily, E.F.	5	Francis, G.C.J.	3	Mariner, P.	13
Baker, J.H.	3	Francis, T.	12	Marsh, R.W.	1
Ball, A.J.	8	Froggatt, J.	2	Matthews, S.	11
Barnes, J.	11	Froggatt, R.	2	*(inc. 8 scored pre-war)*	
Barnes, P.S.	4				
Beardsley, P.A.	8	Gascoigne, P.J.	5	Medley, L.D.	1
Beattie, I.K.	1	Goddard, P.	1	Melia, J.	1
Bell, C.	9	Grainger, C.	3	Merson, P.C.	1
Bentley, R.T.F.	9	Greaves, J.	44	Milburn, J.E.T.	10
Blissett, L.	3			Moore, R.F.	2
Bowles, S.	1	Haines, J.T.W.	2	Morris, J.	3
Bradford, G.R.W.	1	Hancocks, J.	2	Mortensen, S.H.	23
Bradley, W.	2	Hassall, H.W.	4	Mullen, J.	6
Bridges, B.J.	1	Hateley, M.	9	Mullery, A.P.	1
Broadbent, P.F.	2	Haynes, J.N.	18		
Broadis, I.A.	8	Hirst, D.E.	1	Neal, P.G.	5
Brooking, T.D.	5	Hitchens, G.A.	5	Nicholls, J.	1
Brooks, J.	2	Hoddle, G.	8	Nicholson, W.E.	1
Bull, S.G.	4	Hughes, E.W.	1		
Butcher, T.	3	Hunt, R.	18	O'Grady, M.	3
Byrne, J.J.	8	Hunter, N.	2	Own goals	23
		Hurst, G.C.	24		
Carter, H.S.	7	Johnson, D.E.	6	Paine, T.L.	7
(inc. 2 scored pre-war)				Palmer, C.L.	1
		Kay, A.H.	1	Parry, R.A.	1
Chamberlain, M.	1	Keegan, J.K.	21	Peacock, A.	3
Channon, M.R.	21	Kennedy, R.	3	Pearce, S.	3
Charlton, J.	6	Keown, M.R.	1	Pearson, J.S.	5
Charlton, R.	49	Kevan, D.T.	8	Pearson, S.C.	5
Chivers, M.	13	Kidd, B.	1	Perry, W.	2
Clarke, A.J.	10			Peters, M.	20
Connelly, J.M.	7	Langton, R.	1	Pickering, F.	5
Coppell, S.J.	7	Latchford, R.D.	5	Platt, D.	20
Cowans, G.	2	Lawler, C.	1	Pointer, R.	2
Crawford, R.	1	Lawton, T.	22		
Currie, A.W.	3	*(inc. 6 scored pre-war)*		Ramsay, A.E.	3
		Lee, F.	10	Revie, D.G.	4
Dixon, L.M.	1	Lee, J.	1	Robson, B.	26
Dixon, K.M.	4	Lee, S.	2	Robson, R.	4
Douglas, B.	11			Rowley, J.F.	6
				Royle, J.	2

Sansom, K. 1
Sewell, J. 3
Shackleton, L.F. 1
Shearer, A. 2
Smith, A.M. 2
Smith, R. 13
Steven, T.M. 4
Stiles, N.P. 13
Summerbee, M.G. 1

Tambling, R.V. 1
Taylor, P.J. 2
Taylor, T. 16
Thompson, P.B. 1
Tueart, D. 2

Viollet, D.S. 1

Waddle, C.R. 6
Wallace, D.L. 1
Walsh, P. 1
Watson, D.V. 4
Webb, N. 4
Weller, K. 1
Wignall, F. 2
Wilkins, R.G. 3
Wilshaw, D.J. 10
Wise, D.F. 1
Withe, P. 1
Woodcock, T. 16
Worthington, F.S. 2
Wright, I.E. 1
Wright, M. 1
Wright, W.A. 3

SCOTLAND
Aitken, R. 1
Archibald, S. 4

Baird, S. 2
Bannon, E. 1
Bauld, W. 2
Baxter, J.C. 3
Bett, J. 1
Bone, J. 1
Booth, S. 1
Brand, R. 8
Brazil, A. 1
Bremner, W.J. 3
Brown, A.D. 6
Buckley, P. 1
Burns, K. 1

Caldow, E. 4
Campbell, R. 1
Chalmers, S. 3
Collins, J. 3
Collins, R.V. 10
Combe, J.R. 1
Conn, A. 1
Cooper, D. 6
Craig, J. 1
Curran, H.P. 1

Dalglish, K. 30
Davidson, J.A. 1
Docherty, T.H. 1
Dodds, D. 1
Duncan, D.M. 1
Durie, G.S. 4

Fernie, W. 1
Flavell, R. 2
Fleming, C. 2

Gallacher, K.W. 1
Gemmell, T.K
(St Mirren) 1
Gemmell, T.K
(Celtic) 1
Gemmill, A. 8
Gibson, D.W. 3
Gilzean, A.J. 12
Gough, C.R. 1
Graham, A. 2
Graham, G. 3
Gray, A. 7
Gray, E. 3
Gray, F. 1
Greig, J. 3

Hamilton, G. 4
Harper, J.M. 2
Hartford, R.A. 4
Henderson, J.G. 1
Henderson, W. 5
Herd, D.G. 4
Hewie, J.D. 2
Holton, J.A. 2
Houliston, W. 2
Howie, H. 1
Hughes, J. 1
Hunter, W. 1
Hutchison, T. 1

Jackson, C. 1
Jardine, A. 1
Johnston, L.H. 1
Johnston, M. 14
Johnstone, D. 2
Johnstone, J. 4
Johnstone, R. 9
Jordan, J. 11

Law, D. 30
Leggat, G. 8
Lennox, R. 3
Liddell, W. 6
Linwood, A.B. 1
Lorimer, P. 4

Macari, L. 5
McAllister, G. 4
MacDougall, E.J. 3
MacKay, D.C. 4
Mackay, G. 1
MacKenzie, J.A. 1
MacLeod, M. 1
McAvennie, F. 1
McCall, S.M. 1
McCalliog, J. 1
McClair, B. 2
McCoist, A. 15
McGhee, M. 2
McInally, A. 3
McKimmie, S.I. 1
McKinnon, R. 1
McLaren, A. 4
McLean, T. 1
McLintock, F. 1
McMillan, I.L. 2
McNeill, W. 3
McPhail, J. 3
McQueen, G. 5
McStay, P. 9
Mason, J. 1
Masson, D.S. 5
Miller, W. 1
Mitchell, R.C. 1
Morgan, W. 1
Morris, H. 3
Mudie, J.K. 9
Mulhall, G. 1
Murdoch, R. 5
Murray, J. 1

Narey, D. 1
Nevin, P.K.F. 4
Nicholas, C. 5

O'Hare, J. 5
Ormond, W.E. 1
Orr, T. 1
Own goals 7

Parlane, D. 1
Pettigrew, W. 2
Provan, D. 1

Quinn, J. 7
Quinn, P. 1

Reilly, L. 22
Ring, T. 2
Rioch, B.D. 6
Robertson, A. 1
Robertson, J. 2
Robertson, J.N. 8

St John, I. 9
Scott, A.S. 5
Sharp, G. 1
Smith, G. 4
Souness, G.J. 3
Steel, W. 12
Stein, C. 10
Stewart, R. 1
Strachan, G. 5
Sturrock, P. 3

Thornton, W. 1

Waddell, W. 6
Wallace, I.A. 1
Wark, J. 7
Weir, A. 1
White, J.A. 3
Wilson, D. 9

Young, A. 2

WALES

Allchurch, I.J. 23
Allen, M. 3

Barnes, W. 1
Blackmore, C.G. 1
Bodin, P.J. 3
Bowen, D.I. 3
Bowen, M. 2

Boyle, T. 1
Burgess, W.A.R. 1

Charles, J. 1
Charles, M. 6
Charles, W.J. 15
Clarke, R.J. 5
Coleman, C. 1
Curtis, A. 6

Davies, G. 2
Davies, R.T. 8
Davies, R.W. 7
Deacy, N. 4
Durban, A. 2
Dwyer, P. 2

Edwards, G. 2
Edwards, R.I. 4
England, H.M. 3
Evans, I. 1

Flynn, B. 7
Ford, T. 23
Foulkes, W.J. 1

Giggs, R.J. 1
Giles, D. 2
Godfrey, B.C. 2
Griffiths, A.T. 6
Griffiths, M.W. 2

Harris, C.S. 1
Hewitt, R. 1
Hockey, T. 1
Hodges, G. 2
Horne, B. 2
Hughes, L.M. 12

James, L. 10
James, R. 8
Jones, A. 1
Jones, B.S. 2
Jones, Cliff 15
Jones, D.E. 1
Jones, J.P. 1

Kryzwicki, R.I. 1

Leek, K. 5
Lovell, S. 1
Lowrie, G. 2

Mahoney, J.F 1
Medwin, T.C. 6
Moore, G. 1

Nicholas, P. 2

O'Sullivan, P.A. 1
Own goals 5

Palmer, D. 1
Paul, R. 1
Pembroke, M.A. 1
Phillips, D. 1
Powell, A. 1
Powell, D. 1
Price, P. 1

Reece, G.I. 2
Rees, R.R. 3
Roberts, P.S. 1
Rush, I. 25

Saunders, D. 12
Slatter, N. 2
Smallman, D.P. 1

Tapscott, D.R. 4
Thomas, M. 4
Toshack, J.B. 13

Vernon, T.R. 8
Walsh, I. 7
Williams, G.E. 1
Williams, G.G. 1
Woosnam, A.P. 4

Yorath, T.C. 2
Young, E. 1

NORTHERN IRELAND

Anderson, T. 4
Armstrong, G. 12

Barr, H.H. 1
Best, G. 9
Bingham, W.L. 10
Black, K. 1
Blanchflower, D. 2
Blanchflower, J. 1

Brennan, R.A.	1
Brotherston, N.	3
Campbell, W.G.	1
Casey, T.	2
Caskey, W.	1
Cassidy, T.	1
Clarke, C.J.	13
Clements, D.	2
Cochrane, T.	1
Crossan, E.	1
Crossan, J.A.	10
Cush, W.W.	5
D'Arcy, S.D.	1
Doherty, I.	1
Doherty, P.D.	3
(inc. 1 scored pre-war)	
Dougan, A.D.	8
Dowie, I.	2
Elder, A.R.	1
Ferguson, W.	1
Ferris, R.O.	1
Finney, T.	2
Hamilton, B.	4
Hamilton, W.	5
Harkin, J.T.	2
Harvey, M.	3
Hill, C.F.	1
Humphries, W.	1
Hughes, M.E.	1
Hunter, A.	1
Irvine, W.J.	8
Johnston, W.C.	1
Jones, J.	1
Lockhart, N.	3
Magilton, J.	4
McAdams, W.J.	7
McClelland, J.	1
McCrory, S.	1
McCurdy, C.	1
McDonald, A.	3
McGarry, J.K.	1
McGrath, R.C.	4
McIlroy, J.	10
McIlroy, S.B.	5
McLaughlin, J.C.	6
McMordie, A.S.	3
McMorran, E.J.	4
McParland, P.J.	10
Moreland, V.	1
Morgan, S.	3
Neill, W.J.T.	2
Nelson, S.	1
Nicholl, C.J.	3
Nicholl, J.M.	2
Nicholson, J.J.	6
O'Kane, W.J.	1
O'Neill, J.	1
O'Neill, M.	1
O'Neill, M.H.	8
Own goals	4
Peacock, R.	2
Penney, S.	2
Quinn, J.M.	6
Simpson, W.J.	5
Smyth, S.	5
Spence, D.W.	3
Stewart, I.	2
Taggart, G.P.	5
Tully, C.P.	3
Walker, J.	1
Walsh, D.J.	5
Welsh, E.	
Whiteside, N.	9
Wilson, D.J.	1
Wilson, K.J.	6
Wilson, S.J.	7

EIRE

Aldridge, J.	12
Ambrose, P.	1
Anderson, J.	1
Bermingham, P.	1
Bradshaw, P.	4
Brady, L.	9
Brown, D.	1
Byrne, J. (Bray)	1
Byrne, J. (QPR)	4
Cantwell, J.	14
Carey, J.	3
Carroll, T.	1
Cascarino, A.	11
Coad, P.	3
Conroy, T.	2
Conway, J.	3
Coyne, T.	3
Cummings, G.	5
Curtis, D.	8
Daly, G.	13
Davis, T.	4
Dempsey, J.	1
Dennehy, M.	2
Donnelly, J.	3
Donnelly, T.	1
Duffy, B.	1
Duggan, H.	1
Dunne, J.	12
Dunne, L.	1
Eglinton, T.	2
Ellis, P.	1
Fagan, F.	5
Fallon, S.	2
Fallon, W.	2
Farrell, P.	3
Fitzgerald, J.	1
Fitzgerald, P.	2
Fitzsimons, A.	7
Flood, J.J.	4
Fogarty, A.	3
Fullam, J.	1
Fullam, R.	1
Galvin, A.	1
Gavin, J.	2
Geoghegan, M.	2
Giles, J.	5
Givens, D.	19
Glynn, D.	1
Grealish, T.	8
Grimes, A.A.	1
Hale, A.	2
Hand, E.	1
Haverty, J.	3

Holmes, J.	1	Martin, C.	6	Ryan, G.	1
Horlacher, A.	2	Martin, M.	4	Ryan, R.	3
Houghton, R.	3	Mooney, J.	1		
Hughton, C.	1	Moore, P.	7	Sheedy, K.	9
Hurley, C.	2	Moran, K.	6	Sheridan, J.	1
		Moroney, T.	1	Slaven, B.	1
Irwin, D.	1	Mulligan, P.	1	Sloan, W.	1
				Squires, J.	1
Jordan, D.	1	O'Callaghan, K.	1	Stapleton, F.	20
		O'Connor, T.	2	Staunton, S.	5
Kelly, D.	7	O'Farrell, F.	2	Strahan, F.	1
Kelly, J.	2	O'Flanagan, K.	3	Sullivan, J.	1
		O'Keefe, E.	1		
Lacey, W.	1	O'Leary, D.A.	1		
Lawrenson, M.	5	O'Neill, F.	1	Townsend, A.D.	4
Leech, M.	2	O'Reilly, J.	2	Treacy, R.	5
		O'Reilly, J.	1	Tuohy, L.	4
McCann, J.	1	Own goals	6		
McCarthy, M.	2			Waddock, G.	3
McEvoy, A.	6	Quinn, N.	10	Walsh, D.	5
McGee, P.	4			Walsh, M.	3
McGrath, P.	7	Ringstead, A.	7	Waters, J.	1
Madden, O.	1	Robinson, M.	4	White, J.J.	2
Mancini, T.	1	Rogers, E.	5	Whelan, R.	3

11th UEFA UNDER-16 CHAMPIONSHIP 1993

FINAL TOURNAMENT IN TURKEY

Group A
Iceland (2) 6, Northern Ireland (2) 2
Poland (1) 1, Switzerland (1) 1
Poland (1) 2, Iceland (0) 0
Switzerland (0) 1, Northern Ireland (0) 1
Northern Ireland (0) 0, Poland (0) 1
Switzerland (1) 1, Iceland (0) 0

	P	W	D	L	F	A	Pts
Poland	3	2	1	0	4	1	5
Switzerland	3	1	2	0	3	2	4
Iceland	3	1	0	2	6	5	2
Northern Ireland	3	0	1	2	3	8	1

Group B
Hungary (2) 2, Greece (0) 0
Turkey (0) 0, Spain (0) 1
Greece (0) 0, Spain (0) 1
Hungary (0) 0, Turkey (1) 1
Greece (0) 2, Turkey (0) 2
Spain (0) 1, Hungary (1) 2

	P	W	D	L	F	A	Pts
Hungary	3	2	0	1	4	2	4
Spain	3	2	0	1	3	2	4
Turkey	3	1	1	1	3	3	3
Greece	3	0	1	2	2	5	1

Group C
Belgium (0) 1, England (0) 1
Czechoslovakia (1) 2, Republic of Ireland (0) 1
Belgium (0) 0, Czechoslovakia (0) 0
England (0) 1, Republic of Ireland (0) 0
England (0) 0, Czechoslovakia (2) 2
Republic of Ireland (1) 1, Belgium (0) 2

	P	W	D	L	F	A	Pts
Czechoslovakia	3	2	1	0	4	1	5
Belgium	3	1	2	0	3	2	4
England	3	1	1	1	2	3	3
Republic of Ireland	3	0	0	3	2	5	0

Group D
France (0) 1, Russia (1) 1
Portugal (0) 1, Italy (2) 2
France (1) 3, Portugal (0) 1
Russia (0) 1, Italy (1) 2
Italy (1) 1, France (1) 1
Russia (1) 1, Portugal (1) 1

	P	W	D	L	F	A	Pts
Italy	3	2	1	0	5	3	5
France	3	1	2	0	5	3	4
Russia	3	0	2	1	3	4	2
Portugal	3	0	1	2	3	6	1

Quarter-finals
Holland (0) 0, Belgium (0) 0
Poland won on penalties
Czechoslovakia (1) 3, Switzerland (0) 0
Hungary (0) 0, France (1) 3
Italy (0) 0, Spain (0) 0
Italy won on penalties

Semi-finals
Poland (1) 2, France (0) 1 aet
Czechoslovakia (0) 0, Italy (0) 0
Italy won on penalties

Match for third place
France (1) 1, Czechoslovakia (1) 2

Final
Poland (1) 1, Italy (0) 0

9th UEFA UNDER-18 CHAMPIONSHIPS 1992–93

Group 1
Belgium (2) 3, Iceland (0) 2
Iceland (1) 5, Belgium (2) 2

Group 2
Finland (1) 1, Scotland (0) 0
Scotland (0) 2, Finland (0) 1 aet

Group 3
Malta (0) 0, France (0) 0
France (2) 4, Malta (0) 0

Group 4
Albania (0) 0, Spain (2) 4
Spain (2) 3, Albania (1) 1

Group 5
Austria (2) 2, Turkey (2) 3
Turkey (0) 1, Austria (1) 1

Group 6
Cyprus (0) 0, Hungary (1) 2
Hungary (0) 5, Cyprus (1) 2

Group 7
Norway (1) 2, Germany (0) 3
Germany (0) 1, Norway (0) 1

Group 8
Czechoslovakia (0) 1, Denmark (0) 0
Denmark (1) 4, Czechoslovakia (1) 2

Group 9
Greece (2) 2, CIS (2) 2
CIS (1) 3, Greece (0) 1

Group 10
Wales (0) 0, Israel (0) 0
Wales (0), Holland (0) 1
Holland (2) 3, Israel (1) 1
Holland (1) 1, Wales (1) 1
Israel (0) 0, Holland (0) 1
Israel (1) 2, Wales (0) 2

Group 11
Romania (2) 4, Northern Ireland (1) 2
Romania (0) 1, Republic of Ireland (0) 0
Northern Ireland (0) 2, Republic of Ireland (2) 3
Republic of Ireland (0) 1, Romania (0) 1
Northern Ireland (0) 1, Romania (1) 4
Republic of Ireland (2) 3, Northern Ireland (3) 3

Group 12
Liechtenstein (0) 0, Switzerland (3) 8
Switzerland (4) 8, Leichtenstein (0) 0

Group 13
Luxembourg (0) 1, Sweden (2) 2
Luxembourg (0) 0, Portugal (2) 3
Portugal (0) 2, Sweden (0) 1

Group 14
Poland (0) 1, Bulgaria (2) 3
Bulgaria (1) 2, Poland (2) 2
Poland (1) 1, Italy (4) 5
Italy (3) 3, Bulgaria (0) 1
Italy (0) 2, Poland (0) 0
Bulgaria (0) 0, Italy (1) 2

Second Round
Group 1
Holland (1) 2, Denmark (1) 1
Denmark (0) 1, Holland (3) 3

Group 2
Portugal (1) 2, Russia (0) 1
Russia (0) 0, Portugal (0) 0

Group 3
Italy (0) 0, Hungary (1) 2
Hungary (0) 0, Italy (0) 1

Group 4
Turkey (0) 2, Switzerland (1) 1
Switzerland (0) 0, Turkey (0) 1

Group 5
Finland (3) 3, France (1) 4
France (0) 2, Finland (0) 2

Group 6
Romania (0) 0, Iceland (0) 0
Iceland (0) 0, Romania (1) 1

Group 7
Germany (0) 0, Spain (0) 0
Spain (3) 5, Germany (1) 2

274

Group A

Portugal 0, Romania 0
Hungary 1, Turkey 1
Portugal 2, Hungary 0
Romania 0, Turkey 3
Turkey 2, Portugal 0
Romania 0, Hungary 1

Final at Nottingham Forest FC
England 1, Turkey 0 att. 23,381

Group B

England 2, France 0
Holland 2, Spain 3
Spain 4, France 1
England, 4, Holland 1
Spain 1, England 5
France 1, Holland 1

9th UEFA UNDER-21 CHAMPIONSHIP 1992–94

Group 1
Scotland 0, Portugal 0
Italy 1, Switzerland 0
Switzerland 4, Malta 0
Malta 0, Italy 1
Malta 0, Portugal 2
Scotland 3, Malta 0
Portugal 2, Italy 0
Italy 3, Malta 0
Switzerland 1, Portugal 1
Malta 1, Switzerland 4
Portugal 7, Malta 0

Group 2
San Marino 0, Norway 3
Holland 1, Poland 3
England 0, Norway 2
Turkey 4, San Marino 0
England 0, Turkey 1
Turkey 1, Holland 1
England 6, San Marino 0
Holland 0, Turkey 1
San Marino 0, Turkey 2
Holland 3, San Marino 0
Turkey 0, England 1
San Marino 0, Poland 5
Poland 1, England 4
Norway 1, England 4
Holland 2, Norway 1

Group 3
Denmark 3, Republic of Ireland 2
Albania 0, Germany 1
Spain 2, Republic of Ireland 1
Germany 1, Spain 2
Germany 4, Albania 1
Republic of Ireland 0, Germany 1
Germany 8, Republic of Ireland 0
Denmark 0, Spain 1
Denmark 1, Germany 4
Albania 1, Republic of Ireland 1
Denmark 5, Albania 0

Group 4
Belgium 1, Romania 0
Cyprus 2, Wales 4
Romania 1, Czechoslovakia 0
Belgium 3, Wales 1
Cyprus 0, Romania 2
Cyprus 0, Czechoslovakia 2
Wales 0, Belgium 0
Romania 1, Cyprus 0
Czechoslovakia 4, Romania 2

Group 5
Iceland 1, Greece 3
Russia 5, Iceland 0
Russia 2, Luxembourg 1
Greece 2, Hungary 1
Romania 1, Czechoslovakia 0
Greece 6, Luxembourg 0
Hungary 1, Greece 2
Luxembourg 0, Russia 6
Luxembourgg 1, Iceland 3
Russia 1, Greece 1
Iceland 0, Russia 1
Iceland 2, Hungary 1

Group 6
Sweden 6, Bulgaria 0
France 6, Austria 1
Austria 1, Israel 5
Israel 1, Sweden 1
Israel 1, Bulgaria 2
Israel 1, France 2
Austria 0, France 1
Austria 2, Bulgaria 0
Bulgaria 1, Israel 0
Sweden 1, Austria 0
Sweden 4, Israel 1
Finland 1, Israel 0

GM VAUXHALL CONFERENCE 1992–1993

GM VAUXHALL CONFERENCE TABLE 1992–93

| | | Home | | | Goals | | Away | | | Goals | | |
	Pl	W	D	L	F	A	W	D	L	F	A	Pts
Wycombe Wanderers	42	13	5	3	46	16	11	6	4	38	21	83
Bromsgrove Rovers	42	9	7	5	35	22	9	7	5	32	27	68
Dagenham & Redbridge	42	10	5	6	48	29	9	6	6	27	18	67
Yeovil Town	42	13	5	3	42	21	5	7	9	17	28	66
Slough Town	42	12	3	6	39	28	6	8	7	21	27	65
Stafford Rangers	42	7	6	8	22	24	11	4	6	33	23	64
Bath City	42	9	8	4	29	23	6	6	9	24	23	59
Woking	42	9	2	10	30	33	8	6	7	28	29	59
Kidderminster Harriers	42	9	5	7	26	30	5	11	5	34	30	58
Altrincham	42	7	7	7	21	25	8	6	7	28	27	58
Northwich Victoria	42	5	6	10	24	29	11	2	8	44	26	56
Stalybridge Celtic	42	7	10	4	25	26	6	7	8	23	29	56
Kettering Town	42	10	5	6	36	28	4	8	9	25	35	55
Gateshead	42	9	6	6	27	19	5	4	12	26	37	52
Telford United	42	9	5	7	31	24	5	5	11	24	36	52
Merthyr Tydfil	42	4	9	8	26	37	10	1	10	25	42	52
Witton Albion	42	5	9	7	30	34	6	8	7	32	31	50
Macclesfield Town	42	7	9	5	23	20	5	4	12	17	30	49
Runcorn	42	8	3	10	32	36	5	7	9	26	40	49
Welling United	42	8	6	7	34	37	4	6	11	23	35	48
Farnborough Town	42	8	5	8	34	36	4	6	11	34	51	47
Boston United	42	5	6	10	23	31	4	7	10	27	38	40

GM VAUXHALL CONFERENCE LEADING GOALSCORERS 1992–93

GMVC			FAC	VFAT	DC
32	David Leworthy *(Farnborough Town)*	+	1	5	1
23	Mark Whitehouse *(Bromsgrove Rovers)*	+	—	2	1
21	Malcolm O'Connor *(Northwich Victoria)*	+	2	1	3
20	Keith Scott *(Wycombe Wanderers)*	+	1	5	2
19	Paul Cavell *(Dagenham & Redbridge)*	+	8	1	1
	Terry Robins *(Welling United)*	+	1	2	1
	Andy Sayer *(Slough Town)*	+	1	1	—
	Karl Thomas *(Wilson Albion)*	+	—	3	—
17	Gary Abbott *(Welling United)*	+	—	1	1
16	Phil Brown *(Kettering Town)*	+	2	—	—
	Gary Jones *(Boston United)*	+	2	5	1
	Mickey Spencer *(Yeovil Town)*	+	2	1	2
15	Tony Hemmings *(Northwich Victoria)*	+	1	—	4
	Alan Lamb *(Gateshead)*	+	7	1	—

GM VAUXHALL CONFERENCE RESULTS 1992–93

(Home \ Away)	Altrincham	Bath City	Boston United	Bromsgrove R.	D'ham & R'bdge	Farnborough T.	Gateshead	Kettering Town	Kidderminster H.	Macclesfield T.	Merthyr Tydfil	Northwich Vic.	Runcorn	Slough Town	Stafford Rangers	Stalybridge C.	Telford United	Welling United	Witton Albion	Woking	Wycombe W'ers	Yeovil Town
Altrincham	—	1-0	1-1	2-2	1-0	2-2	0-1	3-0	2-2	1-0	0-1	0-5	0-2	1-2	1-5	0-0	0-3	2-0	2-1	1-0	0-2	1-2
Bath City	1-0	—	2-1	1-2	3-1	2-1	2-0	1-0	2-1	1-0	3-1	0-5	0-0	0-0	1-1	1-1	4-1	2-0	2-1	1-0	2-0	0-0
Boston United	3-0	1-2	—	3-1	1-0	0-2	3-0	0-1	0-3	3-1	2-0	3-5	0-0	0-0	0-1	1-1	2-0	2-1	3-2	1-2	0-3	0-0
Bromsgrove R.	4-1	1-2	1-0	—	1-4	1-0	3-3	2-1	1-0	1-2	1-1	0-5	2-1	1-0	2-3	1-1	2-0	1-2	4-3	0-1	1-0	1-1
D'ham & R'bdge	2-2	2-1	2-1	1-1	—	1-0	3-1	1-5	1-2	0-1	1-1	0-1	2-1	0-3	1-2	1-2	0-3	1-2	3-2	2-0	1-2	1-1
Farnborough T.	2-5	1-0	4-0	1-1	5-1	—	6-1	1-3	2-2	1-0	0-1	4-1	5-1	4-4	2-3	1-2	0-1	3-2	3-2	5-1	0-1	2-1
Gateshead	2-0	2-2	2-0	1-3	3-1	1-0	—	1-0	1-0	1-0	4-0	0-3	2-1	1-0	2-1	2-0	2-0	2-4	2-0	0-3	0-1	3-0
Kettering Town	0-1	1-1	3-3	2-1	2-1	3-2	2-4	—	2-1	1-1	4-0	3-3	3-5	5-0	2-0	2-0	2-1	2-4	0-4	1-3	1-4	1-1
Kidderminster H.	0-1	1-0	0-2	0-1	3-0	1-2	0-0	0-0	—	2-1	0-3	5-3	0-3	1-1	0-2	0-0	0-3	1-1	0-2	1-3	1-4	1-1
Macclesfield T.	2-2	2-1	1-0	0-2	1-0	2-1	2-2	2-1	1-3	—	1-2	3-0	1-2	5-0	4-1	1-4	4-0	4-3	2-1	3-0	1-4	3-0
Merthyr Tydfil	1-2	1-0	1-1	1-1	1-1	1-0	0-0	1-1	4-3	1-2	—	1-0	0-3	1-1	1-0	1-3	4-0	1-1	3-0	1-1	2-1	1-1
Northwich Vic.	2-2	0-3	3-3	0-1	0-1	2-2	2-2	2-2	0-1	1-3	3-0	—	1-1	0-3	2-3	2-3	2-0	4-2	4-3	0-1	0-0	0-0
Runcorn	1-2	0-3	3-3	1-1	1-1	2-1	2-0	2-1	1-0	1-3	3-2	0-4	—	1-0	2-1	2-3	4-0	3-0	4-2	1-3	0-1	1-0
Slough Town	0-1	1-3	2-1	0-1	1-4	3-1	3-0	2-0	2-1	2-0	1-1	2-1	1-1	—	0-0	1-0	1-1	1-1	2-2	2-1	2-1	3-0
Stafford Rangers	0-0	3-2	0-0	3-4	2-0	2-1	2-4	3-0	2-2	0-1	2-2	2-1	0-0	1-0	—	0-0	2-0	4-3	2-3	0-0	0-1	1-0
Stalybridge C.	1-0	1-1	2-1	1-3	3-1	3-1	1-0	2-1	0-0	2-2	2-2	0-6	2-1	0-0	0-1	—	0-1	0-1	2-2	3-3	2-2	0-3
Telford United	2-0	2-2	3-2	4-2	0-2	3-1	3-1	1-1	2-1	1-2	2-2	2-1	3-2	0-3	1-0	1-4	—	2-0	2-2	3-0	2-3	1-1
Welling United	1-1	3-1	2-1	1-1	1-1	4-1	1-4	3-2	1-1	4-0	2-5	3-2	4-0	0-1	4-1	1-4	3-3	—	1-0	1-2	3-3	0-0
Witton Albion	0-2	2-0	2-0	0-3	2-2	2-1	1-5	1-2	1-5	2-3	0-3	4-0	4-0	1-1	0-3	4-0	4-0	3-0	—	2-1	0-3	1-0
Woking	0-2	1-1	2-1	1-1	1-1	2-2	1-1	1-2	1-2	1-5	0-1	2-1	1-5	1-0	0-3	0-0	3-2	1-5	2-1	—	0-0	5-1
Wycombe W'ers	0-2	2-0	0-3	1-0	1-2	0-1	0-1	1-4	1-4	1-4	2-1	0-0	0-1	2-1	0-1	2-2	2-3	3-3	0-3	2-3	—	3-0
Yeovil Town	1-0	2-1	2-1	2-2	2-3	1-1	1-1	1-1	1-1	1-1	1-1	1-1	1-1	5-1	2-0	1-1	1-1	1-1	1-0	4-1	3-0	—

BEAZER HOMES LEAGUES 1992–93

Premier Division

	P	W	D	L	F	A	Pts
Dover Athletic	40	25	11	4	65	23	86
Cheltenham Town	40	21	10	9	76	40	73
Corby Town	40	20	12	8	68	43	72
Hednesford Town	40	21	7	12	72	52	70
Trowbridge Town	40	18	8	14	70	66	62
Crawley Town	40	16	12	12	68	59	60
Solihull Borough	40	17	9	14	68	59	60
Burton Albion	40	16	11	13	53	50	59
Bashley	40	18	8	14	60	60	59*
Halesowen Town	40	15	11	14	67	54	56
Waterlooville	40	15	9	16	59	62	54
Chelmsford City	40	15	9	16	59	69	54
Gloucester City	40	14	11	15	66	68	53
Cambridge City	40	14	10	16	62	73	52
Atherstone United	40	13	14	13	56	60	50*
Hastings Town	40	13	11	16	50	55	50
Worcester City	40	12	9	19	45	62	45
Dorchester Town	40	12	6	22	52	74	42
Moor Green	40	10	6	24	58	79	36
V.S. Rugby	40	10	6	24	40	63	36
Weymouth	40	5	10	25	39	82	23 #

(Dartford records expunged.

\# Weymouth 2 points deducted.

* Atherstone United and Bashley 3 points deducted).

LEADING GOALSCORERS

Premier Division

J. Smith (Cheltenham Town)	29
R. Carter (Solihull Borough)	25
K. Bayliss (Gloucester City)	22
C. Burton (Solihull Borough)	22
P. Fishenden (Crawley Town)	22
G. Manson (Dorchester Town)	21
L. O'Connor (Hednesford Town)	21
L. Cormack (Waterlooville)	20
P. Joinson (Halesowen Town)	20
M. Murphy (Corby Town)	20
L. Ryan (Cambridge City)	20

BEAZER HOMES SOUTHERN LEAGUE PREMIER DIVISION RESULTS 1992–93

	Atherstone United	Bashley	Burton Albion	Cambridge City	Chelmsford City	Cheltenham Town	Corby Town	Crawley Town	Dorchester Town	Dover Athletic	Gloucester City	Halesowen Town	Hastings Town	Hednesford Town	Moor Green	Solihull Borough	Trowbridge Town	VS Rugby	Waterlooville	Weymouth	Worcester City
Atherstone United	—	0-1	1-1	2-4	3-1	1-1	0-2	2-1	0-1	0-0	2-1	1-1	2-3	4-2	4-3	4-2	1-1	1-0	4-4	1-0	1-0
Bashley	1-1	—	0-1	1-1	5-3	0-3	1-1	1-3	2-3	0-3	0-3	4-3	0-0	1-5	6-1	2-0	1-1	2-0	2-0	2-0	1-0
Burton Albion	0-3	0-1	—	1-0	3-1	0-3	1-2	2-1	2-0	1-2	6-3	0-2	0-0	0-5	4-4	1-3	3-2	2-1	0-2	2-0	1-0
Cambridge City	2-1	1-0	1-0	—	3-1	0-3	1-2	6-4	4-0	4-0	6-0	0-3	3-0	1-5	4-4	1-3	3-2	2-1	2-2	3-2	2-0
Chelmsford City	2-2	5-2	3-1	3-1	—	2-1	1-0	3-0	1-0	1-2	3-0	1-2	1-1	3-1	5-1	3-1	0-3	1-1	3-0	2-0	2-0
Cheltenham Town	0-1	0-3	0-3	0-3	1-1	—	1-0	2-0	2-0	1-0	1-5	3-0	1-0	2-1	1-0	1-3	1-1	1-3	5-0	4-0	4-1
Corby Town	0-1	1-1	1-2	1-2	3-4	3-0	—	1-3	5-1	0-1	1-0	0-1	1-1	2-2	2-0	2-1	2-0	1-0	1-1	1-0	1-2
Crawley Town	1-3	1-3	1-1	6-4	3-0	1-2	1-3	—	2-3	1-1	2-0	4-1	4-2	2-2	0-0	4-2	2-3	3-0	2-3	2-2	4-0
Dorchester Town	0-1	2-3	2-0	4-0	1-0	2-2	5-1	2-3	—	0-1	1-1	2-0	0-1	1-0	5-1	3-0	5-1	2-0	1-1	0-1	1-1
Dover Athletic	4-0	0-3	1-2	4-0	1-2	1-0	0-1	1-1	0-1	—	2-0	1-1	1-1	0-2	1-1	0-2	0-4	0-4	0-2	2-3	1-2
Gloucester City	2-2	0-3	4-0	6-0	4-0	2-1	1-0	2-0	2-0	2-0	—	6-0	2-1	1-3	5-1	3-1	2-4	2-0	2-2	2-1	4-0
Halesowen Town	1-1	4-3	0-2	0-3	2-1	3-0	3-0	1-0	1-1	3-1	3-1	—	3-1	1-1	1-4	2-3	1-3	1-1	0-3	2-1	1-1
Hastings Town	0-4	3-1	0-0	3-0	1-1	1-1	1-1	5-1	0-1	1-1	2-1	6-2	—	2-3	1-3	3-1	1-3	6-2	3-1	1-1	2-1
Hednesford Town	1-1	0-4	0-5	1-5	3-1	2-1	1-2	3-1	1-0	0-2	1-2	1-1	1-3	—	3-2	1-2	3-2	0-3	0-2	5-2	1-3
Moor Green	5-0	3-0	4-4	4-4	5-1	1-1	1-1	1-2	3-0	1-1	5-1	1-4	1-2	1-2	—	1-2	3-2	0-1	2-1	3-2	2-3
Solihull Borough	1-1	0-1	1-3	1-3	3-1	1-3	2-1	1-2	3-0	0-2	0-1	2-3	2-2	1-2	3-2	—	0-1	4-0	3-2	2-1	2-1
Trowbridge Town	3-3	3-3	3-2	3-2	0-1	1-0	2-0	1-2	3-0	0-4	1-2	1-3	1-1	3-2	3-2	1-3	—	2-1	2-1	1-0	1-0
VS Rugby	1-1	0-1	2-1	2-1	1-1	1-0	2-0	3-0	2-0	0-4	1-5	1-1	4-1	0-3	0-1	4-2	4-0	—	2-1	4-2	3-1
Waterlooville	1-3	0-0	0-2	2-2	3-0	1-0	1-1	1-2	1-1	0-2	2-0	1-1	0-2	0-1	2-1	1-0	2-1	4-2	—	3-0	1-0
Weymouth	1-0	0-2	2-0	3-2	2-0	4-0	1-0	2-2	0-1	1-1	2-1	2-1	1-1	5-2	3-2	2-1	1-0	4-2	3-0	—	2-2
Worcester City	2-1	3-0	1-0	2-0	2-0	4-1	1-2	4-0	1-1	2-1	4-0	1-1	2-1	1-3	2-3	2-1	1-0	3-1	1-3	2-0	—

HFS LOANS LEAGUE 1992–93

PREMIER DIVISION

	P	W	D	L	F	A	Pts
Southport	42	29	9	4	103	31	96
Winsford United	42	27	9	6	91	43	90
Morecambe	42	25	11	6	93	51	86
Marine	42	26	8	8	83	47	86
Leek Town	42	21	11	10	86	51	74
Accrington Stanley	42	20	13	9	79	45	73
Frickley Athletic	42	21	6	15	62	52	69
Barrow	42	18	11	13	71	55	65
Hyde United	42	17	13	12	87	71	64
Bishop Auckland	42	17	11	14	63	52	62
Gainsborough Trinity	42	17	8	17	63	66	59
Colwyn Bay	42	16	6	20	80	79	54
Horwich	42	14	10	18	72	79	52
Buxton	42	13	10	19	60	75	49
Matlock Town **	42	13	11	18	56	79	47
Emley	42	13	6	23	62	91	45
Whitley Bay	42	11	8	23	57	96	41
Chorley	42	10	10	22	52	93	40
Fleetwood Town	42	10	7	25	50	77	37
Droylsden	42	10	7	25	47	84	37
Mossley	42	7	8	27	53	95	29
Goole Town	42	6	9	27	47	105	27

Leading goalscorers

Lge	Cup	Tot.	
33	12	45	John Coleman (Morecambe)
32	12	44	Steve Haw (Southport)
26	15	41	Paul Beck (Accrington Stanley)
24	13	37	Bevan Blackwood (Winsford United)
26	8	34	Chris Camden (Peter Donnelly)
23	11	34	Peter Donnelly (Colwyn Bay)
25	8	33	Brian Ross (Marine)
18	12	30	Peter McCrae (Chorley)
26	-	26	Andy Graham (Hyde United)
24	2	26	Phil Chadwick (Hyde United)
18	8	26	Peter Withers (Southport)
22	3	25	John Brady (Barrow)
21	2	23	Tony McDonald (Horwich)
21	1	22	Stuart Lowe (Buxton)
16	6	22	Bob Clarke (Emley)

HFS LOANS LEAGUE—PREMIER DIVISION RESULTS 1992-93

	Accrington Stanley	Barrow	Bishop Auckland	Buxton	Chorley	Colwyn Bay	Droylsden	Emley	Fleetwood Town	Frickley Ath	Gainsborough Trinity	Goole Town	Horwich RMI	Hyde United	Leek Town	Marine	Matlock Town	Morecambe	Mossley	Southport	Whitley Bay	Winsford United
Accrington Stanley	—	2-0	0-0	0-1	1-0	3-3	0-3	3-2	0-2	1-0	0-1	3-0	2-1	1-1	2-1	1-1	1-0	1-1	1-1	2-2	2-0	1-3
Barrow	2-0	—	0-3	0-4	1-1	5-0	1-3	0-1	2-1	2-1	2-2	4-1	2-1	1-2	1-2	3-1	1-0	0-3	2-2	2-2	0-1	0-0
Bishop Auckland	0-0	4-3	—	0-3	1-0	1-2	2-3	3-0	2-1	0-1	2-2	1-1	0-2	3-3	1-0	1-0	0-1	2-2	0-3	1-3	0-0	2-2
Buxton	0-1	2-1	0-1	—	2-3	4-2	7-3	1-3	3-1	2-0	0-3	1-5	2-2	3-3	2-1	1-5	1-1	4-1	2-2	1-6	0-0	2-3
Chorley	1-0	5-0	2-1	2-1	—	1-0	3-0	1-0	3-1	0-1	2-0	4-2	4-2	2-4	2-3	0-6	3-1	1-2	4-1	2-4	4-4	0-4
Colwyn Bay	3-3	1-2	1-2	0-2	1-1	—	1-1	2-2	4-3	2-0	3-0	1-0	1-3	1-5	1-1	1-3	0-1	0-1	4-2	2-5	1-2	2-3
Droylsden	0-3	3-0	2-3	3-0	1-1	2-0	—	3-0	1-2	1-2	0-2	2-0	2-1	1-1	5-5	3-1	2-2	2-1	0-1	1-2	1-1	0-4
Emley	3-2	0-1	3-0	1-3	0-2	2-1	1-3	—	0-0	3-1	1-1	0-2	2-1	2-0	3-0	0-0	2-3	2-2	1-4	2-1	0-1	1-2
Fleetwood Town	0-2	2-1	2-1	4-3	2-1	1-0	3-1	3-1	—	1-2	1-2	3-1	2-1	2-1	1-4	2-3	1-0	1-2	3-2	2-5	3-0	1-2
Frickley Ath	1-0	2-1	0-1	2-0	1-1	2-1	1-0	0-0	0-0	—	4-0	6-3	2-2	1-1	0-3	0-3	2-0	1-0	2-1	1-1	7-1	1-2
Gainsborough Trinity	0-5	1-0	1-0	1-0	0-2	0-2	2-1	1-3	3-1	1-3	—	3-3	1-2	2-0	2-2	1-2	0-4	2-3	1-2	0-5	3-3	3-1
Goole Town	2-2	1-0	1-1	2-2	0-2	3-3	1-1	0-1	4-1	3-0	3-1	—	4-1	0-1	3-3	0-1	2-4	0-4	3-0	1-1	1-3	2-4
Horwich RMI	2-6	0-2	0-2	4-1	3-0	6-1	2-2	2-0	4-0	0-1	3-3	3-1	—	3-5	4-1	4-1	0-1	1-2	0-2	2-2	4-1	3-3
Hyde United	3-1	2-1	3-3	3-5	5-1	3-0	1-4	3-1	2-0	3-1	6-1	3-3	3-3	—	3-5	3-3	6-0	2-0	5-2	0-1	1-0	0-0
Leek Town	2-0	2-3	1-0	2-4	2-1	1-4	1-1	2-0	2-0	2-4	2-1	1-0	1-2	3-3	—	1-1	1-2	4-3	4-2	2-1	3-0	2-4
Marine	1-2	2-2	1-0	0-1	3-1	2-1	2-2	7-4	0-1	0-1	2-1	3-2	0-1	1-1	1-1	—	2-1	0-3	3-3	1-0	0-1	1-0
Matlock Town	2-0	0-1	3-1	0-4	0-0	1-4	3-1	1-2	4-2	1-2	3-4	2-1	4-0	2-2	0-1	0-1	—	2-1	1-0	0-2	0-0	3-3
Morecambe	2-0	3-1	3-1	2-8	0-0	0-1	0-1	1-2	5-0	2-3	2-1	0-3	0-1	0-2	2-2	1-0	0-0	—	0-3	0-6	3-1	2-4
Mossley	0-5	0-5	0-1	0-2	1-1	1-2	1-2	5-0	1-2	0-2	2-0	0-1	3-1	0-1	2-0	1-0	3-0	0-6	—	3-1	1-0	5-0
Southport	2-2	2-2	1-3	0-5	1-0	2-4	4-0	2-4	2-0	3-2	3-0	2-0	0-2	0-2	0-2	1-5	2-3	2-1	3-1	—	1-0	0-3
Whitley Bay	1-1	1-1	0-0	3-3	2-1	2-4	5-0	2-1	2-0	1-1	3-0	3-1	3-1	1-0	0-2	0-1	0-0	5-0	3-0	0-2	—	6-0
Winsford United	2-0	1-4	2-2	2-3	0-1	3-2	5-2	5-1	2-0	2-1	1-0	3-0	0-1	3-1	2-0	5-1	0-0	2-0	1-0	1-2	1-0	—

DIADORA FOOTBALL LEAGUE 1992–93

Premier Division

	P	Home			Away			Totals			Goals		Pts
		W	D	L	W	D	L	W	D	L	F	A	
Chesham United	42	17	3	1	13	5	3	30	8	4	104	34	98
St Albans City	42	15	5	1	13	4	4	28	9	5	103	50	93
Enfield	42	13	1	7	12	5	4	25	6	11	94	48	81
Carshalton Athletic	42	10	7	4	12	3	6	22	10	10	96	56	76
Sutton United	42	12	5	4	6	9	6	18	14	10	74	57	68
Grays Athletic	42	13	6	2	5	5	11	18	11	13	61	64	65
Stevenage Borough	42	10	2	9	8	6	7	18	8	16	62	60	62
Harrow Borough	42	7	8	6	9	6	6	16	14	12	59	60	62
Hayes	42	7	8	6	9	5	7	16	13	13	64	59	61
Aylesbury United	42	8	8	5	8	10	1	16	18	7	70	77	60
Hendon	42	6	11	4	6	7	8	12	18	12	52	54	54
Basingstoke Town	42	7	10	4	5	7	9	12	17	13	49	45	53
Kingstonian	42	8	5	8	6	5	10	14	10	18	59	58	52
Dulwich Hamlet	42	6	5	10	6	9	6	12	14	16	52	66	50
Marlow	42	4	7	10	8	4	9	12	11	19	72	73	47
Wokingham Town	42	7	9	5	4	4	13	11	13	18	62	81	46
Bromley	42	6	4	11	5	9	7	11	13	18	51	72	46
Wivenhoe Town	42	10	2	9	3	5	13	13	7	22	41	75	46
Yeading	42	5	5	11	6	7	8	11	12	19	58	66	45
Staines Town	42	7	5	9	3	8	10	10	13	19	59	77	43
Windsor & Eton	42	3	4	14	5	3	13	8	7	27	40	90	31
Bognor Regis	42	3	5	13	2	5	14	5	10	27	46	106	25

LEADING GOALSCORERS

Premier Division	Lge	Lge. C	FMC
40 Jimmy Bolton (Carshalton Athletic)	37		3
36 Steve Clark (St. Albans City)	36		
31 Dave Pearce (Kingstonian)	27	3	1
(inc 15 and 3 for Hayes)			
27 Graham Westley (Aylesbury United)	23	4	
(inc 5 and 4 for Enfield)			
26 Darren Collins (Enfield)	23	3	
(inc 8 and 3 for Aylesbury United)			
24 Chris Townsend (Chesham United)	24		
Jon Warden (Carshalton Athletic)	19	1	4
22 Winston Whittingham (Grays Athletic)	19	1	2
21 Tommy Langley (Wokingham Town)	21		
David Lay (Marlow)	13	6	2
20 Martin Gittings (Stevenage Borough)	20		

DIADORA LEAGUE PREMIER DIVISION

Home \ Away	Aylesbury	Basingstoke	Bognor Regis	Bromley	Carshalton Ath	Chesham Utd	Dulwich Hamlet	Enfield	Grays Athletic	Harrow Borough	Hayes	Hendon	Kingstonian	Marlow	St Albans	Staines Town	Stevenage Boro	Sutton Utd	Windsor & Eton	Wivenhoe Town	Wokingham	Yeading
Aylesbury Utd	—	1-1	2-0	6-1	0-0	1-4	0-2	4-0	1-0	2-0	1-0	1-1	2-0	0-3	3-2	5-3	1-2	0-4	3-0	3-0	1-0	1-1
Basingstoke	1-2	—	1-3	0-2	0-0	0-0	2-1	4-1	6-2	1-3	0-0	1-0	0-1	2-1	2-6	2-1	0-1	1-1	3-2	4-1	5-0	0-6
Bognor Regis	4-5	3-0	—	3-2	0-4	0-4	2-2	2-2	2-0	3-3	0-0	3-4	1-5	1-5	2-6	4-1	0-2	1-1	0-1	0-1	0-6	2-4
Bromley	1-0	0-2	0-6	—	0-2	2-2	2-2	0-1	1-0	2-1	1-1	1-0	0-0	2-2	2-0	0-2	0-5	0-2	1-2	2-3	2-2	1-0
Carshalton Ath	2-1	2-2	4-1	0-4	—	1-1	2-2	3-1	2-0	1-2	1-0	3-1	0-2	0-5	1-4	3-2	6-0	0-0	3-2	3-0	2-1	1-0
Chesham Utd	0-1	0-0	2-2	1-4	2-2	—	2-2	0-5	1-2	1-2	0-1	1-0	2-1	3-2	1-3	0-1	0-2	0-1	2-2	2-0	3-1	0-1
Dulwich Hamlet	3-1	4-1	6-2	2-2	2-2	2-2	—	1-2	0-0	2-4	2-3	4-0	1-0	1-2	2-0	0-2	1-0	0-0	1-1	1-0	2-1	0-1
Enfield	3-1	6-2	4-1	2-1	3-1	1-4	1-2	—	3-2	2-0	0-0	4-0	2-1	5-1	1-4	2-1	0-1	0-0	0-0	6-0	3-0	3-0
Grays Athletic	2-3	2-0	2-0	2-4	0-3	1-2	2-1	3-2	—	2-1	0-1	0-2	2-2	1-2	0-3	2-2	1-2	1-0	2-1	1-0	2-0	4-0
Harrow Borough	4-0	1-3	3-3	0-3	0-4	1-2	2-4	2-0	2-1	—	0-0	2-2	1-0	2-5	3-6	3-1	2-1	2-2	4-3	4-1	4-1	3-0
Hayes	1-1	0-0	0-0	1-2	0-2	0-1	0-0	0-0	0-1	0-0	—	1-1	3-0	0-0	1-3	4-0	0-2	1-1	1-1	2-1	1-1	1-3
Hendon	7-1	1-0	3-4	1-0	3-1	1-0	4-0	0-4	0-2	2-2	2-4	—	1-1	5-1	1-3	2-1	1-2	2-1	3-0	3-0	3-2	2-0
Kingstonian	1-0	0-1	1-5	0-2	0-2	2-1	1-0	2-1	2-2	1-0	1-1	1-1	—	1-1	1-0	2-3	2-1	0-2	2-1	2-1	3-1	2-0
Marlow	3-4	2-1	1-5	0-2	0-5	3-2	2-2	2-1	2-1	2-5	1-4	0-0	5-1	—	4-3	1-4	0-2	0-1	2-1	2-1	2-2	1-1
St Albans	1-0	2-6	2-6	3-6	1-4	1-3	3-1	1-4	0-3	3-6	0-2	1-3	1-0	3-4	—	1-3	1-2	0-5	2-1	1-0	0-1	1-0
Staines Town	1-4	2-1	4-1	2-3	3-2	0-1	3-1	2-4	3-1	1-0	1-0	3-3	5-2	2-3	3-2	—	1-3	2-1	2-1	3-0	1-1	2-2
Stevenage Boro	1-3	0-1	0-2	0-5	3-2	0-2	2-4	2-1	0-0	1-2	0-1	3-3	2-3	4-0	0-1	2-4	—	2-2	2-1	2-2	2-0	1-2
Sutton Utd	4-0	1-0	1-1	3-1	3-1	1-0	2-4	2-0	6-1	1-2	1-1	4-1	1-0	2-0	3-1	2-4	0-3	—	5-2	3-0	2-2	1-3
Windsor & Eton	2-3	3-2	1-0	4-1	0-4	3-2	0-1	0-4	2-0	0-2	2-3	2-1	0-3	2-1	2-1	1-1	2-4	1-1	—	3-1	1-0	1-3
Wivenhoe Town	0-2	4-1	1-3	1-0	0-4	2-2	0-1	2-2	2-2	2-1	5-0	0-4	2-3	2-2	2-2	3-1	2-2	3-3	3-1	—	2-0	3-0
Wokingham	0-2	3-1	2-1	1-2	3-2	3-1	2-0	0-3	0-4	1-1	1-2	1-2	0-4	0-0	1-3	0-1	2-0	1-0	1-0	1-0	—	2-2
Yeading	2-1	1-2	2-1	0-0	1-1	0-1	0-2	1-2	2-3	2-0	1-0	1-2	1-2	1-1	1-3	0-1	2-2	4-0	1-0	2-4	2-4	—

THE PONTIN'S LEAGUE

Division One

	P	W	D	L	F	A	Pts
Aston Villa	34	21	8	5	64	32	71
Nottingham Forest	34	20	8	6	77	46	68
Blackburn Rovers	34	18	10	6	60	37	64
Leeds United	34	15	8	11	59	44	53
Bolton Wanderers	34	15	8	11	48	49	53
Manchester United	34	13	13	8	58	50	52
Liverpool	34	13	10	11	47	43	49
Sheffield Wednesday	34	13	10	11	51	48	49
Leicester City	34	12	12	10	42	38	48
Wolverhampton Wanderers	34	13	6	15	46	55	45
Notts County	34	12	8	14	56	52	44
Newcastle United	34	12	7	15	36	43	43
Sheffield United	34	10	10	14	54	59	40
Sunderland	34	11	6	17	57	57	39
Barnsley	34	9	11	14	48	58	38
Stoke City	34	8	8	18	38	56	32
Manchester City A	34	7	9	18	34	68	30
Rotherham United	34	5	6	23	29	69	21

Division Two

	P	W	D	L	F	A	Pts
Derby County	34	26	5	3	103	28	83
Everton	34	21	10	3	78	44	73
Coventry City	34	19	5	10	53	31	62
York City	34	17	8	9	48	31	59
West Bromwich Albion	34	18	5	11	54	50	59
Oldham Athletic	34	17	6	11	70	52	57
Port Vale	34	14	8	12	51	49	50
Bradford City	34	14	7	13	60	58	49
Huddersfield Town	34	15	4	15	61	56	49
Grimsby Town	34	13	7	14	51	45	46
Middlesbrough	34	14	4	16	47	53	46
Blackpool	34	13	6	15	40	55	45
Burnley	34	11	8	15	46	56	41
Mansfield Town	34	11	6	17	41	49	39
Scunthorpe United	34	10	4	20	46	64	34
Hull City	34	7	6	21	33	76	27
Wigan Athletic	34	6	5	23	25	68	23
Preston North End	34	5	6	23	43	85	21

THE NEVILLE OVENDEN FOOTBALL COMBINATION

	P	W	D	L	F	A	Pts
Millwall	38	21	10	7	71	42	73
Chelsea	38	20	11	7	78	49	71
QPR	38	19	11	8	70	46	68
Crystal Palace	38	18	12	8	66	44	66
Southampton	38	18	10	10	56	39	64
Tottenham Hotspur	38	16	15	7	75	38	63
Oxford United	38	16	12	10	58	57	60
Watford	38	15	12	11	62	61	57
Wimbledon	38	15	10	13	60	43	55
Ipswich Town	38	16	7	15	58	62	55
Arsenal	38	12	15	11	57	46	51
Charlton Athletic	38	14	6	18	48	57	48
Luton Town	38	13	9	16	53	64	48
West Ham United	38	13	6	19	56	59	45
Norwich City	38	11	12	15	66	78	45
Swindon Town	38	10	12	16	53	60	42
Bristol City	38	8	12	18	39	60	36
Portsmouth	38	8	10	20	43	73	34
Brighton & Hove Albion	38	9	7	22	38	81	34
Fulham	38	5	7	26	28	76	22

Division Two	P	W	D	L	F	A	Pts
Bristol Rovers	27	18	5	4	61	36	59
Swansea City	27	17	6	4	78	33	57
Birmingham City	27	14	9	4	61	42	51
AFC Bournemouth	27	10	6	11	52	44	36
Yeovil Town	27	9	6	12	48	67	33
Cheltenham Town	27	7	9	11	43	56	30
Cardiff City	27	7	8	12	48	51	29
Exeter City	27	8	4	15	45	62	28
Plymouth Argyle	27	7	6	14	51	65	27
Torquay United	27	7	3	17	30	61	24

SOUTH EAST COUNTIES LEAGUE

Division One

	P	W	D	L	F	A	Pts
Tottenham Hotspur	30	22	2	6	84	27	46
Millwall	30	19	6	5	81	45	44
Arsenal	30	16	6	8	65	36	38
Queens Park Rangers	30	18	1	11	81	55	37
Watford	30	14	9	7	48	37	37
Cambridge United	30	13	5	12	62	59	31
Ipswich Town	30	13	5	12	35	46	31
Chelsea	30	13	3	14	60	56	29
Charlton Athletic	30	10	9	11	54	55	29
Norwich City	30	11	4	15	54	67	26
West Ham United	30	12	2	16	57	71	26
Fulham	30	9	7	14	55	77	25
Southend United	30	8	6	16	45	62	22
Portsmouth	30	8	6	16	33	52	22
Leyton Orient	30	9	3	18	37	67	21
Gillingham	30	6	4	20	36	75	16

Division Two

	P	W	D	L	F	A	Pts
Wimbledon	26	19	3	4	67	26	41
Bristol City	26	16	2	8	55	35	34
Brentford	26	12	8	6	39	26	32
Luton Town	26	14	1	11	57	47	29
Brighton & Hove Albion	26	11	6	9	48	49	28
AFC Bournemouth	26	11	6	9	37	39	28
Tottenham Hotspur	26	11	5	10	48	50	27
Southampton	26	8	9	9	28	31	25
Crystal Palace	26	10	4	12	38	33	24
Oxford United	26	8	4	14	48	52	20
Swindon Town	26	7	6	13	29	45	20
Bristol Rovers	26	6	7	13	36	57	19
Colchester United	26	9	1	16	24	47	19
Reading	26	6	6	14	35	52	18

REPUBLIC OF IRELAND

Qualifying Table 1992–93

	P	W	D	L	F	A	Pts
Bohemians	22	10	10	2	37	12	30
Cork City	22	12	5	5	36	25	29
Derry City	22	9	10	3	17	12	28
Shelbourne	22	10	7	5	42	24	27
Dundalk	22	8	10	4	29	24	26
Limerick City	22	6	11	5	24	18	23
St Patrick's Ath	22	5	13	4	19	17	23
Shamrock Rovers	22	6	6	10	33	27	18
Drogheda U	22	3	11	8	20	32	17
Sligo Rovers	22	4	9	9	10	25	17
Bray Wanderers	22	2	9	11	13	35	13
Waterford U	22	5	3	14	22	51	13

Final Round

	P	W	D	L	F	A	Pts
Bohemians	32	13	14	5	46	19	40
Shelbourne	32	15	10	7	53	29	40
Cork City	32	16	8	8	47	34	40
Dundalk	32	13	13	6	35	28	39
Derry City	32	11	15	6	26	23	37
Limerick City	32	6	15	11	27	31	27

Title Round

	P	W	D	L	F	A	Pts
Shelbourne	4	1	2	1	3	3	4
Bohemians	4	1	2	1	2	2	4
Cork City	4	1	2	1	2	2	4

Play-offs: Cork City 1, Bohemians 0; Cork City 3, Shelbourne 2; Bohemians 2, Shelbourne 1. Cork City champions.

HIGHLAND LEAGUE

	P	W	D	L	F	A	Pts
Elgin City	34	24	5	5	110	35	77
Cove Rangers	34	23	4	7	78	37	73
Lossiemouth	34	21	6	7	104	54	69
Caledonian	34	21	6	7	76	41	69
Ross County	34	19	7	8	87	49	64
Huntly	34	19	5	10	96	55	62
Clachnacuddin	34	17	7	10	47	34	58
Inverness Thistle	34	17	6	11	55	50	57
Buckie Thistle	34	17	4	13	62	55	55
Fraserburgh	34	15	7	12	63	52	52
Deveronvale	34	14	4	16	57	71	46
Keith	34	12	9	13	46	59	45
Brora Rangers	34	11	8	15	72	74	41
Peterhead	34	8	10	16	61	80	34
Rothes	34	4	8	22	42	104	20
Fort William	34	5	4	25	37	89	19
Forres Mechanics	34	4	6	24	40	94	18
Nairn County	34	1	2	31	26	126	5

The result of this competition was declared null and void

Third Qualifying Round

Fleetwood Town v Blyth Spartans	1-3
Goole Town v Bishop Auckland	0-1
Emley v Spennymoor United	2-6
Warrington Town v Stockton	5-2
Morecambe v Southport	2-2, 3-1
Horwich RMI v Winsford United	1-2
Mossley v Frickley Athletic	2-4
Guisborough Town v Shildon	2-0
Whitby Town v South Bank	2-1
Accrington Stanley v Tow Law Town	6-0
Billingham Synthonia v Consett	1-1, 6-2
Northallerton Town v Newcastle Blue Star	2-1
Nuneaton Borough v Burton Albion	0-0, 3-0
Grays Athletic v Atherstone United	2-1
Heybridge Swifts v Halesowen Town	1-0
Wealdstone v Solihull Borough	5-2
St Albans City v Purfleet	2-0
Stourbridge v Leek Town	1-4
Stafford Rangers v Wembley	1-1, 1-0
Harrow Borough v Stevenage Borough	2-2, 0-4
Sutton Coldfield Town v VS Rugby	1-1, 4-5
Chesham United v Leicester United	7-3
Slough Town v Bromley	3-1
Poole Town v Bashley	1-1, 2-2, 2-4
Newport AFC v Sutton United	1-2
Weston-super-Mare v Windsor & Eton	1-0
Basingstoke Town v Dulwich Hamlet	3-0
Abingdon Town v Dorking	2-1
Kingstonian v Canterbury City	5-0
Yeading v Walton & Hersham	3-1

Worcester City v Salisbury	2-1
Hastings Town v Wokingham Town	2-1

First Round

Spennymoor United v Boston United	1-2
Telford United v Northwich Victoria	2-1
Marine v Blyth Spartans	2-0
Hyde United v Runcorn	1-2
Warrington Town v Guisborough Town	2-1
Gateshead v Gretna	3-0
Barrow v Billingham Synthonia	0-1
Winsford United v Altrincham	1-0
Murton v Nuneaton Borough	1-2
Stalybridge Celtic v Accrington Stanley	2-0
Bishop Auckland v Leek Town	1-0
Northallerton Town v Whitby Town	3-0
Morecambe v Frickley Athletic	5-1
Macclesfield Town v Witton Albion	0-0, 0-0, 1-2
Sutton United v Woking	3-0
Basingstoke Town v Kingstonian	1-4
Yeading v Slough Town	1-1, 1-2
Welling United v Aylesbury United	2-1
Grays Athletic v Stafford Rangers	1-0
Merthyr Tydfil v Wivenhoe Town	3-0
Heybridge Swifts v Worcester City	4-0
Yeovil Town v Dagenham & Redbridge	0-0, 1-2
St Albans City v Weston-super-Mare	1-0
Dover Athletic v Hastings Town	1-1, 2-0
Kidderminster Harriers v Enfield	1-3
Wycombe Wanderers v Cheltenham Town	3-1
Stevenage Borough v Bath City	2-0

Kettering Town v
  Bromsgrove Rovers   0-0, 1-4
Wealdstone v Bashley   1-2
Farnborough Town v
  Abingdon Town   4-0
VS Rugby v Chesham
  United   1-6
*Gloucester City received a
bye*

Second Round
Farnborough Town v
  Enfield   4-0
Bishop Auckland v
  Warrington Town   0-1
St Albans City v Witton
  Albion   0-2
Nuneaton Borough v
  Marine   0-1
Northallerton Town v
  Bashley   1-0
Stevenage Borough v
  Grays Athletic   0-1
Billingham Synthonia v
  Winsford United   1-2
Welling United v Boston
  United   1-2
Gateshead v Heybridge
  Swifts   3-1
Kingstonian v Telford
  United   1-2
Morecambe v Wycombe
  Wanderers   1-1, 0-2
Sutton United v Slough
  Town   3-1
Chesham United v Dover
  Athletic   1-0

Bromsgrove Rovers v
  Dagenham & Redbridge   3-1
Gloucester City v Runcorn 3-3, 2-2,
                           0-0, 1-4
Stalybridge Celtic v
  Merthyr Tydfil   1-1, 0-1

Third Round
Telford United v Boston
  United   1-1, 0-4
Grays Athletic v
  Gateshead   1-1, 0-3
Chesham United v Sutton
  United   1-3
Merthyr Tydfil v
  Warrington Town   1-1, 2-3
Wycombe Wanderers v
  Bromsgrove Rovers   2-0
Witton Albion v Marine   1-0
Runcorn v Wnsford
  United   1-0
Northallerton Town v
  Farnborough Town   1-3

Fourth Round
Witton Albion v
  Farnborough Town   3-2
Sutton United v
  Warrington Town   2-1
Wycombe Wanderers v
  Gateshead   1-0
Boston United v Runcorn   0-2

Semi-finals
Wycombe Wanderers v
  Sutton United   2-3, 4-0
Runcorn v Witton Albion   2-0, 0-1

FINAL at Wembley
10 MAY

Wycombe Wanderers (2) 4 *(Cousins, Kerr, Thompson, Carroll)*

Runcorn (1) 1 *(Shaugnessy)* 32,968

Wycombe Wanderers: Hyde; Cousins, Cooper, Kerr, Crossley, Thompson, Carroll,
Ryan, Hutchinson (Hayrettin), Scott, Guppy.
Runcorn: Williams; Bates, Robertson, Hill, Harold (Connor), Anderson, Brady
(Parker), Brown, Shaughnessy, McKenna, Brabin.
Referee: I. Borrett (Norfolk).

FA CHALLENGE VASE 1992–93

Third Round

Bridgnorth Town v Atherton Collieries	4-0
Knowsley United v Flixton	5-2
Hinckley Athletic v Clipstone Welfare	1-0
Bamber Bridge v Cammell Laird	1-2
Curzon Ashton v Chester-le-Street Town	7-1
Burscough v Ponteland United	1-0
Dunston FB v Billingham Town	5-1
Brigg Town v Bridlington Town	1-3
Atherton LR v Ashton United	1-2
Eastwood Hanley v Durham City	2-5
Cray Wanderers v Tring Town	2-3
Stratford Town v Bilston Town	0-2
Buckingham Town v Saffron Walden Town	3-2
Harwich & Parkeston v Banstead Athletic	0-3
Feltham & Hounslow Borough v Tunbridge Wells	1-2
Tilbury v Hoddesdon Town	2-3
Barton Rovers v Diss Town	2-1
Bourne Town v Peacehaven & Telscombe	4-4, 0-4
Norwich United v Harefield United	1-2
Burnham v Gresley Rovers	1-2
Cranleigh v Hailsham Town	1-3
Sittingbourne v Malden Vale	4-2
Walthamstow Pennant v Lowestoft Town	0-1
Littlehampton Town v Pelsall Villa	0-1
Canvey Island v Kings Lynn	1-0
Hartley Wintney v Rothwell Town	0-3
Newport (IW) v Welton Rovers	2-0
Tiverton Town v Almondsbury Picksons	2-1
First Tower United v Paulton Rovers	0-0, 1-5
Clevedon Town v Bemerton Heath Harlequins	2-1
Witney Town v Forest Green Rovers	1-2
Newquay v Evesham United	1-3

Fourth Round

Bridlington Town v Curzon Ashton	5-3
Burscough v Cammell Laird	0-1
Gresley Rovers v Bridgnorth Town	3-0
Hinckley Athletic v Pelsall Villa	2-2, 1-4
Dunston FB v Durham City	3-1
Bilston Town v Ashton United	3-0
Rothwell Town v Knowsley United	1-0
Newport (IW) v Lowestoft Town	4-1
Evesham United v Clevedon Town (ordered to be replayed), 1-3	0-2
Harefield United v Canvey Island	2-2, 0-1
Peacehaven & Telscombe v Sittingbourne	4-1
Tring Town v Banstead Athletic	0-1
Buckingham Town v Paulton Rovers	4-0
Forest Green Rovers v Hailsham Town	6-5
Barton Rovers v Tiverton Town	0-4
Hoddesdon Town v Tunbridge Wells	3-1

Fifth Round

Buckingham Town v Pelsall Villa	1-0 ;
Rothwell Town v Bridlington Town	1-2
Gresley Rovers v Peacehaven & Telscombe	1-0

Banstead Athletic v Newport (IW)	3-0	Gresley Rovers v Dunston FB	2-0
Forest Green Rovers v Tiverton Town	0-6	Buckingham Town v Tiverton Town	1-4
Dunston FB v Cammell Laird	2-1	Canvey Island v Bilston Town	2-0
Bilston Town v Hoddesdon Town	3-2		
Canvey Island v Clevedon Town	1-0		

Semi-finals

Bridlington Town v Gresley Rovers 2-1, 1-1

Sixth Round

Bridlington Town v Banstead Athletic 1-0

Tiverton Town v Canvey Island 2-0, 0-1

FINAL at Wembley

8 MAY

Bridlington Town (0) 0 *(Radford)*

Tiverton Town (0) 0 9061

Bridlington Town: Taylor; Brentano, McKenzie, Harvey, Bottomley, Woodcock, Grocock, Roberts, Jones, Radford (Tyrell), Parkinson.
Tiverton Town: Nott; Smith J, Saunders N, Saunders M, Short (Scott), Steele, Annunziata, Smith K, Everett, Daly, Hynds (Rogers).
Referee: R. Hart (Darlington).

First Round

Carlisle United v York City	1-1, 0-2
Stockport County v Oldham Athletic	2-2, 2-6
Burnley v Barnsley	2-2, 0-3
Blackpool v Tranmere Rovers	1-2
Rotherham United v Blackburn Rovers	2-2, 2-2, 1-2
Bradford City v Darlington	3-1
Sunderland v Preston North End	1-2
Bury v Sheffield United	1-3
Norwich City v Peterborough United	5-0
Derby County v Cambridge United	4-1
Ipswich Town v Leicester City	1-0
Nottingham Forest v Aston Villa	4-2
Northampton Town v Walsall	0-1
Stoke City v Shrewsbury Town	4-1
Scunthorpe United v Bedworth United	4-0
Kidderminster Harriers v Wolverhampton Wanderers	2-7
Luton Town v Port Vale	4-1
Whyteleafe v Fulham (at Fulham)	1-8
Dulwich Hamlet v Carshalton Athletic	3-1
Farnborough Town v Lewes	0-1
Worthing v Sutton United	2-6
Wembley v Boreham Wood	1-1, 1-1, 0-1
St Albans City v Brighton & HA	0-4
Charlton Athletic v Gillingham	1-0
Egham Town v Cambridge City	1-2
Bedfont v Wycombe Wanderers	1-2
Epsom & Ewell v Croydon	1-2
Cardiff City v Bashley	2-2, 3-1
Hungerford Town v Swansea City	0-2
Bristol City v Bristol Rovers	4-1
Exeter City v Southampton	2-5
Swindon Town v Oxford United	3-2
AFC Bournemouth v Hereford United	6-3
Witney Town v Reading (at Witney)	0-4

Second Round

Barnsley v Notts County	1-3
Tranmere Rovers v Liverpool	1-6
Bradford City v Oldham Athletic	4-2
Sheffield Wednesday v Leeds United	1-2
Nottingham Forest v Middlesbrough	2-1
Manchester United v Blackburn Rovers	4-1
Preston North End v Everton	3-2
Crewe Alexandra v Stoke City	1-1, 0-1
Hull City v Manchester City	0-1
Doncaster Rovers v Sheffield United	0-2
York City v Newcastle United	2-0
Scunthorpe United v Derby County	0-0, 1-3
Chelsea v Walsall	3-0
Coventry City v Colchester United	2-1
Southend United v Arsenal	2-4
Birmingham City v Wolverhampton Wanderers	4-4, 1-4
Ipswich Town v Norwich City	0-3
Boreham Wood v Queens Park Rangers	1-7
Leyton Orient v West Ham United	2-1
Watford v Tottenham Hotspur	2-3
Luton Town v West Bromwich Albion	1-2
Wycombe Wanderers v Cambridge City	2-1
Reading v Dulwich Hamlet	2-2, 2-1
Crystal Palace v Cardiff City	2-0
Bristol City v Epsom & Ewell	5-2
Brentford v Lewes	6-1
Wimbledon v Portsmouth	3-3, 2-1
Sutton United v Fulham	2-4

Swansea City v AFC
Bournemouth   2-1

Swindon Town v
Southampton   1-0

Millwall v Plymouth
Argyle   2-2, 5-0

Charlton Athletic v
Brighton & Hove Albion 1-1, 2-3

Third Round

Preston North End v
Manchester City   1-1, 3-1

Derby County v
Nottingham Forest   1-3

Stoke City v Leeds United   2-6

Manchester United v Notts
County   3-1

West Bromwich Albion v
York City   1-1, 0-2

Liverpool v Bradford City 1-1, 1-1,
                               3-1

Sheffield United v
Wolverhampton Wanderers   4-3

Brentford v Leyton Orient   3-5

Tottenham Hotspur v
Norwich City   1-2

Wycombe Wanderers v
Brighton & Hove Albion 1-1, 0-9

Fulham v Wimbledon   2-2, 2-3

Bristol City v Swansea City   2-1

Crystal Palace v Millwall   0-2

Chelsea v Reading   3-2

Queens Park Rangers v
Coventry City   5-3
(at Harrow Borough)

Swindon Town v Arsenal   5-2

Fourth Round

Nottingham Forest v
Preston North End   3-3, 4-3

Leeds United v Queens
Park Rangers   5-1

Norwich City v Chelsea   3-2

Manchester United v
Wimbledon   3-0

Sheffield United v
Liverpool   0-0, 3-2

Millwall v Brighton &
Hove Albion   3-0

Bristol City v Swindon
Town   1-0

York City v Leyton Orient   2-0

Fifth Round

Sheffield United v Leeds
United   2-2, 1-2

Bristol City v Norwich
City   3-4

Manchester United v York
City   5-0

Millwall v Nottingham
Forest   0-0, 3-2

Semi-finals

Manchester United v
Millwall   1-2, 2-0

Norwich City v Leeds
United   1-4, 2-0

FINAL First Leg

10 APR

Manchester United (0) 0

Leeds United (1) 2 *(Forrester, Whelan)* 30,562

Manchester U: Whitmarsh; O'Kane, Riley, Casper, Neville, Gillespie, Butt, Beckham (Savage), Irving (Murdock), Scholes, Thornley.
Leeds United: Pettinger; Couzens, Sharp, Tinkler, Daly, Bowman, Smithard, Ford, Whelan, Oliver, Forrester.
Referee: P. Durkin (Portland).

Second Leg

13 MAY

Leeds United (2) 2 *(Forrester, Smithard)*

Manchester United (1) 1 (Scholes (pen)) 31,037

Leeds United: Pettinger; Couzens, Sharp, Tinkler, Daly, Bowman (Tobin), Smithard, Ford, Whelan, Oliver (Byrne), Forrester.
Manchester United: Whitmarsh; Neville, Riley, Casper, Neville, Gillespie, Scholes, Beckham, Irving (Murdock), Savage, Thornley.
Referee: P. Durkin (Portland).

OTHER AWARDS 1992–93

FOOTBALLER OF THE YEAR

The Football Writers' Association Award for the Footballer of the Year went to Chris Waddle of Sheffield Wednesday and England.

Past Winners
1947–48 Stanley Matthews (Blackpool), 1948–49 Johnny Carey (Manchester U), 1949–50 Joe Mercer (Arsenal), 1950–51 Harry Johnston (Blackpool), 1951–52 Billy Wright (Wolverhampton W), 1952–53 Nat Lofthouse (Bolton W), 1953–54 Tom Finney (Preston NE), 1954–55 Don Revie (Manchester C), 1955–56 Bert Trautmann (Manchester C), 1956–57 Tom Finney (Preston NE), 1957–58 Danny Blanchflower (Tottenham H), 1958–59 Syd Owen (Luton T), 1959–60 Bill Slater (Wolverhampton W), 1960–61 Danny Blanchflower (Tottenham H), 1961–62 Jimmy Adamson (Burnley), 1962–63 Stanley Matthews (Stoke C), 1963–64 Bobby Moore (West Ham U), 1964–65 Bobby Collins (Leeds U), 1965–66 Bobby Charlton (Manchester U), 1966–67 Jackie Charlton (Leeds U), 1967–68 George Best (Manchester U), 1968–69 Dave Mackay (Derby Co) shared with Tony Book (Manchester C), 1969–70 Billy Bremner (Leeds U), 1970–71 Frank McLintock (Arsenal), 1971–72 Gordon Banks (Stoke C), 1972–73 Pat Jennings (Tottenham H), 1973–74 Ian Callaghan (Liverpool), 1974–75 Alan Mullery (Fulham), 1975–76 Kevin Keegan (Liverpool), 1976–77 Emlyn Hughes (Liverpool), 1977–78 Kenny Burns (Nottingham F), 1978–79 Kenny Dalglish (Liverpool), 1979–80 Terry McDermott (Liverpool), 1980–81 Frans Thijssen (Ipswich T), 1981–82 Steve Perryman (Tottenham H), 1982–83 Kenny Dalglish (Liverpool), 1983–84 Ian Rush (Liverpool), 1984–85 Neville Southall (Everton), 1985–86 Gary Lineker (Everton), 1986–87 Clive Allen (Tottenham H), 1987–88 John Barnes (Liverpool), 1988–89 Steve Nicol (Liverpool), 1989–90 John Barnes (Liverpool), 1990–91 Gordon Strachan (Leeds), 1991–92 Gary Lineker (Tottenham H).

THE PFA AWARDS 1993

Player of the Year: Paul McGrath (Aston Villa).
Previous Winners: 1974 Norman Hunter (Leeds U); 1975 Colin Todd (Derby Co); 1976 Pat Jennings (Tottenham H); 1977 Andy Gray (Aston Villa); 1978 Peter Shilton (Nottingham F); 1979 Liam Brady (Arsenal); 1980 Terry McDermott (Liverpool); 1981 John Wark (Ipswich T); 1982 Kevin Keegan (Southampton); 1983 Kenny Dalglish (Liverpool); 1984 Ian Rush (Liverpool); 1985 Peter Reid (Everton); 1986 Gary Lineker (Everton); 1987 Clive Allen (Tottenham H); 1988 John Barnes (Liverpool); 1989 Mark Hughes (Manchester U); 1990 David Platt (Aston Villa); 1991 Mark Hughes (Manchester U); 1992 Gary Pallister (Manchester U).
Young Player of the Year: Ryan Giggs (Manchester U).
Previous Winners: 1974 Kevin Beattie (Ipswich T); 1975 Mervyn Day (West Ham U); 1976 Peter Barnes (Manchester C); 1977 Andy Gray (Aston Villa); 1978 Tony Woodcock (Nottingham F); 1979 Cyrille Regis (WBA); 1980 Glenn Hoddle (Tottenham H); 1981 Gary Shaw (Aston Villa); 1982 Steve Moran (Southampton); 1983 Ian Rush (Liverpool); 1984 Paul Walsh (Luton T); 1985 Mark Hughes (Manchester U); 1986 Tony Cottee (West Ham U); 1987 Tony Adams (Arsenal); 1988 Paul Gascoigne (Tottenham H); 1989 Paul Merson (Arsenal); 1990 Matthew Le Tissier (Southampton); 1991 Lee Sharpe (Manchester U); 1992 Ryan Giggs (Manchester U).

Merit Award: 1968 Manchester United team.

Previous Winners: 1974 Bobby Charlton CBE, Cliff Lloyd OBE; 1975 Dennis Law; 1976 George Eastham OBE; 1977 Jack Taylor OBE; 1978 Bill Shankly OBE; 1979 Tom Finney OBE; 1980 Sir Matt Busby CBE; 1981 John Trollope MBE; 1982 Joe Mercer OBE; 1983 Bob Paisley OBE; 1984 Bill Nicholson; 1985 Ron Greenwood; 1986 The 1966 England World Cup team, Sir Alf Ramsey, Harold Shepherdson; 1987 Sir Stanley Matthews; 1988 Billy Bonds MBE; 1989 Nat Lofthouse; 1990 Peter Shilton; 1991 Tommy Hutchinson; 1992 Brian Clough.

ALEX FERGUSON TAKES BARCLAYS TOP ACCOLADE AS MANAGER OF THE YEAR IN MAN.U's ANNUS MIRABILIS

Alex Ferguson was named unopposed, by a panel of 30 leading football journalists and commentators, as Barclays Bank Manager of the Year in honour of Manchester United's historic success in the inaugural season of the FA Premier League. He received the Barclays trophy, a Silver Eagle memento and a cheque for £5,000.

The presentation was made at the Barclays Bank Managers Awards Luncheon at the Savoy Hotel, London, by Mr Alastair Robinson, group vice-chairman of Barclays Bank.

This is Ferguson's 8th managerial award, following his arrival at old Trafford, in 5 years: six overall Manager of the Month awards (Jan. '89, Jan., Aug., Sept & Dec. '91 & Apr. '93) and a Special Award in 1991, the year of United's Cup-Winners Cup victory).

It is the first time in 25 years the Manager of the Year title has gone to Old Trafford: Matt Busby was the last winner in 1968, the year his side won the European Cup.

This is the sixth time a Scot has claimed the accolade in the past eight years: Kenny Dalglish in '86, '88 & '90 & George Graham in '89 & '91.

BARCLAYS BANK DIVISIONAL MANAGERS OF THE SEASON 1992–93

Kevin Keegan (Newcastle Utd.) in Barclays League Division One; *Lou Macari* (Stoke City) in Division Two; & *Eddie May* (Cardiff City) in Division Three were named by The Football League for the Barclays Bank Divisional Manager of the Season awards. Each received a Silver Eagle memento and a cheque for £1,000.

BARCLAYS BANK ACHIEVEMENT AWARD

Jim Smith of Portsmouth received the Barclays Bank Achievement Award – a Silver Eagle trophy and a cheque for £1,000 – on the vote of the League Managers Association. "The award is designed to highlight the efforts of the manager who, in the opinion of his peers, has worked wonders with the resources available to him," reads the citation.

BARCLAYS BANK SPECIAL AWARD

A special award is being struck by Barclays for Brian Clough listing, and in recognition of, his record number of 25 managerial awards in the 25 years between August '69 and May '93.

BARCLAYS BANK SERVICE TO FOOTBALL ACCOLADE

Stan Cullis, a legendary football figure as a player and manager, prinicipally with Wolverhampton Wanderers, was named for the Barclays Bank Service to Football Award by the members of IFMA (the Institute of Football Management & Administration – which includes managers, secretaries, coaches, trainers, physios, commercial managers and chief executives & directors).

Stan – born at Ellesmere Port in 1916 almost next door to his great friend, the late Joe Mercer – is the 16th winner of this accolade which comprises a silver rosebowl and a Barclays cheque for £1,000.

As a player, pre-war, Stan was described by his manager, Major Frank Buckley as "without doubt the most outstanding of the many great players who have won the Black and Gold."

Between 1937 and 1939 he won 12 international caps for England and like many of his generation was unfortunate to have his career interrupted by the war – although he played in 20 war time internationals, skippering England and the British Army.

As manager at Molineux between 1948 and 1964 he was outstanding: Wolves winning the FA Cup twice and the Football League Championship three times within the space of 12 years. Stan also pioneered floodlight football "on the box" and over 160,000 fans also came through the turnstiles to see Wolves defeat Moscow Spartak, Honved & Moscow Dynamo in those avant-garde fixtures. He spent his final six years as a manager from 1964 with Birmingham City.

BARCLAYS YOUNG EAGLE OF THE YEAR

Ryan Giggs, Manchester Utd's 19 year-old Welsh wizard, was named Barclays Young Eagle of the Year by England manager Graham Taylor and his distinguished panel*. He received his prize – the Barclays Silver Eagle Trophy and a cheque for £5,000 – at the 1992 Barclays Bank Managers Awards luncheon at the Savoy Hotel in London.

THE SCOTTISH PFA AWARDS 1992

Player of the Year: Premier Division: Andy Goram (Rangers); First Division: Gordan Dalziel (Raith R); Second Division: Sandy Ross (Brechin C).

Previous Winners: 1978 Derek Johnstone (Rangers); 1979 Paul Hegarty (Dundee U); 1980 Davie Provan (Celtic); 1981 Sandy Clark (Airdrieonians); 1982 Mark McGhee (Aberdeen); 1983 Charlie Nicholas (Celtic); 1984 Willie Miller (Aberdeen); 1985 Jim Duffy (Morton); 1986 Richard Gough (Dundee U); 1987 Brian McClair (Celtic); 1988 Paul McStay (Celtic); 1989 Theo Snelders (Aberdeen); 1990 Jim Bett (Aberdeen); 1991 Paul Elliott (Celtic); Ally McCoist (Rangers).

Young Player of the Year: Eoin Jess (Aberdeen).

Previous Winners: 1978 Graeme Payne (Dundee U); 1979 Graham Stewart (Dundee U); 1980 John MacDonald (Rangers); 1981 Francis McAvennie (St Mirren); 1982 Charlie Nicholas (Celtic); 1983 Pat Nevin (Clyde); 1984 John Robertson (Hearts); 1985 Craig Levein (Hearts); 1986 Craig Levein (Hearts); 1987 Robert Fleck (Rangers); 1988 John Collins (Hibernian); 1989 Bill McKinlay (Dundee U); 1990 Scott Crabbe (Hearts); 1991 Eoin Jess (Aberdeen); 1992 Phil O'Donnell (Motherwell).

SCOTTISH FOOTBALL WRITERS' ASSOCIATION

Player of the Year 1993 – Andy Goram (Rangers)

1965 **Billy McNeill** (Celtic)	1979 **Andy Ritchie** (Morton)
1966 **John Greig** (Rangers)	1980 **Gordon Strachan** (Aberdeen)
1967 **Ronnie Simpson** (Celtic)	1981 **Alan Rough** (Partick Th)
1968 **Gordon Wallace** (Raith R)	1982 **Paul Sturrock** (Dundee U)
1969 **Bobby Murdoch** (Celtic)	1983 **Charlie Nicholas** (Celtic)
1970 **Pat Stanton** (Hibernian)	1984 **Willie Miller** (Aberdeen)
1971 **Martin Buchan** (Aberdeen)	1985 **Hamish McAlpine** (Dundee U)
1972 **Dave Smith** (Rangers)	1986 **Sandy Jardine** (Hearts)
1973 **George Connelly** (Celtic)	1987 **Brian McClair** (Celtic)
1974 **Scotland's World Cup Squad**	1988 **Paul McStay** (Celtic)
1975 **Sandy Jardine** (Rangers)	1989 **Richard Gough** (Rangers)
1976 **John Greig** (Rangers)	1990 **Alex McLeish** (Aberdeen)
1977 **Danny McGrain** (Celtic)	1991 **Maurice Malpas** (Dundee U)
1978 **Derek Johnstone** (Rangers)	1992 **Ally McCoist** (Rangers)

EUROPEAN FOOTBALLER OF THE YEAR 1992

Marco Van Basten of AC Milan and Holland received the annual *France Football* award for European Footballer of the Year and thus won the honour for the third time. He had previously taken the accolade in 1988 and 1989. But it was not a wholly happy start to 1993 for Van Basten, who suffered an ankle injury and struggled to regain his best form after lengthy absence. He was also honoured as FIFA World Player of the Year.

Past winners

1956 **Stanley Matthews** (Blackpool)	1975 **Oleg Blokhin** (Dynamo Kiev)
1957 **Alfredo Di Stefano** (Real Madrid)	1976 **Franz Beckenbauer** (Bayern Munich)
1958 **Raymond Kopa** (Real Madrid)	
1959 **Alfredo Di Stefano** (Real Madrid)	1977 **Allan Simonsen** (Borussia Moenchengladbach)
1960 **Luis Suarez** (Barcelona)	
1961 **Omar Sivori** (Juventus)	1978 **Kevin Keegan** (SV Hamburg)
1962 **Josef Masopust** (Dukla Prague)	1979 **Kevin Keegan** (SV Hamburg)
1963 **Lev Yashin** (Moscow Dynamo)	1980 **Karl-Heinz Rummenigge** (Bayern Munich)
1964 **Denis Law** (Manchester United)	
1965 **Eusebio** (Benfica)	1981 **Karl-Heinz Rummenigge** (Bayern Munich)
1966 **Bobby Charlton** (Manchester United)	
	1982 **Paolo Rossi** (Juventus)
1967 **Florian Albert** (Ferencvaros)	1983 **Michel Platini** (Juventus)
1968 **George Best** (Manchester United)	1984 **Michel Platini** (Juventus)
1969 **Gianni Rivera** (AC Milan)	1985 **Michel Platini** (Juventus)
1970 **Gerd Muller** (Bayern Munich)	1986 **Igor Belanov** (Dynamo Kiev)
1971 **Johan Cruyff** (Ajax)	1987 **Ruud Gullit** (AC Milan)
1972 **Franz Beckenbauer** (Bayern Munich)	1988 **Marco Van Basten** (AC Milan)
	1989 **Marco Van Basten** (AC Milan)
1973 **Johan Cruyff** (Barcelona)	1990 **Lothar Matthaus** (Inter-Milan)
1974 **Johan Cruyff** (Barcelona)	1991 **Jean-Pierre Papin** (Marseille)

BRITISH FOOTBALL RECORDS

HIGHEST SCORES
First class match
Arbroath 36 Bon Accord 0 *Scottish Cup 1st Rd, 12.9.1885.*
International match
England 13 Ireland 0 *Belfast, 18.2.1882.*
FA Premier League
Blackburn R 7, Norwich C 1, *3.10.1992*

Football League
Tranmere R 13, Oldham Ath 4, *Division 3(N) 26.12.1935*
FA Cup
Preston NE 26 Hyde U 0 *1st Rd, 15.10.1887*
League Cup
West Ham U 10 Bury 0 *2nd Rd, 2nd leg, 25.10.1983*
Liverpool 10 Fulham 0 *2nd Rd, 1st leg, 23.9.1986*
Scottish League
East Fife 13 Edinburgh C 2 *Division 2, 11.12.1937*

MOST GOALS IN A SEASON
FA Premier League
68 in 42 games, Blackburn R, *1992–93*

Football League
128 in 42 games, Aston Villa *Division 1, 1930–31*
128 in 42 games, Bradford C *Division 3(N), 1928–29*
134 in 46 games, Peterborough U *Division 4, 1960–61*
Scottish League
142 in 34 games, Raith R *Division 2, 1937–38*

FEWEST GOALS IN A SEASON
FA Premier League
40 in 42 games, Arsenal, *1992–93*

Football League *(minimun 42 games)*
24 in 42 games, Stoke C *Division 1, 1984–85*
24 in 42 games, Watford *Division 2, 1971–72*
27 in 46 games, Stockport Co *Division 3, 1969–70*
Scottish League *(minimum 30 games)*
18 in 39 games, Stirling A *Division 1, 1980–81*

MOST GOALS AGAINST IN A SEASON
FA Premier League
75 in 42 games, Middlesbrough, *1992–93*

Football League
141 in 34 games, Darwen *Division 2, 1898–99*
Scottish League
146 in 38 games, Edinburgh C *Division 2, 1931–32*

FEWEST GOALS AGAINST IN A SEASON
FA Premier League
31 in 42 games, Manchester U, *1992–93*

Football League *(minimum 42 games)*
16 in 42 games, Liverpool *Division 1, 1978–79*
21 in 46 games, Port Vale *Division 3(N), 1953–54*
Scottish League *(minimum 30 games)*
14 in 38 games, Celtic *Division 1, 1913–14*

MOST POINTS IN A SEASON
Football League *(2 points for a win)*
72 in 42 games, Doncaster R *Division 3(N), 1946–47*
74 in 46 games, Lincoln C *Division 4, 1975–76*
FA Premier League *(3 points for a win)*
84 in 42 games, Manchester U, *1992–93*

Football League *(3 points for a win)*
76 in 38 games, Arsenal *Division 1, 1988–89*
76 in 38 games, Liverpool *Division 1, 1988–89*
90 in 40 games, Liverpool *Division 1, 1987–88*
90 in 42 games, Everton *Division 1, 1984–85*
102 in 46 games, Swindon T *Division 4, 1985–86*
Scottish League
72 in 44 games, Celtic *Premier Division, 1987–88*
72 in 44 games, Rangers *Premier Division, 1991–92*
69 in 38 games, Morton *Division 2, 1966–67*
76 in 42 games, Rangers *Division 1, 1920–21*

FEWEST POINTS IN A SEASON
FA Premier League
40 in 42 games, Nottingham F, *1992–93*

Football League *(minimum 34 games)*
8 in 34 games, Doncaster R *Division 2, 1904–5*
8 in 34 games, Loughborough T *Division 2, 1899–1900*
11 in 40 games, Rochdale *Division 3(N), 1931–32*
17 in 42 games, Stoke C *Division 1, 1984–85*
19 in 46 games, Workington *Division 4, 1976–77*
Scottish League *(minimum 30 games)*
6 in 30 games, Stirling A *Division 1, 1954–55*
7 in 34 games, Edinburgh C *Division 2, 1936–37*
11 in 36 games, St Johnstone *Premier Division, 1975–76*

MOST WINS IN A SEASON
FA Premier League
24 in 42 games, Manchester U, *1992–93*

Football League
33 in 42 games, Doncaster R *Division 3 (N), 1946–47*
Scottish League
27 in 36 games, Aberdeen *Premier Division, 1984–85*
33 in 38 games, Morton *Division 2, 1966–67*
33 in 44 games, Rangers *Premier Division, 1991–92*
35 in 42 games, Rangers *Division 1, 1920–21*
Home
Brentford won all 21 games in Division 3(S) in 1929–30
Away
Doncaster R won 18 out of 21 games in Division 3(N) in 1946–47

FEWEST WINS IN A SEASON
FA Premier League
10 in 42 games, Nottingham F, *1992–93*

Football League *(minimum 34 games)*
1 in 34 games, Loughborough T *Division 2, 1899–1900*
2 in 46 games, Rochdale *Division 3, 1973–74*
Scottish League *(minimum 22 games)*
0 in 22 games, Vale of Leven *Division 1, 1891–92*
1 in 38 games, Forfar Ath *Division 2, 1974–75*

MOST DEFEATS IN A SEASON
FA Premier League
22 in 42 games, Nottingham F, *1992–93*

Football League
33 in 40 games, Rochdale *Division 3(N), 1931–32*
Scottish League
30 in 36 games, Brechin C *Division 2, 1962–63*
31 in 42 games, St Mirren *Division 1, 1920–21*

FEWEST DEFEATS IN A SEASON
FA Premier League
6 in 42 games, Manchester U, *1992–93*

Football League *(minimum 20 games)*
0 in 22 games, Preston NE *Division 1, 1888–89*
0 in 28 games, Liverpool *Division 2, 1893–94*
1 in 38 games, Arsenal *Division 1, 1990–91*
2 in 40 games, Liverpool *Division 1, 1987–88*
2 in 42 games, Leeds U *Division 1, 1968–69*
3 in 46 games, Port Vale *Division 3(N), 1953–54*
Scottish League *(minimum 20 games)*
1 in 42 games, Rangers *Division 1, 1920–21*

MOST DRAWS IN A SEASON
FA Premier League
16 in 42 games, Crystal Palace, *1992–93*
16 in 42 games, Ipswich T, *1992–93*

Football League
23 in 42 games, Norwich C *Division 1, 1978–79*
23 in 46 games, Exeter C, *Division 4, 1986–87*
Scottish League
19 in 44 games, Hibernian *Premier Division, 1987–88*
21 in 44 games, East Fife *Division 1, 1986–87*

MOST GOALS IN A GAME
Football League
10, Joe Payne, for Luton T v Bristol R *Division 3(S), 13.4.1936*
Scottish League
8, Jimmy McGrory, for Celtic v Dunfermline Ath *Division 1, 14.9.1928*
8, Owen McNally, for Arthurlie v Armadale *Division 2, 1.10.1927*
8, Jim Dyet, for King's Park v Forfar Ath *Division 2, 2.1.1930*
8, John Calder, for Morton v Raith R *Division 2, 18.4.1936*

FA Cup
9, Ted MacDougall, for Bournemouth v Margate *1st Rd, 20.11.1971*
Scottish Cup
13, John Petrie, for Arbroath v Bon Accord *1st Rd, 12.9.1885*

MOST LEAGUE GOALS IN A SEASON
Football League
60 in 39 games, W.R. "Dixie" Dean (Everton) *Division 1, 1927–28*
59 in 37 games, George Camsell (Middlesbrough) *Division 2, 1926–27*
Scottish League
66 in 38 games, Jim Smith (Ayr U) *Division 2, 1927–28*
52 in 34 games, William McFadyen (Motherwell) *Division 1, 1931–32*

MOST LEAGUE GOALS IN A CAREER
Football League
434 in 619 games, Arthur Rowley *(WBA, Fulham, Leicester C, Shrewsbury T, 1946–65)*
Scottish League
410 in 408 games, Jimmy McGrory *(Celtic, Clydebank, Celtic, 1922–38)*

MOST CUP WINNERS' MEDALS
FA Cup
5, James Forrest (Blackburn R) *1884, 1885, 1886, 1890, 1891*
5, Hon. A.F. Kinnaird (Wanderers) *1873, 1877, 1878*, (Old Etonians) *1879, 1882*
5, C.H.R. Wollaston (Wanderers) *1872, 1873, 1876, 1877, 1878*
Scottish Cup
7, Jimmy McMenemy, (Celtic) *1904, 1907, 1908, 1911, 1912, 1914*, (Partick T) *1921*
7, Bob McPhail, (Airdrieonians) *1924*, (Rangers) *1928, 1930, 1932, 1934, 1935, 1936*
7, Billy McNeill (Celtic) *1965, 1967, 1969, 1971, 1972, 1974, 1975*

RECORD ATTENDANCES
FA Premier League
44,619, Liverpool v Everton, Anfield, 20.3.1993

Football League
83,260, Manchester U v Arsenal, Maine Road, 17.1.1948
Scottish League
118,567, Rangers v Celtic, Ibrox Stadium, 2.1.1939
FA Cup-tie (other than the final)
84,569, Manchester C v Stoke C, 6th Rd at Maine Road, 3.3.1934 (*a British record for any game outside London or Glasgow*)
FA Cup Final
126,047*, Bolton W v West Ham U, Wembley, 28.4.1923 **The figure stated is the official one. Perhaps as many as 70,000 more got in without paying.*
European Cup
135,826, Celtic v Leeds U, semi-final at Hampden Park, 15.4.1970

TRANSFER MILESTONES
First four-figure transaction
Alf Common: Sunderland to Middlesbrough £1,000, February 1905.
First five-figure transaction
David Jack: Bolton W to Arsenal £10,340, October 1928.

First six-figure transaction
Alan Ball: Blackpool to Everton £112,000, August 1966.
First £200,000 transaction
Martin Peters: West Ham U to Tottenham H £200,000, March 1970
First seven-figure transaction
Trevor Francis: Birmingham C to Nottingham F £1,000,000, February 1979.
First £2,000,000 transaction
Paul Gascoigne: Newcastle U to Tottenham H £2,000,000, July 1988.
Highest British transaction
David Platt: Aston Villa to Bari £5,500,000, July 1991
Paul Gascoigne: Tottenham H to Lazio £5,500,000, May 1992

MOST GOALS IN AN INTERNATIONAL MATCH
England
5, Malcolm Macdonald (Newcastle U) v Cyprus, Wembley, 16.4.1975
5, Willie Hall (Tottenham H) v Ireland, Old Trafford, 16.11.1938
5, G.O. Smith (Corinthians) v Ireland, Sunderland, 18.2.1899
5*, Steve Bloomer (Derby Co) v Wales, Cardiff, 16.3.1896 *(*one of which was credited to him in only some sources)*
5, Oliver Vaughton (Aston Villa) v Ireland, Belfast 18.2.1882
Scotland
5, Charles Heggie (Rangers) v Ireland, Belfast, 20.3.1886
Ireland
6, Joe Bambrick (Linfield) v Wales, Belfast, 1.2.1930
Wales
4, James Price (Wrexham) v Ireland, Wrexham, 25.2.1882
4, Mel Charles (Cardiff C) v N. Ireland, Cardiff, 11.4.1962
4, Ian Edwards (Chester) v Malta, Wrexham, 25.10.1978

MOST GOALS IN AN INTERNATIONAL CAREER
England
49 in 106 games, Bobby Charlton *(Manchester U)*
Scotland
30 in 55 games, Denis Law *(Huddersfield T, Manchester C, Torino, Manchester U)*
30 in 102 games, Kenny Dalglish *(Celtic, Liverpool)*
Ireland
12 in 25 games, Billy Gillespie *(Sheffield U)*
12 in 38 games, Colin Clarke *(Bournemouth, QPR, Southampton, Portsmouth)*
12 in 63 games, Gerry Armstrong *(Tottenham H, Watford, Real Mallorca, WBA, Chesterfield)*
12 in 11 games, Joe Bambrick *(Linfield, Chelsea)*
Wales
24 in 59 games, Ian Rush *(Liverpool, Juventus)*
Republic of Ireland
20 in 70 games, Frank Stapleton *(Arsenal, Manchester U, Ajax, Derby Co, Le Havre, Blackburn R)*

HIGHEST INTERNATIONAL SCORES
World Cup Match: New Zealand 13, Fiji 0, 1981
Olympic Games: Denmark 17, France 1, 1908; Germany 16, USSR 0, 1912
Friendlies: Germany 13, Finland 0, 1940; Spain 13, Bulgaria 0, 1933
European Cup: Feyenoord 12, KR Reykjavik 2, 1969
Cup Winners' Cup: Sporting Lisbon 16, Apoel Nicosia 1, 1963
Fairs/UEFA Cup: 1FC Cologne 13, Union Luxembourg 0, 1965

LEAGUE TITLE WINS

FA PREMIER LEAGUE – Manchester U 1.

LEAGUE DIVISION 1 – Liverpool 18, Arsenal 10, Everton 9, Manchester U 7, Aston Villa 7, Sunderland 6, Newcastle U 5, Sheffield W 4, Huddersfield T 3, Leeds U 3, Wolverhampton W 3, Blackburn R 2, Portsmouth 2, Preston NE 2, Burnley 2, Manchester C 2, Tottenham H 2, Derby Co 2, Chelsea 1, Sheffield U 1, WBA 1, Ipswich T 1, Nottingham F 1 each.

LEAGUE DIVISION 2 – Leicester C 6, Manchester C 6, Sheffield W 5, Birmingham C (one as Small Heath) 4, Derby Co 4, Liverpool 4, Ipswich T 3, Leeds U 3, Notts Co 3, Preston NE 3, Middlesbrough 3, Stoke C 3, Grimsby T 2, Norwich C 2, Nottingham F 2, Tottenham H 2, WBA 2, Aston Villa 2, Burnley 2, Chelsea 2, Manchester U 2, West Ham U 2, Wolverhampton W 2, Bolton W 2, Huddersfield T, Bristol C, Brentford, Bury, Bradford C, Everton, Fulham, Sheffield U, Newcastle U, Coventry C, Blackpool, Blackburn R, Sunderland, Crystal Palace, Luton T, QPR, Oxford U, Millwall, Oldham Ath 1 each.

LEAGUE DIVISION 3 – Portsmouth 2, Oxford U 2, Plymouth Arg, Southampton, Bury, Northampton T, Coventry C, Carlisle U, Hull C, QPR, Watford, Leyton O, Preston NE, Aston Villa, Bolton W, Oldham Ath, Blackburn R, Hereford U, Mansfield T, Wrexham, Shrewsbury T, Grimsby T, Rotherham U, Burnley, Bradford C, Bournemouth, Reading, Sunderland, Wolverhampton W, Bristol R, Cambridge U, Brentford, Cardiff C 1 each.

LEAGUE DIVISION 4 – Chesterfield 2, Doncaster R 2, Peterborough U 2, Port Vale, Walsall, Millwall, Brentford, Gillingham, Brighton, Stockport Co, Luton T, Notts Co, Grimsby T, Southport, Mansfield T, Lincoln C, Cambridge U, Watford, Reading, Huddersfield T, Southend U, Sheffield U, Wimbledon, York C, Swindon T, Northampton T, Wolverhampton W, Rotherham U, Exeter C, Darlington, Burnley 1 each.

To 1957–58

DIVISION 3 (South) – Bristol C 3; Charlton Ath, Ipswich T, Millwall, Notts Co, Plymouth Arg, Swansea T 2 each; Brentford, Bristol R, Cardiff C, Crystal Palace, Coventry C, Fulham, Leyton O, Luton T, Newport Co, Nottingham F, Norwich C, Portsmouth, QPR, Reading, Southampton, Brighton 1 each.

DIVISION 3 (North) – Barnsley, Doncaster R, Lincoln C 3 each; Chesterfield, Grimsby T, Hull C, Port Vale, Stockport Co 2 each; Bradford PA, Bradford C, Darlington, Derby Co, Nelson, Oldham Ath, Rotherham U, Stoke C, Tranmere R, Wolverhampton W, Scunthorpe U 1 each.

LEAGUE ATTENDANCES 1992–93

PREMIER LEAGUE STATISTICS

	Average Gate			Season 1992/93	
	1991/92	1992/93	+/−%	Highest	Lowest
Arsenal	31,905	24,403	−23.5	29,740	18,253
Aston Villa	24,818	29,594	+19.2	39,063	17,120
Blackburn Rovers	13,251	16,246	+22.6	20,305	13,556
Chelsea	18,684	18,787	+0.6	25,157	12,739
Coventry City	13,876	14,951	+7.7	24,410	10,455
Crystal Palace	17,618	15,748	−10.6	30,115	11,224
Everton	23,148	20,445	−11.7	35,827	14,023
Ipswich Town	14,274	18,223	+27.7	22,007	14,053
Leeds United	29,459	29,250	−0.7	34,166	25,774
Liverpool	34,799	37,004	+6.3	44,619	29,574
Manchester City	27,690	24,698	−10.8	37,136	19,524
Manchester United	44,984	35,152	−21.9	40,693	29,736
Middlesbrough	14,703	16,724	+13.7	22,463	12,290
Norwich City	13,858	16,154	+16.6	20,610	12,452
Nottingham Forest	23,721	21,910	−7.6	26,752	17,553
Oldham Athletic	15,087	12,859	−14.8	17,106	10,946
Queens Park Rangers	13,592	15,015	+10.5	21,056	10,677
Sheffield United	22,097	18,801	−14.9	30,039	14,628
Sheffield Wednesday	29,560	27,263	−7.8	38,668	20,918
Southampton	14,070	15,382	+9.3	19,654	10,827
Tottenham Hotspur	27,761	27,740	−0.1	33,709	20,098
Wimbledon	6,905	8,405	+21.7	30,115	3,039

BARCLAYS LEAGUE: DIVISION ONE STATISTICS

	Average Gate			Season 1992/93	
	1991/92	1992/93	+/−%	Highest	Lowest
Barnsley	7,508	6,415	−14.6	13,263	3,855
Birmingham City	12,400	12,328	−0.6	22,234	6,807
Brentford	7,156	8,476	+18.4	11,912	6,334
Bristol City	11,479	11,004	−4.1	21,854	6,755
Bristol Rovers	5,850	5,745	−1.8	7,714	3,921
Cambridge United	7,078	5,545	−21.7	8,077	3,896
Charlton Athletic	6,786	7,005	+3.2	12,945	4,205
Derby County	14,664	15,020	+2.4	21,478	12,166
Grimsby Town	6,921	6,088	+12.0	14,402	4,117
Leicester City	15,202	15,362	+1.1	19,687	10,284
Luton Town	9,715	8,212	−15.5	10,959	6,687
Millwall	7,921	9,188	+16.0	15,821	5,924
Newcastle United	21,148	29,018	+37.2	30,360	26,136
Notts County	10,987	8,151	−25.8	14,841	5,037
Oxford United	5,671	6,356	+12.1	9,499	3,785
Peterborough United	6,279	8,064	+28.4	15,517	5,169
Portsmouth	11,789	13,706	+16.3	24,955	8,943
Southend United	6,733	5,396	−19.9	12,813	2,651
Sunderland	18,390	17,258	−6.2	28,098	13,314
Swindon Town	10,009	10,715	+7.1	17,936	6,090
Tranmere Rovers	8,845	8,071	−8.8	13,118	5,248
Watford	8,511	8,275	−2.8	13,115	5,785
West Ham United	21,342	16,001	−25.0	27,399	10,326
Wolverhampton W	13,743	13,598	−1.1	17,270	10,593

BARCLAYS LEAGUE: DIVISION TWO STATISTICS

	Average Gate			Season 1992/93	
	1991/92	1992/93	+/-%	Highest	Lowest
AFC Bournemouth	5,471	4,454	-18.6	7,129	2,829
Blackpool	4,335	5,501	+26.9	9,386	3,164
Bolton Wanderers	6,030	9,062	+50.3	21,720	4,136
Bradford City	6,115	6,581	+7.6	10,235	3,900
Brighton & Hove Albion	8,002	6,710	-16.1	8,741	4,731
Burnley	10,521	10,537	+0.2	16,667	7,332
Chester City	1,857	2,992	+61.1	5,237	1,614
Exeter City	3,627	3,275	-9.7	6,534	2,393
Fulham	4,492	4,736	+5.4	9,143	3,285
Hartlepool United	3,201	3,144	-1.8	4,396	1,791
Huddersfield Town	7,540	5,918	-21.5	11,089	3,563
Hull City	4,115	4,672	+13.5	9,088	3,167
Leyton Orient	4,460	5,377	+20.6	10,800	3,436
Mansfield Town	3,803	3,730	-19.2	6,820	2,527
Plymouth Argyle	6,739	6,377	-5.4	11,370	4,612
Port Vale	7,382	8,092	+9.6	20,373	5,370
Preston North End	4,722	5,689	+20.5	10,403	3,330
Reading	3,841	4,782	+24.5	8,026	2,491
Rotherham United	4,750	4,769	+0.4	9,021	3,050
Stockport County	4,896	5,504	+12.4	9,402	3,759
Stoke City	13,007	16,579	+27.5	24,334	10,854
Swansea City	3,367	5,199	+54.4	8,366	2,656
West Bromwich Albion	12,711	15,161	+19.3	29,341	12,305
Wigan Athletic	2,862	2,598	-9.2	5,403	1,432

BARCLAYS LEAGUE: DIVISION THREE STATISTICS

	Average Gate			Season 1992/93	
	1991/92	1992/93	+/-%	Highest	Lowest
Barnet	3,643	3,429	-5.9	4,985	2,623
Bury	2,901	2,670	-8.0	4,550	1,739
Cardiff City	6,195	8,560	+38.2	17,253	4,348
Carlisle United	2,554	3,611	+41.4	5,357	2,527
Chesterfield	3,439	3,213	-6.6	5,452	2,271
Colchester United	3,514	3,777	+7.5	5,609	2,774
Crewe Alexandra	3,733	3,455	-7.4	4,549	2,671
Darlington	2,904	1,960	-32.5	3,787	1,366
Doncaster Rovers	2,058	2,411	+17.2	3,350	1,719
Gillingham	3,135	3,301	+5.3	6,985	2,043
Halifax Town	1,633	2,231	+36.6	7,451	1,230
Hereford United	2,735	2,211	-19.2	4,039	1,401
Lincoln City	2,822	3,331	+18.0	4,359	2,689
Northampton Town	2,789	3,234	+16.0	7,504	1,922
Rochdale	2,784	2,312	-17.0	4,500	1,446
Scarborough	1,677	1,929	+15.0	3,863	1,300
Scunthorpe United	3,189	3,147	-1.3	7,407	1,970
Shrewsbury Town	3,456	3,411	-1.3	7,278	1,527
Torquay United	2,734	2,695	-1.4	4,645	1,771
Walsall	3,367	3,628	+7.8	5,573	2,719
Wrexham	2,608	4,987	+91.2	10,852	1,893
York City	2,506	3,946	+57.5	6,568	2,443

GM VAUXHALL CONFERENCE FIXTURES 1993–94

	Altrincham	Bath City	Bromsgrove R	Dagenham/Redbridge	Dover Athletic	Gateshead	Halifax Town	Kettering Town	Kidderminster H
Altrincham	—	28-8	5-2	2-10	26-2	27-11	30-4	2-5	11-9
Bath City	19-2	—	20-11	7-5	26-4	18-9	30-10	2-10	30-8
Bromsgrove R.	30-8	30-4	—	22-3	13-11	16-10	8-1	19-3	27-12
Dagenham/Redbridge	29-1	13-11	12-2	—	25-9	26-3	16-10	27-12	6-11
Dover Athletic	18-9	27-11	1-1	3-1	—	4-9	18-12	12-2	21-8
Gateshead	1-2	16-4	15-1	20-11	30-4	—	4-4	12-3	19-2
Halifax Town	1-1	26-3	6-11	9-4	12-3	27-12	—	21-8	4-12
Kettering Town	30-10	4-12	7-5	26-2	4-4	11-12	23-4	—	8-1
Kidderminster H.	7-5	1-1	4-4	5-2	11-12	5-3	3-1	23-8	—
Macclesfield T.	3-1	12-3	24-8	4-9	28-8	6-11	19-3	18-9	16-4
Merthyr Tydfil	21-8	24-8	2-5	11-12	30-11	29-1	9-10	2-4	1-3
Northwich Vic.	29-3	26-2	12-10	23-4	8-1	23-11	2-4	9-4	29-1
Runcorn	20-11	23-4	26-3	5-3	16-10	15-3	11-9	30-4	12-2
Slough Town	23-4	9-10	26-2	1-1	24-8	2-5	28-8	27-11	30-10
Southport	12-10	11-9	28-8	15-1	30-10	28-9	24-8	5-3	18-12
Stafford Rangers	5-3	15-1	3-1	28-8	19-2	9-4	5-2	9-10	2-10
Stalybridge C.	4-12	29-2	30-10	30-4	16-4	30-8	28-9	6-11	16-10
Telford United	4-4	6-11	25-9	18-12	26-3	8-1	19-2	4-9	15-3
Welling United	4-9	4-4	23-4	9-10	27-12	12-2	29-1	13-11	30-4
Witton Albion	18-12	25-9	4-9	30-10	5-2	24-8	27-11	15-1	14-9
Woking	12-3	11-12	15-3	2-4	12-10	23-4	25-9	3-1	27-11
Yeovil Town	9-10	27-12	11-12	24-8	20-11	30-10	16-4	29-1	2-4

Macclesfield T	Merthyr Tydfil	Northwich Vic	Runcorn	Slough Town	Southport	Stafford Rangers	Stalybridge C	Telford United	Welling United	Witton Albion	Woking	Yeovil Town
27-12	15-1	13-11	12-4	16-10	2-4	25-9	24-8	16-4	11-12	12-2	8-1	19-3
21-8	9-4	18-12	5-2	30-11	8-1	16-10	4-9	2-4	28-9	5-3	19-3	3-1
29-1	27-11	19-2	12-3	2-4	16-4	7-9	18-12	4-12	2-10	9-4	18-9	21-8
8-1	12-3	27-11	16-4	30-8	21-8	2-5	19-2	18-9	25-4	19-3	4-12	4-4
5-3	6-11	2-5	7-5	4-12	9-4	29-1	19-3	15-1	29-3	2-10	30-8	23-4
2-4	19-3	1-1	21-8	2-10	7-5	4-12	3-1	28-8	26-2	27-10	18-12	5-2
26-4	26-2	11-12	15-1	7-5	12-2	30-8	26-10	2-10	20-11	18-9	23-10	4-9
26-3	11-9	28-8	25-9	15-3	20-11	16-4	5-2	1-1	18-12	30-8	19-2	16-10
11-10	25-9	25-10	9-10	4-9	12-3	26-2	18-9	23-4	28-8	20-11	26-3	15-1
—	18-12	5-2	19-2	20-11	2-10	4-4	11-12	26-10	2-5	23-4	15-1	30-4
13-11	—	30-10	18-9	5-2	4-9	20-11	23-4	3-1	16-4	7-5	5-3	1-1
7-5	4-12	—	6-11	18-9	30-8	19-3	5-3	20-11	15-1	27-12	21-8	2-10
30-8	4-4	4-9	—	8-1	4-12	27-12	2-10	24-8	30-10	29-1	9-4	26-2
12-2	12-10	26-3	11-12	—	30-4	11-9	15-1	19-3	3-1	6-11	4-4	21-9
15-3	19-2	3-1	2-5	25-9	—	23-4	4-4	11-12	5-2	26-2	9-10	27-11
30-10	30-4	24-8	1-1	18-12	6-11	—	27-11	12-2	2-4	11-12	4-9	18-9
1-1	8-1	12-2	30-11	21-8	27-12	12-3	—	22-2	7-5	2-4	20-11	9-4
26-2	27-12	30-4	27-11	29-1	16-10	23-11	13-11	—	9-4	21-8	2-5	30-8
27-11	30-8	16-10	19-3	19-2	18-9	21-8	26-3	5-3	—	8-1	1-1	6-11
9-10	28-8	4-4	3-1	16-4	1-1	15-2	2-5	12-10	12-3	—	30-4	19-2
11-9	5-10	16-4	28-8	27-12	29-1	7-5	26-2	30-10	24-8	16-10	—	29-3
25-9	26-4	12-3	23-10	5-3	26-3	8-1	28-8	7-5	14-9	11-9	12-2	—

FA PREMIER LEAGUE FIXTURES 1993–94

	Arsenal	Aston Villa	Blackburn R	Chelsea	Coventry C	Everton	Ipswich T	Leeds U	Liverpool
Arsenal	—	6.11	26.2	16.4	14.8	28.8	11.9	24.8	26.3
Aston Villa	23.4	—	1.1	23.10	11.9	26.2	12.3	30.3	7.5
Blackburn R	1.9	9.4	—	4.12	23.11	29.12	7.5	22.1	5.3
Chelsea	20.11	22.1	14.8	—	12.3	3.1	11.12	23.4	25.9
Coventry C	4.12	5.3	30.4	18.9	—	6.11	23.12	25.9	1.9
Everton	19.2	31.8	4.4	30.3	23.4	—	12.2	23.11	18.9
Ipswich T	5.3	18.9	27.11	21.8	4.4	30.10	—	17.10	1.1
Leeds U	18.12	3.1	23.10	6.11	19.3	30.4	15.1	—	19.2
Liverpool	2.10	28.11	12.9	19.3	26.2	12.3	9.4	28.8	—
Manchester C	15.1	2.4	24.8	30.4	27.8	8.12	3.1	14.8	23.10
Manchester U	19.9	18.12	26.12	5.3	7.5	22.1	24.11	1.1	30.3
Newcastle U	7.5	26.3	29.8	4.4	8.12	25.8	26.2	22.12	21.11
Norwich C	12.2	29.12	8.12	15.1	2.10	19.3	25.8	11.12	24.11
Oldham Ath	23.10	25.9	11.12	12.2	24.8	11.9	14.8	26.2	15.1
QPR	30.3	4.12	6.11	20.12	23.10	16.4	2.10	4.4	18.8
Sheffield U	4.4	16.4	15.1	27.11	12.2	11.12	28.8	13.3	26.12
Sheffield W	21.8	18.8	19.3	19.2	20.11	2.4	23.4	30.10	4.12
Southampton	19.3	30.4	16.4	27.12	15.1	14.8	8.12	11.9	12.2
Swindon T	27.12	30.10	2.10	1.1	30.3	16.10	20.11	7.5	22.8
Tottenham H	16.8	19.2	12.2	1.9	1.1	3.10	19.3	20.11	18.12
West Ham U	24.11	16.10	12.3	2.10	11.12	9.4	2.4	8.12	23.4
Wimbledon	1.1	21.8	29.3	17.8	26.12	27.11	23.10	26.3	4.4

Manchester C	Manchester U	Newcastle U	Norwich C	Oldham Ath	QPR	Sheffield U	Sheffield W	Southampton	Swindon T	Tottenham H	West Ham U	Wimbledon
16.10	12.3	27.11	30.10	22.1	3.1	29.12	11.12	25.9	2.4	7.12	30.4	9.4
27.12	23.8	2.10	4.4	19.3	14.8	20.11	8.12	24.11	12.2	28.8	15.1	11.12
18.12	2.4	19.2	18.8	21.8	23.4	18.10	25.9	20.11	26.3	30.10	18.9	3.1
22.11	11.9	28.12	16.10	30.10	25.8	7.5	28.8	2.4	9.4	26.2	26.3	8.12
19.2	27.11	18.8	26.3	18.12	22.1	31.10	16.4	16.10	3.1	9.4	21.8	2.4
17.8	23.10	18.12	25.9	5.3	20.11	21.8	27.12	4.12	15.1	26.3	1.1	7.5
29.3	30.4	31.8	18.12	4.12	26.3	19.2	6.11	17.8	16.4	26.9	27.12	22.1
4.12	9.4	2.4	21.8	30.8	29.12	18.9	12.2	5.3	27.11	16.4	17.8	2.10
22.1	4.1	16.4	30.4	16.10	8.12	2.4	14.8	30.10	11.12	25.8	6.11	28.12
—	7.11	9.4	16.4	2.10	11.9	19.3	27.11	28.12	26.2	11.12	12.2	12.3
23.4	—	21.8	4.12	4.4	30.10	18.8	26.3	19.2	25.9	16.10	1.9	20.11
1.1	11.12	—	30.3	23.4	16.10	24.11	13.9	22.1	12.3	14.8	25.9	30.10
20.11	15.8	4.1	—	7.5	12.3	28.4	26.2	9.4	28.8	2.4	23.10	11.9
26.3	29.12	6.11	27.11	—	2.4	9.4	30.4	4.1	7.12	12.3	16.4	28.8
5.3	12.2	15.1	18.9	27.12	—	1.9	1.1	21.8	30.4	27.11	19.2	19.3
25.9	7.12	30.4	6.11	1.1	26.2	—	23.10	26.3	14.8	11.9	29.3	24.8
7.5	2.10	5.3	1.9	24.11	9.4	22.1	—	18.9	29.12	3.1	18.12	16.10
4.4	28.8	24.10	1.1	30.3	11.12	2.10	12.3	—	25.8	6.11	27.11	26.2
1.9	19.3	18.9	19.2	18.8	24.11	4.12	4.4	18.12	—	22.1	5.3	23.4
21.8	15.1	4.12	27.12	18.9	7.5	5.3	30.3	23.4	23.10	—	4.4	24.11
1.11	26.2	19.3	22.1	20.11	28.8	3.1	25.8	7.5	11.9	28.12	—	14.8
18.9	16.4	12.2	5.3	19.2	27.9	18.12	15.1	31.8	6.11	30.4	4.12	—

FOOTBALL LEAGUE FIXTURES 1993–94

DIVISION ONE

	Barnsley	Birmingham C	Bolton W	Bristol C	Charlton Ath	Crystal Palace	Derby Co	Grimsby T	Leicester C	Luton T	Middlesbrough
Barnsley	—	28.8	27.11	15.1	9.10	20.11	27.12	6.11	25.9	26.3	24.8
Birmingham C	5.3	—	30.4	16.4	18.12	31.8	4.9	18.9	15.3	25.9	26.3
Bolton W	7.5	19.10	—	26.3	5.3	4.9	30.10	18.12	18.9	15.3	23.4
Bristol C	16.10	2.11	2.10	—	18.9	21.8	5.3	9.4	14.9	19.2	4.12
Charlton Ath	22.1	14.8	28.8	12.3	—	25.9	2.11	5.2	16.10	4.12	7.5
Crystal Palace	23.4	11.12	26.2	22.2	19.3	—	5.2	30.10	22.1	2.11	13.11
Derby Co	2.4	26.2	12.2	28.8	16.4	23.10	—	20.11	28.12	9.10	23.2
Grimsby T	4.12	12.3	14.8	1.1	23.10	12.2	23.4	—	2.11	4.4	29.3
Leicester C	19.3	11.9	12.3	11.12	15.1	9.10	5.4	16.4	—	12.2	26.2
Luton T	2.10	19.3	11.9	11.1	6.11	16.4	22.1	29.12	30.10	—	12.3
Middlesbrough	19.2	2.10	20.11	6.11	27.11	30.4	21.8	3.1	4.9	18.9	—
Millwall	4.9	12.2	15.1	30.4	16.3	1.1	18.9	27.11	5.3	30.3	23.10
Nottingham F	16.3	4.12	19.3	4.4	1.1	19.2	18.8	21.8	5.2	5.3	27.12
Notts Co	28.12	11.1	9.4	9.10	30.4	6.11	25.9	2.4	26.3	15.1	14.8
Oxford U	2.11	29.3	11.12	11.9	12.2	27.12	13.11	2.10	23.4	23.10	1.1
Peterborough U	17.8	23.10	16.4	27.11	20.11	29.3	15.3	4.9	19.12	27.12	12.2
Portsmouth	9.4	23.4	28.12	25.9	17.8	5.3	16.10	19.2	3.1	21.8	2.11
Southend U	5.2	1.1	12.1	26.2	27.12	6.4	7.5	22.1	4.12	13.11	11.9
Stoke C	30.10	27.12	23.2	30.3	4.4	26.3	1.1	16.10	13.11	7.5	11.12
Sunderland	3.1	9.10	2.4	12.2	21.8	15.3	18.12	7.9	9.4	4.9	15.1
Tranmere R	18.9	7.5	9.10	23.10	19.2	18.12	29.3	5.3	21.8	14.9	4.4
Watford	21.8	15.1	23.10	20.11	4.9	27.11	19.2	15.3	2.4	18.12	9.10
WBA	19.12	4.4	6.11	27.12	30.3	18.9	26.3	30.4	19.2	1.1	25.9
Wolverhampton	13.11	22.2	3.1	14.8	2.10	15.1	4.12	19.3	7.5	23.4	28.8

Millwall	Nottingham F	Notts Co	Oxford U	Peterborough U	Portsmouth	Southend U	Stoke C	Sunderland	Tranmere R	Watford	WBA	Wolverhampton W
26.2	11.9	4.4	16.4	11.12	1.1	23.10	12.2	29.3	12.3	22.2	14.8	30.4
30.10	6.11	19.2	3.1	5.2	20.11	9.4	2.4	22.1	27.11	16.10	28.12	22.8
16.10	25.9	1.1	31.8	2.11	4.4	19.2	21.8	27.12	22.1	5.2	4.12	29.3
13.11	28.12	22.1	15.3	7.5	19.3	4.9	3.1	30.10	5.2	23.4	2.4	18.12
11.9	9.4	13.11	30.10	23.4	11.12	2.4	28.12	22.2	24.8	26.2	3.1	26.3
9.4	24.8	5.12	2.4	3.1	28.8	29.12	2.10	11.9	14.8	7.5	12.3	16.10
12.3	11.12	19.3	30.4	11.9	15.1	27.11	9.4	14.8	3.1	12.1	2.10	6.11
7.5	22.2	27.12	26.3	26.2	24.8	9.10	15.1	11.12	28.8	11.9	29.1	25.9
28.8	23.10	2.10	20.11	14.8	30.3	6.11	30.4	1.1	23.2	27.12	12.1	27.11
3.1	28.8	16.10	5.2	2.4	22.2	30.4	27.11	26.2	11.12	14.8	9.4	20.11
5.2	2.4	18.12	9.4	30.10	16.4	15.3	14.9	16.10	28.12	22.1	19.3	5.3
—	16.4	20.10	6.11	19.3	27.12	21.8	19.12	6.4	20.11	2.10	9.10	19.2
3.11	—	30.10	4.9	13.11	2.10	19.12	18.9	7.5	16.10	30.3	23.4	22.1
11.12	12.2	—	27.11	22.2	23.10	3.1	20.11	28.8	26.2	12.3	11.9	16.4
4.12	26.2	7.5	—	12.3	14.8	15.1	9.10	11.1	19.3	28.8	22.2	4.4
25.9	30.4	21.8	18.9	—	9.10	5.3	19.2	26.3	6.11	5.4	15.1	1.1
2.4	26.3	5.2	18.12	22.1	—	18.9	4.9	4.12	30.10	13.11	7.5	15.3
23.2	15.8	30.3	16.10	28.8	12.3	—	19.3	23.4	2.10	3.11	11.12	30.10
14.8	23.4	22.1	12.1	26.2	25.9		—	3.11	11.9	4.12	28.8	5.2
28.12	27.11	5.3	19.2	2.10	6.11	20.11	16.4	—	30.4	19.3	23.10	18.9
23.4	15.1	4.9	25.9	4.12	12.2	26.3	15.3	13.11	—	1.1	2.11	27.12
26.3	3.1	18.9	5.3	28.12	30.4	16.4	6.11	25.9	9.4	—	12.2	7.9
22.1	20.11	16.3	21.8	16.10	27.11	1.9	5.3	5.2	16.4	30.10	—	4.9
24.8	9.10	2.11	28.12	9.4	11.9	12.2	23.10	12.3	2.4	11.12	26.2	—

DIVISION TWO

	Barnet	Blackpool	Bournemouth	Bradford C	Brentford	Brighton & HA	Bristol R	Burnley	Cambridge U	Cardiff C	Exeter C
Barnet	—	26.2	11.9	6.11	29.1	2.4	2.10	29.12	23.10	10.10	3.1
Blackpool	4.9	—	25.9	5.3	21.8	30.10	3.1	9.4	19.12	18.9	5.2
Bournemouth	5.3	19.3	—	21.8	27.12	16.10	18.12	4.9	18.9	15.3	30.10
Bradford C	23.4	11.9	11.12	—	4.4	14.8	22.1	16.10	25.9	7.5	28.8
Brentford	30.10	11.12	2.4	29.12	—	12.3	8.1	20.11	26.3	2.11	14.8
Brighton & HA	27.12	29.1	15.1	18.12	18.9	—	1.9	16.3	1.1	19.2	2.10
Bristol R	26.3	30.3	14.8	9.10	12.2	23.2	—	25.9	27.11	15.1	15.9
Burnley	4.4	1.1	26.2	15.1	30.4	14.9	19.3	—	29.1	12.2	27.11
Cambridge U	5.2	14.8	12.3	19.3	2.10	9.4	7.5	30.10	—	19.11	28.12
Cardiff C	22.1	12.3	14.9	27.11	16.4	28.8	16.10	8.1	30.4	—	22.2
Exeter C	29.3	23.10	29.1	19.2	18.12	26.3	15.3	7.5	4.4	31.8	—
Fulham	15.3	12.2	9.10	4.9	1.1	6.11	19.2	5.3	29.3	21.8	16.4
Hartlepool U	2.11	14.9	28.8	23.10	9.10	11.12	23.4	26.3	15.1	29.1	26.2
Huddersfield T	16.10	30.4	3.1	17.4	27.11	26.2	30.10	5.2	6.11	28.12	11.9
Hull C	18.12	16.4	30.4	2.10	31.8	8.1	4.9	3.1	19.2	5.3	9.4
Leyton O	18.9	27.11	23.10	12.2	15.3	25.9	21.8	19.2	27.12	18.12	6.11
Plymouth Arg	8.1	22.2	9.4	30.4	6.11	3.1	5.2	22.1	16.4	19.3	2.4
Port Vale	21.8	15.1	16.4	3.1	19.3	27.11	5.3	18.12	31.8	4.9	30.4
Reading	1.9	6.11	27.11	16.3	19.2	30.4	2.4	21.8	4.9	9.4	22.1
Rotherham U	7.5	2.10	28.12	2.4	4.9	5.2	18.9	31.8	5.3	3.1	8.1
Stockport Co	1.1	27.12	26.3	31.8	29.3	22.1	20.11	18.9	21.8	23.4	16.10
Swansea C	18.2	9.10	12.2	18.9	5.3	28.12	9.4	2.11	15.3	2.4	19.3
Wrexham	25.9	28.8	6.11	9.4	15.1	16.4	28.12	2.4	9.10	23.10	12.3
York C	20.11	4.4	22.2	29.1	23.10	11.9	2.11	23.4	12.2	2.10	11.12

Fulham	Hartlepool U	Huddersfield T	Hull C	Leyton O	Plymouth Arg	Port Vale	Reading	Rotherham U	Stockport Co	Swansea C	Wrexham	York City
14.9	16.4	15.1	14.8	12.3	12.2	11.12	22.2	27.11	9.4	28.8	19.3	30.4
8.1	15.3	20.11	2.11	7.5	31.8	16.10	23.4	26.3	2.4	22.1	19.2	28.12
22.1	19.2	29.3	20.11	5.2	1.1	2.11	7.5	5.4	2.10	8.1	23.4	31.8
26.2	5.2	3.11	26.3	8.1	20.11	30.3	15.9	27.12	23.2	12.3	1.1	30.10
9.4	22.1	7.5	22.2	14.9	23.4	25.9	28.8	26.2	3.1	11.9	16.10	5.2
23.4	21.8	4.9	12.2	19.3	30.3	7.5	20.11	23.10	9.10	6.4	3.11	5.3
28.8	6.11	29.1	26.2	11.12	23.10	11.9	27.12	12.3	30.4	1.1	4.4	16.4
11.9	2.10	23.10	29.3	28.8	9.10	14.8	11.12	22.2	12.3	16.4	27.12	6.11
3.1	16.10	23.4	28.8	2.4	2.11	22.2	26.2	11.9	11.12	14.9	22.1	8.1
11.12	30.10	4.4	11.9	14.8	25.9	26.2	1.1	29.3	6.11	27.12	5.2	26.3
2.11	4.9	5.3	1.1	23.4	27.12	20.11	9.10	12.2	15.1	25.9	18.9	21.8
—	17.12	19.3	15.1	2.10	4.4	27.12	29.1	30.4	23.10	27.11	31.8	18.9
14.8	—	27.12	4.4	22.2	7.5	12.3	12.2	1.1	11.9	29.3	20.11	25.9
25.9	2.4	—	12.3	9.4	26.3	14.9	14.8	11.12	28.8	22.2	8.1	22.1
16.10	28.12	18.9	—	30.10	21.8	22.1	19.3	6.11	27.11	5.2	15.3	2.4
26.3	31.8	1.1	29.1	—	5.3	4.4	15.1	9.10	16.4	30.4	29.3	4.9
28.12	27.11	2.10	11.12	11.9	—	28.8	12.3	14.9	14.8	26.2	30.10	16.10
2.4	18.9	15.3	9.10	29.12	19.2	—	23.10	29.1	12.2	6.11	2.10	9.4
30.10	8.1	18.12	25.9	16.10	18.9	5.2	—	16.4	28.12	26.3	5.3	3.1
20.11	9.4	21.8	23.4	22.1	15.3	30.10	2.11	—	19.3	16.10	17.12	19.2
5.2	5.3	19.2	7.5	2.11	17.12	8.1	4.4	25.9	—	30.10	4.9	15.3
7.5	3.1	31.8	23.10	20.11	4.9	23.4	1.10	14.1	29.1	—	21.8	18.12
22.2	30.4	12.2	14.9	3.1	29.1	26.3	11.9	14.8	26.2	11.12	—	27.11
12.3	19.3	9.10	27.12	26.2	15.1	1.1	29.3	28.8	14.9	14.8	7.5	—

DIVISION THREE

	Bury	Carlisle U	Chester C	Chesterfield	Colchester U	Crewe Alex	Darlington	Doncaster R	Gillingham
Bury	—	12.2	16.4	6.11	19.3	28.8	27.11	15.1	9.4
Carlisle U	8.1	—	19.3	11.9	7.5	28.12	2.4	11.12	2.10
Chester C	2.11	25.9	—	28.8	9.4	7.5	22.1	14.8	28.12
Chesterfield	23.4	5.3	19.2	—	8.1	30.10	4.9	27.12	18.12
Colchester U	25.9	27.11	1.1	12.2	—	11.12	16.4	30.4	29.1
Crewe Alex	19.2	4.4	27.11	29.1	21.8	—	18.9	1.1	23.10
Darlington	7.5	27.12	9.10	26.2	2.11	12.3	—	4.4	15.1
Doncaster R	16.10	21.8	17.12	2.4	20.11	9.4	28.12	—	3.1
Gillingham	1.1	26.3	4.4	14.8	30.10	5.2	16.10	31.8	—
Hereford U	5.2	1.1	6.11	11.12	16.10	22.1	8.1	27.11	16.4
Lincoln C	18.9	16.4	31.8	23.10	14.12	26.3	21.8	9.10	27.11
Mansfield T	26.3	15.1	23.10	3.1	2.4	26.2	30.4	12.3	6.11
Northampton T	18.12	23.10	30.4	27.11	19.2	3.1	2.10	29.1	2.4
Preston NE	31.8	30.4	27.12	9.10	2.10	14.8	6.11	11.9	12.2
Rochdale	20.11	19.2	4.9	25.9	5.3	23.4	18.12	26.3	21.8
Scarborough	30.10	4.9	18.9	30.4	28.12	16.10	3.1	6.11	19.2
Scunthorpe U	21.8	18.9	5.3	28.12	22.1	8.1	30.10	16.4	19.3
Shrewsbury T	4.9	9.10	15.1	9.4	3.1	2.11	5.3	23.10	18.9
Torquay U	5.4	31.8	29.1	15.1	4.9	25.9	19.2	12.2	5.3
Walsall	27.12	29.1	12.2	12.3	23.4	11.9	19.3	28.8	9.10
Wigan Ath	22.1	6.11	2.10	16.4	5.2	2.4	9.4	26.2	30.4
Wycombe W	5.3	18.12	21.8	26.3	18.9	20.11	5.2	25.9	4.9

Hereford U	Lincoln C	Mansfield T	Northampton T	Preston NE	Rochdale	Scarborough	Scunthorpe U	Shrewsbury T	Torquay U	Walsall	Wigan Ath	Wycombe W
23.10	12.3	2.10	14.8	4.1	30.4	29.1	11.12	26.2	29.12	2.4	9.10	11.9
9.4	2.11	16.10	5.2	20.11	28.8	26.2	12.3	22.1	3.1	30.10	23.4	14.8
23.4	3.1	5.2	20.11	2.4	26.2	12.3	11.9	16.10	30.10	8.1	26.3	11.12
21.8	5.2	31.8	7.5	22.1	19.3	20.11	4.4	1.1	16.10	18.9	2.11	2.10
15.1	14.8	27.12	28.8	26.3	11.9	4.4	9.10	31.8	26.2	6.11	23.10	12.3
9.10	2.10	4.9	31.8	17.12	6.11	15.1	12.2	16.4	19.3	5.3	27.12	30.4
12.2	11.12	17.9	26.3	23.4	14.8	31.8	29.1	11.9	28.8	25.9	1.1	23.10
7.5	22.1	17.9	30.10	4.3	2.10	23.4	1.11	5.2	8.1	19.2	4.9	19.3
2.11	7.5	23.4	27.12	8.1	11.12	28.8	25.9	12.3	11.9	22.1	20.11	26.2
—	28.8	4.4	11.9	30.10	12.3	14.8	26.2	27.12	30.4	26.3	25.9	31.8
19.2	—	5.3	25.9	4.9	29.1	1.1	27.12	4.4	6.11	30.4	12.2	15.1
28.12	11.9	—	11.12	25.9	16.4	9.10	28.8	14.8	9.4	27.11	29.1	12.2
5.3	19.3	12.10	—	29.12	9.4	12.2	15.1	6.11	16.4	4.9	18.9	9.10
29.1	26.2	19.3	4.4	—	23.10	11.12	1.1	28.8	12.3	16.4	15.1	27.11
18.9	30.10	2.11	1.1	5.2	—	26.12	7.5	8.1	22.1	16.10	31.8	4.4
18.12	9.4	22.1	8.1	21.8	2.4	—	26.3	25.9	27.11	5.2	5.3	16.4
4.9	2.4	19.2	16.10	9.4	27.11	2.10	—	30.4	5.2	3.1	18.12	6.11
2.4	28.12	17.12	23.4	19.2	12.2	19.3	20.11	—	2.10	21.8	7.5	29.1
20.11	23.4	1.1	2.11	18.9	9.7	7.5	23.10	26.3	—	18.12	21.8	27.12
2.10	20.11	7.5	26.2	2.11	15.1	23.10	31.8	11.12	14.8	—	5.4	1.1
19.3	8.1	30.10	12.3	16.10	4.1	11.9	14.8	27.11	11.12	28.12	—	28.8
3.1	16.10	8.1	22.1	7.5	28.12	2.11	23.4	30.10	2.4	9.4	19.2	—

OTHER FIXTURES—SEASON 1993–94

August

7	Sat	FA Charity Shield
14	Sat	FA Premier League & Football League Season commences
18	Wed	Coca-Cola Cup 1st Round (1st Leg)
25	Wed	Coca-Cola Cup 1st Round (2nd Leg)
28	Sat	FA Challenge Cup Preliminary Round

September

4	Sat	FA Challenge Vase Extra Preliminary Round
7	Tues	England v Poland (U-21) England v Romania (U-18)
8	Wed	England v Poland (WC)
11	Sat	FA Challenge Cup 1st Qualifying Round FA Youth Challenge Cup Preliminary Round*
15	Wed	European Competitions 1st Round (1st Leg)
18	Sat	FA Challenge Trophy—First Round Qualifying
22	Wed	Coca-Cola Cup Second Round (1st Leg)
25	Sat	FA Challenge Cup Second Qualifying Round
28	Tues	FA XI v Herefordshire FA
29	Wed	European Competitions First Round (2nd Leg)

October

2	Sat	FA Challenge Vase Preliminary Round FA Youth Challenge Cup First Round Qualifying*
6	Wed	Coca-Cola Cup Second Round (2nd Leg)
9	Sat	FA Challenge Cup Third Round Qualifying
10	Sun	FA Sunday Cup Preliminary Round (if required)
12	Tues	Holland v England (U-21)
13	Wed	Holland v England (World Cup) Romania v England (U-18)
16	Sat	FA Challenge Trophy Second Round Qualifying FA Youth Challenge Cup Second Round Qualifying* FA County Youth Challenge Cup First Round*
20	Wed	European Competitions Second Round (1st Leg)
23	Sat	FA Challenge Cup Fourth Round Qualifying
27	Wed	Coca-Cola Cup Third Round France v England (U-18)
30	Sat	FA Challenge Vase First Round
31	Sun	FA Sunday Cup First Round

November

3	Wed	European Competitions Second Round (2nd Leg) FA XI v Southern League
13	Sat	FA Challenge Cup First Round Proper FA Youth Challenge Cup First Round Proper*
16	Tues	San Marino v England (WC) England v France (U-18) FA XI v Northern Premier League
17	Wed	San Marino v England (U-21)
20	Sat	FA Challenge Vase Second Round
21	Sun	FA Sunday Cup Second Round
24	Wed	ECL/UEFA Cup Third Round (1st Leg) Holland v England (U-16)
27	Sat	FA Challenge Trophy Third Round Qualifying FA County Youth Challenge Cup Second Round*

December

1	Wed	Coca-Cola Cup Fourth Round
4	Wed	FA Challenge Cup Second Round Proper
7	Tues	FA XI v Isthmian League
8	Wed	ECL/UEFA Cup Third Round (2nd Leg) Italy v England (U-16)
11	Sat	FA Challenge Vase Third Round FA Youth Challenge Cup Second Round Proper*
12	Sun	FA Sunday Cup Third Round

January

8	Sat	FA Challenge Cup Third Round Proper
10	Mon	FA XI v British Students
11	Tues	FA XI v Combined Services
12	Wed	Coca-Cola Cup Fifth Round
15	Sat	FA Challenge Vase Fourth Round FA Youth Challenge Cup Third Round Proper* FA County Youth Challenge Cup Third Round*
16	Sun	FA Sunday Cup Fourth Round
22	Sat	FA Challenge Trophy First Round Proper
29	Sat	FA Challenge Cup Fourth Round Proper

February

| 2 | Wed | International date England v Italy (U-16) |
| 5 | Sat | FA Challenge Vase Fifth Round FA Youth Challenge Cup Fourth Round Proper* |

12 Sat	FA Challenge Trophy Second Round Proper		April	
13 Sun	Coca-Cola Cup Semi-final (1st Leg)		2 Sat	FA Youth Challenge Cup Semi-final*
	FA Sunday Cup Fifth Round		10 Sun	FA Challenge Cup Semi-final
16 Wed	Coca-Cola Cup Semi-final (1st Leg)		13 Wed	ECL/ECWC and UEFA Cup Semi-final (2nd Leg)
19 Sat	FA Challenge Cup Fifth Round Proper		16 Sat	FA Challenge Trophy Semi-final (1st Leg)
	FA County Youth Challenge Cup Fourth Round*		20 Wed	Germany v England (Friendly)
23 Wed	Coca-Cola Cup Semi-final (2nd Leg)		23 Sat	FA Challenge Trophy Semi-final (2nd Leg)
26 Sat	FA Challenge Vase Sixth Round		27 Wed	ECL Semi-final/UEFA Cup Final (1st Leg)
27 Sun	Coca-Cola Semi-final (2nd Leg)		30 Sat	FA County Youth Challenge Cup Final (fixed date)

March			May	
2 Wed	ECL/ECWC and UEFA Cup Quarter-finals (1st Leg)		4 Wed	European Cup Winners' Cup Final
5 Sat	FA Challenge Trophy Third Round Proper		7 Sat	FA Challenge Vase final—Wembley Stadium
	FA Youth Challenge Cup Fifth Round Proper*			FA Youth Challenge Cup Final*
9 Wed	International date England v Holland (U-16)		8 Sun	FA Sunday Cup Final
12 Sat	FA Challenge Cup Sixth Round Proper		11 Wed	UEFA Cup Final (2nd Leg)
16 Wed	ECL/ECWC and UEFA Cup Quarter-final (2nd Leg)		14 Sat	FA Challenge Cup Final—Wembley Stadium International date
19 Sat	FA Challenge Vase Semi-final (1st Leg)		15 Sun	FL Play-off Semi-final (1st Leg)
	FA County Youth Challenge Cup Semi-final*		18 Web	European Champion Clubs' Cup Final
	Anglo-Italian Cup Final—Wembley Stadium			FL Ply-off Semi-final (2nd Leg)
20 Sun	FA Sunday Cup Semi-final		21 Sat	FA Challenge Trophy Final—Wembley Stadium
26 Sat	FA Challenge Trophy Fourth Round Proper		22 Sun	International date
	FA Challenge Vase Semi-final (2nd Leg)		28 Sat	FL Div 3 Play-off Final—Wembley Stadium
27 Sun	Coca-Cola Cup Final		29 Sun	FL Div 2 Play-off Final—Wembley Stadium
30 Wed	ECL/ECWC and UEFA Cup Semi-final (1st Leg)		30 Mon	FL Div 1 Play-off Final—Wembley Stadium Bank Holiday
			June	
			17 Fri	FIFA World Cup Finals commence (end 17 July)

Key

WC—FIFA World Cup — ECL – European Champions League
ECWC – European Cup Winners' Cup — * *Closing dates of rounds*
N.B. Coca-Cola dates refer to middle of week in which matches can be played. Dates for Autoglass Trophy: w/c 27 Sept, 18 Oct, 8 Nov (Round I), 29 Nov (Round 2), 10 Jan (Q-F), 7 Feb (SF), 28 Feb (Area Finals), 21 March (Area Finals), 24 April (Final)

USEFUL ADDRESSES

The Football Association: R. H. G. Kelly, F.C.I.S., 16 Lancaster Gate, London W2 3LW

Scotland: J. Farry, 6 Park Gardens, Glasgow G3 7YE. *041-332 6372*

Northern Ireland (Irish FA): D. I. Bowen, 20 Windsor Avenue, Belfast BT9 6EG. *0232-669458*

Wales: A. Evans, 3 Westgate Street, Cardiff, South Glamorgan CF1 1JF. *0222-372325*

Republic of Ireland (FA of Ireland): S. Connolly, 80 Merrion Square South, Dublin 2. *0001-766864*

International Federation (FIFA): S. Blatter, FIFA House, Hitzigweg 11, CH-8032 Zurich, Switzerland. *1-384-9595. Fax: 1-384-9696*

Union of European Football Associations: G. Aigner, PO Box 16, CH-3000 Berne 15, Switzerland. *031-321735. Fax: 031-321838.*

The Football League: J. D. Dent, F.C.I.S., The Football League, Lytham St Annes, Lancs FY8 1JG. *0253-729421. Telex 67675*

The Scottish League: P. Donald, 188 West Regent Street, Glasgow G2 4RY. *041-248 384415*

The Irish League: H. Wallace, 87 University Street, Belfast BT7 1HP. *0232-242888*

Football League of Ireland: E. Morris, 80 Merrion Square South, Dublin 2. *0001-765120*

GM Vauxhall Conference: P. D. Hunter, 24 Barnehurst Road, Bexleyheath, Kent DA7 6EZ. *0322-521116*

Northern Premier: R. D. Bayley, 22 Woburn Drive, Hale, Altrincham, Cheshire. *061-980 7007*

Diadora League: N. Robinson, 226 Rye Lane, Peckham SE15 4NL. *081-653 3903*

English Schools FA: M. R. Berry, 4a Eastgate Street, Stafford ST16 2NN. *0785-51142*

National Federation of Football Supporters' Clubs: Registered Office: A. M. Kershaw, 24 South St., Loughborough, Leics. LE11 3EG. *0509-267643* Hon. Secretary: Mark Agate, "The Stadium", 14 Coombe Close, Lordswood, Chatham, Kent ME5 8NU. *0634-863520*

Professional Footballers' Association: G. Taylor, 2 Oxford Court, Bishopsgate, Off Lower Mosley Street, Manchester M2 3W2. *061-236 0575*

Referees' Association: W. J. Taylor, Cross Offices, Summerhill, Kingswinford, West Midlands DY6 9JE. *0384-288386*

Women's Football Association: Miss L. Whitehead, 448/450 Hanging Ditch, The Corn Exchange, Manchester M4 3ES. *061-832 5911*

The Association of Football Statisticians: R. J. Spiller, 22 Bretons, Basildon, Essex SS15 5BY. *0268-416020*

The Football Programme Directory: David Stacey, 'The Beeches', 66 Southend Road, Wickford, Essex SS11 8EN.

England Football Supporters Association: Publicity Officer, David Stacey, 66 Southend Road, Wickford, Essex SS11 8EN.

The Football League Executive Staffs Association: PO Box 52, Leamington Spa, Warwickshire.

The Football Trust: Second Floor, Walkden House, 10 Melton Street, London NW1 2EJ. *071-388 4104*

The Football Supporters Association: PO Box 11, Liverpool L26 1XP. *051-709-2594.*

Beazer Homes League: D. J. Strudwick, 11 Welland Close, Durrington, Worthing, Sussex BN13 3NR.

LIST OF REFEREES FOR SEASON 1993–94

Paul Alcock (S. Merstham, Surrey)
David Allison (Lancaster)
Gerald Ashby, (Worcester)
Mike Bailey, (Impington, Cambridge)
Keren Barratt, (Coventry)
Neil Barry, (Scunthorpe)
Ray Bigger, (Croydon)
Martin Bodenham, (Looe, Cornwall)
Jim Borrett, (Harleston, Norfolk)
John Brandwood, (Lichfield, Staffs.)
Kevin Breen, (Liverpool)
Keith Burge, (Tonypandy)
Billy Burns, (Scarborough)
George Cain, (Bootle)
Vic Callow, (Solihull)
Brian Coddington, (Sheffield)
Keith Cooper, (Pontypridd)
Keith Cooper, (Swindon)
Ian Cruikshanks, (Hartlepool)
Paul Danson, (Leicester)
Alan Dawson, (Jarrowe)
Roger Dilkes, (Mossley, Lancs.)
Phil Don, (Hanworth Park, Middlesex)
Steve Dunn, (Bristol)
Paul Durkin, (Portland, Dorset)
David Elleray, (Harrow)
Alan Flood, (Stockport)
Peter Foakes, (Clacton-on-Sea)
David Frampton, (Poole, Dorset)
Dermot Gallagher, (Banbury, Oxon.)
Rodger Gifford, (Llanbradach, Mid. Glam.)
Ron Groves, (Weston-Super-Mare)
Allan Gunn, (South Chailey, Sussex)
Keith Hackett, (Sheffield)
Paul Harrison, (Oldham)
Robert Hart, (Darlington)
Terry Heilbron, (Newton Aycliffe)
Ian Hemley, (Ampthill, Beds.)
Brian Hill, (Kettering)

John Holbrook (Ludlow)
Terry Holbrook, (Walsall)
Peter Jones, (Loughborough)
John Key, (Sheffield)
Howard King, (Merthyr Tydfil)
John Kirkby, (Sheffield)
Ken Leach, (Wolverhampton)
John Lloyd, (Wrexham)
Stephen Lodge, (Barnsley)
Eddie Lomas (Manchester)
Terry Lunt, (Ashton-in-Makerfield, Lancs)
Ken Lupton, (Stockton-on-Tees)
Kevin Lynch, (Lincoln)
Roger Milford, (Bristol)
Kelvin Morton, (Bury St. Edmunds)
David Orr (Iver)
Jim Parker, (Preston)
Mike Peck, (Kendal)
Micky Pierce, (Portsmouth)
Graham Poll, (Berkhamsted)
Graham Pooley, (Bishops Stortford)
Richard Poulain, (Huddersfield)
Mike Reed, (Birmingham)
Jim Rushton, (Stoke-on-Trent)
Ray Shepherd, (Leeds)
Gurnam Singh, (Wolverhampton)
Arthur Smith, (Rubery, Birmingham)
Paul Vanes, (Warley, West Midlands)
John Watson, (Whitley Bay)
Trevor West, (Hull)
Clive Wilkes, (Gloucester)
Alan Wilkie, (Chester-le-Street)
Gary Willard, (Worthing, W. Sussex)
Jeff Winter, (Middlesbrough)
Roger Wiseman, (Borehamwood, Herts.)
Eddie Wolstenholme, (Blackburn)
Joe Worrall, (Warrington)
Philip Wright, (Northwich)

More bestselling non-fiction
from Headline